Understanding Health Insurance

A Guide to Professional Billing

Understanding Health Insurance

A Guide to Professional Billing

6th Edition

JoAnn C. Rowell
Founder and Former Chairperson, Medical Assisting Department
Anne Arundel Community College, Arnold, MD
Currently, Adjunct Faculty
Community College of Baltimore County—Catonsville Campus
Catonsville, MD

Michelle A. Green, MPS, RHIA, CMA,
Professor, Department of Physical & Life Sciences
Alfred State College
Alfred, NY

Contributing Author

Alice Covell, CMA-A, RMA, CPC
Covell & Harwood Consultants
Kalamazoo, MI

DELMAR
THOMSON LEARNING

Australia   Canada   Mexico   Singapore   Spain   United   Kingdom   United States

DELMAR

★

THOMSON LEARNING

Understanding Health Insurance

6th Edition

by JoAnn Rowell and Michelle Green

Business Unit Director:
William Brottmiller

Executive Editor:
Cathy L. Esperti

Acquisitions Editor:
Maureen Muncaster

Developmental Editor:
Marjorie A. Bruce

Editorial Assistant:
Jill Korznat

Executive Marketing Manager:
Dawn F. Gerrain

Channel Manager:
Tara Carter

Project Editor
Maureen M. E. Grealish

Production Coordinator:
Anne Sherman

Art/Design Coordinator:
Connie Lundberg-Watkins

Technology Project Manager:
Laurie Davis

Library of Congress Cataloging-in-Publication Data
Rowell, JoAnn C., 1934–
   Understanding health insurance : a guide to professional billing /
Jo Ann C. Rowell : contributing author. Michelle A. Green—6th ed.
   p. cm.
   Includes bibliographical references and index.
   ISBN 0-7668-3206-6 (alk. paper)
   1. Health insurance claims—United States. 2. Insurance,
Health—United States.   I. Green, Michelle A. II. Title.
   HG9396 .R68 2001
   368.38'2'00973—dc21
                                                      2001032396

NOTICE TO THE READER

Contents

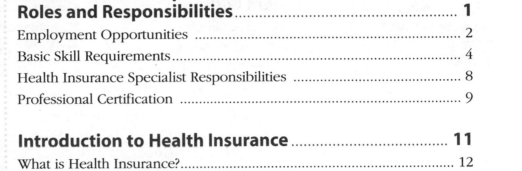

CHAPTER 5

Legal and Regulatory Considerations..............67

CHAPTER 6

ICD-9-CM Coding..............91

CHAPTER 7

CPT Coding..............151

CHAPTER 8

HCPCS Coding System **213**

CHAPTER 9

HCFA Reimbursement Issues **227**

CHAPTER 10

Coding From Source Documents **243**

CHAPTER 11

Essential HCFA-1500 Claim Form Instructions **273**

CHAPTER 12

Filing Commercial Claims... **291**

CHAPTER 13

CHAPTER 14

CHAPTER 15

CHAPTER 16

TRICARE 429

CHAPTER 17

Workers' Compensation 471

Preface

INTRODUCTION

Accurately processing health insurance claims has become more exacting at the same time health insurance plan options have rapidly expanded. These changes, combined with modifications in state and federal regulations affecting the health insurance industry, are a constant challenge to medical office personnel. Those responsible for processing health insurance claims require thorough instruction in all aspects of medical insurance, including plan options, carrier requirements, state and federal regulations, abstracting relevant information from source documents, accurately completing claim forms, and coding diagnoses and procedures. *Understanding Health Insurance, A Guide to Professional Billing*, 6th edition provides the required information in a clear and comprehensive manner.

OBJECTIVES

The objectives of the sixth edition of this text are to:

1. introduce information about major insurance programs and federal health care legislation

2. provide a basic knowledge of national diagnosis and procedure coding systems

3. simplify the process of completing claim forms.

This text is designed to be used by college and vocational school programs to train medical assistants, medical insurance specialists, and health information technicians. It can also be used as an in-service training tool for new medical office personnel and independent billing services, or individually by claims processors in the health care field who want to develop those skills.

FEATURES OF THE TEXT

Major features of this text have been updated and expanded.

● Learning objectives at the beginning of each chapter help to organize the material. They can be used as a self-test for checking comprehension and mastery of the chapter. Key words, abbreviations, and phrases listed in the first objective are bold-faced throughout the chapter to help students master the technical vocabulary associated with claims processing.

- Coding exercises are located within the respective coding chapters: ICD-9-CM Coding, CPT Coding, and HCPCS Coding System. Answers to diagnosis and procedure coding exercises are located in Appendix IV at the back of the text for quick feedback.

- Exercises in other chapters are located after major topics. These exercises provide an opportunity to apply concepts and skills immediately. In Chapters 11 through 17, exercises help develop skills in accurately completing claim forms.

- Numerous examples are provided in each chapter to illustrate the correct application of rules and guidelines.

- Coding Tips provide practical suggestions for mastering the use of the CPT and ICD-9-CM coding manuals.

- End of chapter reviews and challenge exercises reinforce learning and identify topics requiring further study.

- A practice disk (CD-ROM) is provided on the inside back cover. The case studies on the disk are contained in the Clinic Billing Manual (Appendix II) that includes billing data and patient encounter forms with case histories. Appendix V (Using the UHI CD-ROM) provides a brief introduction to setting up and running the CD-ROM. The complete *Disk Procedure Manual* is easily accessed on the CD-ROM and provides complete instructions for working with the software.

THE SIXTH EDITION

- Internet links are included throughout the text so that the latest information about insurance claims processing can be researched.

- The *Legal Considerations* chapter is renamed *Legal and Regulatory Considerations*, and is now located in Chapter 5 (instead of Chapter 2). The following new topics (with examples) are added:

    - confidentiality of patient information

    - retention of patient information and health insurance records

    - Federal False Claims Act

    - Health Insurance Portability and Accountability Act of 1996

- Chapter 6 is renamed *ICD-9-CM Coding* to more appropriately reflect its content. The HCFA ICD-9-CM Coding Guidelines are relocated to the beginning of the chapter. The ICD-9-CM coding rules are rewritten for clarification and to provide additional examples. The coding conventions for the Index to Diseases and the Tabular List are now located in tables within the chapter, and examples of coding book entries are included. The chapter review is updated and includes new coding exercises, which are organized according to the chapters in the ICD-9-CM Tabular List.

- Chapter 7 is renamed *CPT Coding*, and information about tabular conventions is included along with examples from the coding book as chapter figures. The CPT Pathology/Laboratory Section Overview is expanded to include an explanation of each category. The CPT Evaluation and Management Section now contains additional information to assist in the assignment of E&M codes, and an explanation of each category also includes additional examples. The table that includes CPT 2001 modifiers in a quick view format is revised and reformatted to make it easier to use. A discussion of the American Medical Association's CPT-5 Project is added. The chapter review is rewritten and includes new coding exercises, organized by CPT section.

- Content from Chapter 9, *HCFA Reimbursement Issues*, on the correct coding initiative and Medicare compliance plans is now included in Chapter 5, *Legal and Regulatory Issues*. The chapter review contains new challenge exercises.

- Chapter 10, *Coding from Source Documents*, exercises are revised throughout, and tables are added to allow students to organize answers to exercises. A chapter review with evaluation and management coding practice exercises is added.

- Chapter 11, *Essential HCFA-1500 Claim Form Instructions*, has a new chapter title to better reflect its content, and information is added about HCFA's national provider identifier (NPI).

- The step-by-step claim form completion instructions located in Chapters 12–17 are revised according to changes implemented by third-party payers.

- Chapter 14, *Medicare*, contains new information on Medicare Managed Care programs.

- Chapter 15, *Medicaid*, now contains an explanation of mandatory and optional groups and services as well as the relationship between Medicare and Medicaid. Also, instructions for completing mother/baby claims have been added.

- Chapter 16, *TRICARE*, is renamed (dropping the reference to CHAMPUS, which is now called TRICARE Standard). The entire chapter is rewritten to include the historical perspective of CHAMPUS and TRICARE development and an explanation of how TRICARE programs are administered and developed (including demonstration projects). In addition, CHAMPVA is differentiated from CHAMPUS, and instructions for primary TRICARE with supplemental policy claims completion is included.

- Chapter 17, *Workers' Compensation*, now includes a legislative history, expanded information about managed care, and instructions for completing the First Report of Injury form.

- Appendix II, *Clinic Billing Manual and Case Studies: Set Two*, contains a revised partial listing of CPT E&M codes and levels.

- Appendix III, *Forms*, now includes a list of forms located in the appendix. An E&M CodeBuilder form (based on 1995 and 1997 HCFA Documentation Guidelines for E&M) is added. When the 2000 draft documentation guidelines are finalized and adopted, the E&M CodeBuilder form will be revised to incorporate its changes.

- Appendix IV, *Answers to Coding Exercises*, remains a part of the text to facilitate feedback to learners during completion of coding exercises. ***Note:*** Additional coding exercises are included in the Instructor's Manual.

- Appendix V, *Using the UHI CD-ROM*, now contains just the instructions for installing the software. The CD-ROM procedure manual and tutorials are now located only on the CD-ROM and can be accessed by opening the software and clicking on Resources, then Help. The manual and tutorials can be printed from the CD-ROM.

● Appendix VI lists the abbreviations used in the text, both by chapter and in alphabetic order.

● Appendix VII lists common prefixes, suffixes, and combining forms used in medical terminology.

● Appendix VIII summarizes the Web sites listed throughout the chapters in the Internet Link feature. The sites are listed both in alphabetic order and by name of the site.

● Appendix IX introduces the concept of electronic data interchange as it relates to submitting UB-92 (Uniform Bill) claim form information for institutional services (including hospitals and skilled nursing facilities).

● Appendix X is an updated bibliography of references and recommended readings.

SUPPLEMENTS

The following supplements accompany the sixth edition of this text.

Instructor's Manual

The Instructor's Manual consists of two parts, one relating to the text and one relating to the workbook. The Instructor's Manual for the text has been updated, and continues to serve as a guide for a course of study in health insurance claims processing. It provides a grading plan and additional exercises and tests, including case studies not provided in the text that can be used as a final examination. The Instructor's Manual lists ideas that instructors can use to simplify the teaching approach. It also provides answers to coding exercises not included in Appendix IV of the text. Completed claim forms for all case studies in the text, Instructor's Manual, and Student Workbook are also included.

The *Instructor's Manual to Accompany the Workbook* contains answers to all chapter exercises with completed claim forms for the case studies in Chapters 11 through 17.

Student Workbook

The workbook developed for the text follows the text's chapter organization with questions grouped under main topic headings also found in the text. The exercises provide additional practice to reinforce learning and improve skills in basic coding and completion of claim forms. In Chapters 11 through 17, new case studies allow more practice in completing the HFCA-1500 claim form. Each case study consists of an encounter form for a patient and a blank HCFA-1500 claim form.

Computerized Test Bank

The computerized test bank on CD-ROM provides test creation, delivery, and reporting capability. Organized by chapter to follow the text, there are approximately 1,000 questions.

WEBTUTOR

WebTutor is an Internet-based course management and delivery system designed to accompany the text. Its content is available for use in either WebCT or Blackboard. Available to supplement on-campus course delivery or as the course management platform for an on-line course, WebTutor contains:

- On-line quizzes for each chapter
- Discussion topics and learning links
- On-line glossary, organized by chapter
- Answers to textbook challenge exercises

To learn more, visit http://webtutor.delmar.com and complete the Adopt WebTutor form.

REVIEWERS

A special thank you is extended to the reviewers who have provided recommendations and suggestions for improvement throughout the development of the fifth edition. Their experience and knowledge has been a valuable resource for the authors.

Douglas R. Anderson, M. D.
   Bascom Palmer Eye Institute
   University of Miami School of Medicine
   Miami, FL
Susan Pritchard Bailey, MBA, RHIA
   Bailey & Associates
   Lenox, MA
Ann M. Baus
   Insurance Specialist
   Seattle, WA
Carolyn L. Burr, CPC
   Distance Learning Instructor
   Terlingua, TX
Janette Thomas, MPS, RHIA
   Alfred State College
   Alfred, NY

ACKNOWLEDGMENTS

To my husband and son, Michael and Eric, who understand and support my passion for teaching.

   To my students, throughout the world, who motivate me to want to learn everything so I can teach them everything. You are my inspiration.

   To my coauthor, JoAnn Rowell, who provided me with this wonderful opportunity.

   To Ruth Burke, thank you for your attention to detail!

   To my Developmental Editor, Marge Bruce, who has infinite patience for my perfectionism.

   To my Acquisitions Editor, Maureen Muncaster, who listens to my ideas and makes them happen.

   To my sixth and ninth grade English teacher, Mrs. Hourihan, who made me believe I could write, and to Mr. Odum, my tenth grade English teacher, who just expected that I would write.

To Alice, who told an undecided 16-year-old girl, "Pick a career and go to college." So I did, and then during my career as a health information manager, she said, "You could fill out insurance claims for people who don't know how to." So, I did—sort of—in the form of this textbook. Thanks, Mom.

Special appreciation is expressed to Medicode, St. Anthony Publishing, and Ingenix Publishing for granting permission to reprint selected tables and pages from:

● *Medicode 2001 HCPCS*

● *St. Anthony Publishing Illustrated ICD-9-CM Code Book for Physician Payment*

● *St. Anthony Publishing Medicare Correct Coding & Payment Manual*

Health Insurance Specialist— Roles and Responsibilities

OBJECTIVES Upon successful completion of this chapter, you should be able to:

1. Define the following terms, phrases, and abbreviations:

   health insurance claim

   preauthorization

   health care provider

   Health Care Financing Administration (HCFA)

   hold harmless clause

   electronic claims processing

   electronic data interchange (EDI)

   coding

   ICD-9-CM (*International Classification of Diseases, 9th Revision, Clinical Modification*)

   HCPCS (HCFA Common Procedure Coding System)

   CPT (*Current Procedural Terminology*)

   National Codes

   Local Codes

   ethics

2. Explain the reasons for increasing employment opportunities for health insurance specialists.

3. Prepare a list of career paths for health insurance specialists.

4. List and discuss the basic skill requirements for aspiring health insurance specialists.

5. List and discuss twelve responsibilities of health insurance specialists.

6. Name three professional organizations dedicated to working with health insurance specialists who are filing claims for physicians and other health care professionals.

INTRODUCTION The career of a health insurance specialist is a challenging one with new opportunities arising continuously. Job security is high for an individual who understands claims processing and billing regulations, possesses accurate coding skills, and successfully appeals underpaid or denied insurance claims. A review of medical office personnel help wanted advertisements indicates the need for individuals with these skills.

EMPLOYMENT OPPORTUNITIES

Most health care practices in the United States accept responsibility for filing health insurance claims. A **health insurance claim** is the documentation submitted to an insurance plan requesting reimbursement of health care services provided. In the past few years, many practices have increased the number of employees assigned to some aspect of the claims filing process. This increase is due to more patients having some form of health insurance, many of whom require **preauthorization** (prior approval) for treatment by specialists and post-treatment reports. Competitive insurance companies are fine tuning procedures to reduce administrative costs and overall expenditures. This cost-reduction campaign forces closer scrutiny of the entire claims process, which in turn increases the time and effort medical practices must devote to billing and filing claims according to the insurance policy filing requirements. Poor attention to claims requirements will result in lower reimbursement rates to the practices and increased expenses.

An increasing number of managed care contracts are being signed by health care providers. A **health care provider** is a physician or other health care practitioner (e.g., physician's assistant). Each new provider-managed care contract increases the practice's patient base, the number of claims requirements and reimbursement regulations, the time the office staff must devote to fulfilling contract requirements, and the complexity of referring patients for specialty care. Each insurance plan has its own authorization requirements, billing deadlines, claims requirements, and a list of participating providers or networks. If a health care provider has signed ten participating contracts, there are ten different sets of requirements to follow and ten different panels of participating health care providers from which referrals can be made. Rules associated with health insurance processing (especially government programs) change frequently, and to remain up-to-date, insurance specialists should be sure they are on mailing lists to receive newsletters from insurance payers. It is also important to remain current regarding news released from the **Health Care Financing Administration (HCFA)**, the administrative agency within the federal Department of Health and Human Services (DHHS). The Secretary of the DHHS, is often reported by the news media as having announced the implementation of new regulations. If preauthorization requirements are not met, payment of the claim is denied. If the insurance plan has a **hold harmless clause** (patient is not responsible for paying what the insurance plan denies) in the contract, the health care provider cannot collect the fees from the patient. In addition, patients referred to nonparticipating providers (e.g., physician who does not participate in a particular health care plan) have significantly higher out-of-pocket costs than anticipated.

INTERNET LINKS

What's New on hcfa.gov at www.hcfa.gov/whatsnew contains the latest information on federal regulations, payment systems, and more.

■ **NOTE:** Internet links will appear throughout the text, and a comprehensive listing can be found in Appendix VIII. ■

Another reason for the increased hiring of insurance specialists is a direct result of employers attempting to reduce the cost of providing employee health insurance coverage. Employers renegotiate benefits with existing plans or change insurance carriers altogether. The employees often receive retroactive notice of these contract changes and, in some cases, once notified may have to wait several weeks before new health benefit books and new insurance identification cards are issued. These changes in employer-sponsored plans have made it necessary for the health care provider's staff to check on patients' current eligibility and benefit status at the time of each office visit.

Career Opportunities

According to the *Occupational Outlook Handbook* published by the U.S. Department of Labor–Bureau of Labor Statistics, health care facilities and insurance companies will hire claims examiners (insurance specialists) to process routine medical claims at an increased rate of 10 to 20% through the year 2008. As the use of software for processing insurance claims is implemented, insurance specialist positions will become more automated, requiring a background in word processing and other computer applications. Providers who implement **electronic claims processing** send data in a standardized machine-readable format to an insurance company via disk, telephone, or cable. The insurance company receives the data, reviews it, and sends an acknowledgment to the provider. This mutual exchange of data between the provider and insurance company is called **electronic data interchange (EDI)**.

In addition to the increase of insurance specialist positions available in health care practices, opportunities are increasing in other settings for experienced health insurance specialists as:

- Claims benefit advisors in health, malpractice, and liability insurance companies.
- Coding or insurance specialists in state, local, and federal government agencies, legal offices, private insurance billing offices, and medical societies.
- Educators in schools and companies specializing in medical office staff training.
- Writers and editors of health insurance textbooks, newsletters, and other publications.
- Self-employed consultants who provide assistance to medical practices with billing practices and claims appeal procedures.
- Consumer claims assistance professionals, who file claims and appeal low reimbursement for private individuals. In the latter case, individuals may be dissatisfied with the handling of their claims by the health care provider's insurance staff.
- Practices with poorly trained health insurance staff who are unwilling or unable to file a proper claims appeal.
- Private billing practices dedicated to claims filing for elderly or disabled patients.

Coding is the process of reporting diagnoses, procedures, and services as numeric and alphanumeric characters on the insurance claim form. Two systems used are ICD-9-CM and HCPCS. **ICD-9-CM (*International Classification of Diseases, 9th Revision, Clinical Modification*)** is the coding system used to report diagnoses (e.g., diseases, signs, and symptoms) and reasons for encounters (e.g., annual physical examination, and surgical follow-up care) on physician office claims. Codes are reported either numerically or alphanumerically and include a decimal (e.g., 401.9 is the code for hypertension; V20.2 is the code for a well child office visit). **HCPCS (HCFA Common Procedure Coding System)** consists of three levels: (1) **CPT (*Current Procedural Terminology*)**, which is published by the American Medical Association and includes five-digit numeric codes and descriptors for procedures and services performed by providers (e.g., 99203 identifies a detailed office visit for a new patient); (2) **National Codes**, commonly referred to as HCPCS codes, which are published by HCFA and include five-digit alphanumeric codes for procedures, services, and supplies that are not classified in CPT (e.g., J-codes are used to assign drugs administered); and (3) **Local Codes**, which are developed by local insurance companies and include five-digit alphanumeric codes for procedures, services, and supplies that are also not classified in CPT.

■ **NOTE:** HCFA plans to eventually phase out local codes. ■

BASIC SKILL REQUIREMENTS

Anyone who aspires to become a health insurance specialist needs to possess the following:

- Strong foundation in medical terminology
- Basic knowledge of anatomy and physiology
- Knowledge of diagnosis and procedure coding conventions and rules
- Critical reading and comprehension skills
- Sufficient math skills to maintain patient financial records
- Excellent oral and written communication skills
- Ability to enter financial and demographic data into a patient database
- Ability to access information through the Internet
- Strong sense of ethics
- Attention to detail

The Importance of Medical Terminology

Health insurance specialists must be fluent in the language of medicine and have access to a comprehensive medical dictionary as a reference. A background in medical terminology is also important, and individuals can enroll in formal coursework or obtain a medical terminology textbook and complete it as self-paced instruction (e.g., *Medical Terminology for Health Professions, 4th Edition,* by Ann Ehrlich and Carol Schroeder). They are required to take diagnoses, symptoms, and treatments or services reported in the patient's chart and translate them into numerical or alphanumerical codes required by state and federal health care agencies and the commercial health insurance industry. These three-, four-, or five-digit codes are reported on all health insurance claim forms and insurance payment documents without narrative descriptions of the diagnoses, symptoms, or procedures performed.

Frequently, descriptions in the patient record/chart do not match the precise wording found in the coding systems. Therefore, health insurance specialists must draw on their knowledge of medical terminology to assign codes to the written narratives documented by health care providers.

Practice

As a review, or to become familiar with common medical terms, refer to Appendix VII and define common prefixes, suffixes, and combining forms located there.

Basic Knowledge of Anatomy and Physiology

A basic understanding of anatomy and physiology is crucial in recognizing abnormal body conditions. If an insurance program is to pay for medical procedures or services, it must understand the medical necessity for the procedure(s) or service(s) performed. *Every procedure or service reported to the insurance company must be linked to a condition that justifies the necessity for performing that procedure or service.*

EXAMPLE 1

Procedure: Knee X ray

Documented diagnosis: Shoulder pain

In this example, the procedure is not covered because the X ray is not medically justified.

EXAMPLE 2

Procedure: Knee X ray

Documented diagnosis: Fractured patella (knee bone)

In this example, the procedure is covered because it is medically justified.

Knowledge of Diagnosis and Procedure Coding Conventions/Rules

Computerization of the medical practice and insurance claims processing function requires the translation of diagnoses, procedures, and services into logical and systematic coding systems. Working with coded information requires an understanding of the rules, conventions, and applications of these coding systems to ensure proper selection of individual codes.

EXAMPLE

Chief Complaint: Patient is seen for facial laceration.

Procedure: Suture of 3 cm facial laceration, simple.

When referring to the CPT coding manual, there is no listing for "Suture, facial laceration." There is, however, an instructional notation just below the entry for "Suture" that refers the coder to "Repair." When "Repair" is referenced in the Index, the coder must then locate subterm "Skin," and then "Wound" and "Simple." The code range for "Repair, Skin, Wound, Simple" is 12020-12021. The final step is to verify the code selection in the tabular section of the coding manual and to enter it on the insurance claim form.

Critical Reading

Reading and comprehension skills are critical to differentiating the technical description of two different but similar procedures or diagnoses. For example, a skilled coder or biller should be able to readily identify the differences in the following cases:

CASE 1

Ureteral endoscopy through a ureter*otomy* versus ureteral endoscopy through a ureter*ostomy*

Answer: When a ureteral endoscopy is performed via ureterotomy, the physician is examining the kidney and ureteral structures using an endoscope after an incision is made through the skin and the ureter. After the examination, the scope is removed and the surgical wound is sutured.

For a ureteral endoscopy via ureterostomy, the endoscope is passed into the ureter through an ureterostomy tube that has been in place since a previous surgery. After the examination is completed, the scope is removed and the ureterostomy is either left in place or it is removed and the passageway allowed to seal on its own.

CASE 2

Spond*ylosis* versus spondyl*olysis*

Answer: Spondylosis means any condition of the spine. Spondylolysis is a defect (break down) in the interarticular portion of the vertebra.

Misreading or misinterpretating any word or diagnosis may result in assignment of incorrect code numbers and the possibility of a delay in payment or total rejection of a claim. For example, "facial" versus "fascial," as in the example on page 5. The patient has a wound of the face, not the layer of tissue that covers muscle (called fascia). Including, excluding, or substituting one letter in a word can result in misinterpretation (e.g., "golf" versus "gulf"— while friends await your arrival at the golf course, you are expecting to meet them at the beach).

*Excellent
Communication
Skills*

All health insurance specialists must possess excellent oral and written communication skills. They must be comfortable discussing insurance concepts and regulations on several levels. Patients often need assistance in translating complex insurance concepts and regulations into basic terms they can understand. The ability to communicate intelligently with health care providers regarding documentation of services and/or procedures can reduce coding and billing errors. At the same time, the health insurance specialist must communicate effectively with insurance company personnel using the language of the health care industry.

Underpaid claims must be appealed. Some appeals are straightforward and only take a short note to correct the error. Many claims, however, will require long, detailed, written appeals. A poorly written appeal of a complex claim may not get the reconsideration the case deserves. An incorrect diagnosis or procedure code on the original claim may result in a denial. The appeal for reconsideration of the case requires notification that a coding error occurred along with the submission of a corrected claim. Other appeals may be generated because the insurance company recoded a complex case. If the recoding is not justified, an appeal for reconsideration must contain a detailed defense of the original claim's coding and the rationale that supports the original codes submitted.

Data Entry Ability

Because federal legislation will soon require all claims to be electronically submitted, insurance specialists must have good keyboarding skills and the ability to enter basic financial and insurance data into the practice's accounting system. Accurate and precise data entry of the patient's demographic (identification) and account information ensures that required data is electronically placed in proper fields on claim forms generated by the computer. In some computer programs, insurance information screens with different titles otherwise appear identical. For example, primary and secondary insurance screens require the entry of similar information. Electronic claim forms will be rejected by the insurance company for missing or misplaced critical data on the form. Improper payment or charge data entered on the patient account will also result in incorrect data displayed on the claim form.

Internet Access

The ability to access the Internet is rapidly becoming a necessary function of insurance claims processing. Online information sources provide access to a large volume of medical reference materials, insurance carrier manuals, and procedure guidelines that are not accessible in printed form or are too costly for the majority of practices to purchase. In addition, many insurance companies and government agencies use Web sites to release reimbursement and billing changes prior to adoption. By pre-releasing major changes, insurers and government agencies receive feedback from medical practices on how changes will affect operations in the field. When a designated comment period ends, the issue is either re-evaluated or the final rule is adopted and reported. By checking Web sites, practices can anticipate changes and plan for a smooth transition to implementing new rules before the announced effective date of these changes. Access to this resource may allow for several week's advanced notification of the new rule before it is available to practices in newsletters and bulletins. Insurance company Web sites also provide quick access to provider information departments without the long delays caused by the limited number of telephone lines.

The Internet also offers numerous opportunities to network with other health insurance specialists across the country. Access to solutions and insight into billing and coding problems through specialized chat rooms or forums sponsored by the various medical coding and nongovernment insurance information organizations is invaluable.

Strong Sense of Ethics

The *American Heritage® Concise Dictionary* defines **ethics** as the principle of right or good conduct, and rules that govern the conduct of members of a profession. The insurance specialist, upon joining a professional association, is responsible for upholding the code of ethics (see Internet Links—Code of Ethics for Professional Associations).

WWW. INTERNET LINKS

CODE OF ETHICS FOR PROFESSIONAL ASSOCIATIONS

American Association of Medical Assistants   www.aama-ntl.org/mission.html

American Health Information
    Management Association   www.ahima.org/infocenter/guidelines/ethics.html

Attention to Detail

Processing insurance claims requires careful consideration and thorough follow-up. Tasks are completed one at a time, including those that may appear to be unimportant. This attention to detail is an essential characteristic of an insurance specialist.

HEALTH INSURANCE SPECIALIST RESPONSIBILITIES

This section provides an overview of major responsibilities delegated to health insurance specialists. In practices with just one or two persons working with insurance billing, each individual must be capable of performing all of the listed responsibilities. In large multispecialty practices with many insurance department positions, each insurance specialist usually processes claims for a limited number of insurance payers (e.g., an insurance specialist may be assigned to process only Medicare claims). In some practices, there is a clear division of labor with specific individuals accepting responsibility for only a few assigned tasks. Typical tasks are listed in the following job description.

Health Insurance Specialist Job Description

1. Abstract patient records and other source documents to accurately code all diagnoses, procedures, and services using ICD-9-CM for diagnoses, and CPT and HCPCS, pronounced "hick picks", for procedures.

   The accurate coding of diagnoses, procedures, and services rendered to the patient allows a medical practice to:

   • communicate diagnostic and treatment data to a patient's insurance carrier to assist the patient in obtaining maximum benefits from their health insurance plan.

   • facilitate analysis of the practice's patient base to improve patient care delivery and efficiency of practice operations to contain costs.

2. Research and apply knowledge of all insurance rules and regulations for major insurance programs in the local or regional area.

3. Operate the office bookkeeping system properly.

4. Accurately post charges, payments, and adjustments to patient accounts and office accounts receivable records.

5. Prepare or review claims generated by the practice to ensure that all required data is accurately reported.

6. Review all insurance payments and explanation of benefits (EOB) forms generated by the insurance company to ensure proper processing and payment of each claim.

7. Correct all data errors and resubmit all unprocessed or returned claims.

8. Research and prepare appeals for all underpaid, unjustly recoded, or denied claims.

9. Rebill all claims not paid within 30 to 45 days, depending on individual practice policy.

10. Inform health care providers and the staff of changes in fraud and abuse laws, coding changes, documentation guidelines, and insurance carrier requirements that may affect the billing and claims submission procedures.

11. Assist with the timely updating of the practice's internal documents, patient registration forms, and billing forms as required by changes in coding or insurance billing requirements.

12. Maintain an internal audit system to ensure that required pretreatment authorizations have been received and entered into the billing and treatment records.

13. Explain insurance benefits, policy requirements, and filing rules to patients.

PROFESSIONAL CERTIFICATION

The health insurance specialist who becomes affiliated with one or more professional associations receives useful information available in several formats including professional journals and newsletters, access to members-only Web sites, notification of professional development, and so on. A key feature of membership is an awareness of the importance of professional certification.

The American Health Information Association (AHIMA) sponsors two certification exams for coding specialists. The *Certified Coding Specialist (CCS)* demonstrates competence in ICD-9-CM and CPT Surgery coding as well as in patient documentation and data integrity/quality issues, anatomy, physiology, and pharmacology. The *Certified Coding Specialist–Physician-based (CCS-P)* demonstrates expertise in multi-specialty CPT, ICD-9-CM, and HCPCS National (Level II) coding. For information on membership and certification, call AHIMA at (312) 233-1100, or e-mail inquiries to info@ahima.org. Their mailing address is 233 N. Michigan Avenue, Chicago, IL 60611-5519.

The American Academy of Professional Coders offers two certification exams. The *Certified Professional Coder (CPC)* is available for physician practice and clinic coders, and the *Certified Professional Coder–Hospital (CPC–H)* examination is written for outpatient facility coders. Contact the AAPC at (800) 626-8699, or e-mail them at aapc@aapcnatl.org. Their mailing address is 309 West 700 South, Salt Lake City, UT 84101.

The Alliance of Claims Assistance Professionals (ACAP) sponsors two exams for insurance claims specialists, the *Certified Claims Assistance Professional (CCAP)* and the *Certified Electronic Claims Professional (CECP)*. For information on certification and other services, contact ACAP at (630) 588-1260, or e-mail them at askus@claims.org. Their mailing address is 731 Naperville Road, Wheaton, IL 60187-6407.

INTERNET LINKS

American Health Information Management Association (AHIMA)   www.ahima.org

American Academy of Professional Coders (AAPC)   www.aapcnatl.org

Alliance of Claims Assistance Professionals (ACAP)   www.claims.org

REVIEW

CHALLENGE EXERCISE

Answer the following:

1. Describe the basic skills necessary to become a health insurance specialist.

2. Make a list of traditional and developing career opportunities available to health insurance specialists.

3. List two professional organizations dedicated to serving and credentialing health insurance specialists employed in health care provider offices.

Introduction to Health Insurance

OBJECTIVES

Upon successful completion of this chapter, you should be able to:

1. Define the following terms, phrases, and abbreviations:

insurance
medical care
health care
preventive services
health insurance
disability insurance
liability insurance
prepaid health plan
health maintenance organization (HMO)
group practice
Medicare
Medicaid
welfare
CHAMPUS (TRICARE)
fee-for-service plan
deductible
coinsurance
copayment
copay
primary care physician

primary care provider (PCP)
gatekeeper
CHAMPVA
Health Care Financing Administration (HCFA)
Health Care Financing Administration Common Procedure Coding System (HCPCS)
Physician's *Current Procedural Terminology* (CPT)
International Classification of Diseases 9th Revision Clinical Modification (ICD-9-CM)
HCFA-1500 (1-90)
usual and reasonable payments
fee schedule
nonparticipating limited fee
private contract
Correct Coding Initiative (CCI)

Health Insurance Portability and Accountability Act (HIPAA)
third party payers
national health planID (PlanID)
national provider identifier (NPI)
national standard employer identifier number (EIN)
electronic data interchange (EDI)
electronic transaction standards
ANSI ASC X12N 837
health care fraud
ambulatory payment classifications (APCs)
capitation
per capita
PMPM payment (per member per month payment)
fee-for-service reimbursement
managed fee-for-service
episode of care reimbursement
global surgical fee

2. Explain why it was necessary to standardize procedural terminology and develop a procedural coding system.

3. Explain why HCFA regulated the use of the HCFA-1500 claim form for Medicare billing.

4. Explain the purpose of the national Correct Coding Initiative (CCI).

5. List four features of the Health Insurance Portability and Accountability Act of 1996 (HIPAA).

6. List and describe the four types of third-party reimbursement seen in physician practices across the country today.

7. List and describe the four methods of reimbursement seen in today's health care practices.

INTRODUCTION According to the *American Heritage® Concise Dictionary*, **insurance** is a contract that protects the insured from loss. An insurance company guarantees payment to the insured for an unforeseen event (e.g., death, accident, and illness) in return for the payment of premiums. The types of insurance include disability, liability, malpractice, property, life, and health (covered in this text). This chapter includes explanations of terms and concepts as an introduction to health insurance processing. These terms and concepts are covered in greater detail in later chapters of this text.

WHAT IS HEALTH INSURANCE?

To understand the meaning of the term "health insurance" as it is used in this text, differentiation between medical care and health care must be made. **Medical care** includes the identification of disease and the provision of care and treatment as that provided by members of the health care team to persons who are sick, injured, or concerned about their health status. **Health care** expands the definition of medical care to include **preventive services**, which are designed to help individuals avoid health and injury problems. Preventive or proactive examinations may bring about early detection of problems resulting in treatment options that are less drastic and less expensive.

Health care insurance or **health insurance** is a contract between a policy holder and an insurance carrier or government program to reimburse the policy holder for all or a portion of the cost of medically necessary treatment or preventive care rendered by health care professionals. Because both the government and the general public speak of "health insurance," this text will use that term exclusively.

DISABILITY AND LIABILITY INSURANCE

Disability Insurance

Disability insurance, for the purpose of this text, is defined as reimbursement for income lost as a result of a temporary or permanent illness or injury. When patients are treated for disability diagnoses and other medical problems, separate patient records must be maintained. It is also a good idea to organize the financial records separately for these patients. Offices that generate one patient record for the treatment of disability diagnoses and other medical problems often confuse the submission of diagnostic and procedural data for insurance processing. This results in payment delays and claims denials.

■ **NOTE:** Disability insurance generally does not pay for health care services, but provides the disabled person with financial assistance. ■

Liability Insurance

Although liability insurance is not covered in this text, it is important to understand how it influences the processing of health insurance claims. **Liability insurance** is a policy that covers losses to a third party caused by the insured, by an object owned by the insured, or on premises owned by the insured. Liability insurance claims are made to cover the cost of medical care for traumatic injuries, lost wages, and in many cases, remuneration for the "pain and suffering" of the injured party. Most health insurance contracts state that health insurance benefits are secondary to liability insurance. In this situation, the patient is *not* the insured. This means that the insured (e.g., employer) is responsible for payment, and the patient's health insurance plan is billed as secondary (and reimburses only the remaining costs of health care *not* covered by the insured). When negligence by another party is suspected in an injury claim, the health insurance carrier will not reimburse the patient for medical treatment of the injury until one of two factors is established: (1) it is determined there was no third-party negligence, or (2) in cases where third-party negligence did occur, the liability carrier determines the incident is not covered by the negligent party's liability contract.

EXAMPLE

Dr. Small treated Jim Keene in the office for scalp lacerations (cuts) that resulted from a work-related injury. Mr. Keene is covered by an employer-sponsored group health plan called HealthCareUSA, and his employer provides workers' compensation insurance coverage for on-the-job injuries.

The insurance claim for treatment of Mr. Keene's lacerations should be submitted to the employer's workers' compensation insurance carrier (company).

If the claim was submitted to HealthCareUSA, it would be subject to review because the diagnosis code submitted would indicate trauma (injury), which activates the review of patient records by an insurance company. Upon reviewing requested copies of patient records, HealthCareUSA would determine that another insurance plan should have been billed for this treatment. HealthCareUSA would deny payment of the claim, and Dr. Small's office would then submit the claim to the workers' compensation carrier. With this scenario, a delay in payment for treatment has resulted.

To file a claim with a liability carrier, a regular patient billing statement addressed to the liability carrier is often used rather than an insurance claim form. Be sure to include the name of the policy holder and the liability policy identification numbers. If the liability insurer denies payment, a claim is then filed with the patient's health insurance plan. *A photocopy of the written denial of responsibility must accompany the health insurance claim form.*

MAJOR DEVELOPMENTS IN HEALTH INSURANCE

1900 to 1940

Health care, like other aspects of society in this country, has undergone tremendous changes during this past century. For about the first 40 years of the 20th century, medical practices consisted largely of general practitioners in solo practice, and patients were the only responsible party for payment to physicians and hospitals for health care services received. The concept of *physician specialists* also emerged during this period.

In the late 1920s and early 1930s there were isolated instances of groups banding together to explore innovative ways to improve health care in their local community. Several of these efforts resulted in the development of contracts with local hospitals and/or physicians for prepaid health care. These contracts called for the participating hospital or physician to perform specified medical services in exchange for a predetermined fee that would be paid to the provider of care on either a monthly or yearly basis. These early prepaid medical care arrangements were so successful that soon the original policies were expanded to include more individuals and providers in a given region. These **prepaid health plans** were the forerunner of today's **health maintenance organizations (HMO)** or managed care plans.

In the early 1940s, a new concept in prepaid health care began to emerge. This plan stipulated that policyholders of medical care contracts should pay a small amount for each medical service received if their earned income was above a set level. At the same time, policyholders whose earned income fell below the stated level would not have to pay for their medical services.

1940 to Present

The number of prepaid medical insurance plans increased rapidly during World War II. Many employers needed a way to retain good workers and attract new employees at a time when they were operating under government-enforced pay scales. Government restrictions applied only to wages; there were no restrictions on the number or total dollar amount of benefits, other than wages, an employer could offer employees. Many employers began to offer employer-sponsored medical or health insurance policies as an incentive.

Specialty Group Practices Emerge

World War II was also responsible for changes in the structure of medical practices. As the war progressed and the number of wounded increased, the military recognized the need for physicians caring for the wounded to become trained in specific areas of treatment. When the war ended in 1945, the majority of the military doctors discharged from the armed forces elected to use veterans' educational benefits to further their study of the specialized training they had received in the military. A large number became specialists, and fewer entered general practice. When these physicians re-entered civilian practice, many joined together to practice in small groups as they had done in the military, rather than establishing solo practices. The first group practices to emerge were single-specialty groups. Later, some physicians began to form multiple-specialty group practices. A **group practice** is defined by the American Medical Association (AMA) as three or more doctors joining together to deliver health care who agree to make joint use of equipment, supplies, and personnel, and divide income by a prearranged formula.

Employer-Sponsored Health Insurance

In the early 1950s, there was a demand for medical or health care insurance that encouraged many insurance companies to expand into health care and prompted new corporations to enter the market. The upward surge in covered persons or "lives" prompted many changes in medical offices. Patients originally paid their health care bill and submitted receipts to the insurance company for reimbursement. Later, insured patients began to request that the offices bill their health insurance before making payments on their accounts. They agreed to pay the balance due after the carriers determined the insurance portion of the claim. Each insurance company had a unique set of billing requirements. The complexity of the new billing procedures greatly increased paperwork and practices had to, therefore, increase the size of their billing staff.

Coding

By the mid 1950s, the increased demand for filing insurance claims led some persons in the medical community to attempt standardization of the procedural terminology reported on the claims. Almost simultaneously, insurance companies began to use computers for the collection and organization of procedural data on the claim form for statistical purposes. The use of computers led the medical community to develop a numerical coding system that could easily be entered into the computer. By the mid 1960s, some areas of the country had a procedural coding system in place. The system developed by the California Medical Society became the prototype for the *Current Procedural Terminology* (CPT) system published by the AMA and currently reported on all outpatient claims in this country.

The standardization of diagnostic data on claims submitted by physicians was achieved by adopting a diagnosis coding system known as the International Classification of Diseases (ICD). The World Health Organization (WHO) originally developed ICD in 1948 to collect data for statistical purposes. Codes were later reported for hospital inpatient reimbursement purposes, and in 1988, Medicare began requiring physician offices to submit the ICD-9-CM codes on HCFA-1500 claims.

Emergence of Government-Sponsored Programs

The next phase of health insurance dawned between 1965 and 1966 when the U.S. Congress enacted legislation to establish three government-sponsored health care programs: Medicare, Medicaid, and CHAMPUS (now known as TRICARE).

- **Medicare** was originally designed to cover individuals aged 65 or older and retired on either Social Security or the Railroad Retirement program.

- The **Medicaid** program is jointly funded by state and local governments to provide health care benefits to indigent persons on **welfare** (public assistance), the aged, and/or the disabled. Some states expanded this mandate to cover certain other medically needy individuals who met special state-determined criteria.

- **CHAMPUS**, the Civilian Health and Medical Program of the Uniformed Services, was originally designed as a benefit for dependents of personnel serving in the armed forces and the uniformed branches of the Public Health Service and the National Oceanic and Atmospheric Administration. This program relieved the overtaxed armed forces medical services by allowing dependents to seek medical care from civilian health care providers when the necessary care was not available at a nearby government medical treatment facility. In the late 1990s, the program was reorganized and the name was changed to **TRICARE**. The name was chosen to represent the new three-part program, which includes TRICARE Prime, Extra, and Standard.

Billing Complexity Increases

This legislation introduced complexity in the form of government-mandated billing and reimbursement regulations for the three government programs. Another outcome of this legislation was the beginning of investor-owned hospital chains and the growth in university-owned, multiple-specialty medical centers throughout the country.

By the early 1970s, medical practices were dealing with four categories of patients: those enrolled in government programs, workers' compensation, or liability plans; those enrolled in private or commercial plans known as fee-for-service plans; those enrolled in prepaid health maintenance organizations; and those without insurance coverage.

Both the government programs and the private commercial plans operated on a **fee-for-service plan** that allowed for complete freedom in the choice of health care providers. Reimbursement was based on a set fee schedule or the usual and customary charges for a specific service in a given geographic region. Payment was made only for medically necessary treatment, with little or no payment for preventive care. The patient was responsible for payment of a yearly deductible and a coinsurance payment. The **deductible** is a specified amount of annual out-of-pocket expenses for covered health care services the insured must pay for health care before the insurer pays benefits. **Coinsurance** is defined as a specified percentage of each fee for a covered service the patient must pay to the provider. Coinsurance is often confused with copayment. A **copayment**, abbreviated as **copay**, is a fixed fee paid at each visit for each service rendered.

EXAMPLE

Mary Burns' HealthCareUSA insurance plan requires payment of an annual deductible ($250), a copayment for each office visit ($10), a copayment for hospital emergency department visits ($25), a copayment for hospital outpatient services ($15), and coinsurance for hospital inpatient services (20 percent of inpatient charges).

On 6/15, Mary was seen in her physician's office for stomach pain and her doctor prescribed a medication. On 6/16 (Saturday), the stomach pain became much worse and when Mary contacted her physician's answering service, her physician called and instructed her to go to the hospital emergency department for evaluation. Mary was admitted to the hospital from the emergency department and discharged on 6/19; inpatient charges totaled $1500.

Mary is responsible for paying the following:
- $10 copayment for the 6/15 office visit
- $25 copayment for the 6/16 emergency department visit
- $300 coinsurance for the three-day inpatient admission (this amount is 20% of the $1500 inpatient bill)

Health Maintenance Organization Growth

In the early 1970s, Health Maintenance Organizations (HMOs), which lacked support from organized medicine, attracted the attention of employers and the general public due to lower premiums. HMOs were especially attractive because they reintroduced the concept of a general practitioner rendering primary care and helping patients determine when and what type of specialty care was needed. These organizations were able to offer prepaid care at a lower premium than the fee-for-service plans by restricting health care access to its panel of participating providers. HMOs also required the patient's primary care physician to preauthorize all services performed by specialists. A **primary care physician** or **primary care provider (PCP)** usually specializes in family medicine, internal medicine, or pediatrics. The PCP is often referred to as a **gatekeeper** in managed care systems because of the responsibility for managing a patient's health care, including arranging patient referrals to specialists. The HMO patient rarely pays a yearly deductible but may be responsible for a small copayment for each service rendered.

In the late 1960s, many studies were conducted by private agencies comparing the quality of care given by HMOs with the more traditional health care plans. Most of these studies concluded that the quality of HMO care was equal to the traditional plans even though the HMO premiums and out-of-pocket expenses were lower. Congress took note of the results of these studies and moved to encourage the growth of HMOs by enacting the Health Maintenance Organization (HMO) Act of 1973. This legislation allowed the government to assist HMOs if they met specific federal requirements. It also required employers with 25 or more employees sponsoring health insurance plans to offer a choice between a traditional fee-for-service plan and at least one federally funded HMO plan.

Government Program Reorganization

The Veterans Health Care Expansion Act of 1973 authorized the formation of a new government-sponsored program known as **CHAMPVA**, the Civilian Health and Medical Program of the Veterans Administration. This program parallels TRICARE (formerly CHAMPUS) coverage for spouses and children of veterans with 100% service-connected disabilities or who died as a result of a service-connected disability.

In 1977, the Carter administration combined the Medicare and Medicaid programs under a single administrative agency. The administrator of the **Health Care Financing Administration (HCFA)** (pronounced "hic fah") is appointed by the President and reports directly to the Secretary of Health and Human Services. Since then, HCFA has become a powerful influence on the operations of the practice of medicine.

With the Social Security Amendments of 1983, Congress also provided HCFA with the authority to establish a new Medicare prospective payment system for hospital inpatient services. Hospitals are paid a predetermined amount for each person who falls into a diagnosis-related group, better known as the DRG rate.

Procedural Coding Required

In 1984, HCFA began to require standardization of information submitted on Medicare claims. Prior to this, there were many different procedural coding systems used throughout the country on a multitude of different claim forms. HCFA required the use of one standard claim form, known as the HCFA-1500 form, for all Medicare claims. It also created the **Health Care Financing Administration Common Procedure Coding System**, better known as **HCPCS** (pronounced "hic' pics"). HCFA adopted the AMA's existing procedure code system officially titled **Physician's Current Procedural Terminology** (better known as **CPT**) in its entirety as level I in the three-level HCPCS system. HCFA created a set of national (level II) and regional (level III) codes to cover services and reimbursement issues not addressed in CPT. HCPCS codes were initially required on all Medicare and Medicaid claims, and were later required on CHAMPUS claims. Shortly thereafter commercial payers saw the value of using one standard national coding system, and they quickly moved to require the use of CPT on all claims, but were much slower in adopting HCPCS national codes. The rapid growth in computerized billing by medical practices forced the commercial payers to abandon their own customized billing forms in favor of the HCFA-1500 claim form.

Diagnosis Coding Required

In 1988, HCFA officially required the reporting of all diagnoses on claim forms using the United States version of the World Health Organization's *International Classification of Diseases*. The U.S. version is known as the ***International Classification of Diseases-9th Revision-Clinical Modification (ICD-9-CM)***. Beginning in January 1989, HCFA required all physicians to submit claims on behalf of Medicare patients regardless of the physician's participation status in the Medicare program. ICD-10-CM and ICD-10-PCS are scheduled for implementation within the next 3–5 years.

HCFA Dictates Major Changes

In late 1991, HCFA required other major billing changes on claim forms. The AMA and HCFA instigated major revisions of the entire office visit code subsection of CPT, with a new section entitled Evaluation and Management. HCFA also released a new version of the claim form known as **HCFA-1500 (1-90)**, and required its use for all government claims. This new form was quickly adopted by the commercial payers and is still in use today.

HCFA implemented a new fee schedule for Medicare services. The Omnibus Budget Reconciliation Acts (OBRA) of 1989 and 1990 were passed by Congress and mandated that HCFA replace the regional usual and reasonable payment basis used by Medicare with a fixed fee schedule calculated according to the Resource-Based Relative Value Scale system (RBRVS). **Usual and reasonable payments** were determined by Medicare and based on fees typically charged by providers in a particular region of the country. A **fee schedule** includes a list of pre-established payment amounts for health care services provided to patients; for example, a fee is assigned to each CPT code. The resulting payment system created two separate fee schedules, one for participating providers and a separate schedule for nonparticipating providers. The rate of Medicare reimbursement for nonparticipating providers was 5% less than the participating providers fee schedule. Nonparticipating providers were also forbidden to charge the patients more than 15% of the nonparticipating provider's Medicare reimbursement. This is known today as the **nonparticipating limited fee**. (The Medicare Fee Schedule, RBRVS, and limited fees issues are discussed further in Chapter 14.)

Some physicians choose to provide covered services to Medicare beneficiaries under private contracts. A **private contract** is the term Medicare uses to describe situations where a patient and physician agree not to submit a claim for a service that would otherwise be covered and paid by Medicare. These physicians "opt out" of the Medicare program for two years.

National Correct Coding Initiative

In 1996, Medicare's **national Correct Coding Initiative (CCI)** was released. The CCI was developed to correct procedural coding problems. The policies included in this initiative are based on the AMA's CPT coding conventions with additional input from national professional medical societies. Quarterly updates are made to the CCI publication's rules and conventions.

HIPAA Legislation

In the summer of 1996, Congress passed the **Health Insurance Portability and Accountability Act (HIPAA)**, which contains provisions limiting coverage restrictions for pre-existing conditions. The act includes a prohibition on the use of genetic testing information to deny health insurance coverage, and contains tax incentives for the purchase of long-term care insurance. HIPAA also requires the adoption of new standards for financial and administrative electronic transmission of claims, new standards for claims attachments, and standardization of diagnostic and procedure coding. This legislation further requires the large commercial insurers to comply with these standards within 24 months of their release by HCFA. Small health plans will be permitted an additional 12 months to comply. The act also greatly strengthens existing fraud, abuse, and confidentiality issues that are addressed in Chapter 5.

National Identifiers

The administrative simplification (AS) provision of HIPAA requires the establishment of standard identifiers for **third party payers** (e.g., insurance companies, Medicare, and Medicaid), providers, and employers. The **National Health PlanID (PlanID)** will be assigned to third party payers. The **National Provider Identifier (NPI)** will be assigned to health care providers and is proposed as an 8-position alphanumeric identifier with the eighth position serving as a numeric check digit to assist in identifying erroneous or invalid NPIs. *As of the publication of this text, the final rule for implementing the PlanID and the NPI has not been issued.* The **National Standard Employer Identifier Number (EIN)** is assigned to employers who, as sponsors of health insurance for their employees, need to be identified in health care transactions. It is assigned by the Internal Revenue Service (IRS) and has nine digits with a hyphen (00-0000000). EIN assignment by the IRS began in January 1998.

Electronic Data Interchange/Electronic Transaction Standards. **Electronic data interchange (EDI)** is the electronic transfer of health claims in a standardized format that is fast and cost effective. EDI reduces claims processing time as compared with handling paper claims, and the risk of lost paper documents is eliminated. EDI also eliminates inefficiencies associated with handling paper documents, reduces administrative burdens, lowers operating costs, and improves data quality. Approximately 400 formats for the submission of electronic health claims were used in the United States as of September 2000. This lack of standardization made it difficult and expensive to develop and update software and minimized the ability of health care providers and health plans to achieve efficiency and savings.

The Health Insurance Portability and Accountability Act of 1996 (HIPAA) included provisions to address the need for **electronic transaction standards** (a uniform language) for the electronic transmission of health information. The standards were implemented in October 2000. All health care providers and health plans that conduct EDI directly and use other electronic format(s), as well as all health care providers that decide to change from a paper format to an electronic one, must begin to use the standards (referred to by the abbreviation ANSI ASC X12N 837) for submitting electronic health care claims. **ANSI ASC X12N 837** is the abbreviation for the American National Standards Institute (ANSI), Accredited Standards Committee (ASC), Insurance Subcommittee (X12N), Claims validation tables (837).

Coding Compliance Programs

The federal government's Balanced Budget Act of 1997 includes 15 sections addressing **health care fraud** and abuse issues. In 1997, the Office of the Inspector General (OIG) audited Medicare claims and reported finding 30% error rates on claims paid in 1996. The *Department of Health and Human Services/Office of Inspector General (HHS/OIG)* provides investigative and audit services in health care fraud cases. When fraud cases are settled, the HHS/OIG determines whether a provider will be excluded from federal health care programs or if a corporate integrity agreement will be imposed on the provider. In 1999, the federal government won or negotiated more than $524 million for health care fraud cases.

Exclusion from federally sponsored programs involves the government's ability to prohibit companies or individuals from participating in Medicare, Medicaid, or other federally sponsored health care programs. In 1999, 2,976 individuals and entities were excluded.

The *corporate integrity agreement (CIA)* requires a provider to implement compliance measures for a period of five years to ensure the integrity of federal health claims submitted. CIA requires providers to: (1) hire a compliance officer and/or appoint a compliance committee, (2) develop written standards and policies, (3) implement a comprehensive employee training program, (4) audit billings to federal health care programs, (5) establish a confidential disclosure program, (6) restrict employment of ineligible persons, and (7) submit reports to the HHS/OIG. As of January 2000, more than 425 CIAs were being monitored. As a result of this study, the OIG is issuing Coding Compliance Program Guidelines for hospitals, billing agencies, home health agencies, physicians, skilled nursing facilities, and laboratories. (This issue will be addressed further in Chapter 8.)

Ambulatory Payment Classifications

Another major change occurred in 2000 when a new payment system affecting hospital billing of Medicare outpatient claims was implemented. Prospective payment of Medicare and TRICARE claims, using diagnosis related groups (DRGs), have already saved Medicare billions of dollars for inpatient hospital services. Now HCFA anticipates substantial savings in hospital-billed Medicare outpatient claims through the use of **ambulatory payment classifications (APCs)**, formerly called ambulatory patient groups (APGs), to replace fee-for-service payments for outpatient services. APCs are based on procedures performed. The rules and regulations do not affect the claims submitted for outpatient care from physician offices or clinics that are not owned by hospitals. As with other recent HCFA changes, many commercial carriers have already announced that they will adopt APCs if the payment scheme produces the substantial savings Medicare expects.

HEALTH INSURANCE COVERAGE STATISTICS

U.S. Census Bureau data from 1998 estimates that 84% of people in the U.S. are covered by some form of health insurance; and of that percentage:

- 62% are covered by employment-based plans
- 24% are covered by government plans (e.g., Medicare, Medicaid, TRICARE)
- 8% are covered by privately sponsored plans

The reason the insurance coverage percentage breakdown does not total 84% is because approximately 10% of people in the U.S. are covered by more than one insurance plan (e.g., employment-based plan plus Medicare). An estimated 44.3 million people in the U.S. have no health insurance coverage, which represents an increase of 1 million people (16%) as compared with 1997 U.S. Census Data.

THIRD-PARTY REIMBURSEMENT METHODS

The variety of third-party reimbursement schemes seen in health care practices today greatly adds to the complexity of the practice's administrative billing operations. Many practices must work concurrently with three of the following four reimbursement methods: capitation, fee-for-service, managed fee-for-service, and episode of care.

Capitation

Capitation is the method used by HMOs and some other managed care plans to pay the health care provider a fixed amount on a **per capita** (per person) basis as stipulated in the provider's contract. This fee is independent of the number of services rendered to the enrolled patients. Capitation is usually described in the HMO/managed care literature as the **PMPM payment (per member per month payment)**. This reimbursement method was initially provided only to primary care physicians. In some parts of the country capitation is paid to selected health care specialties.

Fee-for-Service Reimbursement

Fee-for-service reimbursement is a traditional form of payment to providers for services performed. Payment for services may be made by the patient or from a third-party payer.

Managed Fee-for-Service

Managed fee-for-service adds prospective (e.g., precertification prior to treatment) and retrospective review of the health care provider's treatment and/or discharge planning (coordination of patient's discharge from inpatient alternate forms of care). These utilization controls are designed to ensure that the patient is given all necessary care in the most appropriate health care setting by the most cost effective method. This reimbursement scheme is most often chosen by employers who elect to cut the cost of health care through managed care. Employers may retain the employee's ability to choose health care providers.

Episode of Care

Episode of care reimbursement is a payment method in which the health care provider receives one lump sum for all services rendered to the patient for a specific illness. One example of such reimbursement is the **global surgical fee** paid to physicians who perform major surgery. These global surgical fee payments cover the following services: a preoperative visit, the surgery, and normal postoperative care. Reimbursement for any surgical complications is usually paid on a strict fee-for-service basis.

Two examples of reimbursement methods that affect hospital payments are diagnosis-related group payments (DRGs) covering inpatient institutional services, and ambulatory payment classification (APCs) payments covering hospital outpatient services. *Neither of these two hospital reimbursement methods affect the services and claims for physician services.*

REVIEW

DEFINITION EXERCISE

Read the definitions carefully. If the statement is true, put a check mark to the left of the item number. If the statement is false, correct it without rewriting the entire statement.

1. *Insurance:* Protection against risk, loss, or ruin by a contract in which an insurance company guarantees to pay a sum of money to the policyholder in the event of some contingency such as death, accident, or illness, in return for the payment of a deductible.

2. *Liability Insurance:* A policy that covers losses to a third party caused by the insured, by an object owned by the insured, or on the premises owned by the insured.

3. *Medical Care:* Diagnostic and therapeutic measures provided by patients to members of the health care team who are sick, injured, or concerned about their health status.

4. *Health Insurance:* A contract between a policyholder and an insurance carrier or government program to reimburse the provider for all or a portion of the cost of medical treatment or preventive care rendered by health care professionals.

CHALLENGE EXERCISE

Answer the following:

1. State the original purpose of the following government programs:

   A. Medicare   **C.** TRICARE

   B. Medicaid   **D.** CHAMPVA

2. Discuss the issues that led to the formation of employer-sponsored health insurance plans in this country.

3. Compare and contrast the difference between the meaning of the terms "health care" and "medical care."

4. Explain the difference between the National Provider Identifier and the PlanID.

5. Match the reimbursement schemes listed in Group One with their correct definitions from Group Two. Place the number of the definition in Group Two to the left of the matching description in Group One.

Group One

_____ **A.** Ambulatory Payment Classification (APC)

_____ **B.** Capitation

_____ **C.** Fee-for-service

_____ **D.** Episode of Care

_____ **E.** Fee-for-service with utilization

Group Two

1. Individual services are itemized, priced, and charged to the patient's account.

2. A lump-sum payment for all services rendered to the patient for a specific illness or injury.

3. Prospective and retrospective review of the patient's records, the treatment/discharge plan, with itemization and pricing of patient services charged to the patient's individual account.

4. A percentage of the cost of each service the patient must pay to a provider to put a health insurance policy in force.

5. Prospective payment system implemented for outpatient care.

6. Provider is paid a fixed amount for all covered lives assigned to the primary care physician.

7. Charge established by payers to reimburse providers for services rendered to patients.

Managed Health Care

OBJECTIVES Upon successful completion of this chapter, you should be able to:

1. Define the following terms, phrases, and abbreviations:

managed health care
managed care
enrollees
Federal Health Maintenance Organization Assistance Act of 1973 (HMO Act of 1973)
federally qualified HMO
Employee Retirement Income Security Act of 1974 (ERISA)
Tax Equity and Fiscal Responsibility Act of 1982 (TEFRA)
Medicare Risk Program
risk contract
competitive medical plan (CMP)
Omnibus Budget Reconciliation Act of 1981 (OBRA)
Preferred Provider Health Care Act of 1985
Consolidated Omnibus Budget Reconciliation Act of 1985 (COBRA)
Amendment to the HMO Act of 1973
Health Plan Employer Data and Information Set (HEDIS)
HCFA's Office of Managed Care
The Health Insurance Portability and Accountability Act of 1996 (HIPAA)
Balanced Budget Act of 1997
managed care organization (MCO)
covered lives
capitation

primary care provider (PCP)
gatekeeper
mandates
quality assurance program
legislation
Quality Improvement System for Managed Care (QISMC)
standards
report card
utilization management (UM)
preadmission review
preadmission certification (PAC)
preauthorization (prior authorization)
concurrent review
discharge planning
utilization review organization (URO)
third-party administrator (TPA)
case management
second surgical opinion
gag clause
physician incentive
Physician Incentive Plan
exclusive provider organization (EPO)
integrated delivery system (IDS)
physician-hospital organization (PHO)
management service organization (MSO)
group practice without walls (GPWW)
integrated provider organization (IPO)

medical foundation
health maintenance organization (HMO)
traditional health insurance coverage
fee-for-service
copayment (copay)
deductible
closed-panel HMO
direct contract model
group model
individual practice association (IPA)
independent practice association (IPA)
network model
staff model
point-of-service plan (POS)
self-referral
preferred provider organization (PPO)
triple option plan
cafeteria plan
adverse selection
risk pool
National Committee for Quality Assurance (NCQA)
accreditation
standards
survey
oversight
Joint Commission on Accreditation of Healthcare Organizations (JCAHO)

2. List the eight principles of managed care.

3. List and describe the six managed care models.

4. List and describe the five HMO models.

5. List the three levels of NCQA accreditation.

6. Describe the influence of managed care programs on medical practice's administrative procedures.

| INTRODUCTION | **Managed health care** (or **managed care**) combines health care delivery with the financing of services provided. The intent was to replace conventional fee-for-service plans with more affordable quality care to health care consumers and providers who agreed to certain restrictions (e.g., patients would receive care only from providers who are members of a managed care organization.) |

HISTORY OF MANAGED HEALTH CARE

Managed health care (or managed care) was developed as a way to provide affordable, comprehensive, prepaid health care services to **enrollees** (employees and dependents who join a managed care plan; known as beneficiaries in private insurance plans). In 1929, the first managed care programs were created when a farmers' cooperative in Elk City, Oklahoma was formed and a California medical group provided prepaid health care services to Los Angeles Department of Water and Power employees and their dependents.

In 1933, Dr. Sidney Garfield established prepaid health care services for Southern California construction workers, and in 1938 he joined businessman Henry Kaiser to create a group-practice prepayment plan for Grand Coulee Dam construction workers, which was open to employees and their families. Dr. Garfield also established group-practice prepayment plans for Kaiser shipyard (California) and steel mill (Washington) employees and their families, eventually serving 200,000 members. In 1955, the nationally recognized health maintenance organization, Kaiser-Permanente, was created.

INTERNET LINK

For more information about Kaiser Permanente, visit www.kaiserpermanente.org.

While Dr. Garfield was establishing a prepayment plan for Kaiser employees during World War II, the federal War Labor Board ruled that employers could offer employees fringe benefits of up to five percent. Consequently, employers began offering health care benefits to employees (who were in short supply during World War II), and the modern U.S. employer-based insurance system was created. During the 1960s, health care costs dramatically increased, which resulted in debates on how to improve the health care delivery system. By 1970, many states had restricted the development and/or operation of HMOs, while some employers and labor unions supported the concept of managed care. In 1971, President Nixon's State of the Union address called for "new programs to encourage preventive medicine by attacking the causes of disease and injury, and by providing incentives for doctors to keep people well, rather than just to treat them when they are sick." Federal legislation was first enacted in 1983 to encourage the growth of privately sponsored managed care systems, and subsequent legislation has been implemented in response to health care industry needs and changes (see Table 3-1).

Table 3-1 *Timeline for managed health care federal legislation*

FEDERAL LEGISLATIVE TIMELINE–MANAGED HEALTH CARE

YEAR	LEGISLATIVE TITLE	LEGISLATIVE SUMMARY
1973	**Federal Health Maintenance Organization Assistance Act of 1973 (HMO Act of 1973)**	▪ authorized grants and loans to develop HMOs under private sponsorship ▪ defined a **federally qualified HMO** (certified to provide health care services to Medicare and Medicaid enrollees) as one that has applied for and met federal standards established in the HMO Act of 1973 ▪ required most employers with more than 25 employees to offer HMO coverage if local plans were available
1974	**Employee Retirement Income Security Act of 1974 (ERISA)**	▪ mandated reporting and disclosure requirements for group life and health plans (including managed care plans) ▪ permitted large employers to self-insure employee health care benefits ▪ exempted large employers from taxes on health insurance premium
1982	**Tax Equity and Fiscal Responsibility Act of 1982 (TEFRA)**	▪ modified the HMO Act of 1973 ▪ created **Medicare Risk Programs**, which allowed federally qualified HMOs and competitive medical plans (CMPs) that met specified Medicare requirements to provide Medicare covered services under a risk contract ▪ defined **risk contract** as an arrangement among providers to provide capitated (fixed, prepaid basis) health care services to Medicare beneficiaries ▪ defined **competitive medical plan (CMP)** as an HMO that meets federal eligibility requirements for a Medicare risk contract, but is not licensed as a federally qualified plan.
1981	**Omnibus Budget Reconciliation Act of 1981 (OBRA)**	▪ provided states with flexibility to establish HMOs for Medicare and Medicaid programs ▪ increased enrollment resulted
1985	**Preferred Provider Health Care Act of 1985**	▪ eased restrictions on preferred provider organizations (PPOs) ▪ allowed subscribers to seek health care from providers outside of the PPO

(Continues)

Table 3-1 *Timeline for managed health care federal legislation (Continued)*

FEDERAL LEGISLATIVE TIMELINE–MANAGED HEALTH CARE

YEAR	LEGISLATIVE TITLE	LEGISLATIVE SUMMARY
1985	**Consolidated Omnibus Budget Reconciliation Act of 1985 (COBRA)**	▪ established an employee's right to continue health care coverage beyond scheduled benefit termination date (including HMO coverage)
1988	**Amendment to the HMO Act of 1973**	▪ allowed federally qualified HMOs to permit members to occasionally use non-HMO physicians and be partially reimbursed
1989	**Health Plan Employer Data and Information Set (HEDIS)** is developed by National Committee for Quality Assurance (NCQA)	▪ created standards to assess managed care systems in terms of membership, utilization of services, quality, access, health plan management and activities, and financial indicators
1994	**HCFA's Office of Managed Care** is established	▪ facilitated innovation and competition among Medicare HMOs
1996	**The Health Insurance Portability and Accountability Act of 1996 (HIPAA)**	▪ limited exclusions for pre-existing condition ▪ created federal standards for insurers, health maintenance organizations (HMOs), and employer plans, including those who self-insure ▪ provided credit for prior health coverage and a process for transmitting certificates and other information concerning prior coverage to a new group health plan ▪ allowed individuals to enroll in health coverage when they lost other health coverage or had a new dependent ▪ prohibited discrimination against employees and their dependents based on health status (in terms of enrollment and establishment of premiums) ▪ guaranteed availability of health insurance coverage for small employers and renewal of health insurance coverage in both small and large group markets ▪ preserved states' traditional role in regulating health insurance (including state flexibility to provide greater protections) by limiting federal pre-emption
1997	**Balanced Budget Act of 1997**	▪ mandated major revision of Medicare and Medicaid programs, which reduced reimbursement to providers ▪ encouraged formation of provider service networks (PSNs) and provider service organizations (PSOs) ▪ allowed physicians, hospitals and other health care professionals to contract directly with the government to offer services to Medicare ▪ initiated funding for the States Children's Health Insurance Program (SCHIP)

MANAGED CARE ORGANIZATIONS

A **managed care organization (MCO)** is responsible for the health of a group of enrollees (called **covered lives**), and an MCO can be a health plan, hospital, physician group, or health system. Unlike traditional fee-for-service plans, which reimburse providers for individual health care services rendered, managed care is financed according to a method called **capitation**, where providers accept pre-established payments for providing health care services to enrollees over a period of time (usually one year). If the physician provides services that cost less than the capitation amount, there is a profit (which the physician keeps). If services provided to subscribers cost more than the capitation amount, the physician loses money.

The concentration of MCOs varies widely across the country (Figure 3-1), with the heaviest concentration occurring in California and Rhode Island.

EXAMPLE

In June, Hillcrest Medical Group received a capitated payment of $15,000 for the 150 members (enrollees) of the ABC Managed Care Health Plan. The Group spent $12,500 of the capitated payment on preventive, chronic, and acute health care services provided to member patients. The services were provided at the Group's office and local hospital, which included inpatient,

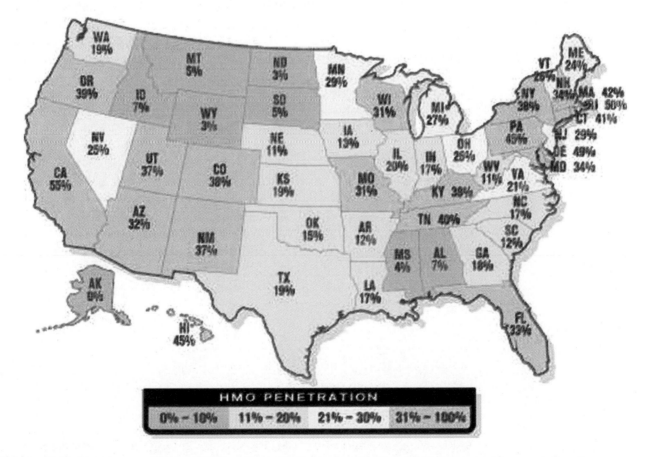

Figure 3-1 2000 Managed Care Profile Map—HMO Penetration Rates (Reprinted with permission from Medical Data International, Inc. Copyright 2000, Medical Data International, Inc., www.medicaldata.com)

outpatient, and emergency department care. (The Group is responsible for paying the enrollees' hospital bills.) In this scenario, health care services provided to enrollees cost less than the capitated payment received. The Hillcrest Medical Group, therefore, made a profit of $2,500. If health care services had cost more than the capitated amount of $15,000, the Group would have experienced a loss.

Gatekeepers

Managed care plan enrollees receive care from a primary care provider that is selected from a list of participating providers. The **primary care provider (PCP)** is responsible for supervising and coordinating health care services for enrollees and preauthorizing referrals to specialists and inpatient hospital admissions (except in emergencies). The PCP serves as a **gatekeeper** by providing essential health care services at the lowest possible cost and avoiding nonessential care.

Quality Assurance

Managed care plans that are "federally qualified" and those that must comply with state quality review **mandates** (laws) are required to establish quality assurance programs. A **quality assurance program** includes activities that assess the quality of care provided in a health care setting. Many states have enacted **legislation** (laws) requiring quality assurance to be conducted by private sector managed care organizations. The types of quality reviews performed include government oversight, patient satisfaction surveys, data collected from grievance procedures, and reviews conducted by independent organizations. Independent organizations that perform reviews include accreditation agencies such as the National Committee for Quality Assurance and Joint Commission on Accreditation of Healthcare Organizations.

Medicare established the **Quality Improvement System for Managed Care (QISMC)** to assure the accountability of managed care plans in terms of objective, measurable **standards** (requirements). Plans are required to meet minimum performance levels and to show demonstrable and measurable improvement in specified broad clinical areas (e.g., preventive services, acute ambulatory care, chronic care, and hospital care) based on performance improvement projects that each plan identifies. The Health Plan Employer Data and Information Set (HEDIS), sponsored by the National Committee for Quality Assurance, consists of performance measures used to evaluate managed care plans (e.g., rate of Pap smears performed among women of a certain age). The National Committee for Quality Assurance (NCQA) reviews managed care plans and develops report cards to allow health care consumers to make informed decisions when selecting a plan. The **report card** contains data regarding a managed care plan's quality, utilization, customer satisfaction, administrative effectiveness, financial stability and cost control.

INTERNET LINK

The NCQA's Web site at www.hprc.ncqa.org allows health care consumers to create a customized report card or to view report cards for all managed care plans.

Utilization Management

Utilization management (UM) involves reviewing the appropriateness and necessity of health care provided to patients. Inpatient hospitalization may require preadmission certification (PAC) or **preadmission review**.

Preadmission certification (PAC) reviews the medical necessity of inpatient care prior to the patient's admission, and a certificate or authorization is issued by the managed care plan. Managed care plans also conduct **preadmission review** of provider recommendations for inpatient care to make certain that an admission is medically necessary and appropriate. These two functions differ from **preauthorization** (or **prior authorization**) performed by a managed care plan that grants prior approval for reimbursement of a health care service (e.g., elective surgery). **Concurrent review** may also occur to ensure the medical necessity of tests and procedures ordered during an inpatient hospitalization. Because a goal of managed care is to discharge inpatients on a timely basis, **discharge planning** is also conducted to arrange health care services required after discharge from the hospital (e.g., nursing facility care or home health care).

A **utilization review organization (URO)**, or **third-party administrator (TPA)**, establishes a utilization review (or utilization management) program to evaluate the medical necessity, appropriateness, and efficient use of health care services, procedures, and facilities. Self-insured plans that do not have the expertise to perform utilization management will contract a URO (or TPA) to oversee the administration of funds set aside to cover employee medical expenses and authorize medically necessary treatments and the payment of legitimate claims for services rendered. The URO (or TPA) also conducts a retrospective utilization review, which reviews the medical necessity and appropriateness of health care services provided to the patient.

Case Management

Case management involves the development of patient care plans for the coordination and provision of care for complicated cases in a cost-effective manner. For example, instead of admitting a patient to the hospital, a managed care plan might authorize 24-hour home health care services when appropriate.

Second Surgical Opinions

Prior to scheduling elective surgery, managed care plans often require a **second surgical opinion** in which a second physician is asked to evaluate the necessity of surgery and recommend the most economical, appropriate facility in which to perform the surgery (e.g., outpatient clinic or doctor's office versus inpatient hospitalization).

Gag Clauses

Medicare and many states prohibit managed care contracts from containing **gag clauses**, which prevent providers from discussing all treatment options with patients, whether or not the plan would provide reimbursement for services. HCFA has stated that Medicare beneficiaries are entitled to advice from their physicians on medically necessary treatment options that may be appropriate for their condition or disease. Since a gag clause would have the practical effect of prohibiting a physician from giving a patient the full range of advice and counsel that is clinically appropriate, it would result in the managed care plan not providing all covered Medicare services to its enrollees, in violation of the managed care plan's responsibilities.

Physician Incentives

Physician incentives include payments made directly or indirectly to health care providers to serve as encouragement to reduce or limit services (e.g., discharge an inpatient from the hospital more quickly) so as to save money for the managed care plan. The federal **Physician Incentive Plan** requires managed care plans that contract with Medicare or Medicaid to disclose information about physician incentive plans to HCFA or State Medicaid agencies, before a new or renewed contract receives final approval.

SIX MANAGED CARE MODELS

Managed care originally focused on cost reductions by restricting health care access through utilization management and availability of limited benefits. Managed care organizations (MCOs) were created to manage benefits and to develop participating provider networks. Managed care can now be categorized according to six models:

1. Exclusive Provider Organization (EPO)

2. Integrated Delivery System (IDS)

3. Health Maintenance Organization (HMO)
   a. direct contract model
   b. group model
   c. individual practice association (IPA)
   d. network model
   e. staff model

4. Point-of-Service Plan (POS)

5. Preferred Provider Organization (PPO)

6. Triple Option Plan

Exclusive Provider Organization (EPO)

An **exclusive provider organization (EPO)** is a managed care plan that provides benefits to subscribers if they receive services from network providers. A network provider is a physician or health care facility under contract to the managed care plan. Usually, network providers sign exclusive contracts with the EPO, which means they cannot contract with other managed care plans. Subscribers are generally required to coordinate health care services through their primary care physician (PCP). EPOs are regulated by state insurance departments (unlike HMOs that are regulated by either the state commerce or department of corporations, depending on state requirements).

Integrated Delivery System (IDS)

An **integrated delivery system (IDS)** is an organization of affiliated providers sites (e.g., hospitals, ambulatory surgical centers, or physician groups) that offer joint health care services to subscribers. Models include physician-hospital organizations, management service organizations, group practices without walls, integrated provider organizations, and medical foundations. A **physician-hospital organization (PHO)** is owned by hospital(s) and physician groups that obtain managed care plan contracts; physicians maintain their own practices and provide health care services to plan members. A **management service organization (MSO)** is usually owned by physicians or a hospital and provides practice management (administrative and support) services to individual physician practices. A **group practice without walls (GPWW)** establishes a contract that allows physicians to maintain their own offices and share services (e.g., appointment scheduling and billing). An **integrated provider organization (IPO)** manages the delivery of health care services offered by hospitals, physicians (who are employees of the IPO), and other health care organizations (e.g., an ambulatory surgery clinic and a nursing facility). A **medical foundation** is a nonprofit organization that contracts with, and acquires the clinical and business assets of physician practices; the foundation is assigned a provider number and manages the practice's business. An integrated delivery system may also be referred to by any of the following names: integrated service network (ISN), delivery system, vertically integrated plan (VIP), vertically integrated system, horizontally integrated system, health delivery network, or accountable health plan.

INTERNET LINK

Go to www.healtheast.org to view information about HealthEast, an integrated care delivery system located in St. Paul, Minnesota, that provides acute care, chronic care, senior services, community-based services, ambulatory/outpatient services, physician clinics, and preventive services.

Health Maintenance Organizations (HMO)

A **health maintenance organization (HMO)** is an alternative to traditional group health insurance coverage, and provides comprehensive health care services to voluntarily enrolled members on a prepaid basis. **Traditional health insurance coverage** is usually provided on a fee-for-service basis, and payment is based on health care services rendered. **Fee-for-service** is a payment system in which reimbursement increases if the health care service fees increase, if multiple units of service are provided, or if more expensive services are provided instead of less expensive services (e.g., brand-name vs. generic prescription medication).

HMOs provide preventive care services to promote "wellness" or good health, thus reducing the overall cost of medical care. Annual physical examinations are encouraged for the early detection of health problems. Health risk assessment instruments (surveys) and resources are also available to subscribers. A primary care provider (PCP) assigned to each subscriber is responsible for coordinating health care services and referring subscribers to other health care providers.

HMOs often require patients to pay a **copayment** (or **copay**), which is a fee paid by the patient to the provider at the time health care services are rendered. Copayments range from $1 to $25 per visit, and some services are exempt because coinsurance payments are required instead. Coinsurance is usually associated with traditional health insurance plans, and can apply to managed care plans when out-of-network (nonparticipating) providers render health care services to plan subscribers. Generally, the coinsurance amount is a fixed percentage (e.g., 50% of mental health care services of an out-of-network provider) for which the subscriber is financially responsible, usually after a deductible has been met. The **deductible** (another term usually associated with traditional health insurance plans) is the amount of money the subscriber must pay before plan benefits are reimbursable.

HMOs must meet the requirements of the HMO Act of 1973 as well as rules and regulations of individual states. There are five HMO models: direct contract model, group model, individual practice association, network model, and staff model. Note that group model and staff model HMOs are referred to as **closed-panel HMOs**, in which health care services are provided in an

HMO-owned health center or satellite clinic or by physicians who belong to a specially formed medical group that serves the HMO. Explanations of each of the five models follows.

- **direct contract model**—contracted health care services are delivered to subscribers by *individual physicians* in the community.

- **group model**—contracted health care services are delivered to subscribers by *participating physicians who are members of an independent multi-specialty group practice.* The HMO reimburses the physician group, which is then responsible for reimbursing physician members and contracted health care facilities (e.g., hospitals). The physician group can be owned or managed by the HMO, or it can simply contract with the HMO. The group model is considered a closed-panel HMO.

- **individual practice association or independent practice association (IPA)**—contracted health care services are delivered to subscribers by *physicians who remain in their independent office settings.* The IPA is an intermediary (e.g., physician association) that negotiates the HMO contract and receives and manages the capitation payment from the HMO so that physicians are paid on either a fee-for-service basis or a capitation basis.

- **network model**—contracted health care services are provided to subscribers by *two or more physician multi-specialty group practices.*

- **staff model**—health care services are provided to subscribers by *physicians employed by the HMO.* Premiums and other revenue are paid to the HMO. Usually, all ambulatory care services are provided within HMO corporate buildings. The staff model is a closed-panel HMO.

Point-of-Service Plan (POS)

To create flexibility in managed care plans, some HMOs and PPOs (preferred provider organizations) have implemented a **point-of-service plan (POS)**, where patients have freedom to use the HMO panel of providers or to self-refer to non-HMO providers. If the enrollee chooses to receive all medical care from the HMO network of health care providers or obtains an authorization from the POS primary care physician for specialty care outside the HMO network, the enrollee pays only the regular copayment, or small visit charges. Also no deductible or coinsurance responsibility applies. If the enrollee sees a non-HMO panel specialist without a referral from the primary care physician, this is known as a **self-referral**. The enrollee will have greater out-of-pocket expenses as they must pay both a large deductible (usually $200 to $250) and the 20% to 25% coinsurance charges similar to those paid by persons with fee-for-service plans.

Preferred Provider Organization

A **preferred provider organization (PPO)** is a network of physicians and hospitals that have joined together to contract with insurance companies, employers or other organizations to provide health care to subscribers for a discounted fee. PPOs do not routinely establish contracts for laboratory or pharmacy services, but they do offer reduced-rate contracts with specific hospitals. Most PPOs are open-ended plans allowing patients to use non-PPO providers in exchange for larger out-of-pocket expenses. Premiums, deductibles, and copayments are usually higher than those paid for HMOs, but lower than regular fee-for-service plans.

Triple Option Plan

A **triple option plan** is usually offered by either a single insurance plan or as a joint venture among two or more insurance carriers, and provides subscribers or employees with a choice of HMO, PPO, or traditional health insurance plans. It is also called a **cafeteria plan** because of different benefit plans and extra coverage options provided through the insurer or third party administrator. Triple option plans are intended to prevent the problem of covering members who are sicker than the general population (called **adverse selection**). A **risk pool** is created when a number of people are grouped for insurance purposes (e.g., employees of an organization); the cost of health care coverage is determined by employees' health status, age, sex, and occupation.

ACCREDITATION OF MANAGED CARE ORGANIZATIONS

Two groups evaluate managed care organizations—the National Committee for Quality Assurance (NCQA) and the Joint Commission on Accreditation of Healthcare Organizations (JCAHO, pronounced jāy cō).

INTERNET LINKS

Visit the NCQA at www.ncqa.org.
Visit the JCAHO at www.jcaho.org.

National Committee for Quality Assurance (NCQA)

The **National Committee for Quality Assurance (NCQA)**, of Washington D.C., is a private, not-for-profit organization that assesses the quality of managed care plans in the United States and releases the data to the public for their consideration when selecting a managed care plan. The NCQA began accrediting managed care programs in 1991 when a need for consistent, independent information about the quality of care provided to patients was originally identified. **Accreditation** is a voluntary process that a health care facility or organization (e.g., hospital or managed care plan) undergoes to demonstrate that it has met standards beyond those required by law. Accreditation organizations develop **standards** (requirements) that are reviewed during a **survey** (evaluation) process that is conducted both off-site (e.g., managed care plan submits an initial document for review) and on-site (at the managed care plan's facilities).

The NCQA's current accreditation process, which involves almost half of the nation's HMOs, evaluates managed care plans according to five areas:

- *access and service* (availability of appropriate health care services)
- *qualified providers* (assessment of provider licensure, training, and patient ratings)
- *staying healthy* (preventive care services provided)
- *getting better* (assessment of care provided to patients who become sick and the evaluation of new procedures, medications and technology to ensure safe and effective patient care)
- *living with illness* (health care provided to chronically ill patients)

In 2000, the NCQA revised its accreditation process to include the evaluation of HEDIS performance measures, which are based on the care and service provided to patients (e.g., diabetes management, immunization rates and member satisfaction). The Health Plan Employer Data and Information Set (HEDIS) contains data elements (e.g., advising smokers to quit) that are collected, evaluated, and published to help people compare the performance of managed health care plans. The NCQA also revised its accreditation status levels, which are assigned by a national **oversight** (supervising) committee of physicians who analyze NCQA accreditation team findings. The new accreditation levels include:

- *excellent* (managed care plan met or exceeded NCQA standards and achieved high-level HEDIS results)
- *commendable* (managed care plan met or exceeded NCQA standards; this status is equivalent to the former "full" accreditation status)
- *accredited* (managed care plan met most NCQA standards; this status is equivalent to the former "one-year" status)
- *provisional* (managed care plan met some, but not all, NCQA basic standards)
- *denied* (managed care plan did not meet NCQA standards)

In addition, the NCQA developed the following levels:

- *suspended* (NCQA withdraws accreditation status of a managed care plan until corrective action is completed)
- *under review* (managed care plan requests review of initial accreditation status awarded; for example, a plan is awarded *accredited* status and the plan requests a review to determine whether the status can be upgraded to *commendable* or *excellent*)
- *discretionary review* (managed care plans that undergo NCQA survey to assess the appropriateness of current accreditation status)
- *initial decision pending* (managed care plan has undergone its first survey but an accreditation status not yet been determined)
- *future review scheduled* (managed care plan is scheduled to undergo an initial survey)

In 2000, the NCQA implemented an accreditation program for preferred provider organizations (PPOs) that incorporates requirements similar to the managed care organization accreditation program. PPO plans are now evaluated according to the following criteria:

- *consumer protection*
- *member services*
- *access to care*
- *provider credentialing*
- *oversight*

Joint Commission on Accreditation of Healthcare Organizations (JCAHO)

The **Joint Commission on Accreditation of Healthcare Organizations (JCAHO),** located in Oakbrook Terrace, Illinois, provides voluntary accreditation of a variety of health care organizations (e.g., hospitals, long-term care and ambulatory care facilities). In 1989, the accreditation program for managed care was implemented as part of the 1990 Ambulatory Care Accreditation Program. In 1997, accreditation for PPOs was created under the Network

Accreditation Program. In that same year, the accreditation program for managed behavioral health care organizations was implemented under the Behavioral Health Care Accreditation Program.

GOVERNMENT MANAGED CARE VENTURES

In an effort to control the upward spiral of health care costs for millions of persons who are enrolled in Medicare, Medicaid, and TRICARE programs, state and federal governments have embraced some form of managed care. Because each one of the programs has developed a unique approach to managed care, these details are discussed within the individual chapters for these programs (Chapters 14 through 16).

EFFECTS OF MANAGED CARE ON ADMINISTRATIVE PROCEDURES IN A PHYSICIAN'S PRACTICE

Managed care programs have tremendous impact on a practice's administrative procedures. A sampling of some procedures that must be in place include:

- Separate bookkeeping systems for each capitated plan to ensure financial viability of the contract.
- A tracking system for primary care physicians for preauthorization of specialty care and documented requests for receipt of the specialist's treatment plan or consultation report.
- A tracking system for specialists for treatment and authorization, their effective dates, and the dates required treatment/discharge reports were forwarded to the primary care physician or case manager.
- Preauthorization and/or precertification for all hospitalizations; and continued certification if the patient's condition requires extension of the number of authorized days.
- Up-to-date lists for referrals to participating health care providers, hospitals, and diagnostic test facilities used by the practice.
- Up-to-date list of special administrative procedures required by each MCO contract.
- Maintenance of up-to-date lists of patient copayments and fees for each plan the providers use.
- Special new patient intake interviews to ensure preauthorization and explain out-of-network requirements if patient is self-referring.
- Additional paperwork for specialists to complete and file with treatment and discharge plans.
- Some case managers require notification if a patient fails to keep a preauthorized appointment.
- Some MCOs require the attachment of preauthorization documentation to all health insurance claim forms.

REVIEW

DEFINITION EXERCISE

Read the definitions carefully. If the statement is true, put a check mark to the left of the item number. If the statement is false, correct it.

1. NCQA: A nonprofit organization that evaluates HMOs according to criteria designed to measure the HMO's ability to deliver good health care.

2. MCO: A system for operating a health insurance program that employs case managers to treat all patients.

CHALLENGE EXERCISE

Answer the following:

1. Describe the function of a utilization review organization (URO).

2. List the characteristics of a managed care organization.

3. Identify the six major MCO models and their characteristics.

4. Describe the function of the JCAHO.

5. List eight ways managed care programs have influenced medical practice administrative procedures.

Life Cycle of an Insurance Claim

4
Four

Upon successful completion of this chapter, you should be able to:

1. Define the following terms, phrases, and abbreviations:

new patient	encounter form	uncovered procedure
established patient	charge slip	noncovered procedure
new patient intake interview	fee ticket	uncovered benefit
participating provider (PAR)	routing form	"not medically necessary service"
PAR provider	superbill	unauthorized service
in-network provider	patient ledger	common data file
nonparticipating provider (nonPAR)	patient account record	allowed charge
	manual daily accounts receivable journal	allowable charge
out-of-network provider		eligible amount
primary care physician (PCP)	day sheet	maximum allowed amount
health care specialist	copayment	deductible
case manager	copay	Explanation of Benefits (EOB) form
primary care referral form	coinsurance payment	
policyholder	coinsurance	source document
subscriber	HCFA-1500	pre-existing condition
primary insurance	accept assignment	beneficiary
birthday rule		

2. Explain the necessity of conducting a new patient intake interview before the patient is scheduled for an initial appointment.
3. Explain how a primary care provider verifies a new patient's eligibility for in-network services.
4. Discuss the authorization process for a patient requesting an initial appointment with a health care specialist.
5. Discuss the process for obtaining authorization for additional treatment by a health care specialist.
6. Discuss the life cycle of an insurance claim from origination of the charge slip to transfer of charges to the ledger card or computer account and subsequently to a claim form.
7. Discuss an insurance company's claims review process.
8. Determine the primary and secondary insurance carriers for adults and children covered by two insurance plans.

This chapter provides an overview of the development of a health insurance claim in the health care provider's office and the major steps taken in processing that claim by the insurance company.

■ **NOTE:** Figures 4-5 (page 48) and 4-8 (page 53) through 4-13 (page 60) are illustrations of documents generated during the life cycle of an insurance claim for a single encounter with the same patient. ■

DEVELOPMENT OF THE CLAIM

The development of an insurance claim begins when the patient contacts a health care provider's office and schedules an appointment. At this time, it is important to determine whether the patient is requesting an initial appointment or is returning to the practice for additional services. The preclinical interview and check-in of a new patient is more extensive than that for an established patient.

A **new patient** to a physician's office is defined as a person who has not received any professional services from the health care provider or another provider of the same specialty in the same group practice within the last 36 months. An **established patient** is a person who has been seen within the last 36 months by the health care provider or another provider of the same specialty in the same group practice.

■ **NOTE:** The definition of a new patient for a hospital is one who does not have an existing patient record because of having never received health care services. ■

The development of a claim consists of three parts:

- Preclinical interview and check-in
- Clinical assessment and treatment
- Postclinical patient check-out

Administrative staff responsibilities for preclinical and postclinical procedures are discussed in this chapter for practices that are not computerized. Each office develops its own procedures. The method described in this chapter is an example. The icon ☑ identifies steps completed for computerized practices.

NEW PATIENT INTERVIEW AND CHECK-IN PROCEDURE

Step 1. Perform a new patient intake interview.

Before scheduling an initial appointment for a new patient, perform a **new patient intake interview** to gather preliminary data. This ensures that the patient has called the appropriate office for an appointment and that the patient's insurance eligibility and benefit status are verified.

The new patient intake interview is a good time to advise the patient to bring to the appointment the appropriate insurance card and any special forms or health insurance policy information.

The following information should be obtained from the patient:

A. Patient's name, address, phone number, and birthdate. In the case of a minor child, obtain the name of the parent or guardian requesting the appointment.

B. The reason the patient is calling for an appointment.

C. Whether the patient is enrolled in an insurance program. If the patient is not enrolled, go directly to Step 3. If the patient is enrolled, identify the insurance company plan, the identification numbers, and the name of the policyholder.

The patient has a right to know whether or not the provider is a participating provider with their insurance plan. A **participating provider (PAR)** (also known as a **PAR provider** or an **in-network provider**) has a contract with the insurance company to provide medical services to subscribers and to accept the insurance company's allowed fee for the procedure and/or service performed.

Patients in managed care plans may elect to see **nonparticipating providers** (also known as **nonPAR** or **out-of-network providers**), but they will incur higher out-of-pocket expenses in doing so. A nonparticipating provider has no contractual relationship with the patient's insurance company and generally has a legal right to expect the patient to pay the difference between the insurance-allowed fee and the amount charged.

Step 2. Verify insurance eligibility and benefit status.

The patient's eligibility for an insurance plan and the plan's benefits need to be verified and clarified before the patient is scheduled for the initial appointment. How this check is performed will depend on the health care provider status as either primary care physician or health care specialist. A **primary care physician (PCP)** is a family practitioner, internist, pediatrician, and in some insurance plans, an obstetrician and/or gynecologist, responsible for providing all routine primary health care for the patient. A **health care specialist** is a health care provider who is not a primary care physician and practices in a specialized area of medicine such as neurology, ophthalmology, and endocrinology.

Patient eligibility for PCP services can be determined by locating the patient's name on the insurance plan's current list of enrollees. Call the insurance company if the name does not appear on the list to determine the patient's eligibility status and policy benefits.

Step 3. Schedule the patient's appointment.

Managed care patients who schedule appointments with a specialist must obtain preauthorization from their PCP or case manager. It is the patient's responsibility to request and obtain the initial preauthorization from the PCP or case manager. This process also requires communication between the physician's office that will provide the service and the authorizing entity (e.g., insurance company). A **case manager** is a nurse or other medically trained person employed by the health insurance company to coordinate the health care of patients with long-term chronic conditions.

Preauthorization generally takes one of two forms:

1. The PCP issues a **primary care referral form**, which is either hand-carried by the patient or faxed to the specialist or ancillary services provider. This form may be a special form provided by the insurance company (see Figure 4-1) or a special form developed by state governments to simplify the referral process by requiring the use of a standard state uniform form (see a sample in Figure 4-2).

Managed Care Insurance Company

PRIMARY CARE PROVIDER PREAUTHORIZATION FORM FOR CONSULTATION

Patient Name	Preauthorization Number	Name of Consulting Physician
Member Identification Number	Member Name (last, First, MI)	Member Birthdate
Primary Care Physician Identification Number	Name of Primary Care Physician (PCP)	PCP Phone Number

This referral authorizes the services listed below. All services must be rendered by provider stated below.

Diagnosis

Medical History

Reason for Referral

Consultant may provide services listed below. All authorized visits must occur within 90 days of date authorized by PCP. If surgical procedure is listed below, Consultant Treatment Plan Is not required. For initial consultation, specialist must submit Consultant Treatment Report of findings and treatment recommendations.

Diagnostic tests indicated:

Procedure(s) to be performed:

Primary Care Physician Signature	Date

Consultant billing procedures for services authorized by Primary Care Physician:

1. Enter Preauthorization Number listed above in Block 23 of the HCFA-1500 form.

2. For first submission, submit HCFA-1500 with original Preauthorization Form for PCP Referral.

3. For subsequent submissions, no attachments are required.

4. Consultant must complete Consultant Treatment Plan to obtain authorization for any surgical procedure not specified on the Preauthorization Form PCP Referral.

Improperly completed forms will be returned.

Figure 4-1 PCP preauthorization form for consultation

Maryland Uniform Consultation Referral Form

Date of Referral:	Carrier Information:

Patient Information:	Name:
Name (Last, First, MI)	Address:
Date of Birth (MM/DD/YYYY) Phone: ( )	
Member #:	Phone Number: ( )
Site #:	Facsimile / Data #: ( )

Primary or Requesting Provider:

Name: (Last, First, MI)		Specialty:
Institution / Group Name:	Provider ID #: 1	Provider ID #: 2 (If Required)
Address: (Street #, City, State, Zip)		
Phone Number: ( )	Facsimile / Data Number: ( )	

Consultant / Facility / Provider:

Name: (Last, First, MI)		Specialty:
Institution / Group Name:	Provider ID #: 1	Provider ID #: 2 (If Required)
Address: (Street #, City, State, Zip)		
Phone Number: ( )	Facsimile / Data Number: ( )	

Referral Information:

Reason for Referral:

Brief History, Diagnosis and Test Results: _____

_____

Services Desired: Provide Care as indicated:

☐ Initial Consultation Only
☐ Diagnostic Test: (specify) _____
☐ Consultation with Specific Procedures: (specify) _____
_____
☐ Specific Treatment: _____
☐ Global OB Care & Delivery
☐ Other: (explain) _____

Place of Service:

☐ Office
☐ Outpatient Medical/Surgical Center*
☐ Radiology   ☐ Laboratory
☐ Inpatient Hospital*
☐ Extended Care Facility*
☐ Other: (explain)
* (Specific Facility Must be Named)

Number of visits: (If blank, 1 visit is assumed)	Authorization #: (If Required)	Referral is Valid Until: (Date) (See Carrier Instructions)
Signature: (Individual Completing This Form)		Authorizing Signature (If Required)

Referral certification is not a guarantee of payment. Payment of benefits is subject to a member's eligibility on the date that the service is rendered and to any other contractual provisions of the plan / carrier.

White: Carrier • Yellow: Primary or Requesting Provider • Pink: Consultant / Facility / Provider • Goldenrod: Patient

See Carrier / Plan Manual For Specific Instructions.

Figure 4-2 Sample state uniform consultation referral form

2. A case manager contacts the specialist's office to provide a verbal preauthorization. The case manager provides a preauthorization number, briefly describes the patient's problem, details services preauthorized, and states the expiration date for the preauthorization. This phone call may or may not be followed by written confirmation (Figure 4-3).

Managed Care Insurance Company

DATE:

RE:
DATE OF BIRTH:
IDENTIFICATION NUMBER:
START TREATMENT DATE:

NAME OF CONSULTANT:
MAILING ADDRESS:

Dear Dr. _____

_____ was referred to you by the Managed Care Insurance Company on
_____. I am authorizing the following medically necessary treatment. This is subject to patient eligibility and contract limitations at the time treatment is performed.

Procedure	Units	From	To	Authorization Number

When filing for reimbursement, please send the HCFA-1500 claim form to me in care of the Managed Care Insurance Company at the above address. In order to expedite payment, please be certain to include in Block 23 all appropriate authorization number(s) as indicated above.

Please note that any services provided beyond those listed in this letter require additional authorization. If you anticipate that the patient will require additional services, you must complete an outpatient treatment report two weeks prior to rendering any additional treatment. If the patient fails to keep appointments, please inform us by telephone. If treatment is discontinued, submit a written discharge summary within two weeks of termination.

Although eligibility and benefit information has been corroborated to the best of our ability, certification for medically necessary care does not guarantee financial reimbursement related to these matters. If you need further information, or if there are any significant changes in the patient's medical status, please contact me at the Managed Care Insurance Company at 800.555.1212, extension 1234. Thank you for your cooperation.

Sincerely,

Case Manager
Original:
cc:

Figure 4-3 Case manager written confirmation order

Managed care programs not only require preauthorization of all services by outside specialists and ancillary providers but specifications of the timeframe during which the authorization is effective.

Always take detailed notes, including name of contact, of all telephone calls from case managers who are preauthorizing services. Written confirmation may not be received prior to the patient's initial appointment.

Services that exceed those included in the preauthorization or performed after the deadline may be disallowed as unauthorized care.

Be sure to enter all authorization numbers on the claim form. (See Block 23 on Figure 4-11 on page 56.)

Step 4. Patient fills out registration form.

Each new patient must complete a Patient Registration Form during their first visit to the practice (see Figures 4-4A and 4-4B on pages 44-45).

The completed Patient Registration Form is used to create the patient's demographic file, patient medical record (chart), financial account, and insurance billing records. When the patient returns the completed form, carefully review it to ensure that all necessary demographic and billing data were supplied. Often patients do not know how to answer the questions, or they feel the requested information does not apply to their particular situation.

■ **NOTE:** It is fraudulent for patients to withhold information regarding other health insurance coverage, and penalties can apply if payer information is *intentionally* omitted. ■

If essential questions are unanswered, the receptionist must query the patient. When the data truly does not apply to the patient, enter "N/A" in any blank that is not applicable.

When the patient reports more than one insurance company, the office staff must check to be sure the patient has correctly determined which policy is primary, secondary, and so on. The determination of primary or secondary status for patients with two or more commercial policies is different for adults than for children.

- *Adult patient named as primary policyholder:* The patient is the **policyholder** or **subscriber**, the person in whose name the insurance policy is issued.

- *Adult patient named as secondary policyholder:* The patient is listed as a dependent on a primary insurance policy.

EXAMPLE

Mary Jones works for Alfred State College and is enrolled in the group health insurance's family plan. She is named as the primary policyholder on this plan. Her husband, Bill, is a full-time college student and is named as the secondary policyholder on Mary's health insurance plan. Bill does not subscribe to any other health insurance policy.

Doctors Group
Main St
Alfred NY 00000

PATIENT REGISTRATION FORM

PAGE 1

Patient Information

Last Name	First Name	Middle Name
Street	City	State/Zip Code
Patient's Date of Birth	Social Security Number	Home Phone Number

Student Status	Employment Status	Marital Status
❑ Full-time ❑ Part-time	❑ Full-time ❑ Part-time ❑ Unemployed	❑ Single ❑ Married ❑ Separated ❑ Divorced ❑ Widowed ❑ Other

Sex	Name/Address of Employer	Occupation
❑ Male ❑ Female		

Employer Phone Number	Referred by:

Emergency Contact	Address	Telephone Number

Visit is related to on-the-job injury	Prior treatment received for injury
❑ No ❑ Yes Date: _____	❑ No ❑ Yes Doctor: _____ WC Number: _____

Visit is related to automobile accident	Name and Address of Insurance Company/Policy Number
❑ No ❑ Yes Date: _____	

Billing Information

Last Name	First Name	Middle Name
Street	City	State/Zip Code
Relationship to Patient	Social Security Number	Home Phone Number
Employer	Employer Address	Employer Phone Number

Figure 4-4A Patient registration form (page 1)

Doctors Group
Main St
Alfred NY 00000

PATIENT REGISTRATION FORM

PAGE 2

Primary Insured Information

Last Name	First Name/Middle Initial
Address	City/State/Zip Code

Relationship to Insured	Sex
❏ Self ❏ Spouse	❏ Male ❏ Female
❏ Child ❏ Other	

Insured's Date of Birth	Home Phone Number
Name of Insurance Company	Address
Insured Identification Number	Group Number

Name of Employer Sponsoring Plan

Effective Date

Secondary Insured Information

Last Name	First Name/Middle Initial
Address	City/State/Zip Code

Relationship to Insured	Sex
❏ Self ❏ Spouse	❏ Male ❏ Female
❏ Child ❏ Other	

Insured's Date of Birth	Home Phone Number
Name of Insurance Company	Address
Insured Identification Number	Group Number

Name of Employer Sponsoring Plan

Effective Date

Third Insured Information

Last Name	First Name/Middle Initial
Address	City/State/Zip Code

Relationship to Insured	Sex
❏ Self ❏ Spouse	❏ Male ❏ Female
❏ Child ❏ Other	

Insured's Date of Birth	Home Phone Number
Name of Insurance Company	Address
Insured Identification Number	Group Number

Name of Employer Sponsoring Plan

Effective Date

Fourth Insured Information

Last Name	First Name/Middle Initial
Address	City/State/Zip Code

Relationship to Insured	Sex
❏ Self ❏ Spouse	❏ Male ❏ Female
❏ Child ❏ Other	

Insured's Date of Birth	Home Phone Number
Name of Insurance Company	Address
Insured Identification Number	Group Number

Name of Employer Sponsoring Plan

Effective Date

I have listed all the medical/health insurance plans from which I may receive benefits.

Signature of Patient

Figure 4-4B Patient registration form (page 2)

- *Primary vs. secondary insurance:* There is a difference between the terms *primary policyholder* and *primary insurance.* **Primary insurance** is associated with how an insurance plan is billed—the insurance plan responsible for paying health care insurance claims first is considered primary. Once the primary insurance is billed and pays the contracted amount (e.g., 80% of billed amount), the secondary plan is billed for the remainder, and so on. Conceivably, an individual could purchase many health insurance policies with an expectation of being paid multiple times for health care services received. While this may be allowed by private health insurance plans, group health insurance reimbursement cannot exceed the total cost of services rendered.

■ **NOTE:** Certain insurance plans are always considered primary to other plans; (e.g., workers' compensation insurance is primary to an employee's group health care plan if the employee is injured on-the-job). These situations are discussed in Chapters 12 through 17. ■

EXAMPLE

Cindy Thomas has two health insurance policies, a group insurance plan through her full-time employer and another group insurance plan through her husband's employer. Cindy's plan through her own employer is primary, while the plan through her husband's employer is secondary. When Cindy receives health care services at her doctor's office, the office first submits the bill (and insurance claim) to Cindy's employer's health plan; once that health plan has paid, the bill (and insurance claim) can be submitted to Cindy's secondary insurance (her husband's group insurance plan).

■ **NOTE:** Total reimbursement cannot exceed the total charges for health care services rendered by Cindy's doctor. ■

- *Child of divorced parents:* The custodial parent's plan is primary. If the parents are remarried, the custodial parent's plan is primary, the custodial step-parent's plan is secondary, and the noncustodial parent's plan is tertiary (third). An exception is made if a court order specifies that a particular parent must cover the child's medical expenses.

- *Child living with both parents:* If each parent subscribes to a different health insurance plan, the primary and secondary policies are determined by applying the **birthday rule**. Physician office staff must obtain the birth date of each policyholder because the birthday rule states that the policyholder whose birth month and day occurs earlier in the calendar year holds the primary policy. The year of birth is not considered when applying the birthday rule determination. If the policyholders have identical birthdays, the policy in effect the longest is considered primary.

EXAMPLE 1

A child is listed as a dependent on each of his father's and mother's group policy. Which policy is primary?

Mother - birthdate 03/06/59 - works for IBM

Father - birthdate 03/20/57 - works for General Motors

> *Answer:* Mother's policy is primary; her birthday is earlier in the calendar year.

EXAMPLE 2

A child has the same coverage as in Example 1; however, in this case the mother was born on 03/04/45 and the father was born on 01/01/56. Which policy is primary?

> *Answer:* Father's policy is primary.

EXAMPLE 3

A dependent child is covered by both parent's group policies. The parents were born on the same day. Which policy is primary?

> Father's policy took effect 03/06/86
>
> Mother's policy took effect 09/06/92
>
> *Answer:* Father's policy is primary because it has been in effect six years longer.

■ **NOTE:** Determination of primary and secondary coverage involving one or more government-sponsored programs is discussed in detail in the respective Medicare, Medicaid, and TRICARE (formerly CHAMPUS) chapters. ■

Step 5. Make a photocopy of the front and back of all insurance identification cards held by the patient. (This photocopy is to be maintained in the patient's financial record.)

■ **NOTE:** Consider maintaining a separate financial record and medical record. ■

Step 6. All patients with insurance must sign an Authorization for Release of Medical Information Form. (See Figure 5-2 on page 71.)

Step 7. Create a new patient's medical record and enter patient demographic information into the practice's computerized patient data base.

Step 8. Generate the patient's encounter form.

The **encounter form** (also known as the **charge slip**, **fee ticket**, **routing form**, or **superbill**) is the financial record source document used by health care providers and other personnel to record treated diagnoses and services rendered to the patient during the current encounter. The minimum information entered on the form at this time is the date of service, patient's name, and balance due on the account. The encounter form may vary in appearance (see Figure 4-5 on page 48).

Clip the encounter form/routing form to the front of the patient's medical record, so that it is available for clinical staff when the patient is escorted to the treatment area.

If all patient scheduling is performed on the computer, generate encounter forms for all patients scheduled on a given day by selecting the "print encounter forms" function from the computer program.

Heeza Friend, M.D.
1 Internal St.
Anywhere, USA

ID # 52-1581586

EVALUATION/MANAGEMENT	NEW	EST.	FEE
		99211	
	99201	99212	
	99202	(99213)	38—
	99203	99214	
	99204		
	99205	99215	
		99211-25	
		99212-25	

CONSULTATION

	99241	
	99242	
	99243	
	99244	
	99245	

HEALTH P.E.

	Adult 18 - 39 Yrs.	99385	99395
	Adult 40 - 64 Yrs.	99386	99396
	Adult 65 +	99387	99397

LABORATORY

	Urinalysis, Micro	81000
	Urine, Colony Count	87087
	Rapid Strep Immuno.	86317
	Mono Spot	86300
	KOH	87220
	Wet Mount	87210
	Sed. Rate	85651
	Gram Stain	87205
	Stool O.B.	82270
	PPD Mantoux	86580
	Tine	86585
	Venipuncture	36415
	Venipuncture-Send Out	99000
	Hematocrit	85014
	Nasal Smear, Eosin	89190
	CBC c Diff	85024
	Blood Smear	85060
	Throat Culture	87060

PROCEDURES

		CPT	FEE
	Flex Sigmoidoscopy	45330	
	Holter Hook Up	93225-QT	
	Holter Analysis	93232-QT	
	Holter Physician Review	93233-QT	
	PFT Spirometry	94010	
	PFT Vapor Inhal.	94664	
	PFT Pre/Post	94060	
	Audio Screen	92551	
	I & D Simple	10060	
	24 Hr. BP Monitor	93784	
	Destruction Face	17000	
	EKG/Interpretation	93000	
	Tympanometry	92567	

INJECTIONS

	Allergy, Single	95115
	Allergy, Multiple	95117
	Td, Adult	90718
	MMR	90707
	Pneumococcal	90732
	Rocephin ____ mg	90788
	Admin, 1 vaccine	90471
	Admin, each additional	90472

MISCELLANEOUS

	Supplies	99070

DIAGNOSIS

	ICD-9		
Abnormal EKG	794.31	Emphysema	492.8
Abnormal Liver Functions	794.8	Epididymitis	604.90
Abrasion	919.0	Erysipelas	035
Abscess Tooth/Dental	522.5	Eustachian Tube Dysfunc.	381.81
Acne Rosacea	695.3	Exanthem Viral	057.9
Anemia Unspecified	285.9	Fibrocystic Breast	610.1
Angina	413.9	Fibroids Uterine	218.9
Angina Unstable	411.1	Fibrositis/Shoulder	726.2
Aphthous Stomatitis	528.2	Gastroenteritis	558.9
Arteritis	447.6	Gastroenteritis Viral	008.8
Arthritis NOS	716.90	GE Reflux/Esophagitis	530.11
Arythma Ventricular NOS	427.41	Gouty Arthropathy/-ritis	274.0
ASCVD	429.2	Headache Migraine	346.10
Asthma Allergic	493.00	Health Supervision	V20.2
Atrial Fibrillation	427.31	Heart Murmur	785.2
Auto Accident	E813.X	Hematemesis	578.0
Bell's Palsy	351.0	Hematuria	599.7
Bronchitis Acute	466.0	Hemorrhoids External	455.3
Bronchitis Asthmatic	493.90	Hemorrhoids Internal	455.0
Burn NOS	949.0	Hernia, Inguinal	550.00
Carotidynia	337.0	Herpes Simplex Genital	054.10
Carpal Tunnel Syndrome	354.0	Herpes Zoster	053.13
Cataract Senile	366.10	Hordeolum (Sty)	373.11
Cellulitis Non Specific	682.9	Hyperglycemia	270.7
Cerumen Impacted	380.4	Hyperlipidemia	272.4
Cervicalgia/Neck Pain	723.1	Hypertension, Benign	401.1
Chest Pain Acute	786.50	Hypertension/Malignant	401.0
Chest Tightness/Pres.	786.59	Hyperthyroidism	242.90
CHF	428.0	Hypothyroidism	244.9
Coagulopathy	286.9	Impetigo	684
Colitis Infectous	009.1	Impotence	302.72
Conjunctivitis	372.00	Insect Bite	919.4
Constipation	564.0	Irritable Bowel/Colitis	564.1
COPD	496	Labyrithitis	386.30
Coronary Artery Disease	414.00	Laryngitis	464.0
Counseling, Tests, Meds	V65.49	Leukocytosis	288.8
Counseling, Diets	V65.3	Leukopenia/Neutropenia	288.0
Cough	786.2	Lipoma	214.1
Deep Vein Thrombo/NOS	451.2	Lithiasis Urinary/Renal	592.9
Deglutition Unspecified	784.9	Lyme Disease	088.81
Dehydration	276.5	Lymphadenitis/Adenitis	289.3
Dementia	290.0	Macrocytosis	289.9
Dermatitis Seborrheic	690.1	Metbolic Disorder	277.9
Diabetes IDDM	250.01	Mitral Valve Prolapse	424.0
Diabetes NIDDM	250.00	Mycardial Infarct. NOS	410.92
Diarrhea/Colitis	558.9	Myeloma	203.00
Disturb Acute/Stress	308.3	Nausea/Vomiting	787.0
Diverticulosis	562.10	Neuritis	729.2
Dyspnea	786.00	Neurodermatitis	698.3
Eczema	691.8	Neuronitis Vestibular	386.12
Edema	782.3	Neuropathy Unspec. NOS	355.9
Elevated BP	796.2	Nevus	448.1
		Nodule Thyroid	241.0

Obesity	278.0
Ophthalmodynia	379.91
Otalgia	388.70
Otitis External	380.10
Otitis Media	382.00
Pain Back Acute	724.2
Palpitations	785.1
Parkinson's Disease	332.0
Peptic Ulcer Disease	533.30
Pharyngitis Acute	462
Pityriasis Rosea	696.3
Pleurisy	511.0
Polyarthopathy/Arthriti NOS	716.50
Polyradicula Neuropathy	357.0
Proctitis	569.49
Prostatitis	601.0
Proteinuria	791.0
Pruritus	698.0
Pyelonephritis	590.00
Rash	782.1
Referral Pt./wo Exam	V68.81
Renal Failure	586
Rhinitis	460
Rhinitis Allergic/Pollen	477.0
Rhinorrhea	478.1
Sacroiliitis	720.2
Sciatica	724.3
Seborrhea	706.3
Sinusitis Acute	461.9
Strep Throat	034.0
Syndrome Restless Leg	333.99
Tachycardia Supraventric	427.0
Tendonitis Elbow	726.30
Thrombocytopenia	287.5
Thrombophleb Superficial	451.0
Thrush Oral/Candidiasis	112.0
TIA	435.9
Tinea Vesicolor	111.0
Tinnitus	388.30
Transaminasemia	790.4
URI	465.0
UTI/Bacteriuria	599.0
Varicocele	456.4
Varicose Veins	454.9
Vertigo Position/Paroxym	386.11
Viral Syndrome	079.99
Vision Blurred	368.8
Vomiting Uncontrollable	536.2
✓ Hypertension NOS	401.9
✓ Hypercholesterolemia familial	272.0

DATE OF APPOINTMENT: 6/25/YYYY	REMARKS

PATIENT		CHART #	SEX	BIRTHDATE
Ima Patient		9804	F	03/08/YYYY

CURRENT	30 DAYS	60 DAYS	90 DAYS	120 DAYS	PATIENT TOTAL	PENDING INSURANCE

TODAY'S CHARGES	PAYMENTS ☐CS ☑CK ☐CS	ADJUSTMENTS	TODAY'S TOTAL			
38.00	− 38.00	− 0	= 0		+	+

BALANCE = 0

=

INSURANCE: BC/BS FEP 123456	

REFERRING PHYSICIAN N/A	ALLERGIES
LAST VISIT	
LAST INSURANCE PAYMENT	CURRENT
LAST PATIENT PAYMENT	
SPECIAL NOTES	PREVIOUS
	PHYSICIAN

Figure 4-5 Preprinted encounter form

■ **NOTE:** At this point, the clinical assessment and/or treatment is performed. After the patient's examination and/or treatment, the provider or clinical assistant will record on the encounter form all current and pertinent diagnoses, services rendered, and special follow-up instructions to be presented during the exit interview. The chart and encounter form are then returned to the staff member responsible for checking out patients. ■

ESTABLISHED PATIENT RETURN VISIT

Step 1. Schedule a return appointment either at the time of the last appointment or later if the patient contacts the office for a return appointment.

Step 2. Check the preauthorization status on all managed care patients.

Approximately one week prior to an appointment with a specialist for nonemergency services, the status of preauthorization for care must be checked to ensure that it is current. If the preauthorization has expired, the patient's nonemergency appointment may have to be postponed until the required treatment reports have been filed with the primary care physician or case manager and a new preauthorization for additional treatment has been obtained (see Figures 4-6 and 4-7 on pages 50 and 51).

Step 3. Check the patient's registration demographics when the patient is at the front desk.

As the cost of health care increases and competition for subscribers escalates among insurers, many employers who pay a portion of health care costs for their employees are purchasing health insurance contracts that cover only a 3- or 6-month period. Therefore, it is important to ask all returning patients if there have been any changes in their demographic data (name, address, phone number, employer, and insurance program). If the answer is yes, a new registration form should be completed and necessary changes made in the computerized patient data base.

Step 4. Generate the encounter form for the patient's current visit.

Clip the encounter form to the front of the patient's chart so it is available for clinical staff when the patient is escorted to the treatment area.

■ **NOTE:** Once the clinical assessment and/or treatment has been completed, the patient enters the postclinical phase of the visit. The services and diagnosis(es) are added to the encounter form, and the patient's record and encounter form are given to the staff member responsible for checking out patients. ■

PROVIDER LETTERHEAD

CONSULTANT TREATMENT REPORT

DATE _____

Case Manager's Name:

Insurance Company Name and Address:

RE: (Patient Name)   (Patient ID)

(Policyholder's Name)

1. INITIAL SYMPTOMS:

2. PAST MEDICAL HISTORY:

3. COURSE OF TREATMENT TO DATE:

4. DIAGNOSTIC TEST RESULTS/DATES:

5. ADDITIONAL TREATMENT REQUESTED:

_____

(NAME AND LICENSE NUMBER OF PROVIDER)

_____

SIGNATURE OF PROVIDER

Figure 4-6 Treatment report

ABC INSURANCE PLAN
Letterhead

CONSULTANT TREATMENT PLAN

TREATMENT PLAN NO. _____   Primary Care Physician Name _____ _____

Patient Name   Patient Birthdate

_____   _____

Member Identification No.   Member Name (Last, First, MI)   Member Birthdate

_____   _____   _____

Consultant Provider ID   Consultant Name   Phone Number

_____   _____   _____

Consultant Address

_____

Consultant Treatment Plans must be completed by the Consultant and approved by the patient's PCP for all surgical procedures or other services not specifically listed on the Primary Care Physician Referral Form. The approved procedures or services must be performed within three months of the date of the PCP approval. All services must be rendered by the consultant stated above.

Diagnosis Description and ICD-9-CM Code

_____

Procedure Code   Services To Be Performed   Estimated Cost

_____
_____
_____
_____

Consultant Signature_____ Date: _____

PRIMARY CARE PHYSICIAN AUTHORIZATION FOR ABOVE PROCEDURES/SERVICES

☐ ACCEPTED   ☐ AS MODIFIED ABOVE   ☐ APPROVAL DENIED

RETROACTIVE TREATMENT PLANS ARE NOT VALID

CONSULTANT INSTRUCTIONS
1. Complete and send the original Consultant Treatment Plan to PCP for signature.
2. Complete a HCFA-1500 form and mail to the ABC Insurance Plan. Enter the Treatment Plan # in Block 23. Attach a copy of the Consultant Treatment Report to the claim form.
3. For subsequent submission(s), no attachment is needed.

IMPROPERLY COMPLETED FORMS WILL BE RETURNED

Figure 4-7 Consultant treatment plan

POST CLINICAL CHECK-OUT PROCEDURES

The following procedures are the same for new and established patients.

Step 1. Code, if necessary, all procedures, services, and diagnoses selected on the encounter form.

Step 2. Enter the charges for procedures and/or services performed, and total the charges on the encounter form.

Step 3. Post all charges to the patient's ledger/account record and the daily accounts receivable journal either manually or on the pertinent computer screens.

The **patient ledger,** known as the **patient account record** in a computerized system, is a permanent record of all financial transactions between the patient and the practice. The charges along with personal or third-party payments are all posted on the patient's account.

Each procedure performed must be individually described and priced on the patient's ledger/account record (See the ledger/account in Figure 4-8).

The **manual daily accounts receivable journal**, also known as the **day sheet**, is a chronological summary of all transactions posted to individual patient ledgers/accounts on a specific day (see Figure 4-9, page 54).

Computer-processed charges and payments are posted simultaneously to the day sheet and the patient's account. See Figure 4-10 (page 55) for a computer-generated patient statement.

Step 4. Collect payment from the patient.

Most health care policies require the patient to pay a portion of the fee at the time services are rendered. The policy may stipulate a copayment and/or coinsurance payment. The **copayment**, commonly called a **copay**, is the amount the patient pays each time a specific service is rendered. Health care providers often require the copayment to be paid at the time of registration because it eliminates costly patient billing for these amounts. A **coinsurance payment**, commonly called **coinsurance**, is the percentage the patient pays for covered services after the deductible has been met and the copayment has been paid. For example, with an 80/20 plan, the insurance company pays 80% and the patient pays 20%.

◆ **HINT:** To save the expense of mailing invoices, ask patients to pay their portion of the bill as they depart the office. ◆

Step 5. Post any payment to the patient's account.

The source of each payment should be identified, either as cash, money order, credit card, insurance, or personal check (see the 5/23/YYYY entry on Figure 4-8).

BC/BS R2345678   **STATEMENT**   PATIENT, IMA

IMA PATIENT
900 RANDELL RD
ANYWHERE MD 20000

DATE	CODE	DESCRIPTION	CHARGE		CREDITS PAYMENTS		ADJ		CURRENT BALANCE	
			BALANCE FORWARD →						30	–
5/23/YYYY		ROA per ck			30	–			0	
6/25/YYYY	99213	OV ROA per ck	38	–	38	–			0	
		Ins billed								

PLEASE PAY LAST AMOUNT IN THIS COLUMN   ⬆

OV — Office Visit	**HOSP** — Hospital Visit	**ROA** — Received on Account
OS — Office Surgery	**HS** — Hospital Surgery	**NC** — No Charge
TC — Telephone Consultation	**SA** — Surgical Assistant	**INS** — Insurance
FA — Failed Appointment	**SC** — Surgical Consultation	
RP — Report	**ER** — Emergency Room	

THIS IS A COPY OF YOUR ACCOUNT AS IT APPEARS ON YOUR LEDGER CARD

Figure 4-8 Patient ledger card

DATE _6/25/yyyy_

DAY SHEET

	PT. NAME	DESCRIPTION	OLD BAL.	CHARGE	PAYMENT	NEW BAL.
1.	Patient, Ima	OV-99213 per ck	0	38 —	38 —	0
2.						
3.						
4.						
5.						
6.						
7.						
8.						
9.						
10.						
11.						
12.						
13.						
14.						
15.						
16.						
17.						
18.						
19.						
20.						
21.						
22.						
		TOTALS				

PROOF

Old Bal.   _____

+ Charges   _____

− Payments   _____

= New Bal.   _____

Figure 4-9 Sample day sheet

```
  Heeza Friend, M.D.          • MAKE CHECK PAYABLE TO PHYSICIAN WHO PROVIDED SERVICES.
  1 Internal Street           • RETAIN LOWER PORTION FOR PERSONAL TAX AND INSURANCE RECORD.
  Anywhere, USA               • RETURN UPPER PORTION WITH PAYMENT TO INSURE PROPER CREDIT.
                                  For Billing Inquiries Call      AMOUNT
                                        (001) 268-2205            REMITTED $ _____
```

Invoice	DATE	ACCT. NUMBER
	06/25/YYYY	9804

```
Bill to:  Ima Patient                   Patient:  Ima Patient
          1 Feelbetter Street                     1 Feelbetter Street
          Anywhere, USA                           Anywhere, USA
```

```
Diagnosis:
401.9 HYPERTENSION                    272.0 HYPERCHOLESTEROLEMIA
```

Date	Code	Procedure/Service	Amount
06/25/YYYY	99213	E/M Service, expanded problem focused	38.00*
06/25/YYYY	CK	PATIENT PAYMENT-THANK YOU	38.00CR

```
Total payment today: $38.00          Total 06/25/YYYY:          $0.00
```

```
PLEASE MAKE AN APPOINTMENT FOR   2 Weeks from today
```

Figure 4-10 Computer-generated statement (or "walkout statement")

Step 6. Complete the insurance claim form.

The insurance claim form used to report professional and technical services is known as the **HCFA-1500** (see Figure 4-11 on page 56). The provider's claim for payment is generated from information located on the patient's encounter form, ledger/account record, and source document (e.g., patient record or chart). Information located on these documents is transferred to the HCFA-1500 claim form. Such information includes patient and insurance policy identification, codes and charges for procedures and/or services, and codes for diagnoses treated and/or managed during the encounter. The selection of codes for procedures, services, and diagnoses are discussed in later chapters.

The HCFA-1500 requires responses to standard questions pertaining to whether the patient's condition is related to employment, auto accident, and/or any other accident; additional insurance coverage; use of an outside lab; and whether or not the provider accepts assignment. To **accept assignment** means the provider accepts as payment in full what is paid by

APPROVED OMB-0938-0008

HEALTH INSURANCE CLAIM FORM

☐☐☐ PICA   PICA ☐☐☐

1.	MEDICARE	MEDICAID	CHAMPUS	CHAMPVA	GROUP HEALTH PLAN	FECA BLK LUNG	OTHER	1a. INSURED'S I.D. NUMBER	(FOR PROGRAM IN ITEM 1)
	☐ (Medicare #)	☐ (Medicaid #)	☐ (Sponsor's SSN)	☐ (VA File #)	☐ (SSN or ID)	☐ (Medicaid #)	☒ (ID)	R0001001	

2. PATIENT'S NAME (Last Name, First Name, Middle Initial)
PATIENT IMA

3. PATIENT'S BIRTH DATE
MM 03 DD 08 YY 1934   SEX M ☐ F ☒

4. INSURED'S NAME (Last Name, First Name, Middle Initial)
PATIENT, H E

5. PATIENT'S ADDRESS (No. Street)
1 FEELBETTER STREET

6. PATIENT RELATIONSHIP TO INSURED
Self ☐ Spouse ☒ Child ☐ Other ☐

7. INSURED'S ADDRESS (No. Street)
SAME

CITY
ANYWHERE USA   STATE

8. PATIENT STATUS
Single ☐   Married ☒   Other ☐

CITY   STATE

ZIP CODE
00001

TELEPHONE (Include Area Code)
(001) 001 3456

Employed ☐   Full-Time Student ☐   Part-Time Student ☐

ZIP CODE   TELEPHONE (INCLUDE AREA CODE)
( )

9. OTHER INSURED'S NAME (Last Name, First Name, Middle Initial)

10. IS PATIENT'S CONDITION RELATED TO:

11. INSURED'S POLICY GROUP OR FECA NUMBER

a. OTHER INSURED'S POLICY OR GROUP NUMBER

a. EMPLOYMENT? (CURRENT OR PREVIOUS)
☐ YES ☒ NO

a. INSURED'S DATE OF BIRTH
MM 12 DD 30 YY YYYY   SEX M ☒ F ☐

b. OTHER INSURED'S DATE OF BIRTH
MM DD YY   SEX M ☐ F ☐

b. AUTO ACCIDENT?   PLACE (State)
☐ YES ☒ NO

b. EMPLOYER'S NAME OR SCHOOL NAME
ANY COMPANY

c. EMPLOYER'S NAME OR SCHOOL NAME

c. OTHER ACCIDENT?
☐ YES ☒ NO

c. INSURANCE PLAN NAME OR PROGRAM NAME
BC/BS

d. INSURANCE PLAN NAME OR PROGRAM NAME

10d. RESERVED FOR LOCAL USE

d. IS THERE ANOTHER HEALTH BENEFIT PLAN?
☐ YES ☒ NO   If yes, return to and complete item 9 a – d.

READ BACK OF FORM BEFORE COMPLETING & SIGNING THIS FORM.
12. PATIENT'S OR AUTHORIZED PERSON'S SIGNATURE I authorize the release of any medical or other information necessary to process this claim. I also request payment of government benefits either to myself or to the party who accepts assignment below.

SIGNED *Ima Patient*   DATE 6/25/YYYY

13. INSURED'S OR AUTHORIZED PERSON'S SIGNATURE I authorize payment of medical benefits to the undersigned physician or supplier for services described below.

SIGNED **SIGNATURE ON FILE**

14. DATE OF CURRENT: ◄ ILLNESS (First symptom) OR INJURY (Accident) OR PREGNANCY (LMP)
MM DD YY

15. IF PATIENT HAS HAD SAME OR SIMILAR ILLNESS, GIVE FIRST DATE MM DD YY

16. DATES PATIENT UNABLE TO WORK IN CURRENT OCCUPATION
MM DD YY   TO   MM DD YY
FROM

17. NAME OF REFERRING PHYSICIAN OR OTHER SOURCE

17a. I.D. NUMBER OF REFERRING PHYSICIAN

18. HOSPITALIZATION DATES RELATED TO CURRENT SERVICES
MM DD YY   TO   MM DD YY
FROM

19. RESERVED FOR LOCAL USE

20. OUTSIDE LAB? $ CHARGES
☐ YES ☒ NO

21. DIAGNOSIS OR NATURE OF ILLNESS OR INJURY. (RELATE ITEMS 1, 2, 3, OR 4 TO ITEM 24E BY LINE)

1. |401 .9   3. |___ .___
2. |272 .0   4. |___ .___

22. MEDICAID RESUBMISSION
CODE   ORIGINAL REF. NO.

23. PRIOR AUTHORIZATION NUMBER

24. A. DATE(S) OF SERVICE						B. Place of Service	C. Type of Service	D. PROCEDURES, SERVICES, OR SUPPLIES (Explain Unusual Circumstances)		E. DIAGNOSIS CODE	F. $ CHARGES	G. DAYS OR UNITS	H. EPSDT Family Plan	I. EMG	J. COB	K. RESERVED FOR LOCAL USE
From MM	DD	YY	To MM	DD	YY			CPT/HCPCS	MODIFIER							
1	06 25 YYYY					11		99213		1 2	38 00	001				
2																
3																
4																
5																
6																

25. FEDERAL TAX I.D. NUMBER   SSN EIN
52 1581586   ☐ ☒

26. PATIENT'S ACCOUNT NO.
9804

27. ACCEPT ASSIGNMENT?
(For govt. claims, see back)
☐ YES ☐ NO

28. TOTAL CHARGE
$ **38 00**

29. AMOUNT PAID
$ **38 00**

30. BALANCE DUE
$ **0 00**

31. SIGNATURE OF PHYSICIAN OR SUPPLIER INCLUDING DEGREES OR CREDENTIALS
(I certify that the statements on the reverse apply to this bill and are made a part thereof.)

SIGNED **HEEZA FRIEND MD**
DATE **0626YYYY**

32. NAME AND ADDRESS OF FACILITY WHERE SERVICES WERE RENDERED (If other than home or office)

33. PHYSICIAN'S SUPPLIER'S BILLING NAME, ADDRESS, ZIP CODE & PHONE #
(001) 001 0101
HEEZA FRIEND MD
1 INTERNAL STREET
ANYWHERE, USA
PIN# **HE0010**   GRP#

(APPROVED BY AMA COUNCIL ON MEDICAL SERVICE 8/88)   *PLEASE PRINT OR TYPE*

FORM HCFA-1500 (U2) (12-90)
FORM OWCP-1500   FORM RRB-1500

Figure 4-11 Completed HCFA-1500 claim form

the insurance company on the claim (except for any copayment and/or coinsurance amounts). The health insurance specialist will also complete portions of the form that identify the type of insurance, patient's sex, patient's relationship to insured, and provider's federal tax ID number. The HCFA-1500 includes several areas that require the signature of the patient and the provider. When electronically submitting claims, *SIGNATURE ON FILE* can be substituted for the patient's signature (as long as the patient's signature is actually on file in the office). The completed claim form is then proofread and double-checked for accuracy (e.g., verification that signature statement is on file, and so on). Any necessary attachments are copied from the patient's chart (e.g., operative report) or developed (e.g., letter delineating unlisted service provided, referred to in the CPT coding manual as a "special report").

The computer generates the claim forms when the "print claim" function is selected. Most computer programs can generate a specific patient's form as well as forms for a number of patients (e.g., patients treated on a particular day). It is essential that office staff responsible for entering patient registration information understand data entry requirements so that the claim forms are formatted properly.

Step 7. ☑ Staple any required attachments to the claim, such as copies of operative reports, pathology reports, and written authorization. For electronic claims, check with the insurance carrier to determine how to submit the attachments (e.g., fax or postal mail).

Step 8. Obtain the provider's signature on the claim form, if manually processed. Special arrangements may be made with some insurance carriers to allow the provider's name to be typed or a signature stamp to be used (see Figure 5-10). No signature is possible on electronic claims.

■ **NOTE:** In July 2000, federal electronic signature legislation was enacted. Physicians who contract with government and/or managed care plans are considered to have valid signatures on file. ■

Step 9. ☑ File a copy of the claim form and copies of the attachment(s) in the practice's insurance files. Electronic claims are stored in the computer.

Step 10. ☑ Log completed claims in an insurance registry if the practice's procedure manual requires this step (see Figure 4-12 on page 58). Be sure to include the date the claim was filed with the insurance carrier. For computerized claims processing, medical office management software should generate a claims log.

Step 11. ☑ Mail or electronically send the claim to the insurance carrier. Paper claims must be generated when attachments are to accompany the claims. Most practices electronically transmit claims, and federal legislation was enacted requiring that government claims be electronically processed (implementation date not yet established). They receive a transmittal notice listing the patient names for claims successfully transmitted. The transmittal notice also con-

INSURANCE CLAIMS REGISTRY

Date Filed	Patient Name	Insurance Company	Unusual Procedure Reported	Amount Due	Amount Paid
6/13/YYYY	Patient, Ima	BC/BS FEP	n/a	$ 38.00	

Figure 4-12 Insurance Claims Registry

tains names of patients whose claims have preliminary processing errors. When the transmittal notice is received, compare it to the list of claims transmitted. If a disruption in service occurred, claims may not have transmitted successfully. Claims reported as not processed must be investigated and data errors corrected. Missing and corrected claims are then transmitted a second time and checked against a second transmittal notice.

INSURANCE COMPANY PROCESSING OF A CLAIM

The processing of paper claims starts in the mailroom, where the envelopes are opened and attachments are unstapled and clipped to the claim. Claims are then scanned into a computer. The processing of electronic claims begins when a file of transmitted claims is opened in the claims processing computer.

Step 1. The computer scans each claim for patient and policy identification for comparison with the computerized data base.

Claims are automatically rejected if the patient and subscriber names do not match exactly with names in the computerized data base. Use of nicknames or typographical errors on claims will cause rejection and return, or delay in reimbursement to the provider because the claim cannot be matched.

Step 2. Procedure codes on the claim form are matched with the policy's list of allowed codes. In the case of a managed care claim, both the procedures and the dates of service are checked to ensure that services performed were preauthorized and performed within the preauthorized timeframe.

Any service determined to be a noncovered benefit is marked either as an **uncovered procedure**, **noncovered procedure**, **uncovered benefit** or **"not medically necessary service,"** and rejected for payment. Services that are provided to a patient without proper authorization or are not covered by a current authorization are marked as **unauthorized services**. Patients may be billed for uncovered or noncovered procedures, but not for unauthorized services.

Step 3. Procedure codes are cross-matched with diagnosis codes to ensure the medical necessity of all services provided.

Any service that is considered not "medically necessary" for the submitted diagnosis code may be disallowed.

Step 4. The claim is checked against the common data file.

The information presented on each claim is checked against the insurer's **common data file**, an abstract of all recent claims filed on each patient. This step determines whether the patient is receiving concurrent care for the same condition by more than one provider. This function further identifies services that are related to recent surgeries, hospitalizations, or liability coverages.

Step 5. A determination is made of "allowed charges."

If no irregularity or inconsistency is found on the claim, the allowed charge for each covered procedure is determined. The **allowed charge**, also known as the **allowable charge**, **eligible amount**, or **maximum allowed amount**, is the maximum amount the insurance company will pay for each procedure or service, according to the patient's policy. The exact amount allowed varies according to the contract and is less than or equal to the fee charged by the provider. Payment is never greater than the fee submitted by the provider (see the total benefit column in Figure 4-13A on page 60). Figure 4-13B is an example of a computer-generated explanation of benefits form sent to the provider by the insurance company.

Step 6. Determination of the patient's annual deductible is made.

The **deductible** is the total amount of covered out-of-pocket medical expenses a policy holder must incur each year before the insurance company is obligated to pay any benefits.

Step 7. The copayment and/or coinsurance requirement is determined.

Step 8. The Explanation of Benefits form (or report) is generated.

The **Explanation of Benefits (EOB) form** (called the Medicare Summary Notice by HCFA) is a statement telling the patient and provider how the insurance company determined its share of the reimbursement (Figure 4-13). The report includes the following:

- Patient and provider identification
- A list of all procedures, dates of service, and charges submitted on the claim form
- A list of any procedures submitted but not considered a benefit of the policy
- A list of allowed charges for each covered procedure
- The amount of the patient deductible, if any, subtracted from the total allowed charges
- The patient's financial cost-sharing responsibility (copayment and/or coinsurance) for this claim
- The total amount payable by the insurance company on this claim

XYZ Insurance Company

P.O. Box 1234
Anywhere USA 00000-0000
(800) 555-1234
(800) 555-1235 TTY

EXPLANATION OF BENEFITS

Insured: Dee Post
Member ID #:   123456789
Group ID #:   1001

10-15-2000

PATIENT: Dee Post
1 Main St
Alfred NY 14802

For Services From To	Type of Service	CPT Code	Total Charges	Disallowed Charges	Deductible (-)	Remaining Covered Charges	Co-Pay	Total Benefit	Patient Responsibility	Comments
PATIENT: Dee Post		**CLAIM:** 89562462-00			**PROVIDER:** Joy Small, MD			**PAYEE:** Joy Small, MD		
0730 073000	Xray	73510	65.00	31.65	.00	0.00	0.00	33.35	0.00	P1
0730 073000	E&M	99203	90.00	.00	.00	0.00	15.00	75.00	15.00	P3
	TOTALS		155.00	31.65	.00	0.00	15.00	108.35	15.00	P2

COMMENTS:

P1   PREFERRED PROVIDER ORGANIZATION DISCOUNT OF $31.65 PROVIDED, PATIENT NOT RESPONSIBLE.
P2   PAYMENT IN THE AMOUNT $108.35 WAS MADE TO JOY SMALL MD ON 10/15/00.
P3   PATIENT IS RESPONSIBLE FOR PAYMENT OF $15.00 TO PROVIDER.

DEE POST   HAS MET $200.00 OF THE $200.00 PATIENT DEDUCTIBLE FOR THE 2000 BENEFIT YEAR.
HAS MET $ 0.00 OF THE OUT-OF-POCKET MAXIMUM FOR THE 2000 BENEFIT YEAR.

THIS IS NOT A BILL. PLEASE SAVE THIS COPY FOR YOUR RECORDS.

Figure 4-13A Explanation of Benefits form sent to patients

Explanation of Benefits

XYZ INSURANCE COMPANY   10-15-2000

Provider ID	Provider Name	Date of Service	Patient Name	Member ID	CPT Code	Total Charge	CoPay Amount	Amount Paid	Total
001	Small, Joy	07/30/00	Dael, Tim	125627	29888	2,400.00	0.00	0.00	0.00
001	Small, Joy	07/30/00	Post, Dee	236594	73510	65.00	0.00	0.00	0.00
001	Small, Joy	07/30/00	Post, Dee	236594	99203	90.00	15.00	75.00	90.00
					Practice Total	2555.00	15.00	75.00	90.00

Figure 4-13B Computer-generated Explanation of Benefits sent to providers

Step 9. EOB and benefit check, if payment is approved, are mailed.

If the claim form stated that direct payment should be made to the provider, the reimbursement check and a copy of the EOB will be mailed to the provider. The EOB (or MSN) is also mailed to the patient. This can be accomplished in one of three ways:

1. The patient signs the authorization of benefits statement, Block 13 on the HCFA-1500 (12-90) form.
2. The provider marks "YES" in Block 27 on the claim form.
3. The provider has signed an agreement with the insurer for direct payment of all claims.

If reimbursement is to be sent to the patient, the policyholder and physician will receive a copy of the EOB. It is the office's responsibility to obtain payment from the patient.

MAINTAINING INSURANCE CLAIM FILES

The federal Omnibus Budget Reconciliation Act of 1987 (OBRA 1987) requires providers to retain copies of any government insurance claim forms and copies of all attachments filed by the provider for a period of six years. HCFA stipulated in March 1992 that "providers and billing services filing claims electronically can comply with this federal regulation by retaining the financial **source document** (routing slip, charge slip, encounter form, or superbill) from which the insurance claim was generated. In addition, the provider should keep the e-mailed report of the summary of electronic claims received from the insurance company.

Claim files should be set up in the following manner:

1. *Open assigned claims* filed by month and insurance company. (These claims have been submitted to the carrier, but processing is not complete.)
2. *Closed assigned claims* filed by year and insurance company. (All processing including appeals is completed.)
3. *Batched EOB* file. (Carrier has reported multiple patient claims on one EOB.)
4. *Unassigned claims* (provider does not accept assignment) filed by year. (Use this file for all unassigned claims for which the provider is *not* obligated to perform any follow-up work.)

EOB Reconciliation

When the EOB and payment are received, pull the claim(s) and review and post the payments to the patient's account. Then make a notation of the date payment was received, the amount of payment, EOB processing date, and applicable EOB batch number on the paper claim form. Claims with no errors are marked "closed" and moved to the closed assigned claims file. Single-payment EOBs may be attached to the claim form before filing the claim in the closed assigned claims file. Batched EOBs are refiled in the EOB file.

If the EOB is received without payment, review the EOB to determine whether an error in processing occurred or payment is denied for another reason. If an error in processing the original claim is found, the following steps should be taken:

Step 1. Write an immediate appeal for reconsideration of payment.

Step 2. Make a copy of the original claim, the EOB, and the written appeal requesting reconsideration.

Step 3. Attach a copy of the original claim and the EOB to the appeal.

If the case was reported on a batched EOB, highlight the specific case.

Step 4. Note the payment (including the check number) on the claim form.

Step 5. Refile the claim form in the appropriate "open file."

Step 6. Mail or fax the appeal to the insurer.

An EOB may indicate that payment was denied for a reason other than a processing error. The reasons for denials may include (1) procedure or service not medically necessary, (2) pre-existing condition not covered, (3) noncovered benefit, (4) termination of coverage, (5) failure to obtain preauthorization, (6) out-of-network provider used, or (7) lower level of care could have been provided. The following steps should be taken for each type of denial.

1. *Procedure or service not medically necessary:* The insurance carrier has determined that the procedure performed or service rendered was not medically necessary based on information submitted on the claim. To respond, first review the original source document (e.g., patient record) for the claim to see if significant diagnosis codes or other important information may have been overlooked. Next, write an appeal letter to the insurance carrier documenting the reasons the provider deemed the treatment to be medically necessary. Emphasize the fact that treatment decisions were made by a provider personally familiar with the patient and based on individual circumstances of the patient's case.

2. *Pre-existing condition:* The insurance carrier has denied this claim based on language of the pre-existing condition clause in the patient's insurance policy. A **pre-existing condition** is any medical condition that was diagnosed and/or treated within a specified period of time immediately preceding the enrollee's effective date of coverage. The wording associated with these clauses varies from policy to policy (e.g., length of time pre-existing condition clause applies or requirement that the condition be diagnosed and treated to trigger the clause). It is possible for an insurance company to cancel a policy (or at least deny payment on a claim) if the patient failed to disclose pre-existing conditions. Respond to this type of denial by determining that the condition associated with treatment for which the claim was submitted was indeed pre-existing. If it is determined that an incorrect diagnosis code was submitted on the original claim, for example, correct the claim and resubmit it for reconsideration of payment.

■ **NOTE:** Office staff must be familiar with federal regulations regarding insurance coverage of pre-existing conditions when a patient changes jobs and/or an employer switches insurance plans. ■

3. *Noncovered benefit:* The claim was denied based on a list developed by the insurance company that includes a description of items covered by the policy as well as those excluded. Excluded items may include procedures such as cosmetic surgery. Respond to this type of denial by determining that the treatment submitted on the claim for payment is indeed excluded from coverage. If it is determined that an incorrect procedure code was submitted, for example, correct the claim and resubmit it for reconsideration of payment.

4. *Termination of coverage:* The insurance carrier has denied this claim because the patient is no longer covered by the insurance policy. Respond to this type of denial by contacting the patient to determine appropriate coverage, and submit the claim accordingly. For example, a patient may have changed jobs and no longer be covered by his former employer's health insurance plan. The office needs to obtain correct insurance carrier information and submit a claim accordingly. This type of denial reinforces the need to interview patients about current address, telephone number, employment, and insurance coverage each time they come to the office for treatment.

5. *Failure to obtain preauthorization:* Many insurance carriers require patients to call a toll-free number located on their insurance card to obtain prior authorization for particular treatments. Problems can arise during an emergency situation when there is a lack of communication between provider and insurance carrier because treatment cannot be delayed while awaiting preauthorization. While the claim is usually paid, payment might be less and/or penalties may apply because preauthorization was not obtained. If failure to obtain preauthorization was due to a medical emergency, it is possible to have penalties waived. Respond to this situation by requesting a retrospective review of a claim, and be sure to submit information explaining special circumstances that might not be evident by reviewing the patient's chart.

6. *Out-of-network provider used:* The insurance carrier has denied payment because treatment was provided outside the provider network. Respond to this denial by writing a letter of appeal explaining why the patient sought treatment from outside the provider network (e.g., medical emergency when patient is out of town). Payment received could be reduced and penalties could also apply.

7. *Lower level of care could have been provided:* This type of denial applies when care rendered on an inpatient basis is normally provided as an outpatient. Respond to this type of denial by writing a letter of appeal explaining why the higher level of care was required. Be prepared to forward copies of the patient's chart for review by the insurance carrier.

Federal Privacy Act

The federal Privacy Act of 1974 prohibits an insurer from notifying the provider regarding payment or rejections of unassigned claims. Providers who do not accept assignment of Medicare benefits do not receive a copy of the Medicare Summary Notice (MSN), previously called an Explanation of Medicare Benefits (EOMB) sent to the Medicare **beneficiary** (the patient). Information that can be released to providers on unassigned claims is limited to telephone inquiries as to whether the claim was received, processed, and approved or denied. Payment amounts and approved payment (e.g., charges) information cannot be disclosed. Nonparticipating providers do receive MSNs on unassigned claims; the unassigned claims are listed in a separate section without summary totals.

To assist in an appeal, the patient must furnish the nonparticipating provider with a copy of the MSN and a letter from the patient stating that the provider is allowed to assist in the appeal of the unassigned claim denial. A copy of the MSN and the letter (signed by the patient and the Medicare beneficiary) must accompany the provider's request for reconsideration of the claim. If the policyholder writes the appeal, the provider must supply the policyholder with the supporting documentation required to have the case reconsidered.

REVIEW

DEFINITION EXERCISE

Read the definitions carefully. If the statement is true, put a check mark next to the number. If the statement is false, correct it without rewriting the entire sentence.

1. Encounter Form: The financial record source document used by health care providers and other personnel to record diagnoses and services rendered to a patient during the current visit.

2. Day Sheet: Summary of services rendered to the patient during one visit.

3. Patient Ledger/Account Record: Written record of all medical services the patient has paid for at the doctor's office.

4. Allowed Charges: The maximum amount the patient will pay for each procedure or service performed.

5. Deductible: The amount of uncovered medical care expenses that must be paid by the policy holder to the health care provider.

6. Copayment: A provision in an insurance policy requiring the policy holder to pay either a specified dollar amount or a percentage of the allowed fee for medical services they receive.

7. Explanation of Benefits form: A statement accompanying all claims payments that explains how the insurance company determined its share of the reimbursement.

8. EOB: Explanation of patient's bill.

CHALLENGE EXERCISE

Answer the following:

1. Listed below are eight steps required for a new patient initial interview and check-in. It is important that the steps be performed in proper sequence.

   Arrange the steps listed below in the proper sequence by placing the correct step number to the left of the statement.

   _____ Create the patient's encounter form.

   _____ Patient fills out registration form.

   _____ Conduct new patient intake interview.

   _____ Schedule patient's appointment.

   _____ Make photocopy of patient insurance cards.

   _____ Verify patient's insurance.

   _____ Patient signs the authorization for release of medical information.

   _____ Create the patient's chart and enter patient demographics in the practice's data base.

2. Listed below are twelve steps covering the period from the postclinical check-out to the generation of the claim form. It is important that the steps be performed in proper sequence.

   Arrange the steps listed below in the proper sequence by placing the correct step number to the left of the statement.

   _____ Collect payments from the patient.

   _____ Log claim in the insurance registry.

   _____ Post all charges and payments to the patient's ledger.

   _____ Provider signs the claim form.

   _____ Mail claim form to insurance company.

   _____ Post all procedures, charges, and payments on the day sheet.

   _____ Generate the claim form.

   _____ File office copy of the claim form.

   _____ Affix any required attachments to the claim.

   _____ Code, if necessary, all procedures and diagnoses.

   _____ Enter and total charges for all procedures performed.

3. Listed below are the nine processing steps performed on a claim form by an insurance company. It is important that the steps be performed in proper sequence.

   Arrange the steps listed below in proper sequence. Place the correct step number to the left of the statement.

   _____ The Explanation of Benefits form is generated.

   _____ Deductible requirements are determined.

   _____ Code numbers are matched with the master benefits list.

   _____ EOB and benefit check are mailed.

   _____ Determination is made of "allowed charges."

   _____ Copayment requirement is determined.

   _____ Procedure codes are cross-matched with diagnosis codes.

   _____ Claim is scanned for patient and policy identification numbers.

   _____ Claim is checked against common data file.

4. Explain how the managed care authorization for specialty care for a new patient is obtained.

5. Discuss how to determine primary and secondary coverage for an adult patient covered by two full benefit policies.

6. Determine the primary carrier for a child in the following scenarios:

   a. Parent A was born on March 13, 1956; Parent B was born on April 13, 1954.

   b. Parent A was born on January 1, 1956, and has had the insurance policy for three years; Parent B was born on January 1, 1960, and has had the policy for six years.

   c. The parents of the patient are divorced and both have remarried. The child is covered under three policies: the father, the stepmother, and the mother, who has custody of the child. The court has not made any stipulation about medical insurance.

   d. Child is covered exactly as described in case 3; however, the court has stipulated the father is responsible for the medical expenses.

Legal and Regulatory Considerations

OBJECTIVES   Upon successful completion of this chapter, you should be able to:

1. Identify or define the following terms, phrases, and abbreviations:

statute	second party	code pairs (edit pairs)
statutory law	verbal contract	modifier
regulation	guardian	black box edits
case law	patient-health care provider	medical savings account (MSA)
common law	contract	identifier
precedent	encrypt	National Provider Identifier (NPI)
Federal Register	Federal False Claims Act	National Health PlanID (PlanID)
Medicare Bulletin	upcoding	National Standard Employer
fiscal intermediary (FI)	self-referral	Identifier
listserv	Health Insurance Portability and	National Individual Identifier
privacy	Accountability Act of 1996	(patient identifier)
confidentiality	(HIPAA)	check digit
security	fraud	electronic data interchange (EDI)
breach of confidentiality	abuse	electronic claim
contract	Correct Coding Initiative (CCI)	electronic explanation of benefits
third party	coding	clearinghouse
first party	unbundling	privacy standards

2. Provide examples of a statute, rule/regulation, and case law.
3. Explain the use of the *Federal Register*.
4. Discuss ways the insurance specialist can obtain information about new laws and regulations.
5. Give examples of breaches of confidentiality.
6. State the importance of obtaining the patient's signature for the "Authorization for Release of Information" statement on the HCFA-1500.
7. Identify two classifications of patients who are not required to sign the "Authorization for Release of Information" statement on the HCFA-1500.
8. Explain how the patient authorization for release of information is obtained for electronic claims.
9. Verify a legitimate telephone request for patient information.
10. Process facsimile (fax) requests for patient information.
11. Prepare a confidentiality notice to serve as the first page of faxed patient information.

12. Establish a patient record retention policy for the physician's office.

13. Summarize the *HCFA Internet Security Policy* and the *Stark II Regulations*.

14. List the components of the Health Insurance Portability and Accountability Act of 1996 (HIPAA), and explain the health care impact of each.

15. Outline the elements of the *Compliance Program Guidance for Physician Practices*.

16. Implement HCFA's *Correct Coding Initiative (CCI)*.

17. Provide an example of *unbundling*.

18. Differentiate among the NPI, PlanID, EIN, and patient identifier.

19. List the scheduled implementation dates for HCFA's *electronic health care standards* and *privacy standards*.

INTRODUCTION

The health insurance specialist must be knowledgeable about the increasing number of laws and regulations for maintaining patient records and processing health insurance claims. This chapter defines legal and regulatory terminology and summarizes laws and regulations that impact health insurance processing. Internet-based links are also included as a resource to the health insurance specialist for remaining up-to-date and obtaining clarification of legal and regulatory considerations.

INTRODUCTION TO LEGAL AND REGULATORY CONSIDERATIONS

The health insurance specialist is responsible for becoming familiar with statutes, rules and regulations, and case law that impact the maintenance of patient records and processing of health insurance claims. Federal and state **statutes** (or **statutory law**) are laws passed by legislative bodies (e.g., federal congress and state legislatures). These laws are then implemented as **regulations**, which are guidelines written by administrative agencies (e.g., HCFA). **Case law** (or **common law**) is based on court decisions that establish a **precedent** (or standard).

INTERNET LINKS

Find your state department of health Web site at www.fsis.usda.gov/ophs/stategov.htm, and use it to search for state public health laws.

Search for federal laws and regulations at www.access.gpo.gov/nara/ (Figure 5-1).

EXAMPLE 1

FEDERAL STATUTE, IMPLEMENTED AS STATE PROGRAM

Congress passed Title XXI of the Social Security Act as part of the Balanced Budget Act of 1997, which called for implementation of the State Children's Health Insurance Program. In response, New York State implemented Child Health Plus, which expanded insurance eligibility to children under age 19 who are not eligible for Medicaid and have limited or no health insurance.

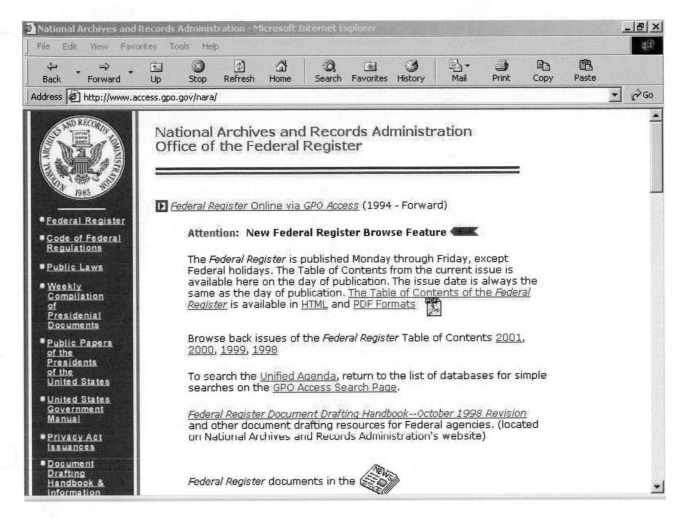

FIGURE 5-1 Web site that allows on-line searches of federal regulations, the *Federal Register*, public laws, and so on (reprinted according to Permissions Notice of the National Archives and Records Administration).

Even if family income is high, children can be eligible to enroll in Child Health Plus; an insurance premium in the form of a monthly family contribution may be required (e.g., a family of two with an income ranging from $24,977-$25,920 pay $15.00 per month per child).

EXAMPLE 2

FEDERAL STATUTE, IMPLEMENTED AS A FEDERAL REGULATION, AND PUBLISHED IN THE FEDERAL REGISTER

Congress passed the Balanced Budget Refinement Act of 1999 (Public Law 106-113), which called for a number of revisions to Medicare, Medicaid, and the State Children's Health Insurance Program. On May 5, 2000, the Department of Health and Human Services' Health Care Financing Administration (HCFA) published a proposed rule in the *Federal Register* to revise the Medicare hospital inpatient prospective payment system for operating costs. This proposed rule was entitled "Medicare Program; Changes to the Hospital Inpatient Prospective Payment Systems and Fiscal Year 2001 Rates; Proposed Rule."

EXAMPLE 3

CASE LAW

When originally passed, New York State Public Health Law (PHL) sections 17 and 18 allowed a *reasonable charge* to be imposed for copies of patient records. Health care facilities, therefore, charged fees for locating the patient's record and making copies. These fees were later challenged in court, and reasonable charge language in the PHL was interpreted in *Hernandez v. Lutheran Medical Center* (1984), *Ventura v. Long Island Jewish Hillside Medical Center* (1985), and *Cohen v. South Nassau Communities Hospital* (1987). The interpretation permitted charges of $1.00 to $1.50 per page, plus a search and retrieval fee of $15.

■ **NOTE:** Sections 17 and 18 of the PHL were amended in 1991 when the phrase, "the reasonable fee for paper copies shall not exceed seventy-five cents per page" was added to the law. ■

To accurately process health insurance claims, especially for government programs like Medicare, Medicaid, and TRICARE, be sure to routinely review legal and regulatory issues found in such publications as the *Federal Register* and *Medicare Bulletin*. The **Federal Register** is a legal newspaper published every business day by the National Archives and Records Administration (NARA) of the federal government. It is available in paper form, on microfiche and online. The **Medicare Bulletin** is a publication produced by your Medicare **fiscal intermediary (FI)**, which is an organization that contracts with HCFA to process Medicare claims.

INTERNET LINKS

The *Federal Register* can be accessed online at www.nara.gov/fedreg/.

HCFA press releases can be viewed at www.hcfa.gov/news/news.htm, and you can subscribe to the HCFA Press mailing list from that site to automatically receive new notices via email.

Medicare bulletins can be viewed at your fiscal intermediary's official Web site. The Trailblazer Health Enterprises, LLC™ Medicare site can be viewed at www.the-medicare.com/ (Figure 5-2).

Consider subscribing to an online service such as CodeCorrect.com located at www.codecorrect.com/ (Figure 5-3), that posts up-to-date billing and coding news. Most online services such as CodeCorrect.com provide a free trial membership to try out their products before actually purchasing them.

Membership in professional associations can also prove helpful in accessing up-to-date information about the health insurance industry (refer to Chapter 1, page 2, for information on joining professional associations). Newsletters and journals published by professional associations routinely include articles that clarify implementation of new legal and regulatory issues. They also provide resources for obtaining the most up-to-date information about such issues. Another way to remain current is to subscribe to a **listserv**, which is a subscriber-based question-and-answer forum that is available through email.

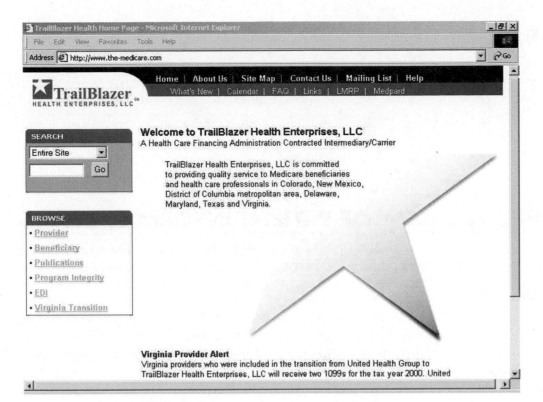

FIGURE 5-2 Online Medicare Part B bulletins can be viewed at The TrailBlazer Health Enterprises, LLC ™ Medicare Web site by selecting "Publications." (Permission to reprint granted by TrailBlazer Health Enterprises, LLC ™)

FIGURE 5-3 Up-to-date billing, coding, and reimbursement news is available on-line from CodeCorrect.com™. Sign up for free e-news and obtain a trial membership account at the Web site. (Permission to reprint granted by CodeCorrect.com™)

WWW. INTERNET LINKS

HCFA offers free subscriptions to outpatient prospective payment system electronic mailing lists at www.hcfa.gov/medlearn/listserv.htm to remain up-to-date with the latest regulations. Notices are sent to your email address.

Join the Medicare Part-B listserv at lyris.ucg.com/cgi-bin/listserv/listserv.pl/partb-l. This listserv is very active (50+ postings per day), and you may want to join the digest version to receive one daily email that contains all postings for that day.

CONFIDENTIALITY OF PATIENT INFORMATION

Confidentiality of patient information includes the related concepts of privacy and security. **Privacy** is the right of individuals to keep their information from being disclosed to others. Once information is disclosed (e.g., for the purpose of obtaining health care), it is essential that confidentiality of the information be maintained. **Confidentiality** involves restricting patient information access to those with proper authorization and maintaining the security of patient information. **Security** involves the safekeeping of patient information by:

- controlling access to hard copy and computerized records (e.g., implementing password protection for computer-based patient records).
- protecting patient information from alteration, destruction, tampering, or loss (e.g., establishing office policies).
- providing employee training in confidentiality of patient information (e.g., conducting annual in-service education programs).
- requiring employees to sign a confidentiality statement that details the consequences of not maintaining patient confidentiality (e.g., employee termination).

Because patient information is readily available through computerized databases and other means, it is essential to take steps to maintain confidentiality. **Breach of confidentiality**, often unintentional, involves the unauthorized release of patient information to a third party. Examples include:

- discussing patient information in public places (e.g., elevators).
- leaving patient information unattended (e.g., computer screen display).
- communicating patient information to family members without the patient's consent.
- publicly announcing patient information in a waiting room or registration area.
- accessing patient information without a job-related reason.

To understand the legality of this issue, it is first necessary to define contract and third party. A **contract** is an agreement between two or more parties to perform specific services or duties. A **third party** is one who has no binding interest in a specific contract. (The **first party** is the person designated in the contract to receive a contracted service. The **second party** is the person or organization providing the service.)

A **verbal contract** is established between the patient and the health care provider when the patient asks a provider to perform medical services. In exchange for services, the patient agrees to promptly pay the provider's customary fee for those services. The parties to this contract are the patient, the health care provider, and the office staff. If the patient is a minor or a legally incompetent adult, parents or stated **guardian(s)** (the person(s) legally designated to be in charge of the patient's affairs) contract for the services of the health care provider on behalf of the patient. The parents or guardians, therefore, become a party to the **patient-health care provider contract**.

For patients to receive proper treatment they must be willing to be examined and touched by medical professionals. Patients must also reveal the reason they sought medical advice and how this problem has affected them. At times, this requires the patient to reveal intimate thoughts and feelings, as well as their bodies. If the patient is to feel comfortable in confiding to a health care provider, the patient must be assured that the office will protect and control the confidential information given to the health care provider. Breach of confidentiality cannot be charged against a health care provider if written permission to release necessary medical information to an insurance company or other third party has been obtained from the patient, the parent, or the guardian. A good maxim to follow is:

"When in doubt, have them write it out."

Authorized Release of Information to Insurance Carriers

To prevent breach of patient confidentiality, all health care professionals involved with processing insurance claim forms should check to be sure the patient has signed an "Authorization for Release of Medical Information" statement before completing the claim form. The release can be obtained in one of two ways:

- Ask the patient to sign block 12, Patient's or Authorized Person's Signature, on the claim form (see Figure 5-4) or

- Ask the patient to sign a special release form that is customized by each practice and specifically names the patient's insurance carrier (see Figure 5-5 on page 74).

The signed customized form is recommended for use by all computerized practices and must be filed in the patient's chart. Copies may be made if the patient's insurance company requests proof of the patient's release of medical information. If this method is used, the computer must be programmed to print the phrase "signature on file," in Block 12 of each claim form filed for that patient (see Figure 5-4). Practices manually preparing claims can ask the patient to sign the release of medical information block on the claim form (see Figure 5-4 and read the authorization statement).

A dated, signed release statement is generally considered to be in force for 1 year from the date entered on the form; therefore, a new signed and dated statement must be obtained annually. Undated signed forms are

---

READ BACK OF FORM BEFORE COMPLETING & SIGNING THIS FORM.	13. INSURED'S OR AUTHORIZED PERSON'S SIGNATURE I authorize payment of medical benefits to the undersigned physician or supplier for services described below.
12. PATIENT'S OR AUTHORIZED PERSON'S SIGNATURE I authorize the release of any medical or other information necessary to process this claim. I also request payment of government benefits either to myself or to the party who accepts assignment below.	
SIGNED ___**SIGNATURE ON FILE**___ DATE _____	SIGNED _____

FIGURE 5-4 Release of medical information (Blocks 12 and 13 on a HCFA-1500 health insurance claim form)

(Practice Letterhead Here)

*Authorization for Release of Medical Information to the Insurance Carrier
and Assignment of Benefits to Physician.*

COMMERCIAL INSURANCE

I hereby authorize release of medical information necessary to file a claim with my insurance company and ASSIGN BENEFITS OTHERWISE PAYABLE TO ME TO _____ (fill in provider's name) _____

I understand that I am financially responsible for any balance not covered by my insurance carrier. A copy of this signature is as valid as the original.

Signature of patient or guardian_____ Date _____

MEDICARE INSURANCE

BENEFICIARY _____ Medicare Number _____

I request that payment of authorized Medicare benefits be made either to me or on my behalf to _____ (fill in provider's name) _____ for any services furnished to me by that provider. I authorize any custodian of medical information about me to release to the Health Care Financing Administration and its agents any information needed to determine these benefits or the benefits payable for related services.

Beneficiary Signature _____ Date _____

MEDICARE SUPPLEMENTAL INSURANCE

BENEFICIARY _____ Medicare Number _____

Medigap ID Number _____

I hereby give ____ (Name of Physician or Practice) ____ permission to bill for Medicare Supplemental Insurance payments for my medical care.

I understand that _____ (Name of Medicare Supplemental Insurance Carrier) _____ needs information about me and my medical condition to make a decision about these payments. I give permission for that information to go to _____ (Name of Medicare Supplemental Insurance Company) _____ .

I request that payment of authorized Medicare Supplemental benefits be made either to me or on my behalf to (Name of Physician or Practice) for any services furnished me by that physician. I authorize any holder of medical information about me to release to (Name of Medicare Supplemental Insurance Company) any information required to determine and pay these benefits.

Beneficiary Signature _____ Date _____

FIGURE 5-5 Model authorization for release of medical information to an insurance company

assumed to be in force until revoked by the patient or guardian. Health Care Financing Administration (HCFA) regulations permit government programs to accept both dated and undated authorizations.

Established medical practices that have previously not maintained authorizations on file, but plan to computerize the practice and/or file some claims electronically, must re-register patients and obtain the necessary authorization forms prior to entering patient information into the computerized databases.

Authorization Exceptions

The federal government allows three exceptions to the required authorization for release of medical information to insurance companies. One exception is for patients covered by Medicaid; another is for patients covered by Workers' Compensation. The federal government has mandated that when a patient enrolls in Medicaid or requests benefits under the Workers' Compensation program, the patient becomes a third-party beneficiary in a contract between the health care provider and the government agency that sponsors the specific program. When health care providers agree to treat either a Medicaid or a Workers' Compensation case, they agree to accept the program's payment as payment in full for covered procedures rendered to these patients. The patient may be billed only for services rendered that are not covered by the specific program, or if the insurance carrier determines the patient was ineligible for benefits on the date(s) of service.

The third exception involves providers who file insurance claims for medical services provided to patients seen at a hospital but who are not expected to receive follow-up care in the physician's office. These patients are required to sign an authorization for treatment and an authorization for release of medical information at the hospital before being seen by the health care provider. If the hospital's medical information release form includes both the authorization for release of information from the hospital and the treating physician's services, claims may be submitted by the physician's office without obtaining a separate medical information release from the patient. The words "Signature on file" are written in the authorization for release of medical information signature block on the health insurance claim form (see Figure 5-4). If, at a later date, proof of the signature authorizing the release of information is requested, a copy of the signed authorization may be obtained from the hospital's files.

Release of HIV/AIDS Status

Patients who undergo screening for the human immunodeficiency virus (HIV) or AIDS infection should be asked to sign an additional authorization statement for release of information regarding their HIV/AIDS status (see Figure 5-6 on page 76). Several states require very specific wording on this form. Be sure to determine if the state you are working in requires a special HIV Status form.

Release of Information to Other Third Parties

The patient's signature on the release of medical information to insurance carrier form restricts the release of information to the insurance company. Release of the same information or copies of the patient medical record to any other third party is not authorized (see Figure 5-7 on page 77 for a sample authorization to release general medical information form).

Most states have special laws covering release of mental health services records. There also are federal laws covering confidentiality when the patient is enrolled in a federally assisted alcohol and drug abuse program. If you work with a substance abuse facility or have a patient receiving mental health services, acquaint yourself with federal and state laws.

(Practice Letterhead here)

Authorization to Release HIV-Related Information

Patient Name _____   Date of Service _____

Address _____   Date of Birth _____

I authorize _____(name of practice)_____ to release HIV-related information to the following organi-zation for the purpose of processing payment for services rendered. I understand that this is a required consent and I voluntarily and knowingly sign this authorization for release of information to:

Name of Requestor _____

Address _____

I understand this consent can be cancelled at any time, but that information already disclosed is exempt. I release _____(name of practice)_____ from any liability arising from the release of information to the individual or agency stated above.

Patient signature: _____   Date: _____

Patient representative signature: _____   Date: _____

Reason patient is unable to sign: _____

Witness signature: _____   Date: _____

Information released shall include a statement prohibiting the requestor from rediscloing patient infor-mation without the prior consent of the patient. Unless otherwise specified, *this authorization will expire one year from date signed.*

FIGURE 5-6 Authorization to release HIV-related information

Need To Know Rule

Confidentiality is breached when a health care professional in the practice releases confidential information to a person who has no demon-strable legal need to receive this information. Persons in this category may include spouses, friends, relatives, other patients, or colleagues working in a practice where the patient has had no previous contact. On the other hand, there is a demonstrable need to provide limited patient information to office personnel when making a referral of a patient to that office.

This does not preclude the sharing of case studies or specific insurance billing problems with colleagues or acquaintances. In these discussions, however, great care must be taken to ensure that a third party (a person or entity not involved in the patient-provider relationship) cannot identify the patient or family involved.

(Practice Letterhead here)

Authorization to Release Medical Information

Patient Name _____   Date of Service _____

Address _____   Date of Birth _____

I authorize _____(name of practice)_____ to release information contained in my medical record
concerning treatment provided from _____ to _____ . I understand that this is
a required consent and I voluntarily and knowingly sign this authorization for release of information to:

Name of Requestor _____

Address _____

I release _____(name of practice)_____ from any liability arising from the release of information to
the individual or agency stated above.

Patient signature: _____   Date: _____

Patient representative signature: _____   Date: _____

Reason patient is unable to sign: _____

Witness signature: _____   Date: _____

Information released shall include a statement prohibiting the requestor from redisclosing patient information without the prior consent of the patient.

FIGURE 5-7 Sample authorization to release general medical information

CLAIMS INFORMATION TELEPHONE INQUIRIES

Another area of concern regarding breach of confidentiality involves the clarification of insurance data by telephone. A signed release statement from the
patient may be on file, but the office has no assurance of the identity or credentials of the inquirer. It is very simple for a curious individual to place a call
to a physician's office and claim to be an insurance company benefits clerk.
The rule to follow here is:

*Never give information over the phone or in person until you have ver-
ified that the party making the request is entitled to the information.*

To verify insurance company telephone inquiries for clarification of claims
data, place the caller on hold until you have the file copy of the patient's
insurance claim form in hand. Ask the caller to read the line on the claim
form that needs clarification. When sufficient information from the caller's

copy is obtained to ensure validity of the inquiry, clarifying statements or data may be released by phone. Be sure to follow up this action by writing a memo detailing the conversation, and file it with the practice's file copy of the claim form. Computerized practices without paper claims on file should access the patient account and/or demographic screens to confirm the data on the claim forms. If an error is detected, it should be corrected and a notation made to explain the change in the message section of the patient's computer file.

If there are multiple questions or if a detailed clarification is needed, it is best to ask for a written request for information. The written request and a copy of the response then become an official addendum to the practice's file copy of the claim.

Another way to verify a caller's identity is to ask how you can return the call. A return call placed through the insurer's switchboard will permit verification that the caller was a valid insurance company employee. If verification cannot be made, the caller must submit a request in writing on company stationery.

Phone Requests From Lawyers

Great care should be taken when attorneys request information over the telephone. Lawyers are well aware that offices must have the patient's signed release of information in the practice's files before answering questions. Never assume that the attorney has a signed release from the patient, and do not submit to pressure from the attorney to breach confidentiality.

Law offices are required to send any patient's authorized release of information statement the lawyers have obtained to the provider. After comparing and matching the signature on the release form sent by the lawyer with the patient's or guardian's signature and handwriting on the registration form, you should respond to the lawyer's request in writing.

FACSIMILE TRANSMISSION

The use of facsimile (fax) machines has become a popular mode of communication. Great care must be taken to ensure that sensitive information sent by fax reaches the intended receiver and is handled properly. It is recommended that health information be faxed only when there is:

1. An urgent need for the health record and mailing the record will cause unnecessary delays in treatment, or

2. Immediate authorization for treatment is required from a primary care physician or other third-party case manager.

In such cases, information transmitted should be limited only to the information required to satisfy the immediate needs of the requesting party. Each transmission of sensitive material should have a cover sheet including the following information:

- Name of the facility to receive the facsimile
- Name and phone number of the person authorized to receive the transmission
- Name and phone number of the sender
- Number of pages being transmitted

IF YOU HAVE RECEIVED THIS TRANSMITTAL IN ERROR, PLEASE NOTIFY THE SENDER IMMEDIATELY.

THE MATERIAL IN THIS TRANSMISSION CONTAINS CONFIDENTIAL INFORMATION THAT IS LEGALLY PRIVILEGED. THIS INFORMATION IS INTENDED ONLY FOR THE USE OF THE INDIVIDUAL OR ENTITY NAMED ABOVE.

IF YOU ARE NOT THE INTENDED RECIPIENT, YOU ARE HEREBY NOTIFIED THAT ANY DISCLOSURE, COPYING, DISTRIBUTION, OR ACTION TAKEN BASED ON THE CONTENTS OF THIS TRANSMISSION IS STRICTLY PROHIBITED.

FIGURE 5-8 Sample fax confidentiality notice

- A confidentiality notice or disclaimer (Figure 5-8)
- Instructions to authorized recipient to send verification of receipt of transmittal to the sender.

The practice should keep a dated log of the transmission of all medically sensitive facsimiles and copies of all "receipt of transmittal" verifications signed and returned by the authorized recipient. Special care must be taken to ensure that proper facsimile destination numbers are keyed into the fax machine prior to transmission.

CONFIDENTIALITY AND THE INTERNET

At the present time there is no guarantee of confidentiality when patient records are transmitted via the Internet or World Wide Web. If time constraints prevent sending sensitive information through a more secure delivery system, special arrangements may be made with the requesting party to transmit the document after deleting specific patient identification information. It is best to call the party requesting the documents to arrange for an identifier code to be added to the document so that the receiving party is assured that the information received is that which was requested. This transmission should be followed by an official unedited copy of the record sent by overnight delivery including specific patient material that was deleted in the previous transmission.

On November 24, 1998, the *HCFA Internet Security Policy* issued guidelines for the security and appropriate use of the Internet for accessing and transmitting sensitive HCFA information (e.g., Medicare beneficiary information). The information must be **encrypted** (information is converted to a secure language format for transmission), and authentication or identification procedures must be implemented to assure that the sender and receiver of data are known to each other and are authorized to send and/or receive such information.

INTERNET LINK

Discussion of encryption models and approaches can be found on HCFA's Web site at http://www.hcfa.gov/security/isecplcy.htm.

RETENTION OF PATIENT INFORMATION AND HEALTH INSURANCE RECORDS

Patient information and health insurance records are to be maintained for five years, unless state law specifies a longer period. The records must be available as references for use by HCFA, fiscal intermediaries, DHHS audit, or as designated for billing review and other references. It is acceptable to microfilm patient information and insurance records (including attachments submitted to insurance companies), if the microfilm accurately reproduces all original documents. All other categories of health insurance records are to be maintained in their original form.

INTERNET LINK

A summary of state record retention laws can be accessed at http://www.ahima.org/journal/pb/99.06.html by scrolling down the page and clicking on Table 4.

FEDERAL FALSE CLAIMS ACT

The federal government passed the **Federal False Claims Act** during the Civil War to regulate fraud associated with military contractors selling supplies and equipment to the Union Army. Since then, this Act has been used by federal agencies to regulate the conduct of any contractor submitting claims for payment to the federal government for any program, including Medicare. Control of fraud and abuse has been a key regulatory interest ever since the hospital prospective payment system legislation (called Diagnosis Related Groups, or DRGs) was passed as part of the Tax Equity & Fiscal Responsibility Act (TEFRA) of 1982. Prior to TEFRA, the cost-based reimbursement system for Medicare claims made fraud almost unnecessary because the system rewarded high utilization of services. The implementation of DRGs resulted in the first serious "gaming" of the system to find ways to maximize revenues for hospitals. Some hospitals engaged in a practice called **upcoding**, which is the assignment of an ICD-9-CM diagnosis code that does not match patient record documentation for the purpose of illegally increasing reimbursement (e.g., assigning the ICD-9-CM code for heart attack code when angina was actually documented in the record). As a result, upcoding became a serious fraud concern under DRGs.

Stark II Regulations

In the 1980's, the issue of self-referral was presented as a serious legislative item in Congress. **Self-referral** involves providers ordering services to be performed for patients by organizations in which they have a financial interest (e.g., laboratories, or durable medical equipment). Commercial laboratories were targeted first, followed by most methods of physician or provider investment in health care delivery entities. Representative Stark led legislative efforts to treat any types of referral practices by physicians to entities in which they had a material financial interest as fraud. Examples of material financial interest include ownership interest and kickbacks to induce referrals (e.g., free or less than fair market value terms for office space, consulting services, and practice management). In 1998, Medicare regulations were released for implementation of "Stark laws" to regulate physician referral for services from which the doctor profits, because studies revealed that when a doctor has an investment interest in a lab, for example, the doctor orders more tests and more expensive services.

In 1996, Congress passed the Health Insurance Portability and Accountability Act (HIPAA) due to additional concerns about fraud (e.g., coding irregularities, medical necessity issues, and waiving of co-pays and deductibles). While the Federal False Claims Act provided HCFA with regulatory authority to enforce fraud and abuse statutes for the Medicare program, HIPAA extends that authority to all federal and state health care programs.

HEALTH INSURANCE PORTABILITY AND ACCOUNTABILITY ACT OF 1996

The **Health Insurance Portability and Accountability Act of 1996 (HIPAA)**, Public Law 104–191, amended the Internal Revenue Code of 1986, to:

- improve the portability and continuity of health insurance coverage in the group and individual markets.
- combat waste, fraud, and abuse in health insurance and health care delivery.
- promote the use of medical savings accounts.
- improve access to long-term care services and coverage.
- simplify the administration of health insurance.
- create standards for electronic health information transactions.
- create privacy standards for health information.
- create unique identifiers for providers, health plans, employers, and individuals.

A discussion on each HIPAA component follows, and although HIPAA standards are still being finalized, health care organizations should develop and implement a response to each component.

INTERNET LINKS

Obtain proposed rules from the DHHS Web sites at aspc.os.dhhs.gov/admnsimp/ and www.hcfa.gov/medicaid/hipaa/default.asp. Then compare them to the way your practice operates.

Go to aspe.os.dhhs.gov/admnsimp/lsnotify.htm and subscribe to the *HIPAA-REGS Listserv* to be notified by email when documents related to HIPAA regulations are published or posted.

Educate your staff about HIPAA and Medicare issues. Download free interactive computer-based training courses and learn about satellite programs designed to teach Medicare billing guidelines at www.medicaretraining.com.

Visit www.mxcity.com, an online gateway to medical reimbursement information. They have compiled thousands of free resources and made them easy to find. Just select your state or clinical specialty and click on GO. You can also subscribe to a free e-newsletter at their Web site.

Portability and Continuity of Health Insurance Coverage

HIPAA provisions were designed to improve the portability and continuity of health coverage by:

- limiting exclusions for pre-existing medical conditions.
- providing credit for prior health coverage and a process for transmitting certificates and other information concerning prior coverage to a new group health plan or issuer.
- providing new rights that allow individuals to enroll for health coverage when they lose other health coverage, change from group to individual coverage, or have a new dependent.
- prohibiting discrimination in enrollment and premiums against employees and their dependents based on health status.
- guaranteeing availability of health insurance coverage for small employers and renewability of health insurance coverage in both the small and large group markets.
- preserving, through narrow preemption provisions, the states' traditional role in regulating health insurance, including state flexibility to provide greater protections.

Fraud and Abuse

HIPAA defines **fraud** as "an intentional deception or misrepresentation that someone makes, knowing it is false, that could result in an unauthorized payment." The attempt itself is considered fraud, regardless of whether it is successful. **Abuse** "involves actions that are inconsistent with accepted, sound medical, business, or fiscal practices. Abuse directly or indirectly results in unnecessary costs to the program through improper payments." The difference between fraud and abuse is the individual's intent; however, both have the same impact in that they steal resources from the Medicare Trust Fund. The most common forms of Medicare fraud include:

- billing for services not furnished.
- misrepresenting the diagnosis to justify payment.
- soliciting, offering, or receiving a kickback.
- unbundling codes.
- falsifying certificates of medical necessity, plans of treatment, and medical records to justify payment.
- billing for a service not furnished as billed.

Examples of Medicare abuse include:

- excessive charges for services, equipment, or supplies.
- submitting claims for items or services that are not medically necessary to treat the patient's stated condition.
- improper billing practices that result in a payment by a government program when the claim is the legal responsibility of another third-party payer.
- violations of participating provider agreements with insurance companies.

When a Medicare provider commits fraud, an investigation is conducted by the Department of Health and Human Services (DHHS) Office of the Inspector General (OIG). The OIG Office of Investigations prepares the case for referral to the Department of Justice for criminal and/or civil prosecution.

A person found guilty of committing Medicare fraud faces criminal, civil, and/or administrative sanction penalties including:

- civil penalties of $5,000 to $10,000 per false claim plus triple damages under the False Claims Act. (The provider pays an amount equal to three times the claim submitted in addition to the civil penalties fine.)
- criminal fines and/or imprisonment of up to ten years if convicted of the crime of health care fraud as outlined in HIPAA or, for violations of the Medicare/Medicaid Anti-Kickback Statute, imprisonment of up to five years and/or a criminal fine of up to $25,000.
- administrative sanctions including up to a $10,000 civil monetary penalty per line item on a false claim, assessments of up to triple the amount falsely claimed, and/or exclusion from participation in Medicare and state health care programs.

In addition to the penalties outlined above, those who commit health care fraud can also be tried for Mail and Wire Fraud.

Compliance Program Guidance for Physician Practices

The DHHS Office of Inspector General issued a draft *Compliance Program Guidance for Individual and Small Group Physician Practices* as published in the June 12, 2000 edition of the *Federal Register*. The intent of the guidance document is to help physicians in solo or small group practices conduct effective voluntary compliance measures to prevent fraud and abuse in government health programs (e.g., Medicare and Medicaid). The draft physician guidance is based on the following seven elements:

1. Implementation of written policies and standards of conduct
2. Designation of a compliance officer or contact
3. Development of training and education programs
4. Creation of accessible lines of communication
5. Performance of internal audits to monitor compliance
6. Enforcement of standards through well-publicized disciplinary directives
7. Prompt corrective action to detect offenses

The guidance suggests ways to implement a compliance plan that is consistent with the size and resources available to the physician practice. For example, if a practice cannot afford a designated compliance officer, the guidance suggests delegating those responsibilities among the practice's staff or outsourcing the compliance officer function to an independent, part-time consultant.

INTERNET LINKS

The full text of the OIG *Final Compliance Program Guidance for Individual and Small Group Physician Practices* is located at www.hhs.gov/progorg/oig/modcomp/webcpg.txt. Other OIG compliance programs (e.g., hospital or hospice compliance) are located at www.hhs.gov/progorg/oig/modcomp.

Correct Coding Initiative

The **Correct Coding Initiative (CCI)** was implemented in 1996 by HCFA to reduce Medicare program expenditures by detecting inappropriate **coding** (a method of assigning numeric or alphanumeric codes to procedures/services; e.g., Current Procedural Terminology or CPT) on claims and to deny payment for them. The CCI was also initiated to address the problem of *unbundling* with regard to physician reporting of services and procedures. **Unbundling** is the reporting of multiple codes to increase reimbursement from the payer, when a single combination code should be reported.

EXAMPLE

A patient presents with a 2.5 centimeter laceration of the forearm. The proper procedure includes cleansing the wound, local infiltration of anesthesia, suturing, and application of a dressing. One code number is reported, and Medicare would pay approximately $80.00. If unbundled, separate charges would be associated with multiple procedures of cleansing of the wound, infiltration of anesthesia, debridement of wound edges, dressing the wound, etc., and Medicare would be billed approximately $140.00.

The CCI is designed to eliminate this practice by establishing **code pairs (edit pairs)** that, if reported together, would either be excluded from payment or would be paid at a reduced rate. Currently, over 90,000 code pairs in the CCI database are applicable to the policy that will return paper or electronic claims to the provider as unprocessable if the claim contains certain incomplete or invalid information. Under these conditions, the claim is not denied but rather rejected and no "initial determination" is made; therefore, no appeal rights are granted to the issuer.

Mutually exclusive code combinations are based on one of two conditions, either (1) the CPT definition or (2) the medical impossibility or improbability that the procedures could have been performed during the same encounter. Violation of the mutually exclusive portion of the CCI can result in much lower reimbursement.

EXAMPLE

The HCFA-1500 reported a laparoscopic cholecystectomy ($750) and an open cholecystectomy ($1,500) on the same patient, with charges totaling $2,250. The claim was denied; upon review of the operative report, it is noted that the surgeon attempted to remove the gallbladder using laparoscopy; however, surgical removal of the gallbladder was required due to the enlarged size of the gallbladder. In this situation, only the open cholecystectomy should be reported on the claim form. The surgeon cannot be paid for both procedures; they are mutually exclusive (in terms of reimbursement).

Some physician practices discovered that attaching a modifier to the code number reported on the HCFA-1500 claim resulted in a bypass of the initial edit and processing of the claim. A denial was issued that provided a detailed explanation and the office had the opportunity to correct the problem and/or appeal the denial. As a result, HCFA created another component of the CCI that indicates whether a modifier reported with a code pair is appropriate. A **modifier** is defined according to the CPT coding manual as "the means by which the reporting physician (or provider) can indicate that a service or procedure that has been performed has been altered by some specific circumstance but not changed in its definition or code."

EXAMPLE

The patient underwent a bilateral procedure. CPT modifier -50 would be reported on the HCFA-1500 claim, and a space would replace the dash. If the procedure code was 12345, the entire procedure would be reported on the HCFA-1500 as 12345 50.

INTERNET LINKS

CCI edits are updated quarterly and are available for purchase through the National Technical Information Services (NTIS) at www.ntis.gov/product/correct-coding.htm.

CCI edits are also available as part of vendor encoder software, including the CodeCorrect.com™ online product at www.codecorrect.com, which is updated as new versions of CCI edits become available.

The Balanced Budget Act of 1996 required further cuts in Medicare spending, and resulted in the establishment of a two-year contract between HCFA and a private company responsible for developing coding edits to be used during claims processing (e.g., to deny a claim because two service or procedure codes were submitted when only one code was allowed under the edit). The private company refused to allow HCFA to publish the coding edits because they considered them proprietary, and these nonpublished code edits became known as **black box edits**. As a result, providers were unable to verify claims denials or ensure that claims submitted had been properly processed. The American Medical Association (AMA) responded by involving its Correct Coding Policy Committee in the review and opposition of black box edits, and HCFA responded by stating that (1) its contract (that expired October 1, 2000) with the private company that created the black box edits would not be renewed and (2) future contracts with private companies would not allow for the restrictions experienced with the black box coding edits. In September 2000, HCFA directed Medicare carriers to discontinue using black box coding edits.

HCFA is continuing the public process established with AdminaStar Federal Inc., an Indiana Medicare carrier, to develop coding edits. These coding edits are published for use by providers submitting claims, and a process was developed by the American Medical Association for physicians and specialty societies to review and comment on proposed coding edits before carriers adopt them for implementation. Commercial software products (e.g., CodeCorrect.com™) incorporate these coding edits so providers can review claims to ensure the accuracy of codes submitted and to expedite payment of the claim.

Medical Savings Accounts

HIPAA permits eligible individuals to establish a **medical savings account (MSA)**, a tax-exempt trust or custodial account established for the purpose of paying medical expenses in conjunction with a high-deductible health plan.

Individuals eligible to establish an MSA include:

- an employee (or spouse of an employee) of a "small employer" that maintains an individual or family "high-deductible health plan" covering that individual (employee or spouse), or

- a self-employed person (or spouse of self-employed person) that maintains an individual or family "high-deductible health plan" covering that individual (self-employed person or spouse).

Access to Long-Term Care Services and Coverage

HIPAA contains tax clarification provisions for long-term care insurance to assure that the tax treatment for private long-term care insurance is the same as for major medical coverage. Insurance companies must also follow certain administrative and marketing practices or face significant fines. For example, consumers must be provided with a description of the policy's benefits and limitations before making a committment to allow consumers to compare policies from different companies. Companies must report annually the number of claims denied, information on policy replacement sales, and policy terminations data. No policy can be sold as a long-term care insurance policy if it limits or excludes coverage by type of treatment, medical condition, or accident. An exception to this rule, however, includes policies that may limit or exclude coverage for pre-existing conditions or diseases, mental or nervous disorders (but not Alzheimer's), or alcoholism or drug addiction. The law also prohibits a company from canceling a policy except for nonpayment of premiums.

Administrative Simplification

HIPAA was part of a Congressional attempt at incremental health care reform, with the *Administrative Simplification* aspect requiring DHHS to develop standards for maintenance and transmission of health information required to identify individual patients. These standards are designed to:

- improve efficiency and effectiveness of the health care system by standardizing the interchange of electronic data for specified administrative and financial transactions.

- protect the security and confidentiality of electronic health information.

The requirements outlined by law and the regulations implemented by DHHS require compliance by *all* health care organizations that maintain or transmit electronic health information (e.g., health plans; health care clearinghouses; and health care providers, from large integrated delivery networks to individual physician offices). After the final standards are adopted, small health plans have 36 months to comply. Others, including health care providers, must comply within 24 months.

The law provides for significant financial penalties for violations.

General penalty for failure to comply:

- each violation: $100

- maximum penalty for all violations of an identical requirement: may not exceed $25,000

Wrongful disclosure of individually identifiable health information:

- wrongful disclosure offense: $50,000; imprisonment of not more than one year; or both

- offense under false pretenses: $100,000; imprisonment of not more than 5 years; or both

- offense with intent to sell information: $250,000; imprisonment of not more than 10 years; or both.

Unique Identifiers

The *Administrative Simplification* aspect of HIPAA mandates the use of unique identifiers for providers, health plans, employers, and individuals receiving health care services (patients). An **identifier** is a series of numerical or alphanumeric characters assigned to providers, health plans, employers, and patients.

The **National Provider Identifier (NPI)** is a unique identification number for health care providers that will be used by all health plans. Health care providers and all health plans and health care clearinghouses will use the NPI in administrative and financial transactions specified by HIPAA. The NPI is proposed as an 8-position alphanumeric identifier; the eighth position is a check digit that can help detect keying errors.

The **National Health PlanID (PlanID)**, formerly known as the PAYERID, is authorized by HIPAA to provide a standard plan identifier for efficient electronic data interchange (EDI) and health care administrative operations. It is expected to have ten numeric positions, with a check digit in the tenth position.

 **INTERNET LINK**

Watch for the NPI & PlanID *Notice of Proposed Rule Making* at www.hcfa.gov.

The **National Standard Employer Identifier** is based on the Employer Identification Number (EIN), which is assigned by the Internal Revenue Service and has nine numeric positions (e.g., 12-3456789).

The most controversial of the proposed identifiers, the **National Individual Identifier (patient identifier)**, is on hold pending privacy legislation. Industry experts speculate that the identifier will consist of approximately ten numeric digits, including a check digit. A **check digit** is a one-digit character (alphabetic or numerical) used to verify the validity of a unique identifier.

INTERNET LINK

Review Administrative Simplification regulations in their entirety at aspe.os.dhhs.gov/admnsimp/.

Electronic Health Care Data Submission Standards

Because no common standard for the transfer of information between health care providers and payers had previously been established, providers submitted insurance claims data to payers based on different criteria. For providers who submit claims to hundreds of payers, programming computer systems to meet these requirements has been a difficult and expensive process. HIPAA changed this practice by requiring payers to implement transaction standards for **electronic data interchange (EDI)**, which is the process of sending data from one party to another using computer linkages. Health care providers submit an **electronic claim**, that contains data submitted on computer tape, diskette, or by computer modem or fax. The payer receives the electronic claim, processes the data, and sends an **electronic explanation of benefits**, which contains the results of processing electronic claims, to the provider. The final rule on transactions and code sets was published in the October 2000 *Federal Register*, and the following standards are to be used for each transaction or code set listed:

- Claims/encounters, eligibility verification, enrollment, and related transactions: *American National Standards Institute ANSI X12N*

- Pharmacy transactions: *National Council for Prescription Drug Programs (NCPDP)*

- Diagnoses and inpatient hospital services: *International Classification of Diseases-9th Revision-Clinical Modification* (ICD-9-CM), which will change to ICD-10-CM when the new system is ready for adoption

- Procedures: *ICD-9-CM* Volume 3 and *HCFA Common Procedure Coding System* (HCPCS)

- Physician services: *Current Procedural Terminology* (CPT)

- Dental services: *Current Dental Terminology* (CDT)

Health plans (except small self-administered plans), health care **clearinghouses** (that perform centralized claims processing for providers and health plans), and health care providers that participate in electronic data interchanges must comply with the final rule within 24 months. Small self-administered plans have 36 months with which to comply.

INTERNET LINK

Free *EDI* downloads are available at hipaa.wpc-edi.com/HIPAA_40.asp.

Privacy Standards

HIPAA required Congress to pass privacy legislation within 36 months of the date the bill was signed into law (October 1996); otherwise, the DHHS was authorized to create and implement final regulations to protect patient privacy. Congress did not meet its deadline, and the DHHS published the final rule establishing standards for the protection of the privacy of patient medical records. The new regulation is scheduled to become effective in 2003, and includes the following components:

- Protecting consumer control over health information
- Setting limits on medical record use and release
- Ensuring security of personal health information
- Establishing accountability for medical record use and release
- Balancing public responsibility with privacy protection

The **privacy standards** outline individual rights for the protection of health information by health care providers, health plans, and health care clearinghouses. Under the rule, health care providers, health plans, and clearinghouses are prohibited from using or disclosing health information except as authorized by the patient or specifically permitted by the regulation. *All* medical records and other individually identifiable health information (electronic, paper, or verbal) are covered by the final rule.

REVIEW

DEFINITION EXERCISE

Read the definitions carefully. If the statement is true, put a check mark to the left of the number. If the statement is false, correct the statement.

1. Breach of confidentiality: Release of confidential patient information to a third party.
2. Fraud: Deception or misrepresentation that an individual makes, knowing it to be false, which could result in some unauthorized benefit.
3. Contract: An agreement between two or more parties to perform specific services or duties.
4. Patient-health care provider contract: A contract between the patient and a health care provider for medical services in exchange for the insurance company's agreement to pay promptly that physician's usual fee for the services performed.
5. Guardian: Person who has legal responsibility for a minor child or incompetent adult.

CHALLENGE EXERCISE

Answer the following:

1. Discuss how an insurance specialist prevents being charged with a "breach of confidentiality" in each of the following cases:
   a. Unauthorized release of medical data to an insurance company.
   b. Unauthorized release of confidential information to a patient's lawyer.
   c. Phone requests for clarification of information on a claim form from an employee of an insurance carrier.
   d. Phone requests concerning diagnostic and treatment data for a competent adult from a "relative" or "spouse."
   e. Discussion of case studies in the classroom.

2. Explain how a health insurance specialist could unwittingly be involved in committing fraud by actions of the following persons:

   Health care provider

   Patient

   Widow/widower of deceased patient

3. Discuss the penalty for committing fraud as stated in the Health Insurance Portability and Accountability Act of 1996.

4. Explain how you can prevent and correct mistakes in filing or processing of insurance claims.

5. List and explain four examples of fraudulent billing practices.

6. Discuss the content of the Confidentiality Notice that should be included on all medical practices' fax cover sheets.

OBJECTIVES Upon successful completion of this chapter, you should be able to:

1. Define the following terms, phrases, and abbreviations:

International Classification of Diseases (ICD)

mortality

International Classification of Diseases-9th revision-Clinical Modification (ICD-9-CM)

morbidity

National Center for Health Statistics (NCHS)

Health Care Financing Administration (HCFA)

medical necessity

Advance Beneficiary Notice (ABN)

HCFA ICD-9-CM Coding Guidelines

outpatient

inpatient

HCFA-1500

UB-92 (HCFA-1450)

primary diagnosis

principal diagnosis

secondary diagnosis

secondary condition

concurrent condition

comorbidity

complication

principal procedure

qualified diagnosis

Tabular List (Volume 1)

V Codes

E Codes

Morphology of Neoplasms (M codes)

morphology

benign

malignant

Glossary of Mental Disorders

Classification of Drugs by AHFS List

Classification of Industrial Accidents According to Agency

List of Three-Digit Categories

Index to Diseases (Volume 2)

Tabular List and Index to Procedures (Volume 3)

HCPCS

main term

nonessential modifier

subterm

essential modifier

coding convention

Index to Diseases Coding Convention

code in slanted bracket

eponym

essential modifier

NEC (not elsewhere classifiable)

nonessential modifier

note

see

see also

see category

chapter heading

major topic heading

category

subcategory

subclassification

Tabular List Coding Conventions

and

bold type

brace

brackets

code first underlying disease

colon

excludes

format

fourth and fifth digits

includes

NOS

note

parentheses

use additional code

with

Index to Procedures and Tabular List (Procedures) Coding Conventions

omit code

code also any synchronous procedures

neoplasm

benign	unspecified nature	indexing
malignant	metastatic	axis of classification
lesion	contiguous sites (overlapping	iatrogenic illness
primary malignancy	sites)	sequelae
secondary malignancy	re-excision	injury
metastasized	adverse effect (reaction)	Final Rule: Standards for
carcinoma (Ca) *in situ*	poisoning	Electronic Transactions
uncertain behavior	late effect	errata

2. Discuss the difference between the terms "primary diagnosis" and "principal diagnosis."

3. Explain the purpose of coding diagnoses on insurance claim forms.

4. List and apply the HCFA guidelines in coding diagnoses using the ICD-9-CM coding system.

5. Identify and properly use the special terms, marks, abbreviations, and symbols used in the ICD-9-CM coding system.

6. Accurately code all diagnoses using the ICD-9-CM coding system.

INTRODUCTION

There are two related classifications of diseases with similar titles. The *International Classification of Diseases* (**ICD**) is used to code and classify **mortality** (death) data from death certificates. The *International Classification of Diseases, Clinical Modification* (**ICD-9-CM**) is used to code and classify **morbidity** (disease) data from inpatient and outpatient records, physician office records, and most statistical surveys. The health insurance specialist assigns ICD-9-CM codes to diagnoses, signs, and symptoms documented by the health care provider. Entering ICD-9-CM codes on the HCFA-1500 results in uniform reporting of medical reasons for health services provided.

INTERNET LINK

If ICD-9-CM coding system is being introduced to you for the first time, consider completing a workbook such as *Understanding Medical Coding: A Comprehensive Guide*, by Sandra J. Johnson, available for purchase from Delmar/Thomson Learning at www.DelmarAlliedHealth.com

ICD-9-CM

ICD-9-CM was sponsored in 1979 as the official system for assigning codes to diagnoses (inpatient and outpatient care, including physician offices) and procedures (inpatient care). The ICD-9-CM is organized into three parts:

- a tabular list that contains a numerical listing of disease code numbers
- an alphabetical index to disease entries
- a classification system for procedures that contains an alphabetic index and a tabular list.

The **National Center for Health Statistics (NCHS)** and the **Health Care Financing Administration (HCFA)** are U.S. Department of Health and Human Services agencies responsible for overseeing all changes and modifications to the ICD-9-CM. The NCHS works with the World Health Organization (WHO) to coordinate official disease classification activities for ICD-9-CM (Index to Diseases and Tabular List), which includes the use, interpretation, and periodic revision of the classification system. HCFA is responsible for creating annual procedure classification updates for ICD-9-CM (Index to Procedures and Tabular List). Updates are available as downloads (DOS, Windows, and Macintosh versions) from the official ICD-9-CM Web site of the NCHS, and a CD-ROM version that contains official coding guidelines as well as the complete, official version of the ICD-9-CM is available for purchase online, by mail, telephone, or fax from the:

> Superintendent of Documents
> U.S. Government Printing Office
> P.O. Box 371954
> Pittsburgh, PA 15250-7954
> (202) 512-1800
> (202) 512-2250 (fax)
> bookstore.gpo.gov

ICD-9-CM coding books are also available from commercial publishing companies and are helpful in manual coding because they contain color-coded entries that identify required additional digits, nonspecific and unacceptable principal diagnoses, and more.

INTERNET LINKS

ICD-9-CM updates are available through a free download at www.cdc.gov/nchs/icd9.htm

Purchase a CD-ROM that contains official coding guidelines and the complete official version of ICD-9-CM at bookstore.gpo.gov

Code books published by the American Medical Association, Medicode, and St. Anthony's Publishing can be viewed at www.delmaralliedhealth.com/ins_cod/index.html

Mandatory Reporting of ICD-9-CM Codes

The Medicare Catastrophic Coverage Act of 1988 mandated the reporting of ICD-9-CM diagnosis codes on Medicare claims, and although the act was largely repealed the following year, the reporting of ICD-9-CM codes is still required. Private insurance carriers adopted similar diagnosis coding requirements for claims submission in subsequent years (reporting procedure codes is discussed in Chapters 7 and 8). Requiring codes to be reported on submitted claims ensures the medical necessity of procedures and services rendered to patients during an encounter (office visit, outpatient visit, or emergency department visit). **Medical necessity** is defined by Medicare as "the determination that a service or procedure rendered is reasonable and necessary for the diagnosis or treatment of an illness or injury." If it is possible that scheduled tests or services/procedures may be found "medically unnecessary" by Medicare, have the patient sign an **Advance Beneficiary Notice (ABN)**, which acknowledges patient responsibility for payment if Medicare denies the claim (the ABN is discussed in greater detail on page 359 of Chapter 14).

■ **NOTE:** Be sure to clarify the definition of *medical necessity* by insurance companies (other than Medicare) because the definition can vary. ■

EXAMPLE

A patient with insulin-dependent diabetes is seen at the physician's office for treatment of a leg injury sustained from a fall. When the physician questions the patient about his general health status since the last visit, the patient admits to knowing that a person on insulin should perform a daily blood sugar level check; the patient also admits to usually skipping this check 1 or 2 times a week and not performing this check today. The physician orders an Xray of the leg, which proves to be positive for a fracture, and a test of the patient's blood glucose level. If the only stated diagnosis on the claim is a fractured tibia, the blood glucose test would be rejected for payment by the insurance company as an unnecessary medical procedure. The diagnostic statement on the claim form should include both the fractured tibia and insulin-dependent diabetes to permit reimbursement consideration for the Xray and the blood glucose test.

ICD-9-CM Annual Updates

HCFA and the NCHS annually update ICD-9-CM, and providers should order new code books no later than September of each year. New diagnosis codes officially go into effect on October 1 of each year, although some Medicare carriers delay reporting requirements until January and some commercial carriers do not require or accept the new codes until March 1.

ICD-10-CM and ICD-10-PCS

In 1992, the World Health Organization (WHO) completed work on the tenth revision, which has a new title: *The International Statistical Classification of Diseases and Related Health Problems* and a new alphanumeric coding system. It is expected that the change from ICD-9-CM to the NCHS-developed ICD-10-CM and the HCFA-developed ICD-10-PCS (Procedure Coding System) will be mandated for 2003 or later. An overview of ICD-10-CM and ICD-10-PCS starts on page 135 of this chapter.

HCFA ICD-9-CM CODING GUIDELINES

The **HCFA ICD-9-CM Coding Guidelines** were developed for use in reporting diagnoses for claims submission. Four cooperating parties are involved in the continued development and approval of the guidelines: (1) American Hospital Association (AHA), (2) American Health Information Management Association (AHIMA), (3) Health Care Financing Administration (HCFA), and (4) National Center for Health Statistics (NCHS). Although the guidelines were originally developed for use in submitting government claims, insurance companies have also adopted them (sometimes with variation).

■ **NOTE:** Because variations may contradict the HCFA guidelines, be sure to obtain each insurance company's official coding guidelines. ■

When reviewing the guidelines, note that the terms *encounter* and *visit* are used interchangeably in describing outpatient services.

Basic Coding Guidelines for Outpatient Services

A. The appropriate code or codes from 001.0 through V82.9 must be used to identify diagnoses, symptoms, conditions, problems, complaints, or any other reason for the encounter/visit.

B. For accurate reporting of ICD-9-CM diagnosis codes, the documentation should describe the patient's condition, using terminology which includes specific diagnoses as well as symptoms, problems, or reasons for the encounter. There are ICD-9-CM codes to describe all of these.

C. The selection of codes 001.0 through 999.9 will frequently be used to describe the reason for the encounter. These codes are from the section of ICD-9-CM for the classification of diseases and injuries (e.g. infectious and parasitic diseases; neoplasms; symptoms, signs, and ill-defined conditions).

D. Codes that describe symptoms and signs, as opposed to diagnoses, are acceptable for reporting purposes when an established diagnosis has not been confirmed by the physician. Chapter 16 of ICD-9-CM, Symptoms, Signs, and Ill-defined Conditions (codes 780.0-799.9) contain many, but not all, codes for symptoms.

E. ICD-9-CM provides codes to deal with encounters for circumstances other than a disease or injury. The Supplementary Classification of Factors Influencing Health Status and Contact with Health Services (V01.0-V82.9) is provided to deal with occasions when circumstances other than a disease or injury are recorded as diagnosis or problems.

F. ICD-9-CM is composed of codes with either 3, 4, or 5 digits. Codes with 3 digits are included in ICD-9-CM as the heading of a category of codes that may be further subdivided by the use of fourth and/or fifth digits which provide greater specificity. A three-digit code is to be used only if it is not further subdivided. Where fourth-digit subcategories and/or fifth-digit subclassifications are provided, they must be assigned. A code is invalid if it has not been coded to the full number of digits required for that code.

G. List first the ICD-9-CM code for the diagnosis, condition, problem, or other reason for encounter/visit shown in the medical record to be chiefly responsible for the services provided. List additional codes that describe any coexisting conditions.

H. Do not code diagnoses documented as "probable," "suspected," "questionable," "rule out," or "working" diagnosis. Rather, code the condition(s) to the highest degree of certainty for that encounter/visit, such as symptoms, signs, abnormal test results, or other reason for the visit.

■ **NOTE:** This is contrary to the coding practices used by hospitals and medical record departments for coding the diagnoses of hospital inpatients. ■

I. Chronic diseases treated on an ongoing basis may be coded and reported as many times as the patient receives treatment and care for the condition(s).

J. Code all documented conditions that coexist at the time of the encounter/visit, and require or affect patient care treatment or management. Do not code conditions that were previously treated and no longer exist. However, history codes (V10-V19) may be used as secondary codes if the historical condition or family history has an impact on current care or influences treatment.

K. For patients receiving diagnostic services only during an encounter/ visit, sequence first the diagnosis, condition, problem, or other reason for encounter/visit shown in the medical record to be chiefly responsible for the outpatient services provided during the encounter/visit. Codes for other diagnoses (e.g., chronic conditions) may be sequenced as additional diagnoses.

L. For patients receiving therapeutic services only during an encounter/visit, sequence first the diagnosis, condition, problem, or other reason for encounter/visit shown in the medical record to be chiefly responsible for the outpatient services provided during the encounter/visit. Codes for other diagnoses (e.g., chronic conditions) may be sequenced as additional diagnoses.

M. The only exception to this rule is for patients receiving chemotherapy, radiation therapy, or rehabilitation. In this instance, the appropriate V code for the service is listed first, and the diagnosis or problem for which the service is being performed is listed second.

N. For patient's receiving preoperative evaluations only, sequence a code from category V72.8, Other specified examinations, to describe the pre-operative consultations. Assign a code for the condition to describe the reason for the surgery as an additional diagnosis. Code also any findings related to the pre-operative evaluation.

O. For ambulatory surgery, code the diagnosis for which the surgery was performed. If the *postoperative* diagnosis is known to be different from the *preoperative* diagnosis at the time the diagnosis is confirmed, select the postoperative diagnosis for coding, since it is the most definitive.

PRIMARY AND PRINCIPAL DIAGNOSIS CODING

Before undertaking the study of diagnosis coding for provider practices, it is necessary to have an understanding of two issues:

1. The definition of *primary diagnosis* versus *principal diagnosis* and how claims submission is impacted by each definition

2. How to deal with diagnostic statements that are qualified by terms and phrases such as: *probable, suspected, rule out*, and *ruled out*

Rules for coding diagnoses on medical insurance claims differ for out-patients and inpatients. An **outpatient** is a person treated in one of three settings:

• Health care provider's office

• Hospital clinic, emergency department, hospital same-day surgery unit, or ambulatory surgical center (ASC) where the patient is released within 23 hours

• Hospital admission solely for observation where the patient is released after a short stay

An **inpatient** is a person admitted to the hospital for treatment with the expectation that the patient will remain in the hospital for a period of 24 hours or more. The inpatient admission status is stipulated by the admitting physician.

The primary diagnosis is reported on physician office claims (HCFA-1500) and hospital outpatient and emergency department claims (UB-92). The principal diagnosis is reported on inpatient hospital claims (UB-92). The **HCFA-1500** is the standard claim form used to report physician office services and procedures. It was originally approved by the American Medical Association in 1975 for group and individual claims processing and was called the *Universal Claim Form*. The HCFA-1500 was revised in 1990 and printed with red ink for optical scanning purposes. In 1992, Medicare required the HCFA-1500 (10/90) to be submitted by physicians and suppliers (except for ambulance services). The **UB-92** (or **HCFA-1450**) is the uniform bill (standard claim form) used to report inpatient admissions and outpatient and emergency department services and procedures. The UB-92 is based on the billing form and standard data set approved for use nationwide by institutional providers and payers in handling health care claims; it was originally called the *UB-82* (because it was implemented in 1982).

INTERNET LINKS

Information about the HCFA-1500 is available at www.nucc.org.

Information about the UB 92 is available at www.nubc.org.

Primary Diagnosis versus Principal Diagnosis

The **primary diagnosis** is the most significant condition for which services and/or procedures were provided, and it is entered first in Block 21 of the HCFA-1500 claim form. The **principal diagnosis** is defined as "the condition determined *after study* that resulted in the patient's admission to the hospital." It is listed in Form Locator 67 on the UB-92 (HCFA-1450).

In addition to reporting the primary diagnosis, up to three **secondary diagnosis** codes may be reported in Block 21 of the HCFA-1500 claim form and linked to services and/or procedures reported in Block 24. If more than four conditions are to be reported, it will be necessary to generate a second HCFA-1500 claim form. A **secondary condition** (or **concurrent condition** or **comorbidity**) coexists with the primary condition, has the potential to affect treatment of the primary condition, and is an active condition for which the patient is treated or monitored. The UB-92 also allows secondary diagnosis codes to be reported (Form Locators 68 through 75); these diagnoses include comorbidities (conditions that coexist with the principal diagnosis) and **complications** (conditions that develop subsequent to inpatient admission).

EXAMPLE 1

A patient seeks care at the health care provider's office for an injury to the right leg that, upon Xray in the office, is diagnosed as a fractured tibia. While in the office, the physician also reviews the current status and treatment of the patient's insulin-dependent diabetes.

Answer: The primary diagnosis is "fracture, shaft, right tibia;" the secondary diagnosis is "insulin-dependent diabetes mellitus." On the HCFA-1500, the health insurance specialist would list the diagnoses codes in Block 21 and enter the diagnosis link in Block 24E for the corresponding service or procedure.

DIAGNOSIS	LINK TO SERVICE OR PROCEDURE
Fracture, shaft, right tibia	of leg
Insulin-dependent diabetes mellitus	Office visit

EXAMPLE 2

The patient has a history of arteriosclerotic heart disease and was admitted to the hospital because of severe shortness of breath. After study, a diagnosis of congestive heart failure is added. What is the principal diagnosis?

Answer. The principal diagnosis is congestive heart failure. (This diagnosis was determined after study to be the cause of the patient's admission to the hospital. Arteriosclerosis alone would not have caused the hospitalization. Shortness of breath is not coded because it is a symptom of the actual condition, congestive heart failure.)

EXAMPLE 3

A patient was admitted with hemoptysis. The following procedures were performed: upper GI series, barium enema, chest , bronchoscopy with biopsy of the left bronchus, and resection of the upper lobe of the left lung. The discharge diagnosis was bronchogenic carcinoma. What is the principal diagnosis?

Answer. The principal diagnosis is bronchogenic carcinoma, left lung. (The hemoptysis precipitated the need for hospitalization, but is a symptom of the underlying problem, bronchogenic carcinoma. After admission to the hospital and after study, the diagnostic tests revealed the carcinoma.)

PRINCIPAL VERSUS SECONDARY PROCEDURES

Hospital coders are required to differentiate between principal and secondary procedures/services rendered using the criteria discussed below. These criteria do not affect coding for health care providers' offices, but are discussed here to introduce the full scope of ICD-9-CM diagnosis and procedure coding.

Hospitals are required to rank all inpatient procedures according to specific criteria for selection of principal and secondary procedures and to code them using the ICD-9-CM procedure index and tabular list.

■ **NOTE:** Outpatient procedures and services, whether performed in the hospital or in the health care provider's office, are coded using the Current Procedural Terminology or CPT coding system. ■

A **principal procedure** is a procedure performed for definitive treatment rather than diagnostic purposes, or one performed to treat a complication, or that which is most closely related to the principal diagnosis. There may be cases in which the only procedures performed are not directly related to the principal diagnosis, but are related to secondary conditions. In such cases, the principal procedure is considered to be the major definitive treatment performed.

EXAMPLE 1

A patient was admitted to the hospital because of a fractured left hip. During the hospital stay, the patient developed a pulmonary embolism. The following procedures were performed: Xrays of the right and left hips, a lung scan, and a surgical pinning of the hip. Which is the principal procedure?

Answer. Pinning of the hip, known as open reduction with internal fixation (ORIF), is the principal procedure; it is the major definitive treatment for the principal diagnosis of fractured hip. The lung scan was a necessary diagnostic procedure for confirmation of a pulmonary embolism. This diagnosis is the most life-threatening problem for the patient, but it does not meet the principal diagnosis criteria: the major cause, determined after study, for the hospitalization.

EXAMPLE 2

A patient entered the hospital with symptoms of profuse sweating, tremors, and polyuria. The patient has an existing problem with control of insulin-dependent diabetes mellitus as well as carpal tunnel syndrome. The diabetes was controlled within 18 hours by adjusting the patient's insulin dosage. A surgical carpal tunnel release was performed. The final diagnoses were carpal tunnel syndrome and uncontrolled insulin dependent diabetes mellitus. What is the principal procedure?

Answer. The principal diagnosis is uncontrolled insulin-dependent diabetes mellitus (IDDM). The principal procedure is the carpal tunnel release. (Carpal tunnel syndrome is not the principal diagnosis because it was not the problem that brought the patient to the hospital. Uncontrolled diabetes caused the admission in this case.)

CODING QUALIFIED DIAGNOSES

Another difference in coding inpatient hospitalizations versus outpatient and/or provider office encounters involves the assignment of codes for qualified diagnoses. A **qualified diagnosis** is a working diagnosis that is not yet proven or established. Terms and phrases associated with qualifying diagnoses include *suspected, rule out, possible, probable, questionable, suspicious for,* and *ruled out.* Do not assign an ICD-9-CM code to qualified diagnoses; instead, code the sign(s) and/or symptom(s) documented in the patient's chart.

EXAMPLE

For Qualified Diagnosis	Code the Sign or Symptom
Suspected pneumonia	Shortness of breath, wheezing, rales, rhonchi
Questionable Raynaud's	Numbness of hands
Rule out wrist fracture	Wrist pain and swelling
Ruled out pneumonia	Influenza (flu)

Qualified diagnoses are a necessary part of the hospital and provider office patient's chart until a specific diagnosis can be determined. While qualified diagnoses are routinely coded for hospital inpatient admissions and reported on the UB-92, HCFA *specifically outlaws the reporting of such diagnoses on the HCFA-1500 submitted by health care provider offices*. HCFA regulations permit the reporting of patients' signs and/or symptoms instead of the qualified diagnoses. This ruling was originally published in the *Health Care Financing Administration, Coding and Reporting Requirements, Medicare Manual 4020.3 1989* and is included in HCFA's official outpatient/physician's office coding guidelines.

An additional incentive for not coding qualified diagnoses resulted from the Missouri case of *Stafford v. Neurological Medicine Inc., 811 F. 2d 470 (8th Cir., 1987)*. In this case, the diagnosis stated in the physician's office chart was "rule out brain tumor." The claim submitted by the office listed the diagnosis code for "brain tumor," although test results were available that proved a brain tumor did not exist. The physician assured the patient, before she left the hospital, that although she had lung cancer, there was no metastasis to the brain. Sometime after the insurance carrier received the provider's claim, it was inadvertently sent to the patient. Upon receipt of the claim, the patient, devastated by the diagnosis, committed suicide. The husband sued and was awarded $200,000 on the basis of "negligent paperwork" because the physician's office was responsible for reporting a "qualified diagnosis."

ICD-9-CM Coding System

The official version of ICD-9-CM was originally published in three volumes:

- Volume 1 (Tabular List)–a numerical listing of diseases and injuries.
- Volume 2 (Index to Diseases)–an alphabetic index to Volume 1.
- Volume 3 (Index to Procedures and Tabular List).

Provider offices and health care facilities use the Tabular List and Index to Diseases (Volumes 1 and 2 of ICD-9-CM) to code diagnoses. The Index to Procedures and Tabular List (Volume 3) is used by hospitals to code inpatient procedures. Many publishers offer their own version of ICD-9-CM, and as a result hospital (Volumes 1, 2 and 3) and outpatient (Volumes 1 and 2) editions of the coding manual are available. In addition, to make the coding procedure easier, publishers often place the Index to Diseases (Volume 2) in front of the Tabular List (Volume 1).

Diseases–Tabular List (Volume 1)

The **Tabular List (Volume 1)** contains 17 chapters that classify diseases and injuries, two supplemental classifications, and five appendices. The 17 chapters are organized as follows:

Chapter 1	Infectious and Parasitic Diseases (001-139)
Chapter 2	Neoplasms (140-239)
Chapter 3	Endocrine, Nutritional and Metabolic Diseases, and Immunity Disorders (240-279)
Chapter 4	Diseases of the Blood and Blood-forming Organs (280-289)
Chapter 5	Mental Disorders (290-319)
Chapter 6	Diseases of the Nervous System and Sense Organs (320-389)

Chapter 7   Diseases of the Circulatory System (390-459)

Chapter 8   Diseases of the Respiratory System (460-519)

Chapter 9   Diseases of the Digestive System (520-579)

Chapter 10   Diseases of the Genitourinary System (580-629)

Chapter 11   Complications of Pregnancy, Childbirth, and the Puerperium (630-677)

Chapter 12   Diseases of the Skin and Subcutaneous Tissue (680-709)

Chapter 13   Diseases of the Musculoskeletal System and Connective Tissue (710-739)

Chapter 14   Congenital Anomalies (740-759)

Chapter 15   Certain Conditions Originating in the Perinatal Period (760-779)

Chapter 16   Symptoms, Signs, and Ill-defined Conditions (780-799)

Chapter 17   Injury and Poisoning (800-999)

The two supplemental classifications include:

V codes   Supplemental Classification of Factors Influencing Health Status and Contact with Health Services (V01-V82)

E codes   Supplementary Classification of External Causes of Injury and Poisoning (E800-E999)

The five appendices include:

Appendix A   Morphology of Neoplasms (M Codes)

Appendix B   Glossary of Mental Disorders

Appendix C   Classification of Drugs by American Hospital Formulary Service List Number and Their ICD-9-CM Equivalents

Appendix D   Classification of Industrial Accidents According to Agency

Appendix E   Three-digit Categories

Supplementary Classifications: V Codes and E Codes

V codes are located in the Tabular List and are assigned for patient encounters when a circumstance other than a disease or injury is present. Examples of V Code assignment include:

- Removal of a cast applied by another physician (V54.8)
- Exposure to tuberculosis (V01.1)
- Personal history of breast cancer (V10.3)
- Well baby check-up (V20.2)
- Annual physical examination (V70.0)

E codes are located in the Tabular List and describe external causes of injury, poisoning, or other adverse reactions affecting a patient's health. They are reported for environmental events, industrial accidents, injuries afflicted by criminal activity, etc. While assignment of these codes does not directly impact reimbursement to the provider, reporting E codes can expedite insurance claims processing because the circumstances related to an injury are indicated.

EXAMPLE 1

A patient who falls at home and breaks his leg would have code E849.0 (preceded by the appropriate fracture code) reported on the insurance claim. This code indicates that the patient's health insurance policy, and not a liability policy, should cover treatment.

EXAMPLE 2

A patient who falls at the grocery store and breaks his leg would have code E849.6 reported on the insurance claim. This code indicates that the store's liability insurance should be billed, not the patient's health insurance.

Appendices

ICD-9-CM appendices serve as a resource in coding neoplasms, mental disorders, adverse effects of drugs and chemicals, and external causes of disease and injury. In addition, the three-digit disease category codes are listed as an appendix. Some publishers (e.g., Medicode's *Hospital & Payor ICD-9-CM Volumes 1, 2, & 3*) include adjunct appendices such as Major Diagnostic Categories (MDCs) (associated with Diagnosis Related Groups), Diagnosis Related Groups (DRG) Categories, valid three-digit ICD-9-CM codes (those that do not require a fourth or fifth digit), and differences and similarities between inpatient and outpatient coding guidelines.

Morphology of Neoplasms (M codes) (found in Appendix A of ICD-9-CM) contains a reference to the World Health Organization publication entitled *International Classification of Diseases for Oncology* (ICD-O). The appendix also interprets the meaning of each digit of the morphology code number. **Morphology** indicates the tissue type of a neoplasm, and while M Codes are *not reported on provider office claims*, they are reported to state cancer registries. A basic knowledge of morphology coding can be helpful to a coder because the name of the neoplasm documented in the patient's chart does not always indicate whether the neoplasm is **benign** (not cancerous) or **malignant** (cancerous).

Referring to the morphology entry in the Index to Diseases helps determine which column in the Neoplasm Table should be referenced to select the correct code. In addition, coding should be delayed until the pathology report is available in the patient's chart for review.

EXAMPLE

The patient's chart documents carcinoma of the breast. The Index to Diseases entry for *Carcinoma* says "*see also* Neoplasm by site, malignant." This index entry directs the coder to the Neoplasm Table, and the code is selected from one of the first three columns (depending on whether the cancer is primary, secondary, or *in situ*—check the pathology report for documentation).

The Glossary of Mental Disorders (found in Appendix B of ICD-9-CM) corresponds to the psychiatric terms that appear in Chapter 5: Mental Disorders, and consists of an alphabetic listing of terms and definitions based on those contained in ICD-9-CM and input from the *American Psychiatric Association's Task Force on Nomenclature and Statistics*. Some definitions are based on those in *A Psychiatric Glossary, Dorland's Illustrated Medical Dictionary*, and *Stedman's Medical Dictionary, Illustrated*.

EXAMPLE

The diagnosis *Chronic Alcoholism* (303.9x) requires the addition of a fifth-digit to completely code the condition. Often providers do not document the term necessary to assign the fifth-digit (e.g., chronic alcoholism that is continuous, episodic, or in remission); therefore, the coder must assign a fifth-digit for "unspecified" (0). The Glossary of Mental Disorders, located in Appendix B of ICD-9-CM, defines alcoholism according to *continuous, episodic,* and in *remission*—if the coder reviewed these definitions, it is likely that the appropriate fifth-digit could be assigned based on documentation in the patient's chart (even though the provider did not specify the term).

The **Classification of Drugs by AHFS List** (found in Appendix C of ICD-9-CM) contains the American Hospital Formulary Services List number and its ICD-9-CM equivalent code number, organized in numerical order according to AHFS List number. The List is published under the direction of the American Society of Hospital Pharmacists.

EXAMPLE

The patient's chart documents that the patient experienced a reaction to *substance 76:00.* By referring to the Classification of Drugs by AHFS List in Appendix C of ICD-9-CM, the coder can determine that *76:00* refers to *oxytocics.* The coder can then turn to the Table of Drugs and Chemicals in the Index to Diseases of ICD-9-CM and look up *Oxytocics* (found in alphabetical order) to locate the reportable codes.

■ **NOTE:** The AHFS List can also be referenced within the Table of Drugs and Chemicals by looking up the word *Drug.* Because providers infrequently document the List number, it *may be* easier for coders to remember to reference the appendix. ■

The **Classification of Industrial Accidents According to Agency** (found in Appendix D of ICD-9-CM) is based on employment injury statistics adopted by the Tenth International Conference of Labor Statisticians. Because it may be difficult to locate the E Code entry in the ICD-9-CM Index to External Causes, coders may find the Industrial Accidents According to Agency appendix more helpful in identifying the category of equipment, etc. for an external cause of injury.

EXAMPLE

The patient sustained an injury as the result of a malfunctioning combine. While the E code for "accident, caused by, combine" can be easily located in the Index to External Causes, if the coder doesn't know what a combine is, the location of the accident cannot be properly coded. The Industrial Accidents According to Agency appendix can be referenced to determine that a combine is categorized as agricultural equipment. Thus, the coder can assign the location E code as "Accident, occurring (at), farm."

The **List of Three-Digit Categories** (found in Appendix E of ICD-9-CM) contains a breakdown of three-digit category codes organized beneath section headings.

> ### EXAMPLE
>
> Acute rheumatic fever (390-392)
>
> 390 Rheumatic fever without mention of heart involvement
>
> 391 Rheumatic fever with heart involvement
>
> 392 Rheumatic chorea

Index to Diseases (Volume 2)

The **Index to Diseases (Volume 2)** contains three sections:

- *The Alphabetical Index of Diseases and Injuries.* This index includes two official tables that make it easier to code hypertension and neoplasms. Some publishers print special editions of ICD-9-CM manuals that contain additional tables to simplify the search for the correct code of other complex conditions.

- *Table of Drugs and Chemicals.* Adverse effects and poisonings associated with medicinal, chemical, and biological substances are coded by referring to this table.

- *Index to External Causes of Injury and Poisoning* (E codes). This separate index is often forgotten; it is helpful to mark it with a tab as a reminder of its usefulness.

Tabular List and Index to Procedures (Volume 3)

The **Tabular List and Index to Procedures (Volume 3)** is included only in the hospital version of commercial ICD-9-CM books. It is a combined alphabetical index and numerical listing of inpatient procedures. Hospital outpatient departments and health care providers' offices use the *Current Procedural Terminology, Fourth Edition* (CPT) published by the American Medical Association (AMA), and/or additional codes created by HCFA to augment CPT codes on Medicare claims. These special HCFA codes are known as HCPCS Level II and III codes. **HCPCS** stands for *Health Care Financing Administration Common Procedure Coding System.* (CPT and HCPCS codes are further discussed in Chapters 7 and 8 of this text.)

DISEASE INDEX ORGANIZATION

The Index to Diseases is an alphabetical listing of main terms or conditions printed in boldface type that may be expressed as nouns, adjectives, or eponyms (Figure 6-1).

Main Terms

Main terms (conditions) are printed in boldface type and are followed by the code number. Main terms may or may not be followed by a listing of parenthetical terms that serve as nonessential modifiers of the main term (see the Main Term in Figure 6-1). **Nonessential modifiers** are qualifying words that do not have to be included in the diagnostic statement for the code number listed at the end of the parenthetical statements to apply.

Subterms

Subterms (or **essential modifiers**) qualify the main term by listing alternate sites, etiology, or clinical status. A list of subterms is indented 2 spaces under the main term. Secondary qualifying conditions are indented 2 spaces under a subterm. Great care must be taken when moving from the bottom of one column to the top of the next column or when turning the page. The main

Dextrocardia (corrected) (false) (isolated)
(secondary) (true)   746.87
   with
      complete transposition of viscera   759.3
      situs invertus 759.3
Dextroversion, kidney (left)   753.3
Dhobie itch   110.3
Main Term ───────────── Diabetes, diabetic (brittle) (congenital)
Nonessential Modifier ──────── (familial) (mellitus) (severe) (slight)
   (without complication)   250.0

> **Note: Use the following fifth-digit subclassification with category 250:**
>
> **0**   **type II [non-insulin dependent type] [NIDDM type] [adult-onset type] or unspecified type, not stated as uncontrolled**
>
> **1**   **type I [insulin dependent type] [IDDM] [juvenile type], not stated as uncontrolled**
>
> **2**   **type II [non-insulin dependent type] [NIDDM type] [adult-onset type] or unspecified type, uncontrolled**
>
> **3**   **type I [insulin dependent type] [IDDM type] [juvenile type], uncontrolled**

   with
Subterm ──────────────── coma (with ketoacidosis) 250.3
Second Qualifier ─────────── hyperosmolar (nonketotic) 250.2
   complication NEC   250.9
     specified NEC   250.8
   gangrene   250.7 *[785.4]*
   ketosis, ketoacidosis   250.1
Bracketed code ──────────── osetomyelitis 250.8 *[731.8]*
(requires second   specified manifestations NEC   250.8
code)   acetonemia   250.1

FIGURE 6-1 ICD-9-CM Index to Diseases layout (Courtesy of *St. Anthony's Illustrated ICD-9-CM*, 2001, (800) 632-0123)

term will be repeated and followed by "*continued.*" Watch carefully to determine if the subterm has changed or new second or third qualifiers appear when moving from one column to another.

EXAMPLE

The ICD-9-CM *Index to Diseases* entries are organized according to main terms, subterms, 2nd qualifiers, and 3rd qualifiers. Refer to the index entry for *Deformity of aortic arch, acquired* (447.8), and note the indented subterm and qualifiers. Notice when the main term continues at the top of a column (or on the next page of the Index to Diseases), the term "*–continued*" appears after the main term, and subterms and qualifiers are indented below the main term.

START OF MAIN TERM IN *INDEX TO DISEASES*	
Main Term	**Deformity** 738.10
Subterm	aortic
2nd Qualifier	arch 747.21
3rd Qualifier	acquired 447.8

CONTINUATION OF MAIN TERM AT TOP OF COLUMN	
Main Term	**Deformity** - *continued*
Subterm	appendix 751.5
Subterm	arm (acquired) 736.89
3rd Qualifier	congenital 755.50

CODING TIP:

1. A subterm or "essential modifier" provides greater specificity when included in the diagnosis. Select the code number stated after the essetial modifier, not the one stated after the main condition. For example, the code to investigate in the Tabular List for *acquired AC globulin deficiency* is 286.7.

2. Always consult the code description in the Tabular List before assigning a code because one or more instructional notes not included in the *Index to Diseases* may change the code selection.

BASIC STEPS FOR USING THE INDEX

Step 1. Locate the main term in the *Index to Diseases (Volume 2)*.

This is accomplished by first locating the condition's bold-faced main term and then reviewing the subterms listed below the main term to locate the proper disorder.

Underlined terms in the following examples are the conditions to locate in the Index to find possible codes.

EXAMPLE

<u>Irritability</u> of the bladder

<u>Impacted</u> feces

Comminuted <u>fracture</u>, left radius

Upper respiratory <u>infection</u>

Table 6-1 is a list of special main terms that should be considered when the main condition is not obvious from the health care provider's diagnostic statement. Those marked with an asterisk are associated with V codes.

Step 2. If the phrase "-*see condition*" is found after the main term, a descriptive term (an adjective) or the anatomic site has been referenced instead of the disorder or the disease (the condition) documented in the diagnostic statement.

EXAMPLE

Diagnostic statement is myocardial infarction.

Look up "myocardial" in the Index.

Locate "**Myocardial** -*see condition*."

The condition that should be located in the Index is "infarction."

Table 6-1 *Special Main Terms*

Abnormal	Infection
Admission*	Injury
Aftercare*	Late Effects
Anomaly	Lesion
Attention to*	Newborn*
Complication	Observation*
Delivery	Outcome*
Disease	Pregnancy
Disorder	Problem With*
Examination*	Puerperal
Exposure to*	Status*
Foreign Body	Syndrome
History (family)*	Vaccination*
History (personal)*	

Step 3. When the condition listed is not found, locate main terms such as syndrome, disease, disorder, derangement of, or abnormal. See Table 6-1, which lists Special Main Terms for additional help.

If unsuccessful in finding a code using the main terms suggested in Table 6-1, turn to Appendix E—Three Digit Categories—in the back of the ICD-9-CM code book. Review the categories listed under the chapter heading to determine which best fits the site of the patient's problem.

If looking for a code that describes an External Cause of Injury, these conditions are found in the separate E Code Index located after the Table of Drugs and Chemicals at the back of the Index.

EXERCISE 6–1 Finding the Condition in the Index

Underline the condition in each of the following items, then, *using only the Index*, locate the main term and the code number. Write the code number on the blank line provided.

■ **NOTE:** Items 6 through 8 are rather uncommon disorders, but are listed in the Index. ■

1. Bronchiole spasm   _____
2. Congenital candidiasis   _____
3. Irritable bladder   _____
4. Earthquake injury   _____
5. Exposure to AIDS   _____

6. Ground itch   _____

7. Nun's knees   _____

8. Mice in right knee joint   _____

After completing this exercise, refer to Appendix IV to check your answers.

Coding Conventions

Coding conventions are rules that apply to the assignment of ICD-9-CM codes. They can be found in the Index to Diseases, Tabular List, and Index to Procedures and Tabular List. (Refer to Table 6-2.)

Table 6-2 *Coding conventions for Index to Diseases. The coding convention is explained in column one, and the coding manual entry is highlighted in column two.*

CODING CONVENTION & EXAMPLE	INDEX TO DISEASES ENTRY
CODES IN SLANTED BRACKETS are always listed as secondary codes because they are manifestations (results) of other conditions. **Example:** *diabetic cataract.*	**Diabetes, diabetic** (brittle) (congenital) (familial) (mellitus) (severe) (slight) (without complication) 250.0 cataract 250.5 *[366.41]*
EPONYMS are diseases (or procedures) named for an individual (e.g., physician who originally discovered the disease, first patient diagnosed with the disease). **Example:** *Barlow's Syndrome.*	**Syndrome** Barlow's (mitral valve prolapse) 424.0

ESSENTIAL MODIFIERS are subterms that are indented below the main term in alphabetical order (except for "with" and "without"). The essential modifier clarifies the main term and must be contained in the diagnostic statement for the code to be assigned. **Example:** *acute necrotizing encephalitis.*	**Encephalitis** (bacterial) (chronic) (hemorrhagic) (idiopathic) (nonepidemic) (spurious) (subacute) 323.9
	 acute—*see also* Encephalitis, viral
	    disseminated (postinfectious) NEC 136.9 *[323.6]*
	      postimmunization or postvaccination 323.5
	    inclusional 049.8
	    inclusion body 049.8
	    necrotizing 049.8

NEC (not elsewhere classifiable) identifies codes to be assigned when information needed to assign a more specific code cannot be located in the ICD-9-CM coding book. **Example:** *disseminated encephalitis.*	**Encephalitis** (bacterial) (chronic) (hemorrhagic) (idiopathic) (nonepidemic) (spurious) (subacute) 323.9
	 acute—*see also* Encephalitis, viral
	    disseminated (postinfectious)
	    NEC 136.9 *[323.6]*

NONESSENTIAL MODIFIERS are subterms that are enclosed in parentheses following the main term. They clarify the code selection, but they do not have to be present in the provider's diagnostic statement. **Example:** *cerebral pseudomeningocele.*	**Pseudomeningocele** (cerebral) (infective) (surgical) 349.2 spinal 349.2 NOTE: Cerebral pseudomeningocele is assigned code 349.2, and pseudomeningocele is also assigned code 349.2

Table 6-2 (Continued)

CODING CONVENTION & EXAMPLE	INDEX TO DISEASES ENTRY

NOTES are contained in boxes to define terms, clarify index entries, and list choices for additional digits (e.g., fourth- and fifth-digits). **Example:** *spontaneous breech delivery.*	**Delivery**
	NOTE: Use the following fifth-digit subclassification with categories 640-648, 651-676
	   0 unspecified as to episode of care
	   1 delivered, with or without mention of antepartum condition
	   2 delivered, with mention of postpartum complication
	   3 antepartum condition or complication
	   4 postpartum condition or complication
	
	   breech (assisted) (spontaneous) 652.2

SEE directs the coder to a more specific term under which the code can be found. **Example:** *traumatic delirium, with spinal cord lesion.*	**Delirium, delirious** 780.09
	   traumatic—*see also* injury, intracranial
	     with
	       lesion, spinal cord—*see* injury, spinal, by site
	The coder is directed to the index entry below, and code 952.9 would be assigned.
	
	Injury
	   Spinal (cord) 952.9

SEE ALSO refers the coder to an index entry that may provide additional information to assign the code. **Example:** *mucus inhalation.*	**Inhalation**
	   mucus (*see also* Asphyxia, mucus) 933.1
	The coder is directed to also check the index entry below; in this case, there is no added information that would change the code.
	
	Asphyxia, asphyxiation (by) 799.0
	   mucus 933.1

SEE CATEGORY refers the coder directly to the Tabular List category (three-digit code) for code assignment. **Example:** *late effect of intracranial abscess.*	**Late**—*see also* condition
	   effect(s) (of)—*see also* condition
	     abscess
	       intracranial or intraspinal (conditions classifiable to 324)—*see* category 326

EXERCISE 6-2 Working with Coding Conventions (Index to Diseases)

Underline the main term (condition) found in the Index to Diseases, and enter the ICD-9-CM code number and index convention on the blank lines.

Condition	ICD-9-CM Code	Index Convention Used
1. Acute purulent <u>sinusitis</u>	461.9	nonessential & essential modifiers
2. Fracture, mandible	_____	_____
3. Actinomycotic meningitis	_____	_____
4. Psychomotor akinetic epilepsy	_____	_____

Condition	ICD-9-CM Code	Index Convention Used
5. 3-cm laceration, right forearm	_____	_____
6. Contusion, abdomen	_____	_____
7. Pneumonia due to _H. influenzae_	_____	_____
8. Delayed healing, open wound, abdomen	_____	_____
9. Bile duct cicatrix	_____	_____
10. Uncontrolled non-insulin dependent diabetes mellitus with osteomyelitis	_____	_____

ORGANIZATION OF THE TABULAR LIST

Numerical System

ICD-9-CM codes for Chapters 1 through 17 (codes 001–999.9) are organized according to three-digit category codes. Specificity is achieved by assigning a decimal point and one or two digits, known as fourth (subcategory codes) and fifth (subclassification codes) digits, to the main three-digit code number (Figure 6-2).

V codes (supplementary classification) are expressed as a three-character alphanumeric code (the letter V plus two digits) that can be subdivided into fourth and fifth digits to provide a more definitive description (Figure 6-3).

E codes (supplementary classification) are expressed as a four-character alphanumeric code (the letter E plus three digits). One additional decimal digit may be required to provide a more specific description of the external cause of the injury or poisoning. (See Figure 6-3 on page 112.) E codes are always secondary diagnostic codes. _They are never reported as the primary code on claim forms._

Chapters

The **chapter heading** is printed in uppercase letters and is preceded by the chapter number. The instructional "Notes" that follow the chapter heading detail general guidelines for code selections within the entire chapter. If the note(s) include an italicized excludes statement, the reference applies to the entire chapter (see Figure 6-2.) For example, the excludes note at the beginning of ICD-9-CM Chapter 3 (see the top of Figure 6-2) states that endocrine and metabolic disturbances of a fetus or newborn should be assigned codes 775.0–775.9, rather than codes 240–279.

Major Topic Heading

ICD-9-CM chapters are subdivided into **major topic headings** printed in bold uppercase letters and followed by a range of codes enclosed in parentheses. Any note or italicized excludes note printed below a major topic heading applies only to the code numbers listed in parentheses after the major topic heading, not to the entire chapter.

EXAMPLE

PSYCHOSES (290-299)
  Excludes: _mental retardation (317-319)_

Categories

Major topics are divided into three-digit categories. The **categories** are printed in bold upper- and lowercase type and are preceded by a three-digit code.

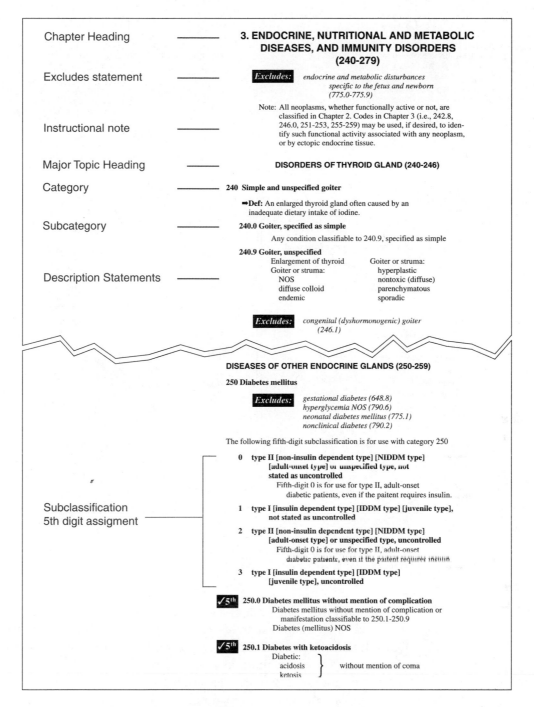

Chapter Heading ———— **3. ENDOCRINE, NUTRITIONAL AND METABOLIC DISEASES, AND IMMUNITY DISORDERS (240-279)**

Excludes statement ———— **Excludes:** *endocrine and metabolic disturbances specific to the fetus and newborn (775.0-775.9)*

Note: All neoplasms, whether functionally active or not, are classified in Chapter 2. Codes in Chapter 3 (i.e., 242.8, 246.0, 251-253, 255-259) may be used, if desired, to identify such functional activity associated with any neoplasm, or by ectopic endocrine tissue.

Instructional note ————

Major Topic Heading ———— **DISORDERS OF THYROID GLAND (240-246)**

Category ———— 240 **Simple and unspecified goiter**

➡**Def:** An enlarged thyroid gland often caused by an inadequate dietary intake of iodine.

Subcategory ———— 240.0 **Goiter, specified as simple**

Any condition classifiable to 240.9, specified as simple

240.9 **Goiter, unspecified**

Enlargement of thyroid	Goiter or struma:
Goiter or struma:	hyperplastic
NOS	nontoxic (diffuse)
diffuse colloid	parenchymatous
endemic	sporadic

Description Statements ————

Excludes: *congenital (dyshormonogenic) goiter (246.1)*

DISEASES OF OTHER ENDOCRINE GLANDS (250-259)

250 **Diabetes mellitus**

Excludes: *gestational diabetes (648.8)
hyperglycemia NOS (790.6)
neonatal diabetes mellitus (775.1)
nonclinical diabetes (790.2)*

The following fifth-digit subclassification is for use with category 250

Subclassification 5th digit assigment ————

0   **type II [non-insulin dependent type] [NIDDM type] [adult-onset type] or unspecified type, not stated as uncontrolled**
    Fifth-digit 0 is for use for type II, adult-onset diabetic patients, even if the paient requires insulin.

1   **type I [insulin dependent type] [IDDM type] [juvenile type], not stated as uncontrolled**

2   **type II [non-insulin dependent type] [NIDDM type] [adult-onset type] or unspecified type, uncontrolled**
    Fifth-digit 0 is for use for type II, adult-onset diabetic patients, even if the paient requires insulin

3   **type I [insulin dependent type] [IDDM type] [juvenile type], uncontrolled**

✓5th 250.0 **Diabetes mellitus without mention of complication**
    Diabetes mellitus without mention of complication or manifestation classifiable to 250.1-250.9
    Diabetes (mellitus) NOS

✓5th 250.1 **Diabetes with ketoacidosis**
    Diabetic:
    acidosis } without mention of coma
    ketosis

FIGURE 6-2 ICD-9-CM Disease Tabular List (Courtesy of *St. Anthony's Illustrated ICD-9-CM*, 2001, (800) 632-0123)

Any italicized excludes note that appears at this point applies to all three-, four-, or five-digit codes in the category.

Subcategories

Fourth-digit **subcategories** are indented and printed in the same fashion as the major category headings (see Figure 6-2). An italicized excludes note found at this level applies only to the specific fourth-digit code.

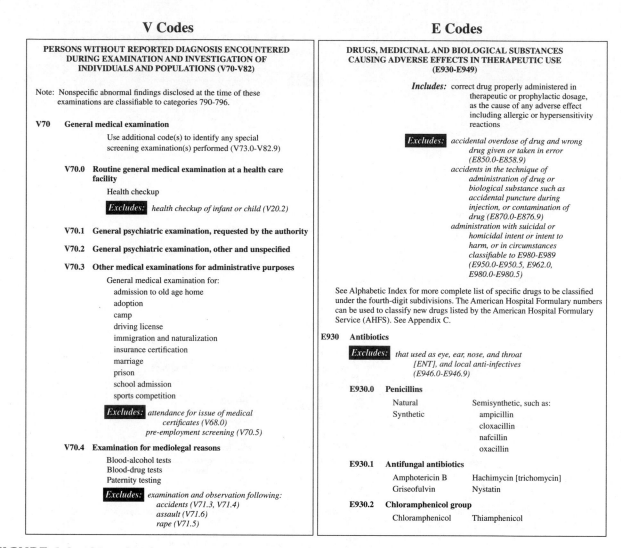

V Codes

PERSONS WITHOUT REPORTED DIAGNOSIS ENCOUNTERED DURING EXAMINATION AND INVESTIGATION OF INDIVIDUALS AND POPULATIONS (V70-V82)

Note: Nonspecific abnormal findings disclosed at the time of these examinations are classifiable to categories 790-796.

V70   General medical examination

Use additional code(s) to identify any special screening examination(s) performed (V73.0-V82.9)

V70.0   Routine general medical examination at a health care facility

Health checkup

Excludes: health checkup of infant or child (V20.2)

V70.1   General psychiatric examination, requested by the authority

V70.2   General psychiatric examination, other and unspecified

V70.3   Other medical examinations for administrative purposes

General medical examination for:
admission to old age home
adoption
camp
driving license
immigration and naturalization
insurance certification
marriage
prison
school admission
sports competition

Excludes: attendance for issue of medical certificates (V68.0)
pre-employment screening (V70.5)

V70.4   Examination for mediolegal reasons

Blood-alcohol tests
Blood-drug tests
Paternity testing

Excludes: examination and observation following:
accidents (V71.3, V71.4)
assault (V71.6)
rape (V71.5)

E Codes

DRUGS, MEDICINAL AND BIOLOGICAL SUBSTANCES CAUSING ADVERSE EFFECTS IN THERAPEUTIC USE (E930-E949)

Includes: correct drug properly administered in therapeutic or prophylactic dosage, as the cause of any adverse effect including allergic or hypersensitivity reactions

Excludes: accidental overdose of drug and wrong drug given or taken in error (E850.0-E858.9)
accidents in the technique of administration of drug or biological substance such as accidental puncture during injection, or contamination of drug (E870.0-E876.9)
administration with suicidal or homicidal intent or intent to harm, or in circumstances classifiable to E980-E989 (E950.0-E950.5, E962.0, E980.0-E980.5)

See Alphabetic Index for more complete list of specific drugs to be classified under the fourth-digit subdivisions. The American Hospital Formulary numbers can be used to classify new drugs listed by the American Hospital Formulary Service (AHFS). See Appendix C.

E930   Antibiotics

Excludes: that used as eye, ear, nose, and throat [ENT], and local anti-infectives (E946.0-E946.9)

E930.0   Penicillins

Natural   Semisynthetic, such as:
Synthetic   ampicillin
                           cloxacillin
                           nafcillin
                           oxacillin

E930.1   Antifungal antibiotics

Amphotericin B   Hachimycin [trichomycin]
Griseofulvin   Nystatin

E930.2   Chloramphenicol group

Chloramphenicol   Thiamphenicol

FIGURE 6-3 ICD-9-CM Supplementary Classifications, Tabular List (Diseases)—V and E codes (partial) (Courtesy of *St. Anthony's Illustrated ICD-9-CM*, 2001, (800) 632-0123)

Subclassifications   Some fourth-digit subcategories contained in codes 001 through V82.9 are further subdivided into **subclassifications** requiring the assignment of a fifth digit. This requirement is indicated at the left margin of each column by the presence of a printer's mark known as a section mark (§), a flag, a red dot or some other identifying mark, depending on the publisher of the code book.

The placement and appearance of fifth digits are not standardized within the code. As you complete Exercise 6-3 you can note the different styles presented. If the fifth-digit listing is preceded by a brief note, be sure to follow the directions as provided. Not all fifth digits are printed immediately below a fourth-digit code. They may appear as a note (usually enclosed in a shaded box) placed after an earlier fourth-digit subcategory. *Fifth digits are required when indicated in the code book.*

EXAMPLE

Codes 651–659 require fifth digits to specify the episode of care.
The fifth digits in this case are located below the major topic heading for codes 650–659 (located above code 650).

Locating
Fifth-digit Entries

1. Locate category code 010 in the Tabular List.

   The listing of fifth digits appears above code 010 and applies only to codes ranging from categories 010–018.

2. Locate code 250.0 in the Tabular List.

   The listing of fifth-digits appears immediately above code 250.0 and applies to all codes in the 250 category.

3. Locate category code 438 in the Tabular List.

   The fifth-digit listing applies to fourth-digit subcategories 438.1–438.8 only; subcategories 438.0 and 438.9 do not require fifth-digit subclassification.

4. Locate category code 634 in the Tabular List.

   Above category code 634, a boxed note lists fourth-digit subdivisions that are styled similarly to fifth-digit subclassification descriptions.

   The fifth digits for category codes 634–637 are located below each three-digit category for each code.

5. Locate category code 710 in the Tabular List.

   No fifth-digits are required for category 710 codes.

6. Locate the fifth-digit note above category code 710.

   This note provides more specificity than is listed for each fifth digit within codes 711-712, 715–716, 718–719, and 730. Refer to this note before assigning fifth digit 8; the health care provider's diagnostic statement may provide more specificity.

7. Locate the Alphabetic Index to External Causes of Injury and Poisoning (E Codes).

   Review the fifth paragraph which provides direction regarding the location of fourth-digits for categories E800–E848. Locate and review the *fourth-digit* listing in the E Code Tabular List.

   Then, locate category E800 to determine whether your version of the code book provides a fourth-digit listing for categories E800–E807.

Overview of the
Tabular List

1. Locate Appendix E, List of Three-Digit Categories in the back of the code book, and scan the list. This Appendix offers an overview of the major categories in the Tabular List.

2. Review the notes located at the beginning of Chapters 1 (Code 001), 2 (Code 140), 3 (Code 240), 5 (Code 290), 13 (Code 710), 15 (Code 760), 16 (Code 780), 17 (Code 800), and the V and E code sections.

BASIC STEPS FOR USING THE TABULAR LIST

Step 1. Locate the first possible code number after reviewing main terms and subterms in the Index to Diseases.

Step 2. Locate the code number in the Tabular List and review the code descriptions. Review any excludes notes to determine whether the condition being coded is excluded.

If the condition is excluded, locate the code number listed as an alternative in the excludes note to determine whether it is the condition to be coded.

Step 3. Assign any required fifth digit.

Step 4. Check to be sure the code number is appropriate for the age and sex of the patient.

Step 5. Return to the Index to Diseases for other possible code selections if the code description in the Tabular List does not appear to fit the condition or reason for the visit.

Step 6. Record the final code selection.

EXERCISE 6-3 Confirming Codes Found in the Index

Using only the Tabular List, verify the following code numbers to determine whether the code matches the stated diagnosis or an excludes statement applies.

Place a "C" on the blank line if the code number is confirmed.

Place an "E" on the blank line if the condition is excluded.

Enter required fifth digits if applicable.

1. 515   Postinflammatory pulmonary fibrosis   _____

2. 250.1   Non-insulin dependent diabetes   _____

3. 727.67 Nontraumatic rupture of Achilles' tendon   _____

4. 422.0   Acute myocarditis due to Coxsackie virus   _____

5. 813.22 Malunion, closed right radial fracture   _____

6. 483.0   Mycoplasmic pneumonia   _____

7. 795.71 Positive HIV test, asymptomatic   _____

8. 796.2   Elevated blood pressure   _____

9. 718.06 Old tear of right knee meniscus   _____

After completing this exercise, refer to Appendix IV to check your answers.

Tabular List (Diseases) Coding Conventions

Tabular List (Diseases) coding conventions apply to disease and condition codes and to supplementary classification codes (e.g., factors influencing health status and contact with health services [V codes], and external causes of injury and poisoning [E codes]). See Table 6-3.

Table 6-3 *Coding conventions for the Tabular List (Diseases). The coding convention is explained in column one, and the coding manual entry is located in column two.*

CODING CONVENTION	TABULAR LIST ENTRY (DISEASES)

AND: when two disorders are separated by the word "and," it is interpreted as "and/or" and indicates that either of the two disorders is associated with the code number.	**466** **Acute bronchitis and bronchiolitis**
	    466.0 **Acute bronchitis**
	    466.1 **Acute bronchiolitis**

BOLD TYPE: all category and subcategory codes and descriptions are printed in bold type.	**421** **Acute and subacute endocarditis**
	    421.0 **Acute and subacute endocarditis**
	    421.1 **Acute and subacute infective endocarditis in diseases classified elsewhere**

BRACES enclose a series of terms, each of which modifies the statement located to the right of the brace.	**478.5** **Other diseases of vocal cords**
	    Abscess
	    Cellulitis
	    Granuloma } of vocal cords
	    Leukoplakia

BRACKETS enclose synonyms, alternate wording, or explanatory phrases.	**428.2** **Pneumonia due to Hemophilus influenzae [H. influenzae]**

CODE FIRST UNDERLYING DISEASE appears when the code referenced is to be sequenced as a secondary code. The code, title, and instructions are italicized.	*366.43* *Tetanic cataract*
	    Code first underlying disease, as:
	      calcinosis (275.4)
	      hypoparathyroidism (252.1)

COLON: used after an incomplete term and is followed by one or more modifiers (additional terms)	**472.0** **Chronic rhinitis**
	    Ozena
	    Rhinitis:
	      NOS
	      atrophic
	      granulomatous
	      hypertrophic
	      obstructive
	      purulent
	      ulcerative

EXCLUDES: an excludes note directs the coder to another location in the codebook for proper assignment of the code	**250** **Diabetes mellitus**
	    EXCLUDES *gestational diabetes (648.8)*
	      hyperglycemia NOS (790.6)
	      neonatal diabetes mellitus (775.1)
	      nonclinical diabetes (790.2)

FORMAT: all subterms are indented below the term to which they are linked, and if a definition or disease requires more than one line, that text is printed on the next line and further indented.	**455.2** **Internal Hemorrhoids with other complications**
	    Internal hemorrhoids:
	      bleeding
	      prolapsed
	      strangulated
	      ulcerated

(Continues)

Table 6-3 *(Continued)*

CODING CONVENTION	TABULAR LIST ENTRY (DISEASES)
FOURTH & FIFTH DIGITS: the assignment of a fourth and/or fifth digit is indicated by an instructional note located below the category or subcategory description	**250 Diabetes mellitus** **EXCLUDES** *gestational diabetes (648.8)* *hyperglycemia NOS (790.6)* *neonatal diabetes mellitus (775.1)* *nonclinical diabetes (790.2)* **The following fifth-digit subclassification is for use with category 250:** **0 type II [non-insulin dependent type] [NIDDM type] [adult-onset type] or unspecified type, not stated as uncontrolled** **1 type I [insulin dependent type] [IDDM] [juvenile type], not stated as uncontrolled** **2 type II [non-insulin dependent type] [NIDDM type] [adult-onset type] or unspecified type, uncontrolled** **3 type I [insulin dependent type] [IDDM] [juvenile type], uncontrolled**
INCLUDES: includes notes appear below a three-digit category code description to further define, clarify, or provide an example.	**244 Acquired hypothyroidism** **INCLUDES** athyroidism (acquired) hypothyroidism (acquired) myxedema (adult) (juvenile) thyroid (gland) insufficiency (acquired)
NOS is the abbreviation for not otherwise specified and indicates that the code is unspecified. Coders should ask the provider for a more specific diagnosis before assigning the code.	**008.8 Other organism, not elsewhere classified** Viral enteritis NOS gastroenteritis **EXCLUDES** influenza with involvement of gastrointestinal tract (487.8)
NOTES define terms, clarify information, and list choices for fourth- and fifth-digits.	**1. INFECTIONS AND PARASITIC DISEASES (001-139)** NOTE: Categories for "late effects" of infectious and parasitic diseases are found at 137-139.
PARENTHESES enclose supplementary words that may be present or absent in the diagnostic statement, without affecting assignment of the code number.	**241.1 Nontoxic multinodular goiter** Multinodular goiter (nontoxic)
USE ADDITIONAL CODE indicates a second code is to be reported to provide more information about the diagnosis.	**510 Empyema** Use additional code to identify infectious organism (041.0-041.9)
WITH: when codes combine one disorder with another (e.g., code that combines primary condition with a complication), the provider's diagnostic statement must clearly indicate that both conditions are present and that a relationship exists between the conditions.	**487 Influenza with bronchopneumonia** **487.0 With pneumonia** **487.1 With other respiratory manifestations** Influenza NOS Influenzal: laryngitis pharyngitis respiratory infection (upper) (acute)

EXERCISE 6-4 Working with Tabular List (Diseases) Coding Conventions

Underline the main term (condition) to be referenced in the Index to Diseases, and apply index coding conventions in locating the code. Verify the code selected in the Tabular List. Enter the ICD-9-CM code number(s) and Tabular List Coding Convention used on the blank lines provided. If more than one code number is assigned, be sure to list the primary condition code first.

	Condition	ICD-9-CM Code(s)	Index Convention(s) Used
1.	<u>Pregnancy</u> complicated by chronic gonorrhea; gonococcal endometritis	647.13, 098.3	fifth-digit required; use additional code
2.	Benign neoplasm, ear cartilage		
3.	Cervicitis, tuberculous		
4.	Uncontrolled Type II diabetes with polyneuropathy		
5.	Congenital hemangioma on face		
6.	Hiss-Russell shigellosis		
7.	Closed fracture, right leg		
8.	Diabetic cataract		
9.	Muscular atrophy, left leg		
10.	Chronic smoker's bronchitis with acute bronchitis		

Index to Procedures and Tabular List (Procedures) Coding Conventions

Although the purpose of this textbook is to cover physician office coding (ICD-9-CM Index to Diseases and Tabular List only), Table 6-4 is included to provide comprehensive coverage of ICD-9-CM coding conventions.

Table 6-4 *Coding conventions for the Index to Procedures and Tabular List. The coding convention is explained in column one and the coding manual entry is located in column two.*

CODING CONVENTION	INDEX TO PROCEDURES ENTRY
OMIT CODE is a term that identifies procedures or services that may be components of other procedures. The *omit code* instruction means that the procedure or service is not coded.	**Laparotomy** NEC 54.19 As operative approach—*omit code*
CODING CONVENTION	**TABULAR LIST (PROCEDURES) ENTRY**
CODE ALSO ANY SYNCHRONOUS PROCEDURES refers to operative procedures that are to be coded to completely classify a procedure.	08.2 **Excision or destruction of lesion or tissue of eyelid** Code also any synchronous reconstruction (08.61- 08.74)

WORKING WITH INDEX TO DISEASES TABLES

Three tables appear in the Index to Diseases: Hypertension and Neoplasm tables, and the Table of Drugs and Chemicals. The discussion that follows provides a basic understanding of how to use each table. Because the official tables consist of three to six columns, it will be helpful if you use a ruler or paper guide when working within a table to ensure that you stay on the same horizontal line as you work with a specific diagnosis.

*Hypertension/
Hypertensive
Table*

The Hypertension/Hypertensive table contains a complete listing of hypertension codes and other conditions associated with it. Column headings are shown in Figure 6-4.

- Malignant—A severe form of hypertension with vascular damage and a diastolic pressure reading of 130 mm Hg or greater. (Hypertension is out of control or there was a rapid change from a benign state for a prolonged period.)
- Benign—Mild and/or controlled hypertension, with no damage to the patient's vascular system or organs.
- Unspecified—No notation of benign or malignant status is found in the diagnosis or in the patient's chart.

CODING TIPS:

1. Always check the Tabular List before assigning a code for hypertension/hypertensive conditions.

2. The table uses all three levels of indentations when the word "with" is included in the diagnostic statement. Be sure you review the subterms carefully. You may need to assign two codes when "with" separates two conditions in the diagnostic statement.

3. Secondary hypertension is a unique and separate condition listed on the table. In this case hypertension was caused by another primary condition (e.g., cancer).

4. Use the fourth digit 9 sparingly.

Most insurance companies insist on conditions being coded to the highest degree of specificity known at the time of the encounter. They will not accept 401.9 Hypertension, unspecified except during the first few weeks of treatment for hypertension. After that point, the physician usually knows whether or not the patient has benign (controlled by medication) or malignant (out-of-control) hypertension. If "benign" or "malignant" is not specified in the diagnosis, ask the physician to document the type of hypertension.

EXERCISE 6–5 Hypertension/Hypertensive Coding

Code the following conditions:

1. Essential hypertension with cardiomegaly _____

2. Transient hypertension due to pregnancy _____

3. Malignant hypertensive crisis _____

4. Renal and heart disease due to hypertension _____

After completing this exercise, refer to Appendix IV to check your answers.

Neoplasm Table

Neoplasms are new growths, or tumors, in which cell reproduction is out of control. For coding purposes, the provider should specify whether the tumor is **benign** (noncancerous, nonmalignant, noninvasive) or **malignant** (cancerous, invasive, capable of spreading to other parts of the body). It is highly advisable that neoplasms be coded directly from the pathology report; however, until the diagnostic statement specifies whether the neoplasm is benign or malignant, coders should code the patient's sign (e.g., breast lump) or report a subcategory code from the "unspecified nature" column of the documented site using the Disease Index Neoplasm table.

	Malignant	Benign	Unspecified
Hypertension, hypertensive (arterial) (arteriolar) (crisis) (degeneration) (disease) (essential) (fluctuating) (idiopathic) (intermittent) (labile) (low renin) (orthostatic) (paroxysmal) (primary) (systemic) (uncontrolled) (vascular)........................	401.0	401.1	401.9
with			
heart involvement (conditions classifiable to 425.8, 428, 429.0–429.3, 429.8, 429.9 due to hypertension) (*see also* Hypertension, heart)	402.00	402.10	402.90
with kidney involvement — *see* Hypertension, cardiorenal			
renal involvement (*only* conditions classifiable to 585, 586, 587) (*excludes conditions classifiable to 584*) (*see also* Hypertension, kidney).............................	403.00	403.10	403.90
renal sclerosis or failure	403.00	403.10	403.90
with heart involvement — *see* Hypertension, cardiorenal			
failure (and sclerosis) (*see also* Hypertension, kidney)...........	403.01	403.11	403.91
sclerosis without failure (*see also* Hypertension, kidney).......	403.00	403.10	403.90
accelerated (*see also* Hypertension, by type, malignant)............	401.0	—	—
antepartum—*see* Hypertension, complicating pregnancy, childbirth, or the puerperium			
cardiorenal (disease)...	404.00	404.10	404.90
with			
heart failure (congestive)	404.01	404.11	404.91
and renal failure...	404.03	404.13	404.93
renal failure	404.02	404.12	404.92
and heart failure (congestive)	404.03	404.13	404.93
cardiovascular disease (arteriosclerotic) (sclerotic)......................	402.00	402.10	402.90
with			
heart failure (congestive)	402.01	402.11	402.91
renal involvement (conditions classifiable to 403) (*see also* Hypertension, cardiorenal)	404.00	404.10	404.90

FIGURE 6-4 ICD-9-CM Hypertension table (partial) (Courtesy of *St. Anthony's Illustrated ICD-9-CM*, 2001, (800) 632-0123)

Another term associated with neoplasms is **lesion**, defined as any discontinuity of tissue (e.g., skin or organ) that may or may not be malignant. Disease Index entries for "lesion" contain subterms according to anatomic site (e.g., organs or tissue), and that term should be referenced if the diagnostic statement does not confirm a malignancy. In addition, the following conditions are examples of benign lesions and are listed as separate Disease Index entries:

- Mass (unless the word "neoplasm" is included in the diagnostic statement)

- Cyst

- Dysplasia

- Polyp

- Adenosis

The Neoplasm Table (see Figure 6-5) is indexed by anatomic site and contains four cellular classifications: malignant, benign, uncertain behavior, and unspecified nature. The malignant classification is subdivided into three divisions: primary, secondary and carcinoma *in situ*. The six neoplasm classifications are defined as follows:

- **Primary malignancy**—The original tumor site. All malignant tumors are considered primary unless otherwise documented as metastatic or secondary.

- **Secondary malignancy**—The tumor has **metastasized** (spread) to a secondary site, either adjacent to the primary site or to a remote region of the body.

- **Carcinoma (Ca) *in situ***—A malignant tumor that is localized, circumscribed, encapsulated, and noninvasive (has not spread to deeper or adjacent tissues or organs).

- **Benign**—A noninvasive, nonspreading, nonmalignant tumor.

- **Uncertain behavior**—It is not possible to predict subsequent morphology or behavior from the submitted specimen. In order to assign a code from this column, the pathology report must specifically indicate the "uncertain behavior" of the neoplasm.

- **Unspecified nature**—A neoplasm is identified, but there is no further indication of the histology or nature of the tumor reflected in the documented diagnosis. Assign a code from this column when the neoplasm was destroyed or removed and a tissue biopsy was performed and results are pending.

To go directly to the Neoplasm Table, you must know the classification and the site of the neoplasm. Some diagnostic statements specifically document "neoplasm" classification; others will not provide a clue.

If the diagnostic statement classifies the neoplasm, the coder can refer directly to the Index to Diseases Neoplasm table to assign the proper code (verifying the code in the Tabular List, of course). Because sufficient information is documented in the diagnostic statements in Example 1, coders can refer directly to the Index to Diseases Neoplasm table.

Neoplasm, neoplastic	Malignant			Benign	Uncertain Behavior	Unspecified Nature
	Primary	Secondary	Ca in situ			
Neoplasm, neoplastic.............................	199.1	199.1	234.9	229.9	238.9	239.9

Notes— 1. *The list below gives the code numbers for neoplasms by anatomical site. For each site there are six possible code numbers according to whether the neoplasm in question is malignant, benign, in situ, of uncertain behavior, or of unspecified nature. The description of the neoplasm will often indicate which of the six columns is appropriate; e.g., malignant melanoma of skin, benign fibroadenoma of breast, carcinoma in situ of cervix uteri.*

Where such descriptors are not present, the remainder of the Index should be consulted where guidance is given to the appropriate column for each morphological (histological) variety listed; e.g., Mesonephroma — see Neoplasm, malignant; Embryoma — see also Neoplasm, uncertain behavior; Disease, Bowen's — see neoplasm, skin, in situ. However, the guidance in the Index can be overwritten if one of the descriptors mentioned above is present; e.g., malignant adenoma of colon is coded to 153.9 and not to 211.3 as the adjective "malignant" overrides the Index entry "adenoma — see also Neoplasm, benign."

*2. Sites marked with the sign * (e.g., face NEC*) should be classified to malignant neoplasm of skin of these sites if the variety of neoplasm is a squamous cell carcinoma or an epidermal carcinoma and to benign neoplasm of skin of these sites if the variety of neoplasm is a papilloma (any type).*

	Primary	Secondary	Ca in situ	Benign	Uncertain	Unspecified
abdomen, abdominal	195.2	198.89	234.8	229.8	238.8	239.8
cavity	195.2	198.89	234.8	229.8	238.8	239.8
organ..	195.2	198.89	234.8	229.8	238.8	239.8
viscera..	195.2	198.89	234.8	229.8	238.8	239.8
wall	173.5	198.2	232.5	216.5	238.2	239.2
connective tissue............................	171.5	198.89	—	215.5	238.1	239.2
abdominopelvic	195.8	198.89	234.8	229.8	238.8	239.8
accessory sinus — *see* Neoplasm, sinus ...						
acoustic nerve...	192.0	198.4	—	225.1	237.9	239.7
acromion (process)	170.4	198.5	—	213.4	238.0	239.2

FIGURE 6-5 ICD-9-CM Neoplasm table(partial) (Courtesy of *St. Anthony's Illustrated ICD-9-CM*, 2001, (800) 632 0123)

EXAMPLE 1

Diagnostic Statement	Neoplasm Table Reference
Tracheal carcinoma in situ	trachea, Malignant, Ca in situ (231.1)
Benign breast tumor, male	breast, male, Benign (217)
Cowpers gland tumor, uncertain behavior	Cowper's gland, Uncertain Behavior (238.0)
Metastatic carcinoma	unknown site or unspecified, Malignant-Secondary (199.1)
Cancer of the breast, primary	breast, Malignant-Primary (174.9)

If the diagnostic statement *does not* classify the neoplasm, the coder must refer to the Index to Diseases entry for the condition documented (instead of the Neoplasm table). That entry will either contain a code number that can be verified in the Tabular List or the coder will be referred to the proper Neoplasm table entry under which to locate the code.

EXAMPLE 2

Diagnostic Statement	Index to Diseases Entry
non-Hodgkin's lymphoma	Lymphoma, non-Hodgkin's type NEC (M9591/3) 202.8
Adrenal adenolymphoma	Adenolymphoma (M8561/0) Specified site-*see* Neoplasm, by site, benign
	Neoplasm (table), adrenal (cortex) (gland) (medulla), benign (227.0)

For *non-Hodgkin's lymphoma*, assign code 202.8 (after verification in the Tabular List) by referring to "lymphoma" in the Index to Diseases. There is no need to go to the Neoplasm table. In fact, referencing the Neoplasm table in this case would have been improper, and the coder would most likely have assigned an incorrect code (e.g., perhaps the coder would have referenced "lymph, lymphatic" within the Neoplasm table and selected code 171.9 from the Malignant-Primary column, the wrong code).

For *Adrenal adenolymphoma*, refer to "adenolymphoma" in the Index to Diseases and because "adrenal" is the site specified in the diagnostic statement, the coder should follow the Index to Diseases instructions to "see Neoplasm, by site, benign." This instructional note refers the coder to the Neoplasm table and the anatomic site for adrenal (cortex) (gland) (medulla). The coder would next refer to the "Benign" column and assign code 227.0 (after verifying the code in the Tabular List).

EXERCISE 6-6 Neoplasm Coding I

Underline the main term found in the Index to Diseases, and enter the code number (after verifying it in the Tabular List) on the blank line.

1. Kaposi's sarcoma _____

2. Lipoma, skin, upper back _____

3. Carcinoma in situ, skin, left cheek _____

4. Scrotum mass _____

5. Neurofibroma _____

6. Cyst on left ovary _____

7. Ganglion right wrist _____

8. Yaws, frambeside _____

9. Breast, chronic cystic disease _____

10. Hurtle cell tumor _____

11. Bile duct cystadenocarcinoma _____

12. Mixed glioma _____

After completing this exercise, refer to Appendix IV to check your answers.

Primary Malignancies

A malignancy is coded as the primary site if the diagnostic statement documents:

- metastatic *from* a site
- spread *from* a site
- *primary neoplasm* of a site
- a malignancy for which no specific classification is documented
- a *recurrent* tumor

EXAMPLES

Carcinoma of cervical lymph nodes, metastatic from the breast
> Primary—breast
> Secondary—cervical lymph nodes

Oat cell carcinoma of the lung with spread to the brain
> Primary—lung
> Secondary—brain

Secondary Malignancies

Secondary malignancies are **metastatic** and indicate that a primary cancer spread (metastasized) to another part of the body. Sequencing of neoplasm codes is dependent on whether the primary or secondary cancer is being managed and/or treated.

■ **NOTE:** Examples in this section consistently sequence the primary first. In practice, the insurance specialist makes the determination as to sequencing of reported codes. ■

To properly code secondary malignancies, consider the following:

- Cancer described as *metastatic from* a site is *primary of* that site. Assign one code to the primary neoplasm and a second code to the secondary neoplasm of the specified site (if secondary site is known) or unspecified site (if secondary site is unknown).

EXAMPLE 1

Metastatic carcinoma from breast to lung

Assign two codes:
> primary malignant neoplasm of breast (174.9)
> secondary neoplasm of lung (197.0)

EXAMPLE 2

Metastatic carcinoma from breast

Assign two codes:
> primary malignant neoplasm of breast (174.9)
> secondary neoplasm of unspecified site (199.1)

- Cancer described as *metastatic to* a site is considered *secondary of* that site. Assign one code to the secondary site and a second code to the specified primary site (if primary site is known) or unspecified site (if primary site is unknown). In the example below, the metastatic site is listed first; in practice, the sequencing of codes depends on the reason for the encounter (e.g., is the primary or secondary cancer site being treated or medically managed).

EXAMPLE 1

Metastatic carcinoma from liver to lung

Assign two codes:
 secondary neoplasm of lung (197.0)
 primary malignant neoplasm of liver (155.0)

EXAMPLE 2

Metastatic carcinoma to lung

Assign two codes as follows:
 secondary neoplasm of lung (197.0)
 primary malignant neoplasm of unspecified site (199.1)

- When anatomical sites are documented as *metastatic*, assign *secondary* neoplasm code(s) to those sites, and assign an *unspecified site* code to the *primary* malignant neoplasm.

EXAMPLE 1

Metastatic renal cell carcinoma of lung

Assign two codes:
 secondary neoplasm of lung (197.0)
 primary renal cell carcinoma (189.0)

EXAMPLE 2

Metastatic osteosarcoma of brain

Assign two codes:
 secondary neoplasm of brain (198.3)
 primary malignant neoplasm of bone (170.9)

EXAMPLE 3

Metastatic melanoma of lung and liver

Assign three codes:
 secondary neoplasm of lung (197.0)
 secondary neoplasm of liver (197.7)
 primary malignant melanoma of unspecified site (172.9)

EXAMPLE 4

Metastatic adenocarcinoma of prostate and vertebra

Assign three codes:
 primary adenocarcinoma of unspecified site (199.1)
 secondary neoplasm of prostate (198.82)
 secondary neoplasm of vertebra (198.5)

- If the diagnostic statement does not specify whether the neoplasm site is primary or secondary, code the site as *primary* unless the documented site is bone, brain, diaphragm, heart, liver, lymph nodes, mediastinum, meninges, peritoneum, pleura, retroperitoneum, spinal cord, or classifiable to 195. These sites are considered *secondary* sites unless the physician specifies that they are primary.

EXAMPLE 1

Lung cancer

Assign one code:

> primary malignant neoplasm of lung (162.9)
>
> ■ **NOTE:** Lung is not included in the above list of secondary (metastatic sites); therefore, this cancer is coded as primary. ■

EXAMPLE 2

Brain cancer

Assign two codes:

> secondary neoplasm of brain (198.3)
> primary malignant neoplasm of unspecified site (199.1)

EXAMPLE 3

Metastatic cancer of hip

Assign two codes:

> secondary neoplasm of hip (198.89)
> primary malignant neoplasm of unspecified site (199.1)

Anatomic Site Is Not Documented

If the cancer diagnosis does not contain documentation of the anatomic site, but the term *metastatic* is documented, assign codes for "unspecified site" for both the primary and secondary sites.

EXAMPLE

Metastatic chromophobe adenocarcinoma

Assign two codes as follows:

> secondary neoplasm of unspecified site (199.1)
> primary chromophobe adenocarcinoma of unspecified site (194.3)

Primary Malignant Site Is No Longer Present

If the primary site of malignancy is no longer present, do not assign the code for primary of unspecified site. Instead, classify the previous primary site by assigning the appropriate code from category V10 "Personal history of malignant neoplasm."

EXAMPLE

Metastatic carcinoma to lung from breast (left radical mastectomy performed last year)

Assign two codes as follows:

> secondary neoplasm of lung (197.0)
> personal history of malignant neoplasm of breast (V10.3)

Contiguous or Overlapping Sites

Contiguous sites (or **overlapping sites**) occur when the origin of the tumor (primary site) involves two adjacent sites. Neoplasms with overlapping site boundaries are classified to the fourth-digit subcategory .8, "Other."

EXAMPLE

Cancer of the jejunum and ileum

Go to the Index to Disease entry for "intestine, small, contiguous sites" in the Neoplasm table. Locate code 152.8 in the Malignant–Primary column, and verify the code in the Tabular List, which appears as:

152   **Malignant neoplasm of small intestine, including duodenum**

      152.8   **Other specified sites of small intestine**

Duodenojejunal junction

Malignant neoplasm of contiguous or overlapping sites of small intestine whose point of origin cannot be determined

Re-excision of Tumors

A **re-excision** of a tumor occurs when the pathology report recommends that the surgeon perform a second excision to widen the margins of the original tumor site. The re-excision is performed to ensure that all tumor cells have been removed and a clear border (margin) of normal tissue surrounds the excised specimen. Use the diagnostic statement found in the report of the original excision to code the reason for the re-excision. The pathology report for the re-excision may not specify a malignancy at this time, but the patient is still under treatment for the original neoplasm.

CODING TIP:

1. Read all notes in the table that apply to the condition you are coding.

2. Never assign a code directly from the table or Index to Diseases.

3. Be certain you are submitting codes that represent the *current status of the neoplasm*.

4. Assign a neoplasm code if the tumor has been excised and the patient is still undergoing radiation or chemotherapy treatment.

5. Assign a V code if the tumor is no longer present or if the patient is not receiving treatment, but is returning for follow-up care.

   EXAMPLES: V10–V15 Personal history of a malignancy

                 V67.X Examination follow-up, no disease found

6. Classification stated on a pathology report overrides the morphology classification stated in the Disease Index.

EXERCISE 6–7 Neoplasm Coding II

Step 1.   Review the notes located at the beginning of the Neoplasm table and at the beginning of Chapter 2 in the Tabular List.

Step 2. Code the diagnostic statements below.

1. Ca of the lung _____
2. Metastasis from the lung _____
3. Abdominal mass _____
4. Carcinoma of the breast (female) with
   metastasis to the axillary lymph nodes _____
5. Carcinoma of axillary lymph nodes and
   lungs, metastatic from the breast (female) _____
6. Astrocytoma _____
7. Skin lesion, left cheek _____

After completing this exercise, refer to Appendix IV to check your answers.

Table of Drugs and Chemicals

The Table of Drugs and Chemicals is used to identify drugs or chemicals that caused poisonings and adverse effects (see Figure 6-6).

The official ICD-9-CM table contains a listing of the generic names of the drugs or chemicals, one column for poisonings, and five separate columns to

		External Cause (E-Code)				
Substance	**Poisoning**	**Accident**	**Therapeutic Use**	**Suicide Attempt**	**Assault**	**Undetermined**
1-propanol	980.3	E860.4	—	E950.9	E962.1	E980.9
2-propanol	980.2	E860.3	—	E950.9	E962.1	E980.9
2, 4-D (dichlorophenoxyacetic acid)	989.4	E863.5	—	E950.6	E962.1	E980.7
2, 4-toluene diisocyanate	983.0	E864.0	—	E950.7	E962.1	E980.6
2, 4, 5-T (trichlorophenoxyacetic acid)	989.2	E863.5	—	E950.6	E962.1	E980.7
14-hydroxydihydromorphinone	965.09	E850.2	E935.2	E950.0	E962.0	E980.0
A						
ABOB	961.7	E857	E931.7	E950.4	E962.0	E980.4
Abrus (seed)	988.2	E865.3	—	E950.9	E962.1	E980.9
Absinthe	980.0	E860.0	—	E950.9	E962.1	E980.9
beverage	980.0	E860.0	E934.2	E950.4	E962.0	E980.4
Acenocoumarin, acenocoumarol	964.2	E858.2	E934.2	E950.4	E962.0	E980.3
Acepromazine	969.1	E853.0	E939.1	E950.3	E962.0	E980.3
Acetal	982.8	E862.4	—	E950.9	E962.1	E980.9
Acetaldehyde (vapor)	987.8	E869.8	—	E952.8	E962.2	E982.8
liquid	989.89	E866.8	—	E950.9	E962.1	E980.9
Acetaminophen	965.4	E850.4	E935.4	E950.0	E962.0	E980.0
Acetaminosalol	965.1	E850.3	E935.3	E950.0	E962.0	E980.0
Acetanilid(e)	965.4	E850.4	E935.4	E950.0	E962.0	E980.0
Acetarsol, acetarsone	961.1	E857	E931.1	E950.4	E962.0	E980.4
Acetazolamide	974.2	E858.5	E944.2	E950.4	E962.0	E980.4
Acetic						
acid	983.1	E864.1	—	E950.7	E962.1	E980.6
with sodium acetate (ointment)	976.3	E858.7	E946.3	E950.4	E962.0	E980.4
irrigating solution	974.5	E858.5	E944.5	E950.4	E962.0	E980.4
lotion	976.2	E858.7	E946.2	E950.4	E962.0	E980.4
anhydride	983.1	E864.1	—	E950.7	E962.1	E980.6
ether						

FIGURE 6-6 ICD-9-CM Table of Drugs and Chemicals (partial) (Courtesy of *St. Anthony's Illustrated ICD-9-CM*, 2001, (800) 632-0123)

indicate the external causes of adverse effects or poisonings. (Some publishers are now adding brand names to the list of drugs and chemicals.)

An **adverse effect** or **reaction** is the appearance of a pathologic condition due to ingestion or exposure to a chemical substance properly administered or taken.

Code first the adverse effect(s) (or manifestations)(e.g., coma) by referring to the Index to Diseases.

The chemical substance is coded by referring to the Therapeutic Use column of the Table of Drugs and Chemicals.

CODING TIP: Never assign a code from the Poisoning column with a code from the Therapeutic Use column.

EXAMPLE

Gastritis due to prescribed tetracycline

In this statement, gastritis (535.50) is the adverse effect (or manifestation) of the properly administered drug, tetracycline (E930.4).

Poisonings occur as the result of an overdose, wrong substance administered or taken, or intoxication (e.g., combining prescribed drugs with nonprescribed drugs or alcohol.) The Table of Drugs and Chemicals categorizes poisonings according to accident, suicide attempt, assault, or undetermined.

Poisonings are coded by referring first to the Poisoning column of the Table of Drugs and Chemicals and then the External Cause (E code) columns within the table (with the exception of the Therapeutic Use column).

EXAMPLE

Accidental overdose of tetracycline

In this statement, the poisoning code is listed first (960.4) followed by the accidental overdose E code (E856).

Review the patient's record to determine the manifestations of the poisoning (e.g., headache, coma); refer to the Index to Diseases and sequence these codes after the codes for the poisoning and external cause.

- **Poisoning** (codes 960–989) is assigned according to classification of the drug or chemical.
- **Accident** (codes E850–E869) is used for accidental overdosing, wrong substance given or taken, drug inadvertently taken, or accidents in the use of drugs and chemical substances during medical or surgical procedures, and to show external causes of poisonings classifiable to 980–989.
- **Therapeutic use** (codes E930–E952) is used for the external effect caused by correct substance properly administered in therapeutic or prophylactic dosages.
- **Suicide attempt** (codes E950–E952) is a self-inflicted poisoning.
- **Assault** (codes E961–E962) is a poisoning inflicted by another person who intended to kill or injure the patient.
- **Undetermined** (codes E980–E982) is used if the record does not state whether the poisoning was intentional or accidental.

<table>
<tr><td>CODING TIP:</td><td>The term "intoxication" is used to indicate that alcohol was involved (e.g., alcohol intoxication) as well as the accumulation of a medication in the patient's bloodstream (e.g., Coumadin intoxication). While the alcohol intoxication would be assigned a code from the Poisoning column, the Coumadin intoxication would be assigned a manifestation code (e.g., dizziness) and an E code from the Therapeutic Use column.</td></tr>
</table>

<table>
<tr><td>CODING TIP:</td><td>E codes are used to explain the cause of the poisoning or the adverse effect. They are not diagnoses but external causes or results of injury. Therefore, E codes are always secondary, never primary, codes.</td></tr>
</table>

EXAMPLE 1

Hives, due to prescribed penicillin

Answer: 708.9 (hives NOS), E930.0 (therapeutic use of penicillin)

EXAMPLE 2

Coma due to overdose of barbiturates, attempted suicide

Answer: 967.0 (poisoning by barbiturates), E950.1 (suicide by barbiturates), 780.01 (coma).

EXERCISE 6–8   Using the Table of Drugs and Chemicals

Code the following statements using ICD-9-CM.

1. Adverse reaction to pertussis vaccine _____

2. Cardiac arrhythmia caused by interaction between prescribed ephedrine and alcohol _____

3. Sinus bradycardia due to correctly prescribed dose of propranolol. _____

4. Stupor, due to overdose of Nytol (suicide attempt) _____

After completing this exercise, refer to Appendix IV to check your answers.

V Codes

V codes are contained in a supplementary classification of factors influencing the person's health status. These codes are used when a person seeks health care but does not have active complaints or symptoms, or when it is necessary to describe circumstances that could influence the patient's health care. These services fall into one of three categories:

1. Problems—issues that could affect the patient's health status

2. Services—Person is seen for treatment that is not caused by illness or injury

3. Factual reporting—used for statistical purposes (e.g., Outcome of delivery or referral of patient without examination)

Refer to Table 6-5 for a list of main terms found in the ICD-9-CM Index to Diseases.

TABLE 6-5 *Common V Code Indicators in the Index to Diseases*

Admission to/for	History, family
Aftercare follow-up	History, personal
Attention to	Maladjustment
Carrier of	Newborn
Checkup for...	Observation
Closure of ...	Outcome
Contact with...	Procedure (not performed because) Prophylactic
Contraception	Removal of
Dialysis	Replacement of
Encounter for	Routine examination
Exposure to	Screening (test) for
Examination of/for	Status
Fitting of	Test (for)
Follow-up (examination)	Vaccination

List V code as the primary diagnosis in the following circumstances:

- Patient was referred for an evaluation of a suspected disorder but has no active symptoms, complaints, prior personal or family history of the disorder, and has received no treatment. (Refer to V71 category code.)
- Patient was seen in a radiology office for an annual radiological examination and no active disease is found. (Assign V72.5)
- A primary V code is needed for a patient seen solely for rehabilitation services (V57.8), chemotherapy services (V58.1), or radiation services (V58.0) followed by a secondary code for the disorder.
- Patient undergoes an examination, with no current symptoms, because the patient has a family history for a disabling disorder and is considered to be a high-risk case. (Select from the V17–V19 series.)
- Patient has a personal history of a disabling disorder, but no current symptoms. (Select from the V10–V15 series.)
- Patient is seen for preoperative evaluation or clearance only. (Assign V72.8 with the appropriate fifth-digit code as the primary code, followed by the reason for the surgery.)
- Patient is seen in the office to receive vaccinations, immunizations, or other prophylactic measures (refer to categories V03–V06).
- Patient encounter is for removal of casts (V54.8), sutures (V58.89), and so on.

CODING TIP: Consult Appendix E (List of Three-Digit Categories) if you have trouble locating a V code category in the Disease Index.

EXERCISE 6–9 Exploring V Codes

Code the following statements using ICD-9-CM.

1. Family history of epilepsy with no evidence of seizures _____

2. Six-week postpartum checkup _____

3. Premarital physical _____

4. Consult with dietitian for patient with diabetes mellitus _____

5. Rubella screening _____

6. Exposure to TB _____

After completing this exercise, refer to Appendix IV to check your answers.

CODING SPECIAL DISORDERS

HIV/AIDS

❋ **CAUTION:** Before entering codes on a claim form or any other official document leaving the office, check to ensure that a signed Authorization for Release of HIV Status form was obtained from the patient. (See Figure 5-6 on page 76 for a sample authorization.) ❋

Code 042 is assigned when a documented diagnosis states the patient is HIV positive and exhibits manifestations associated with AIDS. Secondary codes are assigned to classify the manifestations such as Kaposi's sarcoma, candidiasis, coccidiosis, hemolytic anemia, and so on.

Assign code 079.53 in addition to 042 when HIV type 2 is identified by the provider.

Assign code 795.71 when screening for HIV was reported as nonspecific. For example, this code is used when a newborn tests positive upon HIV screening, but it cannot be determined whether the positive result reflects the true status of the baby or the seropositive status of the mother.

V01.7 is assigned for a patient who was exposed to the virus but not tested for infection.

V08 is assigned when the patient is HIV positive, asymptomatic, and does not exhibit manifestations of AIDS. Once the patient presents with symptoms, V08 can never again be reported.

Assign V65.44 when the reason for the encounter is counseling of a patient who has been tested for HIV. It does not matter whether the patient's HIV status is positive or negative.

Fracture Cases

CODING TIP:

Study the fifth-digit classification note at the beginning of the Musculoskeletal System chapter before coding fractures. This information is extremely helpful in selecting the correct code.

Distinction is required between closed and open fractures. If the diagnostic statement does not specify closed or open, select the appropriate closed fracture code. A list of common types of fractures appears in Table 6-6.

When a patient has suffered multiple injuries, list the injuries in descending order of severity on the claim form.

TABLE 6-6 *Fractures*

COMMON CLOSED FRACTURE TERMS	COMMON OPEN FRACTURE TERMS
Comminuted	Compound
Linear	Missile
Spiral	Puncture
Impacted	Fracture with a foreign body
Simple	Infected Fracture
Greenstick	
Compressed	

EXERCISE 6–10   Coding HIV/AIDS and Fracture Cases

Code the following statements.

1. Patient is HIV positive with no symptoms _____

2. AIDS patient treated for Candidiasis _____

3. Open fracture, maxilla _____

4. Greenstick fracture, 3rd digit right foot _____

5. Multiple fractures, right femur, distal end _____

After completing this exercise, refer to Appendix IV to check your answers.

Late Effect

A **late effect** is a residual effect or sequela of a previous acute illness, injury, or surgery. The patient is currently dealing with long-term chronic effects of the disorder or trauma. The underlying acute condition no longer exists (see Table 6-7).

In most cases, two codes will be required to classify diagnostic statements specifying residual conditions of an original illness or injury. The primary code is the residual (condition currently affecting the patient). The secondary code represents the original condition or etiology of the late effect. Locate the appropriate code by referencing the Index to Diseases under the main term, "Late." If the late effect is also due to an external cause, reference the External Causes Index under the word, "Late." Occasionally, one combination code is used to classify the diagnostic statement.

EXAMPLE

Dysphasia due to CVA 6 months ago
Combination code is 438.12

Occasionally, there will be a reversal of the primary and secondary positions. This occurs when the Index references the late effect first followed by a slanted bracketed residual code.

TABLE 6-7 *Late Effects*

ORIGINAL CONDITION/ETIOLOGY	LATE EFFECT/SEQUELA
Fracture	Malunion
CVA	Hemiplegia
Third-degree burn	Deep scarring
Polio	Contractures
Laceration	Keloid
Breast implant	Ruptured implant

EXAMPLE

Scoliosis due to childhood polio
    Index reads: Scoliosis (acquired) (postural) 737.30
                    Due to or associated with
                        poliomyelitis 138 [*737.43*]
    Primary code is 138
    Secondary code is 737.43 (as dictated by the bracketed code in the index convention)

Burns

Burns require two codes: one for the site and degree and a second for the percentage of body surface (not body part) affected.

The percentage of total body area or surface affected follows the "rule of nines":

- Head and neck = 9%
- Back (trunk) = 18%
- Chest (trunk) = 18%
- Leg (each) = 18%
                                        18%
- Arm (each) = 9%
                                        9%
- Genitalia = 1%

Total Body Surface (TBS)   100%

■ **NOTE:** To achieve the total percentage affected, health professionals add the affected extremities or regions together and state the combined total. ■

EXERCISE 6–11   Coding Late Effect and Burns

1. Malunion due to fracture, right ankle, 9 months ago _____

2. Brain damage due to subdural hematoma, 18 months previously _____

3. 2nd degree burn, anterior chest wall _____

4. Scalding with erythema, right forearm and hand _____

5. 3rd degree burn, back, 18% body surface _____

After completing this exercise, refer to Appendix IV to check your answers.

Use of E Codes

E codes consist of a four-character number (an E followed by three digits) and one digit after a decimal point. The Index to the External Cause of Injuries (E codes) is located separately in the Disease Index, after the Table of Drugs and Chemicals.

Although many states require the reporting of E codes, provider office insurance claims do not. However, reporting E codes on claims can expedite payment by health insurance carriers where no third-party liability for an accident exists. In such cases, it is necessary to report two E codes in addition to the appropriate injury codes (*E codes are never reported as primary codes*).

EXAMPLE

Patient is seen for fractured pelvis sustained when he fell from a ladder while repairing his house. The fractured pelvis is coded and sequenced first on the claim followed by two E codes, one for the external cause and another for the place of occurrence: 808.8, E881.0, and E849.0.

Injury:	**Fracture**	
	pelvis	808.8
External Cause:	**Fall (falling)**	
	from, off	
	ladder	E881.0
Place of Occurrence:	**Accident (to)**	
	occurring (at) (in)	
	home (private) (residential)	E849.0

(Homeowners insurance covers injuries sustained by visitors, but not family members living in the home.)

CODING TIP:

Review the note at the beginning of the E-Code Tabular List before coding External Causes of Injuries and Poisonings.

At the end of the Index to External Causes is a section entitled: "Fourth Digit Subdivisions for the External Cause (E) Codes."

It may be necessary to consult the Appendix E List of Three-digit Categories for assistance in locating possible main terms in the E-Code Index.

EXERCISE 6–12 Coding External Cause of Injury

Code the following statements.

1. Automobile accident, highway, passenger _____

2. Worker injured by fall from ladder _____

3. Accidental drowning, fell from power boat _____

4. Soft tissue injury, right arm, due to snowmobile accident in patient's yard _____

After completing this exercise, refer to Appendix IV to check your answers.

CONSIDERATIONS TO ENSURE ACCURATE ICD-9-CM CODING

1. Preprinted diagnosis codes on encounter forms, routing slips, and coding lists should be reviewed to verify inclusion of fourth and fifth digits.

2. The latest edition codebooks should be purchased each year (new codes are effective each October) because they are annually updated (codes are added/deleted/revised).

3. Providers and insurance specialists should be kept informed of annual coding changes (e.g., newsletter subscription).

4. Diagnosis codes should be reviewed for accuracy when updates are installed in office management software.

5. A policy should be established to address assignment of codes when the office is awaiting the results of laboratory and pathology reports.

6. Reports of diagnostic tests performed at other facilities should be reviewed to ensure accurate coding.

7. The postoperative diagnosis should be coded (not the preoperative diagnosis).

8. Some computer programs automatically generate insurance claims for each encounter. Office staff should intercept these claims to verify diagnosis code(s) assigned (e.g., review for definitive diagnosis).

9. M codes (morphology codes) should not be reported on the HCFA-1500.

10. Diagnosis codes should be proofread to ensure proper entry in the permanent record (e.g., on-screen, paper, and electronic claim forms).

ICD-10-CM: DIAGNOSTIC CODING FOR THE FUTURE

The information presented in this section is excerpted and developed from the copyrighted Medicode publications, *Coders' Desk Reference* and *ICD-9-CM Volumes 1 & 2*. More comprehensive information on ICD-10-CM can be found in the Medicode/St. Anthony publication, *ICD-10 Made Easy*.

The tenth revision of the *International Classification of Diseases* (ICD), and its clinical modification, is expected to replace the ICD-9-CM Index to Diseases and Tabular List between 2003 and 2005. The World Health Organization (WHO) is responsible for revising ICD, and a clinical modification (CM) was developed by the Department of Health and Human Services (DHHS), National Center for Health Statistics (NCHS), for use in the United States.

ICD-10-CM includes more codes and applies to more users than ICD-9-CM because it is designed to collect data on every type of health care encounter (e.g., inpatient, outpatient, hospice, home health care, and long-term care). The ICD structure developed by WHO and clinically modified for use in the United States is also expected to improve the quality of data input into clinical databases and, thereby, provide more information about patients' health care encounters.

History of the ICD

The WHO's original intent for ICD was to serve as a statistical tool for the international collection and exchange of mortality (death) data. A subsequent revision was expanded to accommodate data collection for morbidity (disease) statistics. The seventh revision, published by WHO in 1955, was clinically modified for use in the United States after a joint study was conducted to evaluate the efficiency of **indexing** (cataloging diseases and procedures by code number) hospital diseases. The study participants included the American Hospital Association (AHA) and the American Association of Medical Record Librarians (AAMRL) (now called the American Health Information Management Association, or AHIMA). Results of that study led to the 1959 publication of the *International Classification of Diseases, Adapted for Indexing Hospital Records* (ICDA), by the federal Public Health Service. The ICDA uniformly modified ICD-7, and it gave the United States a way to classify patient operations and treatments.

An eighth edition of ICD, published by WHO in 1965, lacked the depth of clinical data required for America's emerging health care delivery system. In 1968, two widely accepted modifications were published in the United States: the *Eighth Revision of the International Classification of Diseases, Adapted for Use in the United States* (ICDA-8) and the *Hospital Adaptation of ICDA* (H-ICDA). Hospitals used either of these two systems until 1979 when ICD-9-CM was implemented. The ninth revision of the ICD by WHO, in 1975, once again prompted the development of a clinical modification. This time the incentive for creating a clinical modification of the ICD resulted from a process initiated in 1977 by the NCHS for hospital indexing and the retrieval of case data for clinical studies. After more than 30 years since its adoption in the United States, ICD has proven to be indispensable to anyone interested in payment schedules for the delivery of health care services to patients.

ICD-10

The WHO published ICD-10 in 1994 with a new name (*International Statistical Classification of Diseases and Related Health Problems*) and reorganized its three-digit categories (listed below). While the title was amended to clarify content and purpose and to reflect development of codes and descriptions beyond diseases and injuries, the familiar abbreviation "ICD" was kept. ICD-10 contains clinical detail, expands information about previously classified diseases, and classifies diseases discovered since the last revision.

ICD-10 also incorporates organizational changes and new features, but its format and conventions remain largely unchanged. Chapter titles, organization and *includes* and *excludes* notes are similar to ICD-9. The biggest difference is that the new codes are alphanumeric, and there is more detail in ICD-10-CM than in ICD-9-CM.

The ICD-10 coding system consists of 21 chapters:

Chapter 1   (A00–B99)   Certain Infectious and Parasitic Diseases

Chapter 2   (C00–D48)   Neoplasms

Chapter 3 (D50-D89)	Diseases of the Blood and Blood-forming Organs and Certain Disorders Involving the Immune Mechanism
Chapter 4 (E00-E90)	Endocrine, Nutritional, and Metabolic Diseases
Chapter 5 (F01-F99)	Mental and Behavioral Disorders
Chapter 6 (G00-G99)	Diseases of the Nervous System
Chapter 7 (H00-H59)	Diseases of the Eye and Adnexa
Chapter 8 (H60-H95)	Diseases of the Ear and Mastoid Process
Chapter 9 (I00-I97)	Diseases of the Circulatory System
Chapter 10 (J00-J99)	Diseases of the Respiratory System
Chapter 11 (K00-K93)	Diseases of the Digestive System
Chapter 12 (L00-L99)	Diseases of the Skin and Subcutaneous Tissue
Chapter 13 (M00-M99)	Diseases of the Musculoskeletal System and Connective Tissue
Chapter 14 (N00-N99)	Diseases of the Genitourinary System
Chapter 15 (O00-O99)	Pregnancy, Childbirth, and the Puerperium
Chapter 16 (P04-P94)	Certain Conditions Originating in the Perinatal Period
Chapter 17 (Q00-Q94)	Congenital Malformations, Deformations, and Chromosomal Abnormalities
Chapter 18 (R00-R99)	Symptoms, Signs, and Abnormal Clinical and Laboratory Findings, Not Elsewhere Classified
Chapter 19 (S00-T98)	Injury, Poisoning, and Certain Other Consequences of External Causes
Chapter 20 (V01 -Y97)	External Causes of Morbidity
Chapter 21 (Z00-Z99)	Factors Influencing Health Status and Contact with Health Services

Two new chapters added to ICD-10 include Diseases of the Eye and Adnexa (Chapter 7) and Disorders of the Ear and Mastoid Process (Chapter 8). Supplementary classifications of the External Causes of Morbidity (called External Causes of Injury, or E codes, in ICD-9-CM) and Factors Influencing Health Status (or V codes) are incorporated into the core ICD-10 classification system. This means that these codes and descriptions are located throughout all chapters of ICD-10, and they are no longer designated as E codes and V codes.

Some chapter titles are revised for ICD-10. For example, ICD-9-CM Chapter 5 is titled "Mental Disorders" and the ICD-10 Chapter 5 title was changed to "Mental and Behavioral Disorders." The word "certain" was added to the title of Chapter 1, Infectious and Parasitic Diseases, to stress the fact that localized infections are classified to the pertinent body system (e.g., urinary tract infection would be classified to Chapter 14). The title of the ICD-9-CM chapter on congenital anomalies was expanded to include the terms, "deformations" and "chromosomal abnormalities."

ICD-10 chapters were rearranged to allow for expansion in the number of categories for disorders of the immune mechanism by including them in the chapter for diseases of the blood and blood-forming organs. In ICD-9-CM, these disorders are included with Endocrine, Nutritional, and Metabolic Diseases. The chapters on Diseases of the Genitourinary System, Pregnancy, Childbirth and the Puerperium, Certain Conditions Origination in the Perinatal Period, and Congenital Malformations, Deformations, and Chromosomal Abnormalities are sequential in ICD-10.

Some conditions are reassigned to a different chapter because of new knowledge about the disorder. For example, in ICD-9-CM, gout is classified within the Endocrine, Nutritional, and Metabolic Diseases and Immunity Disorders chapter. In ICD-10, gout was moved to Chapter 13, Diseases of the Musculoskeletal System and Connective Tissue.

ICD-10-CM

The NCHS emphasized problems identified in ICD-9-CM as it began to make clinical modifications to ICD-10 for the classification of mortality and morbidity data. In the United States, ICD-10 is being modified to:

- return to or exceed the level of specificity found in ICD-9-CM.
- expand the alphabetic index to diseases.
- provide code titles and language that complement accepted clinical practice.
- remove codes unique to mortality coding.

The modifications applied by the NCHS include:

- increasing ICD-10's five-character structure to six characters.
- incorporating common fourth-digit subcategories and fifth-digit subclassifications.
- creating codes that allow for laterality (e.g., unique code for right arm).
- adding trimesters to obstetric codes.
- creating combined diagnosis/symptoms codes.

Clinical modification does not affect the information reported to the WHO, but it expands that information for specificity purposes.

EXAMPLE 1

ICD-9 and ICD-9-CM Code Descriptions

ICD-9		ICD-9-CM	
140	Malignant neoplasm of the lip	**140.0**	Malignant neoplasm of the upper lip, vermilion border
374.1	Ectropion	**374.13**	Spastic ectropion

EXAMPLE 2

ICD-10 and ICD-10-CM Code Descriptions

ICD-10		ICD-10-CM	
K57.3	Diverticular disease of large intestine without perforation or abscess	**K57.31**	Diverticular disease of large intestine without perforation or abscess with bleeding

ICD-10-CM codes begin with a letter and are followed by up to five numbers. All letters of the alphabet are used, and valid codes can contain three, four, five, or six characters.

EXAMPLE

ICD-10-CM Codes at Highest Level of Specificity

Z66	Do not resuscitate
Q90.1	Down syndrome, Trisomy 21, mosaicism (mitotic nondisjunction)
A69.21	Meningitis due to Lyme disease
J01.01	Acute recurrent maxillary sinusitis

ICD-10 Volumes

ICD-10 is published in three volumes, and publication dates were 1992 for Volume 1, 1993 for Volume 2, and 1994 for Volume 3.

ICD-10 Volume 1: Tabular List

Volume 1 contains a tabular list of alphanumeric disease codes. The same organizational structure in ICD-9 applies to ICD-10 so that all category codes with the same first three digits have common traits, and each digit beyond three adds specificity. In ICD-10, valid codes can contain anywhere from three to five digits; in the clinical modification, valid codes can contain up to six digits.

The ICD-9 organizational structure also applies to ICD-10 notes and instructions. When a note appears under a three-character category code, it applies to all codes within that category. Instructions located under a specific four- or five-character code apply only to that single code.

ICD-10 Volume 2: Instruction Manual

Volume 2 of ICD-10 contains rules and guidelines for mortality and morbidity coding. In ICD-10-CM, it is undecided whether a separate volume will be dedicated to rules, or if they will be organized under a different volume title. If Volume 2 of ICD-10-CM is titled "Instruction Manual," it will be important to remember that it does *not* refer to the Index to Diseases as in ICD-9-CM. HCFA and the NCHS are modifying ICD-10 instructions for use in the United States, and these modifications may be available when the final draft of ICD-10-CM is published.

ICD-10 Volume 3: Alphabetic Index

Volume 3 of ICD-10 is an index to codes classified in the Tabular List. Like the ICD-9-CM Index to Diseases, terms in the ICD-10 index are organized alphabetically according to the name of the disease. The ICD-10-CM Alphabetic Index will consist of a similar arrangement of entities, diseases, and other conditions according to the **axis of classification** (organizing entities, diseases, and other conditions according to etiology, anatomy, or severity). In ICD-10-CM, anatomy is the primary axis of classification, which explains chapter titles like "Diseases of the Circulatory System" and "Diseases of the Genitourinary System."

Organizational Changes in ICD-10 and ICD-10-CM

ICD-10-CM will seem very familiar, but some classification changes include those related to iatrogenic illness, sequelae, and injury. **Iatrogenic illness** results from medical intervention (e.g., adverse reaction to contrast material injected prior to a scan). **Sequelae** (singular form is sequela) are late effects of injury or illness. In ICD-9-CM, these are classified within section 990-995, which is located at the end of the Injury and Poisoning chapter. In ICD-10 these codes appear at the end of each anatomic chapter, as appropriate.

EXAMPLE

H59.2 Cystoid macular edema following cataract surgery (*Eye and Adnexa*)

K91.0 Vomiting following gastrointestinal surgery (*Digestive System*)

M96.2 Postradiation kyphosis (*Musculoskeletal System*)

An **injury** is a traumatic wound or some other damage to an organ. In ICD-9-CM, injuries are initially classified in the Injury and Poisoning chapter by type (e.g., all open wounds are classified in the same chapter). In ICD-10-CM, the axis of classification for injury is the anatomical site of injury. Thus, all injuries to the foot are classified together, as are all injuries to the head. Most of the multiple injury codes have been eliminated from ICD-10-CM, and injuries to the head are subdivided into the following three-digit categories:

Injuries to the head (S00-S09)

S00 Superficial injury of head

S01 Open wound of head

S02 Fracture of skull and facial bones

S03 Dislocation, sprain, and strain of joints and ligaments of head

S04 Injury of cranial nerves

S05 Injury of eye and orbit

S06 Intracranial injury

S07 Crushing injury of head

S08 Traumatic amputation of part of head

S09 Other and unspecified injuries of head

Other Issues of Importance When Comparing ICD-10-CM to ICD-9-CM

ICD-10-CM E codes classify diseases of the endocrine system, not external causes. External causes, currently classified in ICD-9-CM as E codes, will be V codes in ICD-10-CM. V codes, which are included in an ICD-9-CM supplemental classification to report factors influencing health status, have been changed to U Codes and Z Codes in ICD-10-CM.

EXAMPLE

ICD-10-CM EXTERNAL CAUSE AND HEALTH STATUS CODES

V01 Pedestrian injured in collision with pedal cycle

V79.3 Bus occupant (any) injured in unspecified nontraffic accident

W58 Bitten or struck by crocodile or alligator

X81 Confined or trapped in a low-oxygen environment

X39.41 Exposure to radon

X-5 Exposure to ignition or melting of nightwear

Y62.5 Failure of sterile precautions during heart catheterization

Y90.1 Blood alcohol level of 20-30 mg/100 ml

Z45.1   Encounter for adjustment and management of infusion pump

Z91.5   Personal history of self-harm

J Codes, included in the HCPCS Level II (National) coding system, are assigned to report drug administration. In ICD-10-CM, J Codes are used to report disorders of the respiratory system.

Implementing ICD-10-CM

Preparing all professionals—not just coders and insurance specialists—is key to the successful implementation of ICD-10-CM. Consider the following:

- *Create a task force.* Divide implementation of ICD-10-CM responsibilities into major working topics, and assign each member of the task force a job (e.g., coder training, physician training, and identification of software and application elements for information systems).

- *Be vigilant.* Assign one member of the task force to research, read, and summarize articles about ICD-10-CM implementation found in professional journals and newsletters, the Internet, and the *Federal Register.*

- *Alert the entire organization to the change to ICD-10-CM.* Don't wait until the implementation date to speak with information systems managers, vendors, business office, or physicians. The transition to ICD-10-CM affects all departments, so communication with everyone will avoid problems later. Open task force meetings to the entire organization, and invite representatives to become part of the working group.

- *Anticipate problems.* Plan for education and training of personnel, consider the costs associated with implementation of ICD-10-CM, and involve computer information systems personnel in the transition to ICD-10-CM (see Table 6-8 on pages 142 and 143).

- *Train physicians.* The level of detail required in ICD-10-CM emphasizes physician participation. The patient's chart must specify terminology and provide complete documentation according to new standards. For example, in osteoporosis with pathological fracture, the physician must identify the origin of osteoporosis as disuse, drug-induced, idiopathic, menopausal, postmenopausal, postsurgical, or postoophorectomy, along with the specific site.

- *Review patient charts.* Conduct a review of patient charts to identify documentation problems relevant to ICD-10-CM.

INTERNET LINKS

American National Standards Institute (ANSI), Accredited Standards Committee (ASC)—Uniform Standards for Electronic Data Interchange (EDI) (ASC X1 2)–www.x12.org

Department of Health and Human Services (DHHS)—HIPAA Administrative Simplification Provision–aspe.os.dhhs.gov/admnsimp/

National Archives and Records Administration (NARA)—*Federal Register*–www.access.gpo.gov/su-docs/aces/aces140.html

National Center for Health Statistics (NCHS)—ICD-9-CM and ICD-10-CM development–www.cdc.gov/nchs/icd9.htm

National Center for Vital and Health Statistics (NCVHS)—ICD-10-PCS development–www.hcfa.gov/stats/icd10/icd10.htm

World Health Organization (WHO)—ICD-10 development—www.who.int/whosis/icd10

Table 6-8 *Computer Information System (CIS) considerations for ICD-10-CM implementation.*

ICD-9-CM AND ICD-10-CM DIFFERENCES AND IMPLEMENTATION ISSUES FOR CIS

Characteristic	ICD-9-CM	ICD-10-CM	Implementation Issue
Number of characters	3-5	3-6	Fields that read ICD-10-CM codes must accommodate up to 6 characters.
Type of character	Numeric, except for V and E codes	Alphanumeric	Reprogramming may be necessary to distinguish between numbers (0,1) and alphabetic characters (O, I).
			EXAMPLE: Alphabetical characters may need to be capitalized to distinguish between the letter I and the number one (1); a slash may need to be used with the zero to distinguish between the number and the letter (Ø, O).
			Use of the 10-key section of a keyboard is no longer appropriate for data entry.
Decimals	Decimals are used after the third character	Decimals are used after the third character	If your system currently accommodates decimals, make sure that up to three characters can be allowed after the decimal. If your system does not accommodate decimals, there should be no implementation issues, other than the total number of characters required for each field.
			NOTE: If your system accepts both ICD and HCPCS codes, the absence of a decimal may make it difficult for your system to distinguish between HCPCS codes and 5-character ICD-10-CM codes: both have five characters with an alpha character at the first position.
			EXAMPLE:
			E05.00 Thyrotoxicosis with diffuse goiter without thyrotoxic crisis or storm
			E0500 Humidifier, durable for extensive supplemental humidification during IPPB treatments or oxygen delivery
			Your system may need to be reprogrammed to use decimals with ICD-10-CM codes or to otherwise differentiate between those and HCPCS codes.
Hierarchy (organizational position of codes below three-digit categories)	Fourth- and fifth-digit codes have hierarchical relationships within three-digit categories.	Fourth-, fifth-, and sixth-character codes have hierarchical relationships within a three-character category	If your system recognizes ICD-9-CM's hierarchical relationship of fifth- to fourth-digit codes and fourth- to three-digit codes, reprogramming may be necessary to accommodate ICD-10-CM's additional hierarchical relationship–sixth- to fifth-character codes.

(Continued)

Table 6-8 *(Continued)*

ICD-9-CM AND ICD-10-CM DIFFERENCES AND IMPLEMENTATION ISSUES FOR CIS

Characteristic	ICD-9-CM	ICD-10-CM	Implementation Issue
Descriptions of codes	ICD-9-CM uses partial descriptions of codes in the Tabular List instead of restating category and subcategory code description.	Complete descriptions that stand alone.	Although the ICD-9-CM Tabular List uses partial descriptions for codes, data files are available that contain a complete description of each code. If your system uses such a data file, there should be no implementation issues. Some ICD-9-CM data files provide the code description in multiple fields: the three-digit category description, a four-digit subcategory description, and a five-digit subclassification description. If your system uses separate fields for category and subclassification descriptions, reprogramming may be necessary to accept the ICD-10-CM descriptions. Some ICD-9-CM data files contain abbreviated descriptions (e.g., 35-character, 48-character, or 150-character). If your code description field is limited by number of characters, be sure to use a vendor that can provide ICD-10-CM abbreviated descriptions in the length needed.
Coding Conventions	e.g., excludes, includes, notes, essential modifiers, and nonessential modifiers.	e.g., excludes, includes, notes, essential modifiers, and nonessential modifiers.	ICD-10-CM incorporates coding conventions (e.g., includes, excludes, and notes) the same as ICD-9-CM. If your program contains this information, no changes should be necessary.
Quantity of codes	ICD-9-CM contains more than 15,000 Tabular List (Diseases) codes.	ICD-10-CM contains more than 25,000 codes.	ICD-10-CM contains more codes than ICD-9-CM. Reprogramming may be necessary to accommodate the increased number of codes and descriptions. Make sure your system has sufficient memory to handle the additional data. Remember that each ICD-10-CM code description is complete, which means more memory will be required.
Format and availability of data	Codes and descriptions are available both in print and electronic format.	Codes and descriptions are available in print. Access to electronic format has not yet been determined.	Most systems are set up to accept codes and descriptions electronically. Data files commonly provide codes and descriptions in specified formats (e.g., tab-delimited, fixed format, and comma-delimited). Because ICD-10-CM is not widely available, it may be difficult to acquire the codes and descriptions in the electronic format required by your system. Reprogramming may be required to accept a data file in a different format.

Learning from Australia

Australia's transition to ICD-10-Australian Modification (ICD-10-AM) in July 1998 has raised issues that the United States will face during its implementation process: scheduling and budget.

Scheduling

ICD-10-CM is ready to be implemented in the United States, possibly in 2003, but a single procedural system has not been selected. In October 2000, the Department of Health and Human Services (HHS) selected Current Procedural Terminology (CPT) as the standard code set for reporting health care services in electronic transactions. This selection was made as part of the ***Final Rule: Standards for Electronic Transactions***, which implements some requirements of the Administrative Simplification subtitle of the Health Insurance Portability and Accountability Act of 1996 (HIPAA). The *Final Rule* names CPT (codes and modifiers) and the Health Care Financing Administration Common Procedure Coding System (National Codes) as the procedure code set for:

- Physician services
- Physical and occupational therapy services
- Radiological procedures
- Clinical laboratory tests
- Other medical diagnostic procedures
- Hearing and vision services
- Transportation services, including ambulance

In Australia, ICD-10-AM was implemented for one-half of the country in July 1998, and for the second half of the country in July 1999. Australia's National Centre for the Classification of Health (NCCH) was advised to delay the start date until a uniform date could be set since a staggered schedule could increase costs and affect the national data collection. Despite the advice, the NCCH went ahead with an April implementation of ICD-10-AM along with a single procedural classification system, and an **errata** (a published document that contains corrections for errors in the coding manual) was released.

The Australian Bureau of Statistics (ABS) was required to recode two years of past data for ICD-10-AM as a continuum to data collection and to assess trends using the new system. The NCCH believed that a staggered start could improve coding quality because the coders in the initial one-half of the staggered schedule could identify documentation requirements and system flaws prior to national implementation.

Budgeting

In Australia, the NCCH had until July 1998 to produce ICD-10-AM, according to its contractual agreement with the Division of Health and Family Services (DHFS). Government agencies, such as the DHFS and the Classification and Payments Branch, continue to support ICD-10-AM. Workshops, books, and training bring in additional funds. The Health Services Outcomes Branch allocated funds to develop an electronic system for ICD-10-AM at NCCH Sydney, with additional funds for the project being solicited through the national press, according to the July 1998 "Coding Matters." Current funding levels will allow the NCCH to continue its work through June 2000, one month prior to the scheduled second edition of ICD-10-AM.

Planning for the Future

Updating ICD-10-AM is a priority for the Australian NCCH along with stabilizing the classification, although changes are anticipated due to Australian

Coding Standards and typographical corrections. The NCCH will also maintain ICD-10 codes for mortality coding in Australia. For future editions, NCCH anticipates allowing twelve months prior to publication and an additional five months prior to implementation; preparations would begin in the February prior to the July start date for new editions.

Procedures for updating subsequent editions in the United States will probably be similar to the process of updating ICD-9-CM. Revisions to ICD-9-CM are made once a year and are implemented October 1 of each year. Major changes in the time frame are published in the *Federal Register*. The ICD-9-CM Coordination and Maintenance Committee meets twice each year to discuss coding revisions proposed for the subsequent year.

INTERNET LINKS

Medicode will post updates about ICD-10-CM (and the inpatient procedural coding system, ICD-10-PCS) along with other coding issues at www.medicode.com/ingenix/pn/products/icdupdate. asp

REVIEW

The ICD-9-CM Coding review is organized according to the ICD-9-CM chapters and supplemental classifications. To properly code, refer first to the Disease Index (to locate main term and subterm entries) and then to the Disease Tabular List (to review notes and verify the code selected).

■ **NOTE:** Although the review is organized by chapter/supplemental classification, codes from outside a particular chapter/supplemental classification may be required to completely classify a case. ■

Underline the main term in each item; then use Index to Diseases and Tabular List coding rules and conventions to assign the code(s). Enter the code(s) on the line next to each diagnostic statement. Be sure to list the primary code first.

Infectious and Parasitic Diseases (including HIV)

1. Aseptic meningitis due to AIDS   _____
2. Asymptomatic HIV infection   _____
3. Septicemia due to streptococcus   _____
4. Dermatophytosis of the foot   _____
5. Measles; no complications noted   _____
6. Nodular pulmonary tuberculosis; confirmed histologically   _____
7. Acute cystitis due to E. coli   _____
8. Tuberculosis osteomyelitis of lower leg; confirmed by histology   _____
9. Gas gangrene   _____

Neoplasms

10. Malignant melanoma of skin of scalp   _____
11. Lipoma of face   _____
12. Glioma of the parietal lobe of the brain   _____
13. Adenocarcinoma of prostate   _____
14. Carcinoma *in situ* of vocal cord   _____
15. Hodgkin's granuloma of intra-abdominal lymph nodes and spleen   _____
16. Paget's disease with infiltrating duct carcinoma of breast, nipple and areola   _____
17. Liver cancer   _____

18. Metastatic adenocarcinoma from breast to brain
    (right mastectomy performed 5 years ago)   _____
19. Cancer of the pleura (primary site)   _____

Endocrine, Nutritional and Metabolic Diseases, and Immunity Disorders

20. Cushing's Syndrome   _____
21. Hypokalemia   _____
22. Non-insulin dependent diabetes mellitus, uncontrolled, with malnutrition   _____
23. Hypogammaglobulinemia   _____
24. Hypercholesterolemia   _____
25. Nephrosis due to type 2 diabetes   _____
26. Toxic diffuse goiter with thyrotoxic crisis   _____
27. Cystic fibrosis   _____
28. Panhypopituitarism   _____
29. Rickets   _____

Diseases of the Blood and Blood-forming Organs

30. Sickle cell disease with crisis   _____
31. Iron deficiency anemia secondary to blood loss   _____
32. Von Willebrand's disease   _____
33. Chronic congestive splenomegaly   _____
34. Congenital nonspherocytic hemolytic anemia   _____
35. Essential thrombocytopenia   _____
36. Malignant neutropenia   _____
37. Fanconi's anemia   _____
38. Microangiopathic hemolytic anemia   _____
39. Aplastic anemia secondary to antineoplastic medication for breast cancer   _____

Mental Disorders

40. Acute exacerbation of chronic undifferentiated schizophrenia   _____
41. Reactive depressive psychosis due to the death of a child   _____
42. Hysterical neurosis   _____
43. Anxiety reaction manifested by fainting   _____
44. Alcoholic gastritis due to chronic alcoholism (episodic)   _____
45. Juvenile delinquency; patient was caught shoplifting   _____
46. Depression   _____
47. Hypochondria; patient also has continuous laxative habit   _____
48. Acute senile dementia with Alzheimer's disease   _____
49. Epileptic psychosis with generalized grand mal epilepsy   _____

Diseases of the Nervous System and Sense Organs

50. Neisseria meningitis   _____
51. Intracranial abscess   _____
52. Postvaricella encephalitis   _____
53. Hemiplegia due to old CVA   _____
54. Encephalitis   _____
55. Retinal detachment with retinal defect   _____
56. congenital diplegic cerebral palsy   _____
57. tonic-clonic epilepsy   _____
58. infantile glaucoma   _____
59. mature cataract   _____

Diseases of the Circulatory System

60. Congestive rheumatic heart failure _____

61. Mitral valve stenosis with aortic valve insufficiency _____

62. Acute rheumatic heart disease _____

63. Hypertensive cardiovascular disease, malignant _____

64. Congestive heart failure; benign hypertension _____

65. Secondary benign hypertension; stenosis of renal artery _____

66. Malignant hypertensive nephropathy with uremia _____

67. Acute renal failure; essential hypertension _____

68. Acute myocardial infarction of inferolateral wall, initial episode of care _____

69. Arteriosclerotic heart disease (native coronary artery) with angina pectoris _____

Diseases of the Respiratory System

70. Aspiration pneumonia due to regurgitated food _____

71. Streptococcal Group B pneumonia _____

72. Respiratory failure due to myasthenia gravis _____

73. Intrinsic asthma in status asthmaticus _____

74. COPD with emphysema _____

Diseases of the Digestive System

75. Supernumerary tooth _____

76. Unilateral femoral hernia with gangrene _____

77. Cholesterolosis of gallbladder _____

78. Infectious diarrhea _____

79. Acute perforated peptic ulcer _____

80. Acute hemorrhagic gastritis with acute blood loss anemia _____

81. Acute appendicitis with perforation and peritoneal abscess _____

82. Acute cholecystitis with cholelithiasis _____

83. Aphthous stomatitis _____

84. Diverticulosis and diverticulitis of colon _____

85. Esophageal reflux with esophagitis _____

Diseases of the Genitourinary System

86. Vesicoureteral reflux with bilateral reflux nephropathy _____

87. Acute glomerulonephritis with necrotizing glomerulolitis _____

88. Actinomycotic cystitis _____

89. Subserosal uterine leiomyoma, cervical polyp and endometriosis of uterus _____

90. Dysplasia of the cervix _____

Diseases of Pregnancy, Childbirth, and the Puerperium

91. Defibrination syndrome following termination of pregnancy procedure two weeks ago _____

92. Miscarriage at 19 weeks gestation _____

93. Incompetent cervix resulting in miscarriage _____

94. Postpartum varicose veins of legs _____

95. Spontaneous breech delivery _____

96. Triplet pregnancy, delivered spontaneously _____

97. Retained placental without hemorrhage, delivery this admission _____

98. Pyrexia of unknown origin during the puerperium (postpartum), delivery during previous admission _____

99. Late vomiting of pregnancy, undelivered _____

100. Pre-eclampsia complicating pregnancy, delivered this admission _____

Diseases of the Skin and Subcutaneous Tissue

101. Diaper rash _____

102. Acne vulgaris _____

103. Post-infectional skin cicatrix _____

104. Cellulitis of the foot; culture reveals staphylococcus _____

105. Infected ingrowing nail _____

Diseases of the Musculoskeletal System and Connective Tissue

106. Displacement of thoracic intervertebral disc _____

107. Primary localized osteoarthrosis of the hip _____

108. Acute juvenile rheumatoid arthritis _____

109. Chondromalacia of the patella _____

110. Pathologic fracture of the vertebra due to metastatic carcinoma of the bone from the lung _____

Congenital Anomalies

111. Congenital diaphragmatic hernia _____

112. Single liveborn male (born in the hospital) with polydactyly of fingers _____

113. Unilateral cleft lip and palate _____

114. Patent ductus arteriosus _____

115. Congenital talipes equinovalgus _____

Certain Conditions Originating in the Perinatal Period

116. Erythroblastosis fetalis _____

117. Hyperbilirubinemia of prematurity, prematurity (birthweight 2000 grams) _____

118. Erb's palsy _____

119. Hypoglycemia in infant with diabetic mother _____

120. Premature "crack" baby born in hospital to cocaine-dependent mother (birthweight 1,247 grams) _____

Symptoms, Signs, and Ill-defined Conditions

121. Abnormal cervical pap smear _____

122. Sudden infant death syndrome _____

123. Sleep apnea with insomnia _____

124. Fluid retention and edema _____

125. Elevated blood pressure reading _____

Injury and Poisoning

Fractures, Dislocations and Sprains

126. Open frontal fracture with subarachnoid hemorrhage with brief loss of consciousness _____

127. Supracondylar fracture of right humerus and fracture of olecranon process of the right ulna _____

128. Anterior dislocation of the elbow _____

129. Dislocation of the 1st and 2nd cervical vertebra _____

130. Sprain of lateral collateral ligament of knee _____

Open Wounds and Other Trauma

131. Avulsion of eye _____

132. Traumatic below the knee amputation with delayed healing _____

133. Open wound of buttock _____

134. Open wound of wrist involving tendons _____

135. Laceration of external ear _____

136. Traumatic subdural hemorrhage with open intracranial wound; loss of consciousness, 30 minutes _____

137. Concussion without loss of consciousness _____

138. Traumatic laceration of the liver, moderate _____

139. Traumatic hemothorax with open wound into thorax and concussion with loss of consciousness _____

140. Traumatic duodenal injury _____

Burns

141. Third-degree burn of lower leg and second-degree burn of thigh _____

142. Deep third-degree burn of forearm _____

143. Third-degree burns of back involving 20% of body surface _____

144. Thirty percent body burns with 10%, third degree _____

145. First- and second-degree burns of palm _____

Foreign Bodies

146. Coin in the bronchus with bronchoscopy for removal of the coin _____

147. Foreign body in the eye _____

148. Marble in colon _____

149. Bean in nose _____

150. Q-Tip stuck in ear _____

Complications

151. Infected ventriculoperitoneal shunt _____

152. Displaced breast prosthesis _____

153. Leakage of mitral valve prosthesis _____

154. Postoperative superficial thrombophlebitis of the right leg _____

155. Dislocated hip prosthesis _____

V Codes

156. Exposure to tuberculosis _____

157. Family history of colon carcinoma _____

158. Status post unilateral kidney transplant, human donor _____

159. Encounter for removal of cast _____

160. Admitted to donate bone marrow _____

161. Encounter for chemotherapy for patient with Hodgkin's lymphoma _____

162. Reprogramming of cardiac pacemaker _____

163. Replacement of tracheostomy tube _____

164. Encounter for renal dialysis for patient in chronic renal failure _____

165. Encounter for speech therapy for patient with dysphasia secondary to an old CVA _____

166. Encounter for fitting of artificial leg _____

167. Encounter for observation of suspected malignant neoplasm of the cervix _____

168. Visit to radiology department for barium swallow; abdominal pain; findings are negative; barium swallow performed and the findings are negative _____

169. Follow-up examination of colon adenocarcinoma resected one year ago, no recurrence found

170. Routine general medical examination _____

171. Examination of eyes _____

172. Encounter for laboratory test; patient complains of fatigue _____

173. Encounter for physical therapy; status post below the knee amputation six months ago _____

174. Kidney donor _____

175. Encounter for chemotherapy; breast carcinoma _____

Coding Late Effects

Place an X on the line for each diagnostic statement that identifies a late effect of an injury/illness.

176. Hemiplegia due to previous cerebrovascular accident _____

177. Malunion of fracture, right femur _____

178. Scoliosis due to infantile paralysis _____

179. Keloid secondary to injury 9 months ago _____

180. Gangrene, left foot, following third-degree burn of foot 2 weeks ago _____

181. Cerebral thrombosis with hemiplegia _____

182. Mental retardation due to previous viral encephalitis _____

183. Laceration of tendon of finger 2 weeks ago. Admitted now for tendon repair _____

Code the following:

184. Residuals of poliomyelitis _____

185. Sequela of old crush injury to left foot _____

186. Cerebrovascular accident two years ago with late effects _____

187. Effects of old gunshot wound, left thigh _____

188. Disuse osteoporosis due to previous poliomyelitis _____

189. Brain damage following cerebral abscess 7 months ago _____

190. Hemiplegia due to old cerebrovascular accident _____

Adverse Reactions and Poisonings

191. Ataxia due to interaction between prescribed Carbamazepine and Erythromycin _____

192. Vertigo as a result of dye administered for a scheduled IVP _____

193. Accidental ingestion of mother's oral contraceptives (no signs or symptoms resulted) _____

194. Hemiplegia; patient had an adverse reaction to prescribed Enovid one year ago _____

195. Stricture of esophagus due to accidental lye ingestion three years ago _____

196. Listlessness resulting from reaction between prescribed Valium and ingestion of a 6-pack of beer _____

197. Lead poisoning (child had been discovered eating paint chips) _____

198. Allergic reaction to unspecified drug _____

199. Theophylline toxicity _____

200. Carbon monoxide poisoning from car exhaust (suicide attempt) _____

OBJECTIVES   Upon successful completion of this chapter, you should be able to:

1. Define the following terms, phrases, and abbreviations:

Current Procedural Terminology
   (CPT)
Health Care Financing
   Administration Common
   Procedure Coding System
   (HCPCS)
modifiers
symbols
   ●
   ▲
   ►◄
   ;
   *
   +
   ⊘
package concept
global surgery
surgical package
fee-for-service
(Tabular Conventions)
  guidelines
  instructional notes
  blocked indented note
  indented parenthetical note
  boldface type
(Index Conventions)
  See
  inferred words
  boldface type
  italicized type
  descriptive qualifiers

surgical procedure
major surgical procedure
unbundling
fragmented surgery
á la carte billing
itemized pricing
separate procedure
cystourethroscopy
multiple surgical procedures
skin lesion
layered closure
plastic repair
closed fracture treatment
open fracture treatment
percutaneous skeletal fixation
manipulation of a fracture
reduction of a fracture
open treatment of a closed
  fracture
open reduction with internal
  fixation (ORIF)
endoscopic guide-wire dilation
indirect laryngoscopy
direct laryngoscopy
professional component
technical component
radiologic views
laboratory panel
organ panel
disease oriented panel
evaluation and management
  (E&M) section

E&M codes
level of service
place of service
type of service
new patient
established patient
key components
history
extent of history
  problem focused
  expanded problem focused
  detailed
  comprehensive
physical examination
extent of examination
  problem focused
  expanded problem focused
  detailed
  comprehensive
medical decision making
contributory components
counseling
coordination of care
nature of the presenting problem
face-to-face time
unit/floor time
1995 Evaluation and Management
  Documentation Guidelines
  (1995 DGs)
1997 Evaluation and Management
  Documentation Guidelines
  (1997 DGs)

June 2000 DGs (draft version)
hospital observation services
initial hospital care
hospital inpatient
subsequent hospital care
observation or inpatient care
   services
hospital discharge services
consultation
preoperative clearance
confirmatory consultation

emergency department services
critical care services
constant attendance
bundled codes
neonatal intensive care
nursing facility services
comprehensive assessment
subsequent nursing facility care
domiciliary care
home services

prolonged services
direct patient contact
without direct patient contact
physician standby services
case management services
care plan oversight services
preventive medicine services
newborn care
CPT-5
performance measures

2. Discuss the importance of carefully proofreading all code numbers on the claim form.

3. Explain the format of the CPT system.

4. Compare ICD-9-CM to HCPCS.

5. Explain why modifiers were developed for HCPCS.

6. Explain how to determine the level of evaluation and management service.

7. Explain the difference between a new and an established patient.

8. List the requirements for assigning emergency department and critical care codes.

9. Explain the difference between a consultation and a confirmatory consultation.

10. Discuss the qualifications for a "preventative medicine visit."

11. Define "global surgical period" used in CPT as applied by the insurance industry.

12. Explain the significance of the asterisk next to a CPT code (starred procedure).

13. Convert inches to centimeters.

I N T R O D U C T I O N

This chapter introduces the assignment of **Current Procedural Terminology (CPT)** service and procedure codes reported on the HCFA-1500. CPT is published by the American Medical Association and includes codes for procedures performed and services provided to patients. It is level one of the **Health Care Financing Administration Common Procedure Coding System (HCPCS)**, which also contains level two (national codes) and level three (local codes). Because of the introductory nature of this chapter, you are encouraged to obtain a comprehensive textbook that covers CPT principles and practice (e.g., Delmar's *Understanding Medical Coding: A Comprehensive Guide* by Sandra L. Johnson).

CPT CODING SYSTEM

Current Procedural Terminology (CPT) is a listing of descriptive terms and identifying codes for reporting medical services and procedures. It provides a uniform language that describes medical, surgical, and diagnostic services to facilitate communication among providers, patients, and insurers. The American Medical Association (AMA) first published CPT in 1966 and subsequent editions expanded its descriptive terms and codes for diagnostic and therapeutic procedures. Five-digit codes were introduced in 1970, replacing the four-digit classification. In 1983, CPT was adopted as part of the Health Care Financing Administration's (HCFA) Common Procedure Coding System (HCPCS) and its use was mandated for reporting Medicare Part B services. In 1986, HCPCS was required for reporting to Medicaid agencies, and in July 1987, as part of the Omnibus Budget Reconciliation Act (OBRA), HCFA mandated that CPT codes be reported for outpatient hospital surgical procedures.

The AMA prepares an annual update of CPT that is available in late fall of each year preceding its implementation. Federal programs (e.g., Medicare and Medicaid) generally implement the new codes on January 1 of each year; other third-party payers may implement the new codes on the same date or later (e.g., March 1). Be sure to check with each payer to determine when to begin using the new codes. With each update, outdated procedures are deleted, new procedures are added, and narrative descriptions are revised. The ICD and CPT coding manuals are available from Delmar Thomson Learning as the exclusive distributor for Medicode and St. Anthony products. CPT may also be ordered from the AMA by calling (800) 621-8335.

INTERNET LINKS

Order CPT coding books online at www.delmar.com/ or www.ama-assn.org/catalog.

CPT codes are used to report services and procedures performed on patients:
- By providers in offices, clinics, and private homes.
- By providers in institutional settings such as hospitals, nursing facilities, and hospices.
- When the provider is employed by the health care facility (e.g., many of the physicians associated with Veterans Administration Medical Centers are employees of that organization).
- By a hospital outpatient department (e.g., ambulatory surgery, emergency department, and outpatient laboratory or radiographic procedures).

Procedures submitted on a claim must be linked to the ICD-9-CM code that justifies the need for the service or procedure. That ICD-9-CM code must demonstrate medical necessity for the service or procedure to receive reimbursement consideration by insurance payers.

CPT FORMAT

Sections

CPT is organized into the following six sections:

Evaluation and Management	99201 through 99499
Anesthesia	00100 through 01999
Surgery	10040 through 69990
Radiology	70010 through 79999

Pathology and Laboratory 80049 through 89399

Medicine 90281 through 99199

It should be noted that codes 99201 through 99499, Evaluation and Management, are located at the beginning of the book. These codes are used by all specialties for services performed in offices, hospitals, nursing facilities, patient homes, and emergency departments. Also out of sequence in the coding manual are four codes that classify "Qualifying Circumstances" for anesthesia services. While these codes are listed at the end of the Medicine section of CPT, they are to be reported with anesthesia codes.

CPT Appendices

Six appendices are located between the Medicine section and the index. These appendices should be carefully reviewed to become familiar with coding changes that affect the practice annually. Appendix A contains a complete list and detailed description of each CPT modifier.

CODING TIP: Place a marker at the beginning of Appendix A. It is the only place where you will find an overview of all the CPT modifiers. You will be referring to this appendix often.

Appendix B lists annual coding changes (additions, deletions, and revisions) and should be carefully studied upon receiving a current code book. This appendix should be used as the basis for updating interoffice documents and billing tools. Appendix C is a summary of changes made to the CPT computer file. Appendix D provides clinical examples for codes found in the Evaluation and Management section. Appendix E lists add-on codes. These codes are never reported as stand alone codes; they accompany primary procedure codes. (These codes are also individually identified in the numerical section of the code manual by a "**+**" preceding the code number.) Appendix F is a list of codes that are exempt from rules for the use of modifier -51. (These codes are also individually identified in the numerical section of the code manual by a Ø symbol preceding the code number.)

Code Numbers

The CPT coding system is based on five-digit code numbers with descriptions of services and procedures.

EXAMPLE

27780 Closed treatment of proximal fibula or shaft fracture; without manipulation

Modifiers

CPT **modifiers** clarify services and procedures performed by providers, and while the CPT code and description remains unchanged, modifiers indicate that the description of the service or procedure performed has been altered. CPT modifiers are reported as two-digit numeric codes added to the five-digit CPT code.

EXAMPLE

A patient undergoes the repair of a deviated nasal septum for which CPT code 30630 is reported. One year later, a different surgeon performs a repeat repair of the deviated nasal septum because the procedure performed last year was unsuccessful. The CPT code for the repeat repair would be reported with an attached modifier to clarify the situation: 30630-77.

Traditionally, CPT modifiers have applied only to claims submitted for provider office services and procedures performed. However, on April 1, 2000 HCFA began requiring hospitals to report CPT and HCPCS National (Level II) modifiers for outpatient services. An abbreviated listing of CPT modifiers can be found inside the front cover of the coding manual along with an abbreviated listing of CPT and Level II (HCPCS/National) modifiers approved for hospital outpatient reporting purposes.

Detailed information about assignment of CPT modifiers can be found on pages 197-208, and Level II HCPCS/National modifiers are discussed in Chapter 8.

CPT SYMBOLS AND CONVENTIONS

Accurate coding of procedures cannot be accomplished without a thorough understanding of the symbols and conventions used in CPT (Figure 7-1).

Symbol/Convention:	CPT entry:	
Section	**Surgery**	
Category	**Integumentary System**	
Subcategory	**Skin, Subcutaneous and Accessory Structures**	
Heading	**Incision and Drainage**	
Note		(For excision, see 11400, et seq)
		(10000-10020 have been deleted. To report, see 10060, 10061)
Code number/description	**10040***	Acne surgery (eg, marsupialization, opening or removal of multiple milia, comedones, cysts, pustules)
Asterisked/starred procedure	**10060***	Incision and drainage of abscess (eg, carbuncle, suppurative hidradenitis, cutaneous or subcutaneous abscess, cyst, furuncle, or paronychia); simple or single
Use of semicolon	**10061**	complicated or multiple
	11000*	Debridement of extensive eczematous or Infected skin; up to 10% of body surface
Use of plus symbol	**+11001**	each additional 10% of the body surface (List separately in addition to code for primary procedure)
Use of -51 modifier exemption symbol	⊘ **32000***	Thoracentesis, puncture of pleural cavity for aspiration, initial or subsequent
Use of revised instructional note symbol		▶(32001 has been deleted. To report, use 32997)3 ◀

FIGURE 7-1 Selection from CPT that illustrates symbols and conventions (CPT codes, descriptions, and materials only are © 2000 American Medical Association).

Symbols   Seven **symbols** are used in the CPT coding book.

● A bullet located to the left of a code number indicates a new code, neve: before published in CPT.

EXAMPLE (CPT 2001)

● 90743 Hepatitis B vaccine, adolescent (2-dose schedule), for intramuscular use

▲ A triangle located to the left of a code number indicates a code description revision for the current edition of CPT.

EXAMPLE (CPT 2001)

▲ **90744** Hepatitis B vaccine, pediatric/adolescent dosage (3-dose schedule), for intramuscular use

►◄ Horizontal triangles surround revised guidelines and notes. *This symbol is not used for procedure description revisions.*

EXAMPLE (CPT 2001)

11044 skin, subcutaneous tissue, muscle, and bone

► (Do not report 11040-11044 in addition to 97601, 97602) ◄

CODING TIP: A complete list of code additions, deletions, and revisions is found in Appendix B of CPT. Revisions marked with ►◄ are not included in Appendix B, requiring coders to carefully review all CPT guidelines and notes in the new edition.

; The placement of a semi-colon within a CPT description indicates that the portion to the left of the semicolon applies (but is not reprinted) to the indented, shorter descriptions of codes that follow. The unabridged description begins with a capital letter and is indented only two spaces after the code it describes. The abbreviated (or subordinate) descriptions that follow are indented and begin with lower-case letters. This format is used in CPT to save space.

EXAMPLE (CPT 2001)

99315 Nursing facility discharge day management; 30 minutes or less

99316   more than 30 minutes

Code 99316 includes the description located to the left of the semicolon in code 9931. Therefore, code 99316 is interpreted as if written, **99316** Nursing facility discharge day management; more than 30 minutes.

CODING TIP: CPT is printed using proportional spacing, and careful review of code descriptions to locate the semicolon may be necessary.

★ The asterisk (also referred to as a star) is located after minor surgery codes to indicate that variable preoperative and postoperative services are included. This means that the "package" concept for surgical services does not apply. The **"package" concept** (also referred to as **global**

surgery or the **surgical package**) indicates that the listed CPT surgery code includes the procedure, local infiltration, metacarpal/digital block or topical anesthesia when used, and normal, uncomplicated followup care. Asterisked (or starred) procedures are generally paid according to **fee-for-service**, which means that a charge for each service is generated.

EXAMPLE

33010*   Pericardiocentesis; initial

33011*   subsequent

CODING TIP: The asterisk applies only to its assigned code.

A practice's preprinted documents (e.g., Superbill and encounter form) should include the asterisk next to applicable codes. This will remind staff and patients that individual services for these surgical procedures are separately itemized and billed.

+ The plus symbol identifies add-on codes for procedures that are commonly, but not always, performed at the same time and by the same surgeon as the primary procedure. Parenthetical notes, located below add-on codes, often identify the primary procedure to which add-on codes apply. Add-on codes do not stand alone. Do not assign modifier -51 to add-on codes.

⊘ This symbol indicates that modifier -51 is not to be assigned to the code. These codes have not been identified as add-on procedures/services.

EXAMPLE

Primary Procedure

22210 Osteotomy of spine, posterior or posterolateral approach, one vertebral segment; cervical

33496 Repair of nonstructural prosthetic valve dysfunction with cardiopulmonary bypass (separate procedure)

Add-on Procedure

+22216 Each additional vertebral segment (List separately in addition to primary procedure)

+33530 Reoperation, coronary artery bypass procedure or valve procedure, more than one month after original operation (List separately in addition to code for primary procedure)

TABULAR CONVENTIONS

Guidelines

Guidelines are located at the beginning of each of the six sections of the CPT code book. *These guidelines should be carefully reviewed before attempting to code from a section.* **Guidelines** define terms and explain the assignment of codes for procedures and services located in a section (see Figure 7-2 on page 158). Guidelines that precede a particular section apply to that section and, generally, do not apply throughout CPT.

Categories, Subcategories, and Headings

The tabular portion of CPT is organized according to six sections that are subdivided into categories, subcategories, and headings (see Figure 7-3 on page 159).

Surgery Guidelines

Items used by all physicians in reporting their services are presented in the **Introduction.** Some of the commonalities are repeated here for the convenience of those physicians referring to this section on **Surgery**. Other definitions and items unique to Surgery are also listed.

Physicians' Services

Physicians' services rendered in the office, home, or hospital, consultations, and other medial services are listed in the section entitled **Evaluation and Management Services** (99200 series) found in the front of the book, beginning on page 9. "Special Services and Reports" (99000 series) is presented in the **Medicine** section.

Follow-Up Care for Therapeutic Surgical Procedures

Follow-up care for therapeutic surgical procedures includes only that care which is usually a part of the surgical service. Complications, exacerbations, recurrence, or the presence of other diseases or injuries requiring additional services should be reported with the identification of appropriate procedures.

Materials Supplied by Physician

Supplies and materials provided by the physician (eg, sterile trays/drugs), over and above those usually included with the office visit or other services rendered may be listed separately. List drugs, trays, supplies, and materials provided. Identify as 99070.

FIGURE 7-2 Portion of CPT Surgery Guidelines (CPT codes, descriptions, and materials only are © 2000 American Medical Association.)

Notes

Instructional notes appear throughout the CPT tabular to clarify the assignment of codes. They are typeset in two patterns (see Figure 7-3).

1. A **blocked indented note** is located below a subsection title and provides instructions that apply to all codes assigned in that subsection.

2. An **indented parenthetical note** can be found after blocked indented notes, immediately following a code description, or below an indented code description. Parenthetical notes that contain the abbreviation "eg," are considered examples; terminology in the example does not need to appear in the provider's procedural statement.

   Other parenthetical notes within a code series provide information about codes that have been deleted.

Boldface Type

CPT categories, subcategories, headings, and code numbers are printed in **boldface type**.

INDEX CONVENTIONS

See

See is a cross-reference that directs coders to an index entry under which codes are listed. No codes are listed under the original entry.

Cardiovascular System

Blocked unindented note

Selective vascular catheterizations should be coded to include introduction and all lesser order selective catheterizations used in the approach (eg, the description for a selective right middle cerebral artery catheterization includes the introduction and placement catheterization of the right common and internal carotid arteries).

Additional second and/or third order arterial catheterizations within the same family of arteries supplied by a single first order artery should be expressed by 36218 or 36248. Additional first order or higher catheterizations in vascular families supplied by a first order vessel different from a previously selected and coded family should be separately coded using the conventions described above.

Indented parenthetical note located below subsection title

(For monitoring, operation of pump and other Nonsurgical services, *see* 99190-99192, 99291, 99292, 99354-99360)

(For other medical or laboratory related services, *see* appropriate section)

(For radiological supervision and interpretation, *see* 75600-75978)

Heart and Pericardium

Pericardium

33010*   Pericardiocentesis; initial

Indented parenthetical note located below code description

(For radiological supervision and interpretation, use 76930)

Indented parenthetical note located below code description that contains an example

33250   Operative ablation of supraventricular arrhythmogenic focus pathway (eg, Wolff-Parkinson-White, A-V node re-entry), tract(s) and/or focus (foci); without cardiopulmonary bypass

FIGURE 7-3 Selection from CPT that illustrates the two types of instructional notes (CPT codes, descriptions, and materials only are © 2000 American Medical Association.)

EXAMPLE

AV Shunt

See Arteriovenous Shunt

In this example, the coder is directed to the index entry for "Arteriovenous Shunt" because no codes are listed for "AV Shunt."

Inferred Words

To save space in the CPT Index when referencing subterms, the practice of **inferred words** is used.

> ### EXAMPLE
>
> **Abdomen**
>
> Exploration (of) 49000, 49002
>
> In the above example, the word in parentheses (of) is inferred and does not appear in the CPT Index.

Boldface Type

Boldface type is used for main terms in the CPT Index.

Italicized Type

Italicized type is used for the cross reference, *See*, in the CPT Index.

Descriptive Qualifiers

Descriptive qualifiers are terms that clarify the assignment of a CPT code. They can occur in the middle of a main clause or after the semicolon and may or may not be enclosed in parentheses. Read all code descriptions very carefully to properly assign CPT codes that require descriptive qualifiers.

> ### EXAMPLE
>
> **17000*** Destruction by any method, including laser, with or without surgical curettement, all benign or premalignant lesions (eg, actinic keratoses) <u>other than skin tags or cutaneous vascular proliferative lesions</u>, including local anesthesia; <u>first</u> lesion
>
> **+17003** second through 14 lesions, <u>each</u> (List separately in addition to code for first lesion)
>
> ■ **NOTE:** The underlining in the above code descriptions was added to emphasize the descriptive qualifiers in each code description. ■

CODING TIP:

Coders working in a provider's office should highlight all descriptive qualifiers that pertain to the office's specialty. This will help ensure that qualifiers are not overlooked when assigning codes.

EXERCISE 7-1 Working with CPT Symbols and Conventions

If the statement is true, place a "T" in front of the number. If the statement is false, correct it without rewording the entire statement.

_____ **1.** CPT modifiers are reported on outpatient claims at all health care facilities.

_____ **2.** The asterisk following a code number indicates a substantial change in the narrative of a code.

_____ **3.** The major sections of CPT are nuclear medicine, surgery, medicine, pathology, and radiology.

_____ **4.** The triangle is used to indicate a new procedure code number.

_____ **5.** The numerical format for a reported procedure should be expressed with a five-digit main number and a three-digit modifier.

_____ **6.** "Notes" should be applied to all codes located under a heading.

_____ **7.** The semicolon indicates a break between the main and subordinate clauses of procedure descriptions.

_____ **8.** All descriptive qualifiers for a particular code are found in an indented code description.

_____ **9.** When a parenthetical statement within a code description begins with "eg," one of the terms that follows must be included in the provider's description of the surgery for the code number to apply.

_____**10.** The cross-reference that directs coders to refer to a different index entry because no codes are found under the original entry is called "*See.*"

_____**11.** Main terms appear in italics in the CPT Index.

_____**12.** Inferred words appear in the CPT Index to assist coders in assigning appropriate codes.

_____**13.** Horizontal triangles (▶◀) are found in revised guidelines, notes, and procedure descriptions.

_____**14.** The bullet (●) located to the left of a CPT code indicates a new code to that edition of CPT.

_____**15.** Upon review of the CPT tabular listing below, code 50620 would be reported for a *ureterolithotomy performed on the upper or middle one-third of the ureter.*

50610   Ureterolithotomy; upper one-third of ureter

50620   middle one-third of ureter

50630   lower one-third of ureter

After completing this exercise, refer to Appendix IV to check your answers.

CPT INDEX

The CPT index (Figure 7-4 on page 162) is organized by alphabetical main terms printed in boldface. The main terms represent procedures or services, organs, anatomical sites, conditions, eponyms, or abbreviations. The main term may be followed by indented terms that modify the main term; these are called subterms.

Single Codes and Code Ranges

Code numbers for specific procedures may be represented as a single code number, a range of codes separated by a dash, a series of codes separated by commas, or a combination of single codes and ranges of codes. All listed numbers should be investigated before assigning a code for the procedure or service.

EXAMPLE

Liver
Repair
      Abscess....................................47300
      Cyst..47300
    Wound.....47350, 47360, 47361-47362

EXERCISE 7-2 Working with Single Codes and Code Ranges

1. Turn to code number 47300 and review all procedural descriptions through code 47362.

N

Cross-referenced term	**N. Meningitidis** *See* Neisseria Meningitidis
	Naffziger Operation *See* Decompression, Orbit; Section
	Nagel Test *See* Color Vision Examination
Main term Subterm	**Nails** Avulsion 11730-11732
	Biopsy 11755
Range of codes to investigate	Debridement 11720-11721
	Evacuation
	Hematoma, Subungual 11740
	Excision 11750-11752
	Cyst
	Pilonidal 11770-11772
	Removal 11730-11732, 11750-11752
	Trimming 11719

FIGURE 7-4 Selection from CPT Index (CPT codes, descriptions, and materials only are © 2000 American Medical Association.)

2. What does the term marsupialization mean? If you don't know the meaning, look it up in your medical dictionary.

_____

_____

3. How do codes 47350, 47360-47362 differ?

47350 _____

47360 _____

_____

47361 _____

_____

47362 _____

_____

After completing this exercise, refer to Appendix IV to check your answers.

CODING TIP: The descriptions of *all* codes listed for a specific procedure must be carefully investigated before selecting a final code. As with ICD-9-CM, CPT coding must *never* be performed solely from the index.

BASIC STEPS FOR CODING PROCEDURES AND SERVICES

Step 1. Read the Introduction located in the CPT coding manual.

Step 2. Review the guidelines located at the beginning of each CPT section.

Step 3. Review the procedure or service listed on the office's source document (e.g, charge slip, progress note, operative report, laboratory report, or pathology report). Code only what is recorded on the office's source document; do not make assumptions about conditions, procedures, or services not stated. If necessary, obtain clarification from the provider.

Step 4. Refer to the CPT Index, and locate the main term for the procedure or service documented. Main terms can be located by referring to the:

a. *Procedure or service* documented.

> **EXAMPLE:** arthroscopy and consultation.

b. *Organ or anatomic site.*

> **EXAMPLE:** arm, ankle, and backbone.

c. *Condition* documented in the record.

> **EXAMPLE:** emboli, cyst, and chicken pox.

d. *Substance being tested.*

> **EXAMPLE:** blood and urine are tested for cholesterol, chromium, and folic acid.

e. *Synonym* (terms with similar meanings).

> **EXAMPLE:** Intercarpal joint is a finger joint; both are listed in the index.

f. *Eponym* (procedures and diagnoses named for an individual).

> **EXAMPLE:** The Babcock Operation is the ligation of the saphenous vein; both are listed in the index.

g. *Abbreviation*

> **EXAMPLE:** CBC, HAAb, and MRI.

Step 5. Locate necessary subterms, and follow cross references listed in the index.

Step 6. Review the descriptions of service/procedure codes listed in the index. Note and compare all qualifiers in the descriptive statements. (*Hint:* If the last code description you read is located at the bottom of the page, turn the page and check to see if the description continues.)

Step 7. Assign the applicable primary code number and any add-on (**+**) or additional codes needed to accurately classify the statement being coded.

CODING TIP: You may have to refer to synonyms, translate medical terms to ordinary English, or substitute medical words for English terms documented in the provider's statement to find the main term in the index. Some examples are:

Procedure Statement	**Word Substitution**
Placement of a shunt	Insertion of shunt
Pacemaker implantation	Pacemaker insertion
Resection of tumor	Excision or removal of tumor
Radiograph of the chest	Xray of chest
Suture laceration	Repair open wound
Placement of nerve block	Injection of nerve anesthesia

EXERCISE 7-3 Finding Procedures in the Index

Using only the index, find the code or range of codes to be investigated. Note the code or range of codes and any word substitution you made that lead to selected code numbers.

1. Closed treatment of wrist dislocation   _____

2. Dilation of cervix   _____

3. Placement of upper GI feeding tube   _____

4. Radiograph and fluoroscopy of chest, 4 views   _____

5. Magnetic resonance imaging, lower spine   _____

6. Darrach procedure   _____

7. Manual CBC   _____

8. Electrosurgical removal, skin tags   _____

After completing this exercise, refer to Appendix IV to check your answers.

SURGERY OVERVIEW

Definition of Surgery

Most **surgical procedures** in CPT fall into one of the following categories:

- Incision (-otomy)
- Biopsy
- Excision or removal (-ectomy)
- Destruction
- Debridement (cleaning) of a wound
- Repair or reconstruction of a body part (-plasty)
- Insertion of an instrument into an organ (-scopy)

- Suture of a body part or organ (-rrhaphy)
- Application of a cast or strapping of a joint
- Introduction (usually means injection, but can be a special test procedure, such as centesis or aspiration)

The health insurance industry's definition of surgical procedure includes:
- Break in the natural barrier of the skin (injections, suturing)
- Removal of tissue
- Insertion of a scope or instrument beyond the immediate area of an orifice (opening) into the body
- Fracture treatment
- Burn

Some insurers may also include some medical noninvasive testing in the above group.

Surgery Section

The surgery section is organized by body system. Each system is subdivided first by the specific organ or anatomical site and then by procedure categories in the following order:
- Incision
- Destruction
- Excision
- Introduction
- Removal
- Repair
- Endoscopy
- Grafts
- Suture
- Other/miscellaneous procedures

To code surgeries properly, three questions must be asked:
1. What body system was involved?
2. What anatomical site was involved?
3. What type of procedure was performed?

Carefully read the procedure outlined in the operative report. Sometimes the discriminating factor between one code and another will be the surgical approach or type of procedure mentioned.

EXAMPLE 1

Surgical approach

57540 Excision of cervical stump, abdominal approach;

57545   with pelvic floor repair

57550 Excision of cervical stump, vaginal approach;

When reporting the code number for the excision of cervical stump, code 57540 would be reported for an abdominal approach, and code 57550 would be reported for a vaginal approach.

Surgical Package

> **EXAMPLE 2**
>
> Type of procedure
> **11600** Excision, malignant lesion, trunk, arms, or legs; lesion diameter 0.5 cm or less
> **17260*** Destruction, malignant lesion, any method, trunk, arms or legs; lesion diameter 0.5 cm or less

CPT divides surgical procedures into two groups: major surgery and minor surgery. A **major surgical procedure**, one with no asterisk (*) after the code number, is considered by CPT to be a *surgical package* and includes the operation, any local anesthesia administered, and normal, uncomplicated follow-up care. (See Figure 7-5). These are billed as one surgical fee for the services listed.

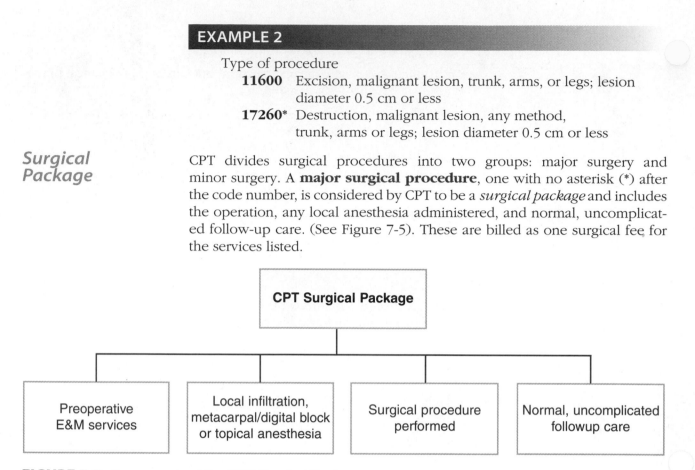

FIGURE 7-5 Components of the CPT Surgical Package

Minor surgical procedures (those with an asterisk (*) following a code number) are considered by CPT to be a "relatively small surgical service too variable to be billed as an all-inclusive package" (see Figure 7-2 on page 158). They are to be billed on a fee-for-service basis; all preoperative and postoperative services and supplies and materials provided over and above those usually included in an office visit are listed and billed separately.

Unbundling (also known as **fragmented surgery, á la carte billing**, or **itemized pricing**) involves assigning multiple codes to procedures/services when just one comprehensive code should be reported to cover all components associated with a procedure or service. Examples of minor procedures that are combined with the surgical package code include:

- Local infiltration of medication
- Closure of surgically created wounds
- Minor debridement
- Exploration of operative area
- Fulguration of bleeding points
- Application of dressings
- Application of splints with musculoskeletal procedures

Read the descriptions of surgical procedures carefully, and remember that the main clause—the narrative to the left of the semicolon (;)—of an indented surgical description is stated only once in a series of related intraoperative procedures. The complexity of the related intraoperative procedures increases as you proceed through the listings of indented code descriptions. *Always report the comprehensive code rather than codes for individual components of a surgery.*

■ **NOTE:** Another indication that a code might not be reportable with another code is the presence of a parenthetical note, (separate procedure) that indicates the procedure is part of a more comprehensive code. ■

EXAMPLE

35001 Direct repair of aneurysm, false aneurysm, or excision (partial or total) and graft insertion, with or without patch graft; for aneurysm and associated occlusive disease, carotid, subclavian artery, by neck incision

35002 for ruptured aneurysm, carotid, subclavian artery, by neck incision

35005 for aneurysm, false aneurysm, and associated occlusive disease, vertebral artery

35011 for aneurysm and associated occlusive disease, axillary-brachial artery, by arm incision

35013 for ruptured aneurysm, axillary-brachial artery, by arm incision

Only one code from this series of five codes should be assigned *if the procedures performed and reported were rendered during the same operative session.*

Exceptions to reporting one combination code occur when the code number is either marked by a + symbol (add-on code) or a parenthetical note indicates that a code should be reported in addition to the primary code number. The following statements appear in CPT code descriptions or as parenthetical notes when it is appropriate to report additional codes:

- List separately in addition to code for primary procedure.
- Use . . . in conjunction with . . ..
- Each additional . . ..
- Each separate/additional . . ..

EXERCISE 7-4 Working with the Surgical Package

Code each statement. If an asterisk appears in a code number include it in your answer (although the asterisk would not be reported on a claim form).

1. Incision and drainage (I&D), finger abscess   _____

2. Percutaneous I&D, abscess, appendix   _____

3. Anesthetic agent injection, L-5 paravertebral nerve   _____

4. Laparoscopic cholecystectomy with cholangiography   _____

5. Flexible esophagoscopy with brushing, specimen collection, removal of foreign body, and radiologic supervision and interpretation   _____

6. Anterior interbody approach, arthrodesis   _____
with minimal diskectomy, L-1 through L-3 vertebrae

After completing this exercise, refer to Appendix IV to check your answers.

**Separate
Procedure**

The parenthetical note, **separate procedure**, follows a code description that identifies procedures that are an integral part of another procedure or service. In addition, a *separate procedure* code is reported if the procedure or service is performed independently of the comprehensive procedure or service or is unrelated to or distinct from another procedure or service performed at the same time. The *separate procedure* code is not reported if the procedure or service performed is included in the description of another reported code.

> **EXAMPLE**

The patient undergoes only a **cystourethroscopy** (passage of an endoscope through the urethra to visualize the urinary bladder). CPT codes for cystourethroscopy include:

52000 Cystourethroscopy (separate procedure)

52005 Cystourethroscopy, with ureteral catheterization, with or without irrigation, instillation, or ureteropyelography, exclusive of radiologic service;

52007   with brush biopsy of ureter and/or renal pelvis

52010 Cystourethroscopy, with ejaculatory duct catheterization, with or without irrigation, instillation, or duct radiography, exclusive of radiologic service

Report code 52000 because only the cystourethroscopy was performed. *A code from among 52005–52010 would be reported only if the operative report documented additional procedures that were included in the code description.* The placement of the phrase "separate procedure" is critical to correct coding. When it appears after the semicolon, it applies to that specific code.

> **EXAMPLE**

57452* Colposcopy (vaginoscopy); (separate procedure)

The phrase that appears to the left of the semicolon applies to all indented code descriptions.

> **EXAMPLE**

32601 Thoracoscopy, diagnostic (separate procedure); lungs and pleural space, without biopsy

32602   lungs and pleural space, with biopsy

EXERCISE 7-5 Coding Separate Procedures

Code the following procedures.

1. Diagnostic arthroscopy, right wrist, with biopsy   _____

2. Simple vaginal mucosal biopsy   _____

3. Diagnostic nasal endoscopy, bilateral,
and a facial chemical peel _____

4. Diagnostic thoracoscopy, pleural space and
biopsy right lung _____

After completing this exercise, refer to Appendix IV to check your answers.

Multiple Surgical Procedures

Great care must be taken when billing **multiple surgical procedures** (two or more surgeries performed during the same operative session). The major surgical procedure (the procedure reimbursed at the highest level) should be listed first on the claim form, and the lesser surgeries listed on the claim form in descending order of expense. Modifier -51 is added to the CPT number for each lesser surgical procedure that does not have the symbol ⊘ or **+** in front of the code. (Appendix F in the CPT coding manual provides a complete list of modifier -51 exemptions.)

The ranking into major and minor procedures is done to accommodate the fact that most insurance companies will reduce the fee for the second surgery by 50 percent of the regular fee and the third, fourth, and so on, by 50 to 75 percent of the regular fee. If a lesser procedure is listed first, it may be paid at 100 percent and the major or most expensive surgery reduced by 50 to 75 percent, resulting in a lower payment for the combined surgeries. Insurance companies reason that when multiple surgical procedures are performed during the same operative session, they share the same pre- and postoperative session; therefore, the fee is reduced because the pre- and postoperative portion is covered in the full payment for the major procedure.

> **BILLING TIP:** Computerized practices must be sure that *multiple surgeries performed during the same operative session are entered into the computer in the proper order* to ensure they are printed correctly on the computer-generated claim form.

Do not confuse multiple procedures with bilateral procedures, which require a -50 modifier. Multiple procedures have different CPT code numbers. Bilateral procedures have the same CPT code number. (A discussion of CPT modifiers begins on page 197.)

CODING SPECIAL SURGERY CASES

Skin Lesions

A **skin lesion** is defined as any discontinuity of the skin. When reporting the excision or destruction of lesions you must know the:

- Site
- Size of the lesion measured before excision (reported in centimeters)
- Number of lesions removed
- Benign or malignant status
- Method used for removal

Read the provider's notes and reports carefully to determine the type of lesion and other qualifying information covered by specific codes. Carefully review the qualifiers for a code number before noting the number of units needed (number of lesions removed) for Item 24G on the claim form (see Figure 7-6).

24.	A							B	C	D		E	F	G	H	I	J	K
	DATE(S) OF SERVICE							Place of Service	Type of Service	PROCEDURES, SERVICES, OR SUPPLIES (Explain Unusual Circumstances)		DIAGNOSIS CODE	$ CHARGES	DAYS OR UNITS	EPSDT Family Plan	EMG	COB	RESERVED FOR LOCAL USE
	From			To						CPT/HCPCS	MODIFIER							
	MM	DD	YY	MM	DD	YY												

FIGURE 7-6 Block 24 on HCFA-1500 claim form

Excision of a lesion requires cutting through the dermal layer of the skin. Destruction (ablation) destroys a lesion, rather than cutting it out, and closure is not required (codes 17000-17286). The diagnosis code reported in Item 24E must match the benign or malignant category used to describe the CPT code.

Simple (nonlayered) closure of skin and subcutaneous tissue is included in the excision of lesions code. If the report describes an excision deeper than the dermal layer (into the subcutaneous tissue), a **layered closure** or **plastic repair** of the excision may be coded. This refers to a separate closure made of deeper structures in addition to closure of the dermis. Layered closure requires two codes: one for the excision and one for an intermediate repair (codes 12031-12057.) Also, if other structures (e.g., nerves, veins, or tendons) are repaired these may be billed as well.

CPT codes for excisions, skin closures, and some destruction procedures are reported in centimeters; if the health care provider reports the size of the lesion in inches, you have to convert the inches to centimeters. One inch equals 2.54 cm.

EXAMPLE

Lesion size is 2 inches
2.54 multiplied by 2 equals 5.08 cm

A biopsy of the lesion is included in the procedure when it is performed after the removal of the lesion. A biopsy performed for the purpose of determining the morphology of the lesion is reported separately. To code a "radical excision" refer to "Excision" in the CPT Index and the specific body site.

Repair of Lacerations

Lacerations are also reported in centimeters. (See the conversion from inches to centimeters above.) The length and depth of lacerations must be documented in the record. *The length of multiple lacerations/wounds falling within the same coding classification (ie, body region) are added together and reported as a single entry.* When multiple lacerations of different classifications are documented, list the code for the most complicated repair first.

EXERCISE 7-6 Coding Lesions and Lacerations

Code the following procedures.

1. Excision, 2.5 cm malignant lesion, left cheek _____

2. Excision, 1-1/2 inch benign lesion, scalp _____

3. Removal of 10 skin tags upper back, 3 right arm, 4 chest, 2 left thigh, 3 abdomen _____

4. Suture of 1 inch simple laceration, left forearm, and 2-1/2 inch simple laceration, right arm _____

5. Excision, 2.5 cm malignant lesion, forehead with intermediate closure _____

After completing this exercise, refer to Appendix IV to check your answers.

Fractures and Dislocations

To code fractures and dislocations correctly, the coder must answer the following questions:

- What is the location of the fracture/dislocation?
- Was manipulation (reduction) documented?
- Was the fracture treatment "open," "closed," or by percutaneous skeletal fixation?

Closed fracture treatment means the fracture site was not surgically opened. **Open fracture treatment** means the fracture site was surgically opened, the bone ends visualized, aligned, and internal fixation may have been applied. **Percutaneous skeletal fixation** is neither an open or closed treatment. In this case the bone fragments are never directly visualized, but fixation (eg, pins) is placed across the fracture site, usually under radiologic guidance.

- Was internal or external fixation required?
- Was skin or skeletal traction applied?
- Was closure of soft tissue required?

Manipulation of a fracture or dislocation and **reduction of a fracture** are the same thing—the application of manually applied forces to restore normal anatomical alignment. Before selecting a code that requires manipulation, be sure the documentation states that either manipulation or a reduction was performed.

The treatment of fractures should be documented in the patient's record as either open or closed. When it cannot be determined from the record whether the fracture was treated as opened or closed, it is assumed to be a closed fracture treatment; that is, no surgery was required to properly align the fracture.

Read the descriptions very carefully. When the description reads "**open treatment of a closed fracture** or dislocation," an incision has been made over the fracture and some type of fixation device applied. Physicians often use the term "**ORIF**" as a shorthand for "**open reduction with internal fixation**." Careful review is also necessary to pick out the terms "single" or "multiple" fractures.

Codes 20692 or 20693 may be reported in addition to the treatment of the fracture when the code description for the fracture procedure does not mention external fixation, but external fixation of a fracture is described in the procedure report.

The first casting, strapping, or traction is included in the fee for code numbers with no asterisk. All subsequent changes of casts or tractions are reported on a fee-for-service basis. Read the note located before code 29000.

Arthroscopy

Differentiation must be made between diagnostic and surgical arthroscopies. A diagnostic arthroscopy is always included in a surgical arthroscopy and should not be listed separately on the claim form. You may bill for a diagnostic arthroscopy separately if the repair cannot be made through the scope. The arthrotomy is considered the primary procedure when it immediately follows an arthroscopy.

EXERCISE 7-7 Coding Fractures, Dislocation, and Arthroscopies

Code the following statements.

1. Exploration of right wrist with removal of deep foreign body   _____

2. Manipulation of right thumb dislocation   _____

3. Reapplication of short leg walking cast   _____

4. Open reduction with screws, compound fracture, shaft, left tibia and fibula, and application of a long leg cast   _____

5. Diagnostic arthroscopy followed by removal of the medial meniscus by arthrotomy   _____

After completing this exercise, refer to Appendix IV to check your answers.

Endoscopy Procedures

Endoscopy codes in CPT are classified according to:

- Anatomic site
- Extent of the examination
- Purpose of the endoscopy—diagnostic versus surgical
- Type of scope used

Carefully review the procedure report, and CPT guidelines, notes, and code descriptions before selecting the final code. Endoscopies of the digestive system are always coded to the furthest site accessed by the scope. CPT codes for diagnostic endoscopies are included in a surgical endoscopy completed during the same operative session. CPT describes a colonoscopy as "examination of entire colon, from rectum to cecum and may include the examination of the terminal ileum." (See the long note above code 45300.)

EXAMPLE

The gastroscope was introduced with ease into the upper esophageal area under direct visualization and advanced to the second portion of the duodenum. No abnormalities were noted.

Code **43235** Upper gastrointestinal endoscopy including esophagus, stomach and either the duodenum and/or jejunum as appropriate; diagnostic, with or without collection of specimen(s) by brushing or washing (separate procedure)

Endoscopic guide-wire dilation involves the passage of a guide-wire through an endoscope into the stomach. The endoscope is removed and dilators, each with a central lumen through which the guide-wire is placed, are used to widen a constricted esophagus. **Indirect laryngoscopy** means the larynx is visualized using a warm laryngeal mirror. **Direct laryngoscopy** is performed by passing a rigid or fiberoptic endoscope into the larynx.

The surgical procedure is an "open procedure," one not performed through a scope, if the CPT code description is not listed under an anatomical site heading of Endoscopy, and the term "endoscopy" or the suffix "-scopy" does not appear in the description of the procedure.

EXERCISE 7-8 Coding Endoscopies

Code the following statements.

1. Laparoscopic cholecystectomy with cholangiography _____

2. Anoscopy with removal of polyp by snare _____

3. Diagnostic flexible bronchoscopy _____

4. Fibroscopic full colonoscopy with removal of polyps by snare _____

5. Nasal endoscopy with partial ethmoidectomy _____

After completing this exercise, refer to Appendix IV to check your answers.

MEDICINE SECTION OVERVIEW

The medicine section starts with code 90281. Noninvasive diagnostic procedures are found in all subsections.

EXAMPLES

92230 Fluorescein angioscopy with interpretation and report

93312 Echocardiography, transesophageal, real time with image documentation (2D) (with or without M-mode recording); including probe placement, image acquisition, interpretation and report

93501 Right heart catheterization

Subsections include the following procedures/services:
- Immune Globulins (90281-90399)
- Immunization Administration for Vaccines/Toxoids (90471-90472)
- Vaccines, Toxoids (90476-90749)
- Therapeutic, Prophylactic or Diagnostic Infusions (90780-90781)
- Therapeutic, Prophylactic or Diagnostic Injections (90782-90799)
- Psychiatry (90801-90899)
- Biofeedback (90901-90911)
- Dialysis (90918-90999)
- Gastroenterology (91000-91299)
- Ophthalmology (92002-92499)
- Special Otorhinolaryngologic Services (92502-92599)
- Cardiovascular (92950-93799)
- Non-Invasive Vascular Diagnostic Studies (93875-93990)
- Pulmonary (94010-94799)
- Allergy and Clinical Immunology (95004-95199)

- Neurology and Neuromuscular Procedures (95805-95999)
- Central Nervous System Assessments/Tests (96100-96117)
- Chemotherapy Administration (96400-96549)
- Photodynamic Therapy (96570-96571)
- Special Dermatological Procedures (96900-96999)
- Physical Medicine and Rehabilitation (97001-97799)
- Osteopathic Manipulative Treatment (98925-98929)
- Chiropractic Manipulative Treatment (98940-98943)
- Special Services, Procedures and Reports (99000-99090)
- Qualifying Circumstances for Anesthesia (99100-99140)
- Sedation With or Without Analgesia (99141-99142)
- Other Services and Procedures (99175-99199)

Cardiovascular System

Invasive procedures of the heart and pericardium are found in the surgery section of CPT; however, cardiac catheterizations, and so on, are located in the Medicine Section beginning with code 93501.

Some codes in this subsection include both the professional and technical components of the test in one code number. Other procedures have specific codes for the combined components and separate codes for the **professional component** (supervision of procedure, interpretation, and writing of the report) or **technical component** (use of equipment and supplies) only. When a physician performs only one component of a test, the CPT modifier -26 (professional component only) or the HCPCS level II modifier -TC (technical component) should be added to the global code to indicate that the full procedure was not performed.

Special Services and Reports

This is a miscellaneous section covering services billable as adjunct to basic services provided to the patient. Carefully read through this entire subsection to become familiar with aspects of coverage found here. The most commonly used codes are:

- 99000-99002   Procurement of specimens to be sent to an outside laboratory.
- 99050-99058   Special codes for E&M services that were performed at times other than the practice's normal hours or under unusual circumstances. These codes may be assigned to augment the regular visitation codes.
- 99080   Special reports such as insurance forms, attorney and insurance reports, and so on.

Infusions and Injections

CPT contains codes to classify injections of antibiotic and intravenous therapy. Refer to codes 90780-90799; review their descriptions and the notes included below the Therapeutic or Diagnostic Infusions subsection.

Because of the variance in cost for therapeutic injections, over 400 HCPCS level II "J" series codes were developed by HCFA to enable computer tracking of specific medications, including immunosuppressive drugs. Because of the potential for a higher level of reimbursement coupled with more accurate descriptions found in HCPCS level II, "J" codes should be used in place of the CPT codes for all medical insurance billings. (A discussion of "J" codes appears in Chapter 8.)

Psychiatry (90801-90899)

The insurance industry usually refers to these services as "mental or behavioral health services." *Psychiatric codes are not reserved for use only by psychiatrists.* They may be used by any physician, clinical psychologist, licensed clinical social worker, mental health counselor, or psychiatric nurse specialist licensed to practice in their state.

Psychological and behavioral testing codes are found in the Central Nervous System Assessments/Tests (96100-96117) subsection of CPT. Psychiatric consultations are reported using E&M consultation codes that are limited to initial and follow-up evaluations and do not allow for psychiatric treatment of the patient. Inpatient or partial hospitalization services of psychiatric patients that are performed by the attending physicians may be reported using codes 99221-99233.

EXERCISE 7-9 Medicine Section Coding

Code the following statements.

1. Cardiac catheterization, right side only, with conscious sedation, IV _____

2. Routine EKG, tracing only _____

3. Spirometry _____

4. CPR, in office _____

5. Diagnostic psychiatric examination _____

6. Influenza vaccine _____

7. Whirlpool and paraffin bath therapy _____

8. WAIS-R and MMPI psychological tests and report, 1 hour _____

9. Office services on emergency basis _____

After completing this exercise, refer to Appendix IV to check your answers.

RADIOLOGY SECTION OVERVIEW

The radiology section includes subsections for diagnostic radiology, diagnostic ultrasound, radiation oncology, and nuclear medicine. These are further subdivided into anatomic categories. Read the category headings and code descriptions carefully.

The number of **radiologic views** (studies taken from different angles) described in the report or on the charge slip determines the code selection in many diagnostic radiologic procedures. The term "complete" in the discussion of views is a reference to the number of views required for a full study of a designated body part. Carefully review code descriptions to understand how many views constitute a "complete study" for a specific type of radiologic procedure.

EXAMPLE

70120 Radiologic examination, mastoids; less than three views per side

70130 complete, minimum of three views per side

70134 Radiologic examination, internal auditory meati, complete

Complete Procedure

Do not confuse the use of the term "complete" found in the description with its use in a parenthetical note.

EXAMPLE

70332 Temperomandibular joint arthrography, radiological supervision and interpretation (70333 (complete procedure) has been deleted, see 21116, 70332)

The above example describes a diagnostic study that has two components: radiologic and surgical.

EXAMPLE

21116 Injection procedure for temporomandibular joint arthrography

(For radiological supervision and interpretation see 70332)

When both components (complete procedure) are performed by the same physician, two codes are reported. If two physicians are involved in performing the procedure, each physician will submit the code only for the portion performed.

Professional Versus Technical Component

Another consideration in radiology coding involves determining which physician is responsible for the professional and technical components of an examination.

The professional component of a radiologic examination covers the supervision of the procedure, and the interpretation and writing of a report describing the examination and its findings. The technical component of an examination covers the use of the equipment, supplies provided, and employment of the radiologic technicians. When the examination takes place in a clinic or private office that owns the equipment and its professional services are performed by a physician employed by the clinic or private office, both the professional and technical components are billed on the same claim. If, on the other hand, the equipment and supplies are owned by a hospital or other corporation and the radiologist performs only the professional component of the examination, two separate billings are generated: one by the physician for the professional component and one by the hospital for the technical component.

When two separate billings are required, the professional component is billed by adding the modifier -26 to the CPT code number. An exception to this rule is when the code description restricts the use of the code to "supervision and interpretation."

EXAMPLE

75710 Angiography, extremity, unilateral, radiologic supervision and interpretation

When the technical component is reported separately from the professional component, the HCPCS modifier -TC is added to the examination code.

Special care must be taken when coding interventional diagnostic procedures that involve injection of contrast media, local anesthesia, or needle localization of a mass. CPT assigns two separate codes to these interventional procedures: a 70000 series supervision and interpretation code, and a surgical code. This is done because these procedures may be performed by two physicians, each billing separately. If only one physician is involved, the claim should still include both codes.

> **CODING TIP:** Use code 76140 when a physician consult is requested to review Xrays produced in another facility and the consultant generates a written report.

EXERCISE 7-10 Radiology Coding

Code the following statements.

1. GI series, with small bowel and air studies, without KUB _____

2. Chest Xray, PA & left lateral _____

3. Cervical spine Xray, complete, with flexion and extension _____

4. Xray pelvis, AP _____

5. Abdomen, flat plate, AP _____

6. BE, colon, with air _____

7. Postoperative radiologic supervision and interpretation of cholangiography by radiologist _____

8. SPECT exam of the liver _____

9. Retrograde pyelography with KUB _____

After completing this exercise, refer to Appendix IV to check your answers.

PATHOLOGY/LABORATORY SECTION OVERVIEW

This section is organized according to the type of pathology or laboratory procedure performed. The major subsections are titled organ or disease oriented panels, drug testing, therapeutic drug assays, evocative/suppression testing, consultations (clinical pathology), urinalysis, chemistry, hematology and coagulation, immunology, transfusion medicine, microbiology, anatomic pathology, cytopathology, cytogenic studies, surgical pathology, and other procedures.

Laboratory Panels   One code number is assigned to a specific **laboratory panel**, (also called **organ panel** or **disease oriented panel**). The panel consists of a series of blood chemistry studies routinely ordered by providers at the same time for the purpose of investigating a specific organ or disorder. The make-up of the panel is very specific; no substitutions are allowed.

EXAMPLE

80055 Obstetric panel

This panel must include the following:

Hemogram, automated, and manual differential WBC count (CBC) (85022) OR

Hemogram and platelet count, automated, and automated complete differential WBC count (CBC) (85025)

Hepatitis B surface antigen (HBsAg) (87340)

Antibody, rubella (86762)

Syphilis test, qualitative (eg, VDRL, RPR, ART) (86592)

Antibody screen, RBC, each serum technique (86850)

Blood typing, ABO (89000), AND

Blood typing, Rh (D) (86901)

The health care provider's laboratory request form may either state a specific panel or individually list all the specific tests.

When the request lists blood chemistry tests individually, check the Organ or Disease Oriented Panel (80048-80090) listing in the code book to determine whether any or all of the tests ordered fit into a specific panel description and, if so, use the panel code. If the request lists chemistry tests in addition to those that fit a specific panel description you will need to report a panel code and a code for each individual test that is not included in the panel.

EXAMPLE

Carbon dioxide, chloride, HDL cholesterol, alkaline phosphatase, potassium and sodium

This would be coded:

80051   for the four tests (carbon dioxide, chloride, potassium and sodium) on the electrolyte panel

83718   for the high-density lipoprotein (HDL) cholesterol

84075   for the alkaline phosphatase

CODING TIP: Refer to "Blood Tests, Panels" in the index for a codes list of panel options. Look up the chemical substance or microbiology specimen in the index to find the code number for the individual substances to be tested (ie, chloride or cytomegalovirus).

Drug Testing

There are four codes in this section used when it is necessary to determine if a drug of a specific classification is present in the blood.

Therapeutic Drug Assays

This section is designed to report tests performed to determine how much of a specific prescribed drug is in the patient's blood.

Evocative/ Suppression Testing

This series of codes is used when specific substances are injected for the purpose of confirming or ruling out specific disorders.

Consultations (Clinical Pathology)

Codes in this subsection are reported by pathologists who, at the request of an attending physician, perform clinical pathology consultations and document written reports.

Urinalysis, Chemistry, Hematology and Coagulation, and Immunology

Codes in these subsections include laboratory tests on bodily fluids (e.g., urine, blood). The tests are ordered by a physician and are performed by technologists under the supervision of a physician (usually a pathologist).

Transfusion Medicine

Codes are reported for procedures associated with blood transfusions (e.g., blood typing, and compatibility testing). Codes for the transfusion of blood and blood components are located in the Surgery Section (36430-36460) except for leukocyte transfusion which is assigned code 86950 from the Pathology and Laboratory Section.

Microbiology

Microbiology codes report procedures for bacteriology, mycology, parasitology, and virology. Procedures performed include taking cultures (e.g., throat culture to test for streptococcus), testing for ova and parasites (e.g., ringworm), and conducting sensitivity studies (e.g., to determine which antibiotic to prescribe).

Anatomic Pathology

This subsection includes codes for postmortem examination (also known as autopsy or necropsy).

Cytopathology and Cytogenic Studies

Cytopathology codes report pathology screening tests (e.g., Pap Smear). Cytogenic Studies codes report tests that involve obtaining tissue cultures for testing purposes and conducting chromosome analysis studies.

Surgical Pathology

Surgical pathology codes are reported when specimens removed during surgery require pathologic diagnosis. The codes are categorized according to level. Code 88300, Level I, is assigned for the gross (or macroscopic) examination of a specimen; no microscopic examination is performed (e.g., kidney stone). Codes reported for Level II through VI surgical pathology are assigned when gross (or macroscopic) and microscopic examinations of a specimen occur (e.g., appendix, or fallopian tube). The CPT Index contains an entry for Pathology, Surgical along with codes assigned according to level. Carefully review the CPT tabular to determine which level categorizes the tissue removed. If multiple specimens were removed that can be classified to more than one level, assign a code for each level.

Other Procedures

Miscellaneous laboratory procedures are included in the Other Procedures subsection.

EXERCISE 7-11 Pathology and Laboratory Coding

Code the following statements.

1. Hepatic function panel _____
2. Hepatitis panel _____
3. TB skin test, PPD _____
4. UA with micro, automated _____
5. CBC with Diff, manual _____

   6. Stool for occult blood   _____

   7. Wet mount, vaginal smear   _____

   8. Glucose/blood sugar, quantitative   _____

   9. Sedimentation rate   _____

  10. Throat culture, bacterial   _____

  11. Urine sensitivity, disk   _____

  12. Hematocrit, spun   _____

  13. Monospot   _____

  14. Strep test, rapid   _____

After completing this exercise, refer to Appendix IV to check your answers.

EVALUATION AND MANAGEMENT SECTION OVERVIEW

The **Evaluation and Management (E&M) Section** (codes 99203-99499) is located at the beginning of CPT because these codes describe services most frequently provided by physicians. Accurate assignment of **E&M codes** is essential to the success of a physician's practice because most of the revenue generated by the office is based on provision of these services. Before assigning codes, carefully review the E&M Section guidelines (located at the beginning of the section) and apply any notes (located below category and subcategory headings).

ASSIGNING EVALUATION AND MANAGEMENT CODES

CPT 1992 introduced Evaluation & Management (E&M) *level of service* codes, which replaced the *office visit* codes that were included in the Medicine Section of past revisions of CPT. The E&M **level of service** reflects the amount of work involved in providing health care to patients. Between three and five levels of service are included in E&M categories and subcategories, and documentation in the patient's chart must support the level of service reported. HCFA often refers to E&M codes by level numbers (e.g., Level I, Level II, and so on).

EXAMPLE

Refer to the Office or Outpatient Services category of E&M, and notice that it contains two subcategories (New Patient and Established Patient). The New Patient subcategory contains four codes, while the Established Patient subcategory contains five codes. Each code represents a level of E&M Service, ranked from lowest to highest level. HCFA would consider E&M code 99201 a Level I code.

Accurate assignment of E&M codes is dependent upon (1) identifying the place and/or type of service provided to the patient, (2) determining whether the patient is new or established to the practice, (3) reviewing the patient's chart for documentation of level of service components, and (4) applying HCFA's *Documentation Guidelines for Evaluation and Management Services* to federal government health care programs.

Place of Service

Place of service refers to the physical location where health care is provided to patients (e.g., office or other outpatient settings, hospitals, nursing facilities, home health care, or emergency departments).

EXAMPLE 1

The provider treated the patient in his office.
Place of Service: Office
E&M Category: Office or Other Outpatient Services

EXAMPLE 2

The patient received care in the hospital's emergency department.
Place of Service: Hospital emergency department
E&M Category: Emergency Department Services

Type of Service

Type of service refers to the kind of health care services provided to patients. It includes critical care, consultation, initial hospital care, subsequent hospital care, confirmatory consultation, and so on.

EXAMPLE 1

The patient underwent an annual physical examination in the provider's office.
Type of Service: Preventive care
E&M Category: Preventative Medicine Services

EXAMPLE 2

The hospital inpatient was transferred to the regular Medical-Surgical Unit where he was recovering from surgery. He suddenly stopped breathing and required respirator management by his physician.
Type of Service: Critical care
E&M Category: Critical Care Services

■ **NOTE:** While this type of care is often administered in a critical care unit, that is not a requirement for code assignment. ■

Sometimes, both the type and place of service must be identified before the proper code can be assigned.

EXAMPLE 1

Dr. Smith completed Josie Black's history and physical examination on the first day of her inpatient admission.
Place of Service: Hospital
Type of Service: Initial care
E&M Category: Hospital Inpatient Services
E&M Subcategory: Initial Hospital Care

EXAMPLE 2

Dr. Charles saw Josie Black in her office to render a second opinion.
Type of Service: Consultation
Place of Service: Office
E&M Category: Consultations
E&M Subcategory: Office or Other Outpatient Consultations

New and Established Patients

A **new patient** is one who *has not* received any professional services from the physician or another physician of the same specialty who belongs to the same group practice, within the past three years. An **established patient** is one who *has* received professional services from the physician or another physician of the same specialty who belongs to the same group practice, within the past three years.

CODING TIP: Professional services may not require a face-to-face encounter with a provider.

EXAMPLE 1

Sally Dunlop had a prescription renewed by Dr. Smith's office on January 1, 2001, but she did not see the physician. She has been Dr. Smith's patient since her initial office visit on March 15, 1998. On December 1, 2001, Dr. Smith treated Sally during an office visit.

New Patient   March 15, 1998

Established Patient   January 1, 2001 & December 1, 2001

Because she received professional services (the prescription renewal) on January 1, 2001, Sally Dunlop is considered an established patient for the December 1, 2001 visit.

EXAMPLE 2

Dr. Charles and Dr. Black share a practice. Dr. Charles is a general surgeon who treated Mary Smith in the office on July 1, 2001. Mary was first seen by the practice on February 15, 2000 when Dr. Black provided preventative care services to her. Mary returned to the practice on November 1, 2001 for her annual physical examination, conducted by Dr. Black.

New Patient: February 15, 2000 & July 1, 2001

Established Patient: January 1, 2001

■ **NOTE:** Review insurance company policies for definitions of new and established patient visits when provided by different specialties and subspecialties in the same group. ■

CRITICAL THINKING

Dr. Corey left Alfred Medical Group to join Buffalo Physician Group as a family practitioner. At Buffalo Physician Group, when Dr. Corey provides professional services to patients, will those patients be considered new or established?

Answer: Patients who have not received professional services from Dr. Corey or another physician of the same specialty at Buffalo Physician Group would be considered new. If the patients had seen another family practitioner at Buffalo Physician Group within the past two years, the patients would be considered established. If any of Dr. Corey's patients from the Alfred Medical Group choose to seek care from him at the Buffalo Physician Group, they are also considered established patients.

Remember! Definitions of new and established patients include professional services rendered by other physicians of the same specialty in the same group practice.

Key Components

Key components include extent of history, extent of examination, and complexity of medical decision making. All three key components must be considered when assigning codes for new patients. For established patients, two of the three key components must be considered. This means that documentation in the patient's chart must support the key components used to determine the E&M code selected.

Extent of History

A **history** is an interview of the patient that includes the following components: history of the present illness (HPI) (including the patient's chief complaint), a review of systems (ROS), and a past/family/social history (PFSH). The **extent of history** is categorized according to four types, listed and defined as follows:

Problem focused: chief complaint, brief history of present illness or problem

Expanded problem focused: chief complaint, brief history of present illness, problem pertinent system review

Detailed: chief complaint, extended history of present illness, problem pertinent system review extended to include a limited number of additional systems, pertinent past/family/social history directly related to patient's problem

Comprehensive: chief complaint, extended history of present illness, review of systems directly related to the problem(s) identified in the history of the present illness plus a review of all additional body systems, complete past/family/social history

Extent of Examination

A **physical examination** is an assessment of the patient's organ (e.g., extremities) and body systems (e.g., cardiovascular). The **extent of examination** is categorized according to four types, listed and defined as follows:

Problem focused: a limited examination of the affected body area or organ system

Expanded problem focused: a limited examination of the affected body area or organ system and other symptomatic or related organ system(s)

Detailed: an extended examination of the affected body area(s) and other symptomatic or related organ system(s)

Comprehensive: general multi-system examination or a complete examination of a single organ system.

Complexity of Medical Decision Making

Medical decision making refers to the complexity of establishing a diagnosis and/or selecting a management option as measured by the:

• Number of diagnoses or management options.

• Amount and/or complexity of data to be reviewed.

• Risk of complications and/or morbidity or mortality.

Once the key components for extent of history and examination are determined, the medical decision making type can be selected: straightforward, low complexity, moderate complexity, or high complexity. The physician is responsible for determining the complexity of medical decision making, and that decision must be supported by documentation in the patient's chart. CPT includes a table in the E&M Guidelines that can assist in determining complexity of medical decision making (see Table 7-1).

Table 7-1 *Complexity of medical decision making.*

COMPLEXITY OF MEDICAL DECISION MAKING			
Number of Diagnoses or Management Options	Amount and/or Complexity of Data to be Reviewed	Risk of Complications and/or Morbidity or Mortality	Type of Decision Making
minimal	minimal or none	minimal	straightforward
limited	limited	low	low complexity
multiple	moderate	moderate	moderate complexity
extensive	extensive	high	high complexity

(CPT codes, descriptions, and materials only are © 2000 American Medical Association).

Contributory Components

Contributory components include counseling, coordination of care, nature of presenting problem, and time. Counseling and/or coordination of care components drive CPT code selection only when they dominate the encounter (e.g., office visit), requiring that more than 50% of the provider's time be spent on such components. In such circumstances, the provider must be sure to carefully document these elements so as to support the higher level code selected.

Counseling

CPT defines **counseling** as it relates to E&M coding as a discussion with a patient and/or family concerning one or more of the following areas:

• Diagnostic results, impressions, and/or recommended diagnostic studies.

• Prognosis.

• Risks and benefits of management (treatment) options.

• Instructions for management (treatment) and/or follow-up.

• Importance of compliance with chosen management (treatment) options.

• Risk factor reduction.

• Patient and family education.

This counseling is not to be confused with psychotherapy. Psychotherapy codes are located in the Medicine Section of CPT and are reported for behavioral health modification or the treatment of mental illness.

Coordination of Care

When the physician makes arrangements with other providers or agencies for services to be provided to a patient, this is called **coordination of care**.

EXAMPLE

Dr. Smith writes a discharge order for inpatient Carol Kane to be discharged home and to receive home health care. Dr. Smith contacts the home health agency to make the appropriate arrangements for the patient and instructs the hospital to send copies of the patient's record to the home health care agency.

Nature of the Presenting Problem

CPT defines **nature of the presenting problem** as a disease, condition, illness, injury, symptom, sign, finding, complaint, or other reason for the encounter, with or without a diagnosis being established at the time of the encounter. Nature of the presenting problem is considered when determining medical decision making complexity. Five types of presenting problems are recognized:

- *minimal:* problem may not require the presence of the physician, but service is provided under the physician's supervision (e.g., patient who comes to the office once a week to have blood pressure taken and recorded)

- *self-limited or minor:* a problem that runs a definite and prescribed course, is transient in nature, and is not likely to permanently alter health status; *or* has a good prognosis with management/compliance (e.g., patient diagnosed with adult-onset diabetes mellitus controlled by diet and exercise)

- *low severity:* a problem where the risk of morbidity without treatment is low; there is little to no risk of mortality without treatment; full recovery without functional impairment is expected (e.g., patient diagnosed with eczema that does not respond to over-the-counter medications)

- *moderate severity:* a problem where the risk of morbidity without treatment is moderate; there is moderate risk of mortality without treatment; uncertain prognosis; *or* increased probability of prolonged functional impairment (e.g., 35-year-old male patient diagnosed with chest pain on exertion)

- *high severity:* a problem where the risk of morbidity without treatment is high to extreme; there is a moderate to high risk of mortality without treatment; *or* high probability of severe, prolonged functional impairment (e.g., infant hospitalized with a diagnosis of respiratory syncytial virus)

Time (Face-to-face vs. Unit/Floor)

Face-to-face time is the amount of time the office or outpatient care provider spends with the patient and/or family. **Unit/floor time** is the amount of time the provider spends at the patient's bedside and managing the patient's care on the unit or floor (e.g., writing orders for diagnostic tests or reviewing test results). Unit/floor time applies to inpatient hospital care, hospital observation care, initial and follow-up inpatient hospital consultations, and nursing facility services.

The key components usually determine the E&M code selected; however, visits that consist *predominantly* of counseling and/or coordination of care are an exception. When counseling and/or coordination of care dominates (more than 50%) the physician-patient and/or family encounter, it can be considered a key factor in selecting a particular E&M code. The extent of counseling must be documented in the patient's chart to support the E&M code selected.

EXAMPLE

Anne Sider sees Dr. Cyrix in the office for her three-month check-up (she has chronic hypertension controlled by diet and exercise). During the visit, Dr. Cyrix notes that the patient seems distracted and stressed, and he asks her about these symptoms. Anne starts to cry and spends 10 minutes telling Dr. Cyrix that her "life is falling apart" and that she wakes up in the middle of the night with a pounding heart, feeling like she's going to die. Dr. Cyrix spends the next 45 minutes counseling Anne about these symptoms. He determines that Anne is suffering from panic attacks, so he prescribes a medication and contacts ABC Counseling Associates to arrange an appointment for mental health counseling.

In this example, a routine three-month check-up (for which code 99212 or 99213 would be selected) evolves into a higher level service (for which code 99215 can be reported).

■ **NOTE:** The provider must carefully document all aspects of this visit to include the recheck for hypertension, counseling and coordination of care provided, and length of time spent face-to-face with the patient. ■

CODING TIP: Add V65.4 to the claim when counseling and/or coordination of care dominates the patient encounter, and is documented by the provider.

HCFAs Documentation Guidelines for Evaluation and Management Services

Although the CPT E&M Section Guidelines included definitions and instructions for selecting level of service codes, HCFA and many physicians believed they were insufficient to guarantee consistent coding by physicians and reliable medical review by carriers. In response, HCFA collaborated with the AMA to develop the **1995 Evaluation and Management Documentation Guidelines** (or **1995 DGs**) that supplemented and clarified the E&M Section Guidelines in CPT. In September 1994, HCFA distributed the 1995 DGs to Medicare carriers, who educated providers in their appropriate use. The educational period concluded on August 31, 1995, and effective September 1, 1995, carriers used the 1995 DGs when performing medical reviews of E&M codes reported.

Some specialists criticized the 1995 DGs because requirements for documenting a complete single system examination were unclear (e.g., ophthalmology exam), and it was felt that medical reviews did not properly reflect the code assignment for complete single system exams. In addition, specialists were concerned that work equivalency for multi- and single-system exams could not be ensured under the 1995 DGs. In response, HCFA and the AMA worked with medical specialty societies to develop the **1997 Evaluation and Management Documentation Guidelines** (or **1997 DGs**), an alternative set of DGs to be used when single-system exams were performed. The 1997 DGs included ten single-system examinations, and definitions for multi-system examinations were clarified (e.g., required elements for determining complexity of medical decision making were significantly changed). The revised DGs were reviewed extensively and approved by representatives of most national medical societies.

HCFA intended to replace the 1995 DGs with the 1997 DGs; however, many physicians objected, stating that the 1997 DGs were confusing, too complicated, and required extensive counting of services and other elements. Therefore, in April 1998, HCFA instructed Medicare carriers to use both the 1995 and 1997 DGs when reviewing records. Physicians could use whichever set of guidelines was most advantageous. In addition, HCFA committed to the evaluation of alternative sets of guidelines, pilot studies of additional draft guidelines before implementation, and the education of physicians and carriers prior to implementation of new DGs. In 2000, HCFA drafted new documentation guidelines based on the 1995 DGs, entitled the **June 2000 DGs** (see Figure 7-7 on page 188).

INTERNET LINKS

1995, 1997, and 2000 *Documentation Guidelines for Evaluation and Management Services* along with implementation updates are available for download at www.hcfa.gov/medicare/mcarpti.htm

To assess the accuracy of reported E&M codes, download forms and score sheets from www.hgsa.com/professionals/scoresheets.shtml and www.donself.com/doc-nomusic.html

To remain up-to-date regarding documentation guideline issues, read online *Family Practice Management* newsletters available from the American Academy of Family Physicians at www.aafp.org/fpm/.

EVALUATION AND MANAGEMENT CATEGORIES

Office or Other Outpatient Services

Report codes 99201-99215 when E&M services are provided in a physician's office, a hospital outpatient department, or another ambulatory care facility (e.g., stand-along ambulatory care center). Office or Other Outpatient Services codes contain patient status subcategories (new vs. established patient).

Hospital Observation Services

E&M codes were created to report encounters that are designated as "observation status" in a hospital. Observation services are furnished in a hospital outpatient setting to determine whether further treatment or inpatient admission is needed. When a patient is placed under observation, the patient is treated as an outpatient. If the duration of observation care is expected to be

HEALTHCARE MANAGEMENT SOLUTIONS, INC.

Solutions for Health Care Providers

Issue 321   **October 2000**

The HCFA targets 2001 for new E&M guidelines

"We view it as a 'back to the future' move." At least, that's what Joette P. Derricks, told her audience at a recent HMS coding seminar, following the HCFA's June 23, 2000 unveiling of the "new" evaluation and management (E&M) guidelines. Joette acknowledges that the E&M guidelines have come full circle with the HCFA's announcement that it plans to ditch the 1997 guidelines and those proposed by AMA's CPT Editorial Panel in 1999 in favor of yet another set it created based on the 1995 guidelines.

Although an advocate of physicians being proactive, she cautioned this is one time to play the "wait and see" game. The HCFA's new draft 2000 guidelines aren't expected to go into effect until early 2002. In the meantime, she stresses that physicians should continue using the 1995 and/or the 1997 E&M guidelines. "Unfortunately, we find that some physicians have never learned the current standards and are at risk for overpayments." Still, Joette notes, "other practices could improve their revenue if they would just take a few hours and learn how to document properly per the existing guidelines."

The new guidelines will use specialty-specific vignettes for multi-system exams, single-organ system exams and medical decision making that the physician will use as a guide, predicating documentation on the exam findings and medical necessity, assessment and plan of treatment. The guidelines also minimize the counting of items, eliminate all references to shaded systems and bullets and base documentation on the review of systems in the history and the physical examination of organ systems/body areas to assign the appropriate level of service. Specifically, the June 2000 E&M draft guidelines:

- Include numbers as a guide under history review of systems.
- Change the levels of review of systems into 3 new levels: brief, extended and complete (expanded problem-focused, detailed or comprehensive history).
- Add another requirement (pertinent, 1 of 3) for past, family, social history to expanded problem-focused history and the detailed and comprehensive PFSH now require complete (2 of 3 or 3 of 3).
- Combine problem-focused and expanded problem-focused into a brief exam, which includes 1-2 body areas. Detailed exam requires 3-8 body areas/organ systems instead of the total number of items examined.
- Eliminate straightforward medical decision-making, leaving low, moderate and high.

HCFA plans to run two pilot tests, which would look at:

- Simplifying the physical exam to three levels that will be based on the number of organ systems, i.e., a detailed exam would have findings from 3-8 organ systems instead of the total number of items examined.
- Giving more weight to medical decision making, with less of a focus on history and physical examination.

FIGURE 7-7 Newsletter article about draft June 2000 DGs (Permission to reprint granted by Healthcare Management Solutions, Inc.)

23 hours or more, the physician must order an inpatient admission. The date the physician orders the inpatient stay is the date of the inpatient admission.

The hospital is not required to establish a physical area of observation; however, patients must be designated as "observation status." Patients initially seen at another place of service (e.g., hospital emergency department) who are later designated as (or admitted to) observation services have the original services incorporated into the reported observation service E&M code.

EXAMPLE

A patient seen in the hospital's emergency department and designated as observation status would have just the observation status code reported.

The **hospital observation services** E&M category includes subcategories for observation care discharge services and initial observation care, and no differentiation is made as to patient status (new vs. established). The initial observation care codes in this category are reported for patients who are admitted for observation on one date and discharged from observation status on a different date. Thus, the insurance specialist reports multiple codes from this category (e.g., 99218 and 99217). To report codes for patients who are admitted and discharged from observation status on the same date, refer to the Observation or Inpatient Care Services (including Admission and Discharge Services) subcategory of Hospital Inpatient Services category in the E&M Section.

CODING TIP: Observation services codes may not be reported for postoperative recovery if the "global surgery" (or surgical package) concept applies to the procedure performed.

CODING TIP: Patients who are admitted as hospital inpatients from observation status on the same date are reported only as initial hospital care. The code assigned should identify both the observation care provided and the initial hospital care admission service. In this circumstance, a code for observation care discharge services does not apply and is not reported.

EXAMPLE

A patient was treated in the hospital's emergency department (ED) for acute asthmatic bronchitis. The ED physician determines that the patient needed to be observed for a period of 6-8 hours after provision of emergency treatment. The patient received a detailed level of observation services and was discharged from observation services the next day.

In this example, the CPT codes to be reported include 99218 and 99217. If the observation care services rendered had been initiated and concluded on the same day, only code 99234 would be reported.

CODING TIP: There is no subsequent day observation code. You must assign a code from Office or Other Outpatient Services, 99212-99215, for a patient who remains designated as observation status for a second calendar day and who is not admitted to inpatient status or discharged from observation services.

Hospital Inpatient Services

Initial hospital care services cover the first inpatient encounter the *admitting/attending physician* has with the patient for each admission. A **hospital inpatient** is someone who is admitted and discharged and has a length of stay (LOS) of one or more days. These codes cover all E&M services performed by that physician as related to the admission, regardless of where other E&M services were performed (e.g., preoperative history and examination performed in the office just days prior to an elective admission). Physicians involved with care of the patient, but not designated as the admitting/attending physician, report services from a different category of E&M depending upon where services were rendered (e.g., emergency department services, and consultations).

Subsequent hospital care includes the review of the patient's chart for changes in the patient's condition, the results of diagnostic studies, and/or the reassessment of the patient's condition since the last assessment performed by the physician.

A code for **observation or inpatient care services** (including admission and discharge services) is assigned only if the patient was admitted to and discharged from observation/inpatient status on the same day. Do not assign an observation care or inpatient discharge services code. Refer to the discussion of hospital observation services on pages 187-189 for the assignment of initial observation care and observation care discharge services codes from the Hospital Observation Services subsection of CPT.

CODING TIP: Assign a code from Observation or Inpatient Care Services, code range 99234-99236, if the patient was admitted and discharged from observation services within the same calendar day.

Hospital discharge services include the final examination of the patient, discussion of the hospital stay with the patient and/or caregiver; instructions for continuing care provided to the patient and/or caregiver; and preparation of discharge records, prescriptions, and referral forms.

CODING TIP: Do not report Subsequent Hospital Care codes (99232-99233) on the day of hospital discharge. Code 99232 indicates the patient has had an inadequate response to therapy or has developed a complication. Code 99233 is reported for an unstable patient or one who has developed a significant complication or new problem.

Consultations

A **consultation** is defined (for general coding purposes) as an examination of a patient by a health care provider, usually a specialist, for the purpose of advising the referring or attending physician in the evaluation and/or management of a specific problem with a known diagnosis. Consultants may initiate diagnostic and/or therapeutic services as necessary during the consultative encounter.

The consultation category of E&M allows the following types of consultations to be reported: office or other outpatient, initial and follow-up inpatient, and confirmatory consultations. *Follow-up office or other outpatient consultation services are not reported; if subsequent office or other outpatient consultation services are performed for a patient, these services are reported by the consultant using office or other patient services codes, established patient (99211-99215).*

INTERNET LINK

For additional information on documentation issues related to consultation reports, check out www.bcm.tmc.edu/compliance/jun99reged.html

EXERCISE 7-12 E&M Coding I

Code the following statements. To determine the appropriate level of service codes, refer to the CPT E&M Code Abstract (Table 4) located in Appendix II.

1. Home visit, problem focused, established patient _____

2. ED service, new patient, low complexity;
   DX: low-grade chest pain _____

3. Hospital care, new patient, initial, high complexity _____

4. Hospital care, subsequent, detailed _____

5. ED care, established patient, problem focused, counseling
   15 minutes; DX: bladder infection _____

6. Patient requested consultation, new patient, moderate
   complexity, no third-party confirmation required _____

7. Office consultation, high complexity, established
   patient, surgery scheduled tomorrow _____

8. Follow-up consultation, office, problem-focused,
   counseling 15 minutes, encounter was 25 minutes _____

9. Follow-up consultation, inpatient, detailed, 35 minutes _____

After completing this exercise, refer to Appendix IV to check your answers.

Codes 99261-99265 cover follow-up inpatient consultation. To assign code numbers 99241-99245 or 99251-99255 the consultation request must be:

- Initiated by the attending physician or other health care provider. (Consultations requested by the patient, the patient's family, or a third party are classified in the Confirmatory Consultation subsection of CPT. See the description on page 192.)
- Referring providers must document all consultation requests in the patient's chart.
- The consultant must document a written report that includes the name of the person requesting the consultation, the reason for the consultation, and how the findings were communicated to the referring health care provider.

Any specifically identifiable diagnostic or therapeutic service performed on the same day as the examination may be billed on a fee-for-service basis. These separate services must be linked to the appropriate diagnosis to ensure that "medical necessity" criteria have been met. Some carriers, including Medicare, may disallow payment when procedures and services are performed during the encounter.

If the consultant assumes responsibility for a portion or all of the management of the case, all subsequent care is to be reported and billed using the appropriate office or other outpatient services, established patient, code or the subsequent hospital care code.

Do not confuse a *consultation* with a *referral*. Patients may report that they were referred by another health care provider, but no direct referral appointments were made for the patients and no written referrals are available. To ensure proper coding of the visit, call the stated health care provider's office to inquire whether a consultation or direct referral was intended.

Preoperative clearance occurs when a surgeon requests that a specialist or other physician (e.g., general practice) examine a patient and certify whether or not that patient can withstand the expected risks of a specific surgery. This is also considered a consultation, even if the referring physician is the patient's primary care physician.

CODING TIP:	Remember the "three Rs" when deciding whether or not to code a visit as a consultation:
	● Request
	● Render opinion
	● Report back

Confirmatory Consultation

A **confirmatory consultation** is an E&M service requested by the patient, the patient's family, or a third party for the purpose of rendering a second or third opinion about the necessity or appropriate nature of a previously recommended diagnosis, surgical or medical procedure. The examination setting or site of service does not enter into the selection of the appropriate confirmatory consultation code. When the confirmatory consultation is mandated by a third-party payer, modifier -32 is used for clarification of circumstances surrounding the encounter. Subsequent services rendered to the patient are reported and billed as an established patient office or other outpatient service or a subsequent hospital care.

Emergency Department Services

Emergency department services are defined by CPT as those provided in an organized hospital-based facility, which is open on a 24-hour basis, for the purpose of "providing unscheduled episodic services to patients requiring immediate medical attention." Code 99288 is reported when the physician is in two-way voice communication contact with ambulance or rescue crew personnel located outside of the hospital.

Critical Care Services

Critical care services are reported when a physician, who is in constant attendance, provides medical care to a critically ill or injured patient. **Constant attendance** means that the physician "devotes his or her full attention to that patient and, therefore, cannot provide services to any other patient during the same period of time." While constant attendance does *not* mean that the physician must remain at the patient's bedside (e.g., physician could be reviewing lab test results), the physician is expected to stay in close proximity to the patient and the time spent providing services is documented in the patient's record.

Critical care service codes include other services and procedures, or **bundled codes**. These other services and procedures are not reported as separate codes when critical care service codes are reported. Services and procedures that are "bundled" with critical care service codes include chest Xrays, blood gas tests, gastric intubation, interpretation of cardiac output measurements, information stored in computers (e.g., ECGs), temporary transcutaneous pacing, ventilator management, and vascular access procedures. Refer to the notes included under the Critical Care Services subsection of CPT for codes that apply to the "includes services and procedures."

■ **NOTE:** The reporting of critical care services is *not* dependent on the patient being located in a critical care unit. ■

The codes are reported for critical care services having been rendered to a patient. Likewise, just because patients are located in a critical care unit does not mean they are receiving critical care; if the patient is stable, report the appropriate level subsequent hospital care or inpatient consultation codes. If, while located in a critical care unit, the patient receives critical care services from a physician in constant attendance, the critical care services codes are reported in addition to hospital care or inpatient consultation codes.

EXAMPLE

Mary Jones is seen in the hospital emergency department (ED) for trauma as the result of an automobile accident; she also receives one hour of critical care services in the ED. Report the appropriate level ED code *and* code 99291 from the critical care services category of the E&M section.

CODING TIP: When critical care services are coded in addition to another E&M service code (e.g., ED care, and initial hospital care), add modifier -25 to the E&M service code to report it as a separately identified service provided to the patient.

Remember! Critical care services are reported based on the total time the physician spends in constant attendance (Table 7-2), and the time does *not* have to be continuous.

EXAMPLE

Dr. Smith was in constant attendance on June 15th providing critical care services to his patient, Lori Burr, from 8:00-9:00 A.M., 10:30-10:45 A.M., and 3:00-3:45 P.M. To code this case, add up the minutes of critical care services provided to the patient, and refer to Table 7-2 to select the codes. The answer is 99291 and 99292 x 2.

Remember! You may have to report other E&M codes (along with modifier -25).

Table 7-2 Critical care services.

TOTAL DURATION OF CRITICAL CARE	CODES
Less than 30 minutes	Assign appropriate E&M code(s)
30-74 minutes	99291
75-104 minutes	99291, 99292
105-131 minutes	99291, 99292, 99292
135-164 minutes	99291, 99292, 99292, 99292

(CPT codes, descriptions, and materials only are © 2000 American Medical Association).

Neonatal Intensive Care

A physician who directs the care of a critically ill newborn (or the very low birth weight infant) provides **neonatal intensive care** services. Codes 99295-99298 are reported for "neonates (30 days of age or less) admitted to an intensive care unit."

■ **NOTE:** If an infant older than 30 days is admitted to an intensive care unit, report services using codes from the critical care services category of the E&M section.

Neonatal intensive care begins on the date of admission, and codes are reported once per day, per patient. The codes are "global 24-hour codes and not reported as hourly services." When the neonate is no longer considered to be critically ill and attains a body weight that exceeds 1500 grams, codes for subsequent hospital care (99231-99233) are reported.

Nursing Facility Services

Nursing facility services are performed at the following sites: skilled nursing facilities (SNFs), intermediate care facilities (ICFs), and long-term care facilities (LTCFs). In addition, E&M services provided to patients in psychiatric residential treatment facilities are also reported from this subsection of CPT.

Each nursing facility providing convalescent, rehabilitative, or long-term care for patients is required to have a **comprehensive assessment** completed on each patient. The comprehensive assessment must include an assessment of the patient's functional capacity, an identification of potential problems, and a nursing plan to enhance, or at least maintain, the patient's physical and psychosocial functions. These assessments are to be written at the time of the patient's admission/readmission to the facility or when a reassessment is necessary owing to a substantial change in the patient's status. Physicians are required to review, amend, and approve these plans. Codes 99301-99303 are used to report this in-depth review.

It is appropriate to report both an acute hospital discharge code (99238-99239), observation discharge (99217), or same day admit/discharge (99221-99223) and a nursing facility services comprehensive assessment code, if a patient is discharged and admitted to a SNF, ICF, or LTCF on the same calendar day.

Subsequent nursing facility care is reported when the evaluation of the patient's assessment plan is not required and/or when the patient has not had a major or permanent change of health status.

For discharge from a nursing facility, refer to codes 99315-99316.

Domiciliary, Rest Home, or Custodial Care Services

Domiciliary care covers E&M services provided to patients who live in custodial care or boarding home facilities that do not provide 24-hour nursing care.

Home Services

Home services are provided in a private residence, and this category of E&M identifies patient status (new vs. established) for the purpose of assigning codes.

Prolonged Services

Prolonged services codes are assigned in addition to other E&M services when treatment exceeds by 30 minutes or more the time included in the CPT description of the service.

This category is divided into three subcategories:

99354-99347   Prolonged physician service with direct (face-to-face) patient contact

99358-99359   Prolonged physician service without direct (face-to-face) patient contact

99360   Physician standby service

Direct patient contact refers to face-to-face patient contact (outpatient or inpatient), and codes 99354-99357 are reported in addition to other physician E&M services provided (e.g., office or other outpatient services).

Without direct patient contact services include non-face-to-face time spent by the physician on an outpatient or inpatient basis and occurring before and/or after direct patient care.

EXAMPLE 1

Review of extensive records and test results

EXAMPLE 2

Communicating with family members or other professionals

Codes 99358 and 99359 are reported in addition to other physician E&M services provided (e.g., subsequent hospital care).

Physician standby services involve a physician spending a prolonged period of time without patient contact waiting for an event to occur that will require the physician's services. Such services must be requested by another physician (e.g., attending physician) and are reported only if they are greater than 30 minutes. In addition, if a physician on standby is called to perform a global surgery service, the standby time is considered part of the surgical package. Examples of standby services include:

- *Operative standby*–A surgeon is requested to stand by in the event surgery is required, perhaps for a trauma case.
- *Pathology standby*–A pathologist is requested to stand by to perform an evaluation of a frozen section while the patient is in the operating room.
- *Diagnostics standby*–A cardiologist is requested to stand by to monitor diagnostics, such as telemetry.
- *Obstetrics standby*–A surgeon is requested to stand by in the event that a cesarean section is needed.
- *Pediatrics standby*–A pediatrician is requested to stand by in the event that services are needed after the delivery of a high-risk newborn.

CODING TIP: Code 99360 may be reported in addition to codes 99431 (history and examination of normal newborn) and 99440 (newborn resuscitation), but not 99436 (attendance at delivery and initial stabilization of newborn).

Case Management Services

Case management services are defined as the process by which an attending physician coordinates and supervises the care provided to a patient by other health care providers. Community organizations can also be considered part of case management conferences when such events are not attended by the patient. This category is further subdivided for reporting telephone calls either with the patient or with other health care providers for the purpose of altering instructions or initiating new procedures and/or medications.

Care Plan Oversight Services

Care plan oversight services cover the physician's time supervising a complex and multidisciplinary care treatment program for a specific patient who is under the care of a home health agency, hospice, or nursing facility. These codes are classified separately from other E&M codes where the physician is involved in direct patient examinations. The billing covers a 30-day period, and only one physician in a group practice may bill for this service in any given 30-day period.

Preventive Medicine Services

Preventive medicine services consist of routine examinations or risk management counseling for children and adults *exhibiting no overt signs or symptoms of a disorder while presenting to the medical office for a preventive medical physical,* that is, "wellness visits." Discussion of risk factors such as diet and exercise counseling, family problems, substance abuse counseling, injury prevention, and so on, are an integral part of preventive medicine. Great care must be taken to select the proper code according to the age of the patient and the patient's status (new vs. established).

This category is not to be used when the patient under treatment for a specific disorder returns to the office for a "recheck of a known problem."

Both the appropriate preventive medicine code and an office or other outpatient services code (99201-99215) may be reported during one encounter when a significant abnormality or pre-existing problem is addressed during the course of a well child or adult preventive medicine annual physical. To qualify for both codes, the preventive medicine portion of the visit must be complete and comprehensive and the work-up for the significant problem must meet the required key components for assignment of codes 99201-99215.

Modifier -25 should be added to codes 99201 through 99215, and the diagnosis code reported to justify the 99201-99215 codes must identify the significant problem(s) addressed.

Newborn Care

The CPT definition of **newborn care** covers examinations of normal or high-risk neonates in the hospital or other locations, subsequent newborn care in a hospital, and resuscitation of high-risk babies. Assign code 99436 for a newborn who was assessed and discharged within the same calendar day.

Special E&M Services

Code 99450 may be used when an insurer requests a baseline evaluation on a patient who has applied for life or disability insurance, and the examining provider does not assume active management of the patient's health problems. Codes 99455 and 99456 are used for insurer-requested examinations of a patient with either a work-related or a medical disability problem.

Other E&M Service

Code 99499 is assigned when the E&M service provided is not described in any other listed E&M codes. The use of modifiers with this code is not appropriate. In addition, a special report must be submitted with the HCFA-1500 claim form.

EXERCISE 7-13   E&M Coding II

Code the following services:

1. New patient, routine preventative medicine, age 11. Risk factor discussion, 20 minutes   _____

2. Critical care, 1.5 hours   _____

3. Nursing facility visit, subsequent visit, expanded problem focused H&PE   _____

4. Medical team conference, 50 minutes   _____

5. Follow-up visit, ICU patient, stable, expanded problem focused H&PE   _____

6. Resuscitation of newborn, initial   _____

7. Telephone call with social worker, brief   _____

8. Custodial care, established patient, detailed H&PE, high complexity   _____

9. Pediatrician on standby, high risk birth, 65 minutes   _____

10. Heart risk factor education, group counseling, nonsymptomatic attendees, 65 minutes   _____

11. Prolonged care of subsequent level III inpatient with CPR, 1 hour 45 minutes   _____

After completing this exercise, refer to Appendix IV to check your answers.

CPT MODIFIERS

The last step in the coding process is to add modifiers to the CPT code when it is necessary to provide additional information to payers about services/procedures which have been altered in some way. Use of modifiers enables the provider to explain that a service provided to the patient varied from the usual code description.

When HCFA developed HCPCS codes to augment services reported in CPT, they also developed two-character modifiers. These modifiers can be attached to CPT codes when necessary. The HCPCS coding system is discussed in Chapter 8.

Not all CPT modifiers apply to every section of CPT. Table 7-3 provides a summary in numerical order. The following case study illustrates how and why modifiers are used.

Mrs. T has a history of gallbladder disease. After several hours of acute pain, she was referred to Dr. S for an evaluation of her condition. Dr. S performed a complete history and physical examination and decided to admit the patient to the hospital for an immediate work-up for cholecystitis. When the results of laboratory tests and sonogram were received, the patient was scheduled for an emergency laparoscopic cholecystectomy. Dr. A was the assistant surgeon.

The surgery was successful. The patient was discharged the next day and told to return to the office in 7 days.

Table 7-4 CPT 2001 modifiers in a quick view format.

KEY

– Shaded boxes that contain an "X" indicate modifiers restricted to a specific CPT Section.
– Shaded boxes that contain "X-S" indicate modifiers restricted to CPT Surgery codes reported by ASC settings.
– Unshaded boxes that contain an "X" indicate modifiers applicable to multiple CPT Sections.

ASC = Ambulatory Surgery Center, and this column is included to indicate CPT modifiers applicable to that setting. ASCs are located in hospital outpatient settings and as stand-alone surgical centers. HCPCS modifiers are located in Chapter 8.

Modifier	Title of Modifier	E&M	Anesthesia	Surgery	Radiology	Pathology & Laboratory	Medicine	Ambulatory Surgical Center (ASC)
-21	Prolonged Evaluation and Management Services	X						
-22	Unusual Procedural Services		X	X	X	X	X	
-23	Unusual Anesthesia		X					
-24	Unrelated Evaluation and Management Service by the Same Physician During a Postoperative Period	X						
-25	Significant, Separately Indentifiable Evaluation and Management Service by the Same Physician on the Same Day of the Procedure or Other Service	X						X
-26	Professional Component			X	X	X	X	
-27	Multiple Outpatient Hospital E/M Encounters on the Same Date	X						X
-32	Mandated Services	X	X	X	X	X	X	
-47	Anesthesia by Surgeon			X				
-50	Bilateral Procedure			X				X
-51	Multiple Procedures		X	X	X		X	
-52	Reduced Services	X		X	X	X	X	X
-53	Discontinued Procedure (Outpatient physician reporting only)			X	X	X	X	
-54	Surgical Care Only			X				
-55	Postoperative Management Only			X			X	
-56	Preoperative Management Only	X		X			X	
-57	Decision for Surgery	X					X	
-58	Staged or Related Procedure or Service by the Same Physician During the Postoperative Period			X	X		X	X
-59	Distinct Procedural Service			X	X	X	X	X
-60	Altered Surgical Field			X				
-62	Two Surgeons			X	X			
-66	Surgical Team			X	X			
-73	Discontinued Outpatient Hospital/Ambulatory Surgery Center (ASC) Procedure Prior to the Administration of Anesthesia							X-S
-74	Discontinued Outpatient Hospital/Ambulatory Surgery Center (ASC) Procedure After Administration of Anesthesia							X-S
-76	Repeat Procedure by Same Physician			X	X		X	X
-77	Repeat Procedure by Another Physician			X	X		X	X
-78	Return to the Operating Room for a Related Procedure During the Postoperative Period			X	X		X	
-79	Unrelated procedure or Service by the Same Physician During the Postoperative Period			X	X		X	
-80	Assistant Surgeon			X	X			
-81	Minimum Assistant Surgeon			X				
-82	Assistant Surgeon (when qualified resident surgeon not available)			X				
-90	Reference (Outside) Laboratory					X		
-91	Repeat Clinical Diagnostic Laboratory Test					X		X
-99	Multiple Modifiers			X	X		X	

(CPT codes, descriptions, and materials only are © 2000 American Medical Association).

Four days later, Mrs. T returned to the surgeon's office complaining of chest pains. The surgeon performed another examination and ordered the necessary tests. After reviewing the test results and confirming with the patient's primary care physician, it was determined that the patient was suffering from mild angina.

Dr. S submitted a claim (see Figure 7-8) for the following services:

Initial hospital visit, comprehensive, with medical decision making of high complexity 99223-57

(Modifier 57 indicates that the decision to perform surgery was made during the hospital evaluation)

Laparoscopic cholecystectomy 47562

Office visit, established patient, expanded problem focused, with medical decision making of low complexity 99213-24

(Modifier 24 indicates that the re-examination of the patient revealed the problem to be unrelated to the normal postoperative care provided to a cholecystectomy patient. The diagnosis linked to this visit is angina.)

24. A DATE(S) OF SERVICE							B Place of Service	C Type of Service	D PROCEDURES, SERVICES, OR SUPPLIES (Explain Unusual Circumstances)		E DIAGNOSIS CODE	F $ CHARGES	G DAYS OR UNITS	H EPSDT Family Plan	I EMG	J COB	K RESERVED FOR LOCAL USE
From MM	DD	YY	To MM	DD	YY				CPT/HCPCS	MODIFIER							
									99223	57							
									47562								
									99213	24							

FIGURE 7-8 Block 24D on HCFA-1500 claim form

Dr. A submits a claim (see Figure 7-9) for the following service:

Laparoscopic cholecystectomy 47562-80

(Modifier 80 indicates Dr. A is the assistant surgeon.)

24. A DATE(S) OF SERVICE							B Place of Service	C Type of Service	D PROCEDURES, SERVICES, OR SUPPLIES (Explain Unusual Circumstances)		E DIAGNOSIS CODE	F $ CHARGES	G DAYS OR UNITS	H EPSDT Family Plan	I EMG	J COB	K RESERVED FOR LOCAL USE
From MM	DD	YY	To MM	DD	YY				CPT/HCPCS	MODIFIER							
									47562	80							

FIGURE 7-9 Completed Block 24D on HCFA-1500 claim form

The list of modifiers was developed by the AMA and HCFA over the course of many years. A presentation that follows strict numerical order makes it difficult to compare modifiers that are related to each other. As new modifiers were added to the list, they were assigned available numbers with no clear relationship to established modifiers. This textbook presents a numerical listing of modifiers along with a narrative discussion of modifiers in functional groups. This should simplify the differences among closely related modifiers.

■ **NOTE:** This text's wording of modifiers (below) does not correspond word-for-word with the description found in the CPT book. The text discussion is presented in an attempt to simplify the CPT description. The initials in parentheses indicate the sections of CPT where the modifier is most often applied (S = surgery, R = radiology, P = pathology and laboratory, M = medicine, A = anesthesia, E = E&M). The "ASC" after the parentheses indicates the modifier applies to Ambulatory Surgical Center and Hospital Outpatient Department settings, not physician offices. ■

Special E&M Cases

-21 (E) This modifier is applied only to the highest level of a specific category of evaluation and management services (E&M). It is to be used when the service provided was prolonged and greater than the average highest reportable level of service required. A report should accompany the claim. This modifier does not affect reimbursement but is used as a data collection and statistical reporting tool.

-24 (E) This modifier is used primarily by a surgeon to indicate an additional E&M service was performed, during the standard postoperative period, for a condition that is completely *unrelated* to the surgery. This procedure must be linked to a diagnosis totally unrelated to the surgical diagnosis previously submitted. Attach documentation explaining the particular circumstances to the claim.

EXAMPLE

Five weeks after the surgical release of a "frozen" shoulder, a patient falls and severely sprains an ankle, requiring strapping immobilization for support and comfort. Report code 29540-24.

According to CPT, notes associated with codes that are reported for the *application of casts and strapping* say, "The listed procedures apply when the . . . strapping is an initial service performed . . . to stabilize . . . and/or afford comfort to a patient."

CODING TIP: Use modifier -57 rather than -24 if the reported E&M service resulted in the decision to perform a surgical procedure.

-25 (E) This modifier is used when a stated E&M service was performed on the same day as another procedure because the patient's condition required the assignment of significant, separately identifiable additional E&M services normally not a part of the other procedure.

EXAMPLE 1

A patient underwent a biopsy of the prostate in an ambulatory surgical center and developed shortness of breath and chest pains while waiting to be discharged.

EXAMPLE 2

During the course of a routine annual preventive medicine examination, it was discovered that the patient had an enlarged liver. This discovery expanded the scope of the physical examination, the patient's present medical, family, and social history, and medical decision making and risk factor discussions.

In these cases, report both the preventive medicine code and established patient outpatient services code (99211-99215). The modifier is attached to the outpatient services code, and a report describing the unusual circumstances that warranted the use of modifier -25 is attached to the claim.

CODING TIP: Assign modifier -57 rather than -25 to an E&M code when the initial decision to perform surgery is made on the same day as the surgery.

-57 (ME) The reported E&M service resulted in the initial decision to perform surgery *within 24 to 48 hours of an examination.* This modifier permits payment of the required physical examination performed within 24 hours of the surgery.

Greater or Reduced Services

-22 (SRPMA) Use this modifier when a procedure *requires greater than normal services,* more time than an average procedure or service reported for this code, and, therefore, a higher than normal fee is reflected in the charge for the procedure. This modifier should not be used if another identifiable HCPCS code would better describe the services performed. Include documentation with the claim of the unusual circumstances and how they compare to the usual procedure.

Key words or phrases found in patient's documentation indicating possible usage of -22 modifier are: difficult, complicated, extensive, unusual, or rare procedure.

EXAMPLE

Blood loss of 600 cc or greater.

Prolonging or extending the operative time by or due to _____

CODING TIP: *This modifier has been greatly overused.* Be sure the special circumstances are fully explained in the documentation, and send a copy of the documentation with the claim.

-52 (SRPME)-ASC To be used when a service has been partially reduced at the physician's discretion and does not completely match the narrative description for the reported CPT code. Attach documentation or an explanation to the claim.

-60 (S) This modifier is used with surgical procedures that involve significantly increased operative complexity and/or time in a *significantly altered surgical field* (resulting from the effects of prior surgery, adhesions, inflammation, trauma, etc).

Discontinued Services

-53 (SRPM) This modifier is used when the physician has elected to terminate a surgery or diagnostic procedure because of extenuating circumstances that threaten the well-being of the patient. This modifier applies only if the surgical prep has started in the operating room or the induction of anesthesia has been initiated.

Do not report procedures electively cancelled prior to induction of anesthesia and/or surgical prep.

EXAMPLE

Procedure started and terminated due to equipment failure.

Patient develops heart arrhythmia during an elective procedure.

CODING TIP: Modifier -53 applies only to physician office settings. Ambulatory Surgical Centers and hospital outpatient department settings report -73 or -74, not -53.

-73 (S) -ASC This modifier describes discontinued surgical or diagnostic procedure *prior to the administration of any anesthesia* because of extenuating circumstances threatening the well-being of the patient. Do not report elective cancellations.

-74 (S) -ASC This modifier describes discontinued surgical or diagnostic procedure *after* the administration of anesthesia owing to extenuating circumstances.

These modifiers are reported only by ambulatory surgical centers and hospital outpatient departments.

Global Surgery

The following three modifiers apply to the four areas related to the CPT surgical package (see Figure 7-10).

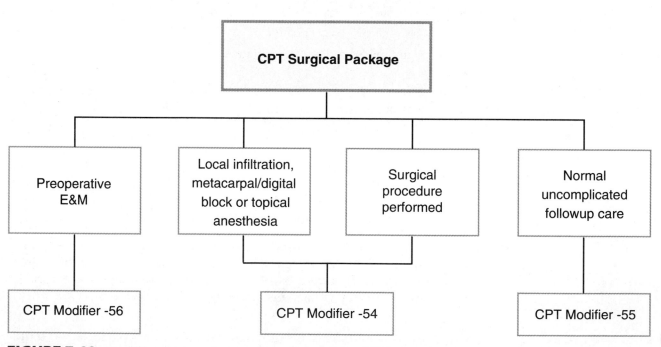

FIGURE 7-10 Modifiers that apply to components of the CPT Surgical Package

-54 (S) This modifier is used when the surgeon performed only the surgical portion of the surgical package and personally administered required local anesthesia. The preoperative evaluation and/or post-operative care was performed by another physician.

The performing surgeon is usually responsible for the patient care until the patient is ready for discharge from the hospital.

✳ **CAUTION:** An exception to the application of this modifier occurs with obstetrical coding, where the CPT description of specific codes clearly describes separate antepartum, postpartum and delivery services for both vaginal and cesarean deliveries (see codes 49426, 59409, 59410, 59425, 59430, 59514, 59515, and so on). ✳

-55 (SM) This modifier is used when a provider other than the surgeon is responsible for only the postoperative management of a surgery performed by another physician.

A note should be placed in the patient's chart detailing the date of the transfer of care to include calculation of the percentage of the fee to be billed for postoperative care. The following items should be included on the HFCA-1500 claim form:

- The date of the surgery in Block 14 (Date of Current Illness)
- The range of dates covered by the transfer of care in Item 24A
- The code number for the surgery performed with modifier 55 in Item 24D

An attachment to the claim providing the name and address of the surgeon is also needed for further clarification of circumstances. This modifier will not apply to cases where a second provider is occasionally covering for the surgeon and where no transfer of care has occurred, or in cases described in the note for modifier -54.

-56 (ESM) Use modifier -56 when a provider other than the operating surgeon performs preoperative clearance for surgery.

CODING TIP:

The primary diagnosis should include any problem found during this examination, followed by the reason for surgery. Code V72.8 for preoperative care should also be added to the claim form as a secondary diagnosis code when using this modifier.

Special Surgery/ Procedure Events

-59 (SRPM) -ASC   Use this modifier when the same physician performs one or more distinctly independent procedures on the same day as other procedures or services, and another more descriptive CPT or HCPCS modifier is not available.

The procedures may be performed at a different session, on a different site or organ, for multiple or extensive injuries, using separate incisions/excisions, for separate lesions, when not ordinarily encountered or not ordinarily performed on the same day, and for that which would otherwise provide the perception of "unbundling" or "fragmenting coding."

The following are samples of HCPCS modifiers to be used when reporting modifier -59 by physician offices, and ambulatory surgical centers and hospital outpatient services. (See Chapter 8 of this textbook for the complete list of HCPCS modifiers).

-RT Right side	-LT Left side
-E1 Upper left eyelid	-E2 Lower left eyelid
-FA Left thumb	-F1 Left second digit
-F2 Left third digit	-F3 Left fourth digit
-TA Left great toe	-T1 Left second toe
-T2 Left third toe	-T3 Left fourth toe
-LC Left circumflex coronary artery	
-LD Left anterior descending coronary artery	

EXAMPLE 1

When a service described as a "separate procedure" in CPT is performed during the same session as a distinctly unrelated procedure report modifier-59.

EXAMPLE 2

The patient has two basal cell carcinomas removed, one from the forehead with a simple closure (11640) and the other from the nose requiring closure by adjacent tissue transfer (14060). Modifier -59 is added to code 11640 (the lesser procedure) to indicate it is a separate procedure performed on a different site from the primary surgery.

-58 (SRM) -ASC Use this modifier to indicate that additional related surgery was required during the postoperative period of a previously completed surgery and was performed by the same physician.

1. The original plan for surgery included additional stages of the surgery to be performed within the postoperative period for the first stage of the procedure;

2. Underlying disease required a second related, but unplanned, procedure to be performed; or additional related therapy is required after the performance of a diagnostic surgical procedure.

EXAMPLE 1

A surgical wound is not healing properly because of the patient's underlying diabetes. Patient was told prior to the original surgery that if this happened, additional surgery would be required to debride or resuture the wound.

EXAMPLE 2

A biopsy of a breast lesion was performed. The pathology report indicates carcinoma and 4 days later a mastectomy will be performed.

EXAMPLE 3

A series of surgical steps was planned to correct a given problem. An enteroscopy was performed with a planned closure of the stoma in 6 to 8 weeks.

Do not use modifier -58 if the CPT code description describes multiple sessions of an event.

EXAMPLE 1

67208 Destruction of localized lesion of retina (e.g., macular edema, tumors), one or more sessions; cryotherapy, diathermy

EXAMPLE 2

17304 Chemosurgery (Mohs' micrographic technique); first stage, fresh tissue technique, up to 5 specimens

⊘**17305** second stage, fixed or fresh tissue, up to 5 specimens

-78 (SRM) Use this modifier to report unplanned circumstances that require the return to the operating room for complications of the initial operation such as a "bleeder" or a surgical wound dehiscence.

Complications arising during the normal postoperative period require the patient to return to the operating room for a procedure directly related to the original surgery. Other acceptable settings may involve cardiac catheterization laboratories, laser or endoscopic suites, and an ICU, if the patient is critical and there is no time to move the patient to the operating room.

EXAMPLE

Surgical sutures did not hold and the wound had to be resutured.

The patient hemorrhaged following surgery and was returned to the OR for open exploration and cauterization of the bleeder.

To ensure payment for the procedure with the -78 modifier, the diagnosis reported to prove medical necessity for the return to operating room must reflect the surgical complication.

-79 (SRM) A new procedure or service is performed by a surgeon during the normal postoperative period of a previously performed but unrelated surgery.

EXAMPLE

Six weeks following cataract surgery performed on the left eye, the patient undergoes a separate and unrelated surgery on the right eye.

Bilateral Procedures

-50 (S)-ASC Bilateral procedures were performed during the same session when the code description does not specify that the procedure is bilateral. This modifier applies to the second procedure only.

The addition of the HCPCS modifiers -LT (left side) and -RT (right side) to the procedures will remove any doubt that a bilateral procedure was performed. Documentation should accompany the submitted claim. Do not use modifier -50 if the CPT description of a code describes a bilateral procedure, "2" or "both." Do not report modifier -50 with modifiers -LT and -RT.

Multiple Procedures and Services

-27 (E) -ASC Multiple outpatient hospital E&M services performed on the same date are to be reported with modifier -27 which was established for Medicare's new hospital outpatient prospective payment system (Ambulatory Payment Classifications). This modifier allows a hospital outpatient facility to report multiple E&M services received by a patient and performed by different physicians.

EXAMPLE

A patient seen in the hospital's emergency department and then in it's outpatient clinic would have two different E&M codes reported. Modifier -27 would be added to each E&M code reported.

■ **NOTE:** Modifier -27 is not used to report multiple E&M services performed by the same physician on the same date. ■

-51 (SRMA) Multiple procedures, other than E&M services, were performed on the same day. This modifier covers multiple surgeries performed through separate incisions, multiple medical procedures, or a combination of medical and surgical procedures. The modifier applies to the secondary or lesser procedures and not to the primary procedure. Documentation should accompany the claim.

CODING TIP:

Do not use modifier -51 if the CPT description or a note includes one of the following:

1. Notes at the beginning of a category instructing the coder to "report additional codes in addition to" .... without the use of modifier -51. (See the note above code 22305.)

2. The code description states "List separately in addition to the code for primary procedure." (See code 22116.)

3. The code description uses the words "each" or "each additional" segment, lesion, and so on. (See codes 22103, 17001, and 17003.)

4. This modifier should not be appended to designated add-on codes—those codes preceded by the symbol **+**. (A complete list of add-on codes appears in Appendix E and a list of -51 exempt codes appears in Appendix F of the CPT coding manual.)

5. This modifier is never used with laboratory/pathology codes in the 80000 series.

◆ **HINT:** To assist in recalling which modifier stands for bilateral procedures and which for multiple services, think alphabetically B (bilateral -50) comes before M (multiple -51). ◆

Repeated Services

-76 (SRM)-ASC The service performed was repeated because of special circumstances involving the original service and performed by the same physician.

-77 (SRM)-ASC The service, which is *not performed by the original physician*, is a repeat procedure required because of special circumstances involving the original study or procedure.

-91 (P) -ASC This modifier is reported if a clinical diagnostic laboratory test is repeated on the same day to obtain subsequent (multiple) test results. This modifier is *not* reported when lab tests are rerun to confirm initial results (e.g., due to equipment problems).

CODING TIP: Diagnosis codes V64.1 or V64.2 should be added to the claim form to document the following conditions:

- V64.1 A procedure was halted due to a patient contraindication or complication.
- V64.2 A procedure was terminated at the patient's request.

Surgical Teams

-62 (SR) Two primary surgeons are required during this operative session, each performing distinct portions of a reportable procedure. Ideally, the surgeons represent different specialties. Both surgeons should report the procedure using the same CPT code. If add-on codes are reported, do not add this modifier to them. The operative reports should clearly detail the extent of the surgery performed by each surgeon. The reported primary diagnosis on the claim should link to and justify the procedure submitted by each physician.

EXAMPLE

An orthopedist creates the surgical approach through a bone and a neurosurgeon repairs the nerve.

CODING TIP: Either surgeon may act as the assistant surgeon on any additional unrelated procedure performed during the same operative session. In these cases, -80 or -81 is added to the additional procedures.

-66 (SR) This surgery is highly complex and requires the services of a highly skilled team of three or more physicians. The procedure listed on the claim for each participating physician must report this modifier. The operative report must document the complexity of the surgery and briefly refer to the actions of the team members.

EXAMPLE

Separation of conjoined twins

Surgical Assistants

-80 (SR) The procedure submitted is for the complete services of an assistant surgeon. If the primary surgeon used modifier -22 because of unusual circumstances in the case, the assistant surgeon should also use modifier -22 when submitting a claim.

-81 (S) Minimal services of an assistant surgeon are required.

-82 (S) An assistant surgeon is needed for surgery in a *teaching hospital* because no qualified surgical resident was available.

Professional versus Technical Components

-26 (SRPM) The procedure fee represents only the physician portion or component (the supervision and interpretation of results and writing the report of a diagnostic procedure) and does not include the cost of the technical component of the test (the equipment and supply cost).

This modifier should not be used when there is a specific separately identifiable code describing just the professional component of a diagnostic procedure; for example, CPT code 93010.

EXAMPLE

Independent radiologist performs the supervision and interpretation for an Xray performed at the community hospital.

Third-Party Payer Mandated Service

-32 (SRPMAE) The services were mandated by a third-party.

Anesthesia Services

-23 (A) Unusual circumstances requiring a general anesthesia for a procedure that usually requires either no anesthesia or only the administration of a local anesthetic.

-47 (S) Regional or general anesthesia, but not local anesthesia, administered personally by the surgeon performing the surgery.

CODING TIP: This modifier is added to the basic surgical service. It is not reported with codes 00100-01999.

Outside Laboratory Bills Physician

-90 (P) The procedure submitted is for laboratory testing and diagnostic procedures performed by an outside laboratory and billed to the treating/reporting physician.

One Service— Multiple Modifiers

-99 (SRM) More than one modifier applies to a procedure or service. The additional modifiers may be listed as part of the service descriptions.

EXERCISE 7-14 Coding Procedures Requiring CPT Modifiers

Code the following procedures:

1. Assistant surgeon, cesarean section, delivery only   _____

2. Cholecystectomy, open, performed within the post-operative period of a leg fracture   _____

3. Level III office visit, Established patient work-up, at time of a preventive medicine visit, age 54   _____

4. Abdominal hysterectomy, surgery only   _____

5. Level II, initial inpatient hospital visit by surgeon, with decision to perform surgery tomorrow   _____

6. Office consult, level IV, preoperative clearance for surgery   _____

7. Postoperative management of vaginal hysterectomy   _____

8. Repeat gallbladder Xray series, same physician _____

9. Reduction of closed fracture, left wrist, followed by diagnostic arthroscopy, right elbow _____

10. Needle core biopsy, right and left breast _____

11. Level II office consult requested by lawyer _____

12. Unrelated level III office visit, by surgeon during postoperative period for an appendectomy _____

After completing this exercise, refer to Appendix IV to check your answers.

CPT-5 PROJECT

In response to the electronic data interchange requirements of the Health Insurance Portability and Accountability Act of 1996 (HIPAA), the American Medical Association is developing a fifth edition of CPT, entitled **CPT-5**, which is scheduled to be implemented no sooner than 2003. Among HIPAA's requirements is that code sets and classification systems be implemented in a cost effective manner that includes the low cost, efficient distribution and application to all users. While CPT was identified as the procedure coding standard for the reporting of physician services in 2000, the May 7, 1998 edition of the *Federal Register* reported that "CPT is not always precise or unambiguous . . . there are no viable alternatives for the year 2000." The CPT 5 project is, therefore, intended to insure that all HIPAA requirements are met and CPT continues to be used for reporting physician services.

Similarities Between CPT-5 and CPT-4

CPT-5 codes will remain 5-digits in length, and code descriptions will continue to reflect health care services and procedures performed in modern medical practice. In addition, the process of periodically reviewing and updating codes and descriptions will continue.

Changes to Be Incorporated into CPT-5

CPT-5 will be revised to support electronic data interchange, the computer-based patient record (or electronic medical record), and reference/research databases. It is likely that CPT-5 codes will also be used to track new technology and **performance measures** (criteria upon which the assessment of providers and facilities is based).

New codes are planned for counseling/preventive medicine services and for non-physician health professional evaluation services (e.g., chiropractors, nurses, nurse practitioners, optometrists, physician assistants, psychologists, social workers, and therapists–occupational, speech, and physical), and code descriptors will be improved in an attempt to eliminate ambiguous terms. CPT guidelines and notes will undergo revision so that they are comprehensive, easy to interpret, and specific. A CPT glossary will be created to standardize definitions and differentiate the use of synonymous terms; and a searchable, electronic CPT index will be developed along with a computerized database that will delineate relationships among CPT code descriptions. Improvements to CPT will also be made to address the needs of hospitals, managed care organizations and long term care facilities.

INTERNET LINKS

For more information about the CPT-5 Project, visit
www.ama-assn.org/ama/pub/category/3883.html

A slide presentation developed by the Workgroup for Electronic Data
Interchange (WEDI) is available at www.wedi.org by conducting a search
for "CPT 5".

REVIEW

Evaluation and Management Section

Refer to the CPT coding manual to answer each of the following items.

1. Which category is used to report services for patients seen in stand-alone
   ambulatory care centers? _____

2. Office or Other Outpatient Services is used to report services rendered by a physician
   to a patient in a hospital observation area. TRUE or FALSE. _____

3. Which category is used to report services provided to patients in a partial hospital setting? _____

4. What is the name of the service provided by a physician whose opinion is requested? _____

5. The service identified in question #4 must be requested by another physician
   (e.g. attending physician). TRUE or FALSE. _____

6. Consultations provided in a physician's office are reported using office
   or other outpatient services codes. TRUE or FALSE. _____

7. Only one initial consultation is to be reported by a consultant per hospital
   inpatient admission. TRUE or FALSE. _____

8. A consultant who participates in an inpatient's management after conducting
   an initial consultation will report services using codes from which subcategory? _____

9. Second or third opinions that are mandated by third party payers are reported
   from which E&M subcategory? What other code would be identified for
   such cases? _____

10. A distinction is made between new and established patients when
    reporting E&M Emergency Department Services. TRUE or FALSE. _____

11. Which code would you assign to report for a physician who provides
    directed emergency care? _____

12. What is meant by the phrase *directed emergency care*? _____

13. Critical care services must be provided in a critical care unit
    area (e.g. ICU). TRUE or FALSE. _____

14. Which code(s) would be assigned to report 2 1/2 hours of critical
    care provided by the attending physician? _____

15. SNFs, ICFs, and LTCFs are referred to as _____ .

16. Which category would be used when reporting a physician's visit
    to a patient residing in a boarding home? _____

17. Services provided by a physician to patients in a private residence
    are reported using codes from which category? _____

18. Which code would be reported when a physician calls a patient
    about recent lab test results? _____

19. A physical examination was performed on an 18-year-old who is scheduled to attend college in the fall. Which code(s) would you assign? _____

20. Assign code(s) to well baby care of 9-month-old that includes the administration of DTP and oral polio vaccines. **HINT:** You'll also need to refer to the Medicine Section of CPT. _____

21. Assign a code for preventive medicine service to a 56 year-old-established-patient. _____

22. Assign code(s) to a patient who was admitted to observation services on June 30th and also discharged from observation services on that date. _____

23. Assign code(s) to a patient who received critical care services for a total of 210 minutes on July 15th. On this date, the patient also underwent an inpatient comprehensive history and examination with medical decision making of high complexity. _____

24. Identify the code to assign to a patient who underwent a medical disability evaluation by his own physician. _____

25-29: Identify the E&M category and subcategory you would use to code each case below. The key components of history, examination and medical decision making are identified in each case, and you are required to assign the correct code based on that information.

25. Dr. Jones is an Internist who performed a hospital admission, examination, and initiation of treatment program for a 67-year-old male with uncomplicated pneumonia who requires IV antibiotic therapy. Dr. Jones completed a comprehensive history & examination; the medical decision making is of low complexity. Minimal patient counseling was provided. The patient's problem was of low severity.

Identify the CPT category and subcategory _____ .

Identify the appropriate CPT code_____ .

26. Dr. Smith completed an office consultation for management of systolic hypertension in a 70-year-old male scheduled for elective prostate resection. Dr. Smith conducted an expanded problem focused history and examination; medical decision making was straightforward. The patient's problem is of low severity. Dr. Smith spent 20 minutes counseling the patient.

Identify the CPT category and subcategory _____ .

Identify the appropriate CPT code _____ .

27. Dr. Choi conducted subsequent hospital care for the evaluation and management of a healthy newborn on the second day of inpatient stay.

Identify the CPT category _____ .

Identify the appropriate CPT code _____ .

28. Dr. Lange saw an established patient in the office for recent syncopal attacks. Comprehensive history & examination were performed. Medical decision making is of high complexity.

Identify the CPT category and subcategory _____ .

Identify the appropriate CPT code _____ .

29. Dr. Doolittle conducted a follow-up hospital visit for a 54-year-old patient, post myocardial infarction, who is out of the CCU but is now having frequent premature ventricular contractions on telemetry. Expanded problem focused interval history and examination were completed. Medical decision making is of moderate complexity. Dr. Doolittle coordinated care with the patient's providers and discussed the case with the patient's immediate family.

Identify the CPT category and subcategory _____ .

Identify the appropriate CPT code _____ .

Surgery Section

Code each procedure using the CPT coding manual.

30. Pneumocentesis; assistant surgeon reporting   _____

31. Electrodesiccation, basal cell carcinoma (1 cm), face   _____

32. Complicated bilateral repair of recurrent inguinal hernia   _____

33. Biopsy of anorectal wall via proctosigmoidoscopy   _____

34. Mastectomy for gynecomastia   _____

35. Open reduction, right tibia/fibula shaft, with insertion of screws   _____

36. Excision, condylomata, penis   _____

37. Replacement of breast tissue expander with breast prosthesis (permanent)   _____

38. Closed reduction of closed fracture, clavicle   _____

39. Incision & drainage infected bursa, wrist   _____

40. Cystourethroscopy with biopsy   _____

41. Endoscopic right maxillary sinusotomy with partial polypectomy   _____

42. Insertion of Hickman catheter (cutdown) (age 70)   _____

43. Avulsion of four nail plates   _____

Radiology, Pathology & Laboratory, and Medicine Sections

Code each procedure/service using the CPT coding manual.

44. Arthrography of the shoulder, supervision and interpretation.   _____

45. Chest Xray, frontal, single view (professional component only).   _____

46. Complete pelvic echography, pregnant uterus (obstetrics) (B Scan).   _____

47. Application of radioactive needles (radioelement), intracavitary of uterus, intermediate.   _____

48. Arthritis panel blood test.   _____

49. Drug screen for opiates (outside laboratory performed drug screen)   _____

50. Hemogram (manual) (complete CBC)   _____

51. Papanicolaou smear, cervical   _____

52. Gross and microscopic examination of gallbladder   _____

53. Echocardiography, complete, M-mode   _____

54. Mumps vaccine immunization   _____

55. Intermittent positive pressure breathing of a newborn   _____

56. Gait training, first 30 minutes   _____

57. Medical psychoanalysis   _____

58. Ultraviolet light is used to treat a skin disorder   _____

59. Chemotherapy, IV infusion technique, 10 hours, requiring use of portable pump (including refill)   _____

60. Combined left & right cardiac catheterization and retrograde left heart catheterization   _____

HCPCS Coding System

OBJECTIVES Upon successful completion of this chapter, you should be able to:

1. Define the following terms, phrases, and abbreviations:

HCFA Common Procedure
   Coding System (HCPCS)
durable medical equipment
   (DME)
durable medical equipment,
   prosthetic and orthotic supplies (DMEPOS) dealers

durable medical equipment
   regional carriers
   (DMERC)
local Medicare carrier (LMC)
Coverage Issues Manual (CIM)
Medicare Carriers Manual (MCM)

waiver of liability
Advance Beneficiary Notice
   (ABN)
Health Personnel Shortage Area
   (HPSA)

2. Discuss code jurisdictions of the Local Medicare Carrier and the DME Regional Carrier.

3. Explain the process for determining the correct carrier for a HCPCS service.

4. Describe the purpose of the Medicare Carrier Manual and the Coverage Issues Manual.

INTRODUCTION This chapter presents the procedure/service coding reference developed by the Health Care Financing Administration (HCFA), the **HCFA Common Procedure Coding System (HCPCS**, pronounced "hick-picks"). HCPCS was introduced in 1983 after Medicare found that its payers used over 100 different coding systems, making it difficult to analyze claim data. HCPCS furnished healthcare providers and suppliers with a standardized language for reporting professional services, procedures, supplies, and equipment. Most state Medicaid programs also use HCPCS.

ORGANIZATION OF HCPCS CODING SYSTEM

There are three levels associated with HCPCS, commonly referred to as level I, II, and III codes.

Level I

Level I contains five-digit Current Procedural Terminology (CPT) codes developed and published by the American Medical Association (AMA) as discussed in Chapter 7. The AMA is responsible for annually updating this coding system, along with its two-digit modifiers.

Level II

Level II, or National, codes describe common medical services and supplies not included in CPT. These HCPCS codes are also five characters in length, but begin with the letters A–V, followed by four numbers. Level II codes identify the services of physician and nonphysician providers (e.g., nurse practitioners and speech therapists), as well as ambulance and durable medical equipment (DME) companies (or durable medical equipment, prosthetic and orthotic supplies [DMEPOS] dealers). Durable medical equipment (DME) is defined by Medicare as equipment that:

- can withstand repeated use.
- is primarily used to serve a medical purpose.
- is used in the patient's home.
- would not be used in the absence of illness or injury.

Durable medical equipment, prosthetic and orthotic supplies (DME-POS) dealers supply patients with durable medical equipment (e.g., canes, crutches, walkers, commode chairs, and blood glucose monitors). DMEPOS claims are submitted to regional **durable medical equipment regional carriers (DMERC)** that were awarded contracts by HCFA. Each DMERC covers a specific geographic region of the country and is responsible for processing DMEPOS claims for their specific region. A large section of level II codes, the J codes, list many commonly used medications by name and dosage. Also, when most people refer to HCPCS codes, they are referring to the level II codes. HCFA is responsible for the annual updates to HCPCS level II codes and the two-character alphanumeric modifiers. Level II codes are further discussed in this chapter.

Level III

Level III HCPCS codes have the same structure as level II codes but are assigned by the **local Medicare carrier (LMC)**. The LMC is the agent responsible for processing Medicare claims in the local area. Level III codes begin with the letters W, X, Y, or Z, and are not found in the HCPCS coding references purchased from the AMA, St. Anthony's, or other companies. Local or level III codes are issued on an as-needed basis, frequently identifying new services or other special procedures. Carriers maintain these level III codes and modifiers and must receive permission from HCFA to create new local codes. The LMC will notify physicians and other providers and suppliers when the local codes are to be used. The carrier's regular bulletins and special coding notices introduce and maintain level III codes and modifiers. Carriers also provide an annual list of acceptable level III codes and modifiers. Because these are local codes, the code X1234 could describe a different service in New York, Nebraska, and Nevada.

Local or level III codes will be eliminated from the Medicare system by October 2002 according to the final rule for administration simplification (IHPPA), published August 2000. Generally, level III codes are used only by Medicare. Other payers, such as Blue Shield, Medicaid, or Workers' Compensation may adopt some level III codes, but they will advise providers of the acceptable codes in their newsletters and bulletins.

HCPCS NATIONAL (LEVEL II) CODES

These codes are developed and maintained by HCFA. Unlike CPT, Medicare's HCPCS level II coding system does not carry the copyright of a private organization. The national codes are in the public domain and many publishers print the annual updates. Each publisher may elect to color code the print or pages, include supplemental explanatory material, or provide information from the Medicare Carriers Manual (MCM) for Part B, or the Medicare Coverage Issues Manual (CIM) (see Figures 8-1A and 8-1B).

Some HCPCS level II references contain general instructions or guidelines for each section; an appendix summarizing additions, deletions, and terminology revisions in level II codes (similar to Appendix B in CPT); or separate tables of drugs or deleted codes. Others use symbols to identify codes excluded from Medicare coverage, codes where payment is left to the discretion of the carrier, or codes with special coverage instructions. In addition, most references provide a complete appendix of current HCPCS national modifiers. HCFA has stated it is not responsible for any errors that might occur in or from the use of these private printings of HCPCS level II codes.

The alphabetic first character identifies the code sections of HCPCS level II. Some are logical, such as D for dental or R for radiology, while others, such as J for drugs, appear to be arbitrarily assigned. For the 2001 HCPCS, level II code ranges are as follows, with an example shown from each section:

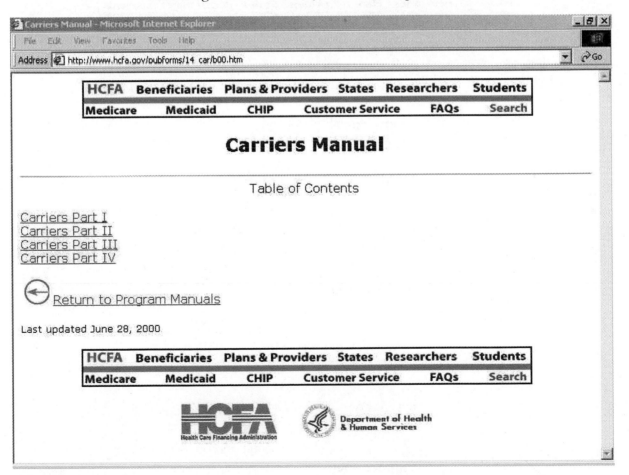

Figure 8-1A Medicare Carriers Manual Web site (Reprinted according to hcfa.gov Web Site Content Reuse policy)

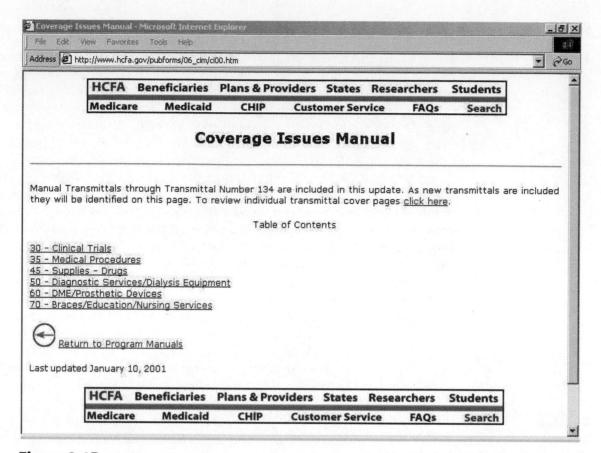

Figure 8-1B Medicare Coverage Issues Manual (Reprinted according to hcfa.gov Web Site Content Reuse policy)

A0000–A0999	Transportation services including ambulance
A0322	Ambulance service, basic life support, emergency transport, supplies included, mileage separately billed
A4000–A4899	Medical and surgical supplies
A4215	Needles only, sterile, any size, each
A9000–A9999	Administrative, miscellaneous, and investigational
A9500	Supply of radiopharmaceutical diagnostic imaging agent, technetium tc 99M sestamibi, per dose
B4000–B9999	Enteral and parenteral therapy
B4164	Parenteral nutrition solution; carbohydrates (dextrose), 50% or less (500 ml = 1 unit)—home mix
D0000–D9999	Dental procedures
D2751	Crown—porcelain fused to predominantly base metal
E0100–E9999	Durable medical equipment
E0660	Nonsegmental pneumatic appliance for use with pneumatic compressor, full leg
G0000–G9999	Procedures/professional services (temporary)
G0108	Diabetes outpatient self-management training services, individual, per session

J0000–J8999	Drugs administered other than oral method
J1530	Injection, gamma globulin, intramuscular, 8 cc
K0000–K9999	K-codes (temporary)
K0113	Trunk support device, vest type, without inner frame, prefabricated
L0000–L4999	Orthotic procedures
L3080	Foot, arch support, nonremovable, attached to shoe, metatarsal, each
M0000–M0302	Medical services
M0064	Brief office visit for the sole purpose of monitoring or changing drug prescriptions used in the treatment of mental, psychoneurotic, and personality disorders
P0000–P9999	Pathology and laboratory services
P9603	Travel allowance, one way, in connection with medically necessary laboratory specimen collection drawn from homebound or nursing home bound patient; prorated miles actually traveled
Q0000–Q9999	Q-codes (temporary)
Q9926	Injection EPO, per 1000 units, at patient HCT of 26
R0000–R5999	Diagnostic radiology services
R0076	Transportation of portable EKG to facility or location, per patient
V0000–V2999	Vision services
V2301	Sphere, trifocal, plus or minus 4.12 to plus or minus 7.00d per lens
V5000–V5999	Hearing services
V5210	Hearing aid, BICROS, in the ear

The American Dental Association (ADA) has copyrighted the D codes and updates the codes in the D series. No codes beginning with the letters C, F, H, I, N, O, S, T, or U are currently in use. It is unlikely that codes will be issued beginning with the letter "O" as they could be confused with "0" (zero) and the CPT anesthesia codes.

HCPCS National Codes (Level II) Index

Because of the wide variety of services and procedures described in HCPCS level II, the alphabetical index is very helpful in finding the correct code. The various publishers of the reference may include an expanded index that lists "alcohol wipes" and "wipes" as well as "Ancef" and "cefazolin sodium," making the search for codes easier and faster (see Figure 8-2). Some references also include a Table of Drugs. The J codes are assigned to medications and list the generic drug name. Some publishers print the brand names underneath the generic description, and some provide a special expanded index of the drug codes. It is important to never code directly from the level II index and to always verify the code in the tabular section of the codebook. You may wish to review the HCPCS references from several publishers and select the one that best meets your needs and is the easiest for you to use.

If the service or procedure cannot be found in CPT, the CPT Index, or the HCPCS Level II Index, review the HCPCS Level II Table of Contents and look in the appropriate section (see Figure 8-3). Read the descriptions there very carefully. You may need to ask the provider to help select the correct code.

Index

Abbokinase, J3364, J3365

Abciximab, J0130

Abdomen
  dressing holder/binder, A4462
  pad, low profile, L1270
  supports, pendulous, L0920, L0930

Abduction control, each, L2624

Abduction rotation bar, foot, L3140–L3170

Abelcet, see Amphotericin B Lipid Complex

ABLC, see Amphotericin B

Absorption dressing, A6251-A6256

Access system, A4301

Accessories
  ambulation devices, E0153–E0159
  artificial kidney and machine (*see also* ESRD), E1510–E1699
  beds, E0271–E0280, E0305–E0326
  wheelchairs, E0950–E1001, E1050–E1298, K0001–K0109

Acetazolamide sodium, J1120

Acetylcysteine, J7610, J7615

Acetylcysteine, inhalation solution, J7608

Achromycin, J0120

ACTH, J0800

Acthar, J0800

Actimmune, J9216

Activase, J2996

Adenocard, J0150, J0151

Adenosine, J0150, J0151

Adhesive, A4364, K0450
  disc or foam pad, A5126
  remover, A4365, A4455, K0451
  support, breast prosthesis, A4280
  tape, A4454, A6265

Administrative, Miscellaneous and Investigational, A9000–A9999

Adrenalin, J0170

Adrenalin Chloride, J0170

Adriamycin, J9000

Adrucil, J9190

Aerosol
  compressor, K0269
  compressor filter, K0178–K0179
  mask, K0180

AFO, E1815, E1830, L1900–L1990, L4392, L4396

Aggrastat, J3245

A-hydroCort, J1710

Air ambulance (*see also* Ambulance), A0030, A0040

Air bubble detector, dialysis, E1530

Air fluidized bed, E0194

Air pressure pad/mattress, E0176, E0186, E0197

Air travel and nonemergency transportation, A0140

Akineton, J0190

Alarm, pressure, dialysis, E1540

Alatrofloxacin mesylate, J0200

Albumin, human, Q0156, Q0157

Albuterol, inhalation solution, concentrated, J7618

Albuterol, inhalation solution, unit dose, J7619

Albuterol sulfate, J7620, J7625

Alcohol, A4244

Alcohol wipes, A4245

Aldesleukin, J9015

Aldomet, J0210

Alferon N, J9215

Alginate dressing, A6196–A6199

Alglucerase, J0205

Alkaban-AQ, J9360

Alkeran, J8600

Alpha-1-proteinase inhibitor, human, J0256

Alprostadil, injection, J0270

Alprostadil, urethral supposity, J0275

Alteplase recombinant, J2996

Alternating pressure mattress/pad, A4640, E0180, E0181, E0277

Alupent, J7670, J7672, J7675

Alveoloplasty, D7310–D7320

Amalgam dental restoration, D2110–D2161

Ambulance, A0021–A0999
  air, A0030, A0040
  disposable supplies, A0382–A0398
  oxygen, A0422

Ambulation device, E0100–E0159

Amcort, J3302

A-methaPred, J2920, J2930

Amifostine, J0207

Aminophylline, J0280

Amitriptyline, HCl, J1320

Figure 8-2 First page from HCPCS 2001 Index (Permission to reprint granted by Medicode)

Contents

Figure 8-3 First page from HCPCS 2001 Table of Contents (Permission to reprint granted by Medicode)

EXERCISE 8–1 The HCPCS Index

Using the Index, find and verify the following codes in the tabular section of the HCPCS coding reference. Indicate the key word(s) used to search the Index.

1. _____ Injection, chlorpheniramine maleate, per 10 mg.

   Key word(s):_____

2. _____ Fern test

   Key word(s):_____

3. _____ Benesch boot, pair, junior

   Key word(s):_____

4. _____ Safety belt/pelvic strap for wheelchair

   Key word(s):_____

5. _____ Sterilizing agent for dialysis equipment, per gallon

   Key word(s):_____

6. _____ Colorectal screening by colonoscopy on high-risk individual

   Key word(s):_____

DETERMINING CARRIER RESPONSIBILITY

The specific HCPCS level II code determines whether the claim is sent to the local Medicare carrier (LMC) or the DME Regional Carrier (DMERC). HCPCS National codes beginning with D, G, M, P, or R fall under the jurisdiction of the LMC. The DMERC is responsible for level II codes beginning with B, E, K, and L. Codes beginning with A, J, Q, and V may be assigned individually to either the LMC or the DMERC. The Local Medicare Carrier and the DMERC distribute annual lists of valid level II codes. They can also give the provider the complete billing instructions for those services.

EXERCISE 8-2 Recognizing Carrier Responsibility

Using the above criteria and the codes and descriptions listed in Exercise 8–1, identify the codes sent to the LMC, the DMERC, or those possibly assigned to either carrier.

Local Medicare Carrier: _____

DMERC: _____

Local Medicare Carrier or DMERC: _____

Because the DMERC is another Medicare carrier, each entity dispensing medical equipment and supplies must register as a provider. When the doctor treats a Medicare patient for a broken ankle and supplies the patient with crutches, two claims are generated. The one for the fracture care, or professional service, is sent to the local Medicare carrier; the claim for the crutches is sent to the DMERC. The physician must register with both carriers, review the billing rules, comply with the claim form instructions, and forward the claims correctly to secure payment for both services. If the doctor is not registered with the DMERC to provide medical equipment and supplies, the patient is given a prescription for crutches to take to a local DMEPOS dealer.

At one time the local Medicare carriers (LMCs) processed all claims for DME. The emphasis on keeping seniors in their own homes led to a rapid expansion in DME services and dealers. Also, many of the larger companies operated in several states and sent their claims to multiple Medicare carriers. Unfortunately, a few companies formed for the sole purpose of collecting as much money as possible from the Medicare program and then closed down. When HCFA began to investigate and pursue fraudulent claims, it became apparent that DME billings were out of control, so HCFA decided to have all DME claims processed by only four regional carriers, the DMERCs. This allowed the LMCs to concentrate on the familiar, traditional claims of providers billing for services, not equipment.

Some services, such as most dental procedures, are excluded as Medicare benefits by law and will not be covered by either carrier. Splints and casts for traumatic injuries have CPT numbers that would be used to report these supplies or services to the LMC. Because the review procedures for adding new codes to level II is a much shorter process, new medical and surgical services may first be assigned a level II code and then incorporated into CPT at a later date.

ASSIGNING HCPCS NATIONAL (LEVEL II) CODES

Some services must be reported by assigning both a CPT and a HCPCS code. The most common scenario uses the CPT code for administration of an injection and the HCPCS code to identify the medication. Most drugs have qualifying terms such as dosage limits that could alter the quantity reported (see Figure 8-4, page 222). If a drug stating "per 50 mg" is administered in a 70-mg dose, the quantity billed would be "2." If you administered only 15 mg of a drug stating "up to 20 mg," the quantity is "1." Imagine how much money providers lose by reporting only the CPT code for injections. Unless the payer or insurance plan advises the provider that they do not pay separately for the medication injected, always report this combination of codes.

It is possible that a particular service would be assigned a CPT code, a level II HCPCS code, and a local code. Which one should you report? The answer is found in the instructions from the payer. Most commercial insurers require the CPT code. Medicare gives HCPCS National (level II) codes the highest priority unless there is a local code for the same service. If the CPT code is general and the HCPCS National (level II) code is more specific, use the level II code.

Most supplies are included in the charge for the office visit or the procedure. CPT provides code 99070 for all supplies and materials exceeding those usually included in the primary service or procedure performed. However, this CPT code may be too general to ensure correct payment. If the office provides additional supplies when performing a service, the HCPCS level II codes may identify the supplies in sufficient detail to secure proper reimbursement.

While HCFA developed this system, some HCPCS level I and II services are not payable by Medicare. Medicare may also place qualifications or conditions on payment for some services. As an example, an EKG is a covered

J

? ☑ **J0475** Injection, baclofen, 10 mg
MCM 2049
Use this code for Lioresal.

? ☑ **J0476** Injection, baclofen, 50 mcg for intrathecal trial
MCM 2049

? ☑ **J0500** Injection, dicyclomine HCl, up to 20 mg
MCM 2049
Use this code for Bentyl, Dilomine, Antispas, Dibent, Di-Spaz, Neoquess, Or-Tyl, Spasmoject.

? ☑ **J0510** Injection, benzquinamide HCl, up to 50 mg
MCM 2049
Use this code for Emete-con.

? ☑ **J0515** Injection, benztropine mesylate, per 1 mg
MCM 2049
Use this code for Cogentin.

? ☑ **J0520** Injection, bethanechol chloride mytonachol or urecholine, up to 5 mg
MCM 2049
Use this code for Urecholine.

? ☑ **J0530** Injection, penicillin G benzathine and penicillin G procaine, up to 600,000 units
MCM 2049
Use this code for Bicillin C-R.

? ☑ **J0540** Injection, penicillin G benzathine and penicillin G procaine, up to 1,200,000 units
MCM 2049
Use this code for Bicillin C-R, Bicillin C-R 900/300.

? ☑ **J0550** Injection, penicillin G benzathine and penicillin G procaine, up to 2,400,000 units
MCM 2049
Use this code for Bicillin C-R.

? ☑ **J0560** Injection, penicillin G benzathine, up to 600,000 units
MCM 2049
Use this code for Bicillin L-A, Permapen.

? **J0570** Injection, penicillin G benzathine, up to 1,200,000 units
MCM 2049
Use this code for Bicillin L-A, Permapen.

? ☑ **J0580** Injection, penicillin G benzathine, up to 2,400,000 units
MCM 2049
Use this code for Bicillin L-A, Permapen.

? ☑ **J0585** Botulinum toxin type A, per unit
MCM 2049

? ☑ **J0590** Injection, ethylnorepinephrine HCl, 1 ml
MCM 2049
Use this code for Bronkephrine

? ☑ **J0600** Injection, edetate calcium disodium, up to 1000 mg
MCM 2049
Use this code for Calcium Disodium Versenate, Calcium EDTA)

? ☑ **J0610** Injection, calcium gluconate, per 10 ml
MCM 2049
Use this code for Kaleinate.

? ☑ **J0620** Injection, calcium glycerophosphate and calcium lactate, per 10 ml
MCM 2049
Use this code for Calphosan.

? ☑ **J0630** Injection, calcitonin-salmon, up to 400 units
MCM 2049
Use this code for Calcimar, Miacalcin.

? ☑ **J0635** Injection, calcitriol, 1 mcg ampule
MCM 2049
Use this code for Calcijex.

? ☑ **J0640** Injection, leucovorin calcium, per 50 mg
MCM 2049
Use this code for Wellcovorin.

? ☑ **J0670** Injection, mepivacaine HCl, per 10 ml
MCM 2049
Use this code for Carbocaine, Polocaine, Isocaine HCl.

? ☑ **J0690** Injection, cefazolin sodium, up to 500 mg
MCM 2049
Use this code for Ancef, Kefzol, Zolicef.

? ☑ **J0694** Injection, cefoxitin sodium, 1 g
MCM 2049
Use this code for Mefoxin.

? ☑ **J0695** Injection, cefonicid sodium, 1 g
MCM 2049
Use this code for Monocid.

? ☑ **J0696** Injection, ceftriaxone sodium, per 250 mg
MCM 2049
Use this code for Rocephin.

? ☑ **J0697** Injection, sterile cefuroxime sodium, per 750 mg
MCM 2049
Use this code for Kefurox, Zinacef.

? ☑ **J0698** Cefotaxime sodium, per g
MCM 2049
Use this code for Claforan.

J

   ☑ Quantity Alert   ● New Code   ▲ Revised Code   **HCPCS 2001**

Figure 8-4 Page from HCPCS 2001 J Section (Permission to reprint granted by Medicode)

service for a cardiac problem but is not covered when performed as part of a routine examination. Also, the payment for some services may be left to the carrier's discretion. Two HCFA publications assist the carriers in correctly processing claims. The **Coverage Issues Manual (CIM)** advises the local Medicare carrier (LMC) whether a service is covered or excluded under Medicare regulations. The **Medicare Carriers Manual (MCM)** directs the LMC to pay a service or reject it using a specific "remark" or explanation code.

There are almost 3000 HCPCS level II codes, but you may find that no code exists for the procedure or service you need to report. Unlike CPT, HCPCS level II does not have a consistent method of establishing codes for reporting "unlisted procedure" services. If the LMC does not provide special instructions for reporting these services in HCPCS, report them with the proper "unlisted procedure" code from CPT. Remember to submit documentation explaining the procedure or service when using the "unlisted procedure" codes.

HCFA developed the level II codes for Medicare, but increasing numbers of commercial insurance companies are adopting them. Very few insurance plans or payers accept the level III (local) codes and modifiers. They do not have access to the codes distributed by the Medicare carriers nor can they price their insurance products to allow for payment of these unknown services.

HCPCS MODIFIERS

Like CPT modifiers, HCPCS level II and level III modifiers tell the payer that the service or supply has been altered in some manner. Level II and level III modifiers are alphanumeric, using two letters or a combination of letters and numbers.

Level I Modifiers Level I two-digit modifiers are developed for use with CPT codes.

Level II Modifiers Level II two-character (alphanumeric) modifiers are developed for use with CPT and level II (national) codes.

Level III Modifiers Level III modifiers are developed by the local Medicare carrier and begin with the letters W–Z. Carriers may also require the use of a CPT modifier with a particular local HCPCS level III code, or a level III modifier with a certain CPT code. These special requirements may be part of national Medicare monitoring or regional data collection and usually do not impact the reimbursement for the service. Updated modifier use rules appear in the carrier bulletins, and a complete list of valid local codes and modifiers is printed and distributed annually by the carrier.

ASSIGNING HCPCS NATIONAL (LEVEL II) MODIFIERS

Some level II modifiers are two letters, others contain a letter and a number, and some modifiers are constructed by using special tables. The 2001 HCPCS includes special modifiers to identify CPT services provided by nonphysicians.

> **EXAMPLE**
>
> A clinical psychologist is identified by the level II modifier -AH, and a clinical social worker uses modifier -AJ. Either care provider can report:

90804 Individual psychotherapy, insight oriented, behavior modifying and/or supportive, in an office or outpatient facility, approximately 20–30 minutes face-to-face with the patient

The clinical psychologist would bill 90804-AH; the clinical social worker would bill 90804-AJ.

Because Physician Assistants, Nurse Practitioners, and Clinical Nurse Specialists are now assigned their own Medicare billing numbers, the modifier -AS added to a surgery code indicates that they served as an assistant at surgery. A physician serving as an assistant at the same surgery would report the surgical code with a modifier in the CPT modifier range of -80 to -82.

Other frequently used National HCPCS modifiers are:

-CC   Procedure code change. (Use CC when the procedure code submitted was changed either for administrative reasons or because an incorrect code was filed.) A -CC on a claim advises the carrier that this is a correction to a previously filed but rejected claim.

-GA   **Waiver of liability** statement on file (protects beneficiaries from liability when they receive services, in good faith, from a Medicare provider for which Medicare payment is subsequently denied as *not reasonable and necessary*). This modifier advises Medicare that the provider has obtained the patient's agreement to pay for a service that is sometimes rejected by Medicare. This agreement is also called an **Advance Beneficiary Notice (ABN)**.

   ■ **NOTE:** Use of -GA is *not* appropriate for services that are never reimbursed by Medicare. ■

-LT   Left side (used to identify procedures performed on the left side of the body).

-RT   Right side (used to identify procedures performed on the right side of the body).

-QB   Physician providing service in a rural **Health Personnel Shortage Area (HPSA)**. This modifier appended to an Evaluation and Management (E&M) service tells the carrier that the patient was seen in a rural area underserved by health care providers (as defined by the Bureau of the Census). Medicare makes an additional payment to the physician for these services.

-QU   Physician providing service in an urban HPSA.

   Modifier -QU reported with E&M services indicates a medically underserved urban area.

Transportation Services have special single-character modifiers to indicate the origin and destination of the service. These are used in pairs; the first character indicates the origin of the transportation service and the second shows the destination.

EXAMPLE

H   Hospital

P   Physician's office

R   Residence

A transportation service from the patient's home to the hospital would be assigned the modifier -RH.

There are situations when level I (CPT) codes and modifiers are used with level II (National HCPCS) codes and modifiers.

EXAMPLE

A Medicare patient undergoes tendon surgery on the right palm and left middle finger:

26170   Excision of tendon, palm, flexor, single (separate procedure), each

26180   Excision of tendon, finger, flexor (separate procedure), each tendon

The coding would be reported as:

26180 -F2

26170 -59 -RT

The finger surgery has a higher relative value and is therefore the major procedure reported on the first line of the claim form. The modifier -F2 identifies the third digit, left hand. Modifier -59 on the second line reports this "separate procedure" code as a distinct procedural service, unrelated to the other procedure; the -RT further clarifies that this service was performed on the right hand.

Although the terminology contained in HCPCS level II is sometimes confusing or unfamiliar, clearly these codes describe necessary medical services and procedures. Unless a coding system is developed that includes all professional services as well as services and procedures performed by all providers, we will continue to use a multilevel procedure coding system.

REVIEW

CHALLENGE EXERCISE

1. Using the current edition of *HCPCS National Codes*, assign the correct codes, HCPCS modifier(s) and quantity to each of the following services.

   a. B-12 injection not covered by Medicare, but patient agrees to pay.

   Code _____   Modifier(s) _____   Quantity _____

   b. Purchase of new rolling chair with 6" wheels. Rental declined.

   Code _____   Modifier(s) _____   Quantity _____

    c. 100 reagent strips for home glucose monitor. Patient not on insulin.

        Code _____ Modifier(s) _____ Quantity _____

    d. Three fecal-occult blood tests, screening for colorectal malignancy at clinic in rural under-served area.

        Code _____ Modifier(s) _____ Quantity _____

    e. Third month rental, high-humidity oxygen concentrator, 1225 cu. ft.

        Code _____ Modifier(s) _____ Quantity _____

2. Using the current editions of *CPT and HCPCS National Codes*, assign the correct code and the HCPCS modifier(s) and quantity to each of the following scenarios.

    a. Metatarsophalangeal synovectomy, third digit, left foot

        Code _____ Modifier(s) _____ Quantity _____

    b. HemoCue 3 sample GTT

        Code _____ Modifier(s) _____ Quantity _____

    c. Closed manipulation, left Potts fracture, by physician who has opted out of Medicare

        Code _____ Modifier(s) _____ Quantity _____

    d. Anesthesiologist provides medical direction of his employee for radical nasal surgery (quantity not required)

        Code _____ Modifier(s) _____

    e. Psychological testing, 2 hours, by clinical psychologist

        Code _____ Modifier(s) _____ Quantity _____

HCFA Reimbursement Issues

OBJECTIVES

Upon successful completion of this chapter, you should be able to:

1. Define the following terms, phrases, and abbreviations:

Resource-Based Relative Value Scale system (RBRVS)

relative value units (RVU)

conversion factor (CF)

geographic practice cost index (GPCI)

Federal Register (FR)

Local Medicare Carrier (LMC)

fee schedule

Medicare Fee Schedule (MFS)

budget neutral

nonparticipating provider (nonPAR)

accept assignment

limiting charge (LC)

Medicare Summary Notice (MSN)

beneficiaries

balance billing

durable medical equipment, prosthetic and orthotic supplies (DMEPOS)

legislation

most favored nation (MFN)

nurse practitioner (NP)

physician assistant (PA)

scope of practice

"incident to"

constant attendance

fraud

false claim

abuse

Diagnosis Related Groups (DRG)

episode of care

site of service differential

managed care organization (MCO)

Coverage Issues Manual (CIM)

Medicare Carriers Manual (MCM)

E&M Documentation Guidelines

type of service (TOS)

place of service (POS)

global service

2. Explain the national Correct Coding Initiative.

3. Identify sources for the Correct Coding Initiative rules.

4. Explain the Billing and Coding Compliance issues.

INTRODUCTION

Since the Medicare program was implemented in 1965, expenditures have increased at an unanticipated rate, and the news media frequently report that the program will be bankrupt in a few years. In 1983, the Health Care Financing Administration (HCFA) implemented the Diagnosis Related Groups (DRG) Prospective Payment System (PPS) to control the cost of inpatient care. In 1992, Congress changed Medicare law to require that physicians be paid according to the **Resource-Based Relative Value Scale system (RBRVS).** This system divides all services into **relative value units (RVUs)** or payment components of physician work and practice expenses, and malpractice costs. Payment limits were also established by adjusting the RVUs and the **conversion factor (CF)**, the dollar multiplier that converts RVUs into payments (the 2001 CF is $38.2581). The **geographic practice cost index (GPCI)** takes into consideration physicians' work and practice expenses and malpractice costs, as compared with national averages for each within various geographic regions of the country. RBRVS specifies that the combined physician fee schedule of payments cannot exceed $20 million over the unadjusted amounts for the same services.

The actual formula is:

$$(RVUw \times GPCIw) + (RVUpe \times GPCIpe) + (RVUm \times GPCIm) \times CF = \text{total payment}$$

where: w = work expense   pe = practice expense
        m = malpractice insurance cost   CF = conversion factor

Using a computer program increases accuracy when calculating this complex formula.

While the RBRVS system is used to determine payment for Medicare Part B (physician) services, anesthesia, radiology, and pathology/laboratory services require special consideration. Payment for anesthesia services is based upon the actual time an anesthesiologist spends with a patient whereas payment for radiology services varies according to place of service (e.g., institutional versus noninstitutional setting). Payment for pathology services varies according to the number of patients served. For example, pathology services that include clinical laboratory management and the supervision of technologists are covered and paid as hospital services. However, a pathology service that is directed to an individual patient in a hospital setting is reimbursable under Medicare Part B physician payment rules.

THE MEDICARE FEE SCHEDULE

Each year new services, changes in technology, and the way procedures are performed result in adjustments to the Medicare fee schedule. HCFA revalues all HCFA Common Procedure Coding System (HCPCS) services for the upcoming year to remain within the $20 million limitation. In late November or early December, the ***Federal Register* (FR)** publishes new payment values for most procedure codes.

INTERNET LINK

The payment schedules are also available as free downloads from www.hcfa.gov/stats/pufiles.htm (see Figure 9-1).

When reviewing the Medicare fee schedule, you may note fees listed for services not commonly billed to Medicare. Examples include obstetrical deliveries or hernia repairs for patients under 5 years of age. Because many private payers and insurance plans have adopted the RBRVS system, fees are available for most CPT/HCPCS codes. Some services inappropriate for Medicare patients (newborn care) or specifically eliminated because of coding manual terminology (under 5 years of age), are prohibited by law as Medicare benefits.

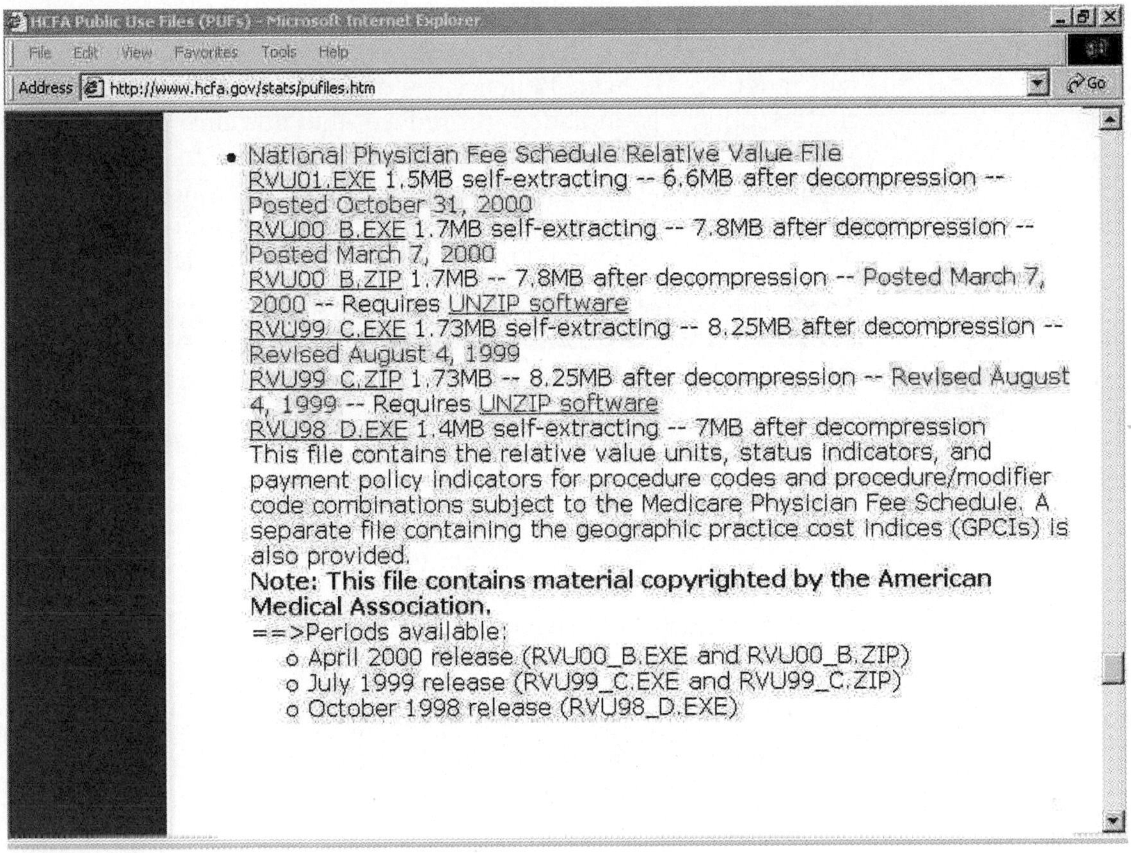

FIGURE 9-1 Web site containing HCFA Public Use Files (Reprinted according to hcfa.gov Web Site Content Reuse Policy)

Local Fee Schedules

Local Medicare Carriers (LMC) translate the HCPCS RVUs, GPCIs, and the CF into a fee schedule and distribute it to enrolled providers. A **fee schedule** is a complete listing of fees used by health plans to pay doctors and other providers. The **Medicare Fee Schedule (MFS)** is a feature of the Physician Payment Reform legislation that was phased in over a five-year period beginning in 1992. MFS amounts are based on Relative Value Units (RVUs), Geographic Practice Cost Indices (GPCIs), and the national Conversion Factor (CF). These locally distributed annual fee schedules also advise the non-participating (NonPAR) physician of the limiting charge (the maximum fee the doctor may charge) for services. Carriers also distribute quarterly updates to the payment schedule for medications, or "J" codes, to reflect actual market costs for these drugs. Throughout the year, LMCs may make adjustments to the fee schedules to keep the Medicare Part B program within the $20 million limit, or **budget-neutral,** as prescribed by the Balanced Budget Act (BBA) of 1997.

Limiting Charge

A **nonparticipating provider (nonPAR)** is a doctor or supplier who does not accept assignment on all Medicare claims. To **accept assignment** means that the provider agrees to accept Medicare's fee as payment in full. When nonPARs do not accept assignment on claims, they are subject to a **limiting charge (LC)**, which is the maximum a patient can be charged for a covered service. The limit is 115% of the Medicare Fee Schedule, and certain services are not subject to the limiting charge (e.g., medical supplies and equipment).

Limiting charge information appears on the **Medicare Summary Notice (MSN)** (previously called an *Explanation of Medicare Benefits*, or *EOMB*) which notifies Medicare beneficiaries of actions taken on claims. The limiting charge policy is intended to reduce the amount patients enrolled in Medicare, referred to as **beneficiaries**, are expected to pay when they receive health care services. If a participating and a nonparticipating physician charge a fee of $45.00 for the same office visit, amounts billed and reimbursement received would be different for each physician.

EXAMPLE

CPT code 99213, E/M visit, has the following reimbursement assignments:

Participating physician fee schedule	$ 41.08
NonPAR fee schedule (41.08 – 5%)	$ 39.03
Limiting charge (39.03 – 115%)	$ 44.88

The Medicare participating physician reports:

Regular fee for office visit	$ 45.00
Medicare 80% payment of $41.08 allowed charge	$ 32.86
Beneficiary is billed for 20% of $41.08	$ 8.22

The NonPAR physician reports:

Regular fee for office visit	$45.00
Limiting charge for office visit	$ 44.88
Medicare 80% payment of $39.03 allowed charge	$ 31.22
Beneficiary is billed the balance of $44.88	$ 13.66
(44.88 – 31.22 = 13.66)	

Generally, participating physicians report their actual fees to Medicare but adjust, or write-off, the uncollectible portion of their charge when they receive payment. NonPAR doctors usually report only the *limiting charge* as their fee. Billing write-off or adjustment amounts to beneficiaries is called **balance billing** and is prohibited by Medicare regulations. In this illustration using CPT code 99213, the write-off amounts are:

Participating physician	$ 3.92
NonPAR physician	$ .12

The participating/nonparticipating provider difference of $5.44 ($13.66 minus $8.22 = $5.44) in this illustration can be significant for people living on a fixed income. Beneficiaries frequently ask, "Does the doctor participate with Medicare?" when calling for an appointment. With very few exceptions, people who qualify for Medicare are not allowed to purchase other primary health insurance. HCFA must be certain that Medicare beneficiaries are not required to pay excessive amounts out-of-pocket for health care services. To protect Medicare enrollees financially, providers must comply with extensive rules and regulations.

Carrier Priced Services

The local Medicare carrier may determine the payment level for some procedures and for drugs. Any services billed to Medicare with a HCPCS level III or local code (beginning with letters W–Z) are paid according to a fee schedule determined by the carrier responsible for issuing and maintaining the specific procedure code. Each **durable medical equipment, prosthetic and orthotic supplies (DMEPOS)** provider or supplier also establishes the payment schedule for supplies and equipment within HCFA specified guidelines.

HCFA REGULATIONS THAT IMPACT REIMBURSEMENT

While Congress enacts Medicare **legislation** (laws), HCFA develops guidelines and regulations to enforce the laws. Remaining up-to-date regarding these rules is critical because medical practices receive much of their income from the Medicare program. Additionally, Medicare regulations state that the provider is responsible for knowing all of the rules that apply to services billed to the program. Fortunately, the local Medicare carrier (LMC) publishes provider manuals and newsletters, in addition to the fee schedule, advising medical practices of these special Medicare rules.

INTERNET LINK

An estimated 17,000 pages of Medicare regulations are published on the Internet at www.hcfa.gov (see Figure 9-2).

Special Payment Policies

The $20 million cost restriction requirement results in continual changes in the ways HCFA limits Medicare payments. One proposal, not implemented in two previous appearances but certain to be proposed again, would require providers to adjust their Medicare billings to the lowest amount they are willing to accept from one of their contracted managed care plans.

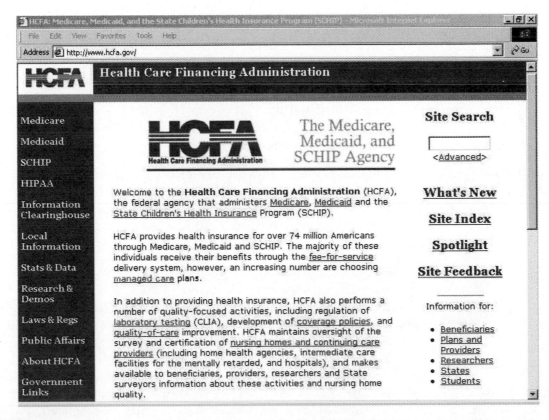

FIGURE 9-2 HCFA's Web site (Reprinted according to hcfa.gov Web Site Content Reuse Policy)

EXAMPLE

Medicare fee allowed for 99213: $ 45.00

The provider participated with
a managed care plan; that plan's
fee allowed for 99213: $ 35.00

Should Congress approve this billing restriction, providers would be limited to charging only $35.00, the fee they are willing to accept from a managed care plan. Participation could no longer be an issue because NonPARs would follow the same rule.

EXAMPLE

All physicians would report:
    Fee for expanded problem-
    focused office visit (99213) $ 35.00
    Medicare 80% payment $ 28.00
    Beneficiary owes 20% $ 7.00

This type of Medicare billing requirement would save the program money and reduce the beneficiary's obligation as well. The Medicare beneficiary who owed either $8.22 or $13.66 in the previous illustration, would now owe the provider only $7.00.

This change would grant Medicare a **most favored nation (MFN)** status, assuring the program of the best price available. An MFN is described as an entity that receives the most beneficial contract or price available to anyone. Clearly this regulation, if approved, could reduce the provider's income.

Consider how this would affect the provider's billing office. This proposed Medicare regulation would require providers to monitor payments from all payers and report to Medicare the lowest allowable amount accepted from any contracted plan. Adding to the problem, many managed care plans do not sell one insurance product but negotiate a separate contract with each insured group. Frequently the employer or group retains their original fee schedule. Payer X could have 100 or more fee schedules associated with individual contracts.

Medicare as a Secondary Payer

Some Medicare beneficiaries are covered by an employer plan if they are still working or if their spouse is employed and the health plan covers family members. Medicare has very specific rules about payment when another insurance is primary. This billing order is discussed in the Medicare chapter of this text.

"Incident to"

Another example of Medicare regulations that affect the reporting of services involves nurse practitioners (NP) and physician assistants (PA). A **nurse practitioner (NP)** has two or more years of advanced training, has passed a special exam, and often works as a primary care provider along with a physician. A **physician assistant (PA)** has two or more years of advanced training, has passed a special exam, works with a physician, and can do some of the same tasks as the doctor. These health care professionals are licensed by the state, and state law defines their **scope of practice**, which means the state determines the health care services that may be practiced, and Medicare restricts payment for services performed by these practitioners. A PA's state license may permit them to care for patients in a hospital, but until recently Medicare did not provide payment when PAs performed hospital services. Medicare now issues special provider numbers for NPs and PAs so that their services can be billed directly to Medicare. NPs and PAs are paid at 85% of the Medicare Fee Schedule.

Before they were issued billing numbers, NP/PA services were billed under the **"incident to"** provision. This Medicare regulation permitted billing Medicare under the physician's billing number for ancillary personnel services when those services were "incident to" a service performed by a physician. Thus, an EKG performed by a medical assistant in the physician's office is billed under the "incident to" provision. Another regulation states that "incident to" services must be those services typically performed in a doctor's office. This excludes services performed in the hospital, so the hospital services of the NP or PA were not payable by Medicare even though they were within the scope of practice in that state. Medicare does not regulate who can perform a service; that is the responsibility of the individual state. However, the program can and does specify conditions that must be present for payment of services to be rendered.

Constant Attendance

Medicare regulations define the *constant attendance* requirement for critical care services. The words alone would imply that the physician must be with the patient constantly to report this service. However, CPT and Medicare define **constant attendance** as including the time spent at the bedside as well as time spent on the hospital floor or unit. Hospital floor or unit time can involve reviewing the patient's laboratory work and other documents or discussing the critically ill patient's care with the medical staff. These activities could occur at the bedside, at the nurse's station, or elsewhere on the floor. Services for a critically ill patient, such as telephone calls from the home or office, are not separately billable because they do not occur at the patient's bedside or on the hospital floor. Other payers, such as Blue Cross and Blue Shield or a managed care plan, may only permit billing "constant attendance" for the time spent at the bedside of a critically ill patient.

MEDICARE REIMBURSEMENT

Some payers adopt Medicare rules almost as soon as they are released. Perhaps they believe that if the rules save money for Medicare, they should save money for their plans as well. Or, they may want to make claim filing as uniform as possible, eliminating billing rules specific to their plans. Providers and billers have difficulty applying the unique but inconsistent payer rules for all of the services that they provide. Medicare has established significant fines and penalties for repeated billing errors that are determined to be fraudulent or *false claims*. Because of these penalties, billers try to remember the Medicare rules and may then erroneously apply them to claims for other payers. This plays a role in the confusion that surrounds Medicare reimbursement issues.

Fraud, False Claims, and Abuse

As discussed in Chapter 5, federal regulations define **fraud** as a deliberate misrepresentation to obtain money the provider is not entitled to receive. For Medicare, this would constitute knowingly reporting a procedure not performed because it pays more money than the procedure actually performed. A **false claim** is created when an incorrect fee is reported or a provider makes no attempt to collect the deductible and coinsurance due from the patient. In both cases, the provider misrepresented the "fee" for service. If the provider is charged and convicted, each false claim service is subject to a $10,000.00 fine plus three times the amount of the claim, a period of exclusion from the Medicare program, and other monetary penalties. The federal government has also implemented regulations that establish the same fines and penalties for **abuse** that involve, for example, errors made when reporting provider charges.

Hospital Inpatient Payment

Since 1983, Medicare has reimbursed hospitals for inpatient care based on the patient's diagnosis. A system called **Diagnosis Related Groups (DRG)**, provides a lump sum payment dependent on the patient's condition or diagnosis. Hospital services are provided during a defined **episode of care**, limited by the admission and discharge dates for that hospitalization, and may relate to a single event such as uncontrolled diabetes or multiple diagnoses. Because the physician might see a patient in the office for many years to control diabetes, for example, the patient's episode of care can last a lifetime.

 **INTERNET LINK**

For information on additional Medicare payment systems (e.g., Home Health PPS and Hospital Outpatient PPS), refer to www.hcfa.gov/medicare/payment.htm (see Figure 9-3).

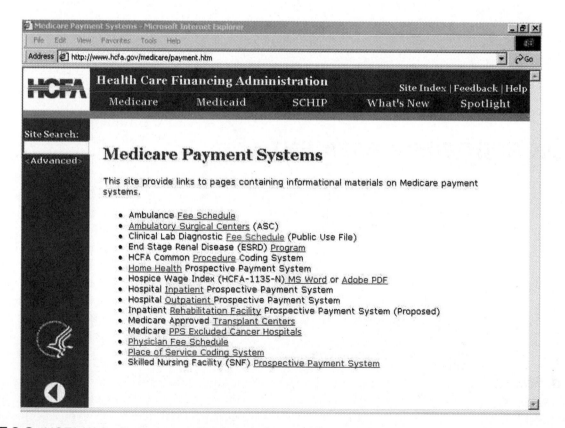

FIGURE 9-3 HCFA Web site that contains descriptions of Medicare Payment Systems (Reprinted according to hcfa.gov Web Site Content Reuse Policy)

Location of Service Adjustment

Physicians are usually reimbursed on a fee-for-service basis with payments established by the RBRVS. When office-based services are performed in a facility, such as a hospital or outpatient setting, payments are reduced because the doctor did not provide supplies, utilities, or the costs of running the facility. This is known as the **site of service differential**. Other rules govern the services performed by hospital-based providers and teaching physicians. This chapter discusses rules that affect private practice physicians billing under the RBRVS.

Managed Care Options

Because of savings associated with **managed care organizations (MCOs)**, Medicare has expanded managed care options to all beneficiaries. Medicare+Choice (Part C) was established as part of the Balanced Budget Act of 1997 (BBA) and expanded options for health care delivery under Medicare. Medicare beneficiaries can continue to receive their benefits through the original fee-for-service program, but most beneficiaries enrolled in both Hospital Insurance (HI) and Supplementary Medical Insurance (SMI) can choose to participate in a Medicare+Choice plan instead. Organizations that contract as Medicare+Choice plans must meet specific organizational and financial requirements. Medicare+Choice is discussed in greater detail in the Medicare chapter of this text.

HCFA must approve a Medicare managed care plan before it is allowed to enroll Medicare beneficiaries. Medicare MCOs must provide coverage that is similar to a fee-for-service program, to include hospital care and office visits. Many plans also offer prescription drug coverage, eyeglasses, hearing aids, and other services that are excluded under the regular Medicare program. These extra features attract patients to managed care plans. The MCO must, however, restrict patient access to any provider the patient chooses.

Because Medicare's managed care plan differs from an insurance company's regular product line, there are additional rules to follow for billing purposes. These are very different from the Medicare fee-for-service rules and the payer's regular business billing manuals.

Fee-for-Service Billing Instructions

Medicare sends carriers the **Coverage Issues Manual (CIM)** and the **Medicare Carriers Manual (MCM)** to assist them in paying claims accurately (see Figure 9-4 on page 236). The CIM identifies services payable by Medicare and conditions eligible for payment. The MCM advises carriers as to the process for paying and denying claims. Portions of these volumes and other HCFA instructions are forwarded to providers as part of the provider manual and bulletins distributed by carriers. Many publications from private organizations, as well as those from the Medicare carrier, attempt to organize and clarify the Medicare billing rules. Perhaps no procedures have been the subject of more instructions than the evaluation and management services.

INTERNET LINK

The Coverage Issues Manual (CIM) and Medicare Carriers Manual (MCM) are also available as downloadable files on HCFA's Web site at www.hcfa.gov/pubforms/p2192toc.htm.

Evaluation and Management Services

HCFA requested a change in CPT "visit" codes for office and hospital services as part of the 1992 RBRVS implementation. When CPT revised the visit codes to create evaluation and management (E&M) services, payers that required

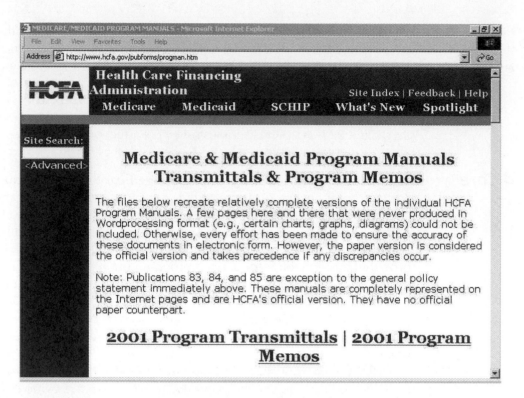

FIGURE 9-4 HCFA Web site that contains downloadable program manuals for Medicare and Medicaid programs (Reprinted according to hcfa.gov Web Site Content Reuse Policy)

the reporting of CPT codes updated the codes. Because physicians report these services, Medicare's requested change had an enormous impact on the entire payment system.

So that Medicare could be certain they were paying for correct levels of service, HCFA released **E&M Documentation Guidelines** developed with the assistance of the American Medical Association (AMA). These guidelines have been revised since their introduction in 1994 and are still being clarified. The guidelines implemented in 1994, and referred to as the 1995 E&M Documentation Guidelines, were criticized because requirements for a complete single system examination were unclear. It was felt that because medical reviewers rarely gave credit for complete single-system exams, specialists were not able to meet the documentation requirements for higher level E&M services. In addition, it was difficult to ensure work equivalency between multi- and single-system exams.

In response, an alternative set of documentation guidelines was developed to include ten single-system examinations and clarification of definitions for multi-system examinations. These guidelines are referred to as the 1997 E&M Documentation Guidelines. The original intent was to replace the 1995 with the 1997 documentation guidelines. However, many physicians objected because they perceived the 1997 documentation guidelines as too complicated and having the potential to detract from patient care. Therefore, in April 1998, HCFA instructed Medicare carriers to use both the 1995 and 1997 documentation guidelines when reviewing records, and physicians could use whichever set of guidelines was most advantageous.

In June 2000, revised draft guidelines were released that represented a simplification of the 1997 E&M Documentation Guidelines (which were based on the physician's performance and documentation of physical examination elements. The draft 2000 E&M Documentation Guidelines reduced the physical examination requirement to three levels, based on the number of organ systems examined (review of systems is also based on number of organ systems). For example, a detailed examination includes findings from three to eight organ systems, rather than the total number of elements examined. Thus, the counting of examination elements is basically eliminated. Medical decision making was also simplified to three levels, with clear requirements that can be cross-referenced to clinical vignettes (currently under development). HCFA will pilot test the draft 2000 E&M Documentation Guidelines, and continuing education will be provided as to their implementation. It is expected that the final guidelines will be adopted in 2002; until then, providers should continue to use either the 1995 or 1997 documentation guidelines, whichever is deemed more advantageous (see Table 9-1).

INTERNET LINK

Go to www.hcfa.gov/medicare/mcarpti.htm and scroll down to the heading *Documentation Guidelines for Evaluation and Management Services* to download all three versions of the Documentation Guidelines and to click on the *Town Hall Presentation*, which was created in MS PowerPoint.

Table 9-1 *Side-by-side comparison of HCFAs E&M Documentation Guidelines (Courtesy of HCFA)*

KEY E&M COMPONENT	1995 E&M GUIDELINES	1997 E&M GUIDELINES	DRAFT 2000 E&M GUIDELINES
History (HPI)	• Specific requirements	• Specific requirements	• Clearer requirements • Explicit recognition of medication monitoring
History (ROS)	• Specific body area or organ system requirements	• Specific body area or organ system requirements	• Less required • Clearer • Examples are provided
History (PFSH)	• Brief information required	• Brief information required	• No difference
Physical Exam	• Specifically referenced general multi-system exam • Description of single-system exams inadequate • 4 levels • Requirements not clear	• 1 general multi-system and 10 single-system exams • 4 levels • Very prescriptive • Confusing shading and bullets format • Requirements often not relevant	• Physician tailors documentation to exam • Only 3 levels • Vignette examples • No bullets, no shading • Minimal counting • No irrelevant facts to record
Medical Decision Making	• 4 levels • Examples not reflective of clinical assessments and plans	• 4 levels • Examples not reflective of clinical assessments and plans	• Only 3 levels • Physician tailors documentation to assessment and plan of treatment • Vignettes (examples)

Regardless of which version of E&M Documentation Guidelines is used, a properly documented patient record is an essential component to providing good clinical care and to supporting the level of E&M service code submitted on a claim. When care is not properly documented (e.g., inadequate or nonexistent documentation), improper payments result. In addition, according to the Office of the Inspector General, audits reveal that it is not unusual for well-intentioned physicians to code as much as two levels apart for identical services due to varying interpretations of definitions of CPT histories, physical examinations, and medical decision making.

Medicare regulations do not permit payment for most preventive medicine services or for screening diagnostic tests. Medicare pays for the treatment of disease; it does not pay for services needed to screen for diseases in asymptomatic individuals. Many Medicare beneficiaries undergo periodic physical examinations to ensure that potential health threats are found early and treated. In fact, routine examinations are advised to detect the early onset of breast or colon cancer. Some patients have Medicare supplemental insurance provided by a former employer that pays for Medicare excluded services. To receive benefits from these plans, it may be necessary to demonstrate that Medicare has rejected charges for such services. If the patient requests it, the office should report these preventive medicine services to Medicare.

A confusing situation occurs if the patient is scheduled for routine physical examination and then, as part of that visit, receives separately identifiable office services for a specific disorder. Medicare has provided the following illustration of how to report such a combination of services.

EXAMPLE

The physician charges $145.00 for an office visit.

Service	Fee	Diagnosis Code
99212-25	$ 35.00	250.10
99397	$ 110.00	V70.0

When Medicare processes this claim, the physician will receive $28.00 (80% of the $35.00 office visit); the patient will owe $117.00, the $7.00 (or 20% of the office visit) plus the full charge for the physical examination. The explanation of Medicare benefits will contain information needed to determine the correct payment to be made by the supplemental insurer.

Because it is better to prevent disease than to cure it, Congress passed legislation that changed regulations so that some screening services are now covered. In addition to pneumonia and flu vaccines, Medicare pays for a screening pap smear every 3 years, a mammogram every 2 years for females, and an annual feces for occult blood (FOB) test. If the patient is at risk for osteoporosis, bone mass screening is covered. Hepatitis B immunizations are also covered for those at risk.

Anesthesia Services

Prior to the 1992 edition of CPT, most payers, including Medicare, required providers to use the appropriate CPT surgery code and indicate a **type of service (TOS)** code "7" for anesthesia services. A combination of the number of "base units" (determined by the complexity of the service) and "time units" (the total anesthesia time for the procedure) were multiplied by a dollar conversion factor to establish the fee and payment for the anesthesia service.

While reimbursement did not always match fees, similar methods were used to calculate both amounts.

Medicare discontinued using the TOS indicators for any service, replacing the information provided by the TOS with procedure code modifiers or expanded two-digit location or **place of service (POS)** codes. Additionally, the annual cost of anesthesia services billed to Medicare, with the usual base and time units multiplied by a per-unit fee, was difficult to predict. While base units could be established, time units varied widely depending on the skill of the surgeon, the patient's condition, and the abilities of the operating room personnel. With the $20 million payment limitation in mind, HCFA determined that the large number of procedure codes involved prevented Medicare from estimating and controlling the expenditures for anesthesia services.

CPT now includes an Anesthesia Section beginning with "0" (zero). These codes contain much more general base units, and the number of anesthesia procedure codes needed has been reduced. Examples of CPT Anesthesia codes include:

00500   Anesthesia for all procedures on esophagus

01200   Anesthesia for all closed procedures involving hip joint

Although included in CPT, very few other payment programs require these codes, and may continue to use the TOS 7 along with the surgery procedure code.

Surgery Services

Medicare defines a **global service** for each surgical code as 0, 10, or 90 days. The global period for each surgery includes all services related to that procedure. Suture removal, postoperative office visits, and dressing changes are all included in the surgical payment and are not separately billable. Because 90 days is a lengthy period of time, an office visit or procedure related to any other condition treated by the surgeon must be billed with modifier -79 to indicate that this procedure or service is not related to the original service. Even if the procedure and diagnosis codes demonstrate that they are unrelated to the surgery, the appropriate modifier must be attached. This extra step serves as the physician's certification that the services are not related. Because these Medicare requested modifiers are CPT modifiers, they are printed in CPT and may be used for other payers to explain how a service was altered in some manner.

Surgical Modifiers

Modifiers explain unique surgical procedures and services provided to Medicare patients. The global period also includes preoperative care. This was a problem for surgeons who were called in for consultation to evaluate a patient's need for surgery. The consultation would be paid only if the consultant did not perform surgery, but was included in the global service if the consultant operated on the patient. Medicare now pays for a preoperative evaluation when the modifier -57 (decision for surgery) is reported with the consultation code.

In some circumstances, the surgeon may not provide any of the postoperative care for a surgical patient. To report this to Medicare, the providers use the surgical procedure code with the modifiers listed below:

xxxxx-54   Surgical care only

xxxxx-55   Postoperative management only

Medicare does not recognize modifier -56 (preoperative management only) because the admitting doctor will report daily medical care services for the condition that required hospital care before surgery was considered. This could involve managing acute abdominal pain before the patient was referred to a surgeon for a cholecystectomy. Perhaps the patient was hospitalized for loss of vision, later diagnosed with a brain tumor, and then treated by a neurosurgeon. This medical care would likely end when the surgeon performed the consultation and reported the consultation code with the modifier -57 indicating this was the decision for surgery.

A physician serving as an assistant surgeon would append the procedure code with -80, the assistant surgeon modifier. If the surgery occurs in a teaching hospital, the surgeon is expected to use a resident physician as an assistant. Another practicing physician serving as the assistant surgeon in a teaching hospital would report the surgical code with -82, indicating that no qualified resident surgeon was available.

EXERCISE 9-1   Reporting Services and Procedures for More Than One Provider

Dr. Jones admits Mrs. Brown on July 8 for severe abdominal pain. Dr. Lake, a gynecologist, sees Mrs. Brown on the 9th and schedules an exploratory laparotomy for the next day. Dr. Jones will assist during surgery and provide postoperative care because Dr. Lake is leaving town on the 11th for a medical conference.

Using the service/procedure codes provided and modifiers -54 and -55, enter the dates of service and the codes and modifiers (explained on page 203) reported for each doctor.

Procedure codes: **99222** Initial hospital care, comprehensive

99232 Subsequent hospital care, expanded problem focused

99252 Initial inpatient consultation, expanded problem focused

49000 Exploratory laparotomy

1. Dr. Jones' billing:

Date	Procedure Code/Modifier

2. Dr. Lake's billing:

Date	Procedure Code/Modifier

Modifiers for related and unrelated procedures are very important and frequently misused.

-**78** Return to the operating room for a related procedure during the postoperative period

-**79** Unrelated procedure or service by the same physician during the postoperative period.

All services related to the original surgery, except a service performed in an operating room, are included in the surgical global service and are not reported separately to Medicare. Such services could include surgery to control internal bleeding or the repair of a wound dehiscence. The Medicare reimbursement would be valued at 50% of the fee schedule for services reported with the -78 modifier. Office surgery, wound debridement, or other outpatient treatments are related to the surgery and are, therefore, included in the global surgical payment.

EXAMPLE

Consider a patient who is recovering from back surgery and cuts his finger while peeling a potato. The laceration repair code is reported with modifier -79 because the repair is unrelated to the original back surgery.

EXAMPLE

A patient undergoes a right carpal tunnel release and then undergoes the same procedure on the left wrist during the postoperative global period for the first procedure. The second procedure will require modifiers -79 and -LT to indicate it is not a repeat of the right wrist surgery.

The use of these modifiers is not limited to reporting to Medicare. However, Medicare rejects surgical services if modifiers are missing or used inappropriately.

REVIEW

CHALLENGE EXERCISE

1. Match the HCFA term with its descriptor.

1. ____ 0, 10, or days	**a.** Coverage Issues Manual
2. ____ reporting an incorrect fee	**b.** Episode of care
3. ____ fee-for-service does not apply	**c.** False claim
4. ____ guarantee of best possible price	**d.** Fraud
5. ____ contains a listing of Medicare covered services	**e.** Global service period
	f. Limiting charge
6. ____ serves as the basis of nonPAR's fee	**g.** Managed care organization
7. ____ fee-for-service payment system	**h.** Most favored nation status
8. ____ applies to an office service provided in a hospital	**i.** RBRVS
	j. Site of service differential
9. ____ deliberate misrepresentation of services provided	
10. ____ defined term of illness	

2. Name three RBRVS components considered when payments are calculated.

3. Calculate the following amounts for a participating provider who bills Medicare:

Submitted charge (based on provider's regular fee for office visit)	$ 75.00
Medicare allowed amount (according to the Medicare Fee Schedule)	$ 60.00
Coinsurance amount (paid by patient or supplemental insurance)	$ 12.00
Medicare payment (80% of the allowed amount)	_____
Medicare write-off (*not* to be paid by Medicare or the beneficiary)	_____

4. Calculate the following amounts for a nonparticipating provider (nonPAR) who bills Medicare:

Submitted charge (based on provider's regular fee)	$ 650.00
NonPAR Medicare Fee Schedule allowed amount	$ 450.00
Limiting Charge (115% of MFS allowed amount)	_____
Medicare Payment (80% of the MFS allowed amount)	_____
Beneficiary is billed 20% plus the balance of the limiting charge	$ 157.50
Medicare write-off (*not* to be paid by Medicare or the beneficiary)	_____

5. Calculate the following amounts for a nurse practitioner (NP) who bills Medicare:

Submitted charge (based on provider's regular fee for office visit)	$ 75.00
Medicare allowed amount (according to the Medicare Fee Schedule)	$ 60.00
Nurse practitioner allowed amount (85% of Medicare Fee Schedule)	_____
Medicare payment (80% of the allowed amount)	_____

6. Congress enacts Medicare legislation, and HCFA interprets that legislation, creating _____ that are to be followed by providers submitting claims.

7. Define *constant-attendance* as it relates to critical care services provided to patients.

8. What is the difference between a nurse practitioner and a physician assistant as related to the provision of patient care services?

9. To bill Medicare for anesthesia services, providers submit codes from the CPT Surgery Section and include a place of service (POS) code on the claim. *True or False.*

10. Providers cannot bill for related services during a procedure's global service period. *True or False.*

CODING FROM SOURCE DOCUMENTS

OBJECTIVES

Upon successful completion of this chapter, you should be able to:

1. Define the following terms, phrases, and abbreviations:

medical necessity	objective	operative report
SOAP note	assessment	op notes
subjective	plan	

2. Abstract and code diagnoses and procedures from source documents for the purpose of completing insurance information on the HCFA-1500 claim form.

INTRODUCTION

In the previous three chapters, the exercises consisted of coding diagnoses and procedures varying in lengths. The next step in learning to code is to learn to take diagnoses and procedures from the same case and link each procedure with an ICD-9 code that justifies the medical necessity for performing the procedure. **Medical necessity** is defined as "proving the necessity for performing a service based on currently accepted standards of medical practice." Without this linkage, third-party payers will not consider payment for the procedure.

The final step in learning to code involves coding directly from the medical record. This chapter will allow you to begin coding from the record by using short clinical scenarios or abstracts to obtain the procedure and diagnosis information that must be coded. Next, we will progress to coding diagnoses and procedures from copies of actual patient records dictated by health care providers. The chart entries include progress notes of various styles, operative reports, and both outpatient and inpatient consultation reports.

APPLYING ICD-9-CM CODING GUIDELINES

In Chapter 6, diagnosis statements were coded according to ICD-9-CM. Now, in preparation for completing the diagnosis blocks on the claim form, it is necessary to apply the HCFA established Official Coding Guidelines for Physician and Outpatient Hospital Services, (see page 93), and to understand the limitations of the HCFA-1500 claim form when billing third-party payers.

- Code and report only those conditions and procedures that are documented in the medical record.

- Use the full range of ICD codes from 001 through 999.9 and V01 through V82.9, and supplement with E-codes when warranted by circumstances.

- Do not code or report tentative (qualified) diagnoses (conditions that are stated as questionable, suspected, or are to be ruled out). Instead, report the documented signs and symptoms.

- Code to the highest level of specificity any disorder or injury that is known and documented at the time of the encounter.

Coding may not be a problem when reviewing short, one-line diagnostic statements such as those that appeared in most of the earlier exercises. When working with clinical scenarios or detailed patient records, abstract the diagnosis and procedure data for the coding and reporting of what was actually documented by the health care provider.

While signs and symptoms are often documented with a qualified diagnosis, they are not coded when a definitive diagnosis is established.

EXAMPLE

1. Sprained ankle with pain, edema, and discoloration
   Code only the sprained ankle (because it is the definitive diagnosis).

2. Pharyngitis, with pain on swallowing, and temperature of 101°F of two day duration.
   Code only the pharyngitis (because it is the definitive diagnosis).

3. Probable tonsillitis. Patient complains of a sore throat, and redness of the pharynx is noted upon exam.
   Code the sore throat and redness of the pharynx (because the tonsillitis is a tentative diagnosis and is not coded).

- V-codes are assigned when there is justification for the patient to seek health care but no disorder currently exists.

- Code only those problems treated during the encounter or that affect the treatment rendered. Questions to consider include:

   1. Does the problem justify a procedure or service performed during this encounter?

   2. Did the provider prescribe a new medication or change a prescription for a condition?

   3. Are there documented positive results of diagnostic tests?

- No more than four diagnoses can be reported on one HCFA-1500 claim form. If more than four conditions are treated during the same encounter, it will be necessary to submit two or more claim forms. Be careful to match the proper diagnosis with the procedure and/or service rendered.

- Health care providers often document past conditions that are not currently active problems for the patient. These conditions are not coded as active, but they could be coded with a V-code. Do not record any codes for inactive problems on the claim form (except when it is medically appropriate to monitor for recurrences).

EXAMPLE

Status post left ankle fracture

Strep throat, 6 months ago

- List the primary diagnosis first, and sequence in descending order additional codes for coexisting (secondary) conditions that affect the treatment of the patient.

  The primary diagnosis is the major reason the patient sought health care today and is coded and reported on the HCFA-1500. Codes for secondary conditions that are treated during the encounter or influence decisions about managing the primary condition are sequenced below the primary diagnosis. There is no designated order for multiple secondary conditions.

- Link each procedure or service with a condition that proves the medical necessity for performing that procedure or service.

  A diagnosis, symptom or sign, or V-code should be linked with each procedure or service on the HCFA-1500. Up to four diagnosis codes are entered next to reference numbers (1-4) in Block 21 of the HCFA-1500. The reference number (1-4) for the diagnosis code reported is linked to the procedure or service code reported in Block 24D. The reference number is entered in Block 24E.

EXAMPLE

Tim Johnson was seen in his primary care physician's office on June 1 where he underwent a detailed history and exam for an upset stomach and vomiting. Mr. Johnson was also evaluated during the visit for his diabetes mellitus. The office drew blood (venipuncture) and performed a blood sugar test, which was within normal limits. Table 10-1 contains a sample form that can be used to link diagnosis and procedure/service codes for entry in the appropriate Blocks (21, 24D, and 24E) on the HCFA-1500 (see Figure 10-1 on page 246).

Table 10-1 *Sample form to be used for linking diagnosis and procedure/service codes for entry in Blocks 21, 24D and 24E of the HCFA-1500 claim form*

DIAGNOSES DOCUMENTED ON PATIENT'S CHART	ICD-9-CM CODE (ENTER IN BLOCK 21 OF HCFA-1500)	REFERENCE NO (ENTER IN BLOCK 24E OF HCFA-1500)	PROCEDURE OR SERVICE RENDERED TO PATIENT	CPT CODE (ENTER IN BLOCK 24D OF HCFA-1500)
Upset Stomach	536.8	1	Office Visit	99213
Vomiting	787.03	2	Office Visit	99213
Diabetes Mellitus	250.00	3	Venipuncture	36415
			Blood Sugar Test	82947

21. DIAGNOSIS OR NATURE OF ILLNESS OR INJURY. (RELATE ITEMS 1,2,3 OR 4 TO ITEM 24E BY LINE)							22. MEDICAID RESUBMISSION CODE	ORIGINAL REF. NO.					

1. | 536 . 8   3. | 250 . 00

2. | 787 . 03   4. | ___ . ___

23. PRIOR AUTHORIZATION NUMBER

24. DATE(S) OF SERVICE From MM DD YY	To MM DD YY	B Place of Service	C Type of Service	D PROCEDURES, SERVICES, OR SUPPLIES (Explain Unusual Circumstances) CPT/HCPCS MODIFIER	E DIAGNOSIS CODE	F $ CHARGES	G DAYS OR UNITS	H EPSDT Family Plan	I EMG	J COB	K RESERVED FOR LOCAL USE
1 06 01 2000				99213	1,2,3						
2 06 01 2000				36415	3						
3 06 01 2000				82947	3						
4											
5											
6											

FIGURE 10-1 Completed Blocks 21, 24A, 24D, and 24E of the HCFA-1500 claim form

EXERCISE 10-1 Choosing the Primary Diagnosis

Review the list of symptoms, complaints, and disorders in each case and underline the primary diagnosis.

1. Occasional bouts of urinary frequency, but symptom free today
   Sore throat with swollen glands and enlarged tonsils
   Acute pharyngitis with negative rapid strep test
   Urinalysis test negative

2. Edema, left lateral malleolus
   Limited range of motion due to pain
   Musculoligamentous sprain, left ankle
   Xray negative for fracture

3. Distended urinary bladder
   Benign prostatic hypertrophy (BPH) with urinary retention
   Enlarged prostate

4. Pale, diaphoretic, and in acute distress
   Bacterial endocarditis
   Limited chest expansion, scattered bilateral wheezes
   Pulse 112 and regular, respiration 22 with some shortness of breath

5. Right leg still weak
   Partial drop foot gait, right
   Tightness in lower back

6. Rule out cervical radiculopathy vs. myofascial pain syndrome
   History of pain in both scapular regions
   Spasms, left upper trapezius muscle
   Limited range of motion neck and left arm
   Xrays show significant cervical osteoarthritis

After completing this exercise, refer to Appendix IV to check your answers.

EXERCISE 10-2 Linking Diagnoses with Procedures/Services

Underline the primary diagnosis in each case scenario. Then, link the diagnosis with the procedure/service by entering just one reference number in the **Ref #** column.

Reminder: *To link the diagnosis with the procedure/service* means to match up the appropriate diagnosis with the procedure/service that was rendered to treat or manage the diagnosis.

EXAMPLE

The patient was seen by the doctor in the office for a fractured thumb, and Xrays were taken. The following diagnoses and procedures were documented in the patient's chart:

1. Diabetes mellitus, noninsulin dependent, controlled
2. Benign essential hypertension
3. <u>Simple fracture, right thumb</u>

REF #	PROCEDURE/SERVICE
1	Office visit
1	Xray, right thumb

Based on the procedure and service delivered, the patient was seen for the thumb fracture. Because the diabetes and hypertension are under control, they require no treatment or management during this visit. Therefore, only the fracture is linked to the procedure and service.

Case Scenario 1

The patient was seen in the office complaining of abdominal cramping. A hemoccult test was positive for blood in the stool. The patient was scheduled for proctoscopy with biopsy two days later, and Duke's C carcinoma of the colon was diagnosed. The patient was scheduled for proctectomy to be performed in seven days. The following diagnoses were documented on the patient's chart:

1. Abdominal cramping
2. Blood in the stool
3. Duke's C carcinoma, colon

REF #	PROCEDURE/SERVICE
	Hemoccult lab test
	Proctoscopy with biopsy
	Proctectomy

Case Scenario 2

The patient was seen in the office complaining of urinary frequency with dysuria, sore throat with cough, and headaches. The urinalysis was negative, and the rapid strep test was positive for streptococcus infection. The patient was placed on antiobiotics and was scheduled to be seen in ten days. The following diagnoses were documented on the patient's chart:

1. Urinary frequency with dysuria
2. Sore throat with cough
3. Headaches
4. Strep throat

REF #	PROCEDURE/SERVICE
	Office visit
	Urinalysis
	Rapid strep test

Case Scenario 3

The patient was seen in the office to rule out pneumonia. She had been experiencing wheezing and congestion, and her respirations were labored. The chest Xray done in the office was positive for pneumonia. The following diagnoses were documented on the patient's chart:

1. Pneumonia
2. Wheezing
3. Congestion
4. Labored respirations

REF #	PROCEDURE/SERVICE
	Office visit
	Chest Xray

Case Scenario 4

The doctor visited the patient in the nursing facility for the second time since she was admitted. The patient complained of malaise and fatigue. It was noted that the patient had a cough as well as a fever of 103°F, and that her pharynx was injected. Tigan, 200 mg, IM, was injected. The following diagnoses were documented on the patient's chart:

1. Malaise
2. Fatigue
3. Cough
4. Fever of 103°F
5. Injected pharynx

REF #	PROCEDURE/SERVICE
	Nursing facility visit
	Injection of Tigan, 200 mg, IM

Case Scenario 5

The patient was seen in the emergency department with chills and fever. The physician noted left lower abdominal quadrant pain and tenderness. The physician diagnosed *acute diverticulitis*. The following diagnoses were documented on the patient's chart:

1. Chills
2. Fever
3. Acute diverticulitis

REF #	PROCEDURE/SERVICE
	Emergency department visit

After completing this exercise, refer to Appendix IV to check your answers.

CPT/HCPCS BILLING CONSIDERATIONS

- Locate the procedure code(s) in CPT; if you cannot find the code, select the appropriate HCPCS code(s).
- Both CPT and HCPCS modifiers can be added to CPT codes.
- CPT procedures indicated with asterisks are reported on a fee-for-service basis because they are generally considered minor. This means the asterisked procedure and any subsequent office visits can be reported and billed separately, depending on the third party payer rules.
- Report only those procedures or services performed by the health care provider or staff during the current medical encounter. Do not report diagnostic procedures (lab work and Xrays) ordered for hospital inpatients unless the provider documents that they performed the test. The hospital will bill for all tests performed by hospital staff or employees.

EXAMPLES

1. "The following tests were ordered" on a hospitalized patient.
2. "Patient was referred to Dr. Cardiac for tests."
3. **"Specimens were sent to the Ames Lab for testing."**
4. "Patient will return tomorrow for tests."

CODING CLINICAL SCENARIOS

Clinical scenarios summarize key medical data from patient records to support issues presented in health care lectures, literature, and seminars. In this text they are used to introduce the student to the process of abstracting key diagnosis and procedure data from the submitted scenario. Once this technique is learned, it will be easier to move on to abstracting from full-length source documents.

Insurance specialists working in the health care arena must be able to abstract and code key clinical and procedural data from the patient record to ensure proper reporting. It is important to abstract only documented procedures and diagnoses in each scenario. Do not yield to temptation to make clinical assumptions that the provider meant something more or less complex than is written.

Steps for Abstracting and Coding Clinical Scenarios

Step 1. Read the entire scenario to obtain an overview of the problems presented and procedures/services performed. Research any word or abbreviation not understood.

Step 2. Reread the problem and highlight the diagnoses, symptoms, or health status that supports, justifies, and/or proves the medical necessity of any procedure or service performed.

 ■ **NOTE:** Do *not* use a highlighter or other marker on an original document. To do so will make copies of the document illegible as highlighter marks copy as a thick, black or gray line. Instead, make a copy of the original document for markup purposes, and then destroy the copy after the abstracting and coding process has been completed. ■

Step 3. List and code the documented procedure(s) or service(s) performed.

Step 4. Assign required modifiers, if applicable.

Step 5. List the diagnosis(es), symptoms, or reasons the patient sought health care that justify performing each procedure.

Step 6. Identify the primary condition.

Step 7. Code the diagnosis(es) or health status listed.

Step 8. Link each procedure or service to a diagnosis, symptom, or health status to communicate the documented medical necessity for performing the procedure.

Sample Clinical Scenarios

Scenario 1

Patient returned to the surgeon's office <u>during postoperative period</u> of surgery on his left arm because of symptoms of <u>shortness of breath, dizzy spells, and pain in the left arm</u>. A level III re-examination (detailed history and examination was documented) of the patient was performed. The wound is healing nicely. There is no abnormal redness or abnormal pain from the incision. A 3-lead EKG rhythm strip was performed which revealed an <u>inversion of the T-wave</u>. The <u>abnormal EKG</u> was discussed with the patient and he agreed to an immediate referral to Dr. Cardiac for a cardiac work-up.

Scenario 1 Answer

Procedure(s) performed	Code	Diagnosis(es)
1. Office visit, established patient, level III	99213-24	**1.** During postoperative status
2. 3-lead EKG rhythm strip	93040	**2.** Shortness of breath and dizziness
		3. Pain in left arm
		4. Abnormal EKG-inverted T wave (794.31)

Rationale

1. The service provided is a level III office visit, established patient.
2. The words "re-examination" and "during postoperative period, by same surgeon" justify the use of the -24 modifier because this examination was conducted during the postoperative period of surgery on the arm.
3. Abnormal EKG illustrates inversion of T-wave, the documented problem.
4. "Shortness of breath, dizzy spells, and pain in the left arm" are symptoms of the abnormal EKG.

Scenario 2

This 72-year-old man with multiple chronic conditions presented to the OR an initial, uncomplicated left <u>inguinal hernia</u> repair. The patient was cleared for surgery by his primary care physician. General anesthesia was administered by the anesthesiologist, after which the incision was made. At this point the patient went into <u>shock</u>, the surgery was halted, and the wound was closed. Patient was sent to Recovery.

Scenario 2 Answer

Procedure(s) performed	Code	Diagnosis(es)
1. Hernia repair, initial	49505-74	1. Inguinal hernia (550.90)
		2. Shock due to surgery (998.0)
		3. Surgery cancelled (V64.1)

Rationale

1. Procedure initiated for uncomplicated, inguinal hernia repair.
2. Modifier -74 indicates surgery was stopped after anesthesia had been administered because of the threat to the patient's well-being from the shock.
3. Primary diagnosis is inguinal hernia, the reason the patient sought health care.
4. Secondary diagnoses include shock due to surgery (explains the discontinuation of the surgery) and cancelled surgery.

EXERCISE 10-3 Coding Clinical Scenarios

A. List and code the procedures and diagnosis(es) for each of the following scenarios.

B. Be sure to include all necessary CPT and/or HCPCS modifiers.

C. Underline the primary condition.

1. A 66-year-old, established Medicare patient came to the office for his annual physical. He had no known health problems and no new complaints. During the course of the examination the physician found BP of 160/130. A detailed history and exam of this established patient was performed in addition to the preventive medicine encounter. Lab work done in the office included automated CBC, automated dipstick UA with microscopy, and chest Xray, 2 views. A screening flexible sigmoidoscopy was performed with negative findings. Patient also received an IM influenza vaccination.

Procedures   **Diagnoses**

_____

_____

_____

_____

_____

2. A 67-year-old woman came to the surgery center for a scheduled diagnostic arthroscopy of her right shoulder because of constant pain on rotation of the shoulder. Prior to entering the OR she told the nurse "I have been feeling weak, depressed, and tired ever since my last visit." The surgeon performs a re-examination with a detailed history, expanded problem focused physical, and moderate complexity decision-making prior to the surgery. The operative findings were negative and the procedure uneventful.

Procedures   **Diagnoses**

_____

_____

_____

_____

_____

3. Cholecystectomy was performed on 5/11 of this year. On 7/10 of this year the patient had an emergency, inpatient admission during which an expanded problem focused history and exam was performed by the same surgeon who performed the cholecystectomy. Open surgery was performed on 7/10 for a ruptured appendix with abscess.

Procedures   **Diagnoses**

_____

_____

_____

_____

_____

4. A surgeon is called to the hospital by the ER physician to see a new patient. The surgeon performs a detailed exam, admits the patient, and schedules an immediate laparoscopic cholecystectomy.

Procedures   **Diagnoses**

_____

_____

_____

_____

_____

5. Dr B performed an expanded problem focused, postoperative examination on an established patient. He also removed the sutures on the patient who returned to her hometown on the opposite coast immediately after discharge from the hospital following an open appendectomy.

Procedures	Diagnoses
_____	_____
_____	_____
_____	_____
_____	_____
_____	

After completing this exercise, refer to Appendix IV to check your answers.

Additional scenarios are found at the end of this chapter and in the workbook that accompanies this text.

CODING MEDICAL REPORTS

This section deals with coding diagnoses and procedures from clinic notes, consultations, and diagnostic reports. The process of coding diagnosis and procedure data is the same process that was used when working with the clinical scenarios. The major difference is that the reports are more detailed.

Abstracting Clinic Notes

There are two major formats that health care providers use for documenting clinic notes. The first of these is the narrative style written in paragraph format.

Narrative Style Clinic Note

> A 21-year-old female patient comes to the office today having been referred by Dr. Bandaid, M.D. for pain in the RLQ of the abdomen, 2 days duration.
>
> Temp: 102°F. Detailed history and physical examination revealed rebound tenderness over McBurney's point with radiation to the RUQ and RLQ. The remainder of the physical examination was normal. For additional information see the complete History and Physical in this chart.
>
> Laboratory data ordered by Dr. Bandaid (oral report given by Goodtechnique Lab) is as follows: WBC 19.1; RBC 4.61; platelets 234,000; hematocrit 42; hemoglobin 13.5; bands 15%, and PMNs 88%. UA and all other blood work was within normal limits. Patient is to be admitted to GoodMedicine Hospital for further work-up and possible appendectomy.
>
> T.J. Stitcher, M.D.

In this style of clinic note, the diagnosis selected for coding may be reported using one of several formats.

1. Impression: Pain, RLQ of abdomen.
2. The patient has pain in the RLQ of the abdomen.
3. On physical exam, I note the patient has pain in the RLQ of the abdomen.
4. Symptoms and Lab data suggest appendicitis. Code the RLQ abdominal pain.

> ■ **NOTE:** A negative diagnostic test result indicates that no disease was identified with certainty. Report symptoms stated by the patient or signs observed by the health care provider to justify performing the test(s). ■

The abstracted clinical data for this case is an office visit and the symptoms of abdominal pain.

While the health care provider is not required to state the level of Evaluation & Management (E&M) service performed in the clinic notes, documentation in the patient's chart must support the E&M code selected.

The E&M service is usually marked on the encounter form (or superbill), which is another legitimate source document (along with the patient's chart). The portion of the encounter form that contains charge data (e.g., date of encounter, E&M service provided with code, and charge) would appear as follows:

01/01/YYYY	New Patient Office Visit, 99203	$70.00

Occasionally, narrative clinic notes are documented in the chart in the form of a letter to the referring physician. In these cases, read the body of the letter and code the diagnoses accordingly.

SOAP Notes

The second style of clinic note uses an outline format, called a **SOAP Note**.

"SOAP" is an acronym derived from the first letter of the topic headings used in progress notes:

S: Subjective
O: Objective
A: Assessment
P: Plan

The **subjective** data contains the chief complaint and the patient's description of the presenting problem. It can also include the response to treatment prescribed earlier, past history, review of symptoms, and relevant family and social history. The subjective note may appear in quotes because it represents the patient's statement verbatim.

1. Patient complains of lack of energy and listlessness.
2. Patient states, "I have resting angina coming on in the morning about 5 to 6 AM, associated with dyspnea, but no palpitations."
3. Patient injured her back when she fell off a ladder cleaning the gutters.

The **objective** data contains documentation of measurable or objective observations made during physical examination and diagnostic testing. Some health care providers may also include historical information obtained from previous encounters in this section.

EXAMPLES

1. "There is tenderness in the right lower quadrant."
2. "Quick Strep test: negative."
3. "The patient had polio at age 3 and walks with a decided limp."
4. "Blood pressure: 114/78."
5. "Xray shows a greenstick fracture of the distal shaft of right radius."
6. "Ordered Xray to determine status of COPD. Chest is clear. No wheeze or rales."
7. "She has marked active synovitis of the right knee."

The **assessment** data contains the diagnostic statement and may include the physician's rationale for the diagnosis.

EXAMPLES

1. "This patient has a resolving rotator cuff adhesive capsulitis of the right shoulder."
2. "Secondary hypertension due to Wilm's tumor."
3. "Benign hypertension and nephrosclerosis."
4. "Patient has active rheumatoid arthritis, not controlled by Prednisone 2 mg bid, Penicillamine 250 mg/day, and Bufferin."
5. "Status quo. No new problems."
6. "I think this man is doing fairly well, except for the continued angina."

If this section is missing from the report, look for positive diagnostic test results documented in the objective data or code the symptoms presented in either the subjective or objective data.

The **plan** is the statement of the physician's future plans for the work-up and medical management of the case. This includes plans for medications, diet and therapy, future diagnostic tests to be performed, suggested life-style changes, items covered in the informed consent discussions, items covered in patient education sessions, and suggested followup care.

EXAMPLES

1. Patient to be seen in the office in 10 days for follow-up.
2. Consultation with Dr. Pulmonary ordered for patient.
3. Repeat chest Xray to be performed on 7/1/YYYY.
4. Arrangements to be made for inpatient admission to the mental health unit to treat patient's severe depression.
5. Patient referred to the pain clinic for management of lower back pain.

EXAMPLE

3/29/YYYY
S: Pt states "no complaints, no new symptoms since last visit."
O: T. 98.6 F; P 80; R 20; BP 120/86, rt arm, sitting, WT 120 lb.
                                        Janet Employee, Medical Assistant
3/29/YYYY
O: Incision, inner aspect of left breast, healing well. No sign of inflammation or infection.
A: Papilloma with fibrocystic changes, no malignancy.
        Size 3.0 X 1.5 X 0.2 cm.
P: 1. Suture removal today.
        2. Return visit, 3 months for follow-up.
        3. Note dictated to Dr. Neckhurts.
                                                    Janet B. Surgeon, M.D.

In this case, the chief complaint (the subjective entry), and the vital signs were written by the medical assistant; then the doctor conducted an examination and recorded her findings. This is the reason for the two objective entries.

The abstracted coding clinical data for this case reveals the following:

Objective section: **1.** This a post surgery visit: "incision is healing well."

2. The surgery site: "inner aspect of the left breast."

Assessment section: **3.** Diagnosis: "Papilloma with fibrocystic changes, no malignancy."

The combination of the documented location and diagnosis results in a very specific diagnostic statement: "Papilloma with fibrocystic changes, inner aspect, left breast."

The plan for this visit is for removal of the sutures. The charge data for the surgical encounter and the present encounter are needed to determine if there is a charge for the current encounter because the papilloma removal was a starred procedure. There may be no charge for the visit because it falls into the postoperative period of a major surgical procedure.

EXERCISE 10-4   Coding SOAP Notes

Review the following SOAP notes, then select and code the diagnoses.

1. S: Patient complains of stomach pain, 3 days duration. She also stated that her legs still get cold and painful from the knees down.

O: Ht 5' 6"; Wt 164; BP 122/86; pulse 92 and regular; Temp 97.0°F, oral; chest normal; heart normal. The doppler arteriogram of lower extremities taken last week at the hospital is reported as within normal limits bilaterally.

A: Another episode of atrophic gastritis.

P: Carafate 1 g. Take 1 tablet qid before meals and at bedtime, #120 tabs.

DIAGNOSES	ICD-9-CM CODE NUMBERS

2. S: Patient seems to be doing quite well, however, the pain that he had prior to his surgery is not gone. He is currently being evaluated for what appears to be metastatic pancreatic carcinoma of his liver. His diabetes is now under control.

O: Incision is well healed. Abdomen is soft and nontender.

A: Pathology revealed chronic cholecystitis and cholelithiasis. Liver biopsy revealed metastatic adenocarcinoma.

P: 1. Lengthy discussion with patient and his wife about treatment in the future. Asked that they call any time they have questions.

2. Return visit here on a prn basis.

DIAGNOSES	ICD-9-CM CODE NUMBERS

3. S: The patient complains of generalized stiffness and being tired. She also notes that her left knee was swollen and felt hot to the touch last week. She was last seen 18 months ago on Penicillamine and 2 mg prednisone bid. Her other meds are loperamide for loose stool and Tagamet 300 mg bid.

O: Examination reveals some swelling of the left knee with active synovitis and minimal fluid. Her present weight is 134 lb, BP 116/72. The hematocrit performed today is 37.5 and her sed rate is 65.

A: This patient has active rheumatoid arthritis.

P: 1. Increase prednisone to 5 mg bid, and Penicillamine to 500 mg bid.

2. Xray of left knee tomorrow.

3. Recheck CBC, sed rate, and urinalysis in 4 weeks.

4 Discussed with her the possibility of injecting steroids into the knee if she shows no improvement.

DIAGNOSES	ICD-9-CM CODE NUMBERS

4. S: Patient returns today for follow-up of chronic angina and dyspnea. She says the angina still appears mainly when she is resting, and particularly just as she is waking up in the morning. This is accompanied by some dyspnea and pain occasionally radiating into the left jaw, but no palpitations. The angina is relieved by nitroglycerin She continues to take Inderal 40 mg qid.

O: BP, left arm, sitting, 128/72; weight is 150 lb. Chest is clear. No wheezing or rales.

A: Unstable angina. Patient again refused to consider a heart catheterization.

P: New RX: Isordil Tembids 40 mg.

Refill nitroglycerine.

DIAGNOSES	ICD-9-CM CODE NUMBERS

5. S: This 17-year-old, single, white female presents to the office with a sore throat, fever, and swollen glands, 2 days duration.

O: Oral temp 102.4°F; pulse 24; respiration 18; BP 118/78; Wt 138 lb. The throat is markedly erythematous with evidence of exudative tonsillitis. Ears show normal TMs bilaterally. Few tender, submandibular nodes, bilaterally.

A: Exudative tonsillitis.

P: 1. Obtained throat culture that was sent to the lab.

2. Patient started on an empiric course of Pen Vee K 250 mg #40 to be taken qid X 10 days

3. Encouraged patient to increase oral fluid intake.

4. Patient to call office in 48 hours to obtain culture results and report her progress.

DIAGNOSES	ICD-9-CM CODE NUMBERS

6. S: This is a 50-year-old widow who comes to the office following a possible seizure. Her friend reports she was seated at her desk, and after a crash was heard, they found her lying on the floor. She had urine incontinence, and now complains of confusion and headache. Patient says this was her first episode and denies ever having chest pain, palpitations, or paresthesias. She cannot recall any recent head trauma or auras. She reports no allergies to medication and currently denies taking a medication.

She does have a history of well-differentiated nodular lymphoma in 1996, which was treated successfully by a course of radiation at the Goodmedicine Hospital in Anywhere, USA. She has had no clinical evidence of recurrence. She reports no hospitalizations except for normal delivery of her son in 1945. She does admit to mild COPD. Her family history is negative for seizures.

O: Review of systems is noncontributory. Wt 155 lb; BP 116/72, both arms; pulse 72 and regular; respirations 18 and unlabored. Head is normocephalic and atraumatic. PERRLA. EOMs are intact. The sclerae are white. Conjunctivae are pink. Funduscopic examination is benign. The ears are normal bilaterally. No evidence of Battle sign. Mouth and throat are normal; tongue is midline and normal. The neck is supple and negative. Chest is clear. Heart rate and rhythm are regular with a grade II/IV systolic ejection murmur along the left sternal border without gallop, rub, click, or other adventitious sounds. Abdomen is soft, nontender, and otherwise negative. Bowel sounds are normal. Pelvic was deferred. There is good rectal sphincter tone. No masses are felt. Hemoccult test was negative. Extremities and lymphatics are noncontributory.

Neurologic exam shows normal mental status. Cranial nerves II–XII are intact. Motor, sensory, cerebellar function, and Romberg are normal. Babinski is absent. Reflexes are 2+ and symmetrical in both upper and lower extremities.

A: New-onset seizure disorder. Rule out metabolic versus vascular etiologies.

P: The patient will be scheduled for MRI of the brain and EEG at Goodmedicine Hospital. Obtain electrolytes, calcium, albumin, LFTs, and CBC with platelet and sed rate at the same visit.

DIAGNOSES	ICD-9-CM CODE NUMBERS

Abstracting Diagnostic Test Data

Diagnostic test data can be found in one of two places: the clinic notes or as a separate report sent to the patient's health care provider from an independent laboratory or diagnostic center.

Refer to the narrative style clinic note on page 253 for an example of how results of laboratory tests are reported. Note that there is no mention of whether or not the individual blood tests reported are normal. Do not make any assumptions about whether the test results are normal or abnormal unless the health care provider specifically states which tests, if any, are elevated or abnormal. The norms of one laboratory can vary considerably from those of another.

■ **NOTE:** Laboratory tests may simply provide quantitative data, while the diagnostic implications are found in clinic notes documented by the primary care provider (e.g., attending physician for hospital inpatient care). For other diagnostic tests (e.g., Xrays and pathology), there is an interpretation and report by the responsible physician (e.g., radiologist or pathologist). ■

EXAMPLES

1. Granulocytes, 88.3% (normal range 42.6–74.5%)
2. Dilantin level, 7.1 µg/mL (therapeutic range 10.0–20.0 µg/mL)

Sample Laboratory Report

PT: Million, Ima   BD: 05/05/YYYY Attending Physician: Erin Helper, M.D.

Group 3: Specimen collected 03/03/YYYY, exam completed 03/03/YYYY 04:50 PM

TEST	RESULT		NORMS
Sodium	142 mEq/L		(135–148)
Potassium	4.4 mEq/L		(3.5–5.1)
Chloride	105 mEq/L		(97–107)
Carbon dioxide	27 mmol/L		(22–29)
Glucose	116 mg/dL	H	(70–110)
BUN	14 mg/dL		(5–20)
Creatinine	1.0 mg/dL		(0.8–1.5)

■ **NOTE:** The glucose reading is marked with an "H" indicating the result is abnormally high. A diagnosis of elevated glucose can be coded to justify performance of this group of tests. ■

Sample Radiology Report

Baseline Mammogram: There are mild fibrocystic changes in both breasts, but without evidence of a dominant mass, grouped microcalcifications, or retractions. Density on the left side is slightly greater and thought to be simply asymmetrical breast tissue. There are some small axillary nodes bilaterally.

IMPRESSION: Class 1 (normal or clinically insignificant findings).

Follow-up in 1 year is suggested to assess stability in view of the fibrocystic asymmetrical findings. Thereafter biannual follow-up if stable. No dominant mass is present particularly in the upper inner quadrant of the left breast.

Maryanne Iona, M.D.

■ **NOTE:** The diagnosis of mild fibrocystic changes of the breast can be used to justify the performance of the test. Also note the recommendation for follow-up in 1 year. ■

CODING OPERATIVE REPORTS

Operative reports (also called **op notes**) will vary from a short narrative description of the minor procedure that is performed in the physician's office to more formal reports dictated by the surgeon in a format required by hospitals and ambulatory surgical centers (ASCs).

Sample Office Surgery Report

12/05/YYYY
Chief Complaint: Postpartum exam and colposcopy
Vitals: Temp: 97.2 F, BP: 88/52, WT:107
Lab: Glucose: negative; Albumin: trace
Patient seems to be doing fine, thinks the bleeding has just about stopped at this point. Her daughter is apparently doing fine; she is to get back chromosomal analysis in a couple of days. No other system defects have been found as of yet.
Breast: Negative. Patient is breast feeding.
Abdomen: Soft, flat, no masses, nontender.
Pelvic: Cervix appeared clear, no bleeding noted. Uterus anteverted, small, nontender. Adnexa negative. Vagina appeared atrophic. Episiotomy was healing well.
Procedure: A colposcopy of the cervix was performed with staining of acetic acid. The entire squamocolumnar junction could not be seen even with the aid of an endocervical speculum. The exam was made more difficult because of very thick cervical mucus which could not be completely removed, and because the vagina and cervix were somewhat atrophic appearing. There was a whitening of the epithelium around the entire circumference of the cervix but no abnormal vasculature was noted. Numerous biopsies were taken from the posterior and anterior lip of the cervix. An endocervical curettage was done. A repeat Pap smear of the cervix was also done. Patient to call at the end of this week for biopsy results. Patient told that she could have intercourse after 5 days, to use condoms, or to come back to the office first to have the size of the diaphragm checked.

_____M.D.

Institutional formats may vary slightly but all contain the following information in outline form.

- Date of the surgery
- Patient identification
- Pre- and postoperative diagnosis(es)
- List of the procedure(s) performed
- Name of primary and secondary surgeons who performed surgery.

The body of the report contains a detailed narrative of:

- Positioning and draping of the patient for surgery
- Achievement of anesthesia
- Detailed description of how the procedure(s) was performed, identification of the incision made, and instruments, drains, dressings, special packs, and so on used during surgery
- Identification of abnormalities found during the surgery
- Description of how hemostasis was obtained and the closure of the surgical site(s)
- Condition of the patient when (s)he left the operating room.
- Signature of surgeon

Sample Hospital Operative Report

	Patient Name
	Room #: 101B
Date:	01/01/YYYY
SURGEON:	Gail R. Bones, M.D.
ASSISTANT SURGEON:	T. J. Stitcher, M.D.
PREOPERATIVE DIAGNOSIS:	Displaced supracondylar frac- ture, left humerus
POSTOPERATIVE DIAGNOSIS:	Same
OPERATION:	Closed reduction and casting, left humeral fracture

FINDINGS AND PROCEDURE: After adequate general anesthesia, the patient's left elbow was gently manipulated and held at 110° of flexion, at which point continued to maintain a good radial pulse. Xrays revealed a good reduction; therefore, a plaster splint was applied, care being taken not to put any constriction in the antecubital fossa. Xrays were taken again, which showed excellent reduction has been maintained. He maintained a good radial pulse, was awake, and taken to Recovery in good condition.

_____
Gail R. Bones, M.D.

Procedure for Coding Operative Reports

Step 1. Make a copy of the operative report.

This will allow you to freely make notations in the margin and highlight special details without marking up the original (which must remain in the patient's record).

Step 2. Review carefully the listing of procedures performed located in the outline section of the report.

Step 3. Read the body of the report and make a note of the procedures you would expect to code.

Key words to look for include:
  Simple versus complicated
  Partial, complete, total, or incomplete
  Unilateral versus bilateral
  Initial versus subsequent
  Incision versus excision
  Open versus closed treatment, surgery, or fracture
  Reconstructive surgery, ___ plasty,
    ___ plastic repair
  Repair, ___ pexy
  Endoscopy
  Biopsy
  Ligation
  Debridement
  Complex, simple, intermediate, repair

Micronerve repair

Reconstruction

Graft (bone, nerve, or tendon needing additional code)

Diagnostic versus surgical procedure

Be alert to the following:

1. Additional procedures documented in the body of the report but not listed in the Operative Procedure or Procedure Performed section of the report.

EXAMPLE

Postoperative Diagnosis: Chronic cholecystitis and cholelithiasis without obstruction

Procedures Performed: Laparoscopic cholecystectomy with cholangiography.

In the body of the operative report the surgeon describes the laparoscopic removal of the gallbladder and a cholangiogram. The surgeon also describes the operative findings along with the biopsy of a suspicious liver nodule.

2. The Procedures Performed section lists procedures performed but the procedure is not described in the body of the operative report. In these cases, the surgeon will have to add a written addendum to the operative report documenting the performance of any listed procedure that should be coded.

EXAMPLE

Procedures performed:

1. Arthroscopy, right knee

2. Open repair, right knee, collateral and cruciate ligaments

In the body of the report, however, the surgeon does not document the removal of the scope.

Step 4. Identify main term(s) and subterms for the procedure(s) to be coded.

Step 5. Underline and research any terms in the report that you cannot define.

Many major coding errors are made when the coder does not understand critical medical terms in the report.

Step 6. Locate the main term(s) in the CPT Index.

Check for the proper anatomic site or organ.

Step 7. Research all suggested codes.

Read all notes and guidelines pertaining to the codes you are investigating. Watch for "add on" procedures described in any notes/guidelines.

Step 8. Return to the index and research additional codes if you cannot find a particular code(s) that matches the description of the procedure(s) performed in the operative report.

Because there is a monetary value for each CPT code, never use multiple, separate codes to describe a procedure if CPT has a single code that classifies all of the individual components of the procedure described by the physician.

Key Words Associated With Global Surgeries (*Remember:* Global surgery includes preoperative assessment, the surgery, and normal uncomplicated postoperative care.)

Exploratory	Anastomosis
Exploration of _____	Transection
Minor lysis of adhesions	Bisection
Temporary _____	Blunt bisection (dissection)
Electrocautery	Sharp dissection
Simple closure	Take down (to take apart)
Minor debridement	Undermining of tissue (to
Wound culture	cut at a horizontal angle)
Intraoperative photo	

Never use a code number described in CPT as a "separate procedure" when it is performed within the same incision as the primary procedure and is an integral part of a greater procedure.

Step 9. Investigate the possibility of adding modifiers to a specific code description to fully explain the procedure(s) performed.

Key Word Indicators for Use of Modifier -22

Extensive debridement/lysis or adhesions

Excessive bleeding (> 500 cc)

Friable tissue

Prolonged procedure due to _____

Unusual, anatomy, findings or circumstances

Very difficult

Step 10. Code the postoperative diagnosis. This should explain the medical necessity for performing the procedure(s). If the postoperative diagnosis does not support the procedure performed, be sure the patient's chart contains documentation to justify the procedure.

EXAMPLE

Patient seen in the emergency department (ED) with right lower quadrant pain, and evaluation reveals elevated temperature and increased white blood count. Preoperative diagnosis is *appendicitis*, and the patient undergoes *appendectomy*; however, the postoperative diagnosis is *normal appendix*. In this situation the documentation of the patient's signs and symptoms in the ED chart justifies the surgery performed.

Look for additional findings in the body of the report if the postoperative diagnosis listed on the operative report does not completely justify the medical necessity for the procedure.

Compare the postoperative diagnosis with the biopsy report on all excised neoplasms to determine whether the tissue is benign or malignant.

When working with the exercises in this text and workbook, use any stated pathology report to determine whether or not excised tissue is benign or malignant if it is not covered in the postoperative diagnosis(es).

When working in a medical practice do not code an excision until the pathology report is received.

Step 11. Review code options with the physician who performed the procedure if the case is unusual.

Before assigning an "unlisted CPT procedure" code, check HCPCS level II and III codes. Remember that a description of the procedure performed must accompany the claim form if an unlisted CPT code is reported.

Step 12. Assign final code numbers for procedures verified in Steps 3 and 4 and any addendum the physician added to the original report.

Step 13. Properly sequence the codes listing first the most significant procedure performed during the episode.

Step 14. Be sure to destroy the copy of the operative report (e.g., shred it) after the abstracting and coding process is completed.

EXERCISE 10-5 Coding Operative Reports

When working with the case studies in this text, rank the procedures as listed on the encounter form. When working in a medical practice, refer to the RBRVS Medicare Fee Schedule or the specific insurance carrier fee schedule to determine which surgical procedure receives the highest reimbursement.

Case 1

Preoperative Diagnosis: Questionable recurrent basal cell carcinoma, frontal scalp.

Postoperative Diagnosis: Benign lesion, frontal scalp.

Operation: Biopsy of granulating area with electrodessication of possible recurrent basal cell carcinoma of frontal scalp.

History: About 1 year ago, the patient had an excision and grafting of a very extensive basal cell carcinoma of the forehead at the edge of the scalp. The patient now has a large granular area at 12 o'clock on the grafted area. This may be a recurrence of the basal cell carcinoma.

Procedure: The patient was placed in the dorsal recumbent position and draped in the usual fashion. The skin and subcutaneous tissues at the junction of the skin grafts of the previous excision and the normal scalp were infiltrated with 1/2% xylocaine containing epinephrine. An elliptical excision of the normal skin and the granulating area was made. After hemostasis was obtained, the entire area of granulating tissue was thoroughly electrodesiccated.

Pathology Report: The entire specimen measures 0.7 x 0.4 x 0.3 cm depth. Part of the specimen is a slightly nodular hemorrhagic lesion measuring 0.3 cm in diameter.

Resected piece of skin shows partial loss of epithelium accompanied by acute and chronic inflammation of granulation tissue from a previous excision of basal cell carcinoma.

Diagnosis: This specimen is benign; there is no evidence of tumor.

Case 2

Preoperative diagnosis: Tumor of the skin of the back with atypical melanocyte cells

Postoperative diagnosis: Same

Operation performed: Wide excision

Anesthesia: General

Indications: The patient had a previous biopsy of a nevus located on the back. The pathology report indicated atypical melanocyte cells in the area close to the margin of the excision. The pathologist recommended that a wide re-excision be performed. The patient was informed of the situation during an office visit last week, and he agreed to be readmitted for a wider excision of the tumor area.

Procedure: The patient was placed on his left side, and general anesthesia was administered. The skin was prepped and draped in a usual fashion. A wide excision, 5.0 cm in length and 4.0 cm wide, was made. The pathologist was alerted and the specimen was sent to the lab. The frozen section was reported as negative for melanocytes on the excisional margin at this time. After the report was received, the wound was closed in layers and a dressing was applied. The patient withstood the procedure well and was sent to Recovery in good condition.

Case 3

Preoperative diagnosis: Colonic polyps

Postoperative diagnosis: Benign colonic polyps
                                    Melanosis coli

Operation performed: Colonoscopy

Anesthesia: An additional 25 mg of Demerol and 2.5 mg of Valium was administered for sedation.

Procedure: The Olympus CF-100 L video colonoscope was passed into the rectum and slowly advanced. The cecum was identified by the ileocecal valve. The prep was suboptimal.

The colonic mucosa had diffuse dark pigmentation suggestive of melanosis coli. The ascending colon, transverse colon, and proximal descending colon appear unremarkable. There were two polyps which were about 8 mm in size adjacent to each other in the sigmoid colon. One was removed for biopsy, and the other was fulgurated with hot wire biopsy forceps. After this, the colonoscope was gradually withdrawn. The patient tolerated the procedure well and was sent to Recovery.

Because of the suboptimal prep, small polyps or arteriovenous malformations could have been missed.

Case 4

Preoperative diagnosis: Serous otitis media

Postoperative diagnosis: Same

Procedure performed: Bilateral myringotomy with insertion of ventilating tubes

Anesthesia: General

Procedure: The patient was placed in a supine position and induction of general anesthesia was achieved by face mask. The ears were examined bilaterally using an operating microscope. An incision was made in the anteroinferior quadrants. A large amount of thick fluid was aspirated from both ears, more so from the left side. Ventilating tubes were introduced with no difficulties. Patient tolerated the procedure well was sent to Recovery in satisfactory condition.

Case 5

Preoperative diagnosis: Lesion, buccal mucosa, left upper lip.
Postoperative diagnosis: Same
Procedure performed: Excisional biopsy of lesion, left buccal mucosa
Anesthesia: Local
Procedure: The patient was placed in the supine position, and a 3 X 4 mm hard lesion could be felt under the mucosa of the left upper lip. After application of 1% xylocaine with 1:1000 epinephrine, the lesion was completely excised. The surgical wound was closed using #4-00 chromic catgut.

The patient tolerated the procedure well and returned to the In & Out Surgery Unit in satisfactory condition.

Case 6

Preoperative diagnosis: Pilonidal cyst
Postoperative diagnosis: Same
Procedure performed: Pilonidal cystectomy
Anesthesia: Local with 4 cc of 1/2% xylocaine.
Estimated blood loss: Minimal
Fluids: 550 cc intraoperatively
Procedure: The patient was brought to the operating room and placed in a jackknife position. After sterile prepping and draping, 40 cc of 1/2% xylocaine was infiltrated into the surrounding tissue of the pilonidal cyst that had a surface opening on the median raphe over the sacrum. After adequate anesthesia was obtained and 1 gram of IV Ancef administered intraoperatively, the surface opening was probed. There were no apparent tracks demonstrated upon probing. Next, a scalpel was used to make an approximately 8 X 8 cm elliptical incision around the pilonidal cyst. The incision was carried down through subcutaneous tissue to the fascia and the tissue was then excised. Attention was turned to achieving hemostasis with Bovie electrocautery. The pilonidal cyst was then opened and found to contain fibrous tissue. The wound was closed with 0 Prolene interrupted vertical mattress. Estimated blood loss was minimal, and the patient received 550 cc of crystalloid intraoperatively. The patient tolerated the procedure well and was sent to the Recovery Room in stable condition.

Case 7

Preoperative diagnosis: Incarcerated right femoral hernia.
Postoperative diagnosis: Same
Procedure performed: Right femoral herniorrhaphy
Anesthesia: General

Procedure: Patient is a 37-year-old male. Initially, the patient was placed in the supine position, and the abdomen was prepped and draped with Betadine in the appropriate manner. Xylocaine (1%) was infiltrated into the skin and subcutaneous tissue. Because of the patient's reaction to pain, general anesthesia was also administered. An oblique skin incision was performed from the anterior superior iliac spine to the pubic tubercle. The skin and subcutaneous tissues were sharply incised. Dissection was carried down until the external oblique was divided in the line of its fibers with care taken to identify the ilioinguinal nerve to avoid injury. Sharp and blunt dissection was used to free the inguinal cord. The cremasteric muscle was transected. Attempts at reduction of the incarcerated femoral hernia from below were unsuccessful. The femoral canal was opened in an inferior to superior manner, and finally this large incarcerated hernia was reduced. The conjoint tendon was then sutured to Cooper's ligament with 0 Prolene interrupted suture. The conjoint tendon was somewhat attenuated and of poor quality. A transition suture was placed from the conjoint tendon to Cooper's ligament and then to the inguinal ligament with care taken to obliterate the femoral space without stenosis of the femoral vein. The conjoint tendon was then sutured laterally to the shelving border or Poupart's ligament. The external oblique was closed over the cord with 0 chromic running suture. 3-0 plain was placed in the subcutaneous tissue and the skin was closed with staples. Sterile dressings were applied. The patient tolerated the operative procedure well and was gently taken to Recovery in satisfactory condition.

After completing this exercise, refer to Appendix IV to check your answers.

REVIEW

Comprehensive Coding Practice

A. Code the following scenarios.

1. A 42-year-old white male was referred to a gastroenterologist by his primary care physician because of a 2-month history of gross rectal bleeding. A new patient was seen, and the doctor performed a comprehensive history and exam. Medical decision making was of moderate complexity. The patient was scheduled for a complete diagnostic colonoscopy 4 days later. The patient was given detailed instructions for the bowel prep that was to be started at home on Friday at 1 PM. On Friday, conscious sedation was administered and the colonoscopy started. The examination had to be halted at the splenic flexure because of inadequate bowel preparation. The patient was rescheduled for Monday and given additional instructions for bowel prep to be performed starting at 3 PM on Sunday. On Monday, conscious sedation was again administered and a successful total colonoscopy was performed. Diverticulosis was noted in the ascending colon and 2 polyps were excised from the descending colon. The pathology report indicated the polyps were benign.
   Code the procedures and link them to the correct diagnosis.

2. Patient underwent an upper GI series, which included both a KUB and delayed films. The request form noted severe esophageal burning daily for the past 6 weeks. The radiology impression was Barrett's esophagus.
   Code the diagnosis and procedure.

3. Patient was referred to a cardiologist for transesophageal echocardiography. Patient suffered a stroke 3 days after a 3-hour session of cardiac arrhythmia. The cardiologist performed conscious sedation and supervised and interpreted the echocardiography. The report stated the "transesophageal echocardiogram showed normal valvular function with no intra-atrial or intraventicular thrombus, and no significant aortic atherosclerosis."
   Code the diagnosis and the procedure.

4. The patient had been seen in the office on the morning of May 5th and a diagnosis of sinusitis was made. Her husband called at 8 PM that same evening to report his wife had become very lethargic and her speech was slightly slurred. The patient was admitted to the hospital at 8:30 PM by the primary care physician. The doctor performed a comprehensive history and examination, and medical decision making was of high complexity. At 9 AM the next day, the patient was comatose and was transferred to the critical care unit. The doctor was in constant attendance from 8:10 AM until the patient expired at 9:35 AM. The attending physician listed CVA as the diagnosis.
   Code the diagnoses and services.

B. Coding Case Studies

1. Make several copies of the Coding Case Studies form found in Appendix III.

2. Review Appendix II for an overview of the Goodmedicine Clinic Billing Manual and Case Study 1-1 in Appendix I.

3. Enter the Case Study number in the appropriate column, then transfer all of the procedures from the Encounter Form to the procedures column of the worksheet.

4. Reread the chart entry for Case Study 1-1 and determine which diagnosis(es) or symptoms to report on the claim form.

5. List the diagnosis(es) in the Diagnosis column on the form.

6. Code the diagnoses, then code the procedures using the CPT and HCPCS systems.
   Leave 2 or 3 blank lines between each case to accommodate any additions or notes.

7. Repeat Steps 3 through 6 for the remaining cases.

8. Save this worksheet. It will be used for completion of claim forms in Chapters 11 through 17.

Evaluation & Management Coding Practice

Review each case, and select the appropriate level of history, examination, and medical decision making (key components) before referring to the CPT E&M Section to assign the code. To assist in the process of selecting the correct level of history, examination, and medical decision making, refer to HCFA's E&M Documentation Guidelines (draft 2000), located in Appendix II.

1. Mary Adams was initially seen by her physician, Dr. Thompson, as an inpatient on May 1st with the chief complaint of having taken an overdose of Ornade. She had been suffering from flu-like symptoms for one week and had been taking the prescribed drug, Ornade, for several

days. She states that she apparently took too many pills this morning and started exhibiting symptoms of dizziness and nausea. She called the office complaining of these symptoms and was told to meet Dr. Thompson at the hospital emergency department. From the emergency department, she was admitted to the hospital.

Past history revealed no history of hypertension, diabetes, or rheumatic fever. The patient denies any chest pain or past history of previously having taken an overdose of Ornade as mentioned above. Social history reveals she does not smoke or drink. She has two healthy children. Family history is unremarkable.

Systemic review revealed HEENT within normal limits. Review of the CNS revealed headache and dizziness. She had a fainting spell this morning. No paresthesias. Cardiorespiratory revealed cough but no chest pain or hemoptysis. GI revealed nausea; she had one episode of vomiting early this morning. No other abdominal distress noted. GU revealed no frequency, dysuria or hematuria.

Physical examination revealed the patient to be stable without any major symptoms upon arrival to the telemetry area. HEAD & NECK EXAM reveal pupil reaction normal to light and accommodation. Funduscopic examination is normal. Thyroid is not palpable. ENT normal. No lymphadenopathy noted. CARDIOVASCULAR EXAM revealed the point of maximum impulse is felt in the left fifth intercostal space in the midclavicular line. No S3 or S4 gallop. Ejection click was heard and grade 2/6 systolic murmur in the left third and fourth intercostal space was heard. No diastolic murmur. CHEST is clear to auscultation. ABDOMEN reveals no organomegaly. NEUROLOGIC EXAM is normal. PERIPHERAL VASCULAR SYSTEM is intact.

EKG reveals a sinus tachycardia and there was no evidence of myocardial ischemia. A pattern of early repolarization syndrome was noted.

ASSESSMENT: Will be briefly observed in the telemetry area to rule out any specific evidence of cardiac arrhythmia. She will also have a routine biochemical and hematological profile, chest Xray, and cardiogram. Estimated length of stay will be fairly short.

IMPRESSION: Rule out dizziness. Rule out cardiac arrhythmias.

Identify the E&M category/subcategory _____

Determine the extent of history obtained _____

Determine the extent of examination performed _____

Determine the complexity of medical decision making _____

CPT E&M code number: _____

2. Sandy White is a 52-year-old white female who was seen in the office by Dr. Kramer on January 15 with the chief complaint of low back pain. The patient has complained of lumbosacral pain off and on for many months, but it has been getting worse for the last two to three weeks. The pain is constant and gets worse with sneezing and coughing. There is no radiation of the pain to the legs.

PAST HISTORY reveals no history of trauma, no history of urinary symptoms and no history of weakness or numbness in the legs. Had measles during childhood. She's had high blood pressure for a few years. Also has a previous history of rectal bleeding from hemorrhoids.

She had appendectomy and cholecystectomy in 1975. She also has diabetes mellitus, controlled by diet alone. FAMILY HISTORY: Mother died postoperatively at the age 62 of an abdominal operation, the exact nature of which is not known. She had massive bleeding. Father died at the age of 75 of a myocardial infarction. He also had carcinoma of the bladder and diabetes mellitus. One sister has high blood pressure. SOCIAL HISTORY: She is widowed. Smokes and drinks just socially. Works at the Evening Tribune which involves heavy lifting.

SYSTEMIC REVIEW reveals no history of cough, expectoration, or hemoptysis. No history of weight loss or loss of appetite. No history of thyroid or kidney disease. The patient has been overweight for many years. HEENT is unremarkable; hearing and vision are normal. CARDIORESPIRATORY reveals no known murmurs. GI reveals no food allergies or chronic constipation. GU reveals no nocturia, enuresis or GI infection. NEUROMUSCULAR reveals no history of paralysis or numbness in the past.

PHYSICAL EXAMINATION in the office reveals a slightly obese middle aged female in acute distress with lower back pain. Pulse is 80, blood pressure is 140/85, respirations 16, temperature 98.4°F. HEENT: PERRLA. Conjunctivae are not pale. Sclerae not icteric. Fundi show arteriolar narrowing. NECK: No thyroid or lymph node palpable. No venous engorgement. No bruit heard in the neck. CHEST: PMI is not palpable. S1, S2 normal. No gallop or murmur heard. Chest moves equally on both sides with respirations. Breath sounds are diminished. No adventitious sounds heard. ABDOMEN: She has scars from her previous surgery. There is no tenderness. Liver, spleen, kidneys not palpable. Bowel sounds normal. EXTREMITIES: Leg raising sign is negative on both sides. Both femorals and dorsalis pedis are palpable and equal bilaterally. There is no ankle edema. CENTRAL NERVOUS SYSTEM: Speech is normal. Cranial nerves are intact. Motor system is normal. Sensory system is normal. Reflexes are equal bilaterally.

The impression is lumbosacral pain. The patient is being referred for physical therapy treatment twice per week. Darvocet-N will be prescribed for the pain.

Identify the E&M category/subcategory _____

Determine the extent of history obtained _____

Determine the extent of examination performed _____

Determine the complexity of medical decision making _____

CPT E&M code number: _____

3. S: Monica Sullivan was seen in the office by Dr. White on 12/13 for the second time. She presents with a chief complaint of dizziness and weakness; she stated that she wanted to have her blood pressure checked.

O: Patient has been on Vasotec 5 mg and Hydrodiuril 25 mg. B/P has been going up at home. Patient has felt ill, weak, and dizzy, with headache for three days. Cardiovascular exam reveals a B/P of 130/110 and pulse rate of 84. Her temperature is 98.6°F and normal.

A: Accelerated hypertension. Bell's palsy.

P: Increase Vasotec to 5 mg a.m. and 2.5 mg p.m. SMA & CBC.

Identify the E&M category/subcategory _____

Determine the extent of history obtained _____

Determine the extent of examination performed _____

Determine the complexity of medical decision making _____

CPT E&M code number: _____

4. Ginny Tallman is a 73-year-old female who is followed in the Alfred State Medical Clinic for COPD. Her medications include Theo-Dur 300 mg p.o. q.a.m. History of present illness reveals that she seems to have adequate control of broncho-spasm using this medication. She also uses an Albuterol inhaler two puffs p.o. q6h. She has no recent complaints of acute shortness of breath, no chest tightness. She has a chronic, dry cough, productive of scanty sputum. At this time she is complaining of shortness of breath.

   PE reveals an elderly female in no real distress. BP in the left arm sitting is 110/84, pulse 74 per minute and regular, respiratory rate 12 per minute and somewhat labored. Lungs reveal scattered wheezes in both lung fields. There is also noted an increased expiratory phase. CV exam reveals no S3, S4, or murmurs.

   The impression is COPD with asthmatic bronchitis. The patient will have present medications increased to Theo-Dur 300 mg p.o. q.a.m. and 400 mg p.o. q.p.m. She should receive follow-up care in the clinic in approximately two months time.

Identify the E&M category/subcategory _____

Determine the extent of history obtained _____

Determine the extent of examination performed _____

Determine the complexity of medical decision making _____

CPT E&M code number: _____

5. Dr. Linde telephoned established patient Mark Jones to discuss the results of his blood glucose level test. The doctor spent a great deal of time discussing the test results and proposed therapy regimen. Mr. Jones had numerous questions that Dr. Linde took the time to answer completely.

Identify the E&M category/subcategory _____

Identify the appropriate code(s)_____

Essential HCFA-1500 Claim Form Instructions

11 Eleven

OBJECTIVES   Upon successful completion of this chapter, you should be able to:

1. Define the following terms, phrases, and abbreviations:

inpatient medical case	Ambulatory Surgical Center (ASC)	employer tax identification
major surgery case	electronic mail (e-mail)	number (EIN)
minor surgery case	optical character reader (OCR)	billing entity
combined medical/surgical case	National Provider Identifier	provider identification number
claim attachment	(NPI)	(PIN)
electronic media claim (EMC)	primary diagnosis(es)	group practice identification
Keep It Short and Simple (KISS)	secondary diagnosis(es)	number (GRP #)
letter	diagnosis reference number	supplemental plan

2. Discuss billing guidelines for the following cases: inpatient medical, inpatient/outpatient global surgery, medical/surgical, and minor surgery.

3. Apply optical scanning guidelines when completing claim forms.

4. Discuss the reporting guidelines and restrictions covering the following claim form items: diagnoses, date entry, procedures, modifiers, charges, diagnostic reference numbers, and units (on Line 24 of the HCFA-1500 claim form).

5. Explain why the billing entity's employer tax identification number (EIN) should appear on the claim rather than the provider's Social Security Number.

6. State the four processing steps that must occur before a completed form can be mailed to the insurance company.

7. Describe how to set up a "tickler" filing system for completed claim forms.

INTRODUCTION

This chapter presents universal instructions that must be considered before entering data on the HCFA-1500 claim form. In addition, there is a discussion of common errors made on claim forms, guidelines for maintaining the practice's insurance claim files, processing assigned claims, and the Federal Privacy Act of 1974.

Before beginning to study how to prepare a claim form, review the following guidelines mentioned in previous chapters:

1. Be sure the patient has signed an "Authorization for Release of Medical Information Statement." (Additional information is found in Chapter 5, page 73.)

2. Distinguish between a patient's primary and secondary insurance policies. Review Step 4 of the New Patient Interview and Check-In Procedures found in Chapter 4, page 43.

GENERAL BILLING GUIDELINES

Here are the general billing guidelines that are common to most carriers:

1. Provider services for **inpatient medical cases** are billed on a fee-for-service basis. Each physician service results in a unique and separate charge designated by a CPT/HCPCS service/procedure code.

EXAMPLE

The patient was admitted on June 1 with a diagnosis of bronchopneumonia. The doctor sees the patient each morning until the patient is discharged on June 5. The billing for this patient will show:

6/1/YYYY	Initial hospital visit (99xxx)
6/2/YYYY–6/4/YYYY	3 subsequent hospital visits (99xxx times 3)
6/5/YYYY	Discharge visit (99xxx)

2. Inpatient or outpatient **major surgery cases** designated by CPT surgery code numbers without an asterisk (*) are billed on a global fee (all-inclusive surgery fee) basis which covers the presurgery work-up, initial and subsequent hospital visits, surgery, the discharge visit, and uncomplicated postoperative follow-up care in the physician's office.

3. Postoperative complications requiring a return to the operating room for surgery related to the original procedure are billed as an additional procedure. (Be sure to use the correct modifier and link the additional procedure to a new diagnosis that describes the complication.)

4. **Minor surgery cases** are designated in CPT by an asterisk (or star) and are billed on a fee-for-service basis. The preoperative service, surgery, and all postoperative care are individually itemized and billed. Starred procedures are coded according to special guidelines delineated in the Surgery Section of CPT.

5. **Combined medical/surgical cases** where the patient was admitted to the hospital as a medical case, but after testing, required surgery, are billed according to the instructions in items 2 through 4.

EXAMPLE

Patient is admitted on June 1st for suspected pancreatic cancer. Tests are performed on June 2 and 3. On June 4, the decision is made to perform surgery. Surgery is performed on June 5. The patient is discharged on June 10.

This case begins as a medical admission.

The billing will show:

6/1/YYYY	Initial hospital visit (99xxx)
6/2/YYYY and 6/3/YYYY	2 subsequent hospital visits (99xxx times 2)
6/4/YYYY	1 subsequent hospital visit with modifier -57 (99xxx –57) (indicating the decision for surgery was made on this day.)

At this point this becomes a surgery case.

The billing continues with:

6/5/YYYY   Pancreatic surgery (99xxx)

■ **NOTE:** No discharge code is billed because pancreatic surgery falls into the major/global surgery category. ■

6. Some claims require attachments such as operative reports, discharge summaries, or clinic notes, to aid in the determination of the fee to be paid by the insurance company. Each **claim attachment** (medical report substantiating the medical condition) should include patient and policy identification information. Instructions are different for **electronic media claims (EMC)** and paper-generated claims:

   • With EMC processing, wait for the carrier to request additional information.

   • For paper-generated claims, required attachments should accompany the original claim.

7. A **"KISS" (Keep It Short and Simple) letter** is written by the provider in clear and simple English rather than "medicalese." The letter describes an unusual procedure, special operation, or a patient's medical condition that warranted performing surgery in a site different from the HCFA-stipulated site for that surgery. It should be used in any of the following circumstances:

   • Surgery defined as an inpatient procedure that is performed at an **Ambulatory Surgical Center (ASC)** or physician's office.

   • Surgery typically categorized as an office procedure that is performed in an ASC or hospital.

   • A patient's stay in the hospital prolonged because of medical or psychological complications.

   • An outpatient or office procedure performed as an inpatient procedure because patient is a high risk case.

   • Explanation of why a fee submitted to an insurance company is higher than the health care provider's normal fee for the coded procedure. (Modifier -22 should be added to the procedure code number.)

   • A procedure submitted with an "unlisted procedure" code number, or a procedure requiring an explanation or report before reimbursement can be determined.

8. A claim requiring attachments for clarification should never be submitted by electronic mail. Such claims must be generated on paper and sent by mail. **Electronic mail (e-mail)** is the transfer of information from one computer to another via an electronic link.

9. For paper-generated claims, great care must be taken to ensure that the data prints well within the boundaries of the properly designated blocks on the form. Data that runs over into the adjacent blocks or appears in the wrong block will cause rejection of claims.

Most computer programs have a claim form test pattern to assist with the alignment of paper in printers. Run this test pattern before printing claim forms. If claim forms must be completed on a typewriter, each claim form must be meticulously aligned in both the horizontal and vertical planes.

OPTICAL SCANNING GUIDELINES

The HCFA-1500 form was designed to accommodate optical scanning of paper claims. Processing time for claims prepared for **optical character readers (OCR)** is much faster than that for claims that must be manually entered into the insurance company's computer; therefore, payments can be generated much faster. The OCR guidelines were established by HCFA when the present claim form was developed. These rules are now used by all insurance carriers processing claims using the official HCFA-1500 form.

■ **NOTE:** If entering patient claim data directly into Practice Management software, such as Medical Manager®, the software may require that all data be entered using upper and lower case and other data to be typed without regard to the HCFA OCR guidelines. In these cases, the computer program converts the data to the HCFA OCR format when claims are printed or electronically transmitted to a carrier. ■

- *All case studies in this text that are prepared using the Delmar computer disk require OCR standards.*

- All data entered on the claim form must fall within the borders of the data field. "X"s must fall completely within the boxes, and no letters or numbers should be printed on vertical solid or dotted lines (see Figure 11-1).

1) Correct placement of "X" in box   1)

2) Incorrect placement   2)

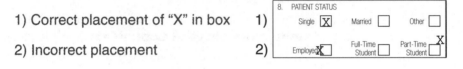

Figure 11-1 Correct placement of the X within a box on the HCFA-1500 claim form

Computer-generated paper claim forms: All claim form programs should have a test pattern program that fills the claim form with "X"s so that you can test the alignment of the forms. This is a critical operation with a pin-fed printer. Check the alignment and make any necessary adjustments each time a new batch of claim forms is inserted into the printer.

When using a typewriter to enter data, proper alignment of the form in the typewriter is critical. The claim form has two test strips printed at the right and left margins of the Health Insurance Claim Form line. To check the horizontal alignment, it is necessary to type "X"s in both the left and the right test patterns.

- Use pica type (10 characters per inch). The equivalent computer font is Courier 10 or OCR 10.

- Type all alpha characters in uppercase (capital letters).

- Do not interchange a zero (0) with the alpha character "O."

- *Substitute a space* for the following key strokes:
  Dollar sign or decimal in all charges or totals
  Decimal point in a diagnosis code number
  Dash in front of a procedure code modifier
  Parentheses surrounding the area code in a telephone number
  Hyphens in social security numbers

- Leave one blank space between the patient or policyholder's last name, first name, and middle initial.
- *Do not* use any punctuation in a patient's, policyholder's, or provider's name, except for a hyphen in a compound name.

EXAMPLE

Gardner-Bey

- *Do not* use a person's title or other designations such as Sr., Jr., II, or III on a claim form unless they appear on the patient's insurance ID card.

EXAMPLE

The name on the ID card reads:
Wm F. Goodpatient, IV

Name on claim form is written:
GOODPATIENT IV WILLIAM F

- Use two zeros in the cents column when a fee or a monetary total is expressed in whole dollars. *Do not* put any leading zeros in front of the dollar amount.

EXAMPLES

Six dollars is expressed as 6 00

Six thousand dollars is expressed as 6 000 00

$ CHARGES	
75	00

- All birth dates should be typed using eight digits with spaces between the digits representing the month, day, and the *four-digit year (MM DD YYYY)*. Care should be taken to ensure that none of the digits fall on the vertical separations within the block (see Figure 11-2). Two-digit code numbers for the months are:

Jan–01	Apr–04	July–07	Oct–10
Feb–02	May–05	Aug–08	Nov–11
Mar–03	June–06	Sept–09	Dec–12

- All corrections to typewriter-generated claim forms must be made using permanent, not removable or lift-off, correction tape, and should be typed/printed using pica type. For an EMC, all corrections must be made within the computer data set. On a computer-generated paper claim, for errors caught before mailing, correct the data in the computer and

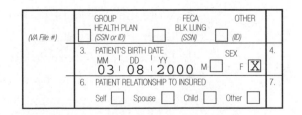

Figure 11-2 Proper entry for birth date

reprint the form. If a paper claim with insufficient or incorrect data is returned by the insurance carrier or contains carrier processing numbers or markings, corrections should be made by typewriter directly on the returned form. Errors should then be corrected in the patient's information in the computer database.

- Claim forms that contain handwritten data, with the exception of the blocks that require signatures, must be manually processed because they cannot be processed by the scanners. This will cause a delay in payment of the claim.

- Extraneous data such as handwritten notes, printed material, or special stamps should be placed on an attachment to the claim.

- The borders of pin-fed claims should be removed evenly at the side perforations, and the claim forms should be separated.

- Nothing should be written or typed in the upper right-hand half of the claim form. Place the name and address of the insurance company in the upper left-hand corner of the form. The words "Do not write in this space" were added for clarification (see Figure 11-3).

- List only one procedure per line starting with line one. Do not skip lines between dates of service (see Blocks 24A-K on page 285).

- Photocopies of claims cannot be optically scanned. All resubmissions must be prepared on an original (red print) claim form.

Figure 11-3 Top of HCFA-1500 claim form

EXERCISE 11-1 Application of Optical Scanning Guidelines

A. On a blank sheet of paper enter the following items in optical scanning format.

1. Patient name: Jeffrey L. Green, DDS
2. Total charge of three hundred dollars
3. Procedure code 12345 with modifiers -22 and -51
4. Write your phone number with area code.
5. Write the ID number using your social security number.
6. Enter your birth date.
7. Illustrate improper marking of boxes.
8. Enter the birth date for a person who was born on March 8, 2000.
9. Write the patient's name. The patient's insurance ID card lists the patient as John W. Green III.

B. Answer the following questions.

1. Your computer always writes the name of the insurance carrier and its mailing address on the claim. Where should this be placed?

2. Your computer uses pin-fed paper. You have just run a batch of 50 claim forms that will be mailed to one insurance company. All claims are properly processed. What must be done to the claim forms before they are placed in the envelope for mailing?

3. What is the rule for placing handwritten material on the claim form?

4. Name the computer/typewriter font style and print size requirements acceptable for optical scanning of claims.

NATIONAL PROVIDER IDENTIFIER

Currently, insurance carriers require provider identification numbers to be reported in Block 17A if a provider is named in Block 17. Individual insurance companies assign these identification numbers. Some insurance companies use the provider's social security number or federal tax identification number, while others assign unique identifier numbers.

The Health Insurance Portability and Accountability Act of 1997 (HIPAA) requires the Department of Health and Human Services (HHS) to adopt standards for specified transactions and data elements (e.g., health care provider identifier). DHHS published a Notice of Proposed Rulemaking (NPRM) in the *Federal Register* on May 7, 1998 that recommended the adoption of the National Provider Identifier (NPI) as the standard health care provider identifier. Public comments are currently being analyzed, and DHHS will publish a Final Rule in a future edition of the *Federal Register* announcing the standard. Compliance with standards is required no later than 24 months after the adoption of the standard (36 months for small health plans).

The **National Provider Identifier (NPI)** will be a unique 8-position alphanumeric identifier (the eighth position is a check digit to help detect keying errors) assigned to health care providers that will be reported to all health plans. Health care providers, health plans, and health care clearinghouses will use the NPI to submit claims or conduct other transactions specified by HIPAA. After the standard is announced as a Final Rule in the *Federal Register*, the NPIs will be assigned to health care providers.

When completing claims for case studies in this text and workbook, follow step-by-step instructions in Chapters 12 through 17.

REPORTING DIAGNOSES: ICD-9-CM CODES

Block 21

Diagnosis codes are placed in Block 21 on the claim form. A maximum of *four* ICD-9-CM codes may be entered on a single claim form.

If more than four diagnoses are required to justify the procedures and/or services on a claim form, use two or more claim forms. In such cases,

21. DIAGNOSIS OR NATURE OF ILLNESS OR INJURY. (RELATE ITEMS 1, 2, 3, OR 4 TO ITEM 24E BY LINE)

1. |___ __| 3. |___ . __|

2. |___ . __| 4. |___ . __|

be sure that the diagnoses listed cover the medical necessity for performing the procedures listed on each claim form. Diagnoses should validate all procedures or services performed.

Sequencing Multiple Diagnoses

The first code listed should be the **primary diagnosis** or the major reason the patient came to the health care provider. **Secondary diagnoses** *codes are placed in numbers 2 through 4 of Block 21, and should be included on the claim form only if they are necessary to justify performing procedures listed in Block 24.* Do not list any diagnoses stated in the patient record that were not treated or addressed during the encounter.

Be sure the code numbers are placed within the designated field on the claim form. The decimal point needed to separate the third and fourth digits is printed on the form. Leave a space; do not type in the decimal points.

When multiple diagnoses are recorded, make sure they are placed in proper sequence on the claim form.

EXAMPLE

1. Primary DX code
2. Secondary DX code
3. Third DX code
4. Fourth DX code

Accurate Coding

Never report a code for tentative diagnoses that include such terms as "rule out," "suspicious for," "probable," "ruled out," "possible," or "questionable." Code either the patient's symptoms or complaints, or suspend completion of this block until a definitive diagnosis is determined.

Be sure all diagnosis codes are reported to the highest degree of specificity known at the time of the treatment.

If the computerized billing system displays a default diagnosis code when entering a patient's claim information, determine if the code validates the current procedure/service reported. It may be necessary to frequently edit this code because, although the diagnosis may still be present, it may not have been treated or managed during each encounter.

■ **NOTE:** Coders should be aware that some chronic conditions always impact patient care and should, therefore, be coded and reported on the HCFA-1500. Examples include diabetes mellitus and hypertension. ■

When completing case studies in this text and workbook, code the reported symptoms documented in the record instead of tentative diagnoses.

REPORTING PROCEDURES AND SERVICES: HCPCS

Instructions in this section are for those blocks that are universally required. All other blocks are discussed individually in Chapters 12 through 17.

24A—Dates of Service

When the claim form was designed, space was allotted for a six-digit date pattern with spaces between the month, day, and two-digit year (MM DD YY). No allowance was made for the year 2000 or beyond and the need for

DATE(S) OF SERVICE					
From			To		
MM	DD	YY	MM	DD	YY
01	02	2000			

a four-digit year. Therefore, an 8-digit date is entered **without spaces** in Blocks 24A and 32 (MMDDYYYY). All other blocks that require dates have room for the OCR required MM DD YYYY pattern as illustrated in Figure 11-2.

All insurance carriers require an entry in the "from column" of Block 24A. A few carriers require entries in both the "from" and the "to" column on all lines when a service is rendered on only one day.

24B—Place of Service

All insurance carriers require a Place of Service (POS) code on the claim form (see Appendix II for POS Codes.) The designated POS must be consistent with the CPT procedure code description.

EXAMPLES

CPT Code		POS Code
99201	Office visit	11 or 3
99221	Initial inpatient service	21 or 1
99301	Annual nursing facility assessment	31 or 8

24D—Procedures and Services

Procedure codes and modifiers are reported in Block 24D. A maximum of six procedures may be submitted on one claim form. Disregard the parenthetical statement to "Explain Unusual Circumstances." This is done either by reporting official CPT or HCPCS modifiers, by including a KISS letter, or by attaching a copy of actual chart documentation to a paper claim form.

Enter only one procedure per line.

Do not include any service or encounter on the claim form if there was no fee charged.

When listing multiple procedures on the claim form, list the surgery with the highest fee first. The secondary procedures along with any required modifiers are then listed in descending order of charges. Complete each horizontal line before starting another. Identical procedures or services may be reported on one line if the following circumstances apply:

- Procedures were performed on consecutive days in the same month.
- Identical code numbers apply to all procedures and/or services.
- Identical charges apply.
- The "Units" block on the claim form is completed.

EXAMPLE

Patient is admitted to the hospital on June 1. The doctor reports detailed subsequent hospital visits on June 2, 3, and 4.

DATE(S) OF SERVICE	
From	To
MM DD YY	MM DD YY
06 01 2000	06 04 2000

If identical consecutive procedures fall within a 2-month span, use two lines, one for the first month and one for the second.

EXAMPLE

Patient is admitted to the hospital on May 30. The doctor reports expanded problem focused visits on May 31, June 1, and June 2.

	DATE(S) OF SERVICE					
	From			To		
	MM	DD	YY	MM	DD	YY
1	05	30	2000	05	31	2000
2	06	01	2000	06	02	2000

When reporting consecutive days on one line, the first date is reported in 24A in the "From" column and the last day in the "To" column. The "Days or Units" column (24G) should reflect the number of days reported in 24A.

Modifiers

Up to three CPT and/or HCPCS modifiers needed to accurately report a procedure or service may be added to the right of the solid vertical line in Block 24D on the claim form. The first modifier is placed between the solid vertical line and the dotted line. Enter two blank spaces between modifiers if multiple modifiers are required. Do not precede modifiers with a hyphen.

D
PROCEDURES, SERVICES, OR SUPPLIES
(Explain Unusual Circumstances)

CPT/HCPCS	MODIFIER
99203	24

Some insurance carriers' optical scanners are not programmed to handle a modifier code on the same line with the procedure code. In this case, the CPT alternate method for reporting modifiers using five digits should be used. Enter the five-digit modifier (099xx) on the line immediately below the CPT number for the procedure that is modified. (Replace the xx with the two-digit CPT modifier.)

When completing exercises and case studies in this text, do not enter modifier –99. Be sure to place all required modifiers on the same line with the CPT code number.

24E—Diagnosis Code

The title of column 24E is a misnomer. HCFA instructions require the use of the diagnosis reference number here, not the ICD code number. **Diagnosis reference numbers** are the item numbers 1 through 4 preprinted in Block 21 on the claim form (see the figure on page 279 and the discussion of sequencing multiple diagnoses in this chapter on page 280; note the parenthetical instructions printed in Block 21 to "Relate Items 1, 2, 3, or 4 to Item 24E by line"). The use of diagnosis reference numbers, rather than ICD code numbers, has become the norm for this block. Insurance companies, however, do not treat Block 24E uniformly. Some require one reference number per horizontal line, whereas others will accept up to two reference numbers separated by one blank space, and a few will accept up to four reference

21. DIAGNOSIS OR NATURE OF ILLNESS OR INJURY. (RELATE ITEMS 1, 2, 3, OR 4 TO ITEM 24E BY LINE)	
1. 794 02	3. 212 4
2. 413 1	4.

E
DIAGNOSIS
CODE
1 2 3

numbers per horizontal line. When working in a health care office, consult the individual insurance carrier manual for specific instructions on how many reference numbers can be included in this block. If more than one reference number is used, the first number placed in this block must reference the diagnosis code that best justifies the procedure or service listed on the same horizontal line in Block 24D.

When working with the case studies in this text, follow the Block 24E instruction for each plan as directed in Chapters 12 through 17.

24F Charges

Careful alignment of the charges in Block 24F, as well as the totals in Blocks 28 through 30, is critical. Precise entry of dollars and cents is also critical. The block has room for five characters in the dollar column and three in the cents column. Dollar amounts and cents must be typed in their own blocks with only one blank space between them (see Figure 11-4 for examples of correct and incorrect placement of charges and totals).

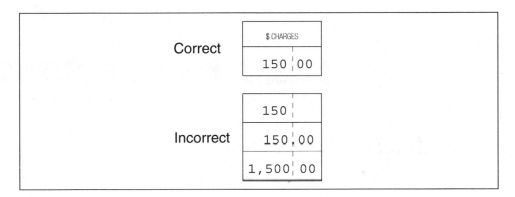

Figure 11-4 Correct entry of charges in Blocks 24F and 28-30

24G Days/Units

Block 24G requires reporting the number of encounters, units of service or supplies, amount of drug injected, and so on, for the procedure reported, on the same line, in Block 24D. This block has room for only three digits.

The most common number used here is "1" for a single procedure.

The number "1" is entered if only one service is performed.

A number greater than "1" is required if identical procedures are reported on one line. *Do not confuse the number of units assigned on one line with the number of days the patient is in the hospital.*

EXAMPLE

Patient is in the hospital 3 days following an open cholecystectomy. The number of units assigned to the line reporting the surgery is "1" (only one cholecystectomy was performed).

When a procedure is performed more than once a day, a "KISS" letter ("Keep It Short and Simple," written in simple terms rather than "medicalese") should be attached to the claim form, explaining why it was necessary to perform the procedure more than once on the same day. Listed below are specific rules that must be followed:

* *Anesthesia time:* Report elapsed time. Convert all hours to minutes.

EXAMPLE

Elapsed time 3 hours and 15 minutes, reported as 195 units.

- *Multiple procedures:* List the primary procedure first, with a "1" in the units column for each procedure. Then add any required modifiers to the secondary procedures in Block 24D (i.e., -51 for multiple procedures).

- *Inclusive dates of similar services:* Report the number of days indicated in the "From" and "To" blocks (Block 24A); the number of days is reported as units in Block 14G.

EXAMPLE

Physician saw Mr. Greenstalk on 01/02 through 01/04 and performed a detailed inpatient, subsequent exam each day. This equals 3 units if reported on one line in Block 24.

- *Radiology services:* Use a number greater than "1" when the same radiology study is performed more than once on the same day. *Do not report the number of Xray views taken for a specific study.*

EXAMPLE

71030 Chest, four views equals one unit

FEDERAL TAX ID NUMBER

Block 25 instructions request information on either the social security number or the employer tax identification number (EIN). All employers are required to have and use either a social security number or a federal **employer tax identification number (EIN)** when they submit quarterly reports on employees' earnings. Use the practice's EIN in this block. In most cases it is typed with the designated hyphen, for example, 11-123456.

25. FEDERAL TAX I.D. NUMBER	SSN	EIN
11-123341	☐	☒

EXERCISE 11-2 Entering Procedures on Line 24

Abstract the following unrelated scenarios and enter the data into columns A, D, F, and G on the following illustration.

If a procedure is performed on consecutive dates enter on one line.

1. 10/10	OV, est pt, detailed	99213	$65.00
2. 10/10	Subsequent hosp visit, expanded problem focused	99232	$45.00
10/10	Subsequent hosp visit, expanded problem focused	99232	$45.00
10/12	Subsequent hosp visit, problem focused	99231	$35.00
3. 10/11	Anesthesia, 1 hour 36 minutes		

4. 10/10	Xray, pelvis, 4 views	72170	$150.00
5. 11/09	Cholecystectomy, open	47600	$900.00
11/09	Diagnostic Arthroscopy, knee	29871-51	$500.00

24. A DATE(S) OF SERVICE From MM DD YY	To MM DD YY	B Place of Service	C Type of Service	D PROCEDURES, SERVICES, OR SUPPLIES (Explain Unusual Circumstances) CPT/HCPCS | MODIFIER	E DIAGNOSIS CODE	F $ CHARGES	G DAYS OR UNITS	H EPSDT Family Plan	I EMG	J COB	K RESERVED FOR LOCAL USE
1											
2											
3											
4											
5											
6											

REPORTING THE BILLING ENTITY

Block 33 calls for the name, address, and phone number of the billing entity. The **billing entity** is the legal business name of the practice; for example, Goodmedicine Clinic. In the case of a solo practitioner, the name of the practice may be entered as the name of the physician followed by initials that designate how the practice is incorporated; for example, Irvin M. Gooddoc, MD, PA. The phone number, including the area code, should be entered on the same line as the printed words "& phone #." Immediately below this line is a blank space for a three-line billing entity mailing address.

The last line of this block is for entering the provider and/or group practice provider numbers, if one is assigned by the insurance carrier or HCFA.

When working with case studies in this text, follow the specific PIN and/or GRP instructions for each plan as directed in the step-by-step instructions in Chapters 12 through 17.

When working in a health care office, consult the individual insurance carrier manual for specific instructions as to whether or not a **PIN (provider identification number)** and **group practice identification number (GRP#)** are required.

■ **NOTE:** The PIN and GRP number will change to the NPI number in the future. ■

EXERCISE 11-3 Completing the Billing Entity Blocks

What is the name of the billing entity in these cases?

1. Dr. Cardiac is employed by Goodmedicine Clinic.
2. Dr. Blank is a solo practitioner. The official name of his practice is Timbuktu Orthopedics.

3. Dr. Jones shares office space with Dr. Blank at Timbuktu Orthopedics·
Dr. Jones, PA and Timbuktu Orthopedics have separate EIN numbers.

PROCESSING SECONDARY CLAIMS

When working in a medical practice, the secondary insurance claim is filed
only after the EOB from the primary claim has been received (see Chapter 4 for
a discussion of how to determine a patient's primary and secondary carriers).

As a general rule, the secondary claim cannot be filed electronically
because the primary EOB must be attached to the secondary claim when sent
to the secondary carrier. Be sure to follow the secondary carrier's format for
filing secondary claims. *Many carriers require primary insurance information in Blocks 11 through 11C.* The secondary policy is identified in Blocks
1 and 1A. Some carriers require the secondary policy to be identified in
Blocks 9–9D (see Figure 11-5).

*When working with claims in this text and the workbook it is necessary to
modify the processing procedure so that two claim forms are completed
when the patient is covered by both a primary and secondary policy. Bill the
primary claim as directed by the primary carrier step-by-step instructions.
The secondary claim is completed by following the secondary claim instructions provided in each chapter.*

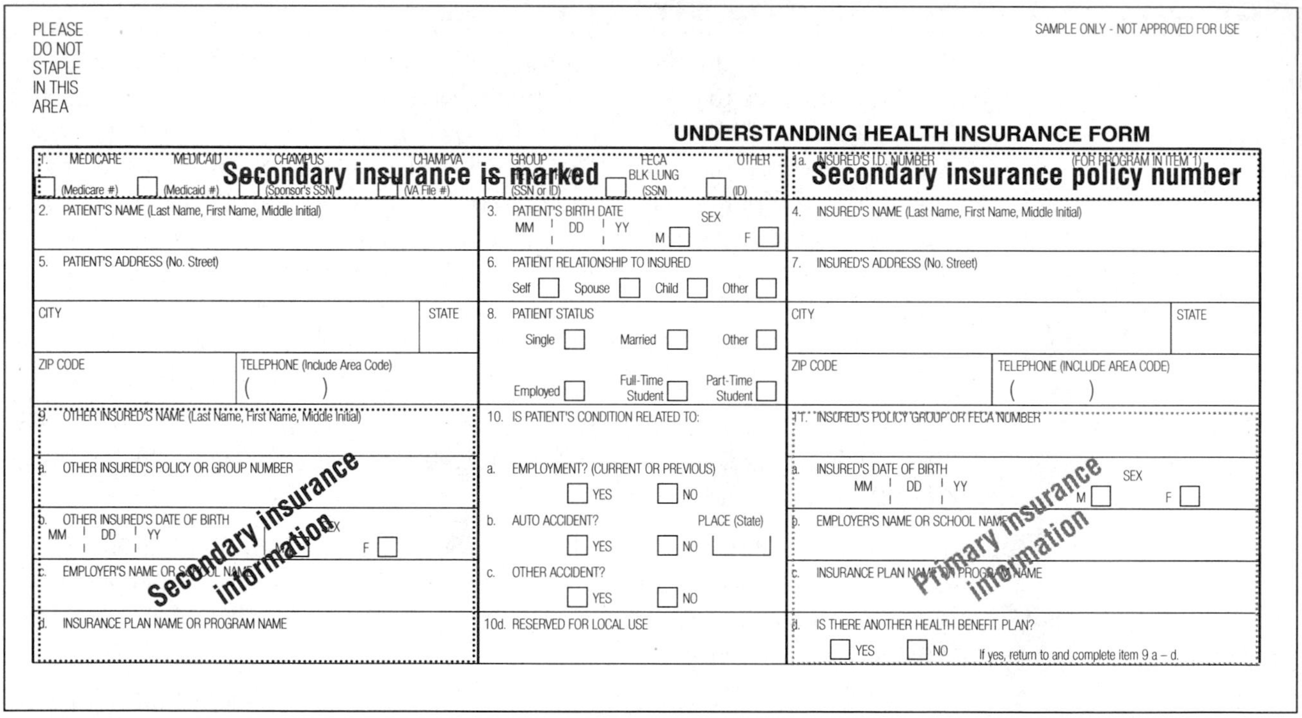

Figure 11-5 Secondary policy information is entered in Blocks 1, 1A, and 9 (primary policy information is
entered in Block 11).

Supplemental Plans   **Supplemental plans** usually cover the deductible and copay or coinsurance
of a primary health insurance policy. Some plans may also cover additional
benefits not included in the primary policy. The best known supplemental
plans are the Medigap plans. These are supplemental plans designed by the

federal government but sold by private commercial insurance companies to "cover the gaps in Medicare." *Supplemental plans are usually noted in Blocks 9 through 9D on the primary insurance claim form (see Figure 11-6).*

9. OTHER INSURED'S NAME (Last Name, First Name, Middle Initial)	
a. OTHER INSURED'S POLICY OR GROUP NUMBER	
b. OTHER INSURED'S DATE OF BIRTH — MM DD YY	SEX — M ☐ F ☐
c. EMPLOYER'S NAME OR SCHOOL NAME	
d. INSURANCE PLAN NAME OR PROGRAM NAME	

Figure 11-6 Supplemental plan information is entered in Block 9

COMMON ERRORS THAT DELAY PROCESSING

After the claim form has been completed, check for these common errors:

1. Typographical errors or incorrect information, as follows:
   - Procedure code number
   - Diagnosis code number
   - Policy identification numbers
   - DOS (Date of service)
   - Practice Employer Tax ID Number
   - Total amount due on a claim form
   - Incomplete or incorrect name of the patient or policyholder (names must match the name on the policy; no nicknames).

2. Omission of the following:
   - Current diagnosis (because of failure to change the patient's default diagnosis in the computer program)
   - Required fourth and/or fifth ICD-9-CM digits
   - Treatment (service) dates
   - Hospital admission and/or discharge dates
   - Name and required identification numbers of the referring provider
   - Required prior treatment authorization numbers
   - Units of service

3. Attachments without patient and policy identification information on each page.

4. Staples or other defacement of the bar code area on the form.

5. Failure to properly align the claim form in the printer to ensure that each item fits within the proper field on the claim.

6. Handwritten items or messages on the claim other than required signatures.

7. Failure to properly link each procedure with the correct diagnosis (Block 24E).

FINAL STEPS IN PROCESSING PAPER CLAIMS

Step 1. Double check each paper claim for errors and omissions.

Step 2. Add any necessary attachments.

Step 3. Obtain the provider's signature on claims to be mailed to the carrier.

Step 4. File a copy of the claim in the practice's claims files.

Step 5. Post the filing of the insurance claim on the patient's account/ledger.

Step 6. Mail the claim to the carrier.

MAINTAINING INSURANCE CLAIM FILES FOR THE PRACTICE

The federal Omnibus Budget Reconciliation Act (OBRA) of 1987 requires physicians to keep copies of any government insurance claim forms and copies of all attachments filed by the provider for a period of five years. HCFA stipulated in March 1992 that "providers and billing services filing claims electronically can comply with the federal regulation by retaining the source documents (routing slip, charge slip, encounter form, superbill) from which they generated the claim, and the daily summary of claims transmitted and received for the five years."

Although there are no specific laws covering retention of commercial or Blue Cross/Blue Shield claims, health care provider contracts with specific insurance carriers may stipulate a specific time frame for all participating providers. It is good business practice to keep these claims until you are sure all transactions have been completed.

Insurance File Set-up

Paper claim files should be organized in the following manner:

1. File *open assigned cases* by month and carrier.

   (These claims have been sent to the carrier, but processing is not complete.)

2. File *closed assigned cases* by year and carrier.

3. File *batched EOBs*.

4. File *unassigned or nonparticipating claims* by year and carrier.

Processing Assigned Paid Claims

When the EOB arrives from the carrier, pull the claim(s) and review the payment(s). Make a notation of the amount of payment, EOB processing date, and applicable EOB batch number on the claim form. Claims with no processing errors and payment in full are marked "closed." They are moved to the Closed Assigned Claims file. Single-payment EOBs may be stapled to the claim form before filing the claim in the Closed Assigned Claims file. Batched EOBs are refiled in the EOB file. If, after comparing the EOB and the claim form, an error in processing is found, the following steps should be taken:

Step 1. Write an immediate appeal for reconsideration of the payment.

Step 2. Make a copy of the original claim, the EOB, and the written appeal.

Step 3. Generate a new HCFA-1500 claim and attach it to the EOB and the appeal. (Black and white copies cannot be read by the insurance carrier's optical scanner.) Make sure the date in Block 31 matches the date on the original claim.

Step 4. Make a notation of the payment (including the check number) on the claim form.

Step 5. Refile the claim form in the appropriate "Open claims file."

Step 6. Mail the appeal to the insurance company.

Federal Privacy Act The Federal Privacy Act of 1974 prohibits an insurance carrier from notifying the provider about payment or rejections of unassigned claims or payments sent directly to the patient/policyholder. If the provider is to assist the patient with the appeal of a claim error, the patient must provide a copy of the EOB and a letter that explains the error. The letter is to be signed by the patient and policyholder giving the carrier permission to permit the provider to appeal the unassigned case. The EOB and letter must accompany the provider's request for reconsideration of the case. If the policyholder writes the appeal, the provider must supply the policyholder with the supporting documentation required to have the claim reconsidered. In recent years, Congress has increased efforts to prevent submission of fraudulent claims to government programs. They are now considering repealing the prohibition from sending EOBs to the provider on unassigned claims. This would allow the provider to appeal processing errors on unassigned government claims.

REVIEW

CHALLENGE EXERCISE

A. Describe the billing rules for the following:
1. Inpatient medical case
2. Major surgery case
3. Minor surgery case

B. Define the following abbreviations:
1. ASC
2. NPI
3. EIN
4. PIN

C. Answer the following questions:
1. A patient is admitted on 10/10 and had an appendectomy on the same day. After postoperative complications, the patient was discharged on 10/12. How many units would appear on the claim form for the surgery entry?
2. The doctor performed a subsequent hospital visit, expanded problem focused (99232), each day on October 29 through November 1. Illustrate the consecutive date entry for Column A, for this case, showing only the proper entry for the dates, procedure code, charge, and units.

3. The social security number for Erin A. Helper, MD is 222-26-9865. Her Blue Cross provider number is EAH1234. She is employed by Goodmedicine Clinic. The clinic's Employer Identification Number is 52-1256789 and the Blue Cross group number is GC1145. Which is the number that should appear in the Tax Identification Number (Block 25) on the HCFA-1500 claim form?

4. What is meant by the "diagnosis reference number?"

5. What is the meaning of the phrase "billing entity?"

6. Compare and contrast the difference between a secondary and a supplemental insurance plan.

D. Listed below are steps required for the final processing of paper claim forms before they are mailed to the carriers. It is important that the steps be performed in proper sequence.

Arrange the steps in proper sequence by placing the correct step number to the left of the statement.

_____ Post the filing of the insurance claim on the patient's account/ledger

_____ File a copy of the claim in the practice's claims file

_____ Obtain the provider's signature on the claim form

_____ Add any necessary attachments

_____ Double-check each paper claim for errors and omissions

Filing Commercial Claims

OBJECTIVES

Upon successful completion of this chapter, you should be able to:

1. Determine the status of primary and secondary commercial claims.
2. Complete commercial primary and secondary fee-for-service claims accurately.
3. Complete commercial primary supplemental fee-for-service claims accurately.
4. Create a comparison chart as an aid to mastering the details of completing claim forms.

INTRODUCTION

This chapter contains instructions for filing fee-for-service claims that are generally accepted nationwide by most commercial health insurance companies, including Aetna, United Health Care, Prudential, Mailhandler's, Cigna, and others. (Instructions for filing Blue Cross/Blue Shield, Medicare, Medicaid, TRICARE/CHAMPUS, CHAMPVA, and Workers' Compensation claims are found in later chapters.)

These step-by-step instructions apply to *all primary commercial and HMO fee-for-service (noncapitated) claims.* Separate instructions are provided when the patient is covered by more than one commercial policy.

■ **NOTE:** Information presented in this chapter builds on the claim form instructions presented in Chapter 11, Essential HCFA-1500 Claim Form Instructions. ■

To supplement the detailed explanation of the step-by-step claim form instructions, the following learning aids have been provided to quickly identify variations on the claim form as required by the six programs discussed in this text:

• Separate instructions for primary and secondary commercial insurance plans.
• Step-by-step instructions broken down into three distinct learning sections with an exercise after each section
• A case study and completed claim form to illustrate each section of the claim form instructions.
• An exercise involving completion of an Insurance Program Comparison Chart to help the student master the instructions and to draw attention to the variations in requirements among the instructions in Chapters 12 through 17.

Permission has been granted by the publisher to make unlimited photocopies of the Comparison Chart. These learning aids may also be tailored to special individual study needs.

INSURANCE PROGRAM COMPARISON CHART

The Insurance Program Comparison Chart assists the reader in mastering the specified blocks on the claim form that require different answers for one or more of the six insurance programs studied in this text. This blank form is located in Appendix III. It is first introduced in Exercise 12-1. The chart allows the student to visually compare the program requirements for commercial, Blue Cross/Blue Shield, TRICARE/CHAMPUS, and Workers' Compensation programs. A separate chart, using the same blank form, is to be created for Medicare and Medicaid.

STEP-BY-STEP INSTRUCTIONS FOR PRIMARY COMMERCIAL CLAIMS

The following instructions are generally recognized nationwide for filing commercial and HMO fee-for-service claims. Some regional carriers may require variations in a few of the blocks, and their requirements should be followed accordingly. Classroom instructors may require the substitution of local requirements for specific blocks. *Write the local instructions in the margins of this text for quick reference when working with the case study assignments.*

Some insurance carriers make frequent billing instruction changes These changes should be available in the latest billing manual or through updates sent by the individual carrier. When filing claims for a medical practice, keep up-to-date by checking for these variations throughout your reading and incorporating changes as they are received. Note modifications and effective dates in the margin of the manual for future reference.

■ **NOTE:** These instructions cover cases in which the patient's insurance plan has primary claim status. The primary claim status is determined by one of the following categories:

- The patient is covered by only one policy.
- The full-benefit employer-sponsored commercial plan is primary if the patient is covered by both a government-sponsored (e.g., Medicare) and an employer-sponsored plan.
- The employer-sponsored plan is primary when the patient is designated as the policyholder of that plan and is also listed as a dependent on another employer-sponsored plan.
- The patient is designated as the policyholder of one employer-sponsored plan and is also listed as a dependent on another employer-sponsored plan.
- The primary policy belongs to the parent with the first birthday in the year (birthday rule) for a child living with both parents who each have commercial policies covering the child. ■

For more details refer to Chapter 4, page 43.

When working with case studies in this text, the primary, secondary, and supplemental status is listed on each case study encounter form (see Figure

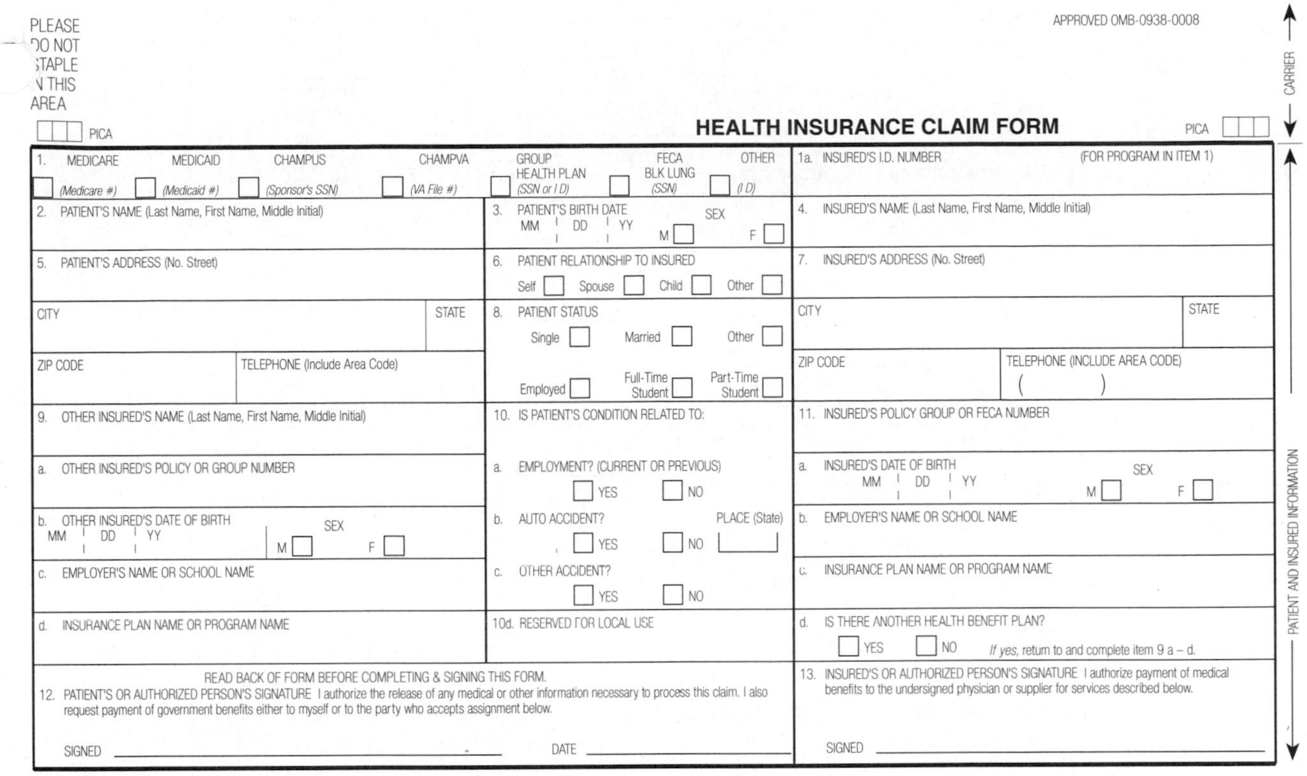
PLEASE DO NOT STAPLE IN THIS AREA

APPROVED OMB-0938-0008

CARRIER

PICA **HEALTH INSURANCE CLAIM FORM** PICA

1. MEDICARE (Medicare #) MEDICAID (Medicaid #) CHAMPUS (Sponsor's SSN) CHAMPVA (VA File #) GROUP HEALTH PLAN (SSN or I D) FECA BLK LUNG (SSN) OTHER (I D)

1a. INSURED'S I.D. NUMBER (FOR PROGRAM IN ITEM 1)

2. PATIENT'S NAME (Last Name, First Name, Middle Initial)

3. PATIENT'S BIRTH DATE MM DD YY SEX M F

4. INSURED'S NAME (Last Name, First Name, Middle Initial)

5. PATIENT'S ADDRESS (No. Street)

6. PATIENT RELATIONSHIP TO INSURED Self Spouse Child Other

7. INSURED'S ADDRESS (No. Street)

CITY STATE

8. PATIENT STATUS Single Married Other

CITY STATE

ZIP CODE TELEPHONE (Include Area Code)

Employed Full-Time Student Part-Time Student

ZIP CODE TELEPHONE (INCLUDE AREA CODE) ( )

9. OTHER INSURED'S NAME (Last Name, First Name, Middle Initial)

10. IS PATIENT'S CONDITION RELATED TO:

11. INSURED'S POLICY GROUP OR FECA NUMBER

a. OTHER INSURED'S POLICY OR GROUP NUMBER

a. EMPLOYMENT? (CURRENT OR PREVIOUS) YES NO

a. INSURED'S DATE OF BIRTH MM DD YY SEX M F

b. OTHER INSURED'S DATE OF BIRTH MM DD YY SEX M F

b. AUTO ACCIDENT? PLACE (State) YES NO

b. EMPLOYER'S NAME OR SCHOOL NAME

c. EMPLOYER'S NAME OR SCHOOL NAME

c. OTHER ACCIDENT? YES NO

c. INSURANCE PLAN NAME OR PROGRAM NAME

d. INSURANCE PLAN NAME OR PROGRAM NAME

10d. RESERVED FOR LOCAL USE

d. IS THERE ANOTHER HEALTH BENEFIT PLAN? YES NO *If yes*, return to and complete item 9 a – d.

READ BACK OF FORM BEFORE COMPLETING & SIGNING THIS FORM.

12. PATIENT'S OR AUTHORIZED PERSON'S SIGNATURE I authorize the release of any medical or other information necessary to process this claim. I also request payment of government benefits either to myself or to the party who accepts assignment below.

SIGNED DATE

13. INSURED'S OR AUTHORIZED PERSON'S SIGNATURE I authorize payment of medical benefits to the undersigned physician or supplier for services described below.

SIGNED

PATIENT AND INSURED INFORMATION

Figure 12-1 Top portion of the HCFA-1500 claim form

12-2). Place a Post-It Note® or other marker on page 294. You will be referring to it frequently when following the step-by-step instructions.

■ **NOTE:** The instructions that follow have been divided into three sections to allow for introduction and mastery of small sections of the claim form. An illustration of a completed section of the claim form is found at the end of each section of instructions (see Figure 12-3 on page 296.) The data for this claim form is located on the John Q. Public encounter form (Figure 12-2). ■

PATIENT AND POLICY IDENTIFICATION

Block 1

Enter an "X" in the "Other" box.

Block 1A

Enter the insurance identification number (and all alpha characters) as it appears on the patient's insurance card. Omit the dashes when completing the claim form.

Block 2

Enter the full name (last name first, followed by the first name and middle initial) of the patient as listed on the patient's insurance identification card. Use of nicknames or typographic errors may result in rejection of the claim.

For case studies in this text, enter the names, minus the punctuation, as they appear on the encounter form. When completing paper claims or claims using the disk that accompanies this text, press the Caps Lock on your keyboard before you start completing the form.

Block 3

Enter the birth date using eight digits in the following format: MM DD YYYY. For the patient's sex, enter an "X" in the appropriate box.

DATE	REMARKS
01/09/YYYY	Authorization Code IG123-45

PATIENT		CHART #	SEX	BIRTHDATE
John Q. Public		12-1	M	03/09/45

MAILING ADDRESS	CITY	STATE	ZIP	HOME PHONE	WORK PHONE
10A Senate Avenue	Anywhere	US	12345	(101) 201 7891	(101) 201 8000

EMPLOYER	ADDRESS	PATIENT STATUS
Legal Research, Inc.	Anywhere US	MARRIED DIVORCED (SINGLE) STUDENT OTHER

INSURANCE: PRIMARY	ID#	GROUP	SECONDARY POLICY
Metropolitan	225120661W	A15	

POLICYHOLDER NAME	BIRTHDATE	RELATIONSHIP	POLICYHOLDER NAME	BIRTHDATE	RELATIONSHIP
		self			

SUPPLEMENTAL PLAN	EMPLOYER

POLICYHOLDER NAME BIRTHDATE RELATIONSHIP	DIAGNOSIS	CODE
	1. Bronchial pneumonia	485
EMPLOYER	2. Urinary frequency	788.41
	3.	
REFERRING PHYSICIAN UPIN/SSN	4.	
Ivan Gooddoc MD 777707070		

PLACE OF SERVICE Office

PROCEDURES	CODE	CHARGE
1. Est Pt OV, level III	99213	$75—
2. Urinalysis, dipstick, automatic microscopy	81001	10—
3. Chest xray, 2 views	71020	50—
4.		
5.		
6.		

SPECIAL NOTES

TOTAL CHARGES	PAYMENTS	ADJUSTMENTS	BALANCE
$135—	$10—	0	$125—

RETURN VISIT	PHYSICIAN SIGNATURE
Prn	*Erin A. Helper, M.D.*

ERIN A. HELPER, M.D.   101 MEDIC DRIVE, ANYWHERE, US 12345
PHONE NUMBER (101) 111-1234
EIN # 11-123452   SSN # 111-22-3333
UPIN EH8888   Medicaid # EBH8881   BC/BS # EH11881 GRP: 1204-P

Figure 12-2 John Q. Public encounter form

Block 4	Enter the word "SAME" if the patient and policyholder are the same person.
	If the patient is not the policyholder, enter the policyholder's full name (last name first, followed by the first name and middle initial).
Block 5	Enter the patient's mailing address on lines 1 and 2 of this block. Enter the five-digit zip code, area code, and phone number in the proper blocks of line 3. Do not type parentheses around the area code as they are preprinted on the HCFA-1500 claim form.
Block 6	Enter an "X" in the appropriate box to indicate the patient's relationship to the policyholder.
Block 7	If the policyholder's address is the same as that stated in Block 5, enter the word "SAME"; otherwise, enter the mailing address of the policyholder.

Block 8

Enter an "X" in the appropriate boxes pertaining to the patient.

■ **NOTE** If the patient is between the ages of 19 and 23, is a dependent on a family policy, and is a full-time student, the claim will not be paid unless the patient can prove full-time student status at the time of the medical encounter. Written acknowledgment of the student's status from the school, college, or university should be filed with the first claim of each semester. ■

Block 9

Enter the word "NONE" and move to Block 10A, leaving 9A-9D blank.

Block 10A

Enter an "X" in the box for "NO" if the reason for the visit is *not* related to an on-the-job injury.

A "YES" indicates the services reported in Block 24D are related to an on-the-job injury, and the previously filed Workers' Compensation claim has been rejected. To receive consideration in these cases from the primary commercial carrier, a copy of the Workers' Compensation Explanation of Benefits and/or letter rejecting the on-job-injury claim must be attached to this commercial claim.

Block 10B

Enter an "X" in the appropriate box.

A "YES" indicates possible third-party liability. The commercial health insurance carrier will return the claim until the issue of third-party liability coverage is settled.

Block 10C

Enter an "X" in the appropriate box.

A "YES" indicates possible third-party liability. If this is not the case, enter one or more E Codes (ICD-9-CM) in Block 21 to indicate the type of injury and its place of occurrence.

Block 10D

This block has been reserved for local use. Consult the appropriate billing manual or the carrier to determine if any action is required for this block.

Leave blank for the purpose of completing case studies in this book and in the workbook.

Block 11

Enter the group policy name or number if one is provided on the patient's card.

Block 11A

Enter the birth date (MM DD YYYY) and sex of the person, if other than the patient, named in Block 4 (policyholder or subscriber).

Block 11B

Enter the name of the employer if the coverage is an employer-sponsored group policy (EGHP is the Employee Group Health Plan) or an organization/union, if one is identified on the patient's ID card.

Block 11C

Enter the name of the carrier for the patient's policy.

Block 11D

Enter an "X" in the "NO" box to indicate the patient is covered by only *one* insurance policy.

Block 12

Enter the words "SIGNATURE ON FILE" if the patient has signed an Authorization for Release of Medical Information form (refer to the discussion in Chapter 5, page 73). Do not enter a date because it is included on the form signed by the patient. If the practice does not have the patient sign a customized form, the patient should date and sign this block on the claim form.

When working with the case studies in this text and workbook, it is assumed that all patients have signed a customized authorization.

Block 13

The patient's signature authorizes direct payment to the physician for the benefits due the patient. "SIGNATURE ON FILE" is acceptable if an assignment statement has been previously signed and is on file (see Figure 12-3).

Figure 12-3 Completed Blocks 1 through 13 for John Q. Public encounter form in Figure 12-2

When working with case studies in this text and workbook, assume the patient has signed a separate authorization for direct payment.

EXERCISE 12-1 Preparing the Comparison Chart

The objective of this assignment is to create a useful reference as an aid to mastering the details of completing claim forms for six major insurance programs.

1. Make five copies of the Comparison Chart in Appendix III.

2. Enter the following titles in the first row of each wide column at the top of each page:

   Commercial

   BC/BS

   TRICARE STANDARD

   Workers' Compensation

3. Enter the following block numbers in the first column of each page as follows:

Page 1	Blocks	1	through	9D
Page 2	Blocks	10	through	16
Page 3	Blocks	17	through	23
Page 4	Blocks	24A	through	24K
Page 5	Blocks	25	through	33

4. Enter abbreviated instructions in Blocks 1-13 of the Commercial column (see a sample in Figure 12-4).

For the purpose of case studies in this text, if the step-by-step instructions in this chapter indicate a particular block is to be left blank, enter the word "Blank."

■ **NOTE:** Arrows indicate that the information or direction from the block to the left or the block above is to be repeated on the claim form. For example, as shown in Figure 12-4, if consecutive blocks are to be left blank, enter the word "Blank" in the first block and draw a vertical arrow down through the other blocks that have similar treatment. ■

ITEM	COMMERCIAL
1 1A	OTHER ID #
2	PATIENT NAME NO PUNCTUATION
3	PT BIRTH DATE/SEX
4	INSURED OR SAME
5	PT ADDRESS
6	RELAT TO INSURED
7	INSURED ADDRESS
8	PATIENT STATUS
9	"NONE"
9A	BLANK
9B	↓
9C	
9D	↓

Figure 12-4 Sample Insurance Comparison Chart, page 1

5. Save this form as it will be used for additional exercises in this chapter and other chapters.

EXERCISE 12-2 HCFA-1500 Blocks 1 through 13

This exercise requires two copies of a blank HCFA-1500 claim form. You may either make photocopies of the form in Appendix III of the text, or print copies of the blank form using the UHI CD-ROM. (Instructions for installing the computer program are located in Appendix V.)

1. Obtain two copies of the HCFA-1500 form.

2. Review instructions for Blocks 1 through 13 on your comparison chart.

3. On the first claim form, complete Blocks 1 through 13 using your own personal data for filing an employer-sponsored claim with a commercial policy. If you do not have a commercial insurance policy, or lack any of the required data use the following information:

Policy ID: Place the prefix ZZX in front of your own Social Security Number

Group number: ZZ34

Policyholder: Yourself

Name of the insurance carrier: MetLife

Employer: Employee International

Other Insurance: None

4. Save this form for use in Exercise 12-8.

5. Review the Mary Sue Patient encounter form (Figure 12-5). Place a page marker at the encounter form.

6. Abstract the information needed for Blocks 1 through 13 from Figure 12-5, and enter the required information on the second claim form using

DATE 01/09/YYYY	REMARKS			
PATIENT Mary Sue Patient		CHART # 12-2	SEX F	BIRTHDATE 10/10/59

MAILING ADDRESS 91 Home Street	CITY Nowhere	STATE US	ZIP 12367	HOME PHONE (101) 201 8989	WORK PHONE

EMPLOYER: Homemaker | ADDRESS | PATIENT STATUS (MARRIED) DIVORCED SINGLE STUDENT OTHER

INSURANCE: PRIMARY Conn General | ID# 222017681 | GROUP AX107 | SECONDARY POLICY

POLICYHOLDER NAME James W. Patient | BIRTHDATE 03/01/48 | RELATIONSHIP spouse | POLICYHOLDER NAME | BIRTHDATE | RELATIONSHIP

SUPPLEMENTAL PLAN | EMPLOYER

POLICYHOLDER NAME | BIRTHDATE | RELATIONSHIP | DIAGNOSIS | CODE

EMPLOYER Anywhere Water Company

1. Abnormal EKG — 794.31
2. Angina, Prinzmetal — 413.1
3. Alpha-lipoproteinemia — 272.4
4.

REFERRING PHYSICIAN UPIN/SSN

PLACE OF SERVICE Goodmedicine Hospital, Anywhere Street, Anywhere, US, 12345

PROCEDURES	CODE	CHARGE
1. Initial Hosp visit, level III 01/07/YYYY	99223	$150—
2. Subsequent Hosp visit, level I 01/08/YYYY	99221	75—
3. Discharge 30 min 01/09/YYYY	99238	75—
4.		
5.		
6.		

SPECIAL NOTES
See Dr. Cardiac for Thallium Stress Test tomorrow and follow-up

TOTAL CHARGES $300—	PAYMENTS 0	ADJUSTMENTS 0	BALANCE $300—

RETURN VISIT | PHYSICIAN SIGNATURE Erin A. Helper, M.D.

ERIN A. HELPER, M.D. 101 MEDIC DRIVE, ANYWHERE, US 12345
PHONE NUMBER (101) 111-1234
EIN # 11-123452 SSN # 111-22-3333
UPIN EH8888 Medicaid # EBH8881 BC/BS # EH11881 GRP: 1204-P

Figure 12-5 Mary Sue Patient encounter form

Optical Scanning Guidelines. This may be completed by handwriting the information, using the Blank Form Mode on the disk found in the text, or entering the data using a typewriter. Instructions for installing the disk are found in Appendix V.

7. Review Blocks 1 through 13 of the claim form to be sure all required blocks are properly completed.

■ **NOTE:** This same encounter form and claim form will be used for Exercise 12-4. ■

DIAGNOSTIC AND TREATMENT DATA

Refer to Figure 12-6 showing Blocks 14 through 23.

Block 14

The arrow in this block indicates that the date refers to either illness, injury, or pregnancy. You could treat this block as if the word "of" were inserted in place of the arrow. Enter the date of the first symptoms or injury. For obstetrical visits, record the date of last menstrual period if available in the documentation. In cases where the history does not document a starting date, but provides an approximation, simply count back to the approximated date and record it on the claim form. Enter the date in MM DD YYYY format.

EXAMPLE

Current date: 03/08/2001, record says "injured 3 months ago." Date in Block 14 would read. 12 08 2000.

Block 15

Enter the date that a prior episode of the same or similar illness began if documented in the patient's record. Date format is MM DD YYYY (enter spaces between month and day, and day and year).

Block 16

Enter the dates the patient was unable to work if documented in the record or on the encounter form. Date format is MM DD Y Y Y Y (with spaces entered as indicated in format).

Block 17

Enter the full name and credentials of the referring/ordering physician(s) or other health care provider if any of the following services are to be listed in Block 24D: consultation, surgery, diagnostic testing, physical or occupational therapy, home health care, or durable medical equipment. For Assistant Surgeon claims, enter the name of the attending surgeon.

14. DATE OF CURRENT: ◄ ILLNESS (First symptom) OR INJURY (Accident) OR PREGNANCY (LMP) MM DD YY	15. IF PATIENT HAS HAD SAME OR SIMILAR ILLNESS, GIVE FIRST DATE MM DD YY	16. DATES PATIENT UNABLE TO WORK IN CURRENT OCCUPATION MM DD YY MM DD YY FROM TO
17. NAME OF REFERRING PHYSICIAN OR OTHER SOURCE	17a. I.D. NUMBER OF REFERRING PHYSICIAN	18. HOSPITALIZATION DATES RELATED TO CURRENT SERVICES MM DD YY MM DD YY FROM TO
19. RESERVED FOR LOCAL USE		20. OUTSIDE LAB? $ CHARGES ☐ YES ☐ NO
21. DIAGNOSIS OR NATURE OF ILLNESS OR INJURY. (RELATE ITEMS 1, 2, 3, OR 4 TO ITEM 24E BY LINE) 1. L___ . __ 3. L___ . __ 2. L___ . __ 4. L___ . __		22. MEDICAID RESUBMISSION CODE ORIGINAL REF. NO.
		23. PRIOR AUTHORIZATION NUMBER

Figure 12-6 Blocks 14 through 23 of the HCFA-1500 claim form

■ **NOTE:** If the health care provider has assumed total care of the patient for a given illness/injury, this block is completed only on the initial claim filed for the condition. ■

Block 17A

PAR Providers: Enter the carrier assigned PIN (provider identification number).

NonPAR Providers: Enter the Social Security Number of the provider, with no spaces or hyphens.

Block 18

Enter the admission date and the discharge date if any procedure/service is rendered to a patient with inpatient status. If the patient is still hospitalized, leave the "TO" block blank. Date format is MM DD YYYY (with spaces entered).

Block 19

This block has been reserved for local use. Consult the appropriate billing manual or the carrier to determine if any action is required for this block.

When working with case studies in the text and workbook, leave this block blank for all commercial cases.

Block 20

Enter an "X" in the "NO" box or leave blank if all laboratory procedures included on this claim form were performed in the provider's office.

Enter an "X" in the "YES" box if laboratory procedures listed on the claim form were performed by an outside laboratory and billed to the referring health care provider. Enter the total amount charged for all tests performed by the outside laboratory. The charge for each test should be entered as a separate line in Block 24D and the name and address of the outside laboratory included in Block 32.

■ **NOTE:** Some local carriers may have other specific instructions for completion of this block. ■

When working with case studies in this text and workbook, enter an "X" in the "NO" box.

Block 21

Enter the ICD-9-CM code number for the diagnoses or conditions treated in this space. Do not enter the decimal. Enter a space instead, as the decimal is preprinted on the HCFA-1500.

■ **NOTE:** Detailed instructions for treatment of this block appear in Chapter 11. ■

When completing case studies in this text and workbook, code the reported symptoms if a qualified diagnosis is documented.

Block 22

Leave blank. (Pertains to Medicaid claims only.)

Block 23

Enter the assigned authorization number when the patient's insurance plan requires specific services to be authorized by the patient's primary physician or the carrier's managed care department before the procedure is performed. Some carriers may also require copies of any written authorization the provider received to be attached to the claim. See Figure 12-7 for completed Blocks 14-23 of the HCFA-1500 form.

14. DATE OF CURRENT: ILLNESS (First symptom) OR INJURY (Accident) OR PREGNANCY (LMP) MM DD YY	15. IF PATIENT HAS HAD SAME OR SIMILAR ILLNESS, GIVE FIRST DATE MM DD YY	16. DATES PATIENT UNABLE TO WORK IN CURRENT OCCUPATION MM DD YY MM DD YY FROM TO
17. NAME OF REFERRING PHYSICIAN OR OTHER SOURCE IVAN GOODDOC, MD	17a. I.D. NUMBER OF REFERRING PHYSICIAN/ 777707070	18. HOSPITALIZATION DATES RELATED TO CURRENT SERVICES MM DD YY MM DD YY FROM TO
19. RESERVED FOR LOCAL USE		20. OUTSIDE LAB? $ CHARGES ☐ YES ☒ NO
21. DIAGNOSIS OR NATURE OF ILLNESS OR INJURY. (RELATE ITEMS 1, 2, 3, OR 4 TO ITEM 24E BY LINE) 1. 485 . __ 3. __ . __ 2. 788 .41 4. __ . __		22. MEDICAID RESUBMISSION CODE ORIGINAL REF. NO. 23. PRIOR AUTHORIZATION NUMBER IG123-45

Figure 12-7 Completed Blocks 14 through 23 for John Q. Public encounter form in Figure 12-2

EXERCISE 12-3 Continuation of Work on Comparison Chart

Reread the instructions for completing Blocks 14 through 23. As you read each block, record a concise description of the instructions in the appropriate block in the Commercial column of the Comparison Chart.

EXERCISE 12-4 Continuation of Exercise 12-2

1. Review the Mary Sue Patient encounter form found in Figure 12-5 to find the diagnostic and treatment data.

2. Abstract the information needed for Blocks 14 through 23, and enter the required information on a new claim form using Optical Scanning Guidelines. This may be completed by handwriting the information, using the Blank Form Mode on the disk, or entering the data using a typewriter. Instructions for installing the disk are found in Appendix V.

3. Review Blocks 14 through 23 of the claim form to be sure all required blocks are properly completed.

4. Compare your claim form with Figure 12-8, page 302.

■ **NOTE:** This same claim form will be used for Exercise 12-6. ■

INSTRUCTIONS FOR BLOCK 24

Refer to Figure 12-9, page 303, for Blocks 24A through 24K.

Block 24A

Enter the date the procedure was performed in the "FROM" column. Do not complete the "TO" column for a single procedure entry unless you have special instructions to do so from a specific carrier. Date format is MMDDYYYY with no spaces.

To list procedures or services that are assigned the same codes and charges because they were performed on consecutive days, indicate the last day the procedure was performed in the "TO" column. Also, enter the number of consecutive days or units in the "DAYS OR UNITS" column" (Block 24G).

Block 24B

Enter the appropriate Place of Service (POS) code number from the following list of codes which identifies where the service reported was performed. Note that POS code numbers vary by carrier.

Inpatient hospital	1
Outpatient hospital	2
Provider's office	3
Patient's home	4
Psychiatric facility—day	5
Inpatient psychiatric facility	6
Nursing home	7
Skilled nursing facility	8
Independent laboratory	A
Other unlisted facility	0

When working with case studies in the text and workbook, use the POS codes listed above.

PLEASE DO NOT STAPLE IN THIS AREA							(SAMPLE ONLY - NOT APPROVED FOR USE)

UNDERSTANDING HEALTH INSURANCE CLAIM FORM PICA

1. MEDICARE ☐ (Medicare #) MEDICAID ☐ (Medicaid #) CHAMPUS ☐ (Sponsor's SSN) CHAMPVA ☐ (VA File #) GROUP HEALTH PLAN ☐ (SSN or ID) FECA BLK LUNG ☐ (SSN) OTHER ☒ (ID)	1a. INSURED'S I.D. NUMBER (FOR PROGRAM IN ITEM 1) 222017681
2. PATIENT'S NAME (Last Name, First Name, Middle Initial) PATIENT MARY SUE	3. PATIENT'S BIRTH DATE MM 10 DD 10 YY 1959 SEX M ☐ F ☒	4. INSURED'S NAME (Last Name, First Name, Middle Initial) PATIENT JAMES W
5. PATIENT'S ADDRESS (No. Street) 91 HOME STREET	6. PATIENT RELATIONSHIP TO INSURED Self ☐ Spouse ☒ Child ☐ Other ☐	7. INSURED'S ADDRESS (No. Street)
CITY NOWHERE STATE US	8. PATIENT STATUS Single ☐ Married ☒ Other ☐	CITY STATE
ZIP CODE 12367 TELEPHONE (Include Area Code) 101 201 8989	Employed ☐ Full-Time Student ☐ Part-Time Student ☐	ZIP CODE TELEPHONE (INCLUDE AREA CODE) ( )
9. OTHER INSURED'S NAME (Last Name, First Name, Middle Initial) NONE	10. IS PATIENT'S CONDITION RELATED TO:	11. INSURED'S POLICY GROUP OR FECA NUMBER AX107
a. OTHER INSURED'S POLICY OR GROUP NUMBER	a. EMPLOYMENT? (CURRENT OR PREVIOUS) ☐ YES ☒ NO	a. INSURED'S DATE OF BIRTH MM 03 DD 01 YY 1948 SEX M ☒ F ☐
b. OTHER INSURED'S DATE OF BIRTH MM DD YY SEX M ☐ F ☐	b. AUTO ACCIDENT? PLACE (State) ☐ YES ☒ NO	b. EMPLOYER'S NAME OR SCHOOL NAME ANYWHERE WATER COMPANY
c. EMPLOYER'S NAME OR SCHOOL NAME	c. OTHER ACCIDENT? ☐ YES ☒ NO	c. INSURANCE PLAN NAME OR PROGRAM NAME CONN GENERAL
d. INSURANCE PLAN NAME OR PROGRAM NAME	10d. RESERVED FOR LOCAL USE	d. IS THERE ANOTHER HEALTH BENEFIT PLAN? ☐ YES ☒ NO If yes, return to and complete item 9 a – d.
READ BACK OF FORM BEFORE COMPLETING & SIGNING THIS FORM. 12. PATIENT'S OR AUTHORIZED PERSON'S SIGNATURE I authorize the release of any medical or other information necessary to process this claim. I also request payment of government benefits either to myself or to the party who accepts assignment below. SIGNED SIGNATURE ON FILE DATE	13. INSURED'S OR AUTHORIZED PERSON'S SIGNATURE I authorize payment of medical benefits to the undersigned physician or supplier for services described below. SIGNED SIGNATURE ON FILE

14. DATE OF CURRENT: MM 01 DD 07 YY YYYY ILLNESS (First symptom) OR INJURY (Accident) OR PREGNANCY (LMP)	15. IF PATIENT HAS HAD SAME OR SIMILAR ILLNESS, GIVE FIRST DATE MM DD YY	16. DATES PATIENT UNABLE TO WORK IN CURRENT OCCUPATION FROM MM DD YY TO MM DD YY
17. NAME OF REFERRING PHYSICIAN OR OTHER SOURCE	17a. I.D. NUMBER OF REFERRING PHYSICIAN	18. HOSPITALIZATION DATES RELATED TO CURRENT SERVICES FROM MM 01 DD 07 YY YYYY TO MM 01 DD 09 YY YYYY
19. RESERVED FOR LOCAL USE		20. OUTSIDE LAB? ☐ YES ☒ NO $ CHARGES
21. DIAGNOSIS OR NATURE OF ILLNESS OR INJURY. (RELATE ITEMS 1, 2, 3, OR 4 TO ITEM 24E BY LINE) 1. 794 31 2. 413 1 3. 272 4 4.		22. MEDICAID RESUBMISSION CODE ORIGINAL REF. NO. 23. PRIOR AUTHORIZATION NUMBER

24. A DATE(S) OF SERVICE From MM DD YY To MM DD YY	B Place of Service	C Type of Service	D PROCEDURES, SERVICES, OR SUPPLIES (Explain Unusual Circumstances) CPT/HCPCS MODIFIER	E DIAGNOSIS CODE	F $ CHARGES	G DAYS OR UNITS	H EPSDT Family Plan	I EMG	J COB	K RESERVED FOR LOCAL USE
1	01 07 YYYY	1	1	99223	1	150 00	1				
2	01 08 YYYY	1	1	99221	1	75 00	1				
3	01 09 YYYY	1	1	99238	1	75 00	1				
4											
5											
6											

25. FEDERAL TAX I.D. NUMBER 11-123341 SSN ☐ EIN ☒	26. PATIENT'S ACCOUNT NO. 12-2	27. ACCEPT ASSIGNMENT? (For govt. claims, see back) ☐ YES ☐ NO	28. TOTAL CHARGE $ 300 00	29. AMOUNT PAID $	30. BALANCE DUE $ 300 00
31. SIGNATURE OF PHYSICIAN OR SUPPLIER INCLUDING DEGREES OR CREDENTIALS (I certify that the statements on the reverse apply to this bill and are made a part thereof.) SIGNED ERIN A. HELPER MD DATE MMDDYYYY	32. NAME AND ADDRESS OF FACILITY WHERE SERVICES WERE RENDERED (If other than home or office) GOODMEDICINE HOSPITAL ANYWHERE STREET ANYWHERE US 12345		33. PHYSICIAN'S SUPPLIER'S BILLING NAME, ADDRESS, ZIP CODE & PHONE # (101) 111 1234 ERIN A HELPER MD 101 MEDIC DRIVE ANYWHERE USA 12345 PIN# GRP#		

(SAMPLE ONLY - NOT APPROVED FOR USE)   *PLEASE PRINT OR TYPE*   SAMPLE FORM 1500 SAMPLE FORM 1500 SAMPLE FORM 1500

Figure 12-8 Completed Mary Sue Patient primary claim form

Figure 12-9 Blocks 24A through 24K of the HCFA-1500 claim form

Block 24C	Enter the Type of Service (TOS) code (if required) from the following list of codes which identify the procedure/medical service classification.

Medical Care	1
Surgery	2
Consultation	3
Diagnostic radiology	4
Diagnostic laboratory	5
Radiation therapy	6
Anesthesia	7
Assistant surgeon	8
Other medical services	9
Pneumococcal vaccine	V
Second surgical opinion	Y

■ **NOTE:** TOS code 9, other medical services, is a miscellaneous category for services that cannot be categorized into any of the other codes, such as rehabilitation or occupational therapy. ■

Block 24D	Enter the correct five-digit CPT or HCPCS Level II/III code number and any required CPT or HCPCS modifiers for the services or procedure reported in this block. Enter a blank space, not a hyphen, to separate the code number from the modifier or multiple modifiers.

Block 24E	Enter the *reference number* (1 through 4) for the ICD code number listed in Block 21 that justifies the medical necessity for each procedure or service listed in Block 24D.

■ **NOTE:** Some local carriers will accept more than one reference number on each line. If more than one reference number is used, the first number stated must represent the primary diagnosis that justifies the medical necessity for performing the procedures on that horizontal line. Unless otherwise directed by the carrier, multiple reference numbers should be separated by blank spaces, not commas or dashes. ■

When working with case studies in the text and workbook, enter only one reference number in this block on commercial claims.

Block 24F	Enter the fee charged to the patient's account for the procedure performed. If identical, consecutive services or procedures are reported on this line, enter the total fee charged for the combined services or procedures.

Block 24G	Enter the number of units/days of services or procedures reported in 24D. (Review the discussion on units in Chapter 11, page 283, if necessary.)
Block 24H	Leave blank. (This block is used to identify all services that are provided under the special Medicaid EPSDT Program. Refer to the Medicaid chapter for more information.)
Block 24I	Enter an "X" in this box when the health care provider's documentation indicates that a medical emergency existed and a delay in treatment in order to obtain authorization would be injurious to the patient. This is especially important when a managed care situation exists and no prior authorization was obtained before the start of emergency treatment.
Block 24J	Leave blank. (COB stands for "coordination of benefits.")

■ NOTE: If the patient has secondary insurance, some payers require an "X" in this block. ■

Block 24K	Leave blank.

See Figure 12-10 for completed Block 24.

24. A DATE(S) OF SERVICE						B Place of Service	C Type of Service	D PROCEDURES, SERVICES, OR SUPPLIES (Explain Unusual Circumstances) CPT/HCPCS	MODIFIER	E DIAGNOSIS CODE	F $ CHARGES		G DAYS OR UNITS	H EPSDT Family Plan	I EMG	J COB	K RESERVED FOR LOCAL USE
From MM	DD	YY	To MM	DD	YY												
1	01 09 YYYY						3	1	99213		1	75	00	1				
2	01 09 YYYY						3	5	81001		2	10	00	1				
3	01 09 YYYY						3	4	71020		1	50	00	1				
4																		
5																		
6																		

Figure 12-10 Completed Block 24 for John Q. Public encounter form in Figure 12-2

EXERCISE 12-5 **Continuation of Work on Comparison Chart**

Reread the instructions for completing Blocks 24A through 24K. As you read each block record a concise description of the instructions in the appropriate block in the Commercial column of the Comparison Chart.

EXERCISE 12-6 **Continuation of Exercise 12-2**

1. Review the procedure data on the Mary Sue Patient encounter form in Figure 12-5.

2. Abstract the information needed for Blocks 24A through 24K and enter the required information on a new claim form using Optical Scanning Guidelines. This may be completed by handwriting the information, using the Blank Form Mode on the disk, or entering the data using a typewriter. Instructions for installing the disk are found in Appendix V.

3. Review Blocks 24A through 24K of the three claim forms to be sure all required blocks are properly completed.

■ NOTE: The same claim forms will be used for Exercise 12-8. ■

PROVIDER/BILLING ENTITY IDENTIFICATION

Refer to Figure 12-11 for Blocks 25 through 33.

25. FEDERAL TAX I.D. NUMBER	SSN EIN	26. PATIENT'S ACCOUNT NO.	27. ACCEPT ASSIGNMENT? (For govt. claims, see back) ☐ YES ☐ NO	28. TOTAL CHARGE $	29. AMOUNT PAID $	30. BALANCE DUE $

31. SIGNATURE OF PHYSICIAN OR SUPPLIER INCLUDING DEGREES OR CREDENTIALS (I certify that the statements on the reverse apply to this bill and are made a part thereof.)

SIGNED

DATE

32. NAME AND ADDRESS OF FACILITY WHERE SERVICES WERE RENDERED (If other than home or office)

33. PHYSICIAN'S SUPPLIER'S BILLING NAME, ADDRESS, ZIP CODE & PHONE #

PIN#   GRP#

(APPROVED BY AMA COUNCIL ON MEDICAL SERVICE 8/88)   *PLEASE PRINT OR TYPE*   FORM HCFA-1500 (12-90)
FORM OWCP-1500   FORM RRB-1500
FORM AMA OP050192

Figure 12-11 Blocks 25 through 33 of the HCFA-1500 claim form

Block 25

Enter the billing entity's Employer Tax Identification Number, if available. Otherwise, enter the provider's Social Security Number. In addition, be sure to enter an "X" in the appropriate box to indicate which is being reported.

■ **NOTE:** While third-party payers will accept the number with or without hyphens, when completing claim forms in this text (and when using the CD-ROM), be sure to enter hyphens. ■

Block 26

Enter the number assigned to the patient's account if the practice uses an identification number to identify the patient's account, ledger card or if the claim is filed electronically. Leave the block blank if the practice files patient accounts by patient name.

When working with the case studies in the text and workbook, enter the case study number in this block. If the case requires completion of primary and secondary carrier claim forms, enter the case study number and a P (for primary) or S (for secondary).

Block 27

To *accept assignment* means that the provider agrees to accept the carrier-determined allowed fee for services performed. This statement is different from the *assignment of benefits* (Block 13) statement, which, when signed by the patient, indicates that payment is to be made directly to the provider. Some payers, however, use Block 27 to indicate whether the patient or provider receives the reimbursement amount. Enter an "X" in the "YES" box if the provider has a participating provider contract with the carrier. Enter an "X" in the "NO" box if the provider has not signed a participating provider contract with the carrier.

When working with the case studies in this text and workbook, enter an "X" in the "NO" box.

Block 28

Total the charges on this claim form, and enter the total in this block. This figure should never reflect negative charges or show that a credit is due to the patient. If multiple claims for one patient are generated by the computer because more than six services were reported, be sure the total charge recorded on each claim form accurately represents the total of the items on each separate claim form submitted.

Block 29

Enter the amount the patient has paid toward the required annual deductible, or any copayment/coinsurance payments collected from the patient for procedures or services listed on this claim. Leave this block blank if no payment is made.

Block 30	Subtract the figure in Block 29 from the figure in Block 28 and enter the total here.
Block 31	PAPER CLAIMS: Most health care providers have arranged with major health insurance carriers to use either a signature stamp or a typed name and professional credential. If these special arrangements have not been made, the provider must sign each claim.

■ **NOTE:** When arrangements are made to transmit claims electronically to an insurance company, a certification letter must be filed with the insurance company to replace the signature usually required in this space. ■

When working with case studies in this text and workbook, enter the provider's full name, credentials, and the date the claim is completed. The date should be entered in MMDDYYYY format.

Block 32	Enter information in this block when the services listed on the claim form were performed at a site other than the provider's office or the patient's home. If the "YES" box in Block 20 contains an "X," enter the name and address of the laboratory that performed the laboratory procedures.
Block 33	The phone number, including the area code, should be entered to the right of the phrase "& PHONE #." It may overlap into the printing above. Enter the official name of the billing entity on the first line below the phone number. Enter the mailing address of the billing entity on the next two lines. The zip code must appear on the same line as the city and state.

OUT-OF-NETWORK PROVIDER CLAIMS: Leave the line with the abbreviations "PIN# and GRP#" blank.

IN-NETWORK PROVIDER CLAIMS: Enter any carrier-assigned participating provider identification number (PIN) and/or group practice identification number (GRP) in the appropriate space.

Refer to Figure 12-12 for completed Blocks 25 through 33.

Some of the case studies in Appendix I may have PAR providers' PINs identified in the provider identification at the bottom of the encounter form. The provider in all other case studies are nonPARs.

EXERCISE 12-7 Continuation of Work on Comparison Chart

Reread the instructions for completing Blocks 25 through 33. As you read each block record a concise description of the instructions in the appropriate block in the Commercial column of the Comparison Chart.

EXERCISE 12-8 Continuation of Exercise 12-2

Additional information needed for this case:

Dr. Helper's Social Security Number is 888 80 8080. She is on the medical staff and admits patients at Goodmedicine Hospital, Anywhere Street, in Anywhere, USA 12345.

1. Review the Mary Sue Patient encounter form (Figure 12-5).
2. Abstract the information needed for Blocks 25 through 33 from the encounter form and the additional data provided above and enter it on the claim form.

PLEASE
DO NOT
STAPLE
IN THIS
AREA

(SAMPLE ONLY - NOT APPROVED FOR USE)

CARRIER

☐☐ PICA   **UNDERSTANDING HEALTH INSURANCE CLAIM FORM** PICA ☐☐

| 1. MEDICARE ☐ (Medicare #) | MEDICAID ☐ (Medicaid #) | CHAMPUS ☐ (Sponsor's SSN) | CHAMPVA ☐ (VA File #) | GROUP HEALTH PLAN ☐ (SSN or ID) | FECA BLK LUNG ☐ (SSN) | OTHER ☒ (ID) | 1a. INSURED'S I.D. NUMBER (FOR PROGRAM IN ITEM 1) 225120661W |

| 2. PATIENT'S NAME (Last Name, First Name, Middle Initial) PUBLIC JOHN Q | 3. PATIENT'S BIRTH DATE MM 03 DD 09 YY 1945 SEX M ☒ F ☐ | 4. INSURED'S NAME (Last Name, First Name, Middle Initial) SAME |

| 5. PATIENT'S ADDRESS (No. Street) 10A SENATE AVENUE | 6. PATIENT RELATIONSHIP TO INSURED Self ☒ Spouse ☐ Child ☐ Other ☐ | 7. INSURED'S ADDRESS (No. Street) SAME |

| CITY ANYWHERE | STATE US | 8. PATIENT STATUS Single ☒ Married ☐ Other ☐ | CITY | STATE |

| ZIP CODE 12345 | TELEPHONE (Include Area Code) 101 201 7891 | Employed ☒ Full-Time Student ☐ Part-Time Student ☐ | ZIP CODE | TELEPHONE (INCLUDE AREA CODE) ( ) |

| 9. OTHER INSURED'S NAME (Last Name, First Name, Middle Initial) NONE | 10. IS PATIENT'S CONDITION RELATED TO: | 11. INSURED'S POLICY GROUP OR FECA NUMBER A15 |

| a. OTHER INSURED'S POLICY OR GROUP NUMBER | a. EMPLOYMENT? (CURRENT OR PREVIOUS) ☐ YES ☒ NO | a. INSURED'S DATE OF BIRTH MM DD YY SEX M ☐ F ☐ |

| b. OTHER INSURED'S DATE OF BIRTH MM DD YY SEX M ☐ F ☐ | b. AUTO ACCIDENT? ☐ YES ☒ NO PLACE (State) | b. EMPLOYER'S NAME OR SCHOOL NAME LEGAL RESEARCH INC. |

| c. EMPLOYER'S NAME OR SCHOOL NAME | c. OTHER ACCIDENT? ☐ YES ☒ NO | c. INSURANCE PLAN NAME OR PROGRAM NAME METROPOLITAN |

| d. INSURANCE PLAN NAME OR PROGRAM NAME | 10d. RESERVED FOR LOCAL USE | d. IS THERE ANOTHER HEALTH BENEFIT PLAN? ☐ YES ☒ NO If yes, return to and complete item 9 a – d. |

READ BACK OF FORM BEFORE COMPLETING & SIGNING THIS FORM.
12. PATIENT'S OR AUTHORIZED PERSON'S SIGNATURE I authorize the release of any medical or other information necessary to process this claim. I also request payment of government benefits either to myself or to the party who accepts assignment below.

SIGNED SIGNATURE ON FILE DATE _____

13. INSURED'S OR AUTHORIZED PERSON'S SIGNATURE I authorize payment of medical benefits to the undersigned physician or supplier for services described below.

SIGNED SIGNATURE ON FILE

| 14. DATE OF CURRENT: ILLNESS (First symptom) OR INJURY (Accident) OR PREGNANCY (LMP) MM 01 DD 09 YY YYYY | 15. IF PATIENT HAS HAD SAME OR SIMILAR ILLNESS, GIVE FIRST DATE MM DD YY | 16. DATES PATIENT UNABLE TO WORK IN CURRENT OCCUPATION FROM MM DD YY TO MM DD YY |

| 17. NAME OF REFERRING PHYSICIAN OR OTHER SOURCE IVAN GOODDOC, MD | 17a. I.D. NUMBER OF REFERRING PHYSICIAN 777707070 | 18. HOSPITALIZATION DATES RELATED TO CURRENT SERVICES FROM MM DD YY TO MM DD YY |

| 19. RESERVED FOR LOCAL USE | 20. OUTSIDE LAB? ☐ YES ☒ NO $ CHARGES |

| 21. DIAGNOSIS OR NATURE OF ILLNESS OR INJURY. (RELATE ITEMS 1, 2, 3, OR 4 TO ITEM 24E BY LINE) 1. 485 2. 788 41 3. 4. | 22. MEDICAID RESUBMISSION CODE ORIGINAL REF. NO. |
| | 23. PRIOR AUTHORIZATION NUMBER IG123-45 |

24. A DATE(S) OF SERVICE From MM DD YY To MM DD YY	B Place of Service	C Type of Service	D PROCEDURES, SERVICES, OR SUPPLIES (Explain Unusual Circumstances) CPT/HCPCS MODIFIER	E DIAGNOSIS CODE	F $ CHARGES	G DAYS OR UNITS	H EPSDT Family Plan	I EMG	J COB	K RESERVED FOR LOCAL USE
1	0109YYYY	3	1	99213	1	75 00	1				
2	0109YYYY	3	5	81001	2	10 00	1				
3	0109YYYY	3	4	71020	1	50 00	1				
4											
5											
6											

| 25. FEDERAL TAX I.D. NUMBER 11-123452 SSN ☐ EIN ☒ | 26. PATIENT'S ACCOUNT NO. 12-1 | 27. ACCEPT ASSIGNMENT? (For govt. claims, see back) ☐ YES ☒ NO | 28. TOTAL CHARGE $ 135 00 | 29. AMOUNT PAID $ 10 00 | 30. BALANCE DUE $ 125 00 |

| 31. SIGNATURE OF PHYSICIAN OR SUPPLIER INCLUDING DEGREES OR CREDENTIALS (I certify that the statements on the reverse apply to this bill and are made a part thereof.) ERIN A. HELPER MD SIGNED DATE MMDDYYYY | 32. NAME AND ADDRESS OF FACILITY WHERE SERVICES WERE RENDERED (If other than home or office) | 33. PHYSICIAN'S SUPPLIER'S BILLING NAME, ADDRESS, ZIP CODE & PHONE # (101) 111 1234 ERIN A HELPER MD 101 MEDIC DRIVE ANYWHERE USA 12345 PIN# GRP# |

(SAMPLE ONLY - NOT APPROVED FOR USE) PLEASE PRINT OR TYPE SAMPLE FORM 1500
SAMPLE FORM 1500 SAMPLE FORM 1500

PATIENT AND INSURED INFORMATION

PHYSICIAN OR SUPPLIER INFORMATION

Figure 12-12 Completed Blocks 25 through 33 of HCFA-1500 claim form. The form is shown in its entirety with all information provided.

3. Review Blocks 25 through 33 of the three claim forms to be sure all required blocks are properly completed.

4. Compare your claim form with the completed claim form in Figure 12-8.

Additional commercial claim case studies are found in Appendix I of this text. Be sure to read through the Insurance Billing Manual in Appendix II to obtain the necessary health care provider and billing entity information for the cases at the end of this chapter and in the workbook.

Case studies in Appendix II require reading the case study chart entries and abstracting and coding the diagnostic information. Necessary clinic, hospital, and physician data is included in the Insurance Billing Manual located in Appendix II.

COMMERCIAL SECONDARY COVERAGE

Modifications are made to the HCFA-1500 claim form when patients are covered by primary and secondary or supplemental health insurance plans. Secondary health insurance plans provide similar coverage to primary plans, while supplemental health insurance plans usually cover just deductible, copayment, and coinsurance expenses.

When the same health insurance carrier issues the primary and secondary or supplemental policies, submit just one HCFA-1500 claim form. If the carriers for the primary and secondary or supplemental policies are different, submit a HCFA-1500 claim to the primary carrier, and generate a second HCFA-1500 claim to send to the secondary carrier.

Modifications to Primary HCFA-1500 Claims

Block 9	Enter the name of the *secondary* or *supplemental policyholder*, if different from the patient; otherwise, enter "SAME."
Block 9a	Enter the ID and group number of the secondary or supplemental policy.
Block 9b	Enter the secondary or supplemental policyholder's date of birth, and enter an "X" in the appropriate box to indicate the insured's sex.
Block 9c	Enter the name of the employer, school, or organization if the secondary or supplemental policy is a group policy.
Block 9d	Enter the name of the secondary or supplemental health insurance plan.
Block 11d	Enter an "X" in the "YES" box.

Modifications to Secondary HCFA-1500 Claims

The instructions below are applicable only when the secondary or supplemental policy carrier is different from the primary carrier.

■ **NOTE:** If the carrier is the same for the primary and secondary or supplemental policies, do not generate a second HCFA-1500 claim. ■

Block 1a	Enter the ID number of the *secondary* or *supplemental policy*.

Block 4	Enter the name of the secondary or supplemental policyholder, if different from the patient; otherwise, enter "SAME."
Block 7	Enter the address of the secondary or supplemental policyholder, if different from the patient; otherwise, enter "SAME."
Block 9	Enter the name of the primary policyholder, if different from the patient; otherwise, enter "SAME."
Block 9a	Enter the ID and group number of the primary policy.
Block 9b	Enter the primary policyholder's date of birth, and enter an "X" in the appropriate box to indicate the insured's sex.
Block 9c	Enter the name of the employer or school, if the primary policy is a group policy; otherwise, leave blank.
Block 9d	Enter the name of the *primary insurance plan.*
Block 11	Enter the group number of the secondary or supplemental policy, if applicable.
Block 11a	Enter the secondary or supplemental policyholder's date of birth, and enter an "X" in the appropriate box to indicate the insured's sex, if different from the patient; otherwise, leave blank.
Block 11b	Enter the name of the employer or school.
Block 11c	Enter the name of the secondary or supplemental insurance plan.
Block 11d	Enter an "X" in the "YES" box.

EXERCISE 12-9   Filing Commercial Secondary Claims

1. Obtain a blank claim form.
2. Underline the Block identifiers on the new claim form for the blocks discussed in the Commercial Claim form instructions.
3. Turn to the encounter form for Mary Sue Patient (Figure 12-5). Enter the following information in the blocks for the secondary policy:

   Conn General ID # 22233544 Group # AA2

   Policyholder: James W. Patient

   Birth date: 03/01/48

   Relationship: Spouse

   Employer: Anywhere Water Company

   Add an "S" to the Patient Chart Number, and include the word "Secondary" in Block 26 on the claim form (e.g., 12-2S Secondary).
4. Complete the secondary carrier's claim form on Mary Sue Patient using the data from the encounter form. Place the secondary information in the blocks highlighted in Step 1.
5. Review the completed claim form to be sure all required blocks are properly completed. Compare your claim form with the completed claim form in Figure 12-13.

PLEASE
DO NOT
STAPLE
IN THIS
AREA

EOB ATTACHED

(SAMPLE ONLY - NOT APPROVED FOR USE)

CARRIER

☐☐☐ PICA

UNDERSTANDING HEALTH INSURANCE CLAIM FORM PICA ☐☐

1. MEDICARE	MEDICAID	CHAMPUS	CHAMPVA	GROUP HEALTH PLAN	FECA BLK LUNG	OTHER	1a. INSURED'S I.D. NUMBER	(FOR PROGRAM IN ITEM 1)
☐ (Medicare #)	☐ (Medicaid #)	☐ (Sponsor's SSN)	☐ (VA File #)	☐ (SSN or ID)	☐ (SSN)	☒ (ID)	222017681	

2. PATIENT'S NAME (Last Name, First Name, Middle Initial)
PATIENT MARY SUE

3. PATIENT'S BIRTH DATE
MM 10 | DD 10 | YY 1959   SEX   M ☐   F ☒

4. INSURED'S NAME (Last Name, First Name, Middle Initial)
PATIENT JAMES W

5. PATIENT'S ADDRESS (No. Street)
91 HOME STREET

6. PATIENT RELATIONSHIP TO INSURED
Self ☐   Spouse ☒   Child ☐   Other ☐

7. INSURED'S ADDRESS (No. Street)
SAME

CITY
NOWHERE

STATE
US

8. PATIENT STATUS
Single ☐   Married ☒   Other ☐

CITY

STATE

ZIP CODE
12367

TELEPHONE (Include Area Code)
101 201 8989

Employed ☐   Full-Time Student ☐   Part-Time Student ☐

ZIP CODE

TELEPHONE (INCLUDE AREA CODE)
(   )

9. OTHER INSURED'S NAME (Last Name, First Name, Middle Initial)
PATIENT JAMES W

10. IS PATIENT'S CONDITION RELATED TO:

11. INSURED'S POLICY GROUP OR FECA NUMBER
AX107

a. OTHER INSURED'S POLICY OR GROUP NUMBER
22335544   AA2

a. EMPLOYMENT? (CURRENT OR PREVIOUS)
☐ YES   ☒ NO

a. INSURED'S DATE OF BIRTH
MM 03 | DD 01 | YY 1948   SEX   M ☒   F ☐

b. OTHER INSURED'S DATE OF BIRTH
MM 03 | DD 01 | YY 1948   SEX   M ☒   F ☐

b. AUTO ACCIDENT?   PLACE (State)
☐ YES   ☒ NO

b. EMPLOYER'S NAME OR SCHOOL NAME
ANYWHERE WATER COMPANY

c. EMPLOYER'S NAME OR SCHOOL NAME
ANYWHERE WATER COMPANY

c. OTHER ACCIDENT?
☐ YES   ☒ NO

c. INSURANCE PLAN NAME OR PROGRAM NAME
CONN GENERAL

d. INSURANCE PLAN NAME OR PROGRAM NAME
CONN GENERAL

10d. RESERVED FOR LOCAL USE

d. IS THERE ANOTHER HEALTH BENEFIT PLAN?
☒ YES   ☐ NO   If yes, return to and complete item 9 a – d.

READ BACK OF FORM BEFORE COMPLETING & SIGNING THIS FORM.
12. PATIENT'S OR AUTHORIZED PERSON'S SIGNATURE   I authorize the release of any medical or other information necessary to process this claim. I also request payment of government benefits either to myself or to the party who accepts assignment below.

SIGNED   SIGNATURE ON FILE   DATE

13. INSURED'S OR AUTHORIZED PERSON'S SIGNATURE   I authorize payment of medical benefits to the undersigned physician or supplier for services described below.

SIGNED   SIGNATURE ON FILE

14. DATE OF CURRENT: ILLNESS (First symptom) OR INJURY (Accident) OR PREGNANCY (LMP)
MM 01 | DD 07 | YY YYYY

15. IF PATIENT HAS HAD SAME OR SIMILAR ILLNESS, GIVE FIRST DATE   MM | DD | YY

16. DATES PATIENT UNABLE TO WORK IN CURRENT OCCUPATION
FROM MM | DD | YY   TO MM | DD | YY

17. NAME OF REFERRING PHYSICIAN OR OTHER SOURCE

17a. I.D. NUMBER OF REFERRING PHYSICIAN ✱

18. HOSPITALIZATION DATES RELATED TO CURRENT SERVICES
FROM MM 01 | DD 07 | YY YYYY   TO MM 01 | DD 09 | YY YYYY

19. RESERVED FOR LOCAL USE

20. OUTSIDE LAB? $ CHARGES
☐ YES   ☒ NO

21. DIAGNOSIS OR NATURE OF ILLNESS OR INJURY. (RELATE ITEMS 1, 2, 3, OR 4 TO ITEM 24E BY LINE)
1. 794 02   3. 212 4
2. 413 1   4. ____ . ____

22. MEDICAID RESUBMISSION CODE   ORIGINAL REF. NO.

23. PRIOR AUTHORIZATION NUMBER

24. A. DATE(S) OF SERVICE		B. Place of Service	C. Type of Service	D. PROCEDURES, SERVICES, OR SUPPLIES (Explain Unusual Circumstances)		E. DIAGNOSIS CODE	F. $ CHARGES	G. DAYS OR UNITS	H. EPSDT Family Plan	I. EMG	J. COB	K. RESERVED FOR LOCAL USE
From MM DD YY	To MM DD YY			CPT/HCPCS	MODIFIER							
01 07 YYYY		1	1	99223		1	150 00	1				
01 08 YYYY		1	1	99221		1	75 00	1				
01 09 YYYY		1	1	99238		1	75 00	1				

25. FEDERAL TAX I.D. NUMBER   SSN ☐   EIN ☒
11-123452

26. PATIENT'S ACCOUNT NO.
12-2S SECONDARY

27. ACCEPT ASSIGNMENT? (For govt. claims, see back)
☐ YES   ☒ NO

28. TOTAL CHARGE
$ 300 00

29. AMOUNT PAID
$

30. BALANCE DUE
$ 300 00

31. SIGNATURE OF PHYSICIAN OR SUPPLIER INCLUDING DEGREES OR CREDENTIALS
(I certify that the statements on the reverse apply to this bill and are made a part thereof.)
ERIN A. HELPER MD
SIGNED   DATE MMDDYYYY

32. NAME AND ADDRESS OF FACILITY WHERE SERVICES WERE RENDERED (If other than home or office)
GOODMEDICINE HOSPITAL
ANYWHERE STREET
ANYWHERE US 12345

33. PHYSICIAN'S SUPPLIER'S BILLING NAME, ADDRESS, ZIP CODE & PHONE #
(101) 111 1234
ERIN A HELPER MD
101 MEDIC DRIVE
ANYWHERE USA 12345
PIN#   GRP#

PATIENT AND INSURED INFORMATION

PHYSICIAN OR SUPPLIER INFORMATION

(SAMPLE ONLY - NOT APPROVED FOR USE)   *PLEASE PRINT OR TYPE*   SAMPLE FORM 1500
SAMPLE FORM 1500   SAMPLE FORM 1500

Figure 12-13 Completed secondary claim form

REVIEW

DEFINITION EXERCISE

Read the definition carefully. If the statement is true, place a check mark to the left of the number. If the statement is false, correct it without rewriting the entire statement.

1. When the patient signs Block 13 of the HCFA-1500 to "assign benefits," the provider accepts, as payment in full, whatever the insurance company reimburses for the service provided.

2. Commercial supplemental policies cover deductibles and copayments/coinsurances associated with primary policies.

3. "SIGNATURE ON FILE" indicates that the patient has signed a special form that has been placed in the financial or medical record.

4. A "place of service" code identifies the classification of the procedure or medical service.

5. To "accept assignment" means that the patient has authorized the provider to be directly reimbursed for services rendered.

CHALLENGE EXERCISE

1. Explain how claims are handled for patients between the ages of 19 and 23, who are full-time students, and are listed as dependents on their family's insurance policy.

2. What is the significance of entering an "X" in the "YES" box in Block 10B?

3. What does the abbreviation EGHP mean?

4. What does it mean when a patient signs Block 12 of the HCFA-1500?

5. What word could be substituted for the arrow in Block 14 of the HCFA-1500?

6. In what circumstances would Block 18 of the HCFA-1500 be completed?

7. What does it mean when an "X" is entered in the "YES" box in Block 20 of the HCFA-1500?

8. When entering the ICD-9-CM codes in Block 21, it is appropriate to enter the decimal. *True or False*

9. What do the abbreviations POS and TOS mean?

10. When entering modifiers in Block 24D of the HCFA-1500, do not enter the hyphen between the CPT code and the modifier. *True or False*

11. In Block 24E, it is acceptable to enter either the reference number from Block 21 or the ICD-9-CM code number. *True or False*

12. How is Block 24F completed when a patient receives identical services during the same encounter (e.g., on the same date)?

13. What does placing an "X" in Block 24I indicate?

14. What does COB mean?

15. When totaling the charges in Block 28, if a credit is due the patient, it is appropriate to indicate this on the claim. *True or False*

Blue Cross and Blue Shield Plans

Upon successful completion of this chapter, you should be able to:

1. Define the following terms, phrases, and abbreviations:

Blue Cross (BC)	special accidental injury rider	Office of Personnel Management
Blue Shield (BS)	medical emergency care rider	(OPM)
prepaid medical plan	National Account	service location
member hospital	BlueCard Program	Government-Wide Service Benefit
American Hospital Association	BlueCard Worldwide	Plan
(AHA)	preferred provider arrangement	Outpatient Pretreatment
Blue Cross/Blue Shield (BCBS)	(PPA)	Authorization Plan (OPAP)
nonprofit corporation	preferred provider organization	prospective authorization
for-profit corporation	(PPO)	precertification
Blue Cross and Blue Shield	exclusive provider organization	mandatory second surgical
Association (BCBSA)	(EPO)	opinion (SSO)
participating provider (PAR)	subscriber	Coordinated Home Health and
Preferred Provider Network	member	Hospice Care Program
(PPN)	guest membership	health maintenance organization
PPN provider	BlueCard PPO	(HMO)
nonparticipating provider	host plan	Away From Home Care Program
(NonPAR)	point-of-service plan (POS)	Medicare Supplemental plans
basic coverage	primary care provider (PCP)	Usual, Customary, and
Major Medical (MM) coverage	Federal Employee Health Benefits	Reasonable (UCR)
durable medical equipment	Program (FEHBP)	assignment of benefits
(DME)	Federal Employee Program	third-party administrator (TPA)
rider	(FEP)	HCFA Place of Service codes

2. Explain the function of the national Blue Cross and Blue Shield Association.

3. List four distinctive features that make the BCBS plans different from other commercial medical insurance programs.

4. Compare and contrast the advantages of being a BCBS participating provider versus being a non-participating provider.

5. Describe the features of BCBS basic benefits.

6. List typical services found in Major Medical coverage.

7. Explain the benefits of special accidental injury riders/clauses.

8. Explain the benefits of a medical emergency rider.

9. Describe the purpose of the BlueCard Program.

10. Explain how a BlueCard patient is identified.

11. Compare and contrast how PARs and NonPARs process BlueCard claims.

12. Compare and contrast the major differences between BCBS, PPA, and POS plans.

13. State the deadline for filing BCBS claims.

14. Complete BCBS claims accurately.

| INTRODUCTION | **Blue Cross (BC)** and **Blue Shield (BS)** plans are perhaps the best known medical insurance programs in the United States. They began as two separate **prepaid medical plans** selling contracts to individuals or groups for coverage of specified medical expenses as long as the premiums were paid.

Claim form instructions in this chapter are devoted to fee-for-service BCBS claims only.

BRIEF HISTORY

Origin of Blue Cross The forerunner of what is known today as the Blue Cross plan began in 1929 when Baylor University Hospital in Dallas, Texas, approached teachers in the Dallas school district with a plan that would guarantee up to 21 days of hospitalization per year for subscribers and each of their dependents in exchange for a $6 annual premium. This plan was accepted by the teachers and worked so well that the concept soon spread across the country. Early plans specified which hospital subscribers and their dependents could use for care. By 1932, some plans modified this concept and organized community-wide programs that allowed the subscriber to be hospitalized in one of several **member hospitals** that had signed contracts to provide services for special rates.

The blue cross symbol was first used in 1933 by the St. Paul, Minnesota plan and was adopted by the **American Hospital Association (AHA)** in 1939 when the association became the approving agency for the accreditation of new prepaid hospitalization plans. Although the AHA became the approving agent, each new plan formed was an independent corporation marketing its own plan contracts. In 1948, the need for additional national coordination among plans arose, and the Blue Cross Association was created. In 1973, the AHA deeded the right to both the name and the use of the blue cross symbol to the Blue Cross Association. At that time, the symbol was updated to the trademark in use today.

Origin of Blue Shield The Blue Shield plans began as a resolution passed by the House of Delegates at an American Medical Association meeting in 1938. This resolution supported the concept of voluntary health insurance that would encourage physicians to cooperate with prepaid health care plans. The first known plan was formed in Palo Alto, California in 1939 and was known as the California Physicians' Service. This plan stipulated that physicians' fees for covered medical services would be paid in full by the plan if the subscriber earned less than $3,000 a year. In cases where the subscriber earned more than $3,000 a year, a small percentage of the physician's fee would be paid by the patient. This patient responsibility for a small percentage of the health care fee is the forerunner of today's industry-wide required patient coinsurance or copay.

The blue shield design was first used as a trademark by the Buffalo, New York plan in 1939. The name and symbol were formally adopted by the Associated Medical Care Plans, formed in 1948, as the approving agency for accreditation of new Blue Shield plans adopting programs created in the spirit of the California Physicians' Service program. In 1951, this accrediting organization changed its name to the National Association of Blue Shield Plans. Like the Blue Cross plans, each Blue Shield plan in the association was established as a separate, nonprofit corporate entity, issuing its own contracts and plans within a specific geographic area.

Early Blue Cross/ Blue Shield Joint Ventures

As shown in this abbreviated history, Blue Cross plans originally covered only hospital bills and Blue Shield plans covered fees for physician services. Over the years, both programs have increased their coverage to include almost all medical services. In many areas of the country there was close cooperation between Blue Cross and Blue Shield plans, culminating in the formation of joint ventures in some states where the two corporations were housed in one building. In these early joint ventures, the **Blue Cross/Blue Shield (BCBS)** corporations shared one building and computer services but maintained separate corporate identities.

The Changing Business Structure

Strong competition among all health insurance companies in the United States emerged during the 1990s. BCBS, a nonprofit agency, reacted to this competition in a variety of ways. Mergers occurred between BCBS regional corporations within a state or with neighboring states, resulting in the creation of names that no longer have regional designations. For example, Care First BCBS is the name for the new corporation that resulted from a merged BCBS of Maryland and the National Capital Area BCBS. Other regional corporations, needing additional capital to compete with commercial for-profit insurance carriers, petitioned their respective state legislatures to allow conversion from their nonprofit status to for-profit corporations. **Nonprofit corporations** are charitable, educational, civic, or humanitarian organizations whose profits are returned to the program of the corporation rather than distributed to shareholders and officers of the corporation. Because no profits of the organization are distributed to shareholders, the government does not tax the organizations' income. **For-profit corporations** pay taxes on profits generated by the corporation's for-profit enterprises and pay dividends to shareholders on after-tax profits.

BCBS plans that have already converted to for-profit companies include:

- Blue Cross of California in 1996 (WellPoint Health Networks)
- Blue Cross Blue Shield of Georgia in 1996
- Blue Cross Blue Shield of Missouri in 1994 (transferred 80% of managed care business into RightChoice, a for-profit subsidiary)
- Trigon Blue Cross Blue Shield in 1997 (Blue Cross Blue Shield of Virginia)
- Triple-S in 1999 (Seguros de Servicio de Salud de Puerto Rico Inc.)

BCBS plans that are undergoing the process of converting to for-profit companies at the time this text was printed include:

- Blue Cross Blue Shield of Colorado
- Blue Cross Blue Shield United of Wisconsin
- Empire (New York) Blue Cross Blue Shield

BCBS ASSOCIATION

In 1977, the membership of the separate Blue Cross and Blue Shield national associations voted to combine personnel under the leadership of a single president, responsible to both boards of directors. Further consolidation occurred in 1986 when the Boards of Directors of the separate national Blue Cross and Blue Shield associations merged into a single corporation, named the **Blue Cross and Blue Shield Association (BCBSA).** The BCBSA is located in Chicago, Illinois and performs the following functions:

- Establishes standards for new plans and programs.
- Assists local plans with enrollment activities, national advertising, public education, professional relations, and statistical and research activities.
- Serves as the primary contractor for processing Medicare hospital, hospice, and home health care claims.
- Coordinates nationwide BCBS plans.

The association is also the registered owner of the BC and BS trademarks (see upper left-hand corner of the ID cards in Figures 13-1 and 13-2).

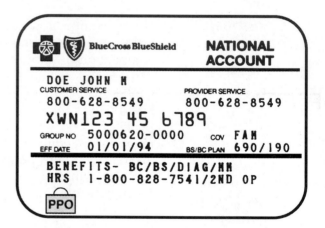

FIGURE 13-1 BCBS National Account identification card (based on identification card, Courtesy of Blue Cross/Blue Shield of Maryland, now known as CareFirst Blue Cross Blue Shield, from the *Guide to Programs and Benefits*)

FIGURE 13-2 BCBS National Account PPO identification card (based on identification card, Courtesy of Blue Cross/Blue Shield of Maryland, now known as CareFirst Blue Cross Blue Shield, from the *Guide to Programs and Benefits*)

BCBS DISTINCTIVE FEATURES

The "Blues" were pioneers in nonprofit, prepaid health care, and they possessed features that distinguished them from other commercial health insurance groups.

1. They maintain negotiated contracts with providers of care. In exchange for such contracts, BCBS agrees to perform the following services: A) make prompt, direct payments of claims; B) maintain regional professional representatives to assist participating providers with claim problems; and C) provide educational seminars, workshops, billing manuals, and newsletters to keep participating providers up-to-date on BCBS insurance procedures.

2. BCBS plans, in exchange for tax relief for their nonprofit status, are forbidden by state law from canceling coverage for an individual because he or she is in poor health or BCBS payments to providers have far exceeded the average. Policies issued by the nonprofit entity can only be canceled, or an individual disenrolled: (1) when premiums are not paid or (2) if the plan can prove that fraudulent statements were made on the application for coverage. For-profit commercial plans have the right to cancel a policy at renewal time if the patient moves into a region of the country where the company is not licensed to sell insurance or if the person is a high user of benefits and has purchased a plan that does not include a noncancellation clause.

3. BCBS plans must obtain approval from their respective state Insurance Commissioner for any rate increases and/or benefit changes that affect all BCBS members within the state. For-profit commercial plans have more freedom to increase rates and modify general benefits, without state approval, when the premium is due for annual renewal (if there is no clause restricting such action in the policy).

4. BCBS plans must allow conversion from group to individual coverage and guarantee the transferability of membership from one local plan to another when a change in residency moves a policyholder into an area served by a different BCBS corporation.

Today, commercial managed care plans have negotiated contracts with participating providers, and a minority of plans have nonprofit status.

PARTICIPATING PROVIDERS

As mentioned earlier, the "Blues" were pioneers in negotiating contracts with providers of care. A **participating provider (PAR)** is a health care provider who enters into a contract with a BCBS corporation and agrees to:

* Submit insurance claims for all BCBS subscribers.
* Provide access to the Provider Relations Department, which assists the PAR provider in resolving claims or payment problems.
* Write off (make a fee adjustment) for the difference or balance between the amount charged by the provider and the approved fee established by the insurer.
* Bill patients for only the deductible and copay/coinsurance amounts that are based on BCBS allowed fees and the full charged fee for any uncovered service.

In return, BCBS corporations agreed to:

* Make direct payments to PARs.
* Conduct regular training sessions for PAR billing staff.
* Provide free billing manuals and PAR newsletters.
* Maintain a provider representative department to assist with billing/payment problems.
* Publish the name, address, and specialty of all PARs in a directory distributed to BCBS subscribers and PARs.

Preferred Providers

PARs can also contract to participate in the plan's **Preferred Provider Network (PPN)**, a program that requires providers to adhere to managed care provisions. In this contractual agreement, the **PPN provider** (a provider who has signed a PPN contract) agrees to accept the PPN allowed rate, which is generally 10% lower than the PAR allowed rate. The provider further agrees to uphold all cost containment, utilization, and quality assurance programs of the PPN program. In return for a PPN agreement, the "Blues" agree to notify PPN providers in writing of new employer groups and hospitals that have entered into PPN contracts, and to maintain a PPN directory.

NONPARTICIPATING PROVIDERS

Nonparticipating providers (NonPAR) have not signed participating provider contracts, and they expect to be paid the full fee charged for services rendered. In these cases, the patient may be asked to pay the provider in full and then be reimbursed by BCBS the allowed fee for each service minus the patient's deductible and copayment obligations. In cases where the provider agrees to file the claim for the patient, the insurance company will send the payment for the claim directly to the patient and not to the provider.

TRADITIONAL FEE-FOR-SERVICE COVERAGE

The "Blues" have always offered a wide variety of fee-for-service plans, the most basic of which is elected by (1) individuals who do not have access to a group plan and (2) many small business employers. Such contracts are divided into two types of coverage within one policy: basic and major medical (MM) benefits.

Basic Coverage Plan The minimum benefits under the BCBS **basic coverage** routinely include the following services:

- Hospitalizations
- Diagnostic laboratory services
- Xrays
- Surgical fees
- Assistant surgeon fees
- Obstetric care
- Intensive care
- Newborn care
- Chemotherapy for cancer

Major Medical (MM) Benefits **Major Medical (MM) coverage** pays benefits for the following services in addition to basic coverage:

- Office visits
- Outpatient nonsurgical treatment
- Physical and occupational therapy
- Purchase of **durable medical equipment (DME)**
- Mental health visits
- Allergy testing and injections
- Prescription drugs
- Private duty nursing (when medically necessary)
- Dental care required as a result of a covered accidental injury

Major medical services are usually subject to patient deductible and copayment requirements, and in a few cases the patient may be responsible for filing claims for these benefits.

Some of the contracts also include one or more **riders**, which are special contract clauses stipulating additional coverage over and above the standard contract. Common riders include special accidental injury and medical emergency care coverage.

The **special accidental injury rider** covers 100% of nonsurgical care sought and rendered within 24 to 72 hours (varies according to the policy) of the accidental injury. Surgical care is subject to any established contract basic plan deductible and patient copayment requirements. Outpatient follow-up care for these accidental injuries is not included in the accidental injury rider, but will be covered if the patient has supplemental coverage.

The **medical emergency care rider** covers *immediate treatment sought and received for sudden, severe, and unexpected conditions* that, if not treated, would place the patient's health in permanent jeopardy or cause permanent impairment or dysfunction of an organ or body part. Chronic or subacute conditions do not qualify for treatment under the medical emergency rider unless the symptoms suddenly become acute and require immediate medical attention. Special attention must be paid to the ICD-9-CM coding (Blocks 21 and 24D) on the HCFA-1500 claim form to ensure that services rendered under the medical emergency rider are linked to diagnoses or reported symptoms generally accepted as conditions that require immediate care. Nonspecific conditions such as "acute upper respiratory infection" or "bladder infection" would not be included on the medical emergency diagnosis list without secondary conditions that would require supporting documentation attachments to the claim to be considered under this medical emergency rider/clause.

NATIONAL ACCOUNTS

Companies with employees located in more than one local plan area may negotiate a National Account that is coordinated through the national Blue Cross and Blue Shield Association. A **National Account** is a health insurance contract that covers company employees who are located in more than one geographic area. The plan is easily identified by the outline of the United States found in the upper right-hand corner of the subscriber's insurance identification card. *Providers file national account claims with local BCBS agencies, not the national Blue Cross and Blue Shield Association in Chicago, IL.*

BLUECARD PROGRAM

The **BlueCard Program** allows Blue Cross and Blue Shield subscribers to receive local Blue Plan health care benefits while traveling or living outside of their Plan's area. More than 85% of U.S. hospitals and physicians contract with independent Blue Cross and Blue Shield Plans, and the BlueCard Program links these health care professionals so that claim information can be electronically processed. Subscribers can call BlueCard Access (800-810-BLUE) to obtain the names and addresses of the participating doctors and hospitals Providers follow the steps listed below:

1. Verify the subscriber's eligibility and coverage by viewing the ID card and calling the BlueCard Eligibility number (800-676-BLUE).

2. Provide the member's three-character alpha prefix to the BlueCard Eligibility operator (prefix is located at the beginning of the subscriber's ID number), so eligibility and coverage information can be verified.

3. Upon providing care to the subscriber, submit the claim (including alpha prefix) to the local Blue Plan for reimbursement. The claim will be electronically routed to the subscriber's local Plan for processing. The provider's Plan pays the provider, and the subscriber's Plan sends an Explanation of Benefits (EOB) to the subscriber.

BlueCard WorldWide

BlueCard Worldwide is a program that allows subscribers who travel or live abroad to receive covered inpatient hospital care and physician services from a network of hospitals and doctors around the world. For emergencies, the subscriber should go directly to the nearest hospital. For referrals, subscribers call 800-810-BLUE to determine names and addresses of participating doctors and hospitals. A medical assistance coordinator, in conjunction with a medical professional, will make an appointment with a doctor or arrange hospitalization, if necessary. Subscribers should contact their Blue Plan for precertification or prior authorization, where necessary, and show their ID card to the hospital to avoid up-front payment for inpatient participating hospital services. Subscribers are responsible for paying out-of-pocket expenses (deductible, copayment, coinsurance, and noncovered services). For outpatient hospital care or physician services, subscribers should pay the hospital or physician, complete an international claim form, and send it to the BlueCard Worldwide Service Center.

INTERNET LINKS

Go to www.bcbs.com to search for a provider by using the BlueCard® Doctor & Hospital Finder.

Go to www.bcbshealthissues.com for health care news.

BCBS & MANAGED CARE

The majority of BCBS plans offer some form of managed care. These plans range from simple precertification for hospitalizations to individual case management of persons with catastrophic injuries or resource-intensive serious illnesses. Most plans also have ventured into either the nonprofit or for-profit Health Maintenance Organization (HMO) market, or both.

Many, but not all, ID cards itemize the specific managed care provisions on the face of the card. Local BCBS manuals specify the managed care requirements in a particular region. A brief overview of the following programs is presented here.

- Preferred Provider Arrangement (PPA)
- Point-of-Service Plan (POS)
- Federal Employee Program (FEP)
- Outpatient Pretreatment Authorization Plan (OPAP)

- Mandatory Second Surgical Opinion (SSO)
- Coordinated Home Health and Hospice Care

A **preferred provider arrangement (PPA)** is a contract between a health care insurer and a health care provider or group of providers who agree to provide services to persons covered under the contract. Examples include preferred provider organizations (PPOs) and exclusive provider organizations (EPOs). A **preferred provider organization (PPO)** offers discounted health care services to subscribers who use designated healthcare providers (who contract with the PPO), but also provides coverage for services rendered by health care providers who are not part of the PPO network. An **exclusive provider organization (EPO)** is a health care benefit arrangement similar to a preferred provider organization in administration, structure, and operation, but it does not cover out-of-network care.

Preferred Provider Arrangement

The BCBS PPO plan is sometimes described as a subscriber-driven program. (BCBS substitutes the term **subscriber** or **member** for the term "policy-holder" used by other commercial carriers.) In this type of plan, the subscriber is responsible for remaining within the network of PPO providers and must, consequently, request referrals to PPO specialists whenever possible. They must also adhere to the managed care requirements of the PPO policy, such as obtaining required second surgical opinions and/or hospital admission review. Failure to adhere to these requirements will result in denial of the surgical claim or reduced payment to the provider. In such cases, the patient is responsible for the difference or balance between the reduced payment and the normal PPO allowed rate.

BCBS offers a **guest membership** plan that allows subscribers and their dependents to become a "guest member" of another local BCBS PPO for a given period of time. This option is appropriate for business travelers on long-term assignments in other regions, college students attending school out-of-state, and children of divorced parents who spend several weeks or months at a time with a parent in another state. The **BlueCard PPO** program offers "guest membership" to subscribers at participating BCBS PPOs. Subscribers select a local PPO that provides benefits similar to those available from their **host plan** (the plan in which the subscriber originally enrolled). The subscriber's identification card contains a "suitcase logo" (see Figure 13-2).

Point-of-Service (POS) Plan

A **point-of-service plan (POS)** allows subscribers to choose, at the time medical services are needed, whether they will go to a provider within the plan's network or outside of the network. When subscribers go outside of the network to seek care, out-of-pocket expenses and copayments generally increase. POS plans provide a full range of inpatient and outpatient services, and subscribers choose a primary care physician (PCP) from the carrier's PCP list. A **primary care provider (PCP)** is a physician or other medical professional who serves as a subscriber's first contact with a plan's health care system. The PCP is also known as a personal care physician or personal care provider.

■ **NOTE:** When subscribers go outside the network for health care, the approval of the PCP is not required. ■

The PCP assumes responsibility for coordinating the subscriber's and dependent's medical care, and the PCP is often referred to as the "gatekeeper" of the patient's medical care. The name and phone number of the PCP appears on all POS ID cards. Written referral notices issued by the PCP must be attached to all paper claims for services, and the written referral is usually mailed to the appropriate local processing address following the transmission of an electronic claim. The PCP is also responsible for obtaining authorization for all inpatient hospitalizations. A specialist's office should contact the PCP when hospitalization is necessary and follow up that call with one to the utilization control office at the local BCBS plan office.

Federal Employee Program

The **Federal Employee Health Benefits Program (FEHBP)**, or **Federal Employee Program (FEP)** is an employer-sponsored health benefits program established by an Act of Congress in 1959. The FEHBP began covering federal employees on July 1, 1960 and now provides benefits to over nine million federal enrollees and dependents through contracts with about 300 insurance carriers. Under its contract with the United States **Office of Personnel Management (OPM)**, the federal government's human resources agency, the FEHBP is underwritten and administered by participating insurance plans (e.g., Blue Cross and Blue Shield Plans). These participating plans are referred to as local plans, and claims are to be submitted to the FEP Local Plan serving the location where the patient was seen (called a **service location**), regardless of the member's FEP Plan affiliation.

FEHBP cards contain the phrase **"Government-Wide Service Benefit Plan"** located under the BCBS trademark. FEP enrollees have identification numbers that begin with the letter "R" followed by eight numeric digits (see Figure 13-3). All ID cards contain the name of the government employee. Dependents' names do *not* appear on the card. A three-digit enrollment code is located on the front of the card to specify the option(s) elected when the government employee enrolled in the program; this code should be entered as the group ID number on BCBS claims. The four enrollment options are:

- 101—Individual, High Option Plan
- 102—Family, High Option Plan
- 104—Individual Standard (Low) Option Plan
- 105—Family Standard (Low) Option Plan

The FEP is considered a "managed fee-for-service program" and has generally operated as a PPO plan. The patient is responsible for ensuring that precertification is obtained for all hospitalizations except routine maternity care, home health and hospice care, and emergency hospitalization within 48

FIGURE 13-3 BCBS FEP PPO identification card (based on identification card, Courtesy of Blue Cross Blue Shield of Maryland, now known as CareFirst Blue Cross Blue Shield, from the *Guide to Programs and Benefits*)

hours of admission. In 1997, a POS product was introduced in specific geographic sections of the country, and gradual expansion to a nationwide POS program is planned. The federal POS program requires that the subscriber select a PCP. This plan offers enhanced benefits and reduced out-of-pocket expenses when PCP referrals are obtained for specialty care.

In accordance with the law *5 U.S.C. 8904 (b)*, the Medicare Fee Schedule and Medicare NonPAR limiting charges (not the local BCBS regional fee schedule) must be adhered to for all *retired federal employees* and enrolled beneficiaries over the age of 65 who are not eligible for Medicare Part B. Medicare Part B, fee schedule, and NonPAR limiting charges are discussed in Chapter 14.

Outpatient Pretreatment Authorization

The **Outpatient Pretreatment Authorization Plan (OPAP)** requires preauthorization of outpatient physical, occupational, and speech therapy services. In addition, OPAP requires periodic treatment/progress plans to be filed. OPAP is a requirement for the delivery of certain health care services and is issued prior to the provision of services. OPAP is also known as **prospective authorization** or **precertification**.

Second Surgical Opinions

The **mandatory second surgical opinion (SSO)** requirement is necessary when a patient is considering elective, non-emergency surgical care. The initial surgical recommendation must be made by a physician qualified to perform the anticipated surgery. If a second surgical opinion is not obtained prior to surgery, the patient's out-of-pocket expenses may be greatly increased. The patient or surgeon should contact the subscriber's BCBS local plan for instructions. In some cases, the second opinion must be obtained from a member of a select surgical panel. In other cases, the concurrence of the need for surgery from the patient's PCP may suffice.

For example, the following list represents procedures that require a second surgical opinion for members of an airline company in the United States:

- Cholecystectomy (removal of the gallbladder)
- Coronary artery bypass
- Hysterectomy (removal of uterus)
- Knee surgery
- Laminectomy or spinal fusion (removal of or welding of parts of the spine)

Coordinated Home Health and Hospice Care

The **Coordinated Home Health and Hospice Care** program allows patients with this option to elect an alternative to the acute care setting. The patient's physician must file a treatment plan with the case manager assigned to review and coordinate the case. All authorized services must be rendered by personnel from a licensed home health agency or approved hospice facility.

Health Maintenance Organizations

All BCBS corporations now offer at least one **Health Maintenance Organization (HMO)** plan, a health care system that assumes or shares the financial and health care delivery risks associated with providing comprehensive medical services to subscribers in return for a fixed, prepaid fee. Some plans were for-profit acquisitions; others were developed as separate nonprofit plans. Examples of plan names are "Capital Care" and "Columbia Medical Plan." Because familiar BCBS names are not always used in the plan name, some HMOs may not be easily recognized as BCBS plans. The BCBS trademarks, however, usually appear on the plan's ID cards and advertisements.

BCBS HMOs offer an **Away From Home Care Program** that offers "guest membership" at participating Blue Cross and Blue Shield HMOs. Subscribers select a local primary care provider in another area and receive health care with the same level of benefits as their host HMO plan.

MEDICARE SUPPLEMENTAL PLANS

BCBS corporations offer several of the federally-designed and regulated **Medicare Supplemental plans** which augment the Medicare program by paying for Medicare deductibles and copayments. These plans are better known throughout the industry as "Medigap Plans." These Medicare Supplemental plans are usually identified by the word "Medigap" on the patient's ID card. (For more information see the discussion of Medicare Supplemental plans in Chapter 14.)

BILLING INFORMATION SUMMARY

A summary follows of the nationwide billing information on traditional BCBS fee-for-service claims. PAR providers are required to file these claims for subscribers.

Fiscal Agent/Carrier   BCBS plans and all other commercial plans process their own claims.

Deadline for Filing Claims   The deadline is customarily one year from the date of service, unless otherwise specified in the subscriber's or provider's contracts.

Forms Used   Most corporations currently accept the HCFA-1500 (12-90) claim form.

Inpatient and Outpatient Coverage   Inpatient and outpatient coverage may vary according to the plan. Many plans require second surgical opinions and prior authorization for elective hospitalizations. Information on the individual program requirements can be found in the BCBS local area manual.

Deductible   The deductible will vary according to the BCBS plan. Consult the local corporation billing manual or eligibility status computerized phone bank for specific patient requirements. Patients enrolled in PPA plans may have no applicable deductibles for certain preventive medicine services.

Patient Copayment/ Coinsurance   Patient copayment/coinsurance requirements will vary according to the patient plan. The most common coinsurance amounts are 20% or 25%, although they may be as high as 50% for mental health services on some policies.

Allowable Fee Determination   The allowable fee will vary according to the program. Many corporations have begun to issue policies that use the Resource-Based Relative Value Scale (RBRVS) system (discussed in Chapter 9) to determine the allowed fees for each procedure. The RBRVS is the basis for the Medicare Fee Schedule. Other plans use a **Usual, Customary, and Reasonable (UCR)** basis, which is the amount commonly charged for a particular medical service by providers within a particular geographic region, for establishing their allowable rates. Participating providers must accept the allowable rate on all covered services, and write off or adjust the difference or balance between the plan determined allowed amount and the amount billed. Patients are responsible for any deductible and copay/coinsurance described in their policy as well as full charges for uncovered services.

The Explanation of Benefits (EOB) sent to PAR and PPN providers clearly states the patient's total deductible and copayment/coinsurance responsibility for each claim submission.

NonPARs may collect the full fee from the patient. BCBS payments are then sent directly to the patient.

Assignment of Benefits

All claims filed by participating providers qualify for an **assignment of benefits** to the provider. This means that payment is made directly to the provider by BCBS.

Special Handling

1. Make it a habit and priority to retain a current photocopy of the front and back of all patient ID cards in the patient's file.
2. Claims for BlueCard patients with more than one insurance policy must be billed directly to the plan from which the program originated. Use HCFA-1500 (12-90) form.
3. NonPARs must bill the patient's plan for all non-national account patients with BlueCards.
4. Rebill claims not paid within 30 days.
5. Some mental health claims are forwarded to a **third-party administrator (TPA)**, a company that provides administrative services to health care plans, specializing in mental health case management rather than mailed directly to the local BCBS corporation. Check the back of the ID card and billing manual for special instructions.

Before working with the BCBS claim forms, turn to page 344 in this chapter and complete the Review.

STEP-BY-STEP INSTRUCTIONS—PRIMARY BCBS CLAIMS

When working with case studies in this text, the primary, secondary, and supplemental status is listed on each case study encounter form. (See Figure 13-4 on page 326.) Place a "Post It Note®" or other marker on pages 326 and 331. You will be referring to them often while following the step-by-step instructions.

The instructions that follow have been divided into three sections to allow for introduction and mastery of small sections of the claim form. See Figure 13-5 (page 327) for Blocks 1-13 of the HCFA-1500 claim form. An illustration of a completed section of the claim form is found at the end of each set of instructions (see Figure 13-6 on page 329). The claims data for this claim form is taken from the John Q. Public encounter form (Figure 13-4).

■ **NOTE:** The information presented in this chapter builds on the universal claim form instructions presented in Chapter 11 Essential Claim Form Instructions. These instructions cover cases where the patient's insurance plan has primary claim status. The primary claim status is determined by one of the following categories:

• The patient is covered by only one policy.

• The full-benefit employer-sponsored BCBS plan, if the patient is covered by both a government-sponsored and an employer-sponsored plan.

DATE 01/12/YYYY	REMARKS					
PATIENT John Q. Public			CHART # 13-1	SEX M	BIRTHDATE 03/09/1945	
MAILING ADDRESS 10A Senate Avenue	CITY Anywhere	STATE US	ZIP 12345	HOME PHONE (101) 210 7891	WORK PHONE	
EMPLOYER Legal Research, Inc.		ADDRESS Anywhere US		PATIENT STATUS (MARRIED) DIVORCED SINGLE STUDENT OTHER		
INSURANCE: PRIMARY Blue Cross Blue Shield US		ID# WWW123456	GROUP A1	SECONDARY POLICY		
POLICYHOLDER NAME	BIRTHDATE	RELATIONSHIP self	POLICYHOLDER NAME	BIRTHDATE	RELATIONSHIP	
SUPPLEMENTAL PLAN			EMPLOYER			
POLICYHOLDER NAME	BIRTHDATE	RELATIONSHIP	DIAGNOSIS		CODE	
EMPLOYER			1. Pneumonia, bronchial		485	
			2. Urinary frequency		788.41	
REFERRING PHYSICIAN UPIN/SSN			3.			
			4.			

PLACE OF SERVICE Office		
PROCEDURES	CODE	CHARGE
1. 01/12/YYYY Est pt office visit level III	99213	$75—
2. Chest xray 2 views	71020	50—
3. Urinalysis, dipstick, automated, with microscopy	81001	10—
4.		
5.		
6.		

SPECIAL NOTES

Date of onset 01/09/YYYY

TOTAL CHARGES $135—	PAYMENTS $15—	ADJUSTMENTS 0	BALANCE $120—
RETURN VISIT 1 week		PHYSICIAN SIGNATURE *Erin A. Helper, M.D.*	

ERIN A. HELPER, M.D.   101 MEDIC DRIVE, ANYWHERE, US 12345
PHONE NUMBER (101) 111-1234
EIN # 11-123341   SSN # 111-22-3333
UPIN EH8888   NPI 00818810   Medicaid # EBH8881   BC/BS # EH11881 GRP: 1204-P

FIGURE 13-4 John Q. Public encounter form

- The employer-sponsored plan, when the patient is also covered by a non–BCBS plan that is not employer-sponsored.
- The patient is designated the policyholder of one employer-sponsored plan and is also listed as a dependent on another employer-sponsored plan. ■

Many insurance carriers frequently change billing rules and instructions. Coding and insurance specialists should be made aware of all changes and can obtain updates from a variety of sources (e.g., professional publications, Internet-based listservs, third-party payer Web sites, and televised proceedings of Congress on C-Span). Providers also receive publications that contain valuable information pertaining to coding and claims processing rules, regulations,

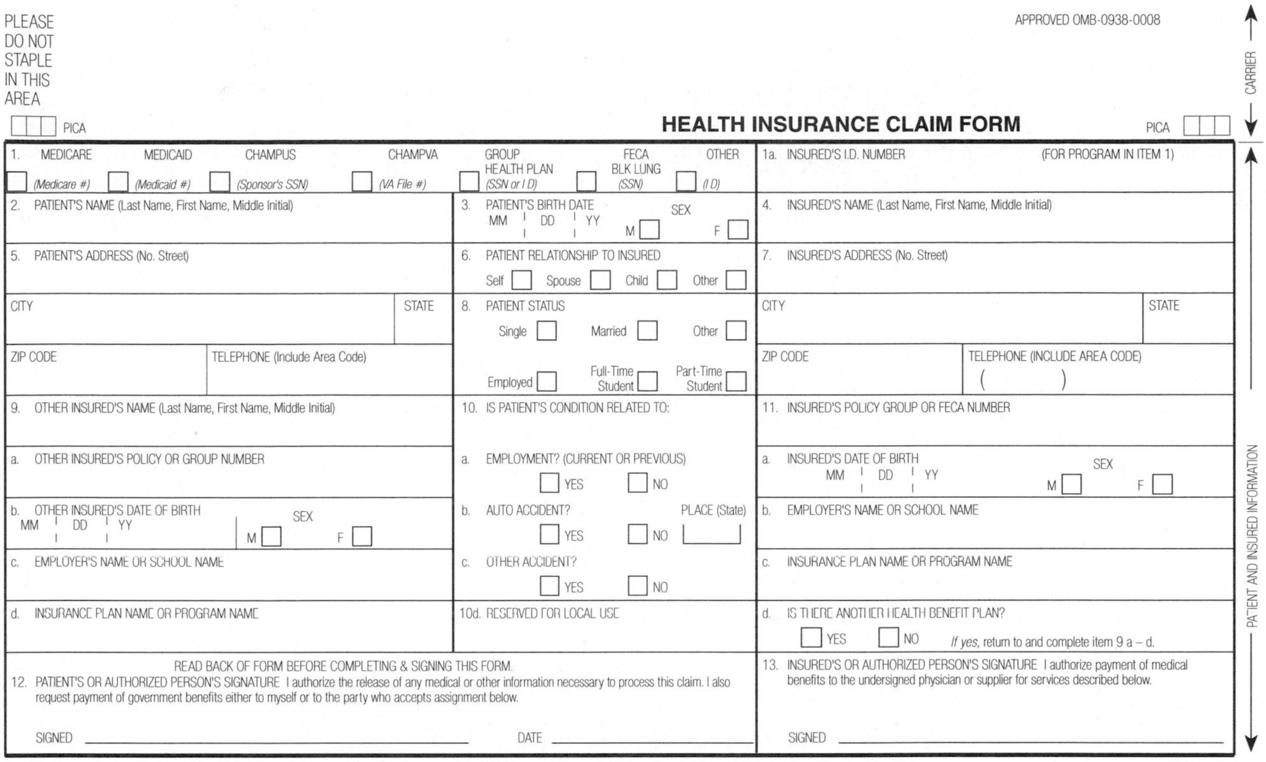
PLEASE DO NOT STAPLE IN THIS AREA

APPROVED OMB-0938-0008

CARRIER

PICA HEALTH INSURANCE CLAIM FORM PICA

1. MEDICARE (Medicare #) MEDICAID (Medicaid #) CHAMPUS (Sponsor's SSN) CHAMPVA (VA File #) GROUP HEALTH PLAN (SSN or I D) FECA BLK LUNG (SSN) OTHER (I D)

1a. INSURED'S I.D. NUMBER (FOR PROGRAM IN ITEM 1)

2. PATIENT'S NAME (Last Name, First Name, Middle Initial)

3. PATIENT'S BIRTH DATE MM DD YY SEX M F

4. INSURED'S NAME (Last Name, First Name, Middle Initial)

5. PATIENT'S ADDRESS (No. Street)

6. PATIENT RELATIONSHIP TO INSURED Self Spouse Child Other

7. INSURED'S ADDRESS (No. Street)

CITY STATE

8. PATIENT STATUS Single Married Other

CITY STATE

ZIP CODE TELEPHONE (Include Area Code)

Employed Full-Time Student Part-Time Student

ZIP CODE TELEPHONE (INCLUDE AREA CODE) ( )

9. OTHER INSURED'S NAME (Last Name, First Name, Middle Initial)

10. IS PATIENT'S CONDITION RELATED TO:

11. INSURED'S POLICY GROUP OR FECA NUMBER

a. OTHER INSURED'S POLICY OR GROUP NUMBER

a. EMPLOYMENT? (CURRENT OR PREVIOUS) YES NO

a. INSURED'S DATE OF BIRTH MM DD YY SEX M F

b. OTHER INSURED'S DATE OF BIRTH MM DD YY SEX M F

b. AUTO ACCIDENT? PLACE (State) YES NO

b. EMPLOYER'S NAME OR SCHOOL NAME

c. EMPLOYER'S NAME OR SCHOOL NAME

c. OTHER ACCIDENT? YES NO

c. INSURANCE PLAN NAME OR PROGRAM NAME

d. INSURANCE PLAN NAME OR PROGRAM NAME

10d. RESERVED FOR LOCAL USE

d. IS THERE ANOTHER HEALTH BENEFIT PLAN? YES NO *If yes*, return to and complete item 9 a – d.

READ BACK OF FORM BEFORE COMPLETING & SIGNING THIS FORM.

12. PATIENT'S OR AUTHORIZED PERSON'S SIGNATURE I authorize the release of any medical or other information necessary to process this claim. I also request payment of government benefits either to myself or to the party who accepts assignment below.

SIGNED DATE

13. INSURED'S OR AUTHORIZED PERSON'S SIGNATURE I authorize payment of medical benefits to the undersigned physician or supplier for services described below.

SIGNED

PATIENT AND INSURED INFORMATION

FIGURE 13-5 Blocks 1 through 13 of the HCFA-1500 claim form

and changes. Be sure these publications are circulated among staff members, to ensure proper updating of databases, comparison charts, and billing/coding manuals.

■ **TIP:** Record new rules on Post-it Notes® and place in the appropriate locations of billing and coding manuals. When new billing and coding manuals are obtained, just transfer the Post-it Notes® (instead of rewriting the information into the new manuals). ■

Classroom instructors may require the substitution of local requirements for specific blocks. *Write these local instructions in the margins of this text for quick reference when working with the case study assignments that are to be graded by the instructor. Follow the instructions in the workbook if you are using the Delmar Understanding Health Insurance computer program for completing claim forms for the case studies and you want the computer to provide feedback as well as score the claims.*

Block 1

Enter an "X" in "OTHER."

Block 1A

Enter the BCBS ID number, two spaces, and the group identifier if provided.

Block 2

Enter the full name (last name first, followed by the first name and middle initial) of the patient listed on the patient's insurance identification card. Use of nicknames or typographic errors may result in rejection of the claim.

For case studies in this text enter the name minus the punctuation, as it appears on the encounter form.

Block 3

Enter the birth date using eight digits in the following format: MM DD YYYY. Sex—Enter an "X" in the appropriate box.

Block 4	Enter the word "SAME" if the patient and policyholder are the same person.
	If the patient is not the policyholder, enter the policyholder's full name (last name first, followed by the first name and middle initial).
Block 5	Enter the patient's mailing address on lines 1 and 2 of this block. Enter the zip code, area code, and phone number in the proper blocks on line 3. Do not type the parentheses around the area code, or a dash in the phone number.
Block 6	Enter an "X" in the appropriate box for the patient's relationship to policyholder.
Block 7	If the policyholder's address is the same as that stated in Block 5, enter the word "SAME"; otherwise, enter the mailing address of the policyholder.
Block 8	Enter an "X" in the appropriate boxes pertaining to the patient.
	■ **NOTE:** If the patient is between the ages of 19 and 23, is dependent on a family policy, and is a full-time student, the claim will not be paid unless the patient can prove full-time student status at the time of the medical encounter. Written acknowledgment of the student's status from the school, college, or university should accompany the first claim filed during each semester. ■
Block 9-9D	Leave blank and proceed to Block 10.
Block 10A	Enter an "X" in the "NO" box, based on documentation reviewed in the patient's record.
	A "YES" indicates the services reported in Block 24D are related to an on-the-job injury and the previously-filed workers' compensation claim has been rejected. To receive consideration in these cases from the primary BCBS carrier, a copy of the Workers' Compensation Explanation of Benefits (EOB) and/or letter rejecting the on-the-job injury claim must be attached to this BCBS claim.
Block 10B	Enter an "X" in the appropriate box.
	A "YES" indicates possible third-party liability. The BCBS health insurance carrier will return the claim until the issue of third-party liability coverage is settled.
Block 10C	Enter an "X" in the appropriate box.
	A "YES" indicates possible third-party liability. If this is not the case, enter one or more E Codes in Block 21 to indicate the type of injury and its place of occurrence.
Block 10D	Leave blank.
Block 11	Leave blank.
Block 11A	Enter the eight-digit birth date (MM DD YYYY) and enter an "X" in the appropriate box to designate the sex of the person, other than the patient, named in Block 4.
Block 11B	Enter the name of the employer if the coverage is an employer-sponsored group policy or an organization/union if one is identified on the patient's ID card.
Block 11C	Enter the name of the carrier for the patient's policy.

FIGURE 13-6 Completed Blocks 1 through 13 for John Q. Public encounter form in Figure 13-4

Block 11D

Enter an "X" in the "NO" box to indicate the patient is covered by only one insurance policy.

Block 12

BCBS recommends that the patient sign an authorization form every year. Enter "SIGNATURE ON FILE." Do not enter the date.

Block 13

Leave blank. Assignment of Benefits is a provision of the subscriber's insurance contract.

Refer to Figure 13-6 for completed Blocks 1 through 13.

EXERCISE 13-1 Preparing the Comparison Charts

■ **NOTE:** Complete all the steps in this exercise if you have not completed Exercise 12-1 prior to working in this chapter. If you have already completed Exercise 12-1 on page 296, take out the Comparison Chart used in that exercise and proceed to Step 4 below. ■

ASSIGNMENT OBJECTIVE: To create a useful reference as an aid to mastering the details of completing claim forms for six major insurance programs.

1. Make five copies of the Comparison Chart in Appendix II.

2. Enter the following titles in the first row of each wide column at the top of each page:

Commercial   TRICARE STANDARD

BCBS   Workers' Compensation

3. Enter the following block numbers in the first column of each page as follows:

Page 1	Blocks	1	through	9D
Page 2		10	through	16
Page 3		17	through	23
Page 4		24A	through	24K
Page 5		25	through	33

4. Enter abbreviated instructions in Blocks 1 through 13 of the BCBS column.

   If the step-by-step instructions in this chapter indicate a particular block is to be left blank, enter the word "Blank."

   Use horizontal arrows to indicate that the instructions in a specific block in the BCBS column are repeated in the next column (see Figure 12-4 on page 297). If consecutive blocks are to be left blank, enter the word "Blank" in the first block and draw a vertical arrow down through the other blocks that have similar treatment.

5. Save this form as it will be used for additional exercises in this chapter and other chapters.

EXERCISE 13-2   BCBS Claim Form Blocks 1 through 13

This exercise requires two copies of a blank HCFA-1500 claim form. You may either make photocopies of the form in Appendix III of this text, or print copies of the blank form using the CD-ROM in the back of the text. Instructions for installing the CD-ROM and printing blank forms are included in Appendix V.

1. Obtain two copies of the HCFA-1500 claim form.

2. Review the instructions for Blocks 1 through 13 on your comparison chart.

3. On the first claim form, complete Blocks 1 through 13 using your personal data for filing an employer-sponsored claim with a BCBS policy. If you do not have a BCBS insurance policy, or lack any of the required data use the following information:

   Policy ID: Place the prefix ZZX in front of your own Social Security Number

   Group number: ZZ34

   Policyholder: Yourself

   Name of the insurance carrier: BCBS

   Employer: Employee International

   Other insurance: None

4. Save this form for use in Exercise 13-8.

5. Review the Mary Sue Patient encounter form (Figure 13-7). Place a page marker on the encounter form.

6. Abstract the information needed for Blocks 1 through 13 from Figure 13-7 and enter the required information on the second claim form using Optical Scanning Guidelines. This may be completed by handwriting

DATE	REMARKS				
01/12/YYYY					

PATIENT			CHART #	SEX	BIRTHDATE
Mary Sue Patient			13-2	F	10/10/1959

MAILING ADDRESS	CITY	STATE	ZIP	HOME PHONE	WORK PHONE
91 Home Street	Nowhere	US	12367	(101) 201 8989	(101) 201 1234

EMPLOYER	ADDRESS	PATIENT STATUS
Happy Farm's Day Care	Anywhere US	(MARRIED) DIVORCED SINGLE STUDENT OTHER

INSURANCE: PRIMARY	ID#	GROUP	SECONDARY POLICY
BC BS US	WWW1023456	HFD6	

POLICYHOLDER NAME	BIRTHDATE	RELATIONSHIP	POLICYHOLDER NAME	BIRTHDATE	RELATIONSHIP
		Self			

SUPPLEMENTAL PLAN	EMPLOYER

POLICYHOLDER NAME	BIRTHDATE	RELATIONSHIP	DIAGNOSIS	CODE
			1. Strep throat	034.0
EMPLOYER			2. IDDM diabetes	250.01
			3.	
REFERRING PHYSICIAN UPIN/SSN			4.	

PLACE OF SERVICE

PROCEDURES	CODE	CHARGE
1. 01/12/YYYY Ofiice visit, Est Pt, level II	99212	$65—
2. 01/12/YYYY Quick Strep test	87880	12—
3.		
4.		
5.		
6.		

SPECIAL NOTES

TOTAL CHARGES	PAYMENTS	ADJUSTMENTS	BALANCE
$72—	0	0	$72—

RETURN VISIT	PHYSICIAN SIGNATURE
	Erin A. Helper, M.D.

ERIN A. HELPER, M.D.   101 MEDIC DRIVE, ANYWHERE, US 12345
PHONE NUMBER (101) 111-1234
EIN # 11-123341   SSN # 111-22-3333
UPIN EH8888   NPI 00818810   Medicaid # EBH8881   BC/BS # EH11881   GRP: 1204-P

FIGURE 13-7 Mary Sue Patient encounter form

the information, using the Blank Form Mode on the disk found in the text, or entering the data using a typewriter. Instructions for installing the disk are found in Appendix V.

7. Review Blocks 1 through 13 of the claim form to be sure all required blocks are properly completed.

■ **NOTE:** This same encounter form and claim form will be used for Exercise 13-4. ■

Refer to Figure 13-4 (John Q. Public encounter form) and to Figure 13-8, Blocks 14-23 of the HCFA-1500 claim form.

FIGURE 13-8 Blocks 14 through 23 of the HCFA-1500 claim form

Block 14	Enter the current date of onset for the primary condition if known, in MM DD YYYY format.
Block 15	Leave blank.
Block 16	Leave blank.
Block 17	Enter the *full name and credentials* of the referring/ordering physician(s) or other health care provider, if any of the following services are to be listed in Block 24D: consultation, surgery, diagnostic testing, physical or occupational therapy, home health care, or durable medical equipment. For Assistant Surgeon claims, enter the name of the attending surgeon. ■ **NOTE:** If the health care provider has assumed total care of the patient for a given illness/injury, this block is completed only on the first claim filed for the condition. ■
Block 17A	Enter the UPIN of any provider named in Block 17. ■ **NOTE:** The Health Insurance Portability and Accountability Act of 1997 (HIPAA) requires use of the National Provider Identification (NPI); however, the final rule for implementation has not been published. ■
Block 18	Hospitalization Enter the eight-digit (MM DD YYYY) admission date and the discharge date *if* any procedure/service is rendered to a patient with inpatient status. If the patient is still hospitalized, leave the "TO" block blank. If the patient has been discharged, enter the 8-digit (MM DD YYYY) discharge date.
Block 19	Enter the name of the lab, procedures performed, and charges if the provider was directly billed for clinical analysis of specimens by an outside laboratory. An entry in this block requires an "X" to be entered in the "YES" box in Block 20 and laboratory procedures reported in Blocks 24A-G. *When working with case studies in this text, leave this block blank and enter an "X" in the "NO" box in Block 20.*
Block 20	Enter an "X" in the "YES" box if the name of a lab is entered in Block 19; otherwise enter an "X" in the "NO" box.
Block 21	Enter up to four diagnoses in priority order (primary diagnosis followed by secondary diagnoses if treated).
Block 22	Leave blank. (Pertains to Medicaid claims only.)

14. DATE OF CURRENT: MM DD YY ILLNESS (First symptom) OR INJURY (Accident) OR PREGNANCY (LMP)	15. IF PATIENT HAS HAD SAME OR SIMILAR ILLNESS, GIVE FIRST DATE MM DD YY	16. DATES PATIENT UNABLE TO WORK IN CURRENT OCCUPATION MM DD YY MM DD YY FROM TO
01 12 YYYY		
17. NAME OF REFERRING PHYSICIAN OR OTHER SOURCE ERIN A HELPER MD	17a. I.D. NUMBER OF REFERRING PHYSICIAN 111223333	18. HOSPITALIZATION DATES RELATED TO CURRENT SERVICES MM DD YY MM DD YY FROM TO
19. RESERVED FOR LOCAL USE		20. OUTSIDE LAB? $ CHARGES ☐ YES ☒ NO
21. DIAGNOSIS OR NATURE OF ILLNESS OR INJURY. (RELATE ITEMS 1, 2, 3, OR 4 TO ITEM 24E BY LINE)		22. MEDICAID RESUBMISSION CODE ORIGINAL REF. NO.
1. 485 . __	3. L___ . __	
2. 788 41	4. L___ . __	23. PRIOR AUTHORIZATION NUMBER

FIGURE 13-9 Completed Blocks 14 through 23 for John Q. Public encounter form in Figure 13-4

Block 23

Enter the assigned authorization number when the patient's insurance plan requires specific services to be authorized by the patient's primary physician or the carrier's managed care department prior to the procedure being performed.

Refer to Figure 13-9 for completed Blocks 14 through 23 of the HCFA-1500 claim form.

EXERCISE 13-3 Continuation of Work on Comparison Chart

Reread the instructions for completing Blocks 14 through 23. As you review each block, enter brief instructions in the appropriate block in the BCBS column of the Comparison Chart.

EXERCISE 13-4 Continuation of Exercise 13-2

1. Review the Mary Sue Patient encounter form in Figure 13-7 and locate the diagnostic and treatment data.
2. Abstract the information needed for Blocks 14-23 and enter the required information on a new claim form using Optical Scanning Guidelines. This may be completed by handwriting the information, using the Blank Form Mode on the disk found in the text, or entering the data using a typewriter. Instructions for installing the disk are found in Appendix V.
3. Review Blocks 14-23 of the claim form to be sure all required blocks are properly completed.
4. Compare your claim forms with the completed form found in Figure 13-14.

■ **NOTE:** This same claim form will be used for Exercise 13-6. ■

Refer to Figure 13-10 for Block 24 of the HCFA-1500 claim form.

Block 24A

Enter the eight-digit (MMDDYYYY) dates in both the "FROM" and the "TO" columns. The same date is to be entered in the "FROM" and "TO" columns if the same procedure was not performed on consecutive dates.

Block 24B

Enter the proper Place of Service (POS) code from the following list:

Provider's office	11
Patient's home	12
Inpatient hospital	21
Outpatient hospital	22

FIGURE 13-10 Block 24 of the HCFA-1500 claim form

Emergency room hospital	23
Ambulatory surgical center	24
Birthing center	25
Military treatment facility or	26
Uniformed service treatment facility	26
Skilled nursing facility	31
Nursing home	32
Custodial care facility	33
Hospice	34
Federally qualified health center	50
Inpatient psychiatric facility	51
Psychiatric facility—day	52
Community mental health center	53
Intermediate care facility/mental retardation	54
Resident substance abuse treatment center	55
Psychiatric residential treatment center	56
Comprehensive inpatient rehabilitation facility	61
Comprehensive outpatient rehabilitation facility	62
End-stage renal disease treatment facility	65
State/local public health clinic	71
Independent laboratory	81
Other unlisted facility	99

■ **NOTE:** This listing is officially known as **HCFA Place of Service Codes**, and is also used in this same block for Medicare, Medicaid, and TRICARE/ CHAMPUS claims. ■

Block 24C   Leave blank.

Block 24D   Enter the correct five-digit CPT code or HCPCS level II/III code number along with any required CPT or HCPCS modifiers for the procedure being reported in this block. Enter a space, not a hyphen, to separate the code number from the modifier or multiple modifiers.

Block 24E   Enter the *reference number* (1 through 4) for the ICD code number listed in Block 21 that justifies the medical necessity for each procedure listed in Block 24D.

   This reference number should be followed by up to three reference numbers for any secondary or concurrent condition that applies to the procedure listed in Block 24D. Do not use commas to separate any multiple reference numbers.

Block 24F   Enter the fee for the procedure charged to the patient's account.

If identical, consecutive procedures are reported on this line, enter the total fee charged for the combined procedures.

Block 24G   Enter the number of units/days in this column. Some BCBS corporations require a three-digit number in all instances in this column; others do not.

The three-digit numbers are created by adding zeros in front of any single- or double-digit number (e.g., a unit of 1 becomes 001; a unit of 10 becomes 010). Special instructions are needed for computer systems not programmed to place three digits in this block. The BCBS manuals from the carriers that require the three-digit numbers say to disregard optical scanning guidelines for this block by placing the first two digits in block 24G and the third digit on the upright line defining the border between blocks 24G and 24H.

When working with case studies in this text, enter a three-digit number for all entries.

Block 24H   Leave blank.

Block 24I   Leave blank.

Block 24J   Leave blank. (COB stands for coordination of benefits.)

Block 24K   Leave blank.

■ **NOTE:** This may be a local field required by some state carriers. ■

When working with case studies in this text and in the workbook, leave this block blank.

Refer to Figure 13-11 for completed Blocks 24A through 24K of the HCFA-1500 claim form.

24.	A DATE(S) OF SERVICE						B Place of Service	C Type of Service	D PROCEDURES, SERVICES, OR SUPPLIES (Explain Unusual Circumstances) CPT/HCPCS	MODIFIER	E DIAGNOSIS CODE	F $ CHARGES		G DAYS OR UNITS	H EPSDT Family Plan	I EMG	J COB	K RESERVED FOR LOCAL USE
	From MM	DD	YY	To MM	DD	YY												
1	0112YYYY			0112YYYY			11		99213		1	75	00	001				
2	0112YYYY			0112YYYY			11		71020		1	50	00	001				
3	0112YYYY			0112YYYY			11		81001		2	10	00	001				
4																		
5																		
6																		

FIGURE 13-11 Completed Block 24 for John Q. Public encounter form in Figure 13-4

EXERCISE 13-5 Continuation of Work on Comparison Chart

Review the instructions for completing Blocks 24A through 24K. As you review each block, enter a brief description of the instructions in the appropriate block in the BCBS column of the Comparison Chart.

EXERCISE 13-6 Continuation of Exercise 13-2

1. Review the procedure data on the Mary Sue Patient encounter form (Figure 13-7).

2. Abstract the information needed for Blocks 24A through 24K and handwrite the required information on a new claim form using Optica Scanning Guidelines. This may be completed by handwriting the information, using the Blank Form Mode on the disk found in the text, or entering the data using a typewriter. Instructions for installing the disk are found in Appendix V.

3. Review Blocks 24A through 24K of the claim form to be sure all required blocks are properly completed.

■ **NOTE:** This same claim form is used for Exercise 13-8. ■

Refer to Figure 13-12 for Blocks 25 through 33 of the HCFA-1500 claim form.

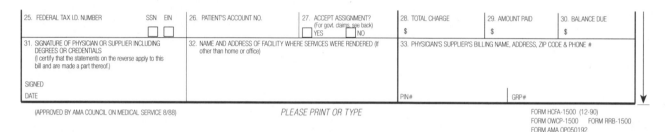

FIGURE 13-12 Blocks 25 through 33 of HCFA-1500 claim form

Block 25 Enter the billing entity's Employer Tax Identification Number (EIN) or Social Security Number (SSN) with the hyphen, and enter an "X" in the appropriate box.

Block 26 Enter the number assigned to the patient's account if the practice uses a numerical identification number to identify the patient's account or ledger card, or if the claim is filed electronically.

Leave this block blank if the practice files patient accounts by patient name.

When working with the case studies in this text and workbook, enter the case study number in this block. If the case requires primary and secondary forms, add the appropriate abbreviation (e.g., "P" for Primary, "S" for Secondary).

Block 27 To accept assignment means the provider has negotiated a participating provider contract and has agreed to accept the carrier-determined, allowed fee for all services performed. Enter an "X" in the "YES" box if the provider has a participating provider contract with the carrier. Enter an "X" in the "NO" box if the provider has not signed a participating provider contract with the carrier.

Block 28 Total all charges on the claim form and enter the sum in this block. This figure should never reflect negative charges or show a credit due to the patient.

If multiple claims for one patient are generated by the computer because more than six services must be reported, be sure the total charge recorded on each claim form accurately represents the total of the items on each separate claim form submitted.

Block 29 Leave blank.

Block 30 Leave blank.

Block 31

Paper Claims: Most health care providers have arranged with major health insurance carriers to use either a signature stamp or a typed name and professional credential. If special arrangements have not been made, the provider must sign each claim.

■ **NOTE:** When arrangements are made to transmit claims electronically to an insurance company, a certification letter must be filed with the insurance company to replace the signature usually required in this space. ■

When working with the case studies in this text and workbook, enter the provider's full name, credential and the date the claim is completed (MMDD YYYY).

Block 32

Complete this item when the services listed on the claim form were performed at a site other than the provider's office or the patient's home.

If the "YES" box in Block 20 contains an "X", enter the name and address of the laboratory that performed the laboratory procedures.

Block 33

Enter the phone number, name, and address of the billing entity. Enter the BCBS PIN number and GRP number. Refer to Figure 13-13 on page 338 showing a completed claim for the encounter form in Figure 13-4.

EXERCISE 13-7 Continuation of Work on Comparison Chart

Review the instructions for completing Blocks 25 through 33. As you read each block, record a brief description of the instructions in the appropriate block in the BCBS column of the Comparison Chart.

EXERCISE 13-8 Continuation of Exercise 13-2

Additional information you need for this case:

Dr. Helper's Social Security Number is 111-22-3333. She is a BCBS PAR provider and her BCBS PIN number is EH11881. The billing entity is Erin A. Helper, M.D. The BCBS group identifier number is 1204-P. She is on the medical staff and admits patients at Goodmedicine Hospital, Anywhere Street, Anywhere US 12345.

1. Review the Mary Sue Patient encounter form (Figure 13-7).
2. Abstract the information needed for Blocks 25 through 33 from the encounter form and the additional data given above and enter it on the claim form.
3. Review Blocks 25 through 33 of the claim form to be sure all required blocks are properly completed.
4. Compare your claim form with the completed claim form in Figure 13-14 on page 339.

TWO BCBS FULL BENEFIT POLICIES

The following modifications are made to the primary claim when the patient is covered by two BCBS plans issued by the same BCBS corporation (see Figure 13-15 on page 340).

Block 9

Enter the secondary policyholder's name, if different from patient; otherwise, enter "SAME".

FIGURE 13-13 Completed claim form shown in its entirety with all information entered for the John Q. Public encounter form shown in Figure 13-4.

PLEASE
DO NOT
STAPLE
IN THIS
AREA

(SAMPLE ONLY - NOT APPROVED FOR USE)

CARRIER

| | PICA | | | | **UNDERSTANDING HEALTH INSURANCE CLAIM FORM** PICA | | |

1. MEDICARE MEDICAID CHAMPUS CHAMPVA GROUP HEALTH PLAN FECA BLK LUNG OTHER	1a. INSURED'S I.D. NUMBER (FOR PROGRAM IN ITEM 1)
☐ (Medicare #) ☐ (Medicaid #) ☐ (Sponsor's SSN) ☐ (VA File #) ☐ (SSN or ID) ☐ (SSN) ☒ (ID)	WWW1023456 HFD6

2. PATIENT'S NAME (Last Name, First Name, Middle Initial)	3. PATIENT'S BIRTH DATE MM DD YY SEX	4. INSURED'S NAME (Last Name, First Name, Middle Initial)
PATIENT MARY SUE	10 10 1959 M☐ F☒	SAME

5. PATIENT'S ADDRESS (No. Street)	6. PATIENT RELATIONSHIP TO INSURED	7. INSURED'S ADDRESS (No. Street)
91 HOME STREET	Self ☒ Spouse ☐ Child ☐ Other ☐	SAME

CITY	STATE	8. PATIENT STATUS	CITY	STATE
NOWHERE	US	Single ☐ Married ☒ Other ☐		

ZIP CODE	TELEPHONE (Include Area Code)		ZIP CODE	TELEPHONE (INCLUDE AREA CODE)
12367	101 201 8989	Employed ☒ Full-Time Student ☐ Part-Time Student ☐		( )

9. OTHER INSURED'S NAME (Last Name, First Name, Middle Initial)	10. IS PATIENT'S CONDITION RELATED TO:	11. INSURED'S POLICY GROUP OR FECA NUMBER
a. OTHER INSURED'S POLICY OR GROUP NUMBER	a. EMPLOYMENT? (CURRENT OR PREVIOUS) ☐ YES ☒ NO	a. INSURED'S DATE OF BIRTH MM DD YY SEX 10 10 1959 M☐ F☒
b. OTHER INSURED'S DATE OF BIRTH MM DD YY SEX M☐ F☐	b. AUTO ACCIDENT? PLACE (State) ☐ YES ☒ NO	b. EMPLOYER'S NAME OR SCHOOL NAME HAPPY FARM'S DAY CARE
c. EMPLOYER'S NAME OR SCHOOL NAME	c. OTHER ACCIDENT? ☐ YES ☒ NO	c. INSURANCE PLAN NAME OR PROGRAM NAME BCBS US
d. INSURANCE PLAN NAME OR PROGRAM NAME	10d. RESERVED FOR LOCAL USE	d. IS THERE ANOTHER HEALTH BENEFIT PLAN? ☐ YES ☒ NO If yes, return to and complete item 9 a – d.

READ BACK OF FORM BEFORE COMPLETING & SIGNING THIS FORM.

12. PATIENT'S OR AUTHORIZED PERSON'S SIGNATURE I authorize the release of any medical or other information necessary to process this claim. I also request payment of government benefits either to myself or to the party who accepts assignment below.

SIGNED   SIGNATURE ON FILE   DATE

13. INSURED'S OR AUTHORIZED PERSON'S SIGNATURE I authorize payment of medical benefits to the undersigned physician or supplier for services described below.

SIGNED

14. DATE OF CURRENT: ILLNESS (First symptom) OR INJURY (Accident) OR PREGNANCY (LMP) MM DD YY 01 12 YYYY	15. IF PATIENT HAS HAD SAME OR SIMILAR ILLNESS, GIVE FIRST DATE MM DD YY	16. DATES PATIENT UNABLE TO WORK IN CURRENT OCCUPATION MM DD YY MM DD YY FROM TO
17. NAME OF REFERRING PHYSICIAN OR OTHER SOURCE	17a. I.D. NUMBER OF REFERRING PHYSICIAN	18. HOSPITALIZATION DATES RELATED TO CURRENT SERVICES MM DD YY MM DD YY FROM TO
19. RESERVED FOR LOCAL USE		20. OUTSIDE LAB? $ CHARGES ☐ YES ☒ NO

21. DIAGNOSIS OR NATURE OF ILLNESS OR INJURY. (RELATE ITEMS 1, 2, 3, OR 4 TO ITEM 24E BY LINE)	22. MEDICAID RESUBMISSION CODE ORIGINAL REF. NO.
1. 034 0 3. __ . __	
2. 250 01 4. __ . __	23. PRIOR AUTHORIZATION NUMBER

24. A. DATE(S) OF SERVICE		B. Place of Service	C. Type of Service	D. PROCEDURES, SERVICES, OR SUPPLIES (Explain Unusual Circumstances)		E. DIAGNOSIS CODE	F. $ CHARGES	G. DAYS OR UNITS	H. EPSDT Family Plan	I. EMG	J. COB	K. RESERVED FOR LOCAL USE
From MM DD YY	To MM DD YY			CPT/HCPCS	MODIFIER							
0112YYYY	0112YYYY	11		99212		1	65 00	001				
0112YYYY	0112YYYY	11		87880		1	12 00	001				

25. FEDERAL TAX I.D. NUMBER SSN EIN	26. PATIENT'S ACCOUNT NO.	27. ACCEPT ASSIGNMENT? (For govt. claims, see back)	28. TOTAL CHARGE	29. AMOUNT PAID	30. BALANCE DUE
11-123341 ☒	13-2	☒ YES ☐ NO	$ 72 00	$	$

31. SIGNATURE OF PHYSICIAN OR SUPPLIER INCLUDING DEGREES OR CREDENTIALS (I certify that the statements on the reverse apply to this bill and are made a part thereof.)	32. NAME AND ADDRESS OF FACILITY WHERE SERVICES WERE RENDERED (If other than home or office)	33. PHYSICIAN'S SUPPLIER'S BILLING NAME, ADDRESS, ZIP CODE & PHONE #
ERIN A HELPER MD SIGNED DATE MMDDYYYY		(101) 111 1234 ERIN A HELPER MD 101 MEDIC DRIVE ANYWHERE, US 12345 PIN# EH1181 GRP# 1204-P

(SAMPLE ONLY - NOT APPROVED FOR USE)   PLEASE PRINT OR TYPE   SAMPLE FORM 1500 SAMPLE FORM 1500 SAMPLE FORM 1500

PATIENT AND INSURED INFORMATION

PHYSICIAN OR SUPPLIER INFORMATION

FIGURE 13-14 Completed claim form for Exercises 13-2, 13-4, 13-6, and 13-8 and the Mary Sue Patient encounter form shown in Figure 13-7.

PLEASE
DO NOT
STAPLE
IN THIS
AREA

(SAMPLE ONLY - NOT APPROVED FOR USE)

CARRIER

| | | | PICA | | |

UNDERSTANDING HEALTH INSURANCE CLAIM FORM PICA | | |

1. MEDICARE MEDICAID CHAMPUS CHAMPVA GROUP HEALTH PLAN FECA BLK LUNG OTHER	1a. INSURED'S I.D. NUMBER (FOR PROGRAM IN ITEM 1)
(Medicare #) (Medicaid #) (Sponsor's SSN) (VA File #) (SSN or ID) (SSN) [X] (ID)	WWW1023456 HFD6

2. PATIENT'S NAME (Last Name, First Name, Middle Initial) PATIENT MARY SUE	3. PATIENT'S BIRTH DATE MM 10 DD 10 YY 1959 SEX M [ ] F [X]	4. INSURED'S NAME (Last Name, First Name, Middle Initial) SAME

5. PATIENT'S ADDRESS (No. Street) 91 HOME STREET	6. PATIENT RELATIONSHIP TO INSURED Self [X] Spouse [ ] Child [ ] Other [ ]	7. INSURED'S ADDRESS (No. Street) SAME

| CITY NOWHERE | STATE US | 8. PATIENT STATUS Single [ ] Married [X] Other [ ] Employed [X] Full-Time Student [ ] Part-Time Student [ ] | CITY | STATE |

| ZIP CODE 12367 | TELEPHONE (Include Area Code) 101 201 8989 | ZIP CODE | TELEPHONE (INCLUDE AREA CODE) ( ) |

9. OTHER INSURED'S NAME (Last Name, First Name, Middle Initial) PATIENT JAMES W	10. IS PATIENT'S CONDITION RELATED TO:	11. INSURED'S POLICY GROUP OR FECA NUMBER

a. OTHER INSURED'S POLICY OR GROUP NUMBER R1527418	a. EMPLOYMENT? (CURRENT OR PREVIOUS) [ ] YES [X] NO	a. INSURED'S DATE OF BIRTH MM DD YY SEX M [ ] F [ ]

b. OTHER INSURED'S DATE OF BIRTH MM 03 DD 01 YY 1948 SEX M [X] F [ ]	b. AUTO ACCIDENT? [ ] YES [X] NO PLACE (State)	b. EMPLOYER'S NAME OR SCHOOL NAME HAPPY FARM'S DAY CARE

c. EMPLOYER'S NAME OR SCHOOL NAME NAVAL STATION	c. OTHER ACCIDENT? [ ] YES [X] NO	c. INSURANCE PLAN NAME OR PROGRAM NAME BCBS US

d. INSURANCE PLAN NAME OR PROGRAM NAME BCBS FEDERAL	10d. RESERVED FOR LOCAL USE	d. IS THERE ANOTHER HEALTH BENEFIT PLAN? [X] YES [ ] NO If yes, return to and complete item 9 a – d.

READ BACK OF FORM BEFORE COMPLETING & SIGNING THIS FORM.

12. PATIENT'S OR AUTHORIZED PERSON'S SIGNATURE I authorize the release of any medical or other information necessary to process this claim. I also request payment of government benefits either to myself or to the party who accepts assignment below. SIGNED SIGNATURE ON FILE DATE	13. INSURED'S OR AUTHORIZED PERSON'S SIGNATURE I authorize payment of medical benefits to the undersigned physician or supplier for services described below. SIGNED

PATIENT AND INSURED INFORMATION

14. DATE OF CURRENT: ILLNESS (First symptom) OR INJURY (Accident) OR PREGNANCY (LMP) MM 01 DD 12 YY YYYY	15. IF PATIENT HAS HAD SAME OR SIMILAR ILLNESS, GIVE FIRST DATE MM DD YY	16. DATES PATIENT UNABLE TO WORK IN CURRENT OCCUPATION FROM MM DD YY TO MM DD YY

17. NAME OF REFERRING PHYSICIAN OR OTHER SOURCE	17a. I.D. NUMBER OF REFERRING PHYSICIAN	18. HOSPITALIZATION DATES RELATED TO CURRENT SERVICES FROM MM DD YY TO MM DD YY

19. RESERVED FOR LOCAL USE	20. OUTSIDE LAB? [ ] YES [X] NO	$ CHARGES

21. DIAGNOSIS OR NATURE OF ILLNESS OR INJURY. (RELATE ITEMS 1, 2, 3, OR 4 TO ITEM 24E BY LINE) 1. 034.0 2. 250.01 3. ____.__ 4. ____.__	22. MEDICAID RESUBMISSION CODE ORIGINAL REF. NO. 23. PRIOR AUTHORIZATION NUMBER

24. A DATE(S) OF SERVICE				B Place of Service	C Type of Service	D PROCEDURES, SERVICES, OR SUPPLIES (Explain Unusual Circumstances) CPT/HCPCS MODIFIER	E DIAGNOSIS CODE	F $ CHARGES	G DAYS OR UNITS	H EPSDT Family Plan	I EMG	J COB	K RESERVED FOR LOCAL USE
From MM DD YY	To MM DD YY												
0112YYYY	0112YYYY			11		99212	1	65 00	001				
0112YYYY	0112YYYY			11		87880	1	12 00	001				

25. FEDERAL TAX I.D. NUMBER 11-123341 SSN [ ] EIN [X]	26. PATIENT'S ACCOUNT NO. 13-2BB	27. ACCEPT ASSIGNMENT? (For govt. claims, see back) [X] YES [ ] NO	28. TOTAL CHARGE $ 72 00	29. AMOUNT PAID $	30. BALANCE DUE $

31. SIGNATURE OF PHYSICIAN OR SUPPLIER INCLUDING DEGREES OR CREDENTIALS (I certify that the statements on the reverse apply to this bill and are made a part thereof.) ERIN A HELPER MD SIGNED DATE MMDDYYYY	32. NAME AND ADDRESS OF FACILITY WHERE SERVICES WERE RENDERED (If other than home or office)	33. PHYSICIAN'S SUPPLIER'S BILLING NAME, ADDRESS, ZIP CODE & PHONE # (101) 111 1234 ERIN A HELPER MD 101 MEDIC DRIVE ANYWHERE, US 12345 PIN# EH1181 GRP#1204-P/

PHYSICIAN OR SUPPLIER INFORMATION

(SAMPLE ONLY - NOT APPROVED FOR USE) *PLEASE PRINT OR TYPE*

SAMPLE FORM 1500
SAMPLE FORM 1500 SAMPLE FORM 1500

FIGURE 13-15 Completed claim form for a patient with two BCBS policies

Block 9A	Enter the secondary policy identification number.
Block 9B	Enter secondary policyholder's eight-digit birth date (MM DD YYYY), and enter an "X" in the appropriate box to indicate the secondary subscriber's gender.
Block 9C	Enter the secondary policyholder's employer name if the policy is an employer-sponsored group policy. Otherwise, leave blank.
Block 9D	Enter the name of the secondary plan.
Block 11D	Enter an "X" in the "YES" box.

EXERCISE 13-9 Filing a Claim When a Patient Has Two BCBS Policies

1. Obtain a blank claim form.
2. Underline the Block identifiers on the new claim form for the blocks discussed in the BCBS Claim form instructions.
3. Review the encounter form for Mary Sue Patient (Figure 13-7). Enter the following information in the blocks for the secondary policy (9-9D):
   BC/BS FEDERAL R1527418 GROUP 101
   Policyholder: James W. Patient
   Birthdate: 03/01/48
   Relationship: Spouse
   Employer: NAVAL STATION
   Add a "BB" to the Patient Chart Number, and include this designation on the claim form in Block 26.
4. Complete the secondary claim form on Mary Sue Patient using the data from the encounter form and placing the secondary information in the blocks highlighted in Step 2.
5. Review the completed claim form to be sure all required blocks are properly completed.

BCBS SECONDARY CLAIMS

These instructions are for claims in which the primary insurer is a commercial or government plan, and the patient is also covered by a BCBS secondary policy. The primary carrier EOB must be attached to the secondary claim.

These instructions do not apply to BCBS policies that are purchased as a supplement to Primary Medicare coverage. Instructions for billing these policies are covered in the Medicare chapter (see Chapter 14).

Block 1A	Enter the patient's BCBS ID and group plan numbers.
Block 11	Enter the *primary policy* identification number.
Block 11A	Enter *primary policyholder's birth date,* and enter an "X" in the appropriate box for gender.
Block 11B	Enter one of two options: Enter the name of the school attended if patient is covered by a school plan, is a full-time student, and is over the age of 19; ***or*** Enter the name of the *primary policyholder's employer.*

Block 11C   Enter the name of the *primary policy carrier.*

Block 29   Enter only payments made by the *primary insurer*

When working with case studies in this text, a notation will be placed in the Notes section of the encounter form indicating any payment from the primary insurer.

Enter the phrase "EOB Attached" at the top of the claim form to simulate the attachment of the EOB on these secondary claims, and add the word "secondary" to Block 26 to show that this is a secondary claim.

EXERCISE 13-10 Filing BCBS Secondary Claims

1. Obtain a blank claim form.
2. Underline the Block identification numbers for the changes discussed above.
3. Review Figure 13-16. Complete the BC/BS secondary claim form for this case using the data from the encounter form.

DATE 01/15/YYYY	REMARKS			
PATIENT Janet B. Cross		CHART # 13-3	SEX F	BIRTHDATE 11/01/1934

MAILING ADDRESS 1901 Beach Head Drive	CITY Anywhere	STATE US	ZIP 12345	HOME PHONE (101) 201 1991	WORK PHONE

EMPLOYER Retired	ADDRESS	PATIENT STATUS (MARRIED) DIVORCED SINGLE STUDENT OTHER

INSURANCE: PRIMARY Medicare	ID# 191 26 6844A	GROUP	SECONDARY POLICY BCBS US WWW191266844

POLICYHOLDER NAME	BIRTHDATE	RELATIONSHIP self	POLICYHOLDER NAME	BIRTHDATE	RELATIONSHIP self
SUPPLEMENTAL PLAN			EMPLOYER		

POLICYHOLDER NAME	BIRTHDATE	RELATIONSHIP	DIAGNOSIS		CODE
			1. Intracranial Hemorrhage		432.9
EMPLOYER			2. Dysphasia		784.5
			3.		
REFERRING PHYSICIAN UPIN/SSN			4.		

PLACE OF SERVICE Goodmedicine Hospital Anywhere Street Anywhere US 12345

PROCEDURES	CODE	CHARGE
1. 01/13/YYYY Initial hospital visit level III	99223	$150—
2. 01/14/YYYY Discharge management, 60 minutes	99239	100—
3.		
4.		
5.		
6.		

SPECIAL NOTES

Patient transferred to University Hospital via advanced life support ambulance

TOTAL CHARGES $250—	PAYMENTS 0	ADJUSTMENTS 0	BALANCE $250—
RETURN VISIT		PHYSICIAN SIGNATURE *Erin A. Helper, M.D.*	

ERIN A. HELPER, M.D.   101 MEDIC DRIVE, ANYWHERE, US 12345
PHONE NUMBER (101) 111-1234
EIN # 11-123341   SSN # 111-22-3333
UPIN EH8888   NPI 00818810   Medicaid # EBH8881   BC/BS # EH11881 GRP: 1204-P

FIGURE 13-16 Encounter form

4. Review the completed claim form to be sure all required blocks are properly completed.

5. Compare your claim form with Figure 13-17.

FIGURE 13-17 Completed claim form for BCBS secondary form

Additional BCBS claim case studies are found in Appendix I and Appendix II.

Case studies in Appendix II require reading the case study chart entries and abstracting and coding the diagnostic information. Necessary clinic, hospital, and physician data is included in the Clinic Billing Manual in Appendix II.

REVIEW

DEFINITION EXERCISE

Read the definitions carefully. If the statement is true, place a check mark to the left of the number. If the statement is false, correct it without rewriting the entire statement.

1. Participating provider (PAR): A physician or other health care provider of medical care who has entered into a contract with BCBS to accept the carrier-determined allowed amount as payment in full.

2. Nonparticipating provider (nonPAR): A health care provider who expects full payment from the carrier for fees charged to patients.

3. FEHBP: Federal Employee Health Benefit Program.

4. Medical emergency care: Treatment sought and received at any time for sudden, severe, and unexpected conditions that, if not treated, would place the patient's health in jeopardy or lead to impairment or permanent dysfunction of an organ or body part.

5. Preferred Provider Network (PPN): A program that requires subscribers to adhere to managed care provisions.

CHALLENGE EXERCISE

Answer the following:

1. State the purpose of the Baylor University plan, which was the precursor of what is now known as Blue Cross.

2. Discuss how the California Physicians' Service Program, established in 1938, differed from the Baylor University plan.

3. BCBS corporations function as independent corporations serving specific regions of the country. Discuss the function of the national BCBSA.

4. List the advantages to the consumer when they select a Blue Shield participating provider.

5. List the advantages of being a Blue Shield participating provider.

6. List the nine distinct types of benefits normally covered by the Blue Shield basic policy.

7. Describe two policy riders that are often added to Blue Shield basic benefits.

8. List eight types of benefits that may appear as Blue Shield major medical benefits.

9. Describe two policy riders that are often added to major medical benefits.

10. Explain how BCBS PARs determine what the deductible, copay/coinsurance, and plan benefits are for a BlueCard patient.

11. State the usual filing deadline for BCBS plans.

12. Indicate where completed paper claims are sent for processing in the following situations:

PAR PROVIDER

A. Patient ID # XYW12345678

B. Patient ID # 332124433

C. Patient has out-of-area BCBS ID XYW12345678 and is also covered by an Aetna full-benefit policy.

D. Patient ID # R12345678

E. The "home plan" is located in California; the "host plan" is located in Virginia.

Medicare

Upon successful completion of this chapter, you should be able to:

1. Define the following terms, phrases, and abbreviations:

fiscal intermediary (FI)

Medicare Part A

Medicare Part B

Social Security Administration (SSA)

disability

Initial Enrollment Period (IEP)

General Enrollment Period (GEP)

Special Enrollment Period

Qualified Medicare Beneficiary (QMB)

Specified Low-income Medicare Beneficiary (SLMB)

benefit period

spell of illness

lifetime reserve days

hospice

respite care

end-stage renal disease (ESRD)

dialysis

hemodialysis

peritoneal dialysis

kidney transplantation

autologous bone marrow transplant

allogenic bone marrow transplant

leukemia

remission

aplastic anemia

severe combined immunodeficiency disease (SCID)

Wiskott-Aldrich syndrome

multiple myeloma

participating provider (PAR)

nonparticipating provider (nonPAR)

limiting charge (LC)

limiting fee

physician extender provider

limited license practitioner (LLP)

Sunshine Law

balance billing

Medicare private contract

Advance Beneficiary Notice (ABN)

medical necessity denial

Resource-Based Relative Value Scale (RBRVS)

Medicare Fee Schedule (MFS)

relative value unit (RVU)

geographic adjustment factor (GAF)

national conversion factor (CF)

Medicare Secondary Payer (MSP)

conditional primary payer status

Original Medicare Plan

Medicare Summary Notice (MSN)

Medicare Supplemental Plan (MSP)

Medigap policy

Employer-Sponsored Retirement Plan

Medicare-Medicaid Crossover (Medi/Medi)

extra coverage plans

Medicare+Choice Program

Coordinated Care Plans

health maintenance organization (HMO)

risk-based HMO

lock-in provision

cost-based HMO

Provider-Sponsored Organization (PSO)

Preferred Provider Organization (PPO)

Medical Savings Accounts Plan (MSA)

Medicare MSA

Medicare MSA Health Policy

Religious Fraternal Benefit Society Plan

Department of Defense (DoD)/TRICARE (demo) Plan

Private Fee-for-Service Plan (PFFS)

Durable Medical Equipment Regional Carrier (DMERC)

ordering physician

Unique Provider Identification Number (UPIN)

Clinical Laboratory Improvement Act (CLIA) certification number

provider identification number (PIN)

plan identification number (PlanID)

National Health PlanID

2. List six categories of persons eligible for Medicare coverage.

3. Describe the coverage for each of the following:

| Medicare Part A | ESRD dialysis cases | hospice care |
| Medicare Part B | heart transplant | kidney donor |

4. List and describe six incentives developed by Congress to encourage providers to become Medicare participating providers.

5. List and describe six restrictions placed on Medicare nonPAR providers.

6. Explain the requirements for use of the Medicare Medical Necessity Statement.

7. Explain requirements governing use of the Surgery Financial Disclosure Statement.

8. List and define seven types of insurance programs that are primary to Medicare.

9. List and define two types of programs that are classified as Medicare Supplemental plans.

10. Explain how a policy falls into the extra coverage category and how it affects Medicare billing.

11. Explain how a Medicare claim is filed for Medicare patients enrolled in Medicare risk-restricted or cost-based HMOs.

12. Explain the billing sequence for Medicare patients with employer-sponsored plans, Medigap, Medicare-Medicaid Crossover plans, and Medicare as secondary coverage.

13. Explain how Medicare's liability as a secondary payer is calculated.

14. State the deadline for filing Medicare claims.

15. Discuss the provider's legal responsibility for collecting the patient's deductible and coinsurance obligations.

16. Explain the procedure health care providers must follow to "opt out" of Medicare

17. Describe the features of Medicare+Choice with regard to the following: private fee-for-service plan, provider-sponsored organizations, and Medicare Savings Accounts.

18. File traditional Medicare or Medicare HMO fee-for-service claims properly.

INTRODUCTION

Medicare, the largest single medical benefits program in the United States, is a federal program authorized by Congress and administered by the Health Care Financing Administration (HCFA). It was enacted as Title 18 of the Social Security Act Amendments of 1965 as a nationwide program to offer identical benefits in all 50 states. HCFA is responsible for the operation of the Medicare program and for the selection of an insurance company to act as the regional Medicare claims processing unit called a **fiscal intermediary (FI)**. Medicare is a two-part program:

- **Medicare Part A** covers institutional providers for inpatient, hospice, and home health services.

- **Medicare Part B** covers noninstitutional health care providers of all outpatient services.

The billing instructions in this chapter cover the filing of Medicare Part B services only. Part A claims are not filed by insurance specialists working in private health care provider offices; they are filed by hospitals, hospices, and home health care providers.

MEDICARE ELIGIBILITY

General Medicare eligibility requires individuals or spouses to:

1. Have worked at least 10 years in Medicare-covered employment.

2. Be a minimum age of 65 years old.

3. Be a citizen or permanent resident of the United States.

Individuals can also qualify for coverage if they are younger than 65 years old and have a disability or chronic kidney disease. The **Social Security Administration (SSA)** (an agency of the Federal Government) bases their definition of **disability** on an individual's inability to work; an individual can be considered disabled if unable to do work as before and it is determined that adjustments cannot be made to do other work because of a medical condition(s). In addition, the disability must last or be expected to last a year or to result in death.

Medicare Part A coverage is available at no cost to individuals *age 65 and over* who:

- Are already receiving retirement benefits from Social Security or the Railroad Retirement Board
- Are eligible to receive Social Security or Railroad benefits but who have not yet filed for them
- Had Medicare-covered government employment

Medicare Part A coverage is available at no cost to individuals *under age 65* who:

- Have received Social Security or Railroad Retirement Board disability benefits for 24 months
- Are kidney dialysis or kidney transplant patients

There is no premium for Part A if individuals meet one of the above conditions; however, they do pay for Part B coverage. The Part B monthly premium changes annually and is deducted from Social Security, Railroad Retirement, or Civil Service Retirement checks.

MEDICARE ENROLLMENT

Medicare enrollment is handled in two ways: individuals are either enrolled automatically or they apply for coverage. In addition, individuals age 65 and over who do not qualify for Social Security benefits may "buy in" to Medicare Part A by paying monthly premiums. The "buy in" premiums for 2001 are $300/month (Part A with less than 30 quarters SSA coverage) or $165/month (Part A with more than 30 quarters SSA coverage), and $50.00 (Part B optional coverage).

Automatic Enrollment

Individuals not yet age 65 who already receive Social Security, Railroad Retirement Board, or disability benefits are automatically enrolled in Part A and Part B effective the month of their 65th birthday. About three months prior to their 65th birthday, or 24th month of disability, individuals are sent an Initial Enrollment Package that contains information about Medicare, a questionnaire, and a Medicare card. If the individual wants both Medicare Part A (hospital insurance) and Part B (supplemental medical insurance), they just sign their Medicare card and keep it in their wallet (or some other safe place).

Individuals who do not want Part B coverage (because there is a monthly premium associated with it) must follow the instructions that accompany their Medicare card requiring the individual to mark an "X" in the refusal box on the back of the Medicare card form, sign the form, and return it *with* the Medicare card to the address indicated. The individual is then sent a new Medicare card showing coverage for Part A only.

Applying for Medicare

Individuals who do not receive Social Security, Railroad Retirement Board, or disability benefits must apply for Medicare Part A and Part B by contacting the Social Security Administration (or Railroad Retirement Board) approximately three months before the month in which they turn 65 or 24th month of disability. Upon applying for Medicare Part A and Part B, a seven month **Initial Enrollment Period (IEP)** begins, which provides an opportunity for the individual to enroll in Medicare Part A and/or Part B. Those who wait until they turn 65 to apply for Medicare will cause a delay in the start of Part B coverage because they will have to wait until the next **General Enrollment Period (GEP)**, which is held January 1 through March 31 of each year; Part B coverage starts on July 1 of that year. The Part B premium is also increased by 10% for each 12-month period that an individual was eligible for Part B coverage, but did not participate.

Under certain circumstances, individuals can delay their Part B enrollment without having to pay higher premiums; examples include individuals age 65 or older who have group health insurance based on their own or their spouse's current employment; or disabled individuals who have group health insurance based on their own or any family member's current employment. If Part B enrollment is delayed for one of these reasons, individuals can enroll anytime during the **Special Enrollment Period**. The Special Enrollment Period is a set time when individuals can sign up for Medicare Part B if they did not enroll in Part B during the Initial Enrollment Period.

Qualified Medicare Beneficiary Program

Under the **Qualified Medicare Beneficiary (QMB)** program, the federal government requires state Medicaid programs to pay Medicare premiums, patient deductibles, and coinsurance for individuals who have Medicare Part A, a low monthly income, and limited resources, but who are not otherwise eligible for Medicaid. See Table 14-1 for programs that help pay Medicare expenses for individuals and couples. In addition to income and assets, an individual or couple may have financial resources and/or own items valued at or below $4,000 for an individual and $6,000 for a couple. Financial resources include bank accounts, stocks, and bonds. Items that are not counted as financial resources include the house the individual/couple lives in, one car, burial plots, furniture, and some life insurance.

Table 14-1 *Programs that help pay Medicare expenses*

Monthly Income Limit (2001)*		Name of Program	Program Will Pay:
$736	Individual (or)	Qualified Medical Beneficiary (QMB)	Medicare Part A and Part B premiums, deductibles, and coinsurance
$988	Couple		
$879	Individual (or)	Special Low-income Medicare Beneficiary (SLMB)	Medicare Part B premiums
$1,181	Couple		
$987	Individual (or)	Qualifying Individual (QI-1)	Medicare Part B premiums
$1,327	Couple		
$1,273	Individual (or)	Qualifying Individual (QI-2)	A small part of the Medicare Part B premiums
$1,714	Couple		
$1,452	Individual (or)	Qualified Disabled Working Individual (QDWI)	Medicare Part B premiums
$1,955	Couple		

*Alaska and Hawaii income limits are slightly higher, and all income limits will increase slightly next year.

Specified Low-Income Medicare Beneficiary Program

Another federally mandated program, the **Specified Low-Income Medicare Beneficiary (SLMB)** program, requires states to cover just the Medicare Part B premium for persons whose income is slightly above the poverty level. See Table 14-1 for monthly income limits for individuals and couples. Assets, house, car, and burial plan requirements are the same as for QMBs.

PART A COVERAGE

Hospital Stays

Medicare pays only a portion of a patient's acute care hospitalization expenses, and the patient's out-of-pocket expenses are calculated on a "benefit period basis." A **benefit period** begins with the first day of hospitalization and ends when the patient has been out of the hospital for 60 consecutive days. (Some Medicare literature uses the term **spell of illness**, formerly called "spell of sickness," in place of "benefit period.") After 90 continuous days of hospitalization, the patient may elect to use their 60-day lifetime reserve days, or they can pay the full daily charges for hospitalization. **Lifetime reserve days** may be used only once during a patient's lifetime and are usually reserved for use during the patient's final, terminal hospital stay. The 2001 Part A deductibles per benefit period are:

Days 1–60	$792 total
Days 61–90	$198/day
Days 91–150	Patient pays total charges, or elects to use lifetime reserve days at $396/day
150+ continuous days	Patient pays total charges

A person who has been out of the hospital for a period of 60 consecutive days will enter a new benefit period if rehospitalized, and the expenses for the first 90 days under this new benefit period are the same as stated above. Persons confined to a psychiatric hospital are allowed 190 lifetime reserve days instead of the 60 days allotted for a stay in an acute care hospital.

Skilled Nursing Facility Stays

Individuals who become inpatients at a skilled nursing facility after a 3-day-minimum acute hospital stay and who meet Medicare's qualified diagnosis and comprehensive treatment plan requirements pay 2001 rates of:

Days 1–20	Nothing
Days 21–100	$99 per day
Days 101+	Full daily rate

Home Health Services

Individuals receiving physician-prescribed, Medicare-covered home health services have no deductible or coinsurance responsibilities for services provided. Patients must be confined to the home, but they do not have to be hospitalized in an acute care hospital before qualifying for home health benefits. The patient is responsible for a 20% deductible of the approved amount for durable medical equipment.

Hospice Care

All terminally ill patients qualify for hospice care. **Hospice** is an autonomous, centrally administered program of coordinated inpatient and outpatient palliative (relief of symptoms) services for terminally ill patients and their families. This program is for patients for whom there is nothing further the provider can do to stop the progression of disease, and the patient is treated only to relieve pain or other discomfort. In addition to medical care, a physician-directed interdisciplinary team provides psychological, sociological, and spiritual care. Medicare limits hospice care to four benefit periods:

- Two periods of 90 days each
- One 30-day period
- A final "lifetime" extension of unlimited duration

The hospice patient is responsible for:

- 5% of the cost of each prescription for symptom management or pain relief, but no more than $5 for any prescription.
- 5% of the Medicare payment amount for inpatient respite care for up to 5 consecutive days at a time.

Respite care is the temporary hospitalization of a hospice patient for the purpose of providing relief from duty for the nonpaid person who has the major day-to-day responsibility for the care of the terminally ill, dependent patient.

A patient who withdraws from the hospice program during the final benefit period is considered to have exhausted their hospice benefits. A patient receiving hospice benefits is not eligible for Medicare Part B services except for those services that are totally unrelated to their terminal illness. When a patient chooses Medicare hospice benefits, all other Medicare benefits stop with the exception of physician services or treatment for conditions not related to the patient's terminal diagnosis.

End-Stage Renal Disease (ESRD) Coverage

For Medicare purposes, **end-stage renal disease (ESRD)** refers to that stage of kidney impairment that appears irreversible and permanent, and requires a regular course of dialysis or kidney transplantation to maintain life. **Dialysis** involves a process by which waste products are removed from the body; two types of renal dialysis are commonly performed:

- **Hemodialysis**, which involves passing the patient's blood through an artificial kidney machine to remove waste products; cleansed blood is subsequently returned to the patient's body.
- **Peritoneal Dialysis**, which involves the passage of waste products from the patient's body through the peritoneal membrane into the peritoneal (abdominal) cavity where a solution is introduced and periodically removed.

A **kidney transplantation** involves surgically inserting a healthy kidney from another person (a kidney donor) into the patient who has ESRD; the new kidney does the work that the patient's kidneys cannot.

This special coverage is available for Medicare-eligible persons in need of renal dialysis or transplant due to ESRD. Medicare coverage for ESRD cases begins with:

- the fourth month of dialysis treatments for (1) individuals who enrolled in Medicare based on their ESRD diagnosis and for (2) individuals who are covered by an employer group health plan (the employer group plan pays first and Medicare pays second for a 30-month coordination period).
- the first month of dialysis treatment for (1) individuals who take part in a home dialysis training program at a Medicare-approved training facility that teaches how to administer dialysis treatments at home, (2) individuals who begin home dialysis training before the third month

of dialysis, (3) individuals who expect to finish home dialysis training and self-administer dialysis treatments.

- the month an individual is admitted to a Medicare-approved hospital for a kidney transplant, or for health care services needed prior to the transplant if the transplant takes place in that same month or within the two following months.

- two months prior to the month of the transplant if the transplant is delayed more than two months after admission to the hospital for the transplant or for health care services needed before the transplant.

EXAMPLE

Mr. Small was admitted to the hospital on January 5 for tests needed prior to a kidney transplant. He was to undergo the transplant on February 5, but it was delayed until June 25. Medicare coverage for Mr. Small starts in April, two months prior to the month of his scheduled kidney transplant.

Coverage continues for individuals who have Medicare because of ESRD for:

- 12 months after the month the patient stops dialysis treatments, or
- 36 months after the month of a successful kidney transplant.

Medicare coverage does not end if:

- the patient starts dialysis again or receives a kidney transplant within 12 months after the month the patient stopped receiving dialysis, or
- the patient continues to receive dialysis or undergoes another kidney transplant within 36 months after a transplant.

Special circumstances can occur for individuals with ESRD and who need a pancreas transplant. Medicare covers pancreas transplants:

- when done at the same time as a kidney transplant, or after a kidney transplant.
- if the pancreas transplant is performed after the kidney transplant, Medicare will pay for immunosuppressive drug therapy for 36 months after the month of the pancreas transplant.

Kidney Donor Coverage

Medicare Parts A and B cover the cost of medical care for a person donating a kidney to a Medicare-eligible ESRD patient. This coverage includes all pre-operative testing, surgery, postoperative services, and any treatment for complications arising from the surgery. Medicare rules state that services furnished to the kidney donor are to be treated as services furnished to the kidney recipient. This stipulation allows Medicare to become the secondary payer when the kidney recipient has large group health insurance covering kidney donors' medical expenses. If the donor's medical expenses are not a covered benefit of the recipient's plan, Medicare will cover the donor's medical expenses for the organ donation. The donor, qualifying under this special Medicare kidney donation program, is not entitled to medical coverage for expenses not directly related to the donation of the kidney. If donors sell their kidneys for transplantation, the purchase price of the donated kidney is not covered by Medicare. All payments for medical expenses incurred by the donor are made directly to the hospital and health care providers.

Heart and Heart-Lung Transplant Coverage

Until 1987, ESRD coverage was the only specified disease and/or transplant coverage in the Medicare program. Heart and heart-lung transplants are now covered if the person is eligible for Medicare and the transplant takes place in a Medicare-certified regional transplant center.

Lung Transplants

The national policy for Medicare coverage of lung transplantation was established in 1995 for hospitals with documented experience and success in performing the procedure. Medicare had been paying for the procedure when approved by Medicare contractors in individual cases. To become an approved Medicare Lung Transplant Center, a hospital must present data (based on HCFA-established criteria) on its lung transplants and outcomes for patients along with documentation of survival rates. In addition, a hospital is required to perform a minimum number of lung transplants each year to retain its status in the Medicare program. This mandate is designed to ensure that the transplant team maintains the skills needed for quality performance. Combined heart-lung transplantation is also covered when performed in a hospital approved for either heart or lung transplants.

Liver Transplants

Liver transplants for adults are covered if the person is eligible for Medicare, does not have a malignancy, and the surgery takes place in a Medicare-certified regional liver transplant center (until 2000, Medicare had not covered liver transplants for patients with hepatitis B). Follow-up care for patients who have received noncovered liver transplants is also available.

Children are covered if they have a diagnosis of biliary atresia or any other form of end-stage liver disease *except* when caused by malignancy that has extended beyond the margins of the liver or those diagnosed with persistent viremia. All transplants must take place in Medicare-certified pediatric liver transplant facilities.

Bone Marrow Transplants

Autologous bone marrow transplants use the patient's own (previously stored) cells and are covered for patients diagnosed with (1) acute leukemia in remission, (2) resistant non-Hodgkin lymphomas, (3) recurrent or refractory neuroblastomas, or (4) advanced Hodgkin disease, only if conventional therapy has failed or there is no HLA-matched (human leukocyte antigen) donor available. Coverage is denied for the following diagnoses: (1) chronic granulocytic leukemia, (2) acute leukemia in relapse, and (3) any solid tumors other than neuroblastoma.

Allogenic bone marrow transplants use a portion of a healthy donor's stem cell or bone marrow as obtained and prepared for intravenous infusion; they are covered for the treatment of:

- **Leukemia** (progressive proliferation of abnormal white blood cells).

- Leukemia in **remission** (symptoms lessen in severity).

- **Aplastic anemia** (decreased formation of red blood cells and hemoglobin) when it is reasonable and necessary.

- **Severe combined immunodeficiency disease (SCID)** (defective immune system due to a defect in the immune mechanism or another disease process).

- **Wiskott-Aldrich syndrome** (x-linked immunodeficiency disorder that occurs in male children).

Allogenic bone marrow transplants are *not* covered as treatment for **multiple myeloma** (a form of bone marrow cancer).

PART B COVERAGE

Medicare Part B is designed to cover outpatient services and professional services provided to inpatients including:

- Physician services, but not routine physicals or strictly cosmetic surgery, unless the result of an injury.
- Professional services provided to inpatients.
- Services of non-physician professionals such as nurses, certified registered nurse anesthetists, nurse practitioners, clinical nurse specialists, certified nurse midwives, and physicians assistants.
- Services of *limited* license personnel such as institutional and independent physical, occupational, and speech therapists, podiatrists, chiropractors, and clinical psychologists.
- Diagnostic testing.
- Radioactive isotope therapy.
- Drugs that are not self-administered.
- Ambulance services.
- Durable medical equipment (DME) and supplies used in the home and certified by a physician.
- Influenza, hepatitis B, and pneumonococcal vaccines.
- Therapeutic shoes and shoe inserts for diabetic patients.
- Home health services for persons enrolled only in Medicare Part B (the benefits, deductible, and coinsurance match those available under Part A).

The following preventive screening services were added to the benefits under the Balanced Budget Act of 1997:

- Annual mammogram screening for women over age 39.
- Annual colorectal screening/fecal-occult blood for patients age 50 and over, if ordered in writing by a physician.
- Colorectal screening/flexible sigmoidoscopies every 4 years for patients age 50 and over (barium enemas may be substituted for the flexible sigmoidoscopy if a physician writes the order).
- Colorectal screening/colonoscopies every 2 years if the patient is at high risk for colorectal cancer (barium enemas may be substituted for the colonscopy if the attending physician determines it is a more appropriate test and issues a written order).
- Screening pelvic and clinical breast examinations every 3 years for women (these tests may be performed annually for certain women of child bearing age or women at high risk for cervical or vaginal cancer).

Deductible and Copay

Medicare Part B costs to the patient include:

- A $100 deductible (payable annually).
- 20% of Medicare allowed charges on all covered benefits, except in the outpatient setting.
- 50% of Medicare allowed charges for most outpatient mental health care.
- 20% of the first $1,500 for all physical or occupational therapy services, and all related charges thereafter.
- 20% of Medicare allowed charges for home health care durable medical equipment.

- No less than 20% of the Medicare allowed payment (after the deductible) for hospital outpatient services.
- The first three pints of blood plus 20% of the Medicare allowed amount for additional pints of blood (after the deductible).

Providers who routinely refrain from collecting the patient's deductible and coinsurance are in violation of Medicare regulations and are subject to large fines and exclusion from the Medicare program.

Special Outpatient Mental Health Benefits

Outpatient mental health treatments are subject to the following special rules. The coinsurance is 50% of allowable charges; however, this is reduced to 20% of allowable outpatient hospital charges if the patient would have required admission to a psychiatric facility if outpatient treatments were not available.

PARTICIPATING PROVIDERS

Medicare has established a **participating provider (PAR)** agreement in which the provider agrees, by annual contract, to accept assignment on all claims submitted to Medicare. In 1999, more than 84% of all physicians, practioners, and suppliers in the United States were PARs. Congress mandated special incentives to increase the number of health care providers signing PAR agreements with Medicare, including:

- Direct payment of all claims.
- A 5% higher fee schedule than that for nonparticipating providers.
- Bonuses provided to carriers for recruitment and enrollment of PARs.
- Publication of an annual, regional PAR directory (MedPARD) made available to all Medicare patients.
- A special message printed on all unassigned explanation of benefits (EOB) forms mailed to patients, reminding them of the reduction in out-of-pocket expenses if they use PARs and stating how much they would save with PARs.
- Hospital referrals for outpatient care that provide the patient with the name and full address of at least one PAR provider each time the hospital provides a referral for care.
- Faster processing of assigned claims.
- Regardless of the type of Medicare Part B services billed, PARs have "one stop" billing for beneficiaries who have nonemployment-related Medigap coverage and who assign both Medicare and Medigap payments to participants. After Medicare has made payment, the claim will be automatically sent to the Medigap insurer for payment of all coinsurance and deductible amounts due under the Medigap policy. The Medigap insurer must pay the participant directly.

NONPARTICIPATING PROVIDER RESTRICTIONS

Medicare **nonparticipating providers (nonPAR)** may elect to accept assignment on a claim-by-claim basis, but several restrictions must be adhered to:

- NonPARs must file all Medicare claims.

- Fees are restricted to no more than the "limiting charge" on nonassigned claims.
- Balance billing of the patient by a nonPAR is forbidden.
- Collections are restricted to only the deductible and coinsurance due at the time of service on an assigned claim.
- Patients must sign a Surgical Disclosure Form for all nonassigned surgical fees over $500.
- NonPARs must accept assignment on clinical laboratory charges.

Limiting Charge

Nonparticipating physicians who do not accept assignment on their Medicare claims are subject to a limit on what can be charged to beneficiaries for covered services. The nonPAR approved rate is 5% below the PAR fee schedule, but the nonPAR physician may charge a maximum of 15% above the nonPAR approved rate (or 10% above the PAR fee schedule). The **limiting charge (LC)** or **limiting fee** is the maximum fee a nonPAR may charge for a covered service. It applies regardless of who is responsible for payment and whether Medicare is primary or secondary. This "limiting charge" or "limiting fee" effectively establishes a dual fee schedule in such practices, one for Medicare patients and a higher one for all other patients.

EXAMPLE

NonPAR charges "limiting fee"	$110.00
NonPAR Medicare allowed charge	95.00
Medicare pays 80% of allowed charge	$ 76.00
Patient owes provider:	
The difference between limiting fee and	
nonPAR Medicare allowed charge	$ 15.00
plus	
20% (copay) of nonPAR approved $95 charge	$19.00
Total payment to provider by patient	$34.00
Total payment to nonPAR	$110.00

Compare the previous example to the following example (patient who is seen by a PAR provider for the same service).

EXAMPLE

PAR charges usual fee	$125.00
PAR Medicare allowed charge	100.00
Medicare pays 80% of allowed charge	$80.00
PAR adjusts the difference between the	
usual charge and Medicare allowed charge	$25.00
Patient pays PAR 20% of $100 approved rate	$20.00
Total payment to PAR	$100.00

With the passage of the Health Insurance Portability and Accountability Act (HIPAA) of 1996, Congress increased the potential fine from $2,000 to $10,000 if a nonPAR does not heed the carrier's warnings to desist from flagrant abuse of the "limiting charge" rules.

Accepting Assignment on a Claim

A nonparticipating provider who agrees to accept assignment on a claim will be reimbursed the Medicare approved charge. The nonPAR may also collect any unpaid deductible and the 20% coinsurance determined from the Medicare Fee Schedule (MFS). If the nonPAR collects the entire fee at the time of the patient's visit, the assigned status of the claim is voided and the nonPAR limiting fee is then in effect. The nonPAR may also be subject to a fine or may be in violation of MFS requirements.

The nonPAR cannot revoke the agreement for an assigned claim *unless* it is by mutual written consent of the provider and the beneficiary. Even then, such an agreement must be communicated to the carrier *before* the carrier has determined the allowed amount. Providers who repeatedly violate the assignment agreement could be charged and found guilty of a misdemeanor, which is punishable by a fine, imprisonment, or both. In addition, a criminal violation may result in suspension from Medicare participation.

Mandatory Assignment

Providers who are *required* to accept assignment on *all* Medicare covered services include:

- **Physician extender providers** (physician assistants, nurse practitioners, nurse midwives, clinical nurse specialists, clinical psychologists, clinical social workers, and Certified Registered Nurse Anesthetists).
- **Limited license practitioners (LLPs)** (psychologists, clinical psychologists, and clinical social workers).

In addition, the following Medicare covered services are paid *only* on an assigned basis:

- Clinical diagnostic laboratory services.
- Physician services provided to Medicaid eligible recipients.
- Ambulatory Surgical Center (ASC) facility fees.

EXAMPLE

A patient undergoes laboratory procedures and sees the physician during an office visit (evaluation and management service). If the nonPAR accepts assignment for just the laboratory procedures, two claims must be submitted: one for the laboratory services and another for the office visit.

Surgery Disclosure Form

Nonparticipating providers must notify beneficiaries in writing of projected out-of-pocket expenses for elective surgery when the charge for surgery is $500 or more. This notification is required of both surgeons and assistant surgeons. For Medicare purposes, "elective surgery" is defined as a surgery that:

- Can be scheduled in advance;
- Is not an emergency; and
- If delayed, *would not* result in death or permanent impairment of health.

The Omnibus Budget Reconciliation Act (OBRA) of 1986 requires the following information to be provided in writing to the patient:

- The anticipated charge for surgery.
- The Medicare approved charge.
- The beneficiary's out-of-pocket expenses.

NonPARs must document the receipt and acknowledgment of the above information by having the beneficiary or his/her representative sign and date a Medical Surgical Financial Disclosure Statement (see Figure 14-1). A copy of the signed and dated statement must be maintained and provided upon request from the carrier. If the nonPAR fails to properly notify the beneficiary

---

Practice Letterhead

Dear Patient:

As previously discussed I do not plan to accept assignment for your surgery. Medicare law requires that I provide a Surgery Financial Disclosure Statement, prior to surgery, to all Medicare patients who are contemplating surgeries that have a fee of $500.00 or more. These estimates assume that you have met the $100.00 annual Medicare Part B deductible.

Type of surgery: _____

Estimated charge: $ _____
Medicare estimated payment: $ _____
Your estimated payment: $ _____

Date: _____   Beneficiary Signature _____

FIGURE 14-1 Sample surgical financial disclosure statement

prior to performing surgery, any money collected from the beneficiary that exceeds the Medicare approved amount must be refunded. Failure to make the appropriate refund could result in civil monetary penalties and/or exclusion from the Medicare program.

Mandatory Claims Submission

Federal law requires that all physicians and suppliers submit claims to Medicare if they provide a Medicare-covered service to a patient enrolled in Medicare Part B. This regulation does not apply if:

- The patient has not enrolled in Part B.
- The patient disenrolled before the service was furnished.
- The patient or the patient's legal representative refuses to sign an authorization for release of medical information.
- The provider opts out of the Medicare program, and those patients enter into private contracts with the provider (see Private Contracting on page 358).

An exception may occur if a patient refuses to sign an authorization for the release of medical information to Medicare. However, if the patient later opts to sign a Medicare authorization and requests that claims for all prior services be filed with Medicare, the request must be honored.

Waiver of Medicare Billing Contracts

Medicare law specifically states that nonPARs are subject to sanctions, including fines and exclusions from the Medicare program, if they require patients to sign agreements stating that the patient waives the right to have the nonPAR provider file the patient's Medicare claims or that the patient agrees to pay for services that are in excess of the nonPAR charge limits.

Privacy Act

In addition to the above restrictions, the Privacy Act of 1979 (also known as the **Sunshine Law**) forbids the regional carrier from disclosing the status of any unassigned claim beyond the following:

- Date the claim was received by the carrier.
- Date the claim was paid, denied or suspended.
- General reason the claim was suspended.

The nonPAR provider will *not* be told payment amounts or approved charge information.

State Law Bans Balance Billing

Many states have passed legislation restricting **balance billing** of patients, which is the act of billing the patient for the difference between the charged fee and the Medicare allowed fee. Balance billing does not affect the patient's deductible and coinsurance obligations. It should be noted that state law takes precedence over HCFA rules.

- Connecticut and Vermont require providers to accept assignment for patients with incomes below the state-established amount.
- Arizona, Florida, Georgia, Massachusetts, Ohio, Pennsylvania, and Rhode Island prohibit balance billing.
- New York restricts billing to 110 percent above the nonPAR fee schedule amount.

In all other states, the nonPAR may collect the difference between the nonPAR approved amount and the limiting fee.

PRIVATE CONTRACTING

Under the Balanced Budget Act of 1997, physicians were provided the option of dropping out of Medicare and entering into a private contract with their Medicare patients. This **Medicare private contract** is an agreement between the Medicare beneficiary and a physician or other practitioner who has "opted out" of Medicare for two years for *all* covered items and services furnished to Medicare beneficiaries. This means that the physician/practitioner will not bill for any service or supplies provided to any Medicare beneficiary for at least 2 years.

Under a private contract:

- No Medicare payment will be made for services or procedures provided to a patient.
- The patient is required to pay whatever the physician/practitioner charges, and there is no limit on what the physician/practitioner can charge for Medicare approved services (the *limiting charge* will not apply).
- Medicare Managed Care Plans will not pay for services rendered under a private contract.
- No claim is to be submitted to Medicare; and Medicare will not pay if a claim is submitted.
- Supplemental Insurance (Medigap) will not pay for services or procedures rendered.
- Other insurance plans may not pay for services or procedures rendered.

The private contract applies only to services and procedures rendered by the physician or practitioner for whom you signed. Patients cannot be asked to sign a private contract when facing an emergency or urgent health situation.

If patients want to pay for services the Original Medicare Plan does not cover, the physician does not have to leave Medicare or ask the patient to sign a private contract. The patient is welcome to obtain noncovered services on their own and to pay for those services.

A physician who enters into a Medicare private contract with one patient will be unable to bill Medicare for any patient for a period of 2 years with the exception of emergency or urgent care provided to a patient who has not signed an agreement with the provider to forego Medicare benefits. In these cases, the claim for urgent or emergency care must be accompanied by an attachment explaining the following: (1) the nature of the emergency or urgent problem, and (2) a statement affirming that this patient has not signed an agreement with the provider to forego Medicare. If a provider submits a nonemergency or urgent care claim for any patient before the "opt out agreement" becomes effective, the provider must submit claims for all Medicare patients thereafter and abide by the "limiting fee" rules. If, however, the patient files the claim, the provider will not be penalized.

ADVANCE BENEFICIARY NOTICES

An **Advance Beneficiary Notice (ABN)** is a written document provided to a Medicare beneficiary by a supplier, physician, or provider prior to rendering a service (see Figure 14-2). The ABN indicates that the service is unlikely to be reimbursed by Medicare, specifies why Medicare denial is anticipated, and requests the beneficiary to sign an agreement that guarantees personal payment for services. A beneficiary who signs an ABN agreement will be held responsible for payment of the bill if Medicare denies payment. ABNs should be generated whenever the supplier, physician, or provider believes that a claim for the services is likely to receive a Medicare **medical necessity denial** (a denial of otherwise covered services that were found to be not "reasonable and necessary").

Advanced Beneficiary Notice

Provider Notice:
Medicare will only pay for services that are determined to be "reasonable and necessary" under section 1862(a)(1) of the Medicare law. If it is determined that a particular service is "not reasonable and necessary" under Medicare program standards, payment will be denied for that service. I believe that, in your case, Medicare is likely to deny payment for _____ for the following reasons: _____

Beneficiary Agreement:
"I have been notified by my provider that Medicare is likely to deny payment for the services identified above, for the reasons stated. If Medicare denies payment, I agree to be personally and fully responsible for payment."

Signed,

_____   _____
Medicare Beneficiary   Date

FIGURE 14-2 Sample Advance Beneficiary Notice (ABN)

■ **TIP:** The purpose of obtaining the ABN is to ensure payment for a procedure or service that might not be reimbursed under Medicare. ■

ABNs are unnecessary for Medicare's "categorically noncovered services" (e.g., cosmetic surgery, hearing aids, routine physicals, and screening tests). In addition, cost estimates are unnecessary when an ABN is generated because the purpose of the ABN is to document that the beneficiary has received notice that a service is unlikely to be reimbursed by Medicare. Hospital ABNs are called "Hospital-Issued Notices of Noncoverage" (HINN) or "Notices of Non-Coverage" (NONC).

✶**CAUTION:** Do not obtain ABNs on every procedure or service to be rendered to a patient "just in case" Medicare denies the claim. To do so is considered fraudulent. ✶

MEDICARE FEE SCHEDULE (MFS)

In 1992, Medicare adopted a **Resource-Based Relative Value Scale (RBRVS)** system, now referred to as the **Medicare Fee Schedule (MFS)** in HCFA literature. Congress commissioned the RBRVS study in the late 1980s as part of a grant to a Harvard research team led by professor, economist, and mathmetician William Hsiao, Ph.D. The RBRVS system integrates three separate unit values for each procedure while factoring regional variations in work, practice, and malpractice expenses, and multiplies these units by a national conversion factor. The annual relative values are published in the *Federal Register* between late October and December. These values become effective on January 1 of the following year. Practices should receive a copy of the MFS along with the annual Medicare Participating Provider enrollment/renewal packet in early December. Practices wishing to change their PAR/nonPAR status must notify the carrier by the first of the next calendar year.

Medicare Fee Schedule amounts are based on:

- Relative value units (RVUs).
- Geographic practice cost indices (GPCIs).
- The national conversion factor (CF).

There are three **relative value units (RVUs)** for each procedure/service code: (1) physician work (RVUw), which includes time required to furnish the service, intensity of effort, and technical skills required, (2) practice expense (RVUpe), which includes costs for office rent, employee salaries, and supplies, and (3) malpractice expense (RVUm), based on historical data and weighted by specialty.

The **geographic adjustment factor (GAF)** accounts for geographic variations in the costs of practicing medicine and obtaining malpractice insurance as well as a portion of the difference in physicians' incomes that is not attributable to these factors. The GAF is the sum of three indices: physician work (GPCIw), practice expense/overhead (GPCIpe), and malpractice insurance (GPCIm).

The **national conversion factor (CF)** is a multiplier that transforms relative values adjusted by the GPCI into payment amounts. Prior to the Balanced Budget Act of 1997, three conversion factors were used in calculating the physician fee schedule: one for primary care services, one for surgical services, and one for all other services. Today, a single conversion factor is used for all physician services.

Medicare Fee Schedule (MFS) Calculation

The payment formula used to calculate a provider's MFS amount is:

$$(\text{work RVU} \times \text{work GPCI}) + (\text{practice expense RVU} \times \text{practice expense GPCI}) + (\text{malpractice RVU} \times \text{malpractice GPCI}) \times \text{conversion factor} = \text{MFS amount}$$

Remember! For each covered service, Medicare allows providers the lesser of the actual charge or Medicare Fee Schedule amount for that service. Medicare's payment is generally 80% of the allowed amount after the $100.00 annual deductible has been met; the remaining 20% is the beneficiary's copayment. NonPAR reimbursement is adjusted 5% below the PAR fee schedule as discussed on page 355 of this chapter.

Experimental and Investigational Procedures

Medicare law allows payment only for services or supplies that are considered reasonable and necessary for the stated diagnosis. Medicare will not cover procedures deemed to be experimental in nature. There are cases in which the provider determines that treatments or services are fully justified and such treatment options are then explained to the patient, who must pay the full cost of the uncovered procedure.

Medicare regulations specify that the provider must refund any payment received from a patient for a service denied by Medicare as investigational, unnecessary, unproved, or experimental, unless the patient agreed in writing prior to receiving the services to personally pay for such services. Figure 14-3 shows a HCFA-approved Medical Necessity Statement. An appeal of the denial of payment must be made in writing, and if the appeal is not granted, a refund must be paid to the patient within 30 days. A refund is not required if the provider "could not have known a specific treatment would be ruled unnecessary."

■ **NOTE:** HCFA has announced that it will consider, for Medicare coverage, certain devices with an FDA-approved Investigational Device (IDE) that are considered nonexperimental or investigational. The FDA categorizes all FDA-approved IDEs into either Category A (experimental) or Category B (nonexperimental/investigational) for Medicare reimbursement consideration. Only those IDEs placed in Category B by the FDA are eligible for Medicare coverage consideration. ■

MEDICARE AS A SECONDARY PAYER

A clarification of the **Medicare Secondary Payer (MSP)** rules was published in 1996 stating that Medicare is secondary when the patient is eligible for Medicare and is also covered by one or more of the following plans:

- An employer-sponsored group health plan (EGHP) that has more than 20 covered employees.
- Disability coverage through an employer-sponsored group health plan that has more than 100 covered employees.
- An ESRD case covered by an employer-sponsored group plan of any size during the first 18 months of the patient's eligibility for Medicare.
- A third-party liability policy, if the Medicare-eligible person is seeking treatment for an injury covered by such a policy (this category includes automobile insurance, no-fault insurance, and self-insured liability plans).
- A Workers' Compensation program; if the claim is contested, the provider should file a Medicare primary claim and include a copy of

the workers' compensation notice declaring that the case is "pending a Compensation Board decision."

● Veterans Administration (VA) preauthorized services for a beneficiary who is eligible for both VA benefits and Medicare.

● Federal Black Lung Program that covers currently or formerly employed coal miners.

Practice Letterhead

To My Medicare Patients:

My primary concern as your physician is to provide you with the best possible care. Medicare does not pay for all services and will only allow those which it determines, under the guidelines spelled out in the Omnibus Budget Reconciliation Act of 1986 Section 1862(a)(1), to be reasonable and necessary. Under this law, a procedure or service deemed to be medically unreasonable or unnecessary will be denied. Since I believe each scheduled visit or planned procedure is both reasonable and necessary, I am required to notify you in advance that the following procedures or services listed below, which we have mutually agreed on, may be denied by Medicare.

Date of Service _____

Description of Service   Charge

_____   _____

_____   _____

_____   _____

Denial may be for the following reasons:

1. Medicare does not usually pay for this many visits or treatments,

2. Medicare does not usually pay for this many services within this period of time, and/or

3. Medicare does not usually pay for this type of service for your condition.

I, however, believe these procedures/services to be both reasonable and necessary for your condition, and will assist you in collecting payment from Medicare. In order for me to assist you in this matter, the law requires that you read the following agreement and sign it.

I have been informed by (fill in the name and title of the provider) that he/she believes, in my case, Medicare is likely to deny payment for the services and reasons stated above. If Medicare denies payment, I agree to be personally and fully responsible for payment.

Beneficiary's Name: _____   Medicare ID# _____ or

Beneficiary's Signature: _____

or

Authorized Representative's Signature _____

FIGURE 14-3 Sample Medicare-approved medical necessity statement

All primary plans, which are collectively described in the Medicare literature as MSP plans, must be billed first. Medicare is billed only after the EOB from the primary plan or plans has been received. (The EOBs must be attached to the Medicare claim when the claim is submitted.)

To avoid fines and penalties for routinely billing Medicare as primary when it is the secondary payer, a more detailed Medicare Secondary Payer (MSP) questionnaire (Figure 14-4) should be provided to all Medicare patients when they register/reregister (update demographic and/or insur-

---

Practice Letterhead

All Medicare Patients

In order for us to comply with the Medicare as Secondary Payer laws you must fill out this Medicare Data Sheet before we can properly process your insurance claim.

Please complete this questionnaire and return it to the desk. We will also need to make photocopies of all your insurance identification cards. Do not hesitate to ask for clarification of any item on this form.

CHECK ALL ITEMS THAT DESCRIBE YOUR HEALTH INSURANCE COVERAGE

1. I am working full time _____ part time_____ I retired on ___/___/___.
   _____ I am enrolled in a Medicare HMO Plan.
2. _____ I am entitled to Black Lung Benefits.
   _____ I had a job-related injury on ___/___/___.
   _____ I have a fee service card from the VA.
   _____ I had an organ transplant on ___/___/___.
   _____ I have been on kidney dialysis since ___/___/___.
   _____ I am being treated for an injury received in a car accident _____.
   _____ other vehicle Other type of accident (please identify) _____
   _____.
3. _____ I am employed/My spouse is employed and I am covered by an employer-sponsored health care program covering more than 20 employees. Name of policy:

4. _____ I/My spouse has purchased a private insurance policy to supplement Medicare. Name of policy:

5. _____ I have health insurance through my/my spouse's previous employer or union. Name of previous employer or union:

6. _____ I am covered by Medicaid and my ID number is: _____

7. _____ I am retired and covered by an employer-sponsored retiree health care plan. Name of plan:

8. _____ I am retired, but have been called back temporarily and have employee health benefits while I am working. Name of plan:

Patient Signature _____ Date ___/___/___

FIGURE 14-4 Sample Medicare secondary payer questionnaire

ance information) with the practice. This form is used to clarify primary and secondary insurance payers and may be substituted for the second page o the Registration Form (see Figures 4-4A and B).

MSP Fee Schedule Rules

- The primary insurance fee schedule overrules the Medicare schedule on *assigned claims only.*
- NonPARs who do not accept assignment are prohibited from collecting amounts above the applicable limiting charge.
- Providers are not required to file Medicare secondary claims unless the patient specifically requests it.

Medicare Primary Rules

Medicare is considered the primary payer under the following circumstances.

- The employee is eligible for a group health plan but has declined to enroll or recently dropped coverage.
- The employee is currently employed, but is not yet eligible for group plan coverage or has exhausted benefits under the plan.
- The health insurance plan is only for self-employed individuals.
- The health insurance plan was purchased as an individual plan and not obtained through a group.
- The patient is also covered by TRICARE (formerly known as CHAMPUS), which provides health benefits to retired members of the uniformed services and spouses/children of active duty, retired, and deceased service members.
- The patient is under 65 and has Medicare due to a disability or ESRD and is not also covered by an employer-sponsored plan.
- The patient is under 65, has ESRD, and has an employer-sponsored plan but has been eligible for Medicare for more than 30 months.
- The patient has left a company and has elected to continue coverage in the group health plan under federal COBRA rules.
- The patient has both Medicare and Medicaid (crossover patient).

The Consolidated Omnibus Budget Reconciliation Act of 1985 requires employers with 20 or more employees to allow employees and their dependents to keep their employer-sponsored group health insurance coverage for up to 18 months for any of the following occurrences:

- Death of the employed spouse.
- Loss of employment or reduction in work hours.
- Divorce.

The employee or dependents may have to pay their share as well as the employer's share of the premium.

Medicare Conditional Primary Payer Status

Medicare will award an assigned claim **conditional primary payer status** and process the claim under the following circumstances:

- A plan that is normally considered to be primary to Medicare issues a denial of payment that is under appeal.
- A patient who is physically or mentally impaired failed to file a claim to the primary carrier.
- A Workers' Compensation claim has been denied, and the case is slowly moving through the appeal process.

- There is no response from a liability carrier within 120 days of filing the claim.

Medicare is to be immediately reimbursed if payment is received from the primary carrier at a later date.

MEDICARE PLANS

Depending on where a Medicare beneficiary lives, up to three choices are available: the Original Medicare Plan, a Medicare managed care plan, or a Private Fee-for-Service plan. The Original Medicare Plan is available throughout the country. Medicare managed care plans are available in many areas of the country and most plans require beneficiaries to go to doctors, specialists, or hospitals on the plan's list. The advantage of these plans is that some offer extras, such as prescription plans. Private insurance companies offer a Private Fee-for-Service plan. It is not the same as the Original Medicare Plan that is offered by the federal government. In this type of plan, Medicare pays a pre-established, monthly rate to the private insurance company for health care coverage to people with Medicare on a pay-per-visit arrangement. The insurance company, rather than the Medicare program, decides how much the beneficiaries pay for services received.

Original Medicare Plan

The **Original Medicare Plan** is also known as "fee-for-service" or "traditional pay-per-visit." Beneficiaries are usually charged a fee for each health care service or supply received. Medicare beneficiaries satisfied with receiving health care in this manner do not have to join a Medicare managed care plan or private fee-for-service plan; they can remain in the Original Medicare Plan. To help cover costs that the Original Medicare Plan does not cover, beneficiaries often purchase supplemental insurance plans (e.g., Medigap or employer-sponsored supplemental plans, explained on page 366).

Beneficiaries of the Original Medicare Plan:

- May go to any doctor, specialist, or hospital that accepts Medicare.
- Pay a monthly Part B premium.
- Pay an annual deductible before Medicare reimbursement is generated.
- Pay a coinsurance (copayment) amount for each health care service received.
- Receive a Medicare Summary Notice (MSN) (previously known as the Explanation of Medicare Benefits or EOMB) in the mail.
- Can obtain additional information about the Original Medicare Plan by calling 1-800-MEDICARE.

INTERNET LINK

Visit www.medicare.gov to obtain consumer information about the Original Medicare Plan. HCFA's Web site for Medicare is www.hcfa.gov/medicare/mcarpti.htm and includes downloadable files.

Medicare Summary Notice (MSN)

The **Medicare Summary Notice (MSN)** is an easy-to-read, monthly statement that clearly lists health insurance claims information. It replaces the Explanation of Medicare Benefits (EOMB), the Medicare Benefits Notice (Part A), and benefit denial letters. Not all Medicare contractors and carriers are issuing the new MSN, but will begin to do so at a future date. Until these con tracts and carriers switch to issuing the MSN, they will continue to send ou current notices.

INTERNET LINK

Go to www.medicare.gov/Basics/SummaryNotice_HowToReadB.asp to view a sample Medicare Summary Notice (MSN) that also explains its components.

Medicare Supplemental Plans

Persons who are eligible for Medicare often purchase additional insurance coverage in one of two forms: (1) Medigap or (2) employer-sponsored **Medicare Supplemental Plans (MSP)**. These plans supplement the Medicare program by covering the patient's Medicare deductible and coinsurance obligations but have no obligation if Medicare does not accept liability for a claim.

Medigap Plans

A **Medigap policy** is a private, commercial plan that meets the federal government standards for Medigap coverage and collects the premiums directly from the patient. It provides coverage to patients for health care costs not paid by Medicare ("fills the gap"). The federal government approved 10 different types of coverage for Medigap policies (Figure 14-5). While Plan A is restricted to the basic benefit package with no additions, all of the other plans (B-J) include the basic package plus one or more additional benefits. In the basic package, the coinsurance coverage begins on the 61st day but does not cover the initial inpatient deductible, the coinsurance for post-hospital skilled nursing facility stays, or the Part B deductible. Other plans cover additional benefits including the Part A deductible, Part B deductible, etc., depending on the plan chosen by the subscriber.

It is important to note that the federal government has standard benefits, not premiums. The premiums can vary widely even within the same geographic area. Beneficiaries should shop around before enrolling in coverage. Patients thinking of enrolling in Medigap coverage are urged to call their local area Council Office on Aging to get a listing of Medigap carriers in a given county or state.

Medigap claims are handled in one of two ways:

1. *PAR claims:* The Medicare carrier electronically transfers the billing and Medicare payment information to the Medigap carrier when the Medigap carrier and policyholder information appears on the Medicare claim in Blocks 9 through 9d and 13. If no response from the Medigap carrier with electronic transfer capability has been received within 30 days of receiving the Medicare MSN, a copy of the Medicare/Medigap claim form with a photocopy of the Medicare MSN attached should be filed with the Medigap insurer.

2. *NonPAR claims:* NonPAR providers are not required to include Medigap information on the claim form. If the nonPAR extends a courtesy to the patient by filing a Medigap claim, the patient must provide a copy of the Medicare MSN to the provider. (MSNs for nonassigned claims go directly to the patient; the provider does not receive an MSN directly from Medicare.)

Basic Benefits required by all Medigap Plans	A	B	C	D	E	F	G	H	I	J
Part A Hospital (Days 61–90)	✓	✓	✓	✓	✓	✓	✓	✓	✓	✓
Lifetime Reserve Days (91–150)	✓	✓	✓	✓	✓	✓	✓	✓	✓	✓
365 Life Hosp. Days—100%	✓	✓	✓	✓	✓	✓	✓	✓	✓	✓
Parts A & B Blood	✓	✓	✓	✓	✓	✓	✓	✓	✓	✓
Part B Coinsurance—20%	✓	✓	✓	✓	✓	✓	✓	✓	✓	✓

Additional Benefits	A	B	C	D	E	F	G	H	I	J
Skilled Nursing Facility Coinsurance (Days 21–100)			✓	✓	✓	✓	✓	✓	✓	✓
Part A Deductible		✓	✓	✓	✓	✓	✓	✓	✓	✓
Part B Deductible			✓			✓				✓
Part B Excess Charges						100%	80%		100%	100%
Foreign Travel Emergency			✓	✓	✓	✓	✓	✓	✓	✓
At-Home Recovery				✓			✓		✓	✓
Prescription Drugs								$1,250	$1,250	$3,000
Preventive Medical Care					✓					✓

FIGURE 14-5 Medigap plans

Employer-Sponsored Retirement Plan

An **Employer-Sponsored Retirement Plan** is a conversion plan offered to employees by certain companies at the time of retirement. These plans are intended to complement the retiree's Medicare coverage, are not regulated by the federal government, and are subject to limitations established in the employer's regular health insurance plans. The premiums are paid to the insurance carrier either by or through the employer. If the employer's regular group plan does not cover office visits, these visits may be excluded by the conversion plan.

These plans do *not* qualify for designation as a Medigap policy; therefore, they should not be entered into Block 9-9d on a Medicare claim. Health care providers are not required to file employer-sponsored retirement plan claims. Some employers send the Medicare carrier monthly data on retirement plan eligibility, which is incorporated into Medicare's database for the purpose of an automatic electronic transfer of Medicare claims data to the retirement plan carrier. If the employer-sponsored retirement claim is not forwarded electronically, the patient will need to file for benefits after the Medicare EOB is received.

Medicare-Medicaid Crossover

In addition to the previously mentioned supplemental plans, the **Medicare-Medicaid Crossover** program is a combination of the Medicare and Medicaid/MediCal programs. The designation "MCD" is used in Medicare Block 10d instructions. This plan is available to Medicare-eligible persons with incomes below the federal poverty level. These cases are generally known as Medi/Medi claims, Care/Caid claims, or 18/19 claims, depending on the individual state's designation. ("18/19" refers to Medicare federal and Medicaid designations as Title 18 and 19, respectively, of the Social Security Act Amendments of 1965.) Persons who are eligible for the SLMB program are also considered eligible for Medicare-Medicaid Crossover claims.

The Medicare carrier will electronically transfer the Medicare claim and the payment information to Medicaid for processing of the patient's Medicare deductible and coinsurance responsibilities and for payment of any service that is covered by Medicaid/MediCal but not Medicare. The Medicaid/MediCal payment should be received within 2 to 4 weeks after the Medicare payment. Care must be taken to submit a Medi/Medi claim before the Medicaid/MediCal deadline for filing claims, referred to as the "timely filing period."

Patients who might qualify for the crossover program should be directed to the local Medicaid/MediCal office to apply for the program. Care must be taken to accept assignment on these claims. If not done, the Medicare payment may be sent to the patient and the Medicaid payment, depending on state policy, may either go to the patient or be denied.

Extra Coverage Plans

To fully delineate all possible billing requests that Medicare patients may present, it is necessary to add another category not presented in HCFA or Medicare literature.

Extra coverage plans are specialized insurance plans that cover specific diagnoses or fall into the special hospital indemnity class. The specified-diseases plan pays only if the provider certifies that the patient has a specified disorder, such as cancer or AIDS. Special hospital indemnity plans are usually advertised in magazines and on the radio and television as a plan that "pays $200 per day for every day hospitalized." Any payment for these claims goes directly to the patient and is not reportable to Medicare or any other primary health insurance plan.

EXERCISE 14-1   Medicare Plan Review

1. Review the five cases in the following example.
2. Record the HCFA-prescribed billing order for each case.

EXAMPLE

Patient retired; covered by Medicare, an employer-sponsored retirement plan, and the spouse's employer-sponsored large group plan.

Billing order is: Employer-sponsored large group plan, Medicare, employer-sponsored retirement plan.

Case 1:   Patient is the policyholder in an employer-sponsored large group plan, has Medicare, a Medigap policy, and a $100/day extra coverage hospital plan.
Billing order is:

Case 2:   Patient has Medicare, an employer-sponsored retirement plan, and is a dependent on the spouse's employer-sponsored large group plan. The claim is for an injury received in a car accident.

Billing order is:

Case 3: The patient has a retirement plan through his former employer, Medicare, and a cancer policy. The spouse is deceased.

Billing order is:

Case 4: Patient is 67, working full-time and is covered by Medicare, an employer-sponsored large group plan, and a Medigap plan. The spouse is retired, 62, and covered by an employer-sponsored plan for 18 employees.

Billing order is:

Case 5: Patient is 50 and disabled, and has Medicare and an employer-sponsored group health plan for 50 employees.

Billing order is:

Medicare Managed Care

The Balanced Budget Act of 1997 established the Medicare+Choice Program, which provides Medicare beneficiaries with the choice to receive benefits through the original fee-for-service program (Original Medicare Program) or through one of the following:

- Health Maintenance Organizations (HMOs)
- Provider-Sponsored Organizations (PSOs)
- Preferred Provider Organizations (PPOs)
- Medical Savings Accounts (MSAs)
- Religious fraternal benefit plans
- Department of Defense (DoD)/TRICARE (demo)
- Private Fee-for-Service Plan

■ **NOTE:** Medicare categorizes HMOs, PSOs, and PPOs as **Coordinated Care Plans**. ■

Newly eligible enrollees who do not choose a Medicare+Choice plan are considered to have selected the original Medicare Fee-for-Service option.

Beneficiaries can select a Medicare+Choice plan at initial eligibility or during an enrollment period. As of 1999, coordinated enrollment periods occur each November, and enrollments are effective the following January 1. Individuals remain enrolled in the option of their choice until they choose another plan. From 1998 through 2001, beneficiaries will be able to enroll (if the plan is open to new enrollees) or disenroll on a monthly basis. In 2002, beneficiaries can enroll or disenroll from plans during the first six months of the year (or the first six months of eligibility in a year), but they can only change plans once during the six-month period. Also, beginning in 2002, newly eligible beneficiaries who elect a Medicare+Choice option may choose to go back to the original Medicare fee-for-service plan any time during the first twelve months of their enrollment. After 2002, beneficiaries will be able to change their enrollment options during the first three months of the year (or the first three months of eligibility in a year) and/or during the annual enrollment period.

Each year prior to the November coordinated enrollment period, beneficiaries will be mailed general information about Medicare and comparative information on the Medicare+Choice plans available in their area. General information includes covered benefits, cost sharing, and balanced billing liability under the original fee-for-service program; election procedures; grievances and appeals; and information on Medigap plans and Medicare SELECT. Comparative information includes extensive information on benefits and beneficiary liability, premiums, service areas, quality and performance, and supplemental benefits. Plans may only disenroll beneficiaries for cause (i.e., failure to pay premiums) or plan termination in the beneficiary's geographic area. Beneficiaries terminated for cause are automatically enrolled in the original Medicare fee-for-service program.

Health Maintenance Organizations (HMOs)

A **health maintenance organization (HMO)** is a provider and insurer of health care. A Medicare HMO is a Medicare-approved, contracted, organized, community-based network of physicians, hospitals, and other health care providers. They provide all Medicare-covered services and receive payment directly from Medicare for the beneficiary's care. All Medicare HMOs offer preventive care, and some offer prescription drugs, dental care, hearing aids, and/or eyeglasses.

Medicare beneficiaries are eligible to enroll if they:

- Live in or are willing to travel to the HMO's service area.
- Are enrolled in Medicare Part B.
- Do not have permanent kidney failure before joining or have not had a kidney transplant within the past 36 months.
- Have not selected the Medicare hospice program.

Beneficiaries who join Medicare HMOs usually must obtain services from the health care professionals and facilities that are part of the HMO's community-based network. A primary care physician is selected to coordinate care by either providing health care or arranging for beneficiaries to see other providers when necessary.

Enrollees must continue to pay the Medicare Part B monthly premium, and they may also be required to make copayments when seeking services as well as a monthly premium to the HMO. In return, the HMO provides all Medicare hospital and medical benefits, if the beneficiary is enrolled in Medicare Part A *and* Part B.

Advantages of Joining a Medicare HMO. According to Medicare, enrollment in an HMO can result in:

- *Additional benefits* (E.g., preventive care, dental care, prescription drugs, hearing aids, and eyeglasses at very little or no additional cost).
- *Lower costs* (HMOs are expected to minimize out-of-pocket payments and charge predictable premium amounts; beneficiaries do not need Medicare Supplemental Insurance.)
- *Less paperwork* (There are no claim forms to complete for services provided by the HMO as beneficiaries usually just show their enrollment card, pay any required copayment, and receive services. The Medicare Summary Form is not mailed to Medicare HMO enrollees.)
- *No "accepting assignment" problems* (Enrollees don't worry about finding a doctor who accepts Medicare assignment.)
- *No health screening requirement* (Enrollment is approved despite health problems, and beneficiaries cannot be denied membership because of a pre-existing medical condition.)

- *Access and convenience* (Care is available on a 24-hour basis through the community-based network.)
- *Preventive care* (There is an emphasis on preventive care, including mammograms, flu shots, and diabetes and hypertension screening.)
- *Educational services* (Health education classes and information is available to encourage healthier lifestyles.)
- *Quality* (Medicare HMOs must meet standards to maintain eligibility; the primary care physician coordinates health care services from other providers, which helps reduce inappropriate care and prevent adverse prescription drug interactions.)
- *Flexibility* (Beneficiaries can return to the Original Medicare Plan, which would be effective the first day of the month following the month in which the request is received.)

Disadvantages of Joining a Medicare HMO. Medicare also lists the following associated with Medicare HMO enrollment:

- *Lack of freedom* (Patients cannot choose any provider from which to seek health care, except perhaps for emergency or out-of-area urgent care).
- *Prior approval required* (Patients need to obtain prior approval of the primary care provider before seeking care from a specialist, scheduling elective surgery, or obtaining equipment or other medical services.)
- *Disenrollment can be lengthy* (Length of time to disenroll from the plan can take up to 30 days, and the patient must continue to use HMO providers until disenrollment is finalized.)

Types of Medicare HMO Plans. There are two types of Medicare HMO plans:

- The **risk-based HMO** (also known as a risk plan), a type of Medicare HMO, is a capitated plan, which requires the HMO to provide all Medicare benefits, but may offer additional benefits not available to regular Medicare patients. A **lock-in provision** may be associated with the risk-restricted HMO, which means that neither the HMO nor Medicare will pay for nonemergency services provided by health care providers who are not part of the HMO's community-based network, unless referred outside the network by the primary care physician. The regular Medicare carrier is not responsible for processing risk-restricted HMO claims, and such claims will be forwarded to the HMO for processing. An MSN will be generated, alerting the practice that the patient is in a risk-restricted HMO plan and that the claim was forwarded to the HMO.
- The **cost-based HMO**, a type of Medicare HMO, allows beneficiaries to receive care through an HMO without the loss of traditional Medicare benefits. When the patient receives care from an HMO provider, the HMO is responsible for paying the claim. If the patient seeks care outside the HMO's community-based network, the claim is submitted to the regular Medicare carrier for processing.

Special Medicare HMO Billing Situations. Medicare HMO patients do not have special Medicare cards that indicate a Medicare HMO; however, they may be issued an HMO card in addition to their regular Medicare card. Each Medicare patient should be asked at each visit whether they are currently enrolled in an HMO program. The practice must be aware of the type of HMO plans offered in the area (risk-restricted versus cost-based).

Capitated providers do not file claims to a Medicare-HMO unless special bookkeeping procedures are required for tracking Medicare patients. In these cases, the HMO's special instructions are followed.

HMO-Authorized Fee-for-Service (FFS) Specialty Care. For HMO-authorized FFS specialty care, the claim is sent directly to the HMO. Medicare has no responsibility for making direct payments to providers for patients enrolled in a risk-based HMO. Medicare providers who perform unauthorized, non-emergency medical care to a risk-based HMO beneficiary may bill the patient directly. NonPARs may charge up to the "limiting fee" for covered services. PARs are instructed to use the regular Medicare Fee Schedule.

All services for emergency care should be billed directly to the HMO on the HCFA-1500 claim form. Because HMOs fall into a commercial claim category, the rules for filing regular commercial claims are followed, not the Medicare claims instructions. These instructions are found in Chapter 12. The patient may be responsible for a copayment (e.g., $5.00 or $10.00), and all providers may bill normal, non-Medicare fees for any noncovered service.

Medicare *will* make payment if the patient receives unauthorized care from a cost-based HMO. *The deadline for filing Medicare-HMO claims is established by the HMO. It may be as short as 45 days after the service is rendered. It is important that the practice's billing department be aware of each HMO's timely filing restrictions.*

HMO Primary Plans. All employer-sponsored group health HMO plans covering 25 or more employees are primary to Medicare when the beneficiary meets Medicare Secondary Payer (MSP) provisions. Medicare secondary payments are possible depending on the amount of payment from the HMO primary insurer. Contact the patient's HMO to determine how to bill the HMO. MSP payments are filed using the normal rules for filing MSP claims (see page 395.)

HMO Supplemental Plan. Medicare recognizes employer-sponsored retiree plans as Medicare supplemental plans. Medicare will pay 80 percent of the allowed amount after the regular annual deductible has been met. Medicare billing rules discussed on page 366 are followed.

Provider-Sponsored Organizations (PSOs)

Provider-Sponsored Organizations (PSOs) are managed care organizations owned and operated by a network of physicians and hospitals, rather than by an insurance company.

Preferred Provider Organizations (PPOs)

Preferred Provider Organizations (PPOs) provide care through a network of doctors and hospitals. The beneficiary does not usually have to select a primary care physician, and can go to any doctor in the plan's network. Insurance claims are processed first by Medicare, then the PPO pays the portion of the Medicare-allowed amount that Medicare does not pay, including Medicare deductibles.

■ **NOTE:** Beneficiaries can also receive care from doctors and hospitals outside the plan's network if they are willing to pay out-of-pocket costs. ■

Medical Savings Accounts Plans (MSAs)

Medicare's **Medical Savings Accounts Plans (MSAs)** were authorized by the Balanced Budget Act of 1997 and are offered on a first-come, first-served basis to beneficiaries; they contain two parts.

- **Medicare MSA** (referred to as an *Account* by Medicare) is a special savings account that is used by the beneficiary to pay medical bills. This money is deposited into a savings account offered through an insurance company or other qualified company, by Medicare, annually. It is not taxed if used for qualified medical expenses and may earn interest or dividends.

- **Medicare MSA Health Policy** (referred to as a *Policy* by Medicare) is a special insurance policy that has a high deductible. Currently, the deductible cannot exceed $6,000.

Together, the *Medicare MSA* and *Medicare MSA Health Policy* comprise a Medicare MSA Plan.

EXAMPLE

Jill selects the Medicare MSA Plan option and establishes an Account. She also selects a Policy with a $5,000 deductible. For this Policy, Medicare deposits $1,200.00 per year into her Account on January 1.

During the first year of the MSA Plan, Jane has an annual physical exam and fills her regular prescriptions (these benefits are not covered by the Original Medicare Plan). She pays for these services using $300 of the $1,200 in her Account. At the end of the year, Jill has $900 remaining in her Account.

On January 1 of the next year, Medicare deposits another $1,200 into her Account; now, Jill has $2,100 for medical expenses. During this year, Jill undergoes surgery that costs $8000.00. She uses the $2,100 in her Account to pay part of the cost; she pays $2,900 of her own money to meet the policy's deductible of $5,000; and the remaining $3,000 is partially paid by the Policy. Jill pays any remaining amount after the Policy has covered some of the costs.

■ **NOTE:** MSA Plan beneficiaries are required to pay the monthly Part B. ■

Religious Fraternal Benefit Society Plans

Religious Fraternal Benefit Society Plans may restrict enrollment to members of the church, convention, or group with which the society is affiliated. Payments to such plans may be adjusted, as appropriate, to take into consideration the actuarial characteristics and experience of plan enrollees.

Department of Defense (DoD)/TRICARE (demo) Plan

The **Department of Defense (DoD)/TRICARE (demo) Plan** is a senior supplement demonstration program to facilitate DoD payments on behalf of Military Health System (MHS) beneficiaries who also receive Medicare benefits while enrolled in TRICARE as a supplement to Medicare. The demonstration program runs from Spring of 2000 to December 31, 2002 and is limited to certain zip codes in California and Texas.

Eligible beneficiaries who enroll pay an enrollment fee. An eligible beneficiary is described as a member or former member of the Uniformed

Services, a dependent of a member or former member of the Uniformed Services, or a dependent of a member of the Uniformed Services who died while on active duty for a period of more than 30 days, who meets the following requirements: (a) is 65 years of age or older; (b) is entitled to hospital insurance benefits under Medicare Part A; (c) is enrolled in the supplemental medical insurance program under Medicare Part B; and (d) who resides in a demonstration program area.

Private Fee-for-Service Plan

A **Private Fee-for-Service Plan (PFFS),** a new health care plan offered by private insurance companies, is available in some areas of the country. Medicare pays a pre-established amount of money each month to a private insurance company and the insurance company, rather than the Medicare program, decides how much it and the beneficiaries will pay for services. Private fee-for-service plans reimburse providers on a fee-for-service basis, and are authorized to charge enrolled beneficiaries up to 115% of the plan's payment schedule (which may be different from the Medicare fee schedule).

Private fee-for-service plans are also required to meet most of the same requirements of other Medicare+Choice plans and will be capitated in exchange for providing enrollees with the full package of Medicare benefits. Unlike coordinated care Medicare+Choice plan options, PFFS plans are prohibited from placing the health care provider at financial risk or from varying payment based on utilization experience.

BILLING NOTES

Following is a summary of nationwide billing information for traditional fee-for-service Medicare claims submission.

Medicare Carriers

The regional carrier for traditional Medicare claims is selected by HCFA through a competitive bidding process. Obtain the name and mailing address of the carrier for your local area.

INTERNET LINK

HCFA's Intermediary-Carrier Directory can be found on their Web site at www.hcfa.gov/medicare/incardir.htm.

Beneficiaries enrolled in Railroad Retirement Medicare have a Medicare card with the words "Railroad Retirement" displayed prominently. The identification (ID) number has an alpha *prefix* in front of the nine-digit number. The processing site for these claims is:

Metrahealth Company
Medicare Claims Office
P.O. Box 669
Augusta, GA 30999-0001
(706) 855-1386

The TRICARE/CHAMPUS Medicare carrier is:

Military Medicare
Mutual of Omaha Insurance Co.
P.O. Box 1298
Omaha, NE 68101-1298

Durable Equipment Claims

Durable Medical Equipment (DME) claims must be sent to one of the Medicare **Durable Medical Equipment Regional Carriers (DMERC)** in the country. Check the Medicare manual for the carrier responsible for processing DME claims for your region. The DMERCs are referred to as DMERCA, DMERCB, DMERCC, and DMERCD.

Coal Miner's Claim

Coal Miner's claims are sent to the:

Federal Black Lung Program
P.O. Box 828
Lanham-Seabrook, MD 20703-0828

Deadline for Filing Claims

The claim filing deadline for both regular Medicare and Railroad Retirement claims is December 31 of the year following the date of service. For example, a claim for services performed late in January of 2001 must be postmarked on or before December 31, 2002. To expedite claims filing, HCFA has directed carriers to apply a 10% penalty for any initial claim filed 13 or more months after services were performed.

Forms Used

All paper claims must be filed on the HCFA-1500 (12-90) form. A minimum of 45 days should pass before an unpaid paper claim is resubmitted. A Surgical Financial Disclosure Statement is required for all nonassigned surgeries totaling $500.00 or more. A Medical Necessity Statement is required if the provider is to collect fees from the patient for procedures deemed by Medicare to be unreasonable, experimental, unproved, or investigational.

Medicare does not differentiate between basic and major medical benefits. Medicare is not the primary carrier for accidental injuries covered by any third-party liability program.

Special Handling

All providers are required to file Medicare claims for their patients. Noncompliance with MSP rules and regulations may result in a substantial penalty or fine. For each infraction, when Medicare is the secondary payer, the primary carrier's EOB must be attached to the Medicare claim.

Two claim forms may be needed to describe one encounter in the following circumstances:

- When multiple referring, ordering, or supervising names and provider identifier numbers are required in Blocks 17-17A.
- When multiple facility names and addresses are required in Block 32.
- When DME is charged to the patient at the same time the patient had a reimbursable medical or surgical encounter.
- When the patient has had covered lab services and other medical or surgical services during an encounter with a nonPAR provider.

When more than one claim form is needed to describe an encounter, be sure that the diagnoses on each claim prove the medical necessity for performing the service, and the proper names and numbers required in Blocks 17, 17A, and 32 appear on the correct claims.

Before continuing with the information in this chapter turn to the Challenge Exercise on page 400 and complete the items.

STEP-BY-STEP CLAIM FORM INSTRUCTIONS

The law requires that all Medicare claims be filed using optical scanning guidelines. Practices must make certain that forms generated by computer software follow Medicare claim form guidelines. Extraneous data on the claim forms or data appearing in blocks not consistent with Medicare guidelines will cause the claim to be rejected.

Chapter 11, Essential HCFA-1500 Claim Form Instructions, should be studied before working with Medicare claim instructions.

Read the following instructions carefully. Medicare requires many details that are not required for other programs in this text. Place Post-It® Notes or other markers on pages 379 and 381. You will be referring to them frequently when following the step-by-step instructions and completing claim form exercises.

Primary Fee-for-Service Medicare

These instructions are for filing primary, traditional Medicare fee-for-service claims when the patient is not covered by additional insurance. (Instructions for filing Medicare-HMO fee-for-service claims are found in the discussion of the step-by-step instructions for filing primary claims in Chapter 12, Filing Commercial Claims.)

See Figure 14-6 for Blocks 1 through 13 of the HCFA-1500 claim form.

Block 1
Enter an "X" in the Medicare box.

Block 1A
Enter the Medicare ID number with its proper numeric/alphanumeric prefix or suffix as it appears on the patient's Medicare Health Insurance Card.

■ **NOTE:** Traditional Medicare ID numbers contain nine digits followed by an alpha one-character suffix. Some ID numbers will contain two additional characters that are either numeric or alphabetic. Patients who are retired railway workers have special Railroad Retirement cards with ID numbers containing an alpha prefix. These claims are to be sent to the regional Railroad Retirement carrier, which is different from the carrier for the regular Medicare cases. ■

Block 2
Enter the patient's name (last name, first name, and middle initial) exactly as it appears on the patient's Medicare card.

Block 3
Enter the patient's birth date (MM DD YYYY format). Enter an "X" in the appropriate box to indicate gender.

Block 4
Leave blank.

Block 5
Enter the patient's current street address on the first line, the city and state on the second line, and the zip code and phone number on the third line.

Block 6
Leave blank.

Block 7
Leave blank.

Block 8
Enter an "X" in the appropriate marital and employment status boxes if known. "Single" is selected if the patient is widowed or divorced. Indicate if the patient is employed or a student.

■ **NOTE:** Young children who are disabled are often covered by Medicare. ■

FIGURE 14-6 Blocks 1 through 13 of the HCFA-1500 claim form

Block 9-9d	Leave blank. This field is used for Medigap policy information.
Block 10a	Enter an "X" in the "NO" box.

■ **NOTE:** If any of Blocks 10a, 10b, or 10c contain an "X" in the "YES" box, Medicare is secondary and not primary. Bill the proper third-party liability or Workers' Compensation carrier first. ■

Block 10b	Enter an "X" in the "NO" box.
Block 10c	Enter an "X" in the "NO" box.
Block 10d	Leave blank. This block is used exclusively for Medicaid information. If the patient is entitled to Medicaid, enter the patient's Medicaid number preceded by the abbreviation, *MCD*.
Block 11	Enter the word "NONE" and proceed to Block 12. *Exception:* If there has been a recent change from Medicare Secondary status to Medicare Primary status, proceed to Block 11b.
Block 11a	Leave blank.
Block 11b	If applicable, enter a brief description of the change from Medicare secondary to Medicare primary status and the date the change was effective. Proceed to Block 12.

EXAMPLES

"Retired 12/31/99."

"Spouse employer plan cancelled 12/31/99."

Block 11c	Leave blank.
Block 11d	Leave blank—not required by Medicare.
Block 12	The patient must either sign and date (MM DD YYYY) the actual claim form or a separate "Authorization for Release of Medicare Information" must be on file.

        If the authorization for release of Medicare information is on file, enter the words "Signature on file" or "SOF" in this block. This block also authorizes payment of Medicare benefits to any provider that accepts assignment in Block 27.

        DME Supplier Assigned Claims Only: Enter "Patient's request for payment on file" if the patient is receiving special rentals or purchases and has signed special authorization statements required by HCFA and outlined in the DMERC manual.

Block 13	PAR providers only: Enter "SIGNATURE ON FILE" or "SOF" if the patient has signed the special Medigap authorization on file. Be sure to complete Block 9-9d.

        NonPAR providers: Leave blank.

When working with case studies in the text and workbook, enter the words "SIGNATURE ON FILE."

        Refer to Figure 14-8 showing completed Blocks 1 through 13 for the encounter form in Figure 14-7.

EXERCISE 14-2 Medicare/Medicaid Comparison Chart

ASSIGNMENT OBJECTIVE: To create a useful reference sheet as an aid to mastering the details of completing claim forms for six major insurance programs.

■ **NOTE:** This is a new chart as compared to those discussed in Exercises 12-1 and 13-1. ■

1. Make five copies of the Comparison Chart in Appendix III.
2. Enter the following titles in the first row of each wide column at the top of each page:
   Medicare Primary
   Medicare Primary/Medigap
   Medicare Secondary
   Medicare/Medicaid
   Medicaid
3. Record the following numbers in the first column:

Page 1	Blocks	1	through	9D
Page 2		10	through	16
Page 3		17	through	23
Page 4		24A	through	24K
Page 5		25	through	33

4. Enter abbreviated instructions in Blocks 1 through 13 of the Medicare column.

DATE 01/20/YYYY	REMARKS			
PATIENT John Q Public		CHART # 14-1	SEX M	BIRTHDATE 09/25/1930

MAILING ADDRESS 10A Senate Street	CITY Anywhere	STATE US	ZIP 12345	HOME PHONE (101) 201 7891	WORK PHONE

EMPLOYER Retired	ADDRESS	PATIENT STATUS MARRIED DIVORCED (SINGLE) STUDENT OTHER

INSURANCE: PRIMARY Medicare	ID# 112 34 9801A	GROUP	SECONDARY POLICY

POLICYHOLDER NAME	BIRTHDATE	RELATIONSHIP self	POLICYHOLDER NAME	BIRTHDATE	RELATIONSHIP

SUPPLEMENTAL PLAN	EMPLOYER

POLICYHOLDER NAME	BIRTHDATE	RELATIONSHIP	DIAGNOSIS		CODE
EMPLOYER			1. Pain RLQ 2 days		No Code-Symptom
			2. Acute appendicitis with rupture		540.0
			3.		
REFERRING PHYSICIAN UPIN/SSN NPI 00717717 IM Gooddoc, MD IG7777			4.		

PLACE OF SERVICE Office/Goodmedicine Hospital Anywhere Street Anywhere, US 1234

PROCEDURES	CODE	CHARGE
1. 01/20/YYYY New Pt Office Visit level III	99203-57	$75—
2. 01/21/YYYY Open Appendectomy	44960	$1200—
3.		
4.		
5.		
6.		

SPECIAL NOTES

Admitted 01/21/YYYY   Discharged 01/23/YYYY   Return 01/25/YYYY Call for appt.

TOTAL CHARGES $1275—	PAYMENTS $10—	ADJUSTMENTS 0	BALANCE $1265—

RETURN VISIT	PHYSICIAN SIGNATURE *Erin A. Helper, M.D.*

ERIN A. HELPER, M.D.   101 MEDIC DRIVE, ANYWHERE, US 12345
PHONE NUMBER (101) 111-1234
EIN # 11-123452   SSN # 111-22-3333
UPIN EH8888   NPI 00818810   Medicaid # EBH8881   BC/BS # EH11881 GRP: 1204-P

FIGURE 14-7 John Q. Public Medicare encounter form

If the step-by-step instructions in this chapter indicate a particular block is to be left blank, write the word "Blank."

Use vertical arrows to indicate that the instructions in a specific block in the Medicare column are repeated in the next column (see Figure 12-4 on page 297).

If consecutive blocks are to be left blank, enter the word "Blank" in the first block and draw a vertical arrow down through the other blocks that have similar treatment.

5. Save this form. It will be used with other exercises in this chapter and in Chapter 15.

APPROVED OMB-0938-0008

☐☐☐ PICA

HEALTH INSURANCE CLAIM FORM

PICA ☐☐☐

1. MEDICARE	MEDICAID	CHAMPUS	CHAMPVA	GROUP HEALTH PLAN	FECA BLK LUNG	OTHER	1a. INSURED'S I.D. NUMBER (FOR PROGRAM IN ITEM 1)
☒ (Medicare #)	☐ (Medicaid #)	☐ (Sponsor's SSN)	☐ (VA File #)	☐ (SSN or ID)	☐ (SSN)	☐ (ID)	112349801A

2. PATIENT'S NAME (Last Name, First Name, Middle Initial)
PUBLIC JOHN Q

3. PATIENT'S BIRTH DATE
MM | DD | YY   SEX
09 | 25 | 1930   M ☒   F ☐

4. INSURED'S NAME (Last Name, First Name, Middle Initial)

5. PATIENT'S ADDRESS (No. Street)
10A SENATE AVENUE

6. PATIENT RELATIONSHIP TO INSURED
Self ☐   Spouse ☐   Child ☐   Other ☐

7. INSURED'S ADDRESS (No. Street)

CITY
ANYWHERE

STATE
US

8. PATIENT STATUS
Single ☒   Married ☐   Other ☐

Employed ☐   Full-Time Student ☐   Part-Time Student ☐

CITY

STATE

ZIP CODE
12345

TELEPHONE (Include Area Code)
101 201 7891

ZIP CODE

TELEPHONE (INCLUDE AREA CODE)
(   )

9. OTHER INSURED'S NAME (Last Name, First Name, Middle Initial)

10. IS PATIENT'S CONDITION RELATED TO:

11. INSURED'S POLICY GROUP OR FECA NUMBER
NONE

a. OTHER INSURED'S POLICY OR GROUP NUMBER

a. EMPLOYMENT? (CURRENT OR PREVIOUS)
☐ YES   ☒ NO

a. INSURED'S DATE OF BIRTH
MM | DD | YY   SEX
M ☐   F ☐

b. OTHER INSURED'S DATE OF BIRTH
MM | DD | YY   SEX
M ☐   F ☐

b. AUTO ACCIDENT?   PLACE (State)
☐ YES   ☒ NO

b. EMPLOYER'S NAME OR SCHOOL NAME

c. EMPLOYER'S NAME OR SCHOOL NAME

c. OTHER ACCIDENT?
☐ YES   ☒ NO

c. INSURANCE PLAN NAME OR PROGRAM NAME

d. INSURANCE PLAN NAME OR PROGRAM NAME

10d. RESERVED FOR LOCAL USE

d. IS THERE ANOTHER HEALTH BENEFIT PLAN?
☐ YES   ☐ NO   *If yes,* return to and complete item 9 a – d.

READ BACK OF FORM BEFORE COMPLETING & SIGNING THIS FORM.
12. PATIENT'S OR AUTHORIZED PERSON'S SIGNATURE I authorize the release of any medical or other information necessary to process this claim. I also request payment of government benefits either to myself or to the party who accepts assignment below.

SIGNED **SIGNATURE ON FILE**

DATE

13. INSURED'S OR AUTHORIZED PERSON'S SIGNATURE I authorize payment of medical benefits to the undersigned physician or supplier for services described below.

SIGNED **SIGNATURE ON FILE**

CARRIER

PATIENT AND INSURED INFORMATION

FIGURE 14-8 Completed Blocks 1 through 13 for John Q. Public encounter form in Figure 14-7

EXERCISE 14-3 Medicare Primary Only Claim Form Blocks 1 through 13

This exercise requires one copy of a blank HCFA-1500 claim. You may either make photocopies of the form in Appendix III of the text, or print copies of the blank form using the CD-ROM in the back of the text. Instructions for installing the CD-ROM and printing blank forms are included in Appendix V.

1. Obtain a copy of the HCFA-1500 form.

2. Review the instructions for Blocks 1 through 13 in the Medicare primary column of the comparison chart created in Exercise 14-2.

3. Review the Mary Sue Patient Encounter Form (Figure 14-9). Place a page marker at the encounter form.

4. Abstract the information needed for Blocks 1-13 from the Encounter Form (Figure 14-9) and enter the required information on the second claim form using Optical Scanning Guidelines. This may be completed by handwriting the information, using the Blank Form Mode on the CD-ROM found in the text, or entering the data with a typewriter.

5. Review Blocks 1 through 13 of the claim form to be sure all required blocks are properly completed.

■ **NOTE:** This same encounter form and claim form will be used for Exercise 14-5. ■

Refer to Figure 14-10 for Blocks 14 through 23 of the HCFA-1500 claim form.

DATE	REMARKS				
01/30/YYYY					

PATIENT			CHART #	SEX	BIRTHDATE
Mary Sue Patient			14-2	F	03/08/1933

MAILING ADDRESS	CITY		STATE	ZIP	HOME PHONE	WORK PHONE
91 Home Street	Nowhere		US	12367	(101) 201 8989	

EMPLOYER	ADDRESS	PATIENT STATUS
None		MARRIED DIVORCED (SINGLE) STUDENT OTHER

INSURANCE: PRIMARY		ID#	GROUP	SECONDARY POLICY
Medicare		001287431D		

POLICYHOLDER NAME	BIRTHDATE	RELATIONSHIP	POLICYHOLDER NAME	BIRTHDATE	RELATIONSHIP
		self			

SUPPLEMENTAL PLAN	EMPLOYER

POLICYHOLDER NAME	BIRTHDATE	RELATIONSHIP

DIAGNOSIS — **CODE**

1. Personal history, pulmonary embolism   V12.51
2. Pleurisy   511.0
3. Tachycardia, atrial   427.89
4.

EMPLOYER

REFERRING PHYSICIAN UPIN/SSN   IG7777

I M Gooddoc MD   NPI 00717717

PLACE OF SERVICE

PROCEDURES 01/30/YYYY	CODE	CHARGE
1. Consult level III	99243	$150—
2. Chest xray 2 views	71020	50—
3. 12 lead EKG with interp and report	93000	50—
4.		
5.		
6.		

SPECIAL NOTES

Date of onset 01/28/YYYY   xray & EKG ordered by Dr. Gooddoc

TOTAL CHARGES	PAYMENTS	ADJUSTMENTS	BALANCE
$250—	0	0	$250—

RETURN VISIT	PHYSICIAN SIGNATURE
	Erin A. Helper, M.D.

ERIN A. HELPER, M.D.   101 MEDIC DRIVE, ANYWHERE, US 12345
PHONE NUMBER (101) 111-1234
EIN # 11-123452   SSN # 111-22-3333
UPIN EH8888   NPI 00818810   Medicaid # EBH8881   BC/BS # EH11881   GRP: 1204-P

FIGURE 14-9 Mary Sue Patient Medicare encounter form

Block 14

All providers except chiropractors: Enter the date (MM DD YYYY), using the eight-digit format, of the beginning of the spell of illness reported on this claim or the date the accident or injury occurred. If the claim includes treatment for an accident or injury, one of Blocks 10a through 10c should contain an "X" in the "YES" box.

14. DATE OF CURRENT: ILLNESS (First symptom) OR INJURY (Accident) OR PREGNANCY (LMP) MM : DD : YY	15. IF PATIENT HAS HAD SAME OR SIMILAR ILLNESS, GIVE FIRST DATE MM : DD : YY	16. DATES PATIENT UNABLE TO WORK IN CURRENT OCCUPATION MM : DD : YY MM : DD : YY FROM TO
17. NAME OF REFERRING PHYSICIAN OR OTHER SOURCE	17a. I.D. NUMBER OF REFERRING PHYSICIAN	18. HOSPITALIZATION DATES RELATED TO CURRENT SERVICES MM : DD : YY MM : DD : YY FROM TO
19. RESERVED FOR LOCAL USE		20. OUTSIDE LAB? $ CHARGES ☐ YES ☐ NO
21. DIAGNOSIS OR NATURE OF ILLNESS OR INJURY. (RELATE ITEMS 1, 2, 3, OR 4 TO ITEM 24E BY LINE) 1. ⌐__ . __ 3. ⌐__ . __ 2. ⌐__ . __ 4. ⌐__ . __		22. MEDICAID RESUBMISSION CODE ORIGINAL REF. NO.
		23. PRIOR AUTHORIZATION NUMBER

FIGURE 14-10 Blocks 14 through 23 of the HCFA-1500 claim form

Chiropractors only: Enter the date (MM DD YYYY) the course of treatment was initiated. (Also requires an entry in Block 19.)

■ **NOTE:** Medicare requires uniformity in the date format in Blocks 14, 16, 18, and 31. Use eight-digit format in all of these blocks. ■

Block 15 Leave blank.

Block 16 Leave blank. An entry in this block may indicate employment-related insurance coverage, if the patient is employed and is unable to work. If so, enter the start date (MM DD YYYY) the patient was unable to work.

Block 17 Enter the full name, but not the credentials, of the referring, ordering, supervising physician if a service on this claim falls into one of the categories below. (An **ordering physician** is a physician who orders diagnostic or clinical laboratory tests, pharmaceutical services, or durable medical equipment.)

GROUP 1—PHYSICIAN SERVICES

Physician services include:

- Consultation
- Surgery
- Independent Diagnostic Radiology Providers
- Independent Diagnostic Laboratory Providers

Enter the name of the referring physician.

GROUP 2—NONPHYSICIAN SERVICES

Nonphysician services include:

- Physical therapy
- Audiology
- Occupational therapy
- DME
- Prosthesis
- Orthotic devices
- Parenteral and enteral nutrition
- Immunosuppressive drug claims
- Portable Xray services

Enter the name of the ordering physician.

GROUP 3—PHYSICIAN EXTENDER/LIMITED LICENSE PRACTITIONERS

Physician extender/limited license practitioners include:

- Physician assistants (PA)
- Nurse practitioners (NP)
- Clinical nurse specialists (CNS)

Limited license practitioners (LLP) include:

- Clinical psychologists
- Licensed clinical social workers (LCS)

- Dentists
- Oral surgeons
- Oral/maxillofacial surgeons
- Podiatrists
- Chiropractors
- Optometrists
- Physical and occupational therapists

Enter the name of the supervising physician.

■ **NOTE:** If multiple names are required in this block, a separate claim form must be used for each service requiring a name in Block 17. ■

A name entered in Block 17 requires entry of the UPIN (soon to be the NPI) in Block 17a.

Block 17a

Enter the Medicare assigned **Unique Provider Identification Number (UPIN)** of the physician named in Block 17. The UPIN is a 6-character (2 alpha, 4 digit) number.

Block 18

Enter the eight-digit admission and discharge dates when services relate to hospitalization or skilled nursing facility stays (MM DD YYYY format for each date).

Block 19

Routine Foot Care claims: Enter the date (MM DD YYYY) the patient was last seen and the UPIN (soon to be NPI) of his/her attending physician when an independent physical or occupational therapist or physician providing routine foot care submits claims. For physical and occupational therapists, entering this information certifies that the required physician certification (or recertification) is on file.

Chiropractor Services: Enter the date (MM DD YYYY) an Xray was taken, for chiropractor services.

■ **NOTE:** Chiropractors are no longer mandated by federal law to have Xrays taken to document the level of subluxation. ■

Pharmaceuticals: Enter the name and dosage of the drug when submitting a claim for "not otherwise classified" (NOC) drugs.

Unlisted Procedure Codes: Enter a concise description of an "unlisted procedure code" if it will fit within the 45 spaces provided in the block. Otherwise, submit an attachment with the claim.

Modifiers: Enter all applicable modifiers when modifier -99 (multiple modifiers) is entered in block 24D. If modifier -99 is reported more than once on a single claim, enter the line number from block 24 followed by an "equals sign" and the modifiers that apply to the referenced line.

EXAMPLE

1 = 20 50 80	(1 refers to line 1 of block 24, and 20 50 80 are the modifiers reported in block 24D of that line)
3 = 20 51 80	(3 refers to line 3 of block 24, and 20 51 80 are the modifiers reported in block 24D of that line)

Homebound: Enter the word "Homebound" when an independent laboratory performs an EKG on, or obtains a specimen from, a homebound or institutionalized patient.

Patient Refuses to Assign Benefits: Enter the statement "Patient refuses to assign benefits" when the beneficiary absolutely refuses to assign benefits to a participating provider. In this case, no payment may be made on the claim until the situation is resolved.

Testing for Hearing Aid: Enter the statement, "Testing for hearing aid" when billing services involve the testing of a hearing aid(s); this is done to obtain intentional denials when other payers are involved.

Dental Examinations: When dental examinations are billed, enter the specific surgery for which the exam is performed.

Low Osmolar Contrast Material: Enter the specific name and dosage amount when low osmolar contrast material is billed, but only if HCPCS codes do not cover them.

Global Surgery: Enter the date (MM DD YYYY) for a global surgery claim when providers share postoperative care.

Hospice Service: Enter the statement "Attending physician, not hospice employee" when a physician renders services to a hospice patient but the hospice providing the patient's care does not employ the attending physician.

National Emphysema Treatment Trial: Enter demonstration ID number "30" for all national emphysema treatment trial claims.

Block 20

A "NO" indicates that no purchased laboratory services are reported on the claim. A "YES" indicates that some diagnostic tests listed on this claim form were performed by an outside laboratory. The provider filing this claim was billed for them and is passing the fee on to the patient. The total purchase price of the tests should be entered in the charge column of this block. (The name and address of the clinical laboratory that performed the test must appear in Block 32.)

Separate claim forms must be used when billing for multiple purchased diagnostic services.

■ **NOTE:** NonPAR providers must accept assignment on all diagnostic laboratory services. ■

When working with the case studies in this text, enter an "X" in the "NO" box.

Block 21

Enter up to four current diagnosis codes, beginning with the primary diagnosis. *Space through the place a decimal point usually appears.*

Block 22

Leave blank. Not required by Medicare.

Block 23

Enter the prior authorization number *if* one was assigned.

If billing for physician care plan oversight services, enter the six-digit Medicare provider number of the home health agency or hospice program that is providing services for the patient.

If clinical laboratory services performed by the practice are reported on this claim, enter the 10-digit HCFA assigned **Clinical Laboratory Improvement Act (CLIA) certification number**.

Enter the Investigational Device Exemption (IDE) number for the non-experimental/investigational device used in an FDA-approved clinical trial. Refer to page 361 for clarification of investigational procedures.

Refer to Figure 14-11 for completed Blocks 14 through 23 based on the encounter form in Figure 14-7.

14. DATE OF CURRENT: MM DD YY ILLNESS (First symptom) OR INJURY (Accident) OR PREGNANCY (LMP) 01 20 YYYY	15. IF PATIENT HAS HAD SAME OR SIMILAR ILLNESS, GIVE FIRST DATE MM DD YY	16. DATES PATIENT UNABLE TO WORK IN CURRENT OCCUPATION MM DD YY MM DD YY FROM TO
17. NAME OF REFERRING PHYSICIAN OR OTHER SOURCE I M GOODDOC	17a. I.D. NUMBER OF REFERRING PHYSICIAN IG7777	18. HOSPITALIZATION DATES RELATED TO CURRENT SERVICES MM DD YY MM DD YY FROM 01 21 YYYY TO 01 23 YYYY
19. RESERVED FOR LOCAL USE		20. OUTSIDE LAB? $ CHARGES ☐ YES ☒ NO
21. DIAGNOSIS OR NATURE OF ILLNESS OR INJURY. (RELATE ITEMS 1, 2, 3, OR 4 TO ITEM 24E BY LINE) 1. 540 .0 3. 2. 4.		22. MEDICAID RESUBMISSION CODE ORIGINAL REF. NO.
		23. PRIOR AUTHORIZATION NUMBER

FIGURE 14-11 Completed Blocks 14 through 23 for John Q. Public encounter form in Figure 14-7

EXERCISE 14-4   Continuation of Work on Comparison Chart

Review the instructions for completing Blocks 14 through 23. As you read each block, record a brief description of the instructions in the appropriate block in Medicare Primary column of the Comparison Chart.

EXERCISE 14-5   Continuation of Exercise 14-3

1. Review the Mary Sue Patient encounter form in Figure 14-9 for the diagnostic and treatment data.

2. Abstract the information needed for Blocks 14 through 23 and complete the required information on the claim form using Optical Scanning Guidelines. This may be completed using the CD-ROM found in the back of the text, or by handwriting or typing the data.

3. Review Blocks 14 through 23 of the claim form to be sure all required blocks are properly completed.

4. Compare your claim forms with the completed form found in Figure 14-16 (page 392).

■ **NOTE:** This same claim form will be used for Exercise 14-7. ■

Refer to Figure 14-12 for Block 24 of the HCFA-1500 claim form.

Block 24A   Enter an eight-digit, with no spaces (MMDDYYYY), date of service in the "FROM" column.

Complete the "TO" column only if reporting consecutive dates for the same service. If the consecutive services extend from one month to the next, make separate line entries for each month.

24. A DATE(S) OF SERVICE From To MM DD YY MM DD YY	B Place of Service	C Type of Service	D PROCEDURES, SERVICES, OR SUPPLIES (Explain Unusual Circumstances) CPT/HCPCS MODIFIER	E DIAGNOSIS CODE	F $ CHARGES	G DAYS OR UNITS	H EPSDT Family Plan	I EMG	J COB	K RESERVED FOR LOCAL USE
1										
2										
3										
4										
5										
6										

FIGURE 14-12 Block 24 of the HCFA-1500 claim form

Block 24B   Enter the proper two-digit Place of Service code from the list below to indicate the location where the item was used or the service performed.

Provider's office	11
Patient's home	12
Inpatient hospital	21
Outpatient hospital	22
Emergency room hospital	23
Ambulatory surgical center	24
Birthing center	25
Military treatment facility or	26
Uniformed service treatment facility	26
Skilled nursing facility	31
Nursing facility	32
Custodial care facility	33
Hospice	34
Ambulance—land	41
Ambulance—air or water	42
Federally qualified health center	50
Inpatient psychiatric facility	51
Psychiatric facility—partial hospitalization	52
Community mental health center	53
Intermediate care facility/mentally retarded	54
Resident substance abuse treatment center	55
Psychiatric residential treatment center	56
Mass immunization center	60
Comprehensive inpatient rehabilitation facility	61
Comprehensive outpatient rehabilitation facility	62
End-stage renal disease treatment facility	65
State or local public health clinic	71
Rural health clinic	72
Independent laboratory	81
Other unlisted facility	99

Block 24C   Leave blank. Not required by Medicare.

Block 24D   Enter the CPT/HCPCS procedure code of the service rendered along with appropriate CPT/HCPCS modifiers if applicable. If more than two modifiers apply to one line, enter the "modifier 99" and follow the instructions in Block 19 for describing multiple modifiers.

Block 24E   Enter the *one diagnosis reference number* from Block 21 that best justifies the medical necessity for the service on this line.

Block 24F   *PAR claim:* Enter the amount charged by the PAR provider for the service on this line.

   NonPAR claim: Enter the amount charged by the nonPAR provider. This must be no more than the Medicare "limiting fee".

   For consecutive services reported on one line on either PAR or nonPAR claims: List the charge for a single service and indicate the number of units in 24G. Do not bill a combined fee for the multiple services.

Block 24G	Enter the number of days or units.
Block 24H	Leave blank. Not required by Medicare.
Block 24I	Leave blank. Not required by Medicare.
Block 24J	*Solo practices:* Leave blank.

Group practices: When the NPI is implemented by Medicare (probably in 2003 or later), enter the first two digits of the NPI of the performing provider of service/supplier if they are a member of a group practice (the remaining six digits of the NPI are entered in Block 24K). When several different service providers or suppliers within a group are billing on the same HCFA-1500 claim form, enter the individual NPI in Blocks 24J and 24K of the corresponding line item.

Block 24K

Solo practices: Leave blank.

Group practices: Enter the carrier assigned Medicare **provider identification number (PIN)** of the provider who performed the service.

When Medicare implements the NPI (probably in 2003 or later), enter the last six digits of the NPI (including the 2-digit location identifier) for the service provider or supplier, if a member of a group practice.

■ **NOTE:** This may be a local field required by some state carriers or fiscal intermediaries. ■

Refer to Figure 14-13 for completed Block 24 based on the encounter form in Figure 14-7.

24. A DATE(S) OF SERVICE		B Place of Service	C Type of Service	D PROCEDURES, SERVICES, OR SUPPLIES (Explain Unusual Circumstances) CPT/HCPCS | MODIFIER		E DIAGNOSIS CODE	F $ CHARGES		G DAYS OR UNITS	H EPSDT Family Plan	I EMG	J COB	K RESERVED FOR LOCAL USE
From MM DD YY	To MM DD YY												
1 0120YYYY		21		99203	57	1	75	00	1				
2 0121YYYY		21		44960		1	1200	00	1				
3													
4													
5													
6													

FIGURE 14-13 Completed Block 24 for John Q. Public encounter form in Figure 14-7

EXERCISE 14-6 Continuation of Work on Comparison Chart

Review the instructions for filing in Blocks 24A through 24K. As you read each block, record a concise description of the instructions in the appropriate block in the Medicare Primary column of the Comparison Chart.

EXERCISE 14-7 Continuation of Exercise 14-3

1. Review the Procedure Data on the Mary Sue Patient encounter form found in Figure 14-9.

2. Abstract the information needed for Blocks 24A through 24K and complete the required information on the claim form using Optical Scanning Guidelines. This may be completed using the CD-ROM found in the back of the text, or handwriting or typing the data.

3. Review Blocks 24A through 24K of the claim form to be sure all required blocks are properly completed.

■ **NOTE:** This same claim form will be used for Exercise 14-9. ■

Refer to Figure 14-14 for Blocks 25 through 33 of the HCFA-1500 claim form.

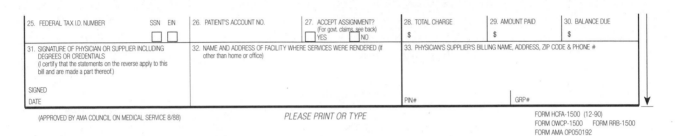

FIGURE 14-14 Blocks 25 through 33 of the HCFA-1500 claim form

Block 25

Enter the billing entity's Employer Tax Identification Number, if available. Otherwise, enter the provider's Social Security Number. In addition, be sure to enter an "X" in the appropriate box to indicate which is being reported.

■ **NOTE:** While third-party payers will accept the number with or without hyphens, when completing claim forms in this text (and while using the CD-ROM), be sure to enter hyphens. ■

Block 26

Optional: Enter the patient account number, if applicable. The number will appear on the EOB and make it easier to identify the patient account when files are indexed numerically rather than alphabetically.

When working with case studies in this text and workbook, enter the case study number here. If the case has both primary and secondary insurance also indicate the primary or secondary status of the claim.

Block 27

Indicate "YES" or "NO" on the accept assignment option.

"YES" must be marked for all PAR claims; nonPAR providers may mark either box. If "YES" is elected, the patient may not be billed for the balance due. Assignment must also be accepted on the following claims:

● Clinical diagnostic laboratory services.

● Medicare-Medicaid Crossover claims.

● Participating physician/supplier services.

● Services of physician assistants, nurse practitioners, clinical nurse specialists, nurse midwives, certified registered nurse anesthetists, clinical psychologists, and clinical social workers.

● Ambulatory surgical center (ASC) services for covered ASC procedures.

● Home dialysis supplies and equipment; check with the local Durable Medical Equipment Regional Carrier (DMERC) for exceptions.

Block 28

Enter the total of all charges on this claim.

■ **NOTE:** Claims will be returned as "unprocessable" if the total on the claim form is incorrect. ■

Block 29

Enter the total amount the patient paid for covered services reported on this claim.

Block 30

Leave blank. Not required by Medicare.

Block 31

Enter the complete name and credentials of the performing provider in the line above the word "Signed." Then enter the date, using the eight-digit no spaces format (MMDDYYYY) on the bottom line of the block.

Block 32

An entry is required here if a Place of Service code in Block 24B is other than 11, 12, 23, or 53, or Block 20-Outside Lab is checked "YES." There is room for only one supplier or facility; if more than one supplier/facility name is required a separate claim is prepared with the services and supplier/facility matched on each claim.

Enter the word "SAME" if the facility's name, address, and billing address are the same as the billing entity's. Otherwise, enter the name, address, and billing address of the facility where the service took place or supplier of DME.

On the bottom line enter the PIN of the facility/supplier. When the facility is a hospital, precede the hospital's PIN with the abbreviation "HSP."

DME claim: Enter the site where the order for equipment or supplies was received.

Certified mammography screening centers: Enter the 6-digit FDA-assigned certification number if mammography services are reported on the claim.

Block 33

Enter the phone number of the practice to the right of "& PHONE #." (This may overlap into the printed explanation for the block.) Enter the official practice name and mailing address on the next three or four lines. Each line should start at the left margin of the block.

PROVIDER IN GROUP PRACTICE: Enter the *billing entity's* PIN billing number (not the UPIN number) in the area to the right of the abbreviation "GRP#." Do not confuse the billing entity's PIN number with the provider UPIN used in Block 17A.

INDIVIDUAL PROVIDER (NONGROUP MEMBER): Enter the individual provider's PIN number to the right of the printed word "PIN#." (Do not confuse the PIN number with the UPIN.)

Refer to Figure 14-15 showing the completed HCFA-1500 form based on the encounter form in Figure 14-7.

EXERCISE 14-8 Continuation of Work on Comparison Chart

Review the instructions for completing Blocks 25 through 33. As you read each block record a brief description of the instructions in the appropriate block in the Medicare Primary column of the Comparison Chart.

PLEASE
DO NOT
STAPLE
IN THIS
AREA

(SAMPLE ONLY - NOT APPROVED FOR USE)

CARRIER

| | PICA | | | **UNDERSTANDING HEALTH INSURANCE CLAIM FORM** | PICA | | |

1. MEDICARE [X] (Medicare #) MEDICAID [ ] (Medicaid #) CHAMPUS [ ] (Sponsor's SSN) CHAMPVA [ ] (VA File #) GROUP HEALTH PLAN [ ] (SSN or ID) FECA BLK LUNG [ ] (SSN) OTHER [ ] (ID) 1a. INSURED'S I.D. NUMBER (FOR PROGRAM IN ITEM 1) **112349801A**

2. PATIENT'S NAME (Last Name, First Name, Middle Initial) **PUBLIC JOHN Q.**

3. PATIENT'S BIRTH DATE MM **09** DD **25** YY **1930** SEX M [X] F [ ]

4. INSURED'S NAME (Last Name, First Name, Middle Initial)

5. PATIENT'S ADDRESS (No. Street) **10A SENATE AVENUE**

6. PATIENT RELATIONSHIP TO INSURED Self [ ] Spouse [ ] Child [ ] Other [ ]

7. INSURED'S ADDRESS (No. Street)

CITY **ANYWHERE** STATE **US**

8. PATIENT STATUS Single [X] Married [ ] Other [ ]

Employed [ ] Full-Time Student [ ] Part-Time Student [ ]

CITY STATE

ZIP CODE **12345** TELEPHONE (Include Area Code) **101 201 7891**

ZIP CODE TELEPHONE (INCLUDE AREA CODE) ( )

9. OTHER INSURED'S NAME (Last Name, First Name, Middle Initial)

10. IS PATIENT'S CONDITION RELATED TO:

11. INSURED'S POLICY GROUP OR FECA NUMBER **NONE**

a. OTHER INSURED'S POLICY OR GROUP NUMBER

a. EMPLOYMENT? (CURRENT OR PREVIOUS) YES [ ] NO [X]

a. INSURED'S DATE OF BIRTH MM DD YY SEX M [ ] F [ ]

b. OTHER INSURED'S DATE OF BIRTH MM DD YY SEX M [ ] F [ ]

b. AUTO ACCIDENT? PLACE (State) YES [ ] NO [X]

b. EMPLOYER'S NAME OR SCHOOL NAME

c. EMPLOYER'S NAME OR SCHOOL NAME

c. OTHER ACCIDENT? YES [ ] NO [X]

c. INSURANCE PLAN NAME OR PROGRAM NAME

d. INSURANCE PLAN NAME OR PROGRAM NAME

10d. RESERVED FOR LOCAL USE

d. IS THERE ANOTHER HEALTH BENEFIT PLAN? YES [ ] NO [ ] If yes, return to and complete item 9 a – d.

READ BACK OF FORM BEFORE COMPLETING & SIGNING THIS FORM.
12. PATIENT'S OR AUTHORIZED PERSON'S SIGNATURE I authorize the release of any medical or other information necessary to process this claim. I also request payment of government benefits either to myself or to the party who accepts assignment below.

SIGNED **SIGNATURE ON FILE** DATE _____

13. INSURED'S OR AUTHORIZED PERSON'S SIGNATURE I authorize payment of medical benefits to the undersigned physician or supplier for services described below.

SIGNED **SIGNATURE ON FILE**

14. DATE OF CURRENT: MM **01** DD **20** YY **YYYY** ILLNESS (First symptom) OR INJURY (Accident) OR PREGNANCY (LMP)

15. IF PATIENT HAS HAD SAME OR SIMILAR ILLNESS, GIVE FIRST DATE MM DD YY

16. DATES PATIENT UNABLE TO WORK IN CURRENT OCCUPATION FROM MM DD YY TO MM DD YY

17. NAME OF REFERRING PHYSICIAN OR OTHER SOURCE **I M GOODDOC**

17a. I.D. NUMBER OF REFERRING PHYSICIAN **IG7777**

18. HOSPITALIZATION DATES RELATED TO CURRENT SERVICES FROM MM **01** DD **21** YY **YYYY** TO MM **01** DD **23** YY **YYYY**

19. RESERVED FOR LOCAL USE

20. OUTSIDE LAB? YES [ ] NO [X] $ CHARGES

21. DIAGNOSIS OR NATURE OF ILLNESS OR INJURY. (RELATE ITEMS 1, 2, 3, OR 4 TO ITEM 24E BY LINE)

1. **540.0**   3. ____.____
2. ____.____   4. ____.____

22. MEDICAID RESUBMISSION CODE ORIGINAL REF. NO.

23. PRIOR AUTHORIZATION NUMBER

| 24. A DATE(S) OF SERVICE | | | | | | B Place of Service | C Type of Service | D PROCEDURES, SERVICES, OR SUPPLIES (Explain Unusual Circumstances) | | E DIAGNOSIS CODE | F $ CHARGES | | G DAYS OR UNITS | H EPSDT Family Plan | I EMG | J COB | K RESERVED FOR LOCAL USE |
From MM	DD	YY	To MM	DD	YY			CPT/HCPCS	MODIFIER								
1	01 20 YYYY					21		99203	57	1	75	00	1				
2	01 21 YYYY					21		44960		1	1200	00	1				
3																	
4																	
5																	
6																	

25. FEDERAL TAX I.D. NUMBER **11-123452** SSN [ ] EIN [X]

26. PATIENT'S ACCOUNT NO. **14-1**

27. ACCEPT ASSIGNMENT? (For govt. claims, see back) YES [X] NO [ ]

28. TOTAL CHARGE $ **1275 00**

29. AMOUNT PAID $

30. BALANCE DUE $

31. SIGNATURE OF PHYSICIAN OR SUPPLIER INCLUDING DEGREES OR CREDENTIALS (I certify that the statements on the reverse apply to this bill and are made a part thereof.)

ERIN A HELPER MD

SIGNED DATE **MMDDYYYY**

32. NAME AND ADDRESS OF FACILITY WHERE SERVICES WERE RENDERED (If other than home or office)
GOODMEDICINE HOSPITAL
ANYWHERE STREET
ANYWHERE US 12345

33. PHYSICIAN'S SUPPLIER'S BILLING NAME, ADDRESS, ZIP CODE & PHONE #
(101) 111 1234
ERIN A HELPER MD
101 MEDIC DRIVE
ANYWHERE US 12345
PIN# GRP#

PATIENT AND INSURED INFORMATION

PHYSICIAN OR SUPPLIER INFORMATION

(SAMPLE ONLY - NOT APPROVED FOR USE) PLEASE PRINT OR TYPE SAMPLE FORM 1500 SAMPLE FORM 1500 SAMPLE FORM 1500

FIGURE 14-15 Completed Blocks 25 through 33 for John Q. Public encounter form in Figure 14-7. The claim is shown in its entirety with all information entered.

EXERCISE 14-9 Continuation of Exercise 14-3

Additional information you need for this case:

Dr. Helper's EIN is 11-123452. She is a Medicare PAR and her Medicare PIN number is H8888. The billing entity is Erin Helper, M.D. The Medicare group identifier number is G1515. She is on the medical staff and admits patients at Anywhere General Hospital, 222 Hospital Drive, in Anywhere US. The hospital PIN is AGH1122 and its NPI is 144123456.

1. Read through the Mary Sue Patient encounter form (Figure 14-9).

2. Abstract the information needed for Blocks 25 through 33 from the encounter form and the additional data given above and enter it on the claim form.

3. Review Blocks 25 through 33 of the claim form to be sure all required blocks are properly completed.

4. Compare your claim form with the completed claim form in Figure 14-16.

PRIMARY MEDICARE WITH A MEDIGAP POLICY

The following modifications must be added to the Medicare primary claim when the health care provider is a Medicare PAR, the patient has a Medigap policy in addition to Medicare, and the patient has signed an Authorization for Release of Medigap Benefits. If a separate Medigap release is on file, the words "SIGNATURE ON FILE" must appear in Block 13. No benefits will be paid to the PAR if Block 27, Accept Assignment, contains an "X" in the "NO" box.

The following modifications are not to be made when the patient is covered by an employer-sponsored supplemental or retirement plan, or when the provider is a nonPAR.

Block 9

Enter the last name, first name, and middle initial of the enrollee in the Medigap policy if it is different from the name listed in Block 2. If the patient is the policyholder, enter "SAME" and proceed to Block 9a.

Block 9a

Enter the word "MEDIGAP" followed by the policy and/or group number.

Block 9b

Enter the Medigap enrollee's birth date and gender.

Block 9c

Disregard the words printed in this block. Leave this block blank if the Medigap **plan identification number (PlanID)** is known. (A Medigap policy is identifiable by the numbers "99" in the seventh and eighth positions of the nine-digit ID number.)

If the PlanID is not known, enter the abbreviated mailing address of the Medigap carrier.

EXAMPLE

111 Anyplace Street, Anywhere, MD 12345 is entered as:
"111 ANYPLACE ST MD 12345".

The **National Health PlanID** is being developed by HCFA, as authorized by the Health Insurance Portability and Accountability Act of 1996, to enumerate health plans and provide a standard plan identifier for efficient electronic data

(SAMPLE ONLY - NOT APPROVED FOR USE)

PLEASE
DO NOT
STAPLE
IN THIS
AREA

CARRIER

☐☐☐ PICA

UNDERSTANDING HEALTH INSURANCE CLAIM FORM   PICA ☐☐☐

1.	MEDICARE	MEDICAID	CHAMPUS	CHAMPVA	GROUP HEALTH PLAN	FECA BLK LUNG	OTHER	1a. INSURED'S I.D. NUMBER	(FOR PROGRAM IN ITEM 1)
	☒ (Medicare #)	☐ (Medicaid #)	☐ (Sponsor's SSN)	☐ (VA File #)	☐ (SSN or ID)	☐ (SSN)	☐ (ID)	001287431D	

2. PATIENT'S NAME (Last Name, First Name, Middle Initial)
PATIENT MARY SUE

3. PATIENT'S BIRTH DATE   SEX
MM 03 DD 08 YY 1933   M ☐ F ☒

4. INSURED'S NAME (Last Name, First Name, Middle Initial)

5. PATIENT'S ADDRESS (No. Street)
91 HOME STREET

6. PATIENT RELATIONSHIP TO INSURED
Self ☐   Spouse ☐   Child ☐   Other ☐

7. INSURED'S ADDRESS (No. Street)

CITY   NOWHERE   STATE US

8. PATIENT STATUS
Single ☒   Married ☐   Other ☐

CITY   STATE

ZIP CODE 12367   TELEPHONE (Include Area Code) 101 201 8989

Employed ☐   Full-Time Student ☐   Part-Time Student ☐

ZIP CODE   TELEPHONE (INCLUDE AREA CODE) (   )

9. OTHER INSURED'S NAME (Last Name, First Name, Middle Initial)

10. IS PATIENT'S CONDITION RELATED TO:

11. INSURED'S POLICY GROUP OR FECA NUMBER
NONE

a. OTHER INSURED'S POLICY OR GROUP NUMBER

a. EMPLOYMENT? (CURRENT OR PREVIOUS)
YES ☐   NO ☒

a. INSURED'S DATE OF BIRTH
MM DD YY   SEX   M ☐ F ☐

b. OTHER INSURED'S DATE OF BIRTH
MM DD YY   SEX   M ☐ F ☐

b. AUTO ACCIDENT?   PLACE (State)
YES ☐   NO ☒

b. EMPLOYER'S NAME OR SCHOOL NAME

c. EMPLOYER'S NAME OR SCHOOL NAME

c. OTHER ACCIDENT?
YES ☐   NO ☒

c. INSURANCE PLAN NAME OR PROGRAM NAME

d. INSURANCE PLAN NAME OR PROGRAM NAME

10d. RESERVED FOR LOCAL USE

d. IS THERE ANOTHER HEALTH BENEFIT PLAN?
YES ☐   NO ☐   If yes, return to and complete item 9 a – d.

READ BACK OF FORM BEFORE COMPLETING & SIGNING THIS FORM.
12. PATIENT'S OR AUTHORIZED PERSON'S SIGNATURE I authorize the release of any medical or other information necessary to process this claim. I also request payment of government benefits either to myself or to the party who accepts assignment below.

SIGNED   SIGNATURE ON FILE   DATE

13. INSURED'S OR AUTHORIZED PERSON'S SIGNATURE I authorize payment of medical benefits to the undersigned physician or supplier for services described below.

SIGNED   SIGNATURE ON FILE

PATIENT AND INSURED INFORMATION

14. DATE OF CURRENT: ILLNESS (First symptom) OR INJURY (Accident) OR PREGNANCY (LMP)
MM 01 DD 28 YY YYYY

15. IF PATIENT HAS HAD SAME OR SIMILAR ILLNESS, GIVE FIRST DATE   MM DD YY

16. DATES PATIENT UNABLE TO WORK IN CURRENT OCCUPATION
FROM MM DD YY   TO MM DD YY

17. NAME OF REFERRING PHYSICIAN OR OTHER SOURCE
I M GOODDOC

17a. I.D. NUMBER OF REFERRING PHYSICIAN
IG7777

18. HOSPITALIZATION DATES RELATED TO CURRENT SERVICES
FROM MM DD YY   TO MM DD YY

19. RESERVED FOR LOCAL USE

20. OUTSIDE LAB? $ CHARGES
YES ☐   NO ☒

21. DIAGNOSIS OR NATURE OF ILLNESS OR INJURY. (RELATE ITEMS 1, 2, 3, OR 4 TO ITEM 24E BY LINE)
1. 511.0
2. 427.89
3. V12.51
4. __.__

22. MEDICAID RESUBMISSION CODE   ORIGINAL REF. NO.

23. PRIOR AUTHORIZATION NUMBER

24.	A. DATE(S) OF SERVICE				B. Place of Service	C. Type of Service	D. PROCEDURES, SERVICES, OR SUPPLIES (Explain Unusual Circumstances)		E. DIAGNOSIS CODE	F. $ CHARGES	G. DAYS OR UNITS	H. EPSDT Family Plan	I. EMG	J. COB	K. RESERVED FOR LOCAL USE
	From MM DD YY		To MM DD YY				CPT/HCPCS	MODIFIER							
1	0130YYYY				11		99243		1	150 00	1				
2	0130YYYY				11		71020		1	50 00	1				
3	0130YYYY				11		93000		2	50 00	1				
4															
5															
6															

25. FEDERAL TAX I.D. NUMBER   SSN ☐ EIN ☒
11-123341

26. PATIENT'S ACCOUNT NO.
14-2

27. ACCEPT ASSIGNMENT? (For govt. claims, see back)
YES ☒   NO ☐

28. TOTAL CHARGE $ 250 00

29. AMOUNT PAID $

30. BALANCE DUE $

31. SIGNATURE OF PHYSICIAN OR SUPPLIER INCLUDING DEGREES OR CREDENTIALS
(I certify that the statements on the reverse apply to this bill and are made a part thereof.)
ERIN A HELPER MD
SIGNED   DATE MMDDYYYY

32. NAME AND ADDRESS OF FACILITY WHERE SERVICES WERE RENDERED (If other than home or office)

33. PHYSICIAN'S SUPPLIER'S BILLING NAME, ADDRESS, ZIP CODE & PHONE #
(101) 111 1234
ERIN A HELPER MD
101 MEDIC DRIVE
ANYWHERE US 12345
PIN#   GRP#

PHYSICIAN OR SUPPLIER INFORMATION

(SAMPLE ONLY - NOT APPROVED FOR USE)   PLEASE PRINT OR TYPE   SAMPLE FORM 1500
SAMPLE FORM 1500 SAMPLE FORM 1500

FIGURE 14-16 Completed Mary Sue Patient primary HCFA-1500 claim form

interchange (EDI) and health care administrative operations. When the National Health PlanID Notice of Proposed Rule Making is published in the *Federal Register*, the public will have an opportunity to comment on HCFA's proposal for this initiative. HCFA's Web site at www.hcfa.gov will announce the publication date of the Rule.

Block 9d

Enter the Medigap PlanID number. If no PlanID number is available, enter the Medigap plan name.

Block 13

The patient's signature or "signature on file" statement authorizes direct payment of Medigap to the PAR providers.

■ **NOTE:** A special authorization with the designated Medigap carrier must be signed. The wording on the claim form is not acceptable to HCFA. ■

EXERCISE 14-10 **Continuation of Comparison Chart**

1. Review the instructions for changes to a primary claim when the patient is also covered by a Medigap policy.

2. Complete the appropriate blocks in the Medigap column of the Medicare Comparison Chart.

3. Draw a horizontal arrow from any block in the Medicare Primary column that remains the same in the Medigap column.

EXERCISE 14-11 **Filing a Claim When the Patient Has Both Medicare Primary and Medigap Insurance Policies**

Additional information needed for this case:

Dr. Helper's EIN is 11-123452. She is a Medicare PAR and her Medicare PIN number is H8888. The billing entity is Erin Helper, M.D. The Medicare group identifier number is G1515.

1. Obtain a blank claim form.

2. Underline the block identifiers on the new claim form for the blocks discussed in the Medigap claim form instructions.

3. Refer to the encounter form for John Q. Public (Figure 14-7 on page 379). Enter the following information in the blocks for the secondary policy:

> Aetna Medigap ID # 22233544   Group # AA2
> PlanID: 11543992
> Policyholder: John Q. Public
> Employer: Retired

4. Complete the Medicare/Medigap claim form using the data from the encounter form.

5. Compare the completed claim form to the claim form in Figure 14-17 to be sure all required blocks are properly completed.

PLEASE
DO NOT
STAPLE
IN THIS
AREA

(SAMPLE ONLY - NOT APPROVED FOR USE)

CARRIER

| | PICA | | **UNDERSTANDING HEALTH INSURANCE CLAIM FORM** PICA | | |

1. MEDICARE MEDICAID CHAMPUS CHAMPVA GROUP HEALTH PLAN FECA BLK LUNG OTHER		1a. INSURED'S I.D. NUMBER (FOR PROGRAM IN ITEM 1)	
[X] (Medicare #) [ ] (Medicaid #) [ ] (Sponsor's SSN) [ ] (VA File #) [ ] (SSN or ID) [ ] (SSN) [ ] (ID)		112349801A	

2. PATIENT'S NAME (Last Name, First Name, Middle Initial)
PUBLIC JOHN Q

3. PATIENT'S BIRTH DATE   SEX
MM | DD | YY
09 | 25 | 1930 M [X] F [ ]

4. INSURED'S NAME (Last Name, First Name, Middle Initial)

5. PATIENT'S ADDRESS (No. Street)
10A SENATE AVENUE

6. PATIENT RELATIONSHIP TO INSURED
Self [ ] Spouse [ ] Child [ ] Other [ ]

7. INSURED'S ADDRESS (No. Street)

CITY ANYWHERE   STATE US

8. PATIENT STATUS
Single [X] Married [ ] Other [ ]
Employed [ ] Full-Time Student [ ] Part-Time Student [ ]

CITY   STATE

ZIP CODE 12345   TELEPHONE (Include Area Code) 101 201 7891

ZIP CODE   TELEPHONE (INCLUDE AREA CODE) ( )

9. OTHER INSURED'S NAME (Last Name, First Name, Middle Initial)
SAME

10. IS PATIENT'S CONDITION RELATED TO:

11. INSURED'S POLICY GROUP OR FECA NUMBER
NONE

a. OTHER INSURED'S POLICY OR GROUP NUMBER
22233544 AA2

a. EMPLOYMENT? (CURRENT OR PREVIOUS)
[ ] YES [X] NO

a. INSURED'S DATE OF BIRTH   SEX
MM | DD | YY   M [ ] F [ ]

b. OTHER INSURED'S DATE OF BIRTH   SEX
MM | DD | YY
09 | 25 | 1935 M [X] F [ ]

b. AUTO ACCIDENT?   PLACE (State)
[ ] YES [X] NO

b. EMPLOYER'S NAME OR SCHOOL NAME

c. EMPLOYER'S NAME OR SCHOOL NAME

c. OTHER ACCIDENT?
[ ] YES [X] NO

c. INSURANCE PLAN NAME OR PROGRAM NAME

d. INSURANCE PLAN NAME OR PROGRAM NAME
11543992

10d. RESERVED FOR LOCAL USE

d. IS THERE ANOTHER HEALTH BENEFIT PLAN?
[ ] YES [ ] NO   If yes, return to and complete item 9 a – d.

READ BACK OF FORM BEFORE COMPLETING & SIGNING THIS FORM.
12. PATIENT'S OR AUTHORIZED PERSON'S SIGNATURE I authorize the release of any medical or other information necessary to process this claim. I also request payment of government benefits either to myself or to the party who accepts assignment below.

SIGNED SIGNATURE ON FILE   DATE _____

13. INSURED'S OR AUTHORIZED PERSON'S SIGNATURE I authorize payment of medical benefits to the undersigned physician or supplier for services described below.

SIGNED SIGNATURE ON FILE

14. DATE OF CURRENT: ILLNESS (First symptom) OR
MM | DD | YY   INJURY (Accident) OR
01 | 09 | YYYY   PREGNANCY (LMP)

15. IF PATIENT HAS HAD SAME OR SIMILAR ILLNESS,
GIVE FIRST DATE MM | DD | YY

16. DATES PATIENT UNABLE TO WORK IN CURRENT OCCUPATION
MM | DD | YY   MM | DD | YY
FROM   TO

17. NAME OF REFERRING PHYSICIAN OR OTHER SOURCE
I M GOODDOC

17a. I.D. NUMBER OF REFERRING PHYSICIAN
IG7777

18. HOSPITALIZATION DATES RELATED TO CURRENT SERVICES
MM | DD | YY   MM | DD | YY
FROM 01 | 21 | YYYY TO 01 | 23 | YYYY

19. RESERVED FOR LOCAL USE

20. OUTSIDE LAB? $ CHARGES
[ ] YES [X] NO

21. DIAGNOSIS OR NATURE OF ILLNESS OR INJURY. (RELATE ITEMS 1, 2, 3, OR 4 TO ITEM 24E BY LINE)
1. 540.0
2. ___.___
3. ___.___
4. ___.___

22. MEDICAID RESUBMISSION
CODE   ORIGINAL REF. NO.

23. PRIOR AUTHORIZATION NUMBER

24. A. DATE(S) OF SERVICE		B. Place of Service	C. Type of Service	D. PROCEDURES, SERVICES, OR SUPPLIES (Explain Unusual Circumstances)		E. DIAGNOSIS CODE	F. $ CHARGES	G. DAYS OR UNITS	H. EPSDT Family Plan	I. EMG	J. COB	K. RESERVED FOR LOCAL USE
From MM DD YY	To MM DD YY			CPT/HCPCS	MODIFIER							
0120YYYY		21		99203	57	1	75 00	0				
0120YYYY		21		44960		1	1200 00	1				

25. FEDERAL TAX I.D. NUMBER SSN [ ] EIN [X]
11-123452

26. PATIENT'S ACCOUNT NO.
14-1MG

27. ACCEPT ASSIGNMENT? (For govt. claims, see back)
[X] YES [ ] NO

28. TOTAL CHARGE
$ 1275 00

29. AMOUNT PAID
$

30. BALANCE DUE
$

31. SIGNATURE OF PHYSICIAN OR SUPPLIER INCLUDING DEGREES OR CREDENTIALS
(I certify that the statements on the reverse apply to this bill and are made a part thereof.)
ERIN A HELPER MD
SIGNED   DATE MMDDYYYY

32. NAME AND ADDRESS OF FACILITY WHERE SERVICES WERE RENDERED (If other than home or office)
GOODMEDICINE HOSPITAL
ANYWHERE STREET
ANYWHERE US 12345

33. PHYSICIAN'S SUPPLIER'S BILLING NAME, ADDRESS, ZIP CODE & PHONE #
(101) 111 1234
ERIN A HELPER MD
101 MEDIC DRIVE
ANYWHERE US 12345
PIN#   GRP#

(SAMPLE ONLY - NOT APPROVED FOR USE)   PLEASE PRINT OR TYPE   SAMPLE FORM 1500
SAMPLE FORM 1500 SAMPLE FORM 1500

PATIENT AND INSURED INFORMATION

PHYSICIAN OR SUPPLIER INFORMATION

FIGURE 14-17 Completed John Q. Public Medicare/Medigap HCFA-1500 claim form

MEDICARE-MEDICAID CROSSOVER CLAIMS

The following modifications must be added to the Medicare Primary claim when the patient is covered by Medicare and also has Medicaid coverage for services rendered on a fee-for-service basis.

Block 1a

Enter an "X" in both the Medicare and the Medicaid boxes.

Block 10d

Enter the abbreviation "MCD" followed by the patient's Medicaid/MediCal ID number.

Block 27

NonPAR must accept assignment on this claim.

EXERCISE 14-12 Continuation of Work on Comparison Chart

1. Review the instructions for completing a Medicare-Medicaid Crossover claim.
2. Complete the appropriate blocks in the Medicare-Medicaid Crossover column of the Medicare Comparison Chart.
3. Draw a horizontal arrow from any block in the Medicare Primary and Medigap columns that remain the same in the Medicare Crossover column.

EXERCISE 14-13 Filing a Medicare-Medicaid Crossover Claim

Additional information needed for this case:

Dr. Helper is a Medicare PAR and her Medicare PIN number is H8888. The billing entity is Erin Helper, M.D. The Medicare group identifier number is G1515.

1. Obtain blank claim form.
2. Underline the Block identifiers on the new claim form for the blocks discussed in the Medicare-Medicaid Crossover claim form instructions.
3. Refer to the Mary Sue Patient encounter form in Figure 14-9 and enter in the additional Medicaid information in the Secondary Policy blocks:

    Insurance policy: Medicaid

    ID #: 101234591XT

    Relationship: Self
4. Complete the Medicare/Medicaid claim form.
5. Compare the completed claim form with the form in Figure 14-18.

WHEN MEDICARE IS THE SECONDARY PAYER

Block 1

Enter an "X" in the "MEDICARE" and "OTHER" boxes.

Block 4

Enter the primary insurance policyholder's name. If the policyholder is the patient, enter "SAME."

Block 6

Indicate the relationship of the patient to the primary insurance policyholder named, if Block 4 is completed.

PLEASE
DO NOT
STAPLE
IN THIS
AREA

(SAMPLE ONLY - NOT APPROVED FOR USE)

CARRIER

| | | PICA | | | **UNDERSTANDING HEALTH INSURANCE CLAIM FORM** PICA | | | |

| 1. MEDICARE [X] (Medicare #) | MEDICAID [X] (Medicaid #) | CHAMPUS [ ] (Sponsor's SSN) | CHAMPVA [ ] (VA File #) | GROUP HEALTH PLAN [ ] (SSN or ID) | FECA BLK LUNG [ ] (SSN) | OTHER [ ] (ID) | 1a. INSURED'S I.D. NUMBER (FOR PROGRAM IN ITEM 1) 001287431D |

| 2. PATIENT'S NAME (Last Name, First Name, Middle Initial) PATIENT MARY SUE | 3. PATIENT'S BIRTH DATE MM DD YY 03 08 1933 SEX M□ F[X] | 4. INSURED'S NAME (Last Name, First Name, Middle Initial) |

5. PATIENT'S ADDRESS (No. Street) 91 HOME STREET
6. PATIENT RELATIONSHIP TO INSURED Self□ Spouse□ Child□ Other□
7. INSURED'S ADDRESS (No. Street)

CITY NOWHERE STATE US
8. PATIENT STATUS Single [X] Married□ Other□
CITY STATE

ZIP CODE 12367 TELEPHONE (Include Area Code) 101 201 8989
Employed□ Full-Time Student□ Part-Time Student□
ZIP CODE TELEPHONE (INCLUDE AREA CODE) ( )

9. OTHER INSURED'S NAME (Last Name, First Name, Middle Initial)
10. IS PATIENT'S CONDITION RELATED TO:
11. INSURED'S POLICY GROUP OR FECA NUMBER NONE

a. OTHER INSURED'S POLICY OR GROUP NUMBER
a. EMPLOYMENT? (CURRENT OR PREVIOUS) YES□ NO[X]
a. INSURED'S DATE OF BIRTH MM DD YY SEX M□ F□

b. OTHER INSURED'S DATE OF BIRTH MM DD YY SEX M□ F□
b. AUTO ACCIDENT? YES□ NO[X] PLACE (State)
b. EMPLOYER'S NAME OR SCHOOL NAME

c. EMPLOYER'S NAME OR SCHOOL NAME
c. OTHER ACCIDENT? YES□ NO[X]
c. INSURANCE PLAN NAME OR PROGRAM NAME

d. INSURANCE PLAN NAME OR PROGRAM NAME
10d. RESERVED FOR LOCAL USE MCD 101234591XT
d. IS THERE ANOTHER HEALTH BENEFIT PLAN? YES□ NO□ If yes, return to and complete item 9 a – d.

READ BACK OF FORM BEFORE COMPLETING & SIGNING THIS FORM.
12. PATIENT'S OR AUTHORIZED PERSON'S SIGNATURE I authorize the release of any medical or other information necessary to process this claim. I also request payment of government benefits either to myself or to the party who accepts assignment below.

SIGNED SIGNATURE ON FILE DATE _____

13. INSURED'S OR AUTHORIZED PERSON'S SIGNATURE I authorize payment of medical benefits to the undersigned physician or supplier for services described below.

SIGNED SIGNATURE ON FILE

PATIENT AND INSURED INFORMATION

14. DATE OF CURRENT: MM DD YY 01 28 YYYY ▶ ILLNESS (First symptom) OR INJURY (Accident) OR PREGNANCY (LMP)
15. IF PATIENT HAS HAD SAME OR SIMILAR ILLNESS, GIVE FIRST DATE MM DD YY
16. DATES PATIENT UNABLE TO WORK IN CURRENT OCCUPATION MM DD YY FROM TO MM DD YY

17. NAME OF REFERRING PHYSICIAN OR OTHER SOURCE I M GOODDOC
17a. I.D. NUMBER OF REFERRING PHYSICIAN IG7777
18. HOSPITALIZATION DATES RELATED TO CURRENT SERVICES MM DD YY FROM TO MM DD YY

19. RESERVED FOR LOCAL USE
20. OUTSIDE LAB? YES□ NO[X] $ CHARGES

21. DIAGNOSIS OR NATURE OF ILLNESS OR INJURY. (RELATE ITEMS 1, 2, 3, OR 4 TO ITEM 24E BY LINE)
1. 511.10
2. 427.89
3. V12.51
4. _____

22. MEDICAID RESUBMISSION CODE ORIGINAL REF. NO.
23. PRIOR AUTHORIZATION NUMBER

| 24. A DATE(S) OF SERVICE | | B Place of Service | C Type of Service | D PROCEDURES, SERVICES, OR SUPPLIES (Explain Unusual Circumstances) | | E DIAGNOSIS CODE | F $ CHARGES | G DAYS OR UNITS | H EPSDT Family Plan | I EMG | J COB | K RESERVED FOR LOCAL USE |
From MM DD YY	To MM DD YY			CPT/HCPCS	MODIFIER							
0130YYYY		11		99243		1	150 00	1				
0130YYYY		11		71020		1	50 00	1				
0130YYYY		11		93000		2	50 00	2				

| 25. FEDERAL TAX I.D. NUMBER 11-123452 SSN□ EIN[X] | 26. PATIENT'S ACCOUNT NO. 14-2MM | 27. ACCEPT ASSIGNMENT? (For govt. claims, see back) YES[X] NO□ | 28. TOTAL CHARGE $ 250 00 | 29. AMOUNT PAID $ | 30. BALANCE DUE $ |

31. SIGNATURE OF PHYSICIAN OR SUPPLIER INCLUDING DEGREES OR CREDENTIALS (I certify that the statements on the reverse apply to this bill and are made a part thereof.) ERIN A HELPER MD

SIGNED _____ DATE MMDDYYYY

32. NAME AND ADDRESS OF FACILITY WHERE SERVICES WERE RENDERED (If other than home or office)

33. PHYSICIAN'S SUPPLIER'S BILLING NAME, ADDRESS, ZIP CODE & PHONE # (101) 111 1234 ERIN A HELPER MD 1201 MEDIC DRIVE ANYWHERE US 12345
PIN# GRP#

PHYSICIAN OR SUPPLIER INFORMATION

(SAMPLE ONLY - NOT APPROVED FOR USE)
PLEASE PRINT OR TYPE
SAMPLE FORM 1500
SAMPLE FORM 1500 SAMPLE FORM 1500

FIGURE 14-18 Completed Mary Sue Patient Medicare/Medicaid HCFA-1500 claim form

Block 7	Enter the address and telephone number of the policyholder named in Block 4, if different from the patient. If the patient is the policyholder or the address of the policyholder is the same as that in Block 5, enter "SAME."
Block 11	Enter the complete policy/group number of the primary plan. (Blocks 4 and 7 must also be filled out.)
Block 11a	Enter the primary policyholder's date of birth (MM DD YYYY format) and gender, if the patient is not the policyholder.
Block 11b	Enter the employer's name for the large group health plan that is primary to Medicare.
Block 11c	Enter the complete primary insurance plan name or the PlanID number. (The primary EOB must be attached to this claim form. If the EOB does not contain the preprinted claims processing address of the primary insurance carrier, enter it.) *Enter "EOB attached" at the top of the claim form for case studies in this text.*
Block 16	Enter dates if patient is employed full time and unable to work.
Block 29	Enter only patient payment for services on this claim form. The attached EOB from primary insurers will indicate the primary carrier's payments.

EXERCISE 14-14 Continuation of Work on Comparison Chart

1. Review the instructions for completing a Medicare-Medicaid Crossover claim.
2. Complete the appropriate blocks in the Medicare Secondary column of the Medicare Comparison Chart.
3. Draw a horizontal arrow from any block in the Medicare Primary, Medigap, and Medicare/Medicaid columns that remains the same in the Medicare Secondary column.

EXERCISE 14-15 Filing a Medicare Secondary Claim

Additional information needed for this case:

Dr. Helper is a Medicare PAR and her Medicare PIN number is H8888. The billing entity is Erin Helper, M.D. The Medicare group identifier number is G1515. The PIN for the Ambulatory Surgical Center is ASC 1000.

1. Obtain a blank claim form.
2. Underline the Block identification numbers for the changes discussed above.
3. Refer to the Jackie L. Neely encounter form (Figure 14-19) and complete the Medicare Secondary claim form for this case using the data from the encounter form.
4. Review the completed claim form to be sure all required blocks are filled in.
5. Compare your claim form with Figure 14-20 found on page 399.

Additional Medicare case studies are found in Appendix I and Appendix II.

Case Studies require reading the case study chart entries and abstracting and coding the diagnostic information. Necessary hospital and physician data is included in the Goodmedicine Clinic Billing Manual in Appendix II.

DATE 01/08/YYYY		REMARKS				
PATIENT Jackie L. Neely				CHART # 14-3	SEX M	BIRTHDATE 09/09/1929

MAILING ADDRESS 329 Water Street	CITY Nowhere	STATE US	ZIP 12367	HOME PHONE (101) 201 1278	WORK PHONE

EMPLOYER Retired	ADDRESS	PATIENT STATUS (MARRIED) DIVORCED SINGLE STUDENT OTHER

INSURANCE: PRIMARY BCBS Federal	ID# R1234567	GROUP 103	SECONDARY POLICY Medicare 111 22 3344A

POLICYHOLDER NAME Mary Neely	BIRTHDATE 03/19/1935	RELATIONSHIP wife	POLICYHOLDER NAME	BIRTHDATE	RELATIONSHIP

SUPPLEMENTAL PLAN	EMPLOYER

POLICYHOLDER NAME	BIRTHDATE	RELATIONSHIP	DIAGNOSIS	CODE
			1. Rectal bleeding (3 days)	569.3
EMPLOYER Federal Department of Investigative Services			2. History polyps ascending colon (1999)	V10.05
			3.	
REFERRING PHYSICIAN UPIN/SSN AY9999 Arnold Younglove MD NPI 00919919			4.	

PLACE OF SERVICE Anywhere Surgical Center, 101 Park Street, Anywhere, US, 12345

PROCEDURES	CODE	CHARGE
1. 01/08/YYYY Colonoscopy, flexible to ileum	45378	$700—
2.		
3.		
4.		
5.		
6.		

SPECIAL NOTES

TOTAL CHARGES $700—	PAYMENTS 0	ADJUSTMENTS 0	BALANCE $700—

RETURN VISIT	PHYSICIAN SIGNATURE *Erin A. Helper, M.D.*

ERIN A. HELPER, M.D.   101 MEDIC DRIVE, ANYWHERE, US 12345
PHONE NUMBER (101) 111-1234
EIN # 11-123452   SSN # 111-22-3333
UPIN EH8888   NPI 00818810   Medicaid # EBH8881   BC/BS # EH11881 GRP: 1204-P

FIGURE 14-19 Jackie L. Neely Medicare Secondary Payer encounter form

PLEASE
DO NOT
STAPLE
IN THIS
AREA

EOB ATTACHED

(SAMPLE ONLY - NOT APPROVED FOR USE)

| | PICA

UNDERSTANDING HEALTH INSURANCE CLAIM FORM   PICA | |

1. MEDICARE	MEDICAID	CHAMPUS	CHAMPVA	GROUP HEALTH PLAN (SSN or ID)	FECA BLK LUNG (SSN)	OTHER (ID)	1a. INSURED'S I.D. NUMBER (FOR PROGRAM IN ITEM 1)
[X] (Medicare #)	[ ] (Medicaid #)	[ ] (Sponsor's SSN)	[ ] (VA File #)	[ ]	[ ]	[ ]	111223344A

2. PATIENT'S NAME (Last Name, First Name, Middle Initial)
NEELY JACKIE L

3. PATIENT'S BIRTH DATE   MM 09 DD 09 YY 1929   SEX M [X] F [ ]

4. INSURED'S NAME (Last Name, First Name, Middle Initial)
NEELY MARY

5. PATIENT'S ADDRESS (No. Street)
329 WATER STREET

6. PATIENT RELATIONSHIP TO INSURED
Self [ ] Spouse [ ] Child [ ] Other [ ]

7. INSURED'S ADDRESS (No. Street)
SAME

CITY
NOWHERE   STATE US

8. PATIENT STATUS
Single [ ] Married [X] Other [ ]

CITY   STATE

ZIP CODE 12367   TELEPHONE (Include Area Code) 101 201 1278

Employed [X]   Full-Time Student [ ]   Part-Time Student [ ]

ZIP CODE   TELEPHONE (INCLUDE AREA CODE) ( )

9. OTHER INSURED'S NAME (Last Name, First Name, Middle Initial)

10. IS PATIENT'S CONDITION RELATED TO:

11. INSURED'S POLICY GROUP OR FECA NUMBER
R1234567   103

a. OTHER INSURED'S POLICY OR GROUP NUMBER

a. EMPLOYMENT? (CURRENT OR PREVIOUS)
[ ] YES   [X] NO

a. INSURED'S DATE OF BIRTH   MM 03 DD 19 YY 1935   SEX M [ ] F [X]

b. OTHER INSURED'S DATE OF BIRTH   MM DD YY   SEX M [ ] F [ ]

b. AUTO ACCIDENT?   PLACE (State)
[ ] YES   [X] NO

b. EMPLOYER'S NAME OR SCHOOL NAME
FEDERAL DEPT INVESTIGATIVE SERVI

c. EMPLOYER'S NAME OR SCHOOL NAME

c. OTHER ACCIDENT?
[ ] YES   [X] NO

c. INSURANCE PLAN NAME OR PROGRAM NAME
BCBS FEDERAL

d. INSURANCE PLAN NAME OR PROGRAM NAME

10d. RESERVED FOR LOCAL USE

d. IS THERE ANOTHER HEALTH BENEFIT PLAN?
[ ] YES   [X] NO   If yes, return to and complete item 9 a – d.

READ BACK OF FORM BEFORE COMPLETING & SIGNING THIS FORM.
12. PATIENT'S OR AUTHORIZED PERSON'S SIGNATURE I authorize the release of any medical or other information necessary to process this claim. I also request payment of government benefits either to myself or to the party who accepts assignment below.

SIGNED   SIGNATURE ON FILE   DATE _____

13. INSURED'S OR AUTHORIZED PERSON'S SIGNATURE I authorize payment of medical benefits to the undersigned physician or supplier for services described below.

SIGNED   SIGNATURE ON FILE

14. DATE OF CURRENT: MM 01 DD 05 YY YYYY ◄ ILLNESS (First symptom) OR INJURY (Accident) OR PREGNANCY (LMP)

15. IF PATIENT HAS HAD SAME OR SIMILAR ILLNESS, GIVE FIRST DATE   MM DD YY

16. DATES PATIENT UNABLE TO WORK IN CURRENT OCCUPATION
FROM MM DD YY   TO MM DD YY

17. NAME OF REFERRING PHYSICIAN OR OTHER SOURCE
ARNOLD YOUNGLOVE

17a. I.D. NUMBER OF REFERRING PHYSICIAN
AY9999

18. HOSPITALIZATION DATES RELATED TO CURRENT SERVICES
FROM MM DD YY   TO MM DD YY

19. RESERVED FOR LOCAL USE

20. OUTSIDE LAB? $ CHARGES
[ ] YES   [X] NO

21. DIAGNOSIS OR NATURE OF ILLNESS OR INJURY. (RELATE ITEMS 1, 2, 3, OR 4 TO ITEM 24E BY LINE)
1. 569 . 3
2. V10 . 05
3. ____ . ____
4. ____ . ____

22. MEDICAID RESUBMISSION CODE   ORIGINAL REF. NO.

23. PRIOR AUTHORIZATION NUMBER

24. A. DATE(S) OF SERVICE						B. Place of Service	C. Type of Service	D. PROCEDURES, SERVICES, OR SUPPLIES (Explain Unusual Circumstances) CPT/HCPCS MODIFIER	E. DIAGNOSIS CODE	F. $ CHARGES	G. DAYS OR UNITS	H. EPSDT Family Plan	I. EMG	J. COB	K. RESERVED FOR LOCAL USE
From MM	DD	YY	To MM	DD	YY										
01 08 YYYY						24		45378	1	700 00	1				

25. FEDERAL TAX I.D. NUMBER   SSN [ ] EIN [X]
11-123452

26. PATIENT'S ACCOUNT NO.
14-3 SECONDARY

27. ACCEPT ASSIGNMENT? (For govt. claims, see back)
[X] YES   [ ] NO

28. TOTAL CHARGE $ 700 00

29. AMOUNT PAID $

30. BALANCE DUE $

31. SIGNATURE OF PHYSICIAN OR SUPPLIER INCLUDING DEGREES OR CREDENTIALS (I certify that the statements on the reverse apply to this bill and are made a part thereof.)
ERIN A HELPER MD
SIGNED   DATE MMDDYYYY

32. NAME AND ADDRESS OF FACILITY WHERE SERVICES WERE RENDERED (If other than home or office)
ANYWHERE SURGICAL CENTER
101 PARK STREET
ANYWHERE US 12345

33. PHYSICIAN'S SUPPLIER'S BILLING NAME, ADDRESS, ZIP CODE & PHONE #
(101) 111 1234
ERIN A HELPER MD
101 MEDIC DRIVE
ANYWHERE US 12345
PIN#   GRP#

(SAMPLE ONLY - NOT APPROVED FOR USE)   PLEASE PRINT OR TYPE   SAMPLE FORM 1500   SAMPLE FORM 1500 SAMPLE FORM 1500

FIGURE 14-20 Completed Jackie L. Neely Medicare secondary HCFA-1500 claim form

REVIEW

DEFINITION EXERCISE

Review the definition carefully. If the statement is true, put a T to the left of the number. If the statement is false, correct it.

1. Specified Low-Income Medicare Beneficiary Program: A Medicare program that requires states to cover premiums, deductibles, and copayments for Medicare-eligible persons with incomes that are slightly above the federal poverty line.

2. Medicare Part B: Covers services provided by institutions and outpatient health care providers.

3. Medicare Part A: Covers inpatient hospital, hospice, skilled nursing facility, and home health care services.

4. Balance Billing: Billing the patient for the entire amount included on the Medical claim.

5. Hospice: Autonomous, centrally-administered program coordinating inpatient and outpatient services for terminally ill patients and their families.

6. ESRD: End-stage renal disorder.

7. Limiting Charge: The maximum charge a PAR provider may charge a Medicare patient.

8. MCD: The initials indicating the Medicare-Medicaid Crossover Program.

CHALLENGE EXERCISE

Answer the following:

1. List six *separate and distinct classifications* of persons who are automatically eligible for full Medicare coverage.

2. List two classifications of persons who could qualify for Medicare coverage under special circumstances.

3. Explain how persons over age 65, who otherwise do not qualify for Medicare coverage, may buy into the program.

4. Describe six *distinctly different* categories of coverage a person can receive under Medicare Part B.

5. Discuss the limitations in Medicare coverage for a kidney donor.

6. Explain how a Medicare-eligible person, who needs a heart or liver transplant, can obtain Medicare to cover the cost of the transplant.

7. List seven incentives developed by the federal government to encourage health care providers to become PARS.

8. List five insurance programs that are considered primary to Medicare.

9. List the advantages for a Medicare beneficiary to sign up for a Medicare-HMO plan.

10. Explain the steps a provider must take to "opt out" of Medicare.

11. Explain how a patient would use a Medicare Savings Account/high deductible insurance plan combination.

12. List four combinations of services performed during one encounter that would require two separate claim forms to fully report the encounter when only two diagnoses and four services were performed.

Medicaid

Upon successful completion of this chapter, you should be able to:

1. Define the following terms, phrases, and abbreviations:

medical assistance program
Medicaid
MediCal
Aid to Families with Dependent
    Children (AFDC) (Welfare)
Personal Responsibility and
    Work Opportunity
    Reconciliation Act of 1996
Temporary Assistance for
    Needy Families (TANF)
State Children's Health
    Insurance Program (SCHIP)
Olmstead v. L.C.
Americans with Disabilities Act
    of 1990 (ADA)
mandatory categorically needy
    eligibility groups

federal poverty level
    (FPL)
Supplemental Security Income
    (SSI)
optional categorically needy
    eligibility groups
special income level
medically needy (MN) optional
    groups
spend down
excess income
Spousal Impoverishment
    Protection Legislation
liquid assets
community spouse

Early and Periodic Screening,
    Diagnostic, and Treatment
    services (EPSDT)
Federal Medical Assistance
    Percentage (FMAP)
dual eligibles
payer of last resort
Qualified Medicare Beneficiary
    (QMB)
Specified Low-Income Medicare
    Beneficiary (SLMB)
Qualifying Individual (QI)
Qualified Disabled and Working
    Individual (QDWI)
medically indigent
subrogation

2. List Medicaid federal guidelines.
3. List services covered under the federal portion of Medicaid assistance.
4. List services covered in your state that are not federally mandated services.
5. Explain how to verify a patient's Medicaid eligibility.
6. State the deadline for filing claims (timely filing period).
7. Explain the importance of the spousal impoverishment protection legislation.
8. Describe the preauthorization procedure for services.
9. File a Medicaid claim using the rules for the HCFA-1500 (12-90) claim form.

In 1965, Congress passed Title 19 of the Social Security Act establishing a federally-mandated, state-administered **medical assistance program** for persons with incomes below the national poverty level. The federal name for this program is **Medicaid**; several states assign local designations (e.g., California uses the title **MediCal**). Unlike Medicare, a nationwide entitlement program, the federal government mandated national requirements for Medicaid and gave the states latitude to develop eligibility rules and additional benefits if they assumed responsibility for the program's support.

LEGISLATIVE BACKGROUND OF MEDICAID

While the federal government later expanded the federally-mandated Medicaid requirements, some of which are funded by the federal government, Congress required states to pay the entire cost of others. The states almost immediately experienced a Medicaid budget crisis because the new mandates became effective at the same time the country entered into an economic slowdown. This resulted in a rapid increase in the number of Medicaid enrollments (national Medicaid enrollments were 33.6 million in 1994 at a cost of $138 billion to the states). The budget crisis prompted state governors to appeal for additional federal funds to cover the cost of the new federally-mandated benefits.

Pilot Programs

In 1993, the Health Care Financing Administration (HCFA) began to look favorably upon requests from individual states for waivers of certain Medicaid requirements. States would be allowed to establish pilot programs to study new ways of reducing the cost of Medicaid to the states. One of the most popular waiver requests was for the formation of statewide Medicaid managed care programs. If the state's request for a waiver was granted, the state would use any resulting savings to fund a higher earned-income ceiling for Medicaid eligibility that would permit more of the currently uninsured, low-income population to be covered.

For example, Oregon performed an extensive study of the cost effectiveness of treating specific disorders and, through an extensive series of town meetings, prioritized disorders to be treated and cases that will receive only palliative care. This unique proposal for a waiver was accepted.

Other innovative waiver proposals have been considered. One example established a statewide purchasing alliance that would negotiate with insurers for the lowest priced health plans rather than permit free choice of physicians. Another establishes limits on the length of time beneficiaries receive assistance. In addition, new rules allowing for Medicaid-HMO programs are now in effect. To qualify for federal funds to provide services to Medicaid beneficiaries, the HMO must agree to specific criteria: (1) no more than 75% of enrollees could be eligible for Medicaid and (2) the HMO must agree to defined standards for disenrollment, grievance procedures, information disclosure, and payment for emergency care received outside the network.

Welfare Reform

In the 1994 general election, the public called for a complete overhaul of the entire Welfare/Medicaid system. Congressional support for this overhaul was strong. By 1995, President Clinton announced that states proposing changes to work requirements or increased child support enforcement would be quickly approved to make such changes. By May 1996, 37 states were granted waivers allowing flexibility in administering **Aid to Families with Dependent Children (AFDC) (Welfare)** programs, the basic cash welfare program.

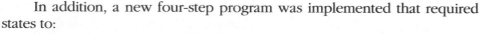

In addition, a new four-step program was implemented that required states to:

1. Enforce school attendance for teenaged mothers by denying benefits to those who drop out and do not take steps to obtain a GED.
2. Pay a bonus to teenaged parents who stay in school.
3. Require all unmarried, teenaged mothers on welfare and/or under the age of eighteen who have previously dropped out of school to sign a personal responsibility plan and agree to the following: (A) live at home with a legal guardian except in cases of abuse in the home or other special mitigating circumstances; (B) help establish paternity and obtain child support from the father; and (C) in some cases, attend parenting classes.
4. Require all teenaged mothers on welfare to live at home or with a responsible adult.

In August 1996, the **Personal Responsibility and Work Opportunity Reconciliation Act of 1996** was implemented, halting open-ended federal entitlement programs for persons who qualified for the AFDC program. Also, the **Temporary Assistance for Needy Families (TANF)** act provided block grants to states offering time-limited cash assistance. The first act also discontinued federal Medicaid eligibility for legal and illegal immigrants and narrowed the definition of disability as it applies to eligibility of children. States can modify their plans if they use the following guidelines to raise or lower income standards:

- States may lower income standards for eligibility, as long as the level does not go below the state income level used in May 1988.
- States may increase income or resources standards up to the percentage increase in the Consumer Price Index (CPI).
- States are allowed to deny Medicaid benefits to adults and heads of households who lose TANF benefits for refusing to work. An exception to this rule is made for children and pregnant women who have continuing Medicaid eligibility.

Balanced Budget Act of 1997 Provisions

In the Balanced Budget Act (BBA) of 1997, Congress added several amendments to the TANF Act:

- Restoration of Medicaid eligibility for legal immigrants who entered the country on or before August 22, 1996, and who since have qualified for Social Security Disability.
- Restoration of benefits to certain disabled children who would lose eligibility through Welfare reform.

In addition, the following changes to the overall Medicaid program were implemented:

- Awarding grants to states for the **State Children's Health Insurance Program (SCHIP)** to expand coverage to uninsured low-income children who live in households where the family income exceeds the state Medicaid level by no more than 150%. The age limit for SCHIP eligibility is 19.
- Allowing states to pay Medicaid rates to providers for persons who are Qualified Medicare Beneficiaries (QMBs).
- Allowing states to mandate managed care enrollment for Medicaid beneficiaries except for Medicaid recipients in the following categories

who can, but do not have to, participate in managed care: (1) Native Americans; (2) persons in alcohol or substance abuse residential programs; (3) those with developmental or physical disabilities receiving home- and community-based services or care-at-home services; (4) persons receiving services provided by an intermediate care facility that cares for the mentally retarded; and (5) Medicaid/Medicare dually eligible individuals.

The Olmstead Decision

In July 1999, the Supreme Court issued the ***Olmstead v. L.C.*** decision that challenges federal, state, and local governments to develop more accessible systems of cost-effective community-based services for individuals with disabilities. HCFA has begun consultation with states to review relevant federal Medicaid regulations, policies, and guidelines to ensure compatibility with requirements of the **Americans with Disabilities Act of 1990 (ADA)** (prohibits discrimination of individuals with disabilities) and the *Olmstead* decision. HCFA is also working with other involved federal agencies to ensure that reviews are consistent with requirements of the statute and are focused on the needs of persons with disabilities.

■ **NOTE:** While Medicaid is an important resource and will assist states in meeting the requirements of the ADA and the *Olmstead* decision, compliance is not limited to Medicaid beneficiaries or to services financed by the Medicaid program. ■

INTERNET LINK

Go to www.hcfa.gov/medicaid/mcaidpti.htm to download and view Medicaid publications, including new legislation.

FEDERAL ELIGIBILITY REQUIREMENTS

States have some discretion in determining Medicaid coverage policies as well as establishing financial criteria for Medicaid eligibility. To be eligible for federal funds, however, states must provide Medicaid coverage to most individuals who receive federally assisted income maintenance payments, as well as to related groups who do not receive cash payments. Federal funds are not provided for state-only programs.

Mandatory Categorically Needy Eligibility Groups

The following represents **mandatory categorically needy eligibility groups** for which federal matching funds are provided:

- Individuals who meet the requirements for the Aid to Families with Dependent Children (AFDC) program in effect in their state as of July 16, 1996.
- Children under age 6 whose family income is at or below 133% of the **federal poverty level (FPL)** (income guidelines established annually by the federal government).
- Pregnant women whose family income is below 133% of the FPL (services to these women are limited to those related to pregnancy, complications of pregnancy, delivery, and postpartum care).
- **Supplemental Security Income (SSI)** recipients in most states (some states use more restrictive Medicaid eligibility requirements that predate SSI).

- Recipients of adoption or foster care assistance under Title IV of the Social Security Act.
- Special protected groups (typically individuals who lose their cash assistance due to earnings from work or from increased Social Security benefits, but who may keep Medicaid for a period of time).
- All children born after September 30, 1983 who are under age 19, in families with incomes at or below the FPL (this process phases in coverage, so that by the year 2002 all such poor children under age 19 will be covered).
- Certain Medicare beneficiaries (described later in this chapter).

Optional Categorically Needed Eligibility Groups

States can provide Medicaid coverage to **optional categorically needy eligibility groups**, which share characteristics with the mandatory groups (that is, they fall within defined categories), but eligibility criteria are more liberally defined. Optional categorically needy eligibility groups for which states will receive federal matching funds under the Medicaid program include the following:

- Infants up to age 1 and pregnant women not covered under the mandatory rules whose family income is no more than 185% of the FPL (this percentage can be modified by each state).
- Children under age 21 who meet the AFDC income and resources requirements that were in effect in their state on July 16, 1996.
- Institutionalized individuals eligible under a **special income level** (the amount established by each state—up to 300% of the SSI federal benefit rate).
- Individuals who would be eligible if institutionalized, but who are receiving care under home- and community-based services waivers.
- Certain aged, blind, or disabled adults who have incomes above those requiring mandatory coverage, but below the FPL.
- Recipients of state supplementary income payments.
- Certain working-and-disabled persons with family income less than 250% of the FPL who would qualify for SSI if they did not work.
- TB-infected persons who would be financially eligible for Medicaid at the SSI income level if they were within a Medicaid-covered category (coverage is limited to TB-related ambulatory services and TB drugs).
- "Optional targeted low-income children" included within the State Children's Health Insurance Program (SCHIP) established by the Balanced Budget Act of 1997 (BBA).
- "Medically needy" individuals (discussed next).

Medically Needy (MN) Optional Groups

Medically needy (MN) optional groups include those eligible for Medicaid under one of the mandatory or optional groups, except that their income and/or resources are above the eligibility level established by their state. They may qualify immediately or "spend down" by incurring medical expenses that reduce their income to or below their state's *medically needy* income level. To **spend down** means to (1) determine an individual's **excess income** (the difference between the individual's income and the amount allowed for Medicaid eligibility) and (2) demonstrate that the individual's medical expenses are equal to or greater than the excess income. If this is proved, the individual can become eligible for Medicaid but for a limited time only, and they will still have to personally pay for some medical bills.

In 1989, **Spousal Impoverishment Protection Legislation** (originally part of the Medicare Catastrophic Coverage Act and later incorporated into the Social Security Act) was enacted to prevent married couples from being required to *spend down* income and other **liquid assets** (cash and property immediately convertible to cash) before one of the partners can be declared eligible for Medicaid coverage for nursing facility care. Spousal impoverishment provisions apply when one spouse resides in a nursing home and the other lives at home. The spouse remaining at home is referred to as the **community spouse** (which has nothing to do with community property). That spouse's monthly income from joint resources, along with minimums for other resources, is established each year by the state in which the individual resides. The spousal allowance is *in addition* to the value of the home, car, burial fund and other exempt assets. The noninstitutionalized spouse may also retain any income that is solely in his or her name.

States may also allow families to establish eligibility as *medically needy* by paying monthly premiums in an amount equal to the difference between family income (reduced by unpaid expenses, if any, incurred for medical care in previous months) and the income eligibility standard. States that elect to implement a medically needy program are required to include certain children under age 18 and pregnant women who, except for income and resources, would be eligible as *categorically needy*. States may also choose to provide coverage to other medically needy persons: aged, blind, and/or disabled persons; certain relatives or children deprived of parental support and care; and certain financially eligible children up to age 21.

Confirming Medicaid Eligibility

Any time a patient states they receive Welfare, Medicaid, or medical assistance, the patient must present a valid Medicaid identification card. Eligibility, in many cases, will depend on the monthly income of the patient. Since eligibility may fluctuate from one month to the next, most states have a dedicated telephone line for verification of eligibility. Confirmation of eligibility should be obtained for each visit; failure to do so may result in a denial of payment. If residing in one of these states, be sure to access the Medicaid verification line. Some states have a "swipe box" similar to those used by credit card companies. Beneficiaries carry plastic cards containing encoded data strips. When the card is swiped, the printout indicates eligibility or noneligibility data.

Retroactive eligibility is sometimes granted to patients whose income has fallen below the state-set eligibility level and who had high medical expenses prior to filing for Medicaid. When a patient notifies the practice that they have become retroactively eligible for Medicaid benefits, confirm this information before proceeding. A refund of any payments made by the patient during the retroactive period must be made, and Medicaid billed for these services.

MEDICAID SERVICES

Medicaid allows considerable flexibility within state plans, but some federal requirements are mandatory if federal matching funds are to be received. A state's Medicaid program *must* offer medical assistance for certain *basic* services to most categorically needy populations.

Mandatory Services

To receive federal matching funds, states must offer the *mandatory categorically needy eligibility group* the following basic services:

- Inpatient hospital services.
- Outpatient hospital services.
- Physician services.
- Medical and surgical dental services.
- Nursing facility (NF) services for individuals aged 21 or older.
- Home health care for persons eligible for nursing facility services.
- Family planning services and supplies.
- Rural health clinic and ambulatory services offered by a rural health clinic, otherwise covered under the state plan.
- Laboratory and Xray services.
- Pediatric and family nurse practitioner services.
- Federally-qualified health center and ambulatory services offered by a federally-qualified health center, otherwise covered under the state plan.
- Nurse-midwife services (to the extent authorized by state law).
- Early and periodic screening, diagnosis, and treatment (EPSDT) services for individuals under age 21.
- If a state chooses to provide to the *medically needy* population, the following services must be offered:
  - Prenatal care and delivery services for pregnant women.
  - Ambulatory services to individuals under age 18 and individuals entitled to institutional services.
  - Home health services to individuals entitled to nursing facility services.

Optional Services

To receive federal funding for the provision of optional services, states commonly offer the following:

- Clinic services.
- Nursing facility services for those under age 21.
- Intermediate care facility/mentally retarded services.
- Optometrist services and eyeglasses.
- Prescribed drugs.
- TB-related services for TB infected persons.
- Prosthetic devices.
- Dental services.

Waiver Services

States may provide home- and community-based care waiver services to certain individuals who are eligible for Medicaid. The services to be provided to these persons may include case management, personal care services, respite care services, adult day health services, homemaker/home health aide, rehabilitation, and other requested services that are approved by HCFA.

EPSDT Services

In 1989, Congress updated the **Early and Periodic Screening, Diagnostic, and Treatment services (EPSDT)** which was originally launched in 1967. Original EPSDT legislation mandated that if states were to receive federal funds, they would be required to provide routine pediatric checkups to all children enrolled in Medicaid. Section 6403 of the Omnibus Budget Reconciliation Act of 1989 strengthened the program by providing a statutory definition of such terms as "screening services," "vision services," "dental services," and "hearing services," considered a regular part of a routine pediatric checkup. A new requirement was added that states,

> "Such other necessary health care, diagnostic services, treatment, and other measures . . . to correct or ameliorate defects and physical and mental illnesses and conditions discovered by the screening services, whether or not such services are covered under the State plan."

Cost Containment

As a cost-containment measure, most states require preauthorization for many services provided to Medicaid patients, especially for nonemergency or elective hospital admissions. Additionally, there are limitations on billing for comprehensive-level examinations and consultations.

Many states also implemented a monitoring system to track over-utilization of services. Some states instituted a copayment requirement for certain Medicaid recipients; for example, the copayment may be as low as fifty cents per visit. In cases of persons classified as *medically needy*, larger copayments may be required, depending on the individual patient's income.

Preauthorized Services

Most states that have not placed all Medicaid beneficiaries into a prepaid HMO have some form of prior approval or preauthorization for recipients. Examples of preauthorization guidelines include:

1. Elective admission
   a. Explanation of the reason why inpatient treatment is necessary
   b. Admission diagnosis and outline of treatment plan

2. Emergency admission
   a. Medical justification for treatment to be provided on an inpatient basis
   b. Date of admission
   c. Admission diagnosis and outline of treatment plan

3. More than one preoperative day
   a. Explanation of reason(s) why surgery cannot be performed within twenty-four hours of the time the surgeon indicates an established need for surgery and the patient's condition is deemed satisfactory for surgery
   b. Number of additional preoperative day(s) requested

4. Outpatient procedure(s) to be performed in an inpatient setting
   a. Code and description of surgical procedure
   b. Medical justification for performing the surgery on an inpatient basis

5. Days exceeding state hospital stay limitation due to complication(s)
   a. Diagnosis stated on original preauthorization request
   b. Beginning and ending dates originally authorized
   c. Statement describing the complication(s)
   d. Day complication(s) presented
   e. Diagnosis for first illness
   f. Diagnosis for secondary disorder

6. Extension of inpatient days
   a. Medical necessity for the extension
   b. Number of additional days requested
   c. The basis for approval of more than one preoperative day
   d. The performance of multiple procedures that, when combined, necessitate a length of stay in excess of that required for any one individual procedure
   e. The development of postoperative complication(s) or a medical history that dictates longer-than-usual postoperative observation by skilled medical staff

Payment for Medicaid Services

Medicaid makes payment directly to the providers, and those participating in Medicaid must accept the reimbursement level as payment in full. States determine their own reimbursement methodology and rates for services, with three exceptions: (1) for institutional services, payment may not exceed amounts that would be paid under Medicare payment rates; (2) for disproportionate share hospitals (DSHs), different limits apply; and (3) for hospice care services, rates cannot be lower than Medicare rates.

States can require deductibles, coinsurance, or copayments for certain services performed for some Medicaid recipients. Emergency services and family planning services are exempt from copayments. Certain Medicaid recipients are also excluded from this cost sharing, including pregnant women, children under age 18, hospital or nursing home patients who are expected to contribute most of their income to institutional care, and *categorically needy* HMO enrollees.

The portion of the Medicaid program paid by the federal government is known as the **Federal Medical Assistance Percentage (FMAP)** and is determined annually for each state using a formula that compares the state's average per capita income level with the national average. Wealthier states receive a smaller share of reimbursed costs, and the federal government shares in administration expenses (50% match).

RELATIONSHIP BETWEEN MEDICAID AND MEDICARE

Certain eligible Medicare beneficiaries may also receive help from the Medicaid program. For those eligible for *full* Medicaid coverage, Medicare coverage is supplemented by services available under a state's Medicaid program. These additional services may include, for example, nursing facility care beyond the 100-day limit covered by Medicare, prescription drugs, eyeglasses, and hearing aids.

Dual Eligibles

Medicare beneficiaries with low incomes and limited resources may receive help with out-of-pocket medical expenses from state Medicaid programs. Various benefits are available to **dual eligibles**, individuals entitled to Medicare and eligible for some type of Medicaid benefit. Individuals eligible for full Medicaid coverage receive program supplements to their Medicare coverage via services and supplies available from the state's Medicaid program. Services covered by both programs are paid first by Medicare and the difference by Medicaid, up to the state's payment limit. Medicaid also covers the following additional services:

- nursing facility care beyond the 100 day limit covered by Medicare.
- prescription drugs.

- eyeglasses.
- hearing aids.

For individuals enrolled in both programs, any services covered by Medicare are paid for by the Medicare program before any payments are made by the Medicaid program, since Medicaid is always the **payer of last resort**.

Qualified
Medicare
Beneficiaries

Limited Medicaid benefits are also available to pay for out-of-pocket Medicare cost-sharing expenses for certain other Medicare beneficiaries. **Qualified Medicare Beneficiaries (QMBs)** have resources at or below twice the standard allowed under the SSI program and income at or below 100% of the federal poverty level (FPL); they do not have to pay their monthly Medicare premiums, deductibles, and coinsurance.

Specified
Low-Income
Medicare
Beneficiaries

Specified Low-Income Medicare Beneficiaries (SLMBs) have resources at or below twice the standard allowed under the SSI program and an income that exceeds the QMB level, but less than 120% of the FPL; they do not have to pay the monthly Medicare Part B premiums.

Qualifying
Individuals

Qualifying Individuals (QIs), not otherwise eligible for full Medicaid benefits and with resources at or below twice the standard allowed under the SSI program, receive assistance with all or a small part of their monthly Medicare Part B premiums, depending on whether their income exceeds the SLMB level, but is less than 135% of the FPL, or their income is at least 135%, but less than 175% of the FPL.

Qualified Disabled
and Working
Individuals

Individuals eligible for Medicare due to disability, but lost Medicare entitlement because they returned to work, may purchase Part A of Medicare. If the individual's income is below 200% of the FPL and resources are at or below twice the standard allowed under the SSI program, and they are not otherwise eligible for Medicaid benefits, they may qualify for Medicaid to pay their monthly Medicare Part A premiums as **Qualified Disabled and Working Individuals (QDWIs)**.

MEDICAID'S FUTURE

Medicaid was created as the medical portion of federally funded income maintenance programs for the poor, with an emphasis on the aged, the disabled, and children dependent on families unable to provide for medical needs. Medicaid has diverged from its origins, and recent legislation has expanded Medicaid coverage to include a number of low-income pregnant women, poor children, and Medicare beneficiaries who are not eligible for cash assistance programs and who would have been ineligible for Medicaid under previous laws. The focus today is on outreach toward specific groups (e.g., pregnant women and children), increased access to care, and improved quality of care. In addition to an increase in the number of beneficiaries, Medicaid has increased its expenditures for acute, home health, and nursing facility care for the aged and disabled. Medicaid has also joined the trend toward managed care enrollment by allowing states increased flexibility to research health care delivery alternatives (to control costs) and to implement managed care delivery systems.

MEDICAID AS A SECONDARY PAYER

Medicaid is always the **payer of last resort**. If the patient is covered by another medical or liability policy, including Medicare, TRICARE (formerly CHAMPUS), CHAMPVA, or Indian Health Services (IHS), this coverage must be billed first. Medicaid is billed only if the other coverage denies responsibility for payment, pays less than the Medicaid fee schedule, or if Medicaid covers procedures not covered by the other policy.

PARTICIPATING PROVIDERS

Any provider who accepts a Medicaid patient must accept the Medicaid-determined payment as payment in full. Providers are forbidden by law to bill (balance billing) patients for Medicaid-covered benefits. A patient may be billed for any service that is not a covered benefit; however, some states have historically required providers to sign formal participating Medicaid contracts. Other states do not require contracts.

MEDICAID AND MANAGED CARE

As stated before, many states have requested federal permission to integrate persons receiving Medicaid assistance into HMO programs. Most programs of this type offer capitated services to the healthier members of the Medicaid populations. Managed care fee-for-service programs are available for the chronically ill and for all patients in rural communities where HMO penetration is extremely low or nonexistent. Some states have a mixture of existing HMOs serving Medicaid. All Medicaid HMO patients have a primary care physician or a case manager responsible for authorizing all specialty care and hospital services.

If the provider is not a member of the HMO managed care network, consult the appropriate state Medicaid manual for instructions on how to bill for unauthorized emergency care.

BILLING INFORMATION NOTES

Following is information on nationwide fee-for-service billing. Consult the HMO billing manual to bill for noncapitated HMO services.

Fiscal Agent

The name of the state's Medicaid fiscal agent will vary from state to state. Contact the local county government for information about the Medicaid program in your area.

Underwriter

Underwriting responsibility is shared between state and federal governments. Federal responsibility rests with HCFA, an agency of the United States Department of Health and Human Services (HHS). The name of the state agency will vary according to state preference.

Form Used

HCFA-1500 (12-90) claim form is the required form, unless residing/working in one of the few states that received a special waiver from HCFA to continue using a state-developed special optical scanning form. (See Michigan form in Figure 15-1). If residing/working in one of the waivered states, consult the local Medicaid office to obtain copies of the special form and billing instructions.

LAST NAME OF INSURED/SUBSCRIBER	FIRST NAME	PHYSICIAN OR PROVIDER NAME, ADDRESS, ZIP CODE	OMB 0938-0008

GROUP NO.   SERVICE CODE

**MICHIGAN
HEALTH
BENEFITS
CLAIM**

| 4 | 8 | 5 |

INSURED'S/SUBSCRIBER IDENTIFYING NO. (INCLUDE ANY LETTERS)   PROVIDER CODE

→ THESE AREAS BLANK FOR MEDICAID CLAIMS

TYPEWRITER — ALIGNMENT   TYPEWRITER ALIGNMENT

PICA   ELITE   RECIPROCITY   BC/BS   MEDICARE   COMP.   FEP   CHAMPUS   MEDICAID   CRIPPLED CHILDREN   OTHER   22   ELITE   PICA

1. PATIENT'S LAST NAME	2. MID. INIT.	3. FIRST NAME	4. PATIENT'S BIRTH DATE	5. INSURED'S NAME (LAST, FIRST, MID. INIT.)
SELL		THOMAS	050550	

6. PATIENT'S STREET ADDRESS	7. CITY	8. PATIENT'S SEX	9. INSURED'S I.D., MEDICARE OR PATIENT'S I.D. NO.
		M F	35227788

| 10. STATE | 11. ZIP CODE | 12. AREA CODE & TELEPHONE NO. | 13. INSURED'S GROUP NO. OR GROUP NAME |

| 14. OTHER INS. COVERAGE POLICYHOLDER NAME | 15. PLAN NAME | 16. PATIENT'S REL. TO INSURED SELF SPOUSE DEP. | 17. INSURED'S STREET ADDRESS |

| 18. PLAN ADDRESS | 19. POLICY NO. | 20. WAS CONDITION RELATED TO EMP. AUTO OTHER | 21. CITY | 22. STATE | 23. ZIP CODE |

24. DATE OF	ILLNESS (FIRST SYMPTOM) OR INJURY (ACCIDENT) OR PREGNANCY (LMP)	25. INJURY CODE	26. DATE FIRST CONSULTED YOU FOR THIS CONDITION	27. HAS PATIENT EVER HAD SAME OR SIMILAR SYMPTOMS? YES NO	28. EMERGENCY
		1			2

29. DATE PATIENT ABLE TO RETURN TO WORK   30. DATES OF TOTAL DISABILITY FROM THROUGH   31. DATES OF PARTIAL DISABILITY FROM THROUGH

32. NAME OF REFERRING PROVIDER OR OTHER SOURCE (E.G. PUBLIC HLTH. AGENCY)   33. I.D. NO.   34. TYPE   35. FOR SERVICES RELATED TO HOSPITAL GIVE DATES ADMITTED DISCHARGED

36. NAME OF FACILITY WHERE SERVICES RENDERED (IF OTHER THAN HOME OR OFFICE)   37. I.D. NO.   38. ADDRESS (CITY, STATE)

39. DIAGNOSIS OR NATURE OF ILLNESS OR INJURY
1.
2.
3.

40. EPSDT YES NO
41. FAMILY PLANNING YES NO
42. PRIOR AUTHORIZATION NO.

BE

43.	A. DATE OF SERVICE	B. DIAGNOSIS CODE	C. PLACE	D. TYPE	E. PROCEDURE CODE	F. QUANTITY	G. CHARGES	H. BCBSM/MEJDICARE USE/ TITLE-XVIII PAID	I. MISC. DATE/ OTHER INS. PAID	J. I.C.	K. EXPL. CD. / DELETE
1.	1201YY	81314	3	2	29075	1	75.00				
2.											
3.											
4.											
5.											
6.											

44. DATE	45. NO ATTACH.	46. ADJ.	47. CO-INSURANCE	48. DEDUCTIBLE	49. TOTAL CHARGES	50. AMOUNT PAID	51. AMOUNT PAID	52. BALANCE DUE
1210YY					75.00			75 00

53. ORIG. CLAIM REFERENCE NO.	54. NO.	55. PROVIDER I.D.	56. TYPE	57. LOC.	58. I ACCEPT ASSIGNMENT/ I PARTICIPATE YES NO	59. PROVIDER NAME
		7654321	10	0		JOE BONES MD

60. MED. STATUS	61. RESOURCES	62. OTHER INS.	63. DATE OTHER INS. CLM. SUBMITTED	64. PHYSICIAN SOC. SEC. NO.	65. PROVIDER STREET ADDRESS	66. CITY
1	1					

| 67. MULT. DIAG. | 68. RELATED TO PHYS. EXAM | 69. PATIENT ACCOUNT NO. | 70. | 71. STATE | 72. ZIP CODE | 73. AREA CODE & TELEPHONE NO. |

74. REMARKS - **DO NOT WRITE OR TYPE IN THIS AREA FOR BCBSM CLAIMS**

CERTIFICATION - READ REVERSE SIDE CAREFULLY BEFORE SIGNING

75. SIGNATURE OF PATIENT OR AUTHORIZED PERSON   (I AUTHORIZE THE RELEASE OF ANY MEDICAL INFORMATION NECESSARY TO PROCESS THIS CLAIM AND REQUEST PAYMENT OF BENEFITS EITHER TO MYSELF OR THE PARTY WHO ACCEPTS ASSIGNMENT/PARTICIPATES BELOW.)   DATE

76. **BCBSM MEMBER READ CAREFULLY AND REFER TO BOX 58.** IF THE **"YES"** BLOCK IS CHECKED PAYMENT WILL BE SENT TO THE **PHYSICIAN/ PROVIDER.** YOUR SIGNATURE IS NOT NECESSARY. IF THE **"NO"** BLOCK IS CHECKED, PAYMENT WILL BE SENT TO THE SUBSCRIBER. YOUR SIGNATURE IS NOT REQUIRED TO RECEIVE BCBSM BENEFITS. THE CONTRACTUAL PROVISIONS CONCERNING PAYMENT OF BENEFITS EXPLAIN YOUR RIGHTS AND OBLIGATIONS. THIS IS REPRODUCED ON THE REVERSE SIDE OF THIS FORM. YOUR SIGNATURE IS REQUIRED ONLY IF YOU AGREE TO THE FOLLOWING CERTIFICATION STATEMENT WHICH MAY OBLIGATE YOU TO MAKE AN ADDITIONAL PAYMENT FOR SERVICES. **"I UNDERSTAND THE PROVIDER'S CHARGE MAY EXCEED THE BCBSM PAYMENT AND IF GREATER THAN SUCH PAYMENT, I WILL RESPONSIBLE FOR THAT AMOUNT."**   DATE

77. SIGNATURE OF PROVIDER (I CERTIFY THAT THE STATEMENTS ON THE REVERSE SIDE APPLY TO THE BILL AND ARE MADE A PRT THEREOF.)   DATE   **12-10-YYYY**

FIGURE 15-1 Michigan Medicaid form

Timely Filing Deadline

Deadlines vary from state to state. Check with your local Medicaid office. It is important to file a Medicaid fee-for-service claim as soon as possible. The only time a claim should be delayed is when the patient does not identify their Medicaid eligibility or if the patient has applied for retroactive Medicaid coverage.

Medicare-Medicaid Crossover claims follow the Medicare, not Medicaid, deadlines for claims. (See page 375 for details of the Medicare claim filing deadline.)

Allowable Determination

The state establishes the maximum reimbursement payable for each non-managed care service. It is expected that Medicaid programs will use the new HCFA Resource-Based Relative Value Scale (RBRVS) system for these services, with each state establishing its own conversion factor. Medicaid recipients can be billed for any noncovered procedure performed. However, because most Medicaid patients have incomes below the poverty level, collection of fees for uncovered services is difficult.

Accept Assignment

If Accept Assignment is not marked on the HCFA-1500 claim form, reimbursement (depending on state policy) may either be denied or forwarded to the patient. It is illegal to attempt collection of the difference between the Medicaid payment and the fee the provider charged, even if the patient did not reveal at the time the procedure was performed that he or she was a Medicaid recipient.

Deductibles

There may be a deductible for persons in the **medically indigent** classification. In such cases, eligibility cards usually are not issued until after the stated deductible has been met. No other eligibility classifications have deductible requirements.

Copayments

Copayments are required for some categories of Medicaid recipients.

Premiums

The Medicaid recipient does not pay a premium for medical coverage.

Inpatient Benefits

All nonemergency hospitalizations must be preauthorized. If the patient's condition warrants an extension of the authorized inpatient days, the hospital must seek an authorization for additional inpatient days.

Major Medical/ Accidental Injury Coverage

There is no special treatment for either of these categories. Medicaid will conditionally subrogate claims when there is liability insurance to cover a person's injuries. **Subrogation** is the assumption of an obligation for which another party is primarily liable.

Because Medicaid eligibility is determined by income, patients can be eligible one month and not the next. Check eligibility status on each visit. New work requirements may change this, as beneficiaries will continue coverage for a specific time even if their income exceeds the state eligibility levels. Prior authorization is required for many procedures and most nonemergency hospitalizations. Consult the current Medicaid Handbook for a listing of the procedures that must have prior authorization. When in doubt, contact the state agency for clarification.

Cards may be issued for the "Unborn child of . . ." (the name of the pregnant woman is inserted in the blank space). These cards are good only for services that promote the life and good health of the unborn child.

Because other health and liability programs are primary to Medicaid, the EOB from the primary coverage must be attached to the Medicaid claim.

A combined Medicare-Medicaid claim should be filed by the Medicaid deadline on the HCFA-1500 (12-90) claim form.

STEP-BY-STEP CLAIM FORM INSTRUCTIONS

Medicaid Fee-for-Service Claims

■ **NOTE:** These instructions are for Medicaid only. If the patient is covered by Medicare and Medicaid, follow the instructions for Medicare-Medicaid Cross-over claims on page 367. ■

Place Post-It® Notes or other markers on pages 000 and 000. You will be referring to them frequently.

Refer to Figure 15-2 for Blocks 1 through 13 of the HCFA-1500 claim form.

Block 1

Enter an "X" in the MEDICAID box.

Block 1a

Enter the insured's Medicaid ID number.

Block 2

Enter the complete name (last name first, followed by the first name and middle initial) of the patient listed on the patient's insurance identification card. Use of nicknames or typographic errors will cause rejection of the claim.

For case studies in this text enter the name, minus the punctuation, as it appears on the encounter form.

Block 3

Enter the birthdate using eight digits in the following format MM DD YYYY. Sex—Enter an "X" in the appropriate box.

FIGURE 15-2 Blocks 1 through 13 of the HCFA-1500 claim form

Block 4	Leave blank.
Block 5	Enter the patient's full mailing address on lines 1 and 2 of this block. Enter the zip code, area code, and phone number in the proper blocks of line 3. Do not type parentheses surrounding the area code.
Blocks 6 through 9d	Leave blank.
Block 10a	Enter an "X" in the "NO" box.
Block 10 b	Enter an "X" in the "NO" box.
Block 10 c	Enter an "X" in the "NO" box.
Block 10d	Leave blank.

■ **NOTE:** In some Medicaid programs, managed care recipients treated for emergency or urgent care may be indicated by entering an "E" or "U" in Block 10d, respectively. ■

Blocks 11–11d	Leave blank.
Block 12	Leave blank. The patient's signature or the statement, "SIGNATURE ON FILE," is not required on Medicaid claims.

■ **NOTE:** If Medicaid *waiver services* (discussed on page 407) are provided, enter " SIGNATURE ON FILE," and maintain the original patient signature on file. ■

Block 13	Leave blank.

Refer to Figure 15-3 for the John Q. Public encounter form and Figure 15-4 for completed Blocks 1 through 13 (based on the encounter form in Figure 15-3) of the HCFA-1500 claim form.

EXERCISE 15-1 Continuation of Medicare/Medicaid Comparison Form

1. Record abbreviated instructions in Blocks 1 through 13 of the Medicaid column.

   If the step-by-step instructions in this chapter indicate a particular block is to be left blank, record the word "Blank."

   Use horizontal arrows to indicate that the instructions in a specific block in the Medicaid column are repeated in the next column.

   If consecutive blocks are to be left blank, enter the word "Blank" in the first block and draw a vertical arrow down through the other blocks that receive similar treatment.

2. Save this form; it will be used for other exercises in this chapter.

DATE 01/26/YYYY	REMARKS Preauthorization # YY8301			

PATIENT John Q. Public		CHART # 15-1	SEX M	BIRTHDATE 10/10/1959

MAILING ADDRESS 10A Senate Avenue	CITY Anywhere	STATE US	ZIP 12345	HOME PHONE (101) 201 9871	WORK PHONE

EMPLOYER	ADDRESS	PATIENT STATUS MARRIED DIVORCED SINGLE STUDENT OTHER

INSURANCE: PRIMARY Medicaid	ID# 99811948	GROUP	SECONDARY POLICY

POLICYHOLDER NAME	BIRTHDATE	RELATIONSHIP	POLICYHOLDER NAME	BIRTHDATE	RELATIONSHIP

SUPPLEMENTAL PLAN	EMPLOYER

POLICYHOLDER NAME	BIRTHDATE	RELATIONSHIP

DIAGNOSIS — CODE

1. Benign cyst, sebaceous — 706.2
2. Malignant lesion trunk — 173.5
3.
4.

EMPLOYER

REFERRING PHYSICIAN UPIN/SSN

PLACE OF SERVICE

PROCEDURES		CODE	CHARGE
1. 01/21/YYYY	Excision 2.1 cm benign cyst from back	11403	$50—
2. 01/21/YYYY	Excision 1.4 malignant lesion, trunk	11602	$75—
3.	with intermediate repair	12031	$75—
4.			
5.			
6.			

SPECIAL NOTES

TOTAL CHARGES $200—	PAYMENTS 0	ADJUSTMENTS 0	BALANCE $200—

RETURN VISIT 3 days	PHYSICIAN SIGNATURE *Erin A. Helper, M.D.*

ERIN A. HELPER, M.D.   101 MEDIC DRIVE, ANYWHERE, US 12345
PHONE NUMBER (101) 111-1234
EIN # 11-123341   SSN # 111-22-3333
UPIN EH8888   NPI 00818810   Medicaid # EBH8881   BC/BS # EH11881 GRP: 1204-P

FIGURE 15-3 John Q. Public encounter form

EXERCISE 15-2 Medicaid Primary Only Claim Form Blocks 1 through 13

This exercise requires one copy of a blank HCFA-1500 claim form. You may either make photocopies of the form in Appendix II of the text, or print copies of a blank form using the computer disk in the workbook. (Instructions for installing the computer program and printing blank forms are printed in the workbook.)

1. Obtain a copy of the HCFA-1500 claim form.

2. Review the instructions for Blocks 1 through 13 in the Medicare primary column of the comparison chart created in Exercise 14-2.

PLEASE
DO NOT
STAPLE
IN THIS
AREA

APPROVED OMB-0938-0008

CARRIER

☐ ☐ PICA

HEALTH INSURANCE CLAIM FORM

PICA ☐ ☐

| 1. MEDICARE ☐ (Medicare #) | MEDICAID ☒ (Medicaid #) | CHAMPUS ☐ (Sponsor's SSN) | CHAMPVA ☐ (VA File #) | GROUP HEALTH PLAN ☐ (SSN or I D) | FECA BLK LUNG ☐ (SSN) | OTHER ☐ (I D) | 1a. INSURED'S I.D. NUMBER 99811948 | (FOR PROGRAM IN ITEM 1) |

2. PATIENT'S NAME (Last Name, First Name, Middle Initial)
PUBLIC JOHN Q

3. PATIENT'S BIRTH DATE
MM 10 | DD 10 | YY 1959 M ☐ SEX F ☐

4. INSURED'S NAME (Last Name, First Name, Middle Initial)

5. PATIENT'S ADDRESS (No. Street)
10A SENATE AVENUE

6. PATIENT RELATIONSHIP TO INSURED
Self ☐ Spouse ☐ Child ☐ Other ☐

7. INSURED'S ADDRESS (No. Street)

CITY
ANYWHERE

STATE
US

8. PATIENT STATUS
Single ☐ Married ☐ Other ☐

CITY

STATE

ZIP CODE
12345

TELEPHONE (Include Area Code)
101 201 9871

Employed ☐ Full-Time Student ☐ Part-Time Student ☐

ZIP CODE

TELEPHONE (INCLUDE AREA CODE)
( )

9. OTHER INSURED'S NAME (Last Name, First Name, Middle Initial)

10. IS PATIENT'S CONDITION RELATED TO:

11. INSURED'S POLICY GROUP OR FECA NUMBER

a. OTHER INSURED'S POLICY OR GROUP NUMBER

a. EMPLOYMENT? (CURRENT OR PREVIOUS)
☐ YES ☒ NO

a. INSURED'S DATE OF BIRTH
MM | DD | YY
SEX M ☐ F ☐

b. OTHER INSURED'S DATE OF BIRTH
MM | DD | YY
SEX M ☐ F ☐

b. AUTO ACCIDENT?
☐ YES ☒ NO PLACE (State) ☐

b. EMPLOYER'S NAME OR SCHOOL NAME

c. EMPLOYER'S NAME OR SCHOOL NAME

c. OTHER ACCIDENT?
☐ YES ☒ NO

c. INSURANCE PLAN NAME OR PROGRAM NAME

d. INSURANCE PLAN NAME OR PROGRAM NAME

10d. RESERVED FOR LOCAL USE

d. IS THERE ANOTHER HEALTH BENEFIT PLAN?
☐ YES ☐ NO *If yes,* return to and complete item 9 a – d.

READ BACK OF FORM BEFORE COMPLETING & SIGNING THIS FORM.
12. PATIENT'S OR AUTHORIZED PERSON'S SIGNATURE I authorize the release of any medical or other information necessary to process this claim. I also request payment of government benefits either to myself or to the party who accepts assignment below.

SIGNED _____ DATE _____

13. INSURED'S OR AUTHORIZED PERSON'S SIGNATURE I authorize payment of medical benefits to the undersigned physician or supplier for services described below.

SIGNED _____

PATIENT AND INSURED INFORMATION

FIGURE 15-4 Completed Blocks 1 through 13 for the John Q. Public encounter form in Figure 15-3

3. Review Figure 15-5, the Mary Sue Patient encounter form. Place a page marker on the encounter form.

4. Abstract the information needed for Blocks 1 through 13 from Figure 15-5. Enter the required information on the second claim form using Optical Scanning Guidelines. This form may be completed by handwriting the information, using the Blank Form Mode on the computer disk or typing the data.

5. Review Blocks 1 through 13 of the claim form to be sure all required blocks are properly completed.

■ **NOTE:** This same encounter form and claim form will be used for Exercise 15-4. ■

Refer to Figure 15-6 for Blocks 14 through 23 of the HCFA-1500 claim form.

Blocks 14–16   Leave blank.

Block 17   Enter the complete name and/or degree of referring, requesting, ordering, or prescribing provider, if applicable.

Block 17a   Enter the Medicaid ID number of the provider named in Block 17, if any.

■ **NOTE:** Medicaid will switch from using a state ID number to using the NPI (national provider identifier) when required by HCFA. ■

DATE	REMARKS			
01/05/YYYY	Authorization # YY8345			

PATIENT		CHART #	SEX	BIRTHDATE
Mary Sue Patient		15-2		10/10/1959

MAILING ADDRESS	CITY	STATE	ZIP	HOME PHONE	WORK PHONE
91 Home Street	Nowhere	US	12367	(101) 201 8989	

EMPLOYER	ADDRESS	PATIENT STATUS
		MARRIED DIVORCED SINGLE STUDENT OTHER

INSURANCE: PRIMARY	ID#	GROUP	SECONDARY POLICY
Medicaid	99811765		

POLICYHOLDER NAME	BIRTHDATE	RELATIONSHIP	POLICYHOLDER NAME	BIRTHDATE	RELATIONSHIP

SUPPLEMENTAL PLAN	EMPLOYER

POLICYHOLDER NAME BIRTHDATE RELATIONSHIP	DIAGNOSIS	CODE
	1. Annual Exam	V70.0
EMPLOYER	2. Hypertension	401.9
	3.	
REFERRING PHYSICIAN UPIN/SSN	4.	

PLACE OF SERVICE Office

PROCEDURES	CODE	CHARGE
1. 01/05/YYYY Preventive Medicine	99386	$150—
2. 01/05/YYYY Est Office Visit Level III	99213-25	75—
3. 01/05/YYYY Urinalysis, with microscopy	81001	10—
4. 01/05/YYYY Venipuncture, routine	36415	8—
5.		
6.		

SPECIAL NOTES   Pt to go to radio diagnostics for chest x-ray, mammogram

Blood work — Amer Labs

TOTAL CHARGES	PAYMENTS	ADJUSTMENTS	BALANCE
$243—	0	0	$243—

RETURN VISIT	PHYSICIAN SIGNATURE
Return 10 days	*Erin A. Helper, M.D.*

ERIN A. HELPER, M.D.   101 MEDIC DRIVE, ANYWHERE, US 12345
PHONE NUMBER (101) 111-1234
EIN # 11-123341   SSN # 111-22-3333
UPIN EH8888   NPI 00818810   Medicaid # EBH8881   BC/BS # EH11881 GRP: 1204-P

FIGURE 15-5 Mary Sue Patient encounter form

14. DATE OF CURRENT: ◄ ILLNESS (First symptom) OR MM DD YY INJURY (Accident) OR PREGNANCY (LMP)	15. IF PATIENT HAS HAD SAME OR SIMILAR ILLNESS, GIVE FIRST DATE MM DD YY	16. DATES PATIENT UNABLE TO WORK IN CURRENT OCCUPATION MM DD YY MM DD YY FROM TO
17. NAME OF REFERRING PHYSICIAN OR OTHER SOURCE	17a. I.D. NUMBER OF REFERRING PHYSICIAN	18. HOSPITALIZATION DATES RELATED TO CURRENT SERVICES MM DD YY MM DD YY FROM TO
19. RESERVED FOR LOCAL USE		20. OUTSIDE LAB? $ CHARGES ☐ YES ☐ NO
21. DIAGNOSIS OR NATURE OF ILLNESS OR INJURY. (RELATE ITEMS 1, 2, 3, OR 4 TO ITEM 24E BY LINE) 1. ⌊___.___⌋ 3. ⌊___.___⌋ 2. ⌊___.___⌋ 4. ⌊___.___⌋		22. MEDICAID RESUBMISSION CODE ORIGINAL REF. NO. 23. PRIOR AUTHORIZATION NUMBER

FIGURE 15-6 Blocks 14 through 23 of the HCFA-1500 claim form

Block 18

Enter the admission date and the discharge date (MM DD YYYY), if a procedure/service is rendered to the patient with inpatient status.

If the patient is still hospitalized, leave the "TO" block blank.

Block 19

Reserved for local use. Some Medicaid programs require entry of the Medicaid provider number of the practitioner rendering the service. Others require a description to be entered if an unlisted procedure or service code is reported.

■ **NOTE:** If the description does not fit in Block 19, attach documentation to the claim describing unlisted services/procedures and enter "SEE ATTACHMENT" in Block 19. ■

Block 20

Enter an "X" in the appropriate box to indicate whether lab work was sent out to be processed.

■ **NOTE:** Medicaid law forbids billing for services rendered by another provider. Providers should bill only for services they performed. ■

Block 21

Enter the ICD-9-CM code number for up to four diagnoses or conditions treated.

When completing case studies in this text and workbook, code the reported symptoms instead of qualified diagnoses.

Block 22

Enter the Medicaid Resubmission code if it applies to this claim.

When working with case studies in this text and the workbook leave this block blank.

Block 23

Enter the prior authorization (preauthorization) number if applicable. If written authorization was obtained, attach a copy to the paper claim.

Refer to Figure 15-7 for completed Blocks 14 through 23 for the encounter form in Figure 15-3.

EXERCISE 15-3 Continuation of Work on Comparison Chart

Reread the instructions for completing Blocks 14 through 23. As you read each block, enter a concise description of the instructions in the appropriate block in the Medicaid column of the Comparison Chart.

---

14. DATE OF CURRENT: ILLNESS (First symptom) OR MM DD YY INJURY (Accident) OR PREGNANCY (LMP)	15. IF PATIENT HAS HAD SAME OR SIMILAR ILLNESS, GIVE FIRST DATE MM DD YY	16. DATES PATIENT UNABLE TO WORK IN CURRENT OCCUPATION MM DD YY MM DD YY FROM TO
17. NAME OF REFERRING PHYSICIAN OR OTHER SOURCE	17a. I.D. NUMBER OF REFERRING PHYSICIAN	18. HOSPITALIZATION DATES RELATED TO CURRENT SERVICES MM DD YY MM DD YY FROM TO
19. RESERVED FOR LOCAL USE EBH8881		20. OUTSIDE LAB? $ CHARGES ☐ YES ☒ NO
21. DIAGNOSIS OR NATURE OF ILLNESS OR INJURY. (RELATE ITEMS 1, 2, 3, OR 4 TO ITEM 24E BY LINE) 1. 706 . 2 2. 173 . 5 3. ⌊__ . __ 4. ⌊__ . __		22. MEDICAID RESUBMISSION CODE ORIGINAL REF. NO. 23. PRIOR AUTHORIZATION NUMBER YY8301

FIGURE 15-7 Completed Blocks 14 through 23 for the John Q. Public encounter form in Figure 15-3

EXERCISE 15-4 Continuation of Exercise 15-2

1. Review the Mary Sue Patient encounter form found in Figure 15-5 and locate the Diagnostic and Treatment Data.

2. Abstract the information needed for Blocks 14 through 23 and record the required information on a new claim form using Optical Scanning Guidelines. This may be completed using the disk or by handwriting or typing the data.

3. Review Blocks 14 through 23 of the claim form to be sure all required blocks are properly completed.

4. Compare your claim form with the completed form in Figure 15-12 (page 426).

■ **NOTE:** The same claim form will be used for Exercise 15-6. ■

Refer to Figure 15-8 for Block 24 of the HCFA-1500 claim form.

Block 24A Medicaid rules do not permit the billing of consecutive dates. Enter the date (MMDDYYYY) of service for each service rendered.

Block 24B Use the appropriate HCFA Place of Service (POS) code listed below.

Provider's office	11
Patient's home	12
Inpatient hospital	21
Outpatient hospital	22
Emergency department hospital	23
Ambulatory surgical center	24
Birthing center	25
Military treatment facility or	26
Uniformed service treatment facility	26
Skilled nursing facility	31
Nursing facility	32
Custodial care facility	33
Hospice	34
Ambulance—land	41
Ambulance—air or water	42
Federally-qualified health center	50
Inpatient psychiatric facility	51
Psychiatric facility—partial hospitalization	52
Community mental health center	53
Intermediate care facility/mentally retarded	54
Resident substance abuse treatment center	55
Psychiatric residential treatment center	56
Mass immunization center	60
Comprehensive inpatient rehabilitation facility	61
Comprehensive outpatient rehabilitation facility	62
End-stage renal disease treatment facility	65
State or local public health clinic	71
Rural health clinic	72
Independent laboratory	81
Other unlisted facility	99

24.	A						B	C	D		E	F	G	H	I	J	K
	DATE(S) OF SERVICE						Place of Service	Type of Service	PROCEDURES, SERVICES, OR SUPPLIES (Explain Unusual Circumstances)		DIAGNOSIS CODE	$ CHARGES	DAYS OR UNITS	EPSDT Family Plan	EMG	COB	RESERVED FOR LOCAL USE
	From			To					CPT/HCPCS	MODIFIER							
	MM	DD	YY	MM	DD	YY											
1																	
2																	
3																	
4																	
5																	
6																	

FIGURE 15-8 Block 24 of the HCFA-1500 claim form

Block 24C	Use the appropriate Type of Service (TOS) code listed below.

Medical care	1
Surgery	2
Consultation	3
Diagnostic Xray	4
Diagnostic laboratory	5
Radiation therapy	6
Anesthesia	7
Assistant surgeon	8
Other medical services	9
Pneumococcal vaccine	V
Second surgical opinion	Y

Block 24D Enter the CPT/HCPCS procedure code for the service rendered and the appropriate CPT/HCPCS modifiers.

Block 24E Enter the *one diagnosis reference number* from Block 21 that best proves the medical necessity for the service rendered.

Block 24F Enter the amount charged for the service entered in 24D.

Block 24G Enter the number of units. Units represent the number furnished in a single visit or day. Services listed on different days must be listed on separate lines in Block 24.

Block 24H Enter an "E" if the service is rendered under the Early and Periodic Screening, Diagnosis, and Treatment (EPSDT) program. Enter an "F" if the service is known to be for family planning. Enter "B" if service(s) rendered can be categorized as both EPSDT and family planning. Otherwise, leave blank.

Block 24I Enter an "X" or an "E" (depending on which is required by the Medicaid carrier) if the service was for a medical emergency, regardless of where it was rendered.

Blocks 24J & 24K Leave blank.

Refer to Figure 15-9 for completed Block 24 based on the encounter form in Figure 15-3.

24. A DATE(S) OF SERVICE						B Place of Service	C Type of Service	D PROCEDURES, SERVICES, OR SUPPLIES (Explain Unusual Circumstances)		E DIAGNOSIS CODE	F $ CHARGES		G DAYS OR UNITS	H EPSDT Family Plan	I EMG	J COB	K RESERVED FOR LOCAL USE
	From			To				CPT/HCPCS	MODIFIER								
	MM	DD	YY	MM	DD	YY												
1	01	21	YYYY				11	2	11602		2	75	00	1				
2	01	21	YYYY				11	2	12031		2	75	00	1				
3	01	21	YYYY				11	1	11403		1	50	00	1				
4																		
5																		
6																		

FIGURE 15-9 Completed Block 24 for the John Q. Public encounter form in Figure 15-3

EXERCISE 15-5 Continuation of Work on Comparison Chart

Reread the instructions for completing Blocks 24A through 24K. As you read each block, record a concise description of the instructions in the appropriate block in the Medicaid column of the Comparison Chart.

EXERCISE 15-6 Continuation of Exercise 15-2

1. Review the Procedure Data on the Mary Sue Patient encounter form in Figure 15-5.
2. Abstract the information needed for Blocks 24A through 24K and record the required information on a new claim form using Optical Scanning Guidelines. This may be completed using the disk or by handwriting or typing the data.
3. Review Blocks 24A through 24K of the claim form to be sure all required blocks are properly completed.

■ **NOTE:** This same claim form will be used for Exercise 15-8. ■

Refer to Figure 15-10 for Blocks 25 through 33 of the HCFA-1500 claim form.

Block 25

Enter the billing entity's Tax Identification Number, if available. Otherwise, enter the provider's Social Security Number. In addition, be sure to enter an "X" in the appropriate box to indicate which is being reported.

■ **NOTE:** While third-party payers will accept the number with or without hyphens, when completing claim forms in this text (and while using the CD-ROM), be sure to enter hyphens. ■

Block 26

Enter the number assigned to the patient's account if the practice uses a numerical identification number to identify the patient's account, ledger card, or if the claim is filed electronically.
Leave blank if the practice files patient accounts by patient name.

When working with case studies in this text and workbook, enter the case study number in this block. If the case requires primary and secondary forms, add the appropriate term (e.g., "primary").

Block 27

Enter an "X" in the "YES" box.

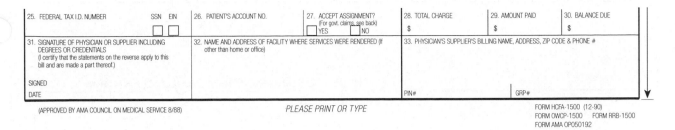

FIGURE 15-10 Blocks 25 through 33 of the HCFA-1500 claim form

Block 28

Total all charges listed on the claim form and enter the total in this block. This figure should never reflect negative charges or show a credit is due to the patient.

If multiple claims for one patient are generated by the computer because more than six services were reported, be sure the total charge entered on each claim form accurately represents the total of the items on each separate claim form submitted.

Blocks 29 and 30

Leave blank.

Block 31

PAPER CLAIMS: Most health care providers have arranged with major health insurance carriers to permit either a signature stamp to be used or a typed name and professional credential. If these special arrangements have not been made, the provider must sign each claim.

■ **NOTE:** When arrangements are made to transmit claims electronically to an insurance company, a certification letter must be filed with the insurance company to replace the signature usually required in this space. ■

When working with case studies in this text and workbook, enter the provider's full name, credential, and the date (MMDDYYYY) the claim is completed.

Block 32

Enter the name and address of the facility where services were rendered, if other than the provider's office or patient's home. Enter the Medicaid provider number on the last line of this block.

Block 33

Enter the provider's billing name, billing address, and phone number. Enter the Medicaid provider number in the lower right-hand section of the block where the word "PIN" appears.

Refer to Figure 15-11 for completed Blocks 25 through 33 for the encounter form in Figure 15-3.

EXERCISE 15-7   Completion of Work on the Medicare/Medicaid Comparison Chart

Review the instructions for completing Blocks 25 through 33. As you read each block enter a concise description of the instructions in the appropriate block in the Medicaid Primary column of the Comparison Chart.

PLEASE
DO NOT
STAPLE
IN THIS
AREA

(SAMPLE ONLY - NOT APPROVED FOR USE)

CARRIER

UNDERSTANDING HEALTH INSURANCE CLAIM FORM

1. MEDICARE MEDICAID CHAMPUS CHAMPVA GROUP HEALTH PLAN FECA BLK LUNG OTHER	1a. INSURED'S I.D. NUMBER (FOR PROGRAM IN ITEM 1)
☐ (Medicare #) ☒ (Medicaid #) ☐ (Sponsor's SSN) ☐ (VA File #) ☐ (SSN or ID) ☐ (SSN) ☐ (ID)	998119848

2. PATIENT'S NAME (Last Name, First Name, Middle Initial)	3. PATIENT'S BIRTH DATE SEX	4. INSURED'S NAME (Last Name, First Name, Middle Initial)
PUBLIC JOHN Q	MM DD YY 10 10 1959 M☐ F☐	

5. PATIENT'S ADDRESS (No. Street)	6. PATIENT RELATIONSHIP TO INSURED	7. INSURED'S ADDRESS (No. Street)
10A SENATE DRIVE	Self☐ Spouse☐ Child☐ Other☐	

CITY	STATE	8. PATIENT STATUS	CITY	STATE
ANYWHERE	US	Single☐ Married☐ Other☐		

ZIP CODE	TELEPHONE (Include Area Code)		ZIP CODE	TELEPHONE (INCLUDE AREA CODE)
12345	101 201 9871	Employed☐ Full-Time Student☐ Part-Time Student☐		( )

9. OTHER INSURED'S NAME (Last Name, First Name, Middle Initial)	10. IS PATIENT'S CONDITION RELATED TO:	11. INSURED'S POLICY GROUP OR FECA NUMBER
a. OTHER INSURED'S POLICY OR GROUP NUMBER	a. EMPLOYMENT? (CURRENT OR PREVIOUS) ☐YES ☒NO	a. INSURED'S DATE OF BIRTH MM DD YY SEX M☐ F☐
b. OTHER INSURED'S DATE OF BIRTH MM DD YY SEX M☐ F☐	b. AUTO ACCIDENT? PLACE (State) ☐YES ☒NO	b. EMPLOYER'S NAME OR SCHOOL NAME
c. EMPLOYER'S NAME OR SCHOOL NAME	c. OTHER ACCIDENT? ☐YES ☒NO	c. INSURANCE PLAN NAME OR PROGRAM NAME
d. INSURANCE PLAN NAME OR PROGRAM NAME	10d. RESERVED FOR LOCAL USE	d. IS THERE ANOTHER HEALTH BENEFIT PLAN? ☐YES ☐NO If yes, return to and complete item 9 a – d.

READ BACK OF FORM BEFORE COMPLETING & SIGNING THIS FORM.

12. PATIENT'S OR AUTHORIZED PERSON'S SIGNATURE I authorize the release of any medical or other information necessary to process this claim. I also request payment of government benefits either to myself or to the party who accepts assignment below.

SIGNED _____ DATE _____

13. INSURED'S OR AUTHORIZED PERSON'S SIGNATURE I authorize payment of medical benefits to the undersigned physician or supplier for services described below.

SIGNED _____

PATIENT AND INSURED INFORMATION

14. DATE OF CURRENT: MM DD YY ◄ ILLNESS (First symptom) OR INJURY (Accident) OR PREGNANCY (LMP)	15. IF PATIENT HAS HAD SAME OR SIMILAR ILLNESS, GIVE FIRST DATE MM DD YY	16. DATES PATIENT UNABLE TO WORK IN CURRENT OCCUPATION MM DD YY MM DD YY FROM TO

17. NAME OF REFERRING PHYSICIAN OR OTHER SOURCE	17a. I.D. NUMBER OF REFERRING PHYSICIAN	18. HOSPITALIZATION DATES RELATED TO CURRENT SERVICES MM DD YY MM DD YY FROM TO

19. RESERVED FOR LOCAL USE	20. OUTSIDE LAB? $ CHARGES
EBH8881	☐YES ☒NO

21. DIAGNOSIS OR NATURE OF ILLNESS OR INJURY. (RELATE ITEMS 1, 2, 3, OR 4 TO ITEM 24E BY LINE)

1. 706.2   3. ___.___
2. 173.5   4. ___.___

22. MEDICAID RESUBMISSION CODE   ORIGINAL REF. NO.
23. PRIOR AUTHORIZATION NUMBER YY8301

24. A. DATE(S) OF SERVICE		B. Place of Service	C. Type of Service	D. PROCEDURES, SERVICES, OR SUPPLIES (Explain Unusual Circumstances) CPT/HCPCS MODIFIER	E. DIAGNOSIS CODE	F. $ CHARGES	G. DAYS OR UNITS	H. EPSDT Family Plan	I. EMG	J. COB	K. RESERVED FOR LOCAL USE
From MM DD YY	To MM DD YY										
0121YYYY		11	2	11602	2	75 00	1				
0121YYYY		11	2	12031	2	75 00	1				
0121YYYY		11	2	11403	1	50 00	1				

25. FEDERAL TAX I.D. NUMBER SSN EIN	26. PATIENT'S ACCOUNT NO.	27. ACCEPT ASSIGNMENT? (For govt. claims, see back)	28. TOTAL CHARGE	29. AMOUNT PAID	30. BALANCE DUE
11-123341 ☐ ☒	15-1	☒YES ☐NO	$ 200 00	$	$

31. SIGNATURE OF PHYSICIAN OR SUPPLIER INCLUDING DEGREES OR CREDENTIALS (I certify that the statements on the reverse apply to this bill and are made a part thereof.) ERIN A HELPER MD SIGNED _____ DATE MMDDYYYY	32. NAME AND ADDRESS OF FACILITY WHERE SERVICES WERE RENDERED (If other than home or office)	33. PHYSICIAN'S SUPPLIER'S BILLING NAME, ADDRESS, ZIP CODE & PHONE # (101) 111 1234 ERIN A HELPER MD 101 MEDIC DRIVE ANYWHERE US 12345 PIN# EBH8881 GRP#

PHYSICIAN OR SUPPLIER INFORMATION

(SAMPLE ONLY - NOT APPROVED FOR USE)   PLEASE PRINT OR TYPE

SAMPLE FORM 1500
SAMPLE FORM 1500 SAMPLE FORM 1500

FIGURE 15-11 Completed Blocks 25 through 33 for the John Q. Public encounter form in Figure 15-3. The form is shown in its entirety with all information provided.

EXERCISE 15-8 Continuation of Exercise 15-2

Additional information you need for this case:

Dr. Helper's EIN is 11-123452. Her Medicaid provider number is EBH8881. Her NPI is 008188180. The billing entity is Erin A. Helper, M.D. She is on the medical staff and admits patients at Anywhere General Hospital, 222 Hospital Drive, in Anywhere, US.

1. Review the Mary Sue Patient encounter form found in Figure 15-5.

2. Abstract the information needed for Blocks 25 through 33 from the encounter form and the additional data provided above, and enter it on the claim form.

3. Review Blocks 25 through 33 of the three claim forms to be sure all required blocks are properly completed.

4. Compare your claim form with the completed claim form in Figure 15-12.

Additional Medicaid case studies are provided in Appendix II.

Case studies require reading the case study chart entries and abstracting and coding the diagnostic information. Necessary clinic, hospital, and physician data is included in the Clinic Billing Manual in Appendix II.

SECONDARY MEDICAID CLAIMS

These instructions are for cases when the patient is covered by a commercial or liability insurance policy. These instructions are for reference purposes; there are no case studies provided.

The instructions do not apply to Medicare-Medicaid Crossover cases which are discussed in the Medicare chapter on page 367.

These instructions are modifications of the primary Medicaid instructions.

Block 4	Enter the name of the policyholder holding the primary insurance.
Block 9d	Enter the primary ID and any group number.
Blocks 10a-10c	Enter an "X" in the appropriate boxes.
Block 11	Enter the appropriate rejection code from Table 15-1 if the patient has other third-party insurance coverage and the claim was rejected.
Block 29	Enter any payment from the primary insurer. If the other insurance denied claim, enter 0 00.
Block 30	Enter the balance due.

MOTHER/BABY CLAIMS

These instructions are for mother/baby claims and are for reference purposes; there are no case studies provided. These instructions are modifications of the primary Medicaid instructions.

Block 1a	Enter the mother's Medicaid ID number.

PLEASE
DO NOT
STAPLE
IN THIS
AREA

(SAMPLE ONLY - NOT APPROVED FOR USE)

CARRIER

UNDERSTANDING HEALTH INSURANCE FORM

1. MEDICARE	MEDICAID	CHAMPUS	CHAMPVA	GROUP HEALTH PLAN	FECA BLK LUNG	OTHER	1a. INSURED'S I.D. NUMBER (FOR PROGRAM IN ITEM 1)
☐ (Medicare #)	☒ (Medicaid #)	☐ (Sponsor's SSN)	☐ (VA File #)	☐ (SSN or ID)	☐ (SSN)	☐ (ID)	99811765

2. PATIENT'S NAME (Last Name, First Name, Middle Initial)
PATIENT MARY SUE

3. PATIENT'S BIRTH DATE
MM 10 | DD 10 | YY 1959   SEX M ☐ F ☒

4. INSURED'S NAME (Last Name, First Name, Middle Initial)

5. PATIENT'S ADDRESS (No. Street)
91 HOME STREET

6. PATIENT RELATIONSHIP TO INSURED
Self ☐ Spouse ☐ Child ☐ Other ☐

7. INSURED'S ADDRESS (No. Street)

CITY **NOWHERE**   STATE **US**

8. PATIENT STATUS
Single ☐ Married ☐ Other ☐

CITY   STATE

ZIP CODE **12367**   TELEPHONE (Include Area Code) **101 201 8989**

Employed ☐ Full-Time Student ☐ Part-Time Student ☐

ZIP CODE   TELEPHONE (INCLUDE AREA CODE) ( )

9. OTHER INSURED'S NAME (Last Name, First Name, Middle Initial)

10. IS PATIENT'S CONDITION RELATED TO:

11. INSURED'S POLICY GROUP OR FECA NUMBER

a. OTHER INSURED'S POLICY OR GROUP NUMBER

a. EMPLOYMENT? (CURRENT OR PREVIOUS)
☐ YES ☒ NO

a. INSURED'S DATE OF BIRTH
MM | DD | YY   SEX M ☐ F ☐

b. OTHER INSURED'S DATE OF BIRTH
MM | DD | YY   SEX M ☐ F ☐

b. AUTO ACCIDENT?   PLACE (State)
☐ YES ☒ NO

b. EMPLOYER'S NAME OR SCHOOL NAME

c. EMPLOYER'S NAME OR SCHOOL NAME

c. OTHER ACCIDENT?
☐ YES ☒ NO

c. INSURANCE PLAN NAME OR PROGRAM NAME

d. INSURANCE PLAN NAME OR PROGRAM NAME

10d. RESERVED FOR LOCAL USE

d. IS THERE ANOTHER HEALTH BENEFIT PLAN?
☐ YES ☐ NO   If yes, return to and complete item 9 a – d.

READ BACK OF FORM BEFORE COMPLETING & SIGNING THIS FORM.
12. PATIENT'S OR AUTHORIZED PERSON'S SIGNATURE I authorize the release of any medical or other information necessary to process this claim. I also request payment of government benefits either to myself or to the party who accepts assignment below.

SIGNED _____   DATE _____

13. INSURED'S OR AUTHORIZED PERSON'S SIGNATURE I authorize payment of medical benefits to the undersigned physician or supplier for services described below.

SIGNED _____

PATIENT AND INSURED INFORMATION

14. DATE OF CURRENT:
MM | DD | YY ◄ ILLNESS (First symptom) OR INJURY (Accident) OR PREGNANCY (LMP)

15. IF PATIENT HAS HAD SAME OR SIMILAR ILLNESS, GIVE FIRST DATE MM | DD | YY

16. DATES PATIENT UNABLE TO WORK IN CURRENT OCCUPATION
MM | DD | YY FROM   TO   MM | DD | YY

17. NAME OF REFERRING PHYSICIAN OR OTHER SOURCE

17a. I.D. NUMBER OF REFERRING PHYSICIAN

18. HOSPITALIZATION DATES RELATED TO CURRENT SERVICES
MM | DD | YY FROM   TO   MM | DD | YY

19. RESERVED FOR LOCAL USE
EBH8881

20. OUTSIDE LAB? $ CHARGES
☐ YES ☒ NO

21. DIAGNOSIS OR NATURE OF ILLNESS OR INJURY. (RELATE ITEMS 1, 2, 3, OR 4 TO ITEM 24E BY LINE)
1. **V70 0**
2. **401 9**
3. ___
4. ___

22. MEDICAID RESUBMISSION CODE   ORIGINAL REF. NO.

23. PRIOR AUTHORIZATION NUMBER
YY8345

24. A DATE(S) OF SERVICE From MM DD YY	To MM DD YY	B Place of Service	C Type of Service	D PROCEDURES, SERVICES, OR SUPPLIES (Explain Unusual Circumstances) CPT/HCPCS	MODIFIER	E DIAGNOSIS CODE	F $ CHARGES	G DAYS OR UNITS	H EPSDT Family Plan	I EMG	J COB	K RESERVED FOR LOCAL USE
1	0105YYYY		11	1	99386		1	150 00	1				
2	0105YYYY		11	1	99213	25	2	75 00	1				
3	0105YYYY		11	5	81001		2	10 00	1				
4	0105YYYY		11	1	36415		1	8 00	1				
5													
6													

25. FEDERAL TAX I.D. NUMBER   SSN ☐ EIN ☒
11-123341

26. PATIENT'S ACCOUNT NO.
15-2

27. ACCEPT ASSIGNMENT? (For govt. claims, see back)
☒ YES ☐ NO

28. TOTAL CHARGE
$ **243 00**

29. AMOUNT PAID
$

30. BALANCE DUE
$

31. SIGNATURE OF PHYSICIAN OR SUPPLIER INCLUDING DEGREES OR CREDENTIALS (I certify that the statements on the reverse apply to this bill and are made a part thereof.)
ERIN A HELPER MD
SIGNED _____   DATE **MMDDYYYY**

32. NAME AND ADDRESS OF FACILITY WHERE SERVICES WERE RENDERED (If other than home or office)

33. PHYSICIAN'S SUPPLIER'S BILLING NAME, ADDRESS, ZIP CODE & PHONE #
(101) 111 1234
ERIN A HELPER MD
101 MEDIC DRIVE
ANYWHERE US 12345
PIN# **EBH8881**   GRP#

PHYSICIAN OR SUPPLIER INFORMATION

(SAMPLE ONLY - NOT APPROVED FOR USE)

PLEASE PRINT OR TYPE

SAMPLE FORM 1500
SAMPLE FORM 1500 SAMPLE FORM 1500

FIGURE 15-12 Completed Mary Sue Patient claim for the encounter form in Figure 15-5

Block 2   Enter the mother's last name followed by the word "newborn."

> **EXAMPLE**
>
> VANDERMARK NEWBORN

Block 3   Enter the infant's date of birth.

Block 4   Enter the mother's name, followed by "MOM," as the responsible party.

> **EXAMPLE**
>
> VANDERMARK JOYCE (MOM)

Block 21   Enter secondary diagnosis codes in fields 2, 3 and/or 4.

REVIEW

DEFINITION EXERCISE

Read the definitions carefully. If the statement is true, place a check mark to the left of the number. If the statement is false, correct it without completely rewriting the sentence.

1. Medicaid: Local government program designed to help the poor with medical expenses.

2. MediCal: Title the state of California assigns to its Medicare program.

3. Medically needy: Special medical coverage to persons who have extremely high medical bills but can cover some of their other expenses.

4. Medically indigent: Special medical coverage to persons who have extremely high medical bills but can cover all routine living expenses.

5. Medical assistance: Medical coverage provided by Medicare programs.

6. SSI: Social Security Income: Government program for the aged, blind, and disabled.

CHALLENGE EXERCISE

Answer the following:

1. List and define four *distinct and separate* categories of individuals eligible for Medicaid coverage as stated in the federal guidelines.

2. List six medical services covered by federal funding for Medicaid.

3. State the range of timely filing deadlines for Medicaid claims.

4. Explain how to verify a patient's Medicaid eligibility.

5. Explain the meaning of the abbreviation AFDC.

TRICARE

16

OBJECTIVES Upon successful completion of this chapter, you should be able to:

1. Define the following terms, phrases, and abbreviations:

TRICARE

CHAMPUS

Civilian Health and Medical
Program of the Uniformed
Services

uniformed services

CHAMPUS Reform Initiative (CRI)

Lead Agent (LA)

Military Health Services System
(MHSS)

Health Affairs (HA)

TRICARE Management Activity
(TMA)

military treatment facility (MTF)

TRICARE Prime

Preferred Provider Network
(PPN)

primary care manager (PCM)

Point-of-Service option

catastrophic cap benefit

TRICARE Extra

balance billing

TRICARE Standard

deductible

cost-share

Defense Enrollment Eligibility
Reporting System (DEERS)

TRICARE Program Management
Organization (PMO)

demonstration project

TRICARE Retiree Dental Program

TRICARE Selected Reserve Dental
Program

National Mail Order Pharmacy
(NMOP)

TRICARE Retail Network
Pharmacy

Base Realignment and Closure
(BRAC) Pharmacy Benefit

TRICARE Prime Remote (TPR)

catchment area

TRICARE Senior Prime

Medicare subvention

Federal Employee Health Benefit
Program (FEHBP)

Demonstration Program for
Retirees

Pharmacy Redesign Pilot Program

TRICARE Senior Supplement
Demonstration Program
(TSSD)

Department of Defense/National
Cancer Institute (DoD/NCI)
Cancer Prevention and
Treatment Clinical Trials
Demonstration Project

clinical trial

TRICARE Service Center (TSC)

Beneficiary Services
Representative (BSR)

health care finder (HCF)

preauthorization

referral

Nurse Advisor

Beneficiary Counseling and
Assistance Coordinator (BCAC)

nonavailability statement (NAS)

emergency

computed tomography (CT) scan

computerized axial tomography
(CAT) scan

radiographic

magnetic resonance imaging
(MRI)

TRICARE contractor

fiscal intermediary (FI)

durable medical equipment
(DME)

diagnosis related group (DRG)
payment

hospice care

palliative care

respite care

individual case management

case management

same day surgery (ambulatory
surgery)

partial hospitalization

cochlear implant

Program for Persons with
Disabilities (PFPWD)

custodial care

Civilian Health and Medical
Program of the Department of
Veterans Affairs (CHAMPVA)

Other Health Insurance (OHI)

Federal Medical Care Recovery
Act of 1970

fiscal year

2. List TRICARE eligibility categories.

3. State the TRICARE definition for the phrases "medical emergency" and "urgent medical problem."

4. State the TRICARE outpatient coverage for mental health and substance abuse.

5. Explain the meaning of catastrophic coverage.

6. List six services that are not covered by TRICARE.

7. List the types of health insurance that are primary to the TRICARE program.

8. List and define the three levels of TRICARE coverage.

9. State the deductibles and cost-share responsibility for TRICARE Extra, Standard, and the Point of Service options.

10. File TRICARE Standard and Extra claims properly.

INTRODUCTION

TRICARE is a health care program for (1) active duty members of the military and their qualified family members, (2) CHAMPUS-eligible retirees and their qualified family members, and (3) eligible survivors of members of the uniformed services. **CHAMPUS** (now called TRICARE Standard) is an abbreviation for the **Civilian Health and Medical Program of the Uniformed Services**, a federal program created in 1966 (and implemented in 1967) as a benefit for dependents of personnel serving in the **uniformed services** (US military branches that include the Army, Navy, Air Force, Marines, and Coast Guard), Public Health Service, and the North Atlantic Treaty Organization (NATO). TRICARE was created to expand health care access, ensure quality of care, control health care costs, and improve medical readiness.

HISTORY OF CHAMPUS AND DEVELOPMENT OF TRICARE

CHAMPUS (now called TRICARE Standard in most of the country) was created in 1967 as the result of an initiative to provide military medical care for families of active-duty members. The original budget was $106 million, and by 1996 expenditures totaled more than $3.5 billion. In the 1980s, the Department of Defense (DoD) began researching ways to improve access to quality care while controlling costs, and demonstration projects were authorized. One demonstration project, the **CHAMPUS Reform Initiative (CRI)** carried out in California and Hawaii, offered military families a choice of how their health care benefits could be used. The DoD noted the successful operation and high levels of patient satisfaction associated with the CRI, and it was determined that its concepts should be expanded to a nationwide uniform program.

TRICARE

This new program became known as TRICARE, a regionally managed health care program that joins the health care resources of the uniformed services (e.g., Army and Navy) and supplements them with networks of civilian health care professionals to provide access and high quality service while maintaining the capability to support military operations. TRICARE is a health care program for members of the uniformed services and their families, and survivors and retired members and their families.

There are eleven TRICARE Regions in the U.S. (see Figure 16-1) plus TRICARE Europe, and TRICARE Latin America. Each is managed by a Lead Agent staff that is responsible for the military health system in that region. Commanders of selected military treatment facilities (MTFs) are selected as **Lead Agents (LA)** for the TRICARE regions. The Lead Agent staff serves as a federal health care team created to work with regional military treatment facility commanders, uniformed service headquarters' staffs, and Health Affairs (HA) to support the mission of the Military Health Services System (MHSS). The **Military Health Services System (MHSS)** is the entire health care system of the U.S. uniformed services and includes military treatment facilities (MTFs) as well as various programs in the civilian health care market, such as TRICARE. **Health Affairs (HA)** refers to the Office of the Assistant Secretary of Defense for Health Affairs, which is responsible for (1) military readiness and (2) peacetime health care.

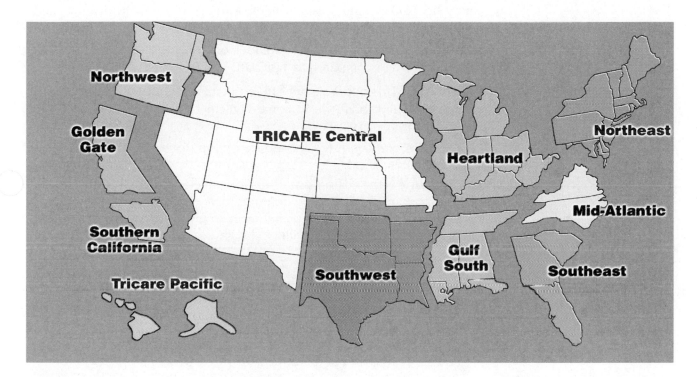

FIGURE 16-1 Map of TRICARE regions

TRICARE ADMINISTRATION

The **TRICARE Management Activity (TMA)** (formerly known as OCHAMPUS) is the office that coordinates and administers the TRICARE program and is accountable for quality health care provided to members of the uniformed services and their families. The TMA also serves as arbitrator for denied claims submitted for consideration by TRICARE beneficiaries; its offices are located in Aurora, Colorado.

■ **NOTE:** Do not submit TRICARE claims to the TMA; claims are processed by TRICARE contractors (similar to Medicare carriers and fiscal intermediaries) for different regions of the country and overseas. ■

INTERNET LINK
TRICARE manuals can be downloaded from www.tricare.osd.mil/tricaremanuals/. TRICARE fact sheets are available at www.tricare.osd.mil/factsheets/.

TRICARE OPTIONS

TRICARE offers three health care options:

1. *TRICARE Prime:* A voluntary enrollment option similar to a civilian health maintenance organization (HMO) in that a primary care manager (PCM) is assigned to each enrollee and designated military treatment facilities (MTFs) and participating providers render health care services. A **military treatment facility (MTF)** is a health care facility (e.g., military hospital or clinic) established for the purpose of furnishing medical and/or dental care to eligible individuals.

2. *TRICARE Extra:* A preferred provider organization (PPO) option that costs less when compared to TRICARE Prime and TRICARE Standard.

   ■ **NOTE:** This option is not offered in all regions because of the limited availability of PPOs in some civilian markets; instead, TRICARE Standard is available. ■

3. *TRICARE Standard:* A fee-for-service option (formerly CHAMPUS).

TRICARE Prime

TRICARE Prime is the option that offers low, fixed copayments, health care from a primary care manager, easy referrals, preventive care benefits, and no deductibles. Enrollment in TRICARE Prime also guarantees priority access to care at the Military Treatment Facilities (MTF).

Features of TRICARE Prime

- Guaranteed access to timely medical care.
- Priority for care at military treatment facilities.
- Assignment of a primary care manager.
- Lowest cost option of the three TRICARE options.
- Requires enrollment for one year.
- Retired military pay enrollment fee.
- Care sought outside of TRICARE Prime is costly.
- May be unavailable in some TRICARE regions.

TRICARE Prime Eligibility

TRICARE Prime provides comprehensive health care benefits at the lowest cost of the three options. Eligible individuals are required to enroll in TRICARE Prime so that adequate professional staffing and resources are available in military treatment facilities and supporting civilian facilities. Individuals eligible for TRICARE Prime include (1) active duty military personnel, (2) family members of active duty sponsors (no enrollment fee), and (3) retirees and their family members, all of whom are under 65. See Tables 16-1 and 16-2, which contain out-of-pocket costs for TRICARE Prime.

Table 16-1 TRICARE out-of-pocket expenses for family members of active duty military personnel

	TRICARE PRIME E1 THRU E4	TRICARE PRIME E5 AND ABOVE	TRICARE EXTRA	TRICARE STANDARD
Annual deductible	$0	$0	$50/individual or $100/family for E-4 and below $150/individual or $300/family for E-5 and above	
Civilian outpatient visit (nonmental health)	$6	$12	15% of negotiated fee	20% of allowable charges
Civilian outpatient visit (mental health)	$10	$20		
Civilian mental health group therapy visits	$6	$12		
Civilian inpatient visit	$11 per day ($25 minimum)	$11 per day ($25 minimum)	Greater of $25 or $10.85 per day	Greater of $25 or $10.85 per day
Civilian inpatient mental health	$25 per admission or $20 per day	$25 per admission or $20 per day	$20 per admission or $20 per day	$20 per admission or $20 per day

(Reprinted according to Security and Provide Notice at www.tricare.osd.mil/main/privacy.html)

Table 16-2 TRICARE out-of-pocket expenses for retirees and their family members

	TRICARE PRIME	TRICARE EXTRA	TRICARE STANDARD
Annual deductible	$0	$150 individual $300 family	$150 Individual $300 family
Annual enrollment fees	$230 individual/ $460 family	$0	$0
Civilian Provider Copays			
Outpatient visit	$12	20% of negotiated fees	25% of allowed charges
Emergency care	$30	20% of negotiated fees	25% of allowed charges
Mental health visit	$25	20% of negotiated fees	25% of allowed charges
Mental health visit (family or group therapy)	$17	20% of negotiated fees	25% of allowed charges
Civilian inpatient cost share (nonmental health)	$11 per day ($25 minimum)	Lesser of $250/day or 25% of billed charges plus 20% of negotiated professional fees	Lesser of $390/day or 25% of billed charges plus 25% of allowed professional charges
Civilian inpatient mental health	$40 per day $40 per day	20% of institutional and professional charges	Lesser of $144 per day or 25% of institutional and professional charges

(Reprinted according to Security and Provide Notice at www.tricare.osd.mil/main/privacy.html)

TRICARE Prime Coverage

TRICARE Prime health care services have been compared to civilian health maintenance organizations (HMOs) because services are provided by designated military treatment facilities and contracted **Preferred Provider Networks (PPNs)** (groups of civilian practitioners organized by TRICARE contractors to supplement military direct care). In addition, a primary care manager (PCM) is assigned to each enrollee. A **primary care manager (PCM)** is a doctor or medical clinic that is part of the TRICARE provider network. The PCM guides TRICARE Prime members through the health care system and coordinates all specialty medical needs. Prime members can choose a PCM from the Military Treatment Facility or the TRICARE Provider Directory. Note that certain TRICARE regions only allow a military doctor or medical clinic to serve as a PCM.

The PCM provides nonemergency care to eligible beneficiaries and arranges referrals for specialty care if needed, usually through a military hospital. If military specialty care is unavailable, the PCM authorizes care from a civilian specialist. For beneficiaries to receive coverage for specialty care, the PCM must make these arrangements. TRICARE Prime guarantees enrollees access to care, and urgent care is rendered within one day while less urgent care is provided within one week. In addition, beneficiaries should not be required to travel more than 30 minutes to see the PCM. Preventive care is emphasized, and the following services are provided at no additional charge: eye exams, immunizations, hearing screenings, mammograms, pap smears, prostate exams, and other cancer-prevention and early diagnosis exams.

TRICARE Prime covers nonemergency care if the beneficiary is away from home and receives prior approval from the PCM. Such authorization is required for all routine medical care provided out of the area or at another facility. If the beneficiary seeks medical care without prior approval, the **Point-of-Service option** is activated, requiring payment of a $300 annual deductible for an individual enrollee or $600 per family, plus 50% or more of visit or treatment fees.

Beneficiaries who require emergency care should seek that care at the nearest civilian or military treatment facility.

Catastrophic Cap Benefit

The **catastrophic cap benefit** protects TRICARE beneficiaries from devastating financial loss due to serious illness or long-term treatment by establishing limits over which payment is not required. Under TRICARE Prime, the maximum out-of-pocket cost per year for covered medical services is $1,000 for active duty family members and $3,000 for retirees and their families per enrollment year.

TRICARE Extra

TRICARE Extra allows TRICARE Standard users to save 5% of their TRICARE Standard cost-shares by using health care providers in the TRICARE network. No enrollment is required to be covered by TRICARE Extra; enrollees simply go to any network doctor, hospital, or other provider and show a military ID card. Care is also available at the Military Treatment Facility on a space-available basis.

Features of TRICARE Extra

- Choice of any physician in the network.
- Less costly than TRICARE Standard.
- May be more expensive than TRICARE Prime.
- Annual enrollment is not required.
- Lower priority for care provided at military treatment facilities.

TRICARE Extra Eligibility

Unlike for TRICARE Prime, individuals eligible for TRICARE Extra do not have to enroll or pay an enrollment fee. They can use the option whenever they choose by selecting any health care provider from within the TRICARE Extra provider network. When a TRICARE Extra network provider renders care, it's just like using TRICARE Standard (formerly CHAMPUS), with the bonus of a 5% discount on most cost-shares.

TRICARE Extra offers enrollees the choice of receiving health care services from participating civilian hospitals, physicians, and other medical providers who have agreed to charge an approved fee for medical treatment and procedures. Two groups that usually prefer TRICARE Extra include (1) individuals and families whose regular physician is a participating member of the TRICARE Extra network, and (2) individuals who do not have convenient access to military treatment facilities who want reduced health care costs as compared with TRICARE Standard.

Those eligible for TRICARE Extra coverage include: (1) family members of active duty sponsors (no enrollment fee), and (2) retirees (except most Medicare-eligible beneficiaries) and their family members under 65.

■ **NOTE:** All active duty members are enrolled in TRICARE Prime and are not eligible for TRICARE Extra. ■

TRICARE Extra Coverage

Individuals eligible to enroll in TRICARE Extra are not required to pay an annual fee, can seek care from a network provider, receive a discount on services, and usually pay reduced copayments (5% less than TRICARE Standard; participating providers are reimbursed the approved rate plus 5%). In addition, network providers file insurance claims for enrollees and are prohibited from balance billing. **Balance billing** refers to the practice of a provider billing a patient for all charges not reimbursed by a health plan.

TRICARE Extra enrollees can also seek health care services from a military treatment facility (MTF) on a space-available basis, and they can select between TRICARE Extra and TRICARE Standard options on a visit-by-visit basis. Tables 16-1 and 16-2 contain out-of-pocket costs for TRICARE Extra.

Catastrophic Cap Benefit

Under TRICARE Extra, active duty family members are responsible for up to $1,000 and retirees for up to $7,500 per year in out-of-pocket costs for covered services.

TRICARE Standard **TRICARE Standard** is the basic TRICARE health care program. To use this option, enrollees either make an appointment at a military treatment facility (MTF) or seek care from any TRICARE-certified civilian health care provider (fee-for-service option). Enrollees are responsible for annual deductibles and cost-shares. A **deductible** is the amount the member pays each year toward outpatient care before TRICARE begins sharing the cost of medical care. **Cost-share** is the percentage the member pays (e.g., copayment) along with the part TRICARE pays of the allowable charges for care submitted on each claim. The cost-share is paid in addition to the annual deductible, and the amount is determined by the sponsor's status (active vs. retired military). TRICARE Standard was formerly called the Civilian Health and Medical Program of the Uniformed Services, or CHAMPUS. It provides beneficiaries with the greatest freedom in selecting civilian providers; however, it has the highest out-of-pocket costs of the three plans. There is no enrollment requirement for TRICARE Standard; however, as with the other TRICARE options, prospective enrollees must be listed as eligible in the **Defense Enrollment Eligibility Reporting System (DEERS)**, the Department of Defense's computerized database that contains information about active and retired military sponsors and all family members eligible for military health care benefits.

Features of TRICARE Standard

- Greatest flexibility in selecting health care providers.
- Most convenient when traveling or away from home.
- Potentially most expensive of all options.
- Enrollment not required.
- Space-available care in military treatment facilities is a provision (low priority is assigned to TRICARE Standard enrollees).

TRICARE Standard Eligibility

Individuals eligible for TRICARE Standard include:

- Eligible family members of active duty service members.
- Military retirees and their eligible family members.
- Surviving eligible family members of deceased active or retired service members.
- Medicare-eligible retirees who are under age 65 and enrolled in Part B.
- Wards and preadoptive children, and some former spouses of active or retired service members who meet certain length-of-marriage rules and other requirements.
- Eligible family members of active duty service members who were court-martialed and separated for spouse or child abuse.
- Certain abused spouses, former spouses, or dependent children of service members who were retirement-eligible but lost that eligibility as a result of abuse of spouse or child.
- Spouses and children of North Atlantic Treaty Organization (NATO) and "Partners for Peace" (PFP) nation representatives. (NATO and PFP family members are not eligible to enroll in TRICARE Prime).
- Husbands, wives, and unmarried children of reservists who are ordered to active duty for more than 30 consecutive days (they are covered only during the reservist's active duty tour) or of reservists who die on active duty.
- Husbands, wives, and unmarried children of reservists who are injured or aggravate an injury, illness, or disease during, or on the way to, active duty training for a period of 30 days or less, or a period of inactive duty training, and who die as a result of the specific injuries, illnesses, or diseases.
- Former spouses of active or retired military who were married to a service member or former member who had performed at least 20 years of creditable service for retirement purposes at the time the divorce or annulment occurred.

TRICARE Standard Coverage

Annual deductibles, cost-shares, and benefits are the same as they were for CHAMPUS. Under TRICARE Standard, enrollees can select their health care provider; however, out-of-pocket costs are higher when compared with other TRICARE options.

Also, enrollees who seek care from nonparticipating providers may have to file their own claim forms and, perhaps, pay more for care (up to 15% more than the allowable charge). Participating providers accept the TRICARE Standard allowable charge as payment in full for care rendered and they will file insurance claims for enrollees.

■ **NOTE:** TRICARE Standard does not enroll participating providers; they participate voluntarily, and may do so on a case-by-case basis. When using TRICARE Standard, enrollees should ask the selected provider whether they participate in TRICARE Standard. ■

Catastrophic Cap Benefit

Under TRICARE Standard, active duty family members are responsible for up to $1,000 and retirees for up to $7,500 per year in out-of-pocket costs for covered services.

TRICARE PROGRAMS AND DEMONSTRATION PROJECTS

The **TRICARE Program Management Organization (PMO)** manages TRICARE programs and demonstration projects. A **demonstration project** tests and establishes the feasibility of implementing a new program during a trial period, after which the program is evaluated, modified, and/or abandoned. If, upon evaluation, it is determined that program implementation criteria are met (e.g., cost-effectiveness and meets intended needs of a population), the demonstration project is approved as a program, and enrollment is expanded to include all eligible individuals.

TRICARE programs include:

- Dental programs.
- Pharmacy options.
- TRICARE Prime Remote (TPR).
- TRICARE Overseas.

TRICARE demonstration projects include:

- TRICARE Senior Prime.
- FEHBP Demonstration Program for Retirees.
- Pharmacy Redesign Pilot Program.
- TRICARE Senior Supplement Demonstration Program.
- Department of Defense/National Cancer Institute (DoD/NCI) Cancer Prevention and Treatment Clinical Trials Demonstration Project.

TRICARE Programs ### Dental Programs

The **TRICARE Retiree Dental Program** was established to provide dental care coverage for uniformed service retirees, certain surviving spouses, and their family members. The Federal Services division of Delta Dental Plan of California administers this voluntary dental plan.

The **TRICARE Selected Reserve Dental Program** provided dental care coverage for uniformed service, National Guard, and Reserve personnel who were also members of the Selected Reserve. This program was combined with the TRICARE Family Member Dental Plan in 2001 to create the TRICARE Dental Program (TDP).

INTERNET LINK

For DeltaSelect USA TRICARE Retiree Dental Program eligibility and coverage details, visit www.ddpdelta.org/.

Pharmacy Options

Individuals registered in the Defense Enrollment Eligibility Reporting System (DEERS) can obtain up to a 90-day supply of prescribed medications, at no cost, from any military treatment facility (MTF) pharmacy.

The **National Mail Order Pharmacy (NMOP)** program allows enrollees to receive a 90-day supply of non-narcotic medications or a 30-day supply of narcotic medications mailed to the enrollee's permanent or temporary home address. This service is free for all active duty members and $4.00 (per prescription) for their family members. All others must pay $8.00 per prescription.

The **TRICARE Retail Network Pharmacy** provides discount prescription drugs to enrollees and is a member of a network of civilian pharmacies established as part of the TRICARE Prime and TRICARE Extra options.

The **Base Realignment and Closure (BRAC) Pharmacy Benefit** is available to Medicare-eligible beneficiaries and their eligible family members who had been using pharmacies at bases closed under BRAC. Beneficiaries can obtain prescription medications from TRICARE network retail pharmacies or from the National Mail Order Pharmacy Program (NMOP).

TRICARE Prime Remote (TPR)

TRICARE Prime Remote (TPR) was initiated in October 1999 to provide benefits (similar to TRICARE Prime) to active duty service members who reside and work outside of a military treatment facility (MTF) **catchment area** (region defined by code boundaries within a 40-mile radius of an MTF). Active duty service members under full-time orders qualify for this program if located more than 50 miles, or a one-hour drive, from an MTF. Family members of TRICARE Prime Remote beneficiaries are not currently eligible for this program. To improve access to health care, TRICARE Prime Remote is being expanded to include family members of beneficiaries and to eliminate copays for active duty family members.

TRICARE Overseas

Active duty military families who live overseas can choose either TRICARE Prime or TRICARE Standard. Military retirees and their families who live overseas can not enroll in TRICARE Prime, but they can use TRICARE Standard.

Under TRICARE Prime, active duty, eligible families who live overseas must enroll as they would stateside. Active duty families pay no enrollment fees, cost-shares, or deductibles while overseas. TRICARE Prime enrollees have access to military treatment facilities and to networks of local civilian providers; primary care managers (PCMs) provide most of the care. When necessary, enrollees will have access to specialized care as recommended by the PCM. If an overseas family member enrolled in TRICARE Prime uses a non-network provider without getting advance authorization, point-of-service copays and deductibles will apply.

Overseas TRICARE Prime enrollees who receive civilian care while traveling in the U.S. are responsible for cost-shares, while advance authorization for urgent or emergency care is unnecessary. In addition, enrollees have the same priority for available appointments at military medical facilities as TRICARE Prime enrollees who live near these facilities.

TRICARE Standard is available to overseas families who choose not to enroll in TRICARE Prime, and the benefits and procedures are the same as in the U.S.

TRICARE Demonstration Projects

TRICARE Senior Prime

TRICARE Senior Prime is a managed care demonstration project designed to better serve the medical needs of military retirees, dependents, and survivors who are age 65 and over. It is also referred to as **Medicare subvention** because the program provides a financial benefit to enrollees in the form of expanded health care coverage. TRICARE Senior Prime is offered at selected sites across the country, and provides enrollees with all of the benefits available under Medicare, plus additional benefits under TRICARE Prime that are currently offered to eligible retired military beneficiaries under age 65. To be eligible for TRICARE Prime Senior, an individual must:

- Be eligible for Medicare and for care within a military treatment facility.
- Be age 65 or older.
- Have received services at a military hospital or clinic as a dual-eligible beneficiary prior to July 1, 1997, or have become eligible for Medicare on or after July 1, 1997.
- Live in a participating military treatment facility's service area.
- Agree to obtain covered services only through TRICARE Senior Prime.
- Have both Medicare Part A and Part B coverage.

The benefits of enrolling in TRICARE Senior Prime include:

- Expanded access to health care services.
- Provisions for preventive health care services.
- Access to a national mail order pharmacy.
- Use of a primary care manager (PCM).
- Reduced out-of-pocket costs.
- Access to a provider network.
- Access to a 24-hour health care information line.
- 24-hour assistance in arranging appointments.

FEHBP Demonstration Program for Retirees

In January 2000, the Department of Defense began a three-year **Federal Employee Health Benefit Program (FEHBP) Demonstration Program**

for Retirees in which uniformed services retirees and their families in select-ed areas enrolled and received health care. Eligible requirements for enroll-ment include:

- Medicare-eligible military retirees and their family members.
- Family members of deceased active or retired military members.
- Certain un-remarried former spouses of military service members or former members.

■ **NOTE:** Persons who enroll in the FEHBP demonstration may *not* use mil-itary medical facilities, TRICARE benefits, or pharmacy services. ■

Pharmacy Redesign Pilot Program

Individuals eligible for the **Pharmacy Redesign Pilot Program** include:

- Members or former members of the uniformed services.
- Dependents of a member or former member of the uniformed services.
- Dependents of a member of the uniformed services who died while on active duty for a period of more than 30 days and who are (a) age 65 or older, (b) entitled to Medicare Part A benefits (c) enrolled in Medicare Part B, and (d) residents in a pilot area.

The benefit for Pharmacy Redesign Pilot Program enrollees is equiva-lent to the TRICARE Extra pharmacy benefit, which includes access to MTF pharmacies (free prescriptions are filled for medications carried by the MTF), TRICARE Retail Network Pharmacies, and the National Mail Order Pharmacy Program. A $200 enrollment fee plus applicable copayments is also required.

TRICARE Senior Supplement Demonstration Program

The **TRICARE Senior Supplement Demonstration Program (TSSD)** offers affordable coverage, secondary to Medicare, and includes a pharmacy benefit for enrollees. Eligible persons include retired members of the uni-formed services, their family members, and surviving family members of deceased uniformed service members who died while on active duty for a period of more than 30 consecutive days. Enrollees must also be age 65 or older, eligible for Medicare Part A, enrolled in Medicare Part B, and must live within one of the demonstration sites. TSSD offers benefits similar to TRI-CARE Extra and TRICARE Standard, which include access to the National Mail Order Pharmacy, use of TRICARE retail network pharmacies, coverage for certain diagnostic and preventive services, extended mental health coverage, and coverage for health care services delivered outside the continental U.S. Enrollment cost is $576 per person, per year, and annual deductibles and copays are required.

DoD/NCI Cancer Clinical Trials Demonstration Project

The **Department of Defense/National Cancer Institute (DoD/NCI) Cancer Prevention and Treatment Clinical Trials Demonstration Project** offers TRICARE beneficiaries the latest in cancer preventive care and treatment. **Clinical trials** are research studies that help find ways to prevent, diagnose, or treat illnesses and improve health care. The Department of Defense (DoD) joined forces with the National Cancer Institute (NCI) through an interagency agreement, known as the DoD/NCI Cancer Clinical

Trials Demonstration Project. Under this agreement, beneficiaries can participate in NCI-sponsored cancer prevention and treatment studies as part of their TRICARE health care benefits. Clinical trials can offer people at risk for cancer and people diagnosed with cancer some of the most promising advances in cancer research. For some TRICARE beneficiaries with cancer, the DoD/NCI Clinical Trials project offers choices when few treatment options exist.

The DoD/NCI Cancer Clinical Trials Demonstration Project was expanded in 1999 to include cancer prevention strategies, which permits eligible patients who meet clinical criteria to participate in NCI-sponsored Phase II and Phase III clinical trials in cancer prevention, in addition to cancer treatment.

TRICARE SERVICE CENTERS

TRICARE regions are served by one or more **TRICARE Service Centers (TSC)** that are business offices staffed by one or more Beneficiary Services Representatives and health care finders who assist with health care needs and answer questions about the TRICARE program. A Beneficiary Service Office offers the same assistance as a TRICARE Service Center, but there are no health care finders onsite.

Beneficiary Services Representatives

Beneficiary Services Representatives (BSRs) are employed at TRICARE Service Centers, and provide information about using the three TRICARE options. They also assist with other matters affecting access to health care, including appointment scheduling.

Health Care Finders

A **health care finder (HCF)** is a registered nurse or physician's assistant who assists primary care managers with preauthorizations and referrals to health care services in the military treatment facility or the civilian provider network. A **preauthorization** is formal approval obtained from a health care finder before certain specialty procedures and inpatient care are rendered. A **referral** is a request for a member to receive treatment from another provider.

Nurse Advisors

In most TRICARE regions, **Nurse Advisors** are available 24 hours per day, 7 days per week for advice and assistance with treatment alternatives and to discuss whether an enrollee should see a provider based on a discussion of symptoms. Nurse advisors will also discuss preventative care and ways to improve a family's health.

BENEFICIARY COUNSELING AND ASSISTANCE COORDINATOR

Beneficiary Counseling and Assistance Coordinators (BCACs) are located at every Lead Agent office and at every MTF worldwide. BCACs serve as the beneficiary advocate and problem solver. They interface with MTF staff, managed care support contractors, and claims processors to resolve beneficiary concerns and questions regarding the TRICARE program. BCACs have been known as health benefits advisors, patient advocates, or ombudsmen at MTFs for many years. To create uniformity, those titles will change to BCAC.

TRICARE PREAUTHORIZATION

A **nonavailability statement (NAS)** is a certificate issued by an MTF that states it cannot provide needed care. TRICARE Prime members must obtain an NAS before TRICARE Prime will cost-share medical expenses for services delivered by civilian providers. For members who reside outside a catchment area, the primary care manager must obtain preauthorization from the health care finder for hospitalization, except in an emergency.

TRICARE Extra members must obtain an NAS if they reside in the catchment area of a military treatment facility with inpatient capability and for certain procedures that require an NAS.

Nonavailability statements are not obtained for emergency hospital admissions or when members have other primary health insurance. TRICARE defines an **emergency** as the sudden and unexpected onset of a medical or mental health condition that is threatening to life, limb, or sight.

COVERED SERVICES—TRICARE STANDARD

Generally, TRICARE Standard covers most health care that is medically necessary. However, special rules or limits may apply to certain types of care, and other types of care are not covered at all. A summary of special benefits and limits on the provision of certain health care services follows.

Special Benefits and Certain Limits

Ambulance Services

TRICARE Standard will cost-share ambulance services when medically necessary (e.g., patient's condition does not allow use of private transportation and ambulance service is necessary for a TRICARE Standard covered medical condition). Ambulance service coverage includes the cost for transfer between any two points determined to be medically necessary for the covered medical condition (e.g., hospitals).

■ **NOTE:** If the military treatment facility (MTF) orders ambulance services, the MTF must pay. ■

Cardiac Rehabilitation Services

Inpatient and outpatient cardiac rehabilitation services are covered; however, services and supplies must be provided by TRICARE network hospitals and ordered by physicians as treatment for patients who have experienced certain conditions during the 12 months prior to services being rendered.

CT Scans and Magnetic Resonance Imaging (MRI) Procedures

Computed tomography (CT) or **computerized axial tomography (CAT) scans** gather anatomical information from the body and the **radiographic** (Xray) data is presented as a likeness generated by a computer. CT scans are cost-shared by TRICARE Standard if the provider has first ordered other diagnostic tests that provide the desired medical information and are less expensive and noninvasive (no instruments or foreign materials are inserted or injected into the body). If the CT scan is considered the most appropriate diagnostic test, TRICARE will cost-share without the other tests having been performed. **Magnetic resonance imaging (MRI)** uses nuclear magnetic resonance technology where the patient is placed in a magnetic field and high quality images of cross-sections of the body are produced to identify internal abnormalities and diseases. TRICARE Standard cost-sharing of MRI procedures is limited to medically necessary and appropriate use of the procedure on soft tissue areas within the body. TRICARE Standard will not cost-share MRI procedures for pregnant women or acutely ill patients on certain types of life-support systems.

Dental Care Services

TRICARE Standard covers dental care services only when such care is a medically necessary part of treatment that is covered by TRICARE Standard. In addition, preauthorization from the TRICARE contractor is required before care is rendered.

■ **NOTE:** Oral surgery does not need preauthorization. ■

A **TRICARE contractor**, or **fiscal intermediary (FI)**, processes TRICARE claims for services rendered within a particular state or region.

In 1998, the TRICARE Retiree Dental Program (a program paid for, in total, by enrollees) was implemented for retired military members, eligible family members, and nonremarried surviving spouses of deceased military retirees (no age limits on eligibility). The program features a variety of services at specified levels of cost-sharing.

In February 2001, two dental programs combined to provide improved coverage for military sponsors and their families: TRICARE Selected Reserve Dental Plan and the TRICARE Family Member Dental Plan (for active duty families). The new plan is known as the TRICARE Dental Program (TDP).

Durable Medical Equipment (DME)

Durable medical equipment (DME) includes wheelchairs, hospital beds, respirators, and so on; they are cost-shared with TRICARE Standard. DME can be rented, leased, or purchased (whichever method is least expensive), and a provider's order specifying the type of equipment needed, reason for the equipment, and length of time needed must be submitted with the claim.

Eye Examinations

One annual screening eye examination per person performed by an ophthalmologist or optometrist is authorized for active duty families only. In addition, eye exams related to a covered medical condition (e.g., eye injury) are authorized for TRICARE Standard members.

Family Planning Services, Genetic Testing, and Maternity Care

TRICARE Standard covers:

- Certain family planning services (e.g., infertility diagnosis and treatment; however, the active duty sponsor is not covered).
- Genetic tests for unborn children (certain criteria apply to the pregnant woman).
- Maternity care (except if an active duty member is discharged from the service while his wife is pregnant).
- Inpatient delivery.

- Certain inpatient maternity care based on **diagnosis related group (DRG) payment** (a pre-established reimbursement amount based on documented diagnoses and procedures.

  ■ **NOTE:** Remember that separate claims must be submitted for mother and infant. ■

- Hospital birthing rooms or centers (TRICARE Standard will cost-share the delivery and maternity care).

- Outpatient deliveries and maternity care; home delivery if a certified nurse midwife provides services.

  ■ **NOTE:** Be sure to determine whether the military treatment facility in your catchment area provides maternity and delivery services because if a patient should have to be admitted to a civilian hospital for maternity and/or delivery care, she will need to submit a non-availability statement to TRICARE Standard so cost-sharing of maternity care costs can occur. ■

- Approved freestanding birthing centers that participate in TRICARE Standard.

- Ambulance services related to maternity care.

- Routine newborn care.

  ■ **NOTE:** Separate claims are submitted after the first three days of care; also be sure the baby is enrolled in DEERS. ■

- Well baby and well child care for children under age six (previously limited to children up to age two).

- Immunizations for children age six and older.

Hospice Care Services

TRICARE Standard covers the cost of hospice care provided to terminally ill patients who are expected to live less than six months if the illness runs its normal course. **Hospice care** is defined as the provision of compassionate and supportive services and includes **palliative care** (relief, such as pain medication, with no attempt to prolong life). There are no limits on custodial care and personal comfort items under hospice care rules as compared with other types of care. TRICARE Standard pays the full cost of covered hospice care services, except for cost-shares collected for medications and inpatient **respite care** (patient stays overnight for a period of 2-3 days in the hospice or on the hospice unit of a military treatment facility to provide a break in care for primary caregivers who reside with the patient).

Individual Case Management

Since 1999, an **individual case management** benefit has been available that allows TRICARE-eligible persons with extraordinary medical or psychological disorders to receive health care benefits that would normally be limited or not covered. Individual case management is intended to address the complex health care needs of catastrophically ill or injured persons, and serves as a "bridge" between acute care and long-term care services.

■ **NOTE:** Individual case management differs from **case management**, which occurs when TRICARE benefits are monitored and coordinated to meet the individual's health needs. ■

Mammograms and Pap Smears

Routine mammograms and pap smears are covered as diagnostic or preventive health care measures. Certain rules regarding how often the procedures can be performed, and who may perform the services, apply.

Medical Equipment and Supplies

To obtain reimbursement for medical supplies (e.g., needles and syringes) as well as medical equipment that costs less than $100 (e.g., crutches), a provider's prescription must be submitted with the claim. (Durable medical equipment worth more than $100 also needs a prescription, and is discussed under the Durable Medical Equipment heading earlier in this chapter).

Mental Health Care

TRICARE Standard helps pay for inpatient and outpatient psychotherapy (including residential treatment center care), and the number of sessions per week are limited (e.g., five inpatient psychotherapy sessions per a week or two outpatient psychotherapy sessions per week). If additional sessions are needed, a TRICARE contractor will review the medical necessity for the care. In addition, if more than eight outpatient psychotherapy sessions in a fiscal year are needed, preauthorization is required from the regional TRICARE contractor.

■ **NOTE:** Psychotherapy sessions are allowed only for treatment of mental disorders (e.g., depression), not for issues such as marital problems. ■

Obesity Treatment

TRICARE Standard coverage is limited to surgical treatment for obesity (gastric bypass, gastric stapling, and gastroplasty, including "vertical banded" gastroplasty) when certain criteria are met (e.g., at least 100 pounds over the ideal weight for height and body structure).

Organ Transplants

TRICARE Standard covers the following organ transplants: cornea, kidney, liver, liver-kidney, heart, lung, heart-lung, small intestine, small intestine-liver, pancreas-kidney, and some bone marrow. There are limits associated with some circumstances (e.g., bone marrow transplants are not covered for treatment of ovarian cancer).

Plastic or Reconstructive Surgery

TRICARE Standard cost-shares plastic or reconstructive surgery for:

- Correction of a serious birth defect (e.g., cleft lip).
- Restoration of body form or function after an accidental injury.
- Improvement in appearance after severe disfiguration or extensive scarring from cancer surgery.
- Reconstruction of the breast after a mastectomy.
- Constructive breast surgery if a medical condition of the breast has existed since birth or was caused by an accident.
- Reduction of the breast under limited circumstances (e.g., intractable pain that does not respond to other treatments).

Private Duty or Visiting Nurses

TRICARE Standard carries limited coverage for private duty, skilled nursing care, in the hospital or at home, that only a professional can provide (e.g., administering certain medications, treatment or therapy). Claims being submitted for reimbursement must include a copy of all nurses' notes along with the name of the provider who ordered the care and the fact that the care is being supervised by the provider. In addition, a copy of the provider's treatment plan must accompany the first TRICARE Standard claim submitted.

Same Day (or Ambulatory) Surgery

Same day surgery (ambulatory surgery) is performed in ambulatory surgery centers, hospitals, or special centers; the operation is performed and the patient is sent home the same day. TRICARE enrollees should check with a Health Benefits Advisor (HBA), Beneficiary Counseling and Assistance Coordinator (BCAC), TRICARE Service Center (TSC), or regional TRICARE contractor, to determine if preauthorization is required before scheduling surgery.

Substance Abuse Treatment

Treatment for alcoholism or the abuse of other substances is considered mental health treatment by TRICARE Standard and is subject to the same preauthorization requirements as mental health care. Alcoholism (or other substance use disorder) treatment includes inpatient hospital and rehabilitation care (including **partial hospitalization**, which involves the patient spending a minimum of three hours on-site at the treatment facility, five days per week, including weekends and/or evenings; the patient then goes home overnight), outpatient for alcoholism or other substance abuse disorders (including outpatient rehabilitation), and family therapy.

Surgical Implants

Surgical implants are covered if approved by the Food and Drug Administration:

- Intraocular lenses, implanted in the eye after cataract surgery.
- **Cochlear implants**, electronic instruments surgically implanted in the ear to assist in hearing.
- Breast implants, for reconstructive surgery following surgical removal of the breast.
- Penile implants, inserted to correct malformation of the male sex organ which has existed since birth, to correct organic impotency, or to correct what the medical profession calls "ambiguous" reproductive organs.

Wigs for Radiation and Chemotherapy Treatment Patients

For patients who suffer hair loss due to cancer treatment, TRICARE Standard will cost-share one wig or hairpiece during a person's lifetime. TRICARE Standard will not cost-share a wig if the enrollee has previously obtained one through the Department of Veterans Affairs (formerly known as the Veterans Administration) or a uniformed service military treatment facility.

PROGRAM FOR PERSONS WITH DISABILITIES

The **Program for Persons with Disabilities (PFPWD)** is a financial assistance program for active duty dependents with severe physical disabilities or moderate-to-severe mental retardation who cannot obtain specialized training or care through public resources. Active duty family members receive benefits from TRICARE and PFPWD at the same time. The program is offered concurrently with any of the three TRICARE options (Prime, Extra, and Standard) and authorization for PFPWD benefits does not affect enrollment in TRICARE Prime.

A cost-share is required of PFPWD participants; however, the beneficiary's cost-share is reduced if multiple children participate in the program so that the family is responsible only for the cost-share of one child. The government pays the total cost of additional children. In addition, cost-share is prorated by military pay grade (e.g., E1 through E5). Authorized PFPWD benefits include:

- Durable medical equipment (DME).
- Diagnostic services.
- Rehabilitation.
- Training and special education.
- Institutional care.
- Transportation (medically necessary).
- Hearing aids.
- Exclusions.
- Custodial care.
- Dental care.
- Camping, field trips, etc.
- Alterations to living spaces and vehicles.

NONCOVERED SERVICES—TRICARE

The following services are *not* usually covered by TRICARE:

- Abortions (except when the mother's life is in danger).
- Acupuncture.
- Artificial insemination (or any form of artificial conception).
- Autopsy services or post mortem examination.
- Birth control (nonprescription).
- Bone marrow transplants for treatment of ovarian cancer.
- Camps for diabetics or obese individuals.
- Care or supplies furnished or prescribed by a person in the immediate family.
- Chiropractic and naturopathic services.
- Christian Science absent treatment (treatment through prayer and spiritual means; the patient is not present).
- Chronic fatigue syndrome (CFS) because there are no generally accepted standards for treatment and existing treatments have not

been consistently shown to be effective; legitimate treatment is limited to relieving symptoms (e.g., prescribing medications for headaches or muscle pain).

- Cosmetic, plastic, or reconstructive surgery, except as described in the Plastic or Reconstructive Surgery section discussed earlier in this chapter.

- Counseling services: nutritional, diabetic self-help, diabetic self-education programs, stress management, life-style modifications, and marriage counseling (marriage counseling isn't the same as treatment by a marriage and family therapist, which is covered under TRICARE Standard).

- Custodial care in an institution or home. **Custodial care** involves caring for daily needs (e.g., eating and dressing) as opposed to caring for medical needs.

- Dental care and dental Xrays, except as provided in the dental care section discussed earlier in this chapter.

- Education or training, except under the Program for Persons with Disabilities.

- Electrolysis.

- Experimental procedures (also called "unproven" procedures).

- Eyeglasses and contact lenses, except under very limited circumstances (e.g., corneal lens removal).

- Food, food substitutes or supplements, or vitamins provided outside of a hospital, except for home parenteral nutrition therapy, such as prescribed for cancer patients.

- Foot care, except when a medical problem or injury is diagnosed.

- Genetic tests not ordered by a provider.

- Hearing aids, except under the Program for Persons with Disabilities.

- Hearing examinations, unless in connection with surgery or a medical problem, or under the Program for Persons with Disabilities.

- Megavitamins and orthomolecular psychiatric therapy.

- Mind expansion or elective psychotherapy (e.g., Erhard Seminar Training (EST), transcendental meditation and Z-therapy).

- Orthodontia, except in limited cases, such as when related to the surgical correction of a cleft palate.

- Orthopedic shoes and arch supports, except when part of a brace.

- Over-the-counter drugs (those not requiring a prescription by a provider).

- Private hospital rooms, unless ordered by the provider for medical reasons or a semi-private room is not available.

- Rest cure.

- Retirement homes.

- Self-help courses and relaxation therapy.

- Sex change procedures.

- Speech therapy, except when related to a specific illness or injury.

- Sexual inadequacy treatment (the prescription medication, Viagra, is covered, within certain limits, if determined by the provider to be medically necessary for treatment of a TRICARE-covered medical problem).

- Surgical sterilization reversals.
- Telephone services or advice (except in TRICARE regions) except for telephonic monitoring of pacemakers.
- Weight control or weight reduction services and supplies, except for certain surgical procedures when specific conditions have been met.
- Workers' compensation.

MEDICAL REVIEW

A national medical review organization, under contract to TRICARE, reviews care that is categorized under the TRICARE diagnosis related groups (DRG) payment system along with outpatient care. Providers and health care facilities are required to participate in a TRICARE contractor's medical review program, which ensures that care is reasonable, necessary, and appropriate. Special rules apply in situations where medical review organizations evaluate care. Requests for reconsideration of review decisions should be submitted directly to the review organization by following the appeal instructions contained in the initial determination letter.

CHAMPVA

Although similar to TRICARE Standard with regard to coverage, the **Civilian Health and Medical Program of the Department of Veterans Affairs (CHAMPVA)** is a separate program from TRICARE Standard. CHAMPVA is a health care benefits program for (1) dependents of veterans who have been rated by VA as having a total and permanent disability, (2) survivors of veterans who died from VA-rated service-connected conditions, or who at the time of death, were rated permanently and totally disabled from a VA rated service-connected condition, and (3) survivors of persons who died in the line of duty and not due to misconduct. Under CHAMPVA, the VA shares the cost of covered health care services and supplies with eligible beneficiaries. The administration of CHAMPVA is centralized at the Health Administration Center in Denver, Colorado.

INTERNET LINK

More information about CHAMPVA can be found at www.va.gov/hac/champva/champva.html.

TRICARE AS A SECONDARY PAYER

Beneficiaries who have **Other Health Insurance (OHI)** (an insurance policy that is considered primary to TRICARE) are required to submit documentation (e.g., explanation of benefits generated by primary insurance carrier) when filing TRICARE claims. TRICARE is the secondary payer to civilian insurance plans, workers' compensation, and liability insurance plans, but not Medicaid or TRICARE supplemental policies.

TRICARE is also secondary to employer-sponsored health maintenance organization (HMO) plans, and TRICARE will not cover services received outside the HMO network if (1) the HMO could have provided the service, and (2) the beneficiary elected to obtain services from a non-network (or out-of-network) provider without a referral by the primary care provider.

Personal injury claims for treatment must be submitted to TRICARE along with a "Personal Injury–Possible Third-Party Liability Statement DD Form 2527." The **Federal Medical Care Recovery Act of 1970** requires the government to pursue repayment of medical expenses reimbursed by TRICARE when third-party liability insurance was available or the injured party successfully sued for damages. ICD-9-CM codes 800 through 959 may indicate possible third-party involvement in an injury claim and will trigger review for TRICARE secondary status.

The following is a list of documentation that must be submitted when a claim is filed with OHI:

- A copy of the OHI's Explanation of Benefits (EOB) or a letter from the OHI documenting the amount paid on the claim.

- For OHI noncovered services that TRICARE will cover, a copy of the insurance policy or benefit handbook page(s) demonstrating noncoverage.

- An itemized letter from the provider attached to the claim explaining exactly what the OHI paid and the amount due from TRICARE.

  ■ **NOTE:** Should this information be incomplete, the claim is returned to the provider for additional information; this rule does not apply to Medicare patients because an EOB must be submitted when Medicare is the primary payer. ■

- If the OHI does not routinely generate an EOB, as may be the case with health maintenance (HMO) and preferred provider organization (PPO) plans, the following may be accepted:
  - Documentation that the beneficiary is enrolled in a PPO.
  - Documentation that there is a liability beyond the amount paid by the OHI.
  - Documentation that the liability is specified in the PPO contract.
  - Documentation of total liability on a prescription plan.

- For pharmacy claims, a copy of itemized pharmacy statements and insurance booklets demonstrating beneficiary liability can be submitted instead of an OHI's EOB.

TRICARE LIMITING CHARGES

All TRICARE nonPAR providers are subject to a limiting charge of 15% above the TRICARE Fee Schedule for PAR providers. Patients can no longer be billed for the difference between the provider's normal fee and the TRICARE limiting fee. Exceptions to the 15% limiting fee are claims from independent laboratory and diagnostic laboratory companies, durable medical equipment, and medical supply companies.

TRICARE SUPPLEMENTAL PLANS

Several commercial companies and veterans organizations offer supplemental insurance to cover the TRICARE deductible and cost-shares where available. There is no direct transfer of claims information between TRICARE and the supplemental carriers. Supplemental policy information should not appear on the TRICARE claim form. The health care provider is not required to file these claims.

TRICARE BILLING INFORMATION

The following is a summary of the nationwide billing information for TRICARE Standard and TRICARE Extra out-of-network services. Providers of services are required to file these claims.

TRICARE Carrier Groupings

In recent years, TRICARE carrier contracts were grouped in large regional districts covering many states. Each regional carrier assigned post office box numbers and an associated nine-digit zip code for each state served. Be sure to use and proofread carefully both the post office box number and its associated zip code when submitting claims or correspondence to the carrier. Contact the HBA at the nearest military facility to obtain the current address of the carrier assigned to your area, or access the TRICARE Web site of the U.S. Department of Defense Military Health System at www.tricare. osd.mil.

Underwriter

TRICARE is based in Colorado. Changes in general benefits are enacted by the United States Congress.

Forms Used

1. HCFA-1500 (12-90) claim form.

2. A nonavailability statement must be obtained for all civilian nonemergency inpatient care.

3. *Mental health cases only:* A TRICARE Treatment Report must be filed with a claim for more than twenty-three outpatient visits in any calendar year. Inpatient care requires a Treatment Report every thirty days.

4. *Personal injury claims:* A "Personal Injury-Possible Third-Party Liability Statement" must accompany a claim for treatment of personal injury covering services rendered for diagnostic codes between 800 and 959.

Filing Deadline

Claims will be denied if they are filed more than one year after the date of service for outpatient care or more than one year from the date of discharge for inpatient care.

Allowable Fee Determination

TRICARE follows the principles of the HCFA RBRVS system, but has made some adjustments to the geographic regions and assigned a slightly higher conversion factor. Fee schedules are available from the fiscal intermediary (FI). The TRICARE fee schedule must still be followed when TRICARE is a secondary payor.

Enrollment Fees

There is an enrollment fee for TRICARE Prime, but none for TRICARE Standard or TRICARE Extra (refer back to Table 16-2).

Deductibles

All deductibles are applied to the government's **fiscal year**, which runs from October 1 of one year to September 30 of the next. This is different from other insurance programs, for which deductibles are usually calculated on a calendar year basis (refer back to Tables 16-1 and 16-2).

Confirmation of Eligibility

Confirmation of TRICARE eligibility and nonavailability statement requirements may be obtained from the area health benefits advisor (HBA) or military treatment facility Outpatient Services Department. Ask them to make a "DEERS check" of the sponsor's Social Security number (DEERS is the nationwide computerized Defense Enrollment Eligibility Reporting System).

Accepting Assignment

Accepting assignment for NonPARs is determined on a claim-by-claim basis. Be sure to indicate the provider's choice in Block 27 of the claim form. All deductibles and cost-shares may be collected at the time service is rendered. When assignment is elected, the local HBA can assist if there are problems collecting the deductible and cost-share (copayment) from the patient. The carrier's provider representative can assist with claims review or intervene when a claim payment is overdue.

TRICARE has established a "Good Faith Policy" for assigned claims when the copy of the front and back of the patient's ID card on file turns out to be invalid. If copies of the card are on file and TRICARE provides notification that the patient is ineligible for payment, the local HBA can help in the investigation of the claim. If the investigation reveals that the ID card is invalid, refile the claim with a note stating: "We treated this patient in good faith. Please note the enclosed copy of the ID that was presented at the time the treatment was rendered." *Do not send* your file copy of the ID card. You should receive payment of the TRICARE-approved fee for these services.

Major Medical or Special Accidental Injury Benefits

There is no separate billing procedure necessary for accidental injury claims. There is no differentiation between basic benefits and major medical benefits.

Special Handling

1. Always make a copy of the front and back of the ID card.
2. Check to determine whether the patient knows the date of his or her next transfer. If it is within six months, it would be wise to accept assignment on the claim to avoid interstate collection problems.
3. Make sure the patient has obtained the necessary nonavailability statement for all nonemergency civilian inpatient care and specified outpatient surgeries if the sponsor lives within a catchment area.
4. Nonemergency inpatient mental health cases require preauthorization, and a nonavailability statement must be obtained.
5. TRICARE Mental Health Treatment Reports should be submitted to TRICARE every 30 days for inpatient cases and on or about the 48th outpatient visit and every 24th visit thereafter. This report should cover the following points:
   - Date treatment began.
   - Age, sex, and marital status of patient.
   - Diagnosis and DSM-IV axis information.
   - Presenting symptoms.
   - Historical data.
   - Prior treatment episodes.

- Type and frequency of therapy.
- Explanation of any deviation from standard treatment for the diagnosis.
- Mental status and psychological testing.
- Progress of patient.
- Physical examination and/or pertinent laboratory data.
- Future plans and treatment goals.

6. A Personal Injury-Possible Third-Party Liability Statement will be required for all injuries that have been assigned ICD codes in the 800 to 959 range. If there is no third-party liability, call the HBA for information on how to file the claim.

7. When filing a claim for services that fall under the special handicap benefits, write the words "DEPENDENT DISABILITY PROGRAM" in red ink across the top of the claim form.

8. Contact the area FI representative if there has been no response within 45 days of filing the claim.

9. For hospice claims, write the words "HOSPICE CLAIMS" on the envelope to ensure the claim arrives at the regional carrier's hospice desk.

TRICARE PRIMARY CLAIM INSTRUCTIONS

Place Post-It® Notes or other markers on pages 455 and 458. You will be referring to them frequently.

Refer to Figure 16-2 for Blocks 1 through 13 of the HCFA-1500 claim form. The following instructions cover claims submitted to TRICARE Extra and TRICARE Standard.

Block 1	Enter an "X" in the CHAMPUS box.
Block 1a	Enter the sponsor's Social Security Number (SSN).
Block 2	Enter the complete name (last name first, followed by the first name and middle initial) of the patient as listed on the patient's insurance identification card. Use of nicknames or typographic errors will cause rejection of the claim.
	For case studies in this text enter the names, minus the punctuation, as they appear on the encounter form.
Block 3	Enter the patient's birth date using eight digits in the following format: MM DD YYYY.
	Sex—Enter an "X" in the appropriate box.
Block 4	*Active Duty:* Enter the sponsor's complete name (last name, first name, middle initial). Enter SAME if the patient is the sponsor.
	Retired: Enter the sponsor's name, if other than the patient. Enter SAME, if the patient is the sponsor.
Block 5	Enter the patient's residence (address) at the time services were rendered along with day and evening phone numbers; if a rural address, include route and box number; APO/FPO address may be used if the patient resides overseas.

FIGURE 16-2 Blocks 1 through 13 of the HCFA-1500 claim form

Block 6	Indicate the patient's relationship to sponsor by entering an "X" in the appropriate box. If "OTHER" is selected, enter the relationship (e.g., parent).
Block 7	*Active-duty sponsor:* Enter the sponsor's duty station address. Enter SAME if the sponsor's address is the same as the patient's.
	Retired sponsor: Enter the sponsor's mailing address. Enter SAME if the sponsor's address is the same as the patient's.
Block 8	Enter an "X" in the appropriate box to indicate marital status, and an "X" in the appropriate box to indicate employment and/or student status.
Block 9	Enter the word NONE.
Blocks 9a-9d	Leave blank.
Blocks 10a-10c	If "YES" is selected for any of these boxes, the sponsor must complete and file a DD Form 2527, "Statement of Personal Injury-Possible Third-Party Liability," with the TRICARE carrier before payment will be received.
Block 10d	Leave blank.
Block 11	Enter the word "NONE."
Blocks 11a-c	Leave blank.
Block 11d	Enter an "X" in the appropriate box.
Block 12	Enter "SIGNATURE ON FILE."

When working with case studies in this text, enter the words "SIGNATURE ON FILE."

Block 13   Leave blank.

Refer to Figure 16-4 for completed Blocks 1 through 13 for the encounter form in Figure 16-3.

DATE 01/14/YYYY		REMARKS					
PATIENT John Q. Public				CHART # 16-1	SEX M		BIRTHDATE 03/09/1945
MAILING ADDRESS 10A Senate Street	CITY Anywhere		STATE US	ZIP 12345	HOME PHONE (101) 201 7891		WORK PHONE
EMPLOYER Retired		ADDRESS		PATIENT STATUS (MARRIED) DIVORCED SINGLE STUDENT OTHER			
INSURANCE: PRIMARY TRICARE Standard		ID# 100 23 9678		GROUP	SECONDARY POLICY		
POLICYHOLDER NAME	BIRTHDATE	RELATIONSHIP self		POLICYHOLDER NAME		BIRTHDATE	RELATIONSHIP
SUPPLEMENTAL PLAN				EMPLOYER			

POLICYHOLDER NAME	BIRTHDATE	RELATIONSHIP	DIAGNOSIS	CODE
			1. Mycoplasma pneumonia	483.0
EMPLOYER			2. Insulin dependent diabetes	250.03
			3. uncontrolled	
REFERRING PHYSICIAN UPIN/SSN			4.	

PLACE OF SERVICE   Goodmedicine Hospital, Anywhere Street, Anywhere, US 12345

PROCEDURES	CODE	CHARGE
1. 01/09/YYYY Initial Hosp visit Level III	99223	$150—
2. 01/10/YYYY Subs. Hosp Level II	99232	75—
3. 01/11/YYYY Subs. Hosp Level II	99232	75—
4. 01/12/YYYY Subs. Hosp Level II	99232	75—
5. 01/13/YYYY Subs. Hosp Level I	99231	50—
6. 01/14/YYYY Discharge, 30 min.	99238	50—

SPECIAL NOTES

TOTAL CHARGES $475—	PAYMENTS	ADJUSTMENTS 0	BALANCE $475—
RETURN VISIT 1 week		PHYSICIAN SIGNATURE *Erin A. Helper, M.D.*	

ERIN A. HELPER, M.D.   101 MEDIC DRIVE, ANYWHERE, US 12345
PHONE NUMBER (101) 111-1234
EIN # 11-123452   SSN # 111-22-3333
UPIN EH8888   NPI 00818810   Medicaid # EBH8881   BC/BS # EH11881   GRP: 1204-P   TRICARE: 12345678

FIGURE 16-3 John Q. Public encounter form

EXERCISE 16-1   Preparing the Comparison Chart

■ **NOTE:** Complete all steps in this exercise if you have not completed Exercise 12-1 or 13-1 prior to working with this chapter. If you have already completed Exercise 12-1 and/or 13-1, refer to the Comparison Chart you used in that exercise and proceed to Step 4. ■

PLEASE
DO NOT
STAPLE
IN THIS
AREA

APPROVED OMB-0938-0008

CARRIER

| | PICA | | **HEALTH INSURANCE CLAIM FORM** | PICA | | |

1. MEDICARE ☐ (Medicare #) MEDICAID ☐ (Medicaid #) CHAMPUS [X] (Sponsor's SSN) CHAMPVA ☐ (VA File #)	GROUP HEALTH PLAN ☐ (SSN or I D) FECA BLK LUNG ☐ (SSN) OTHER ☐ (I D)	1a. INSURED'S I.D. NUMBER (FOR PROGRAM IN ITEM 1) 100239678

2. PATIENT'S NAME (Last Name, First Name, Middle Initial)
PUBLIC JOHN Q

3. PATIENT'S BIRTH DATE
MM | DD | YY
03 | 09 | 1945   SEX   M [X]   F ☐

4. INSURED'S NAME (Last Name, First Name, Middle Initial)
SAME

5. PATIENT'S ADDRESS (No. Street)
10A SENATE AVENUE

6. PATIENT RELATIONSHIP TO INSURED
Self [X]   Spouse ☐   Child ☐   Other ☐

7. INSURED'S ADDRESS (No. Street)
SAME

CITY
ANYWHERE   STATE US

8. PATIENT STATUS
Single ☐   Married [X]   Other ☐

CITY   STATE

ZIP CODE
12345   TELEPHONE (Include Area Code)
101 201 7891

Employed ☐   Full-Time Student ☐   Part-Time Student ☐

ZIP CODE   TELEPHONE (INCLUDE AREA CODE)
( )

9. OTHER INSURED'S NAME (Last Name, First Name, Middle Initial)
NONE

10. IS PATIENT'S CONDITION RELATED TO:

11. INSURED'S POLICY GROUP OR FECA NUMBER
NONE

a. OTHER INSURED'S POLICY OR GROUP NUMBER

a. EMPLOYMENT? (CURRENT OR PREVIOUS)
☐ YES   [X] NO

a. INSURED'S DATE OF BIRTH
MM | DD | YY   SEX   M ☐   F ☐

b. OTHER INSURED'S DATE OF BIRTH
MM | DD | YY   SEX   M ☐   F ☐

b. AUTO ACCIDENT?   PLACE (State)
☐ YES   [X] NO

b. EMPLOYER'S NAME OR SCHOOL NAME

c. EMPLOYER'S NAME OR SCHOOL NAME

c. OTHER ACCIDENT?
☐ YES   [X] NO

c. INSURANCE PLAN NAME OR PROGRAM NAME

d. INSURANCE PLAN NAME OR PROGRAM NAME

10d. RESERVED FOR LOCAL USE

d. IS THERE ANOTHER HEALTH BENEFIT PLAN?
☐ YES   [X] NO   If yes, return to and complete item 9 a – d.

READ BACK OF FORM BEFORE COMPLETING & SIGNING THIS FORM.
12. PATIENT'S OR AUTHORIZED PERSON'S SIGNATURE I authorize the release of any medical or other information necessary to process this claim. I also request payment of government benefits either to myself or to the party who accepts assignment below.

13. INSURED'S OR AUTHORIZED PERSON'S SIGNATURE I authorize payment of medical benefits to the undersigned physician or supplier for services described below.

SIGNED   SIGNATURE ON FILE   DATE

SIGNED

PATIENT AND INSURED INFORMATION

FIGURE 16-4 Completed Blocks 1 through 13 for John Q. Public encounter form in Figure 16-3

ASSIGNMENT OBJECTIVE: To create a reference as an aid to mastering the details of completing claim forms for the six major insurance programs.

1. Make five copies of the Comparison Chart in Appendix III.

2. Enter the following titles in the wide columns at the top of each page:
Commercial
BCBS
TRICARE Standard
Workers' Compensation

3. Enter the following numbers in the first column:

Page 1	Blocks	1	through	9D
Page 2		10	through	16
Page 3		17	through	23
Page 4		24A	through	24K
Page 5		25	through	33

4. Record abbreviated instructions in Blocks 1 through 13 of the TRICARE column. If the step-by-step instructions in this chapter indicate a particular block is to be left blank, write in the word "Blank."

Use horizontal arrows to indicate that the instructions in a specific block in the TRICARE column are repeated in the next column (see Figure 12-4).

If consecutive blocks are to be left blank, enter the word "Blank" in the first block and draw a vertical arrow down through the other blocks that have similar treatment.

5. Save this form; it will be used for additional exercises in this chapter and in other chapters.

EXERCISE 16-2 TRICARE Claim Form Blocks 1 through 13

This exercise requires a copy of a blank HCFA-1500 claim form. You may either make photocopies of the form in Appendix III of the text or print copies of the blank form using the computer disk located at the back of the text. Instructions for installing the computer program and printing blank forms are included with the text.

1. Obtain a copy of the HCFA-1500 claim form.
2. Review the instructions for Blocks 1 through 13 on your comparison chart.
3. Review Figure 16-5 Mary Sue Patient encounter form. Place a page marker at the encounter form.
4. Abstract the information needed for Blocks 1 through 13 from Figure 16-5 and enter the required information on the claim form using Optical Scanning Guidelines. This may be completed by recording the information by using the Blank Form Mode on the disk, or handwriting, or typing the data.
5. Review Blocks 1 through 13 of the claim form to be sure all required blocks are properly completed.
6. Compare your claim form with the completed form in Figure 16-12.

■ **NOTE:** This same encounter form and claim form will be used for Exercises 16-4. ■

Refer to Figure 16-6 for Blocks 14 through 23 of the HCFA-1500 claim form.

Block 14	Information appreciated, but not required. Enter the date (MM DD YYYY) of current illness, injury, or pregnancy.
Block 15	Information appreciated, but not required. Enter the first date (MM DD YYYY) patient had same or similar illness/injury.
Block 16	Information appreciated, but not required. Enter dates (MM DD YYYY) patient was unable to work.
Block 17	Enter the name of the referring provider. If the patient was referred from a military treatment facility, enter the name of the facility.
Block 17a	Enter the referring physician's EIN.
Block 18	Enter the 8 digit (MM DD YYYY) admission date and the discharge date if any procedure/service is rendered to a patient with inpatient status. If the patient is still hospitalized, leave the "TO" block blank.
Block 19	Leave blank.
Block 20	Enter an "X" in the "NO" box.
Block 21	Enter up to four ICD-9-CM codes in priority order.

DATE 01/10/YYYY	REMARKS Dept 07 Naval Station Nowhere US 12367			
PATIENT Mary Sue Patient		CHART # 16-2	SEX F	BIRTHDATE 10/10/1959

MAILING ADDRESS 91 Home Street	CITY Nowhere	STATE US	ZIP 12367	HOME PHONE (101) 201 8989	WORK PHONE

EMPLOYER	ADDRESS	PATIENT STATUS (MARRIED) DIVORCED SINGLE STUDENT OTHER

INSURANCE: PRIMARY TRICARE Standard	ID# 101 23 9945	GROUP	SECONDARY POLICY

POLICYHOLDER NAME James L. Patient	BIRTHDATE 08/22/44	RELATIONSHIP spouse	POLICYHOLDER NAME	BIRTHDATE	RELATIONSHIP

SUPPLEMENTAL PLAN	EMPLOYER

POLICYHOLDER NAME BIRTHDATE RELATIONSHIP	DIAGNOSIS	CODE
	1. Fx distal radius	813.42
EMPLOYER US Navy (see duty address in remarks)	2. @ Home	E849.0
	3. fell down stairs	E880.9
REFERRING PHYSICIAN UPIN/SSN	4.	

PLACE OF SERVICE   Office

PROCEDURES 01/10/YYYY	CODE	CHARGE
1. Closed manipulation distal radius	25600	$300—
2. Xray wrist 3 views	73110	50—
3. Xray forearm 1 view	73090-52	25—
4.		
5.		
6.		

SPECIAL NOTES

Fell on stairs today

TOTAL CHARGES $375—	PAYMENTS $150—	ADJUSTMENTS 0	BALANCE $225—

RETURN VISIT One week	PHYSICIAN SIGNATURE *Erin A. Helper, M.D.*

ERIN A. HELPER, M.D.   101 MEDIC DRIVE, ANYWHERE, US 12345
PHONE NUMBER (101) 111-1234
EIN # 11-123452   SSN # 111-22-3333
UPIN EH8888   NPI 00818810   Medicaid # EBH8881   BC/BS # EH11881   GRP: 1204-P   TRICARE: 12345678

FIGURE 16-5 Mary Sue Patient encounter form

14. DATE OF CURRENT: MM DD YY ◄ ILLNESS (First symptom) OR INJURY (Accident) OR PREGNANCY (LMP)	15. IF PATIENT HAS HAD SAME OR SIMILAR ILLNESS, GIVE FIRST DATE MM DD YY	16. DATES PATIENT UNABLE TO WORK IN CURRENT OCCUPATION MM DD YY MM DD YY FROM TO
17. NAME OF REFERRING PHYSICIAN OR OTHER SOURCE	17a. I.D. NUMBER OF REFERRING PHYSICIAN	18. HOSPITALIZATION DATES RELATED TO CURRENT SERVICES MM DD YY MM DD YY FROM TO
19. RESERVED FOR LOCAL USE		20. OUTSIDE LAB? $ CHARGES ☐ YES ☐ NO
21. DIAGNOSIS OR NATURE OF ILLNESS OR INJURY. (RELATE ITEMS 1, 2, 3, OR 4 TO ITEM 24E BY LINE) 1. ⌐__ . __ 3. ⌐__ . __ 2. ⌐__ . __ 4. ⌐__ . __		22. MEDICAID RESUBMISSION CODE ORIGINAL REF. NO. 23. PRIOR AUTHORIZATION NUMBER

FIGURE 16-6 Blocks 14 through 23 of the HCFA-1500 claim form

Block 22   Leave blank. This block is reserved for Medicaid resubmissions.

Block 23   Enter prior authorization (or preauthorization) number. Attach a copy of any preauthorization required (e.g., heart-lung transplant authorization).

Refer to Figure 16-7 for completed Blocks 14 through 23 for the encounter form in Figure 16-3.

FIGURE 16-7   Completed Blocks 14 through 23 for John Q. Public encounter form in Figure 16-3

EXERCISE 16-3   Continuation of Work on Comparison Chart

Reread the instructions for completing Blocks 14 through 23. As you review each block, record a concise description of the instructions in the appropriate block in the TRICARE column of the Comparison Chart.

EXERCISE 16-4   Continuation of Exercise 16-2

1. Review the Mary Sue Patient encounter form found in Figure 16-5 to locate the diagnostic and treatment data.

2. Abstract the information needed for Blocks 14 through 23 and enter the required information on a new claim form using Optical Scanning Guidelines. This may be completed using the disk, or handwriting or typing the data.

3. Review Blocks 14 through 23 of the claim form to be sure all required blocks are properly completed.

4. Compare your claim form with the completed form in Figure 16-12.

■ **NOTE:** This same claim form will be used for Exercise 16-5. ■

Refer to Figure 16-8 for Block 24 of the HCFA-1500 claim form.

Block 24A   Enter the eight-digit date with no spaces (MMDDYYYY) for the procedure performed in the "FROM" column. Do not fill in the "TO" column for a single procedure entry.

To list procedures with the same codes and charges performed on consecutive days, indicate the last day the procedure was performed in the "TO" column. Also, enter the number of consecutive days or units in the "days/units column," Block 24G.

24.	A					B	C	D		E	F	G	H	I	J	K
	DATE(S) OF SERVICE					Place of Service	Type of Service	PROCEDURES, SERVICES, OR SUPPLIES (Explain Unusual Circumstances)		DIAGNOSIS CODE	$ CHARGES	DAYS OR UNITS	EPSDT Family Plan	EMG	COB	RESERVED FOR LOCAL USE
	From			To												
	MM	DD	YY	MM	DD	YY			CPT/HCPCS	MODIFIER						
1																
2																
3																
4																
5																
6																

FIGURE 16-8 Block 24 of the HCFA-1500 claim form

Block 24B   Use the appropriate two digit code from the list below.

Provider's office	11
Patient's home	12
Inpatient hospital	21
Outpatient hospital	22
Emergency department—hospital	23
Ambulatory surgical center	24
Birthing center	25
Military treatment facility or	26
Uniformed service treatment facility	26
Skilled nursing facility	31
Nursing facility	32
Custodial care facility	33
Hospice	34
Ambulance—land	41
Ambulance—air or water	42
Inpatient psychiatric facility	51
Psychiatric facility—partial hospitalization	52
Community mental health center	53
Intermediate care facility/mentally retarded	54
Residential substance abuse treatment facility	55
Psychiatric residential treatment center	56
Comprehensive inpatient rehabilitation facility	61
Comprehensive outpatient rehabilitation facility	62
End-stage renal disease treatment facility	65
State/local public health clinic	71
Rural health clinic	72
Independent laboratory	81
Other unlisted facility	99

Block 24C   Use the appropriate code from the list below.

Medical care	1
Surgery	2
Consultation	3
Diagnostic Xray	4
Diagnostic laboratory	5

Radiation therapy	6
Anesthesia	7
Assistant at surgery	8
Other medical services	9
Durable medical equipment rental/purchase	A
Drugs	B
Ambulatory surgery	C
Hospice	D
Second opinion on elective surgery	E
Maternity	F
Dental	G
Mental health care	H
Ambulance	I
Program for persons with disabilities	J

Block 24D

Enter the appropriate five-digit CPT code or HCPCS Level II/III code number and any required CPT or HCPCS modifiers for the procedure reported in this block. Enter a blank space, not a hyphen, to separate the code number from the modifier or multiple modifiers.

Block 24E

Enter the *reference numbers* (1 through 4) for the ICD code number listed in Block 21 that justifies the medical necessity for each procedure listed in Block 24D.

■ **NOTE:** Some local carriers will accept more than one reference number on each line. If more than one reference number is used, the first number stated must represent the primary diagnosis that justifies the medical necessity for performing the procedures on that horizontal line. Unless otherwise directed by the carrier, multiple reference numbers should be separated by blank spaces, not commas or dashes. ■

When working with case studies in this text and workbook, enter up to four reference numbers in this block.

Block 24F

Enter the fee for procedures/services listed.

If identical, consecutive procedures are reported on this line, enter the total fee charged for the combined procedures.

Block 24G

Enter the number of units/days for services reported in 24D. (Review the discussion on units in Chapter 11, if necessary.)

Block 24H

Leave blank.

Block 24I

Enter an "X" in this block to indicate services provided in a hospital emergency department.

Block 24J

Leave blank if all services on this claim are performed by one provider.

Block 24K

Leave blank if all services on this claim are performed by one provider.

Multiple providers from group practice: Enter the provider's name and specialty using Blocks 24H through 24J for this purpose.

Refer to Figure 16-9 for completed Block 24 for the John Q. Public encounter form in Figure 16-3.

24. A DATE(S) OF SERVICE						B Place of Service	C Type of Service	D PROCEDURES, SERVICES, OR SUPPLIES (Explain Unusual Circumstances)		E DIAGNOSIS CODE	F $ CHARGES	G DAYS OR UNITS	H EPSDT Family Plan	I EMG	J COB	K RESERVED FOR LOCAL USE
From MM	DD	YY	To MM	DD	YY			CPT/HCPCS	MODIFIER							
1	01 09 YYYY					21	1	99223		1 2	150 00	1				
2	01 10 YYYY		01 12 YYYY			21	1	99232		1 2	225 00	3				
3	01 13 YYYY					21	1	99231		1 2	50 00	1				
4	01 14 YYYY					21	1	99238		1 2	50 00	1				
5																
6																

FIGURE 16-9 Completed Block 14 for John Q. Public encounter form in Figure 16-3

EXERCISE 16-5 Continuation of Work on Comparison Chart

Review the instructions for filing in Blocks 24A through 24K. As you read each block, record a concise description of the instructions in the appropriate block in the TRICARE column of the Comparison Chart.

Refer to Figure 16-10 for Blocks 25 through 33 of the HCFA-1500 claim form.

Block 25

Enter the billing entity's Employer Tax Identification Number, if available. Otherwise, enter the provider's Social Security Number. In addition, be sure to enter an "X" in the appropriate box to indicate which is being reported.

■ **NOTE:** While third-party payers will accept the number with or without hyphens, when completing claim forms in this text (and while using the CD-ROM), be sure to enter hyphens. ■

Block 26

Enter the number assigned to the patient's account if the practice uses a numerical identification number to identify the patient's account or ledger card, or if the claim is filed electronically.
Leave blank if the practice files patient accounts by patient name.

When working with case studies in this text and workbook, enter the case study number in this block. If the case requires primary and secondary forms, add the appropriate term.

Block 27

Enter an "X" in the appropriate box. The nonPAR provider may elect to accept assignment on a case-by-case basis.

When working with case studies in this text, enter an "X" in the "NO" box.

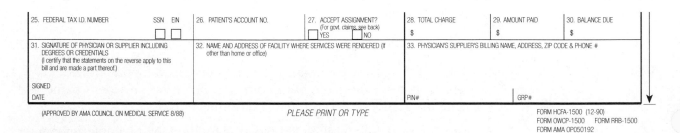

FIGURE 16-10 Blocks 25 through 33 of the HCFA-1500 claim form

Block 28	Total all charges on this claim form and enter in this block. This figure should never reflect negative charges or show a credit is due to the patient.
	If multiple claims for one patient are generated by the computer because more than six services must be reported, be sure the total charge recorded on each claim form accurately represents the total of the items indicated on each separate claim form submitted.
Block 29	Enter the amount received from other health insurance; attach the other insurance EOB. Do not include payment from patient or beneficiary.
Block 30	Enter the balance due.
Block 31	*Paper claims:* Enter the complete name of the provider and credentials. TRICARE requires the provider/supplier to personally sign the claim unless special arrangements have been made with the carrier.
	When working with case studies in this text, sign the claim for the providers. They are nonPARs; therefore, no special arrangements have been made with the carrier.
Block 32	Enter this item when the services listed on the claim form were performed at a site other than the provider's office or the patient's home.
	If the "YES" box in Block 20 contains an "X," enter the name and address of the laboratory that performed the laboratory procedures.
Block 33	Enter the billing entity's name, mailing address, and phone number. Enter the TRICARE provider number.
	Refer to Figure 16-11 for completed HCFA-1500 claim form based on the encounter form in Figure 16-3.

EXERCISE 16-6 Continuation of Exercise 16-2

1. Review the Mary Sue Patient encounter form found in Figure 16-5.
2. Abstract the information needed for Blocks 24 through 33 and enter the required information on a new claim form using Optical Scanning Guidelines. This may be completed using the disk found in the workbook, or by handwriting or typing the data.
3. Review Blocks 24 through 33 of the claim form to be sure all required blocks are properly completed.
4. Compare your claim form with the completed claim form in Figure 16-12.

PRIMARY TRICARE WITH A SUPPLEMENTAL POLICY

The following modifications must be made to the TRICARE primary claim when the health care provider is a TRICARE participating provider and the patient has a supplemental policy in addition to TRICARE.

Block 9a	Enter the policy or group number of other insured's policy.
Block 9b	Enter the other insured's date of birth (MM DD YYYY) and mark an "X" in the appropriate box for sex.

PLEASE
DO NOT
STAPLE
IN THIS
AREA

(SAMPLE ONLY - NOT APPROVED FOR USE)

CARRIER

| | PICA | **UNDERSTANDING HEALTH INSURANCE CLAIM FORM** PICA | | |

| 1. MEDICARE ☐ (Medicare #) | MEDICAID ☐ (Medicaid #) | CHAMPUS ☒ (Sponsor's SSN) | CHAMPVA ☐ (VA File #) | GROUP HEALTH PLAN ☐ (SSN or ID) | FECA BLK LUNG ☐ (SSN) | OTHER ☐ (ID) | 1a. INSURED'S I.D. NUMBER (FOR PROGRAM IN ITEM 1)
100239678 |

| 2. PATIENT'S NAME (Last Name, First Name, Middle Initial)
PUBLIC JOHN Q | 3. PATIENT'S BIRTH DATE
MM 03 DD 09 YY 1945 SEX M ☒ F ☐ | 4. INSURED'S NAME (Last Name, First Name, Middle Initial)
SAME |

| 5. PATIENT'S ADDRESS (No. Street)
10A SENATE STREET | 6. PATIENT RELATIONSHIP TO INSURED
Self ☒ Spouse ☐ Child ☐ Other ☐ | 7. INSURED'S ADDRESS (No. Street)
SAME |

| CITY
ANYWHERE | STATE
US | 8. PATIENT STATUS
Single ☐ Married ☒ Other ☐ | CITY | STATE |

| ZIP CODE
12345 | TELEPHONE (Include Area Code)
101 201 7891 | Employed ☒ Full-Time Student ☐ Part-Time Student ☐ | ZIP CODE | TELEPHONE (INCLUDE AREA CODE)
( ) |

| 9. OTHER INSURED'S NAME (Last Name, First Name, Middle Initial)
NONE | 10. IS PATIENT'S CONDITION RELATED TO: | 11. INSURED'S POLICY GROUP OR FECA NUMBER
NONE |

| a. OTHER INSURED'S POLICY OR GROUP NUMBER | a. EMPLOYMENT? (CURRENT OR PREVIOUS)
☐ YES ☒ NO | a. INSURED'S DATE OF BIRTH
MM DD YY SEX M ☐ F ☐ |

| b. OTHER INSURED'S DATE OF BIRTH
MM DD YY SEX M ☐ F ☐ | b. AUTO ACCIDENT? PLACE (State)
☐ YES ☒ NO | b. EMPLOYER'S NAME OR SCHOOL NAME |

| c. EMPLOYER'S NAME OR SCHOOL NAME | c. OTHER ACCIDENT?
☐ YES ☒ NO | c. INSURANCE PLAN NAME OR PROGRAM NAME |

| d. INSURANCE PLAN NAME OR PROGRAM NAME | 10d. RESERVED FOR LOCAL USE | d. IS THERE ANOTHER HEALTH BENEFIT PLAN?
☐ YES ☒ NO If yes, return to and complete item 9 a – d. |

READ BACK OF FORM BEFORE COMPLETING & SIGNING THIS FORM.
12. PATIENT'S OR AUTHORIZED PERSON'S SIGNATURE I authorize the release of any medical or other information necessary to process this claim. I also request payment of government benefits either to myself or to the party who accepts assignment below.

SIGNED SIGNATURE ON FILE DATE

13. INSURED'S OR AUTHORIZED PERSON'S SIGNATURE I authorize payment of medical benefits to the undersigned physician or supplier for services described below.

SIGNED

| 14. DATE OF CURRENT: ILLNESS (First symptom) OR INJURY (Accident) OR PREGNANCY (LMP)
MM 01 DD 09 YY YYYY | 15. IF PATIENT HAS HAD SAME OR SIMILAR ILLNESS, GIVE FIRST DATE MM DD YY | 16. DATES PATIENT UNABLE TO WORK IN CURRENT OCCUPATION
FROM MM DD YY TO MM DD YY |

| 17. NAME OF REFERRING PHYSICIAN OR OTHER SOURCE | 17a. I.D. NUMBER OF REFERRING PHYSICIAN | 18. HOSPITALIZATION DATES RELATED TO CURRENT SERVICES
FROM MM 01 DD 09 YY YYYY TO MM 01 DD 14 YY YYYY |

| 19. RESERVED FOR LOCAL USE | 20. OUTSIDE LAB? ☐ YES ☒ NO $ CHARGES |

| 21. DIAGNOSIS OR NATURE OF ILLNESS OR INJURY. (RELATE ITEMS 1, 2, 3, OR 4 TO ITEM 24E BY LINE)
1. 483 . 0   3. ____ . ____
2. 250 . 03   4. ____ . ____ | 22. MEDICAID RESUBMISSION CODE ORIGINAL REF. NO.
23. PRIOR AUTHORIZATION NUMBER |

24. A DATE(S) OF SERVICE		B Place of Service	C Type of Service	D PROCEDURES, SERVICES, OR SUPPLIES (Explain Unusual Circumstances)		E DIAGNOSIS CODE	F $ CHARGES	G DAYS OR UNITS	H EPSDT Family Plan	I EMG	J COB	K RESERVED FOR LOCAL USE
From MM DD YY	To MM DD YY			CPT/HCPCS	MODIFIER							
0109YYYY		21	1	99223		1 2	150 00	1				
0110YYYY	0112YYYY	21	1	99232		1 2	225 00	3				
0113YYYY		21	1	99231		1 2	50 00	1				
0114YYYY		21	1	99238		1 2	50 00	1				

| 25. FEDERAL TAX I.D. NUMBER SSN ☐ EIN ☒
11-123452 | 26. PATIENT'S ACCOUNT NO.
16-1 | 27. ACCEPT ASSIGNMENT? (For govt. claims, see back)
☐ YES ☒ NO | 28. TOTAL CHARGE
$ 475 00 | 29. AMOUNT PAID
$ | 30. BALANCE DUE
$ 475 00 |

| 31. SIGNATURE OF PHYSICIAN OR SUPPLIER INCLUDING DEGREES OR CREDENTIALS (I certify that the statements on the reverse apply to this bill and are made a part thereof.)
ERIN A HELPER MD
SIGNED DATE MMDDYYYY | 32. NAME AND ADDRESS OF FACILITY WHERE SERVICES WERE RENDERED (If other than home or office)
GOODMEDICINE HOSPITAL
ANYWHERE STREET
ANYWHERE US 12345 | 33. PHYSICIAN'S OR SUPPLIER'S BILLING NAME, ADDRESS, ZIP CODE & PHONE #
(101) 111 1234
ERIN A HELPER MD
101 MEDIC DRIVE
ANYWHERE US 12345
PIN# 12345678 GRP# |

(SAMPLE ONLY - NOT APPROVED FOR USE)

PLEASE PRINT OR TYPE

SAMPLE FORM 1500
SAMPLE FORM 1500 SAMPLE FORM 1500

PATIENT AND INSURED INFORMATION

PHYSICIAN OR SUPPLIER INFORMATION

FIGURE 16-11 Completed Blocks 25 through 33 for John Q. Public encounter form in Figure 16-3

PLEASE
DO NOT
STAPLE
IN THIS
AREA

(SAMPLE ONLY - NOT APPROVED FOR USE)

| | | PICA

UNDERSTANDING HEALTH INSURANCE CLAIM FORM PICA | | |

1. MEDICARE MEDICAID CHAMPUS CHAMPVA GROUP HEALTH PLAN FECA BLK LUNG OTHER	1a. INSURED'S I.D. NUMBER (FOR PROGRAM IN ITEM 1)
☐ (Medicare #) ☐ (Medicaid #) ☒ (Sponsor's SSN) ☐ (VA File #) ☐ (SSN or ID) ☐ (SSN) ☐ (ID)	101239945

2. PATIENT'S NAME (Last Name, First Name, Middle Initial)	3. PATIENT'S BIRTH DATE SEX	4. INSURED'S NAME (Last Name, First Name, Middle Initial)
PATIENT MARY SUE	MM 10	DD 10	YY 1959 M ☐ F ☒	JAMES L PATIENT

5. PATIENT'S ADDRESS (No. Street)	6. PATIENT RELATIONSHIP TO INSURED	7. INSURED'S ADDRESS (No. Street)
91 HOME STREET	Self ☐ Spouse ☒ Child ☐ Other ☐	DEPT 07 NAVAL STATION

CITY NOWHERE STATE US	8. PATIENT STATUS Single ☐ Married ☒ Other ☐	CITY NOWHERE STATE US
ZIP CODE 12367 TELEPHONE (Include Area Code) 101 201 8989	Employed ☐ Full-Time Student ☐ Part-Time Student ☐	ZIP CODE 12367 TELEPHONE (INCLUDE AREA CODE) ( )

9. OTHER INSURED'S NAME (Last Name, First Name, Middle Initial)	10. IS PATIENT'S CONDITION RELATED TO:	11. INSURED'S POLICY GROUP OR FECA NUMBER
NONE		NONE
a. OTHER INSURED'S POLICY OR GROUP NUMBER	a. EMPLOYMENT? (CURRENT OR PREVIOUS) ☐ YES ☒ NO	a. INSURED'S DATE OF BIRTH MM DD YY SEX M ☐ F ☐
b. OTHER INSURED'S DATE OF BIRTH MM DD YY SEX M ☐ F ☐	b. AUTO ACCIDENT? PLACE (State) ☐ YES ☒ NO	b. EMPLOYER'S NAME OR SCHOOL NAME
c. EMPLOYER'S NAME OR SCHOOL NAME	c. OTHER ACCIDENT? ☐ YES ☒ NO	c. INSURANCE PLAN NAME OR PROGRAM NAME
d. INSURANCE PLAN NAME OR PROGRAM NAME	10d. RESERVED FOR LOCAL USE	d. IS THERE ANOTHER HEALTH BENEFIT PLAN? ☐ YES ☒ NO If yes, return to and complete item 9 a - d.

READ BACK OF FORM BEFORE COMPLETING & SIGNING THIS FORM.

12. PATIENT'S OR AUTHORIZED PERSON'S SIGNATURE I authorize the release of any medical or other information necessary to process this claim. I also request payment of government benefits either to myself or to the party who accepts assignment below.

SIGNED   SIGNATURE ON FILE   DATE

13. INSURED'S OR AUTHORIZED PERSON'S SIGNATURE I authorize payment of medical benefits to the undersigned physician or supplier for services described below.

SIGNED

14. DATE OF CURRENT: MM DD YY ILLNESS (First symptom) OR INJURY (Accident) OR PREGNANCY (LMP)	15. IF PATIENT HAS HAD SAME OR SIMILAR ILLNESS, GIVE FIRST DATE MM DD YY	16. DATE PATIENT UNABLE TO WORK IN CURRENT OCCUPATION FROM MM DD YY TO MM DD YY
01 10 YYYY		

17. NAME OF REFERRING PHYSICIAN OR OTHER SOURCE	17a. I.D. NUMBER OF REFERRING PHYSICIAN	18. HOSPITALIZATION DATES RELATED TO CURRENT SERVICES FROM MM DD YY TO MM DD YY

19. RESERVED FOR LOCAL USE		20. OUTSIDE LAB? ☐ YES ☒ NO $ CHARGES

21. DIAGNOSIS OR NATURE OF ILLNESS OR INJURY. (RELATE ITEMS 1, 2, 3, OR 4 TO ITEM 24E BY LINE)

1. 813.42   3. E880.9

2. E849.0   4.

22. MEDICAID RESUBMISSION CODE   ORIGINAL REF. NO.

23. PRIOR AUTHORIZATION NUMBER

24. A. DATE(S) OF SERVICE From MM DD YY / To MM DD YY	B. Place of Service	C. Type of Service	D. PROCEDURES, SERVICES, OR SUPPLIES (Explain Unusual Circumstances) CPT/HCPCS / MODIFIER	E. DIAGNOSIS CODE	F. $ CHARGES	G. DAYS OR UNITS	H. EPSDT Family Plan	I. EMG	J. COB	K. RESERVED FOR LOCAL USE
1	0110YYYY	11	1	25600	1	300 00	1				
2	0110YYYY	11	4	73110	1	50 00	1				
3	0110YYYY	11	4	73090	52	1	25 00	1				
4											
5											
6											

25. FEDERAL TAX I.D. NUMBER SSN EIN	26. PATIENT'S ACCOUNT NO.	27. ACCEPT ASSIGNMENT? (For govt. claims, see back)	28. TOTAL CHARGE	29. AMOUNT PAID	30. BALANCE DUE
11-123452 ☐ ☒	16-2	☐ YES ☒ NO	$ 375 00	$	$ 375 00

31. SIGNATURE OF PHYSICIAN OR SUPPLIER INCLUDING DEGREES OR CREDENTIALS (I certify that the statements on the reverse apply to this bill and are made a part thereof.)	32. NAME AND ADDRESS OF FACILITY WHERE SERVICES WERE RENDERED (If other than home or office)	33. PHYSICIAN'S SUPPLIER'S BILLING NAME, ADDRESS, ZIP CODE & PHONE #
ERIN A HELPER MD SIGNED DATE MMDDYYYY		(101) 111 1234 ERIN A HELPER MD 101 MEDIC DRIVE ANYWHERE US 12345 PIN# 12345678 GRP#

(SAMPLE ONLY - NOT APPROVED FOR USE)   *PLEASE PRINT OR TYPE*   SAMPLE FORM 1500 SAMPLE FORM 1500 SAMPLE FORM 1500

FIGURE 16-12 Completed Mary Sue Patient HCFA-1500 claim form

Block 9c	Enter the name of the employer or name of the school.
Block 9d	Enter the name of the insurance plan or program name of the patient's other insurance coverage. On an attached sheet, provide a complete mailing address for the insurance plan or program. Enter the word "ATTACHMENT" in Block 10d.
	Enter the name of the supplemental insurance plan or program in Block 11c.

TRICARE AS SECONDARY PAYER CLAIM INSTRUCTIONS

Block 11	Enter the insured's policy, group, or FECA number if the patient has other insurance that is primary to TRICARE. If the patient is covered by Medicare, enter "MEDICARE" in this block.
Block 11a	If different from information in Block 3, enter the insured's date of birth (MM DD YYYY) and enter an "X" in the appropriate box to indicate sex.
Block 11b	Enter the name of the employer or school, if applicable.
Block 11c	Enter the name of the insurance plan or program.
	■ **NOTE:** For patients covered by a health maintenance organization (HMO), attach a copy of the HMO brochure showing that services submitted on this claim are not covered by the HMO. TRICARE will be able to process the claim more quickly if provided with this information. ■
Block 11d	Enter an "X" in the YES or NO box to indicate if there is, or is not, another primary insurance or health plan (e.g., patient may be covered by spouse's health plan).
	■ **NOTE:** Blocks 9a through 9d are also completed to report additional insurance coverage. For example, the patient may have primary insurance coverage through an employer, insurance coverage through the spouse's employer, and TRICARE Standard coverage. TRICARE Standard pays last in this situation because the spouse's insurance is considered primary to TRI-CARE Standard. ■
Block 29	Enter only direct payments from other insurances, not from the patient.
	■ **NOTE:** All secondary claims must be accompanied by the primary EOB, worksheet, or denial. Add the name of the policyholder to the EOB if is not included on the form. ■

EXERCISE 16-7 Completion of TRICARE Secondary Claim

1. Obtain a blank claim form.
2. Refer to Figure 16-13, the John R. Neely encounter form.
3. Complete the TRICARE secondary form for this case.
4. Review the completed claim form to be sure all required blocks are properly completed. Refer to Figure 16-14.

DATE 03/10/YYYY	REMARKS 0010670198 (TRICARE ID#)				
PATIENT John R. Neely			CHART # 16-3	SEX M	BIRTHDATE 10/25/1945

MAILING ADDRESS 1 Military Drive	CITY Anywhere	STATE US	ZIP 12345	HOME PHONE (101) 111 9941	WORK PHONE

EMPLOYER Retired Navy Captain	ADDRESS	PATIENT STATUS (MARRIED) DIVORCED SINGLE STUDENT OTHER

INSURANCE: PRIMARY BC BS	ID# WXY 7031	GROUP AS 101	SECONDARY POLICY TRICARE

POLICYHOLDER NAME Janet B. Neely	BIRTHDATE 09/09/45	RELATIONSHIP spouse	POLICYHOLDER NAME	BIRTHDATE	RELATIONSHIP

SUPPLEMENTAL PLAN	EMPLOYER Retired Navy Captain

POLICYHOLDER NAME	BIRTHDATE	RELATIONSHIP

DIAGNOSIS — **CODE**

EMPLOYER Anywhere School District	

DIAGNOSIS	CODE
1. Abnormal EKG	794.31
2. Coronary Artery Disease	414.00
3. Family History, Heart Disease	V17.4
4.	

REFERRING PHYSICIAN UPIN/SSN

PLACE OF SERVICE Office

PROCEDURES 03/10/YYYY	CODE	CHARGE
1. OV, Est Pt Level III	99213	$75—
2. EKG 12 lead with interpretation and report	93000	60—
3.		
4.		
5.		
6.		

SPECIAL NOTES Authorization BC/BS 1056W
Date of onset 03/09

TOTAL CHARGES $135—	PAYMENTS $12—	ADJUSTMENTS 0	BALANCE $123—

RETURN VISIT Schedule Stress Test tomorrow	PHYSICIAN SIGNATURE *Erin A. Helper, M.D.*

ERIN A. HELPER, M.D.   101 MEDIC DRIVE, ANYWHERE, US 12345
PHONE NUMBER (101) 111-1234
EIN # 11-123341   SSN # 111-22-3333
UPIN EH8888   NPI 00818810   Medicaid # EBH8881   BC/BS # EH11881 GRP: 1204-P   TRICARE: 12345678

FIGURE 16-13 John R. Neely encounter form

Additional TRICARE case studies are found in Appendix I and II of this text and in the workbook.

Case studies require reading the case study chart entries, and abstracting and coding the diagnostic information. Necessary hospital, clinic, and physician data are included in the Clinic Billing Manual in Appendix II.

PLEASE
DO NOT
STAPLE
IN THIS
AREA

(SAMPLE ONLY - NOT APPROVED FOR USE)

↑ CARRIER

| PICA | | **UNDERSTANDING HEALTH INSURANCE CLAIM FORM** | PICA | |

| 1. MEDICARE ☐ (Medicare #) | MEDICAID ☐ (Medicaid #) | CHAMPUS ☒ (Sponsor's SSN) | CHAMPVA ☐ (VA File #) | GROUP HEALTH PLAN ☐ (SSN or ID) | FECA BLK LUNG ☐ (SSN) | OTHER ☐ (ID) | 1a. INSURED'S I.D. NUMBER (FOR PROGRAM IN ITEM 1) 0010670198 |

| 2. PATIENT'S NAME (Last Name, First Name, Middle Initial) NEELY JOHN R | 3. PATIENT'S BIRTH DATE MM 10 DD 25 YY 1945 SEX M ☒ F ☐ | 4. INSURED'S NAME (Last Name, First Name, Middle Initial) NEELY JANET B |

| 5. PATIENT'S ADDRESS (No. Street) 1 MILITARY DRIVE | 6. PATIENT RELATIONSHIP TO INSURED Self ☐ Spouse ☒ Child ☐ Other ☐ | 7. INSURED'S ADDRESS (No. Street) SAME |

| CITY ANYWHERE | STATE US | 8. PATIENT STATUS Single ☐ Married ☒ Other ☐ | CITY | STATE |

| ZIP CODE 12345 | TELEPHONE (Include Area Code) 101 111 9941 | Employed ☐ Full-Time Student ☐ Part-Time Student ☐ | ZIP CODE | TELEPHONE (INCLUDE AREA CODE) ( ) |

| 9. OTHER INSURED'S NAME (Last Name, First Name, Middle Initial) NONE | 10. IS PATIENT'S CONDITION RELATED TO: | 11. INSURED'S POLICY GROUP OR FECA NUMBER WXY7031 AS101 |

| a. OTHER INSURED'S POLICY OR GROUP NUMBER | a. EMPLOYMENT? (CURRENT OR PREVIOUS) ☐ YES ☒ NO | a. INSURED'S DATE OF BIRTH MM 09 DD 09 YY 1945 SEX M ☐ F ☒ |

| b. OTHER INSURED'S DATE OF BIRTH MM DD YY SEX M ☐ F ☐ | b. AUTO ACCIDENT? PLACE (State) ☐ YES ☒ NO | b. EMPLOYER'S NAME OR SCHOOL NAME ANYWHERE SCHOOL DISTRICT |

| c. EMPLOYER'S NAME OR SCHOOL NAME | c. OTHER ACCIDENT? ☐ YES ☒ NO | c. INSURANCE PLAN NAME OR PROGRAM NAME BLUE CROSS BLUE SHIELD |

| d. INSURANCE PLAN NAME OR PROGRAM NAME | 10d. RESERVED FOR LOCAL USE | d. IS THERE ANOTHER HEALTH BENEFIT PLAN? ☐ YES ☒ NO If yes, return to and complete item 9 a – d. |

READ BACK OF FORM BEFORE COMPLETING & SIGNING THIS FORM.
12. PATIENT'S OR AUTHORIZED PERSON'S SIGNATURE I authorize the release of any medical or other information necessary to process this claim. I also request payment of government benefits either to myself or to the party who accepts assignment below.

SIGNED SIGNATURE ON FILE DATE _____

13. INSURED'S OR AUTHORIZED PERSON'S SIGNATURE I authorize payment of medical benefits to the undersigned physician or supplier for services described below.

SIGNED _____

↕ PATIENT AND INSURED INFORMATION

| 14. DATE OF CURRENT: MM 03 DD 09 YY YYYY ILLNESS (First symptom) OR INJURY (Accident) OR PREGNANCY (LMP) | 15. IF PATIENT HAS HAD SAME OR SIMILAR ILLNESS, GIVE FIRST DATE MM DD YY | 16. DATES PATIENT UNABLE TO WORK IN CURRENT OCCUPATION FROM MM DD YY TO MM DD YY |

| 17. NAME OF REFERRING PHYSICIAN OR OTHER SOURCE | 17a. I.D. NUMBER OF REFERRING PHYSICIAN | 18. HOSPITALIZATION DATES RELATED TO CURRENT SERVICES FROM MM DD YY TO MM DD YY |

| 19. RESERVED FOR LOCAL USE | 20. OUTSIDE LAB? ☐ YES ☒ NO $ CHARGES |

| 21. DIAGNOSIS OR NATURE OF ILLNESS OR INJURY. (RELATE ITEMS 1, 2, 3, OR 4 TO ITEM 24E BY LINE) 1. 794.31 3. V17.4 2. 414.00 4. | 22. MEDICAID RESUBMISSION CODE ORIGINAL REF. NO. |
| | 23. PRIOR AUTHORIZATION NUMBER |

24. A DATE(S) OF SERVICE From MM DD YY To MM DD YY	B Place of Service	C Type of Service	D PROCEDURES, SERVICES, OR SUPPLIES (Explain Unusual Circumstances) CPT/HCPCS MODIFIER	E DIAGNOSIS CODE	F $ CHARGES	G DAYS OR UNITS	H EPSDT Family Plan	I EMG	J COB	K RESERVED FOR LOCAL USE
1 03 10 YYYY	11	1	99213	1 2 3	75 00	1				
2 03 10 YYYY	11	9	93000	1	60 00	1				
3										
4										
5										
6										

| 25. FEDERAL TAX I.D. NUMBER 11-123341 SSN ☐ EIN ☒ | 26. PATIENT'S ACCOUNT NO. 16-3 SECONDARY | 27. ACCEPT ASSIGNMENT? (For govt. claims, see back) ☐ YES ☒ NO | 28. TOTAL CHARGE $ 135 00 | 29. AMOUNT PAID $ | 30. BALANCE DUE $ 135 00 |

| 31. SIGNATURE OF PHYSICIAN OR SUPPLIER INCLUDING DEGREES OR CREDENTIALS (I certify that the statements on the reverse apply to this bill and are made a part thereof.) ERIN A HELPER MD SIGNED DATE MMDDYYYY | 32. NAME AND ADDRESS OF FACILITY WHERE SERVICES WERE RENDERED (If other than home or office) | 33. PHYSICIAN'S SUPPLIER'S BILLING NAME, ADDRESS, ZIP CODE & PHONE # (101) 111 1234 ERIN A HELPER MD 101 MEDIC DRIVE ANYWHERE US 12345 PIN# 12345678 GRP# |

↕ PHYSICIAN OR SUPPLIER INFORMATION

(SAMPLE ONLY - NOT APPROVED FOR USE) PLEASE PRINT OR TYPE SAMPLE FORM 1500 SAMPLE FORM 1500 SAMPLE FORM 1500

FIGURE 16-14 Completed TRICARE secondary form for John R. Neely encounter form in Figure 16-13

REVIEW

DEFINITION EXERCISE

Read the definitions carefully. If the statement is true, place a check mark to the left of the number. If the statement is false, correct it without rewriting the statement.

1. CHAMPUS: Civilian Health and Medical Program for the Uniformed Services. This program covers medical care for the members of the Armed Services when they need health care in the civilian community.

2. OCHAMPUS: Administrative headquarters of the TRICARE program and the fiscal agent responsible for processing claims.

3. Uniformed services: Army, Navy, Air Force, Marines, and Coast Guard only.

4. Armed Forces: Army, Navy, Marines, Coast Guard, Air Force, and NOAA.

5. TRICARE sponsor: Uniformed service personnel, either active duty, retired, or deceased.

6. Catchment area: An area defined by postal zip codes that fits roughly within a 40-mile radius of a government treatment facility.

7. Nonavailability statement: A form authorizing dependent medical care by the nearest military or public health treatment facility when the needed care is not available in the catchment area.

8. Active-duty personnel: Service personnel on current assignment with one of the Armed Forces.

9. Fiscal Year: January 1 through December 31 of a given year.

10. HBA: Health Benefits Advisor.

CHALLENGE EXERCISE

Answer the following:

1. State the TRICARE Standard outpatient deductibles for the following categories:
   A. Retired person
   B. CHAMPVA dependent child
   C. Spouse of active-duty sponsor

2. State the inpatient deductible for the following categories:
   A. Spouse of a retired person
   B. Dependent child of an active-duty sponsor
   C. Dependent child of a retired sponsor
   D. Active-duty personnel

3. Explain how a health care provider can check on the TRICARE eligibility of a military dependent.

4. State the requirements for filing a treatment report for mental health cases.

5. Explain the circumstances that require a Nonavailability Statement before claims will be processed for services rendered in the civilian community.

6. List the types of services covered under the TRICARE Mental Health Program.

7. List six separate and distinct types of services that are not covered benefits of TRICARE.

8. Compare and contrast the differences in the terms "policyholder" for a commercial insurance program and "sponsor" for TRICARE.

9. Explain why the government established the TRICARE program.

10. Explain how the function of the TRICARE Management Activity differs from that of the TRICARE Service Center.

Workers' Compensation

OBJECTIVES

Upon successful completion of this chapter, you should be able to:

1. Define the following terms, phrases, and abbreviations:

workers' compensation

Federal Employment
   Compensation Act (FECA)

Federal Employment Liability Act
   (FELA)

Merchant Marine Act (or Jones
   Act)

Longshore and Harbor Workers'
   Compensation Act (LHWCA)

Black Lung Benefits Act

State Compensation Fund

employer self-insured programs

private, commercial workers'
   compensation programs

combination programs

State Compensation
   Board/Commission

State Compensation Fund

on-the-job injury

medical claims with no
   disability

temporary disability

permanent disability

partial disability

total disability

vocational rehabilitation

death of the worker claims

Occupational Safety and Health
   Administration (OSHA)

Material Safety Data Sheet
   (MSDS)

First Report of Injury

2. List the categories of workers covered by the federal compensation program.

3. List and describe the types of workers' compensation available at the state level.

4. List and describe the classifications of workers' compensation cases as stipulated by federal law.

5. Select the proper terminology to describe the employee's "diminished capacity" in cases describing: pulmonary, heart, abdominal weakness, or spinal disorders; lower extremity disorders; levels of pain.

6. Identify final destinations for the required copies of the First Report of Injury form.

7. Describe correct billing procedures for workers' compensation cases.

8. Explain the necessity for separating treatment data for work-related injuries from health care data for treatment of diseases and disorders not related to the patient's employment.

9. List the forms necessary for the proper filing of compensation claims.

10. File First Report of Injury Reports and claim forms accurately.

INTRODUCTION

Before the enactment of workers' compensation laws, many employers seemed to have little concern for the health, welfare, and safety of their employees. Workers assigned to hazardous duties were expected to carry the full responsibility for avoiding injury; there were few precautions taken to guard the health of employees working with toxic substances.

If employees were involved in accidents at work or became too ill to work after long exposure to toxic substances, they were often laid off without compensation, until able to return to work. Early **workers' compensation** coverage provided by some employers was designed to provide some benefits to injured employees for medical expenses and lost wages when they were injured while performing their assigned duties.

After the federal government mandated that states establish workers' compensation laws that would meet minimum standards, a majority of employees were covered for medical expenses and lost wages for work-related injuries or illnesses provided the employee was not negligent in performing their assigned duties. Some states elected to exclude employers with only three to five full-time employees, temporary workers, domestic help, babysitters, volunteers for charitable organizations, and so on.

The philosophy behind the establishment of the workers' compensation laws was threefold: (1) to speed the injured worker's return to the work force; (2) to reduce the chances of the worker needing to apply for welfare or to a private charitable organization to meet their basic needs while they were unable to earn a living; and (3) to decrease employer liability for work-related injuries.

FEDERAL COMPENSATION PROGRAMS

The federal government retained sole responsibility for covering employees of the federal government, coal miners, longshoremen, and harbor workers. Until 1979, workers employed by the District of Columbia were also covered.

Federal employees injured at work are usually instructed to report to a government or military treatment facility for initial treatment, if available. In cases where it is not feasible to report to such a treatment facility, the initial care may be rendered by civilian providers. Contact the employee's human resources office for instructions on where to send the necessary reports and/or records.

Federal Legislation

The **Federal Employment Compensation Act (FECA)** provides workers' compensation coverage for nonmilitary, federal employees, and provisions are typical of most workers' compensation laws. **The Federal Employment Liability Act (FELA)** mandates that railroads engaged in interstate commerce are liable for injuries to employees if negligent. **The Merchant Marine Act (or Jones Act)** provides seamen with protection from employer negligence. The **Longshore and Harbor Workers' Compensation Act (LHWCA)** provides workers' compensation to specified employees of private maritime employers. The **Black Lung Benefits Act** provides workers' compensation for miners suffering from "black lung" (pneumoconiosis).

The injured worker or the company human resources department can provide the mailing address of the district office for submission of injury reports and claims.

STATE-SPONSORED COVERAGE

Four distinct types of coverage emerged from the state legislatures.

1. **State Compensation Fund:** A state government agency that functions as the insuring body to cover workers' compensation claims. Employers pay premiums to the state compensation fund to cover all employees of the company.

2. **Employer Self-insured Programs:** Some employers with sufficient capital to qualify can self-insure. State regulations require them to set aside a specific percentage of capital funds to cover medical expenses and wage compensation for all on-the-job injuries to their employees.

3. **Private, Commercial Workers' Compensation Programs:** Employers are permitted to purchase policies from commercial insurance companies interested in meeting state-determined requirements for workers' compensation coverage.

4. **Combination Programs:** Some states allow employers to choose a combination of any of the aforementioned programs. In these states, companies with a majority of workers at high risk for injury generally find the state compensation fund has the least expensive premium for high-risk workers.

The cost of workers' compensation benefits has skyrocketed along with other kinds of health care. This has forced many employers to look for concrete ways to control costs by turning long-term cases over to managed care programs, which require preauthorization of services and strict deadlines for filing claims.

Each state has also established a **State Compensation Board** or **Commission**, which is the government agency responsible for administering the law and handling appeals for denied claims or cases where a worker feels the compensation offered is too low. Care must be taken to differentiate between the State Compensation Board or Commission and a **State Compensation Fund**, which functions as a state-owned compensation insurance company.

ELIGIBILITY

To qualify for workers' compensation benefits, the employee is either injured while working within the scope of the job description, injured while performing a service required by the employer, or succumbs to a disorder that can be directly linked to employment, such as asbestosis or mercury poisoning. In some states, coverage has been awarded for stress-related disorders to workers in occupations that include emergency services personnel, air traffic controllers, and persons involved in hostage situations at work.

The worker does not have to be physically on company property to qualify for workers' compensation. An **on-the-job injury** would include, for example, a medical assistant who is injured while picking up reports for the office at the local hospital or a worker who is making a trip to the bank to deposit checks. These both qualify as job-related assignments. An employee sent to a workshop in another state who falls during the workshop would also be eligible for compensation, but not if they were injured while sightseeing.

CLASSIFICATION OF ON-THE-JOB INJURIES

The federal law mandated the following classification of cases:
- Medical claims with no disability
- Temporary disability
- Vocational rehabilitation
- Permanent disability
- Death of the worker

Medical claims with no disability are the easiest to process. Such claims are filed for minor injuries when the worker is treated by a health care provider and is able to continue working or return to work within a few days. These claims are easily adjusted to the full satisfaction of the worker.

Temporary disability claims cover medical treatment for injuries and disorders as well as payment for lost income. Each state has a specific waiting period before compensation for lost wages begins. Compensation for lost income in some states may be as much as two-thirds of the worker's normal salary. This payment is not subject to federal or state income taxes at present.

Temporary disability claims may be somewhat difficult to adjudicate. What may first appear to be a minor injury may require weeks for full recovery. Temporary disability status ends when the worker is able to be gainfully employed, although this may not be in the same position held before the injury.

Permanent disability is a legal term referring to the injured employee's diminished capacity to return to the work force. Not all persons who would be considered medically disabled meet the legal standards required for "permanent disability compensation." In cases meeting the legal definition, the physician determines that the injury has stabilized, the employee has been permanently impaired, and the employee is unable to return to the position held before the injury.

The problem with permanent disability claims is establishing fair compensation for lost earning capacity. Severity of the injury, amount of permanent loss, age of the employee, occupation before injury, and chances for rehabilitation all must be factored into determining the percentage of disability and amount of compensation due the worker. There are **partial disability** assignments (ie, 20%, 60%, or 95% loss) and **total disability** (100% loss) assignments. Examples of partial disability cases include the loss of part or all of a hand, arm, or leg or the presence of a neurologic disorder preventing return of full use of the injured area. A rating of 100% permanent disability means that the worker will not be able to be employed in any capacity.

Vocational rehabilitation claims cover the expense of vocational retraining for both temporary and permanent disability cases. Retraining allows an injured worker to return to the work force, although the worker is incapable of resuming the position held before the injury.

Disability Terminology

Specialized terminology has been developed and accepted by compensation carriers and the compensation commission to describe an employee's diminished capacity. The following terminology should be incorporated into the physician's report.

For cases describing injurious effects of pulmonary disease, heart disease, abdominal weakness, or spinal disabilities use the following terms:

- *"Disability resulting in limitation to light work"*: Patient is capable of working in a standing or walking position that demands minimum effort.

- *"Disability precluding heavy work"*: Patient has lost approximately 50% capacity to perform bending, stooping, lifting, pushing, pulling, and climbing activities.

- *"Disability precluding heavy lifting, repeated bending, and stooping"*: Patient has lost 50% capacity to perform the activities listed in the statement.
- *"Disability precluding heavy lifting"*: Patient has lost 50% capacity for lifting.
- *"Disability precluding very heavy work"*: Patient has lost 25% capacity for bending, pulling, climbing, or other comparable activities.
- *"Disability precluding very heavy lifting"*: Patient has lost 25% lifting capacity.

For lower extremity cases, use the following phrases.

- *"Disability resulting in limitation to sedentary work"*: Patient is able to work while sitting with minimal demands for physical effort, and may do some standing and walking.
- *"Disability resulting in limitation to semisedentary work"*: Patient can work at a position that allows for half-time sitting and half-time standing or walking with minimal demand for physical effort while standing, walking, or sitting.

For terminology describing pain use the following terms.

- *Minimal pain"*: The pain is an annoyance but will not handicap the performance of the patient's work.
- *"Slight pain"*: The pain is tolerable, but there may be some limitations in performance of assigned duties.
- *"Moderate pain"*: The pain is tolerable, but there may be marked handicapping of performance.
- *"Severe pain"*: This precludes any activity that precipitates pain.

For **death of the worker claims**, death benefits are computed according to the earning capacity of the worker at the time of the injury. Benefits are paid to the worker's dependents.

OSHA ACT OF 1970

The **Occupational Safety and Health Administration (OSHA) Act of 1970** was enacted by Congress to protect employees against injuries from occupational hazards in the work place. This act has special significance to those employed in the medical setting. Any worker who might come into contact with human blood and infectious materials must be provided specific training in the handling of infectious materials and the strict use of standard precautions to avoid contamination. In addition, each person who might be exposed to these infectious materials must be offered hepatitis B vaccinations. Comprehensive records of all vaccinations given and any accidental exposure incidences such as needle sticks must be kept for 20 years.

INTERNET LINK

The Occupational Safety and Health Administration Web site is located at www.osha.gov/ where you can click on the *Job Safety and Health Quarterly* link to view online versions of the magazine. There is also a link to the OSHA Expert Advisors page that answers questions on how OSHA regulations apply to work settings.

Under OSHA regulations, all employers are required to obtain and retain the manufacturer's **Material Safety Data Sheets (MSDS)** for any chemicals and hazardous substances used on site. Training employees in the safe handling of these substances is also required.

SPECIAL HANDLING OF WORKERS' COMPENSATION CASES

The health care provider is required to accept the workers' compensation–allowable fee as payment in full for covered services rendered on cases involving on-the-job injuries. An adjustment to the patient's account must be made if the amount charged for the treatment is greater than the approved reimbursement for the treatment.

The Compensation Board/Commission and appropriate insurance carriers are entitled by law to review only history and treatment data pertaining to a patient's on-the-job injury or disorder. This requires a provider who treats an established patient for a work-related disorder to create a compensation file (separate from the established medical record file/chart) for entering all notes related to the work-related disorder. This can be accomplished in one of two ways: (1) two separate and distinct files may be maintained; or (2) one file with two distinctly separated sections may be maintained. If two folders or charts are used, it is suggested that the compensation file folder be a different color from regular chart folders. In both cases, the file folder(s) prominently indicate the need for separation of the compensation information. Caution must be used to ensure that treatment data, progress notes, diagnostic test reports, and other pertinent chart entries pertaining to non-work-related disorders or injuries are not combined with notes and reports covering work-related disorders.

EXAMPLE

Patient A has been seen by the doctor for the past 2 years for treatment of diabetes. The patient was then treated for a broken ankle after falling at her place of employment. The patient was told to return in 5 days for a check-up. Three days after the original treatment for the broken ankle, the patient is seen in the office for "strep throat." The doctor also checks on the ankle. The treatment for the throat condition should be reported in the patient's regular chart; the progress report on the broken ankle will be recorded in the workers' compensation file or chart.

Out-of-State Treatment

Billing regulations vary from state to state. Contact the workers' compensation Board/Commission in the state where the injury occurred for billing instructions if an injured worker presents for treatment of a work-related injury that occurred in another state.

WORKERS' COMPENSATION AND MANAGED CARE

Workers and employers have benefited from incorporating managed care into workers' compensation programs since the late 1980s and early 1990s by improving the quality of medical benefits and services provided. For employers, managed care protects human resources and reduces workers' compensation costs. For workers, the benefits include:

- More comprehensive coverage because states continue to eliminate exemptions under current law (e.g., small businesses, and temporary workers).

- Expanded health care coverage if the injury or illness is work-related and the treatment/service is reasonable and necessary.

- Provision of appropriate medical treatment to facilitate healing and promote prompt return-to-work (since lack of treatment can result in increased permanent disability, greater wage replacement benefits, and higher total claim costs).

- Internal grievance and dispute resolution procedures involving the care and treatment provided by the workers' compensation program along with an appeals process to the state workers' compensation agency.

- Coordination of medical treatment and services with other services designed to get workers back to work (research by the Florida Division of workers' compensation suggests that managed care may reduce the time it takes an injured worker to return to work).

- No out-of-pocket costs for coverage or provision of medical services and treatment, and cost/time limits do not apply when an injury or illness occurs.

FIRST REPORT OF INJURY

First Report of Injury forms should be completed when the patient first seeks treatment for a work-related injury (Figure 17-1). This report must be completed in quadruplicate with one copy distributed to each of the following parties.

- One copy to the state Workers' Compensation Board/Commission.
- One copy to the employer-designated compensation carrier.
- One copy to the injured party's employer.
- One copy filed in the patient's work-related injury chart.

■ **NOTE:** There is no patient signature line on this form. The law says that when a patient requests treatment for a work-related injury or disorder the patient has given consent for the filing of compensation claims and reports. The required state forms may be obtained from the state Compensation Board/Commission. Necessary forms for filing federal forms may be obtained from the personnel office where the employee works or from the workers' compensation Federal District Office listed under the United States Government listings in the phone book. ■

The time limit for filing this form varies from 24 hours to 14 calendar days, depending on state requirements. It is best to make a habit of completing the form immediately, thus ensuring that the form is filed on time and not overlooked.

The First Report of Injury form requires some information that is not automatically furnished by a patient. When the patient tells you this was a work-related injury, it will be necessary to obtain the following information:

- Name and address of present employer.
- Name of immediate supervisor.

INSTRUCTIONS

1. Type answers to All questions and file original with the Workers' Compensation Commission within 72 hours after first treatment.
2. DO NOT FAIL to forward to the Workers' Compensation Commission PROGRESS REPORTS and FINAL REPORT upon discharge of patient.

DO NOT WRITE IN THIS SPACE

WCC CLAIM #

EMPLOYER'S REPORT Yes ☐ No ☐

WORKERS' COMPENSATION COMMISSION
6 NORTH LIBERTY STREET, BALTIMORE, MD. 21201-3785
SURGEON'S REPORT

This is First Report ☐ Progress Report ☐ Final Report ☐

EVERY QUESTION MUST BE ANSWERED AND FORM SIGNED

1. Name of Injured Person: | Soc. Sec. No. | D.O.B. | Sex M ☐ F ☐
2. Address: (No. and Street) (City or Town) (State) (Zip Code)
3. Name and Address of Employer:
4. Date of Accident or Onset of Disease: | Hour: A.M. ☐ P.M. ☐ | 5. Date Disability Began:
6. Patient's Description of Accident or Cause of Disease:
7. Medical description of Injury or Disease.
8. Will Injury result in:
(a) Permanent defect? Yes ☐ No ☐ If so, what? (b) Disfigurement Yes ☐ No ☐
9. Causes, other than injury, contributing to patients condition:
10. Is patient suffering from any disease of the heart, lungs, brain, kidneys, blood, vascular system or any other disabling condition not due to this accident?
Give particulars:
11. Is there any history or evidence present of previous accident or disease? Give particulars:
12. Has normal recovery been delayed for any reason? Give particulars:
13. Date of first treatment: | Who engaged your services?
14. Describe treatment given by you:
15. Were X-Rays taken: Yes ☐ No ☐ | By whom? — (Name and Address) | Date
16. X-Ray Diagnosis:
17. Was patient treated by anyone else? Yes ☐ No ☐ | By whom? — (Name and Address) | Date
18. Was patient hospitalized? Yes ☐ No ☐ | Name and Address of Hospital | Date of Admission: Date of Discharge:
19. Is further treatment needed? Yes ☐ No ☐ | For how long? | 20. Patient was ☐ will be ☐ able to resume regular work on: Patient was ☐ will be ☐ able to resume light work on:
21. If death ensued give date: | 22. Remarks: (Give any information of value not included above)
23. I am a qualified specialist in: | I am a duly licensed Physician in the State of: | I was graduated from Medical School (Name) | Year

Date of this report: (Signed)

(This report must be signed PERSONALLY by Physician)

Address: Phone.

FIGURE 17-1 First Report of Injury form (Courtesy of Maryland Workers' Compensation Commission)

- Date and time of the accident or onset of the disease.
- Site location where injury took place.
- Patient's description of the onset of the disorder; if the patient is claiming injury due to exposure to hazardous chemicals or compounds, these should be included in the patient's description of the problem.

In addition, the patient's employer must be contacted to obtain the name and mailing address of the firm's compensation carrier. Ask for a faxed confirmation from the employer of the worker with the on-the-job injury. If the employer disputes the legitimacy of the claim, you should still file the First Report of Injury. The employer must also file an injury report with the Compensation Commission/Board.

■ **NOTE:** The *physician* is responsible for completing this form. ■

Completing the First Report of Injury Form

Item 1

Enter the employee's full name as shown on personnel files (last, first, middle). Enter the employee's social security number and date of birth (MMDD YYYY). Indicate the employee's gender by entering an "X" in the appropriate box.

Item 2

Enter the employee's complete home address. This is very important, since workers' compensation disability payments, when due, will be mailed to this address. An incorrect address will delay their receipt.

Item 3

Enter the complete name and address of the employer.

Item 4

Enter the date (MMDDYYYY) on which the accident or onset of disease occurred. Enter the time of the day at which the accident or onset of disease occurred, and check the appropriate box to indicate A.M. or P.M.

■ **NOTE:** The date of the claimed accident must be specific. For example, if an employee was lifting heavy boxes on Tuesday (11/6) and called in sick on Thursday (11/8) due to a sore back, the date that is entered in Item 4 is 11/6. ■

Item 5

Enter the last date the employee worked after having the accident. If no time was lost from work, enter "STILL WORKING."

Item 6

Enter the employee's description of the accident, word-for-word. A complete description of the accident is required. Attach an additional page if space provided on the First Report of Injury is insufficient.

Item 7

Enter the description of the injury or disease. Explain the physical injuries or disease (e.g.,laceration, fracture, or contusion). Enter the anatomical part(s) of the body that required medical attention. Be specific, and indicate the location of the injured part when necessary (e.g., left middle finger, right thumb, or left shoulder). Enter the location and address where the accident occurred.

Items 8-12

Enter as appropriate.

Item 13

Enter the date (MMDDYYYY) the patient initially received services and/or treatment.

Items 14-19

Enter as appropriate.

Item 20

Enter an "X" in the appropriate box.

Item 21

If the employee died as a result of the injury sustained, enter the date of death (MMDDYYYY). Notify the appropriate state agency immediately upon the work-related death of an employee.

Item 22

Enter additional information of value that was not previously documented on the form.

Item 23

Enter the physician's specialty (e.g., internal medicine), the state in which the physician is licensed, the name of the medical school from which the physician graduated, along with the year of graduation (YYYY).

Be sure the physician dates and signs the report (MMDDYYYY). Enter the physician's office address and phone number.

Appeals

Because of the escalating cost of coverage for work-related injuries, some employers may deny that the injury or disorder reported by the patient qualifies for compensation. Other cases are denied because the worker failed to report the injury to his or her supervisor. The patient must be informed immediately of the employer's rejection of the patient's on-the-job injury claim. Employers are required by law to post the name and address of the compensation carrier along with a statement of employees' right to workers' compensation in a prominent place where it will be seen by all workers. Quite often, this information is posted at the designated sign-in or time clock area. This information should include the name and address of the compensation carrier. If the employer refuses to provide the carrier information to the physician's office, the employee can obtain this information for the provider from the posted notices and the First Report of Injury can then be filed as described.

When the patient receives written notice of denial of the claim from the employer, the patient is required to file an appeal with the State Commission/Board. The patient will have to pay the medical expenses for the alleged on-the-job injury until the Compensation Board/Commission agrees that the injury qualifies for compensation. If the patient's appeal is successful, the Commission/Board will notify the health care provider to refund payments made by the patient covering the medical expenses for the on-the-job injury and to bill the employer's compensation carrier.

PROGRESS REPORTS

A detailed narrative progress/supplemental report (Figure 17-2) should be filed to document any significant change in the worker's medical or disability status. This report should include the following information:

- Patient's name and compensation file/case number.

- Treatment and progress report.

- Work status at the present time.

- Statement of further treatment needed.

- Estimate of the future status with regard to work or permanent loss or disability.

- Copies of substantiating Xray, laboratory, or consultation reports.

The physician should personally sign the original and all photocopies of these reports. No patient signature is required for the release of any report to the compensation carrier or Commission/Board. These reports should be made in duplicate:

- One copy is sent to the compensation carrier.

- One copy is retained in the patient's file.

The physician is required to answer all requests for further information sent from the compensation carrier or the Commission/Board. Acknowledgment of receipt of a claim will be made by the carrier or the Commission/Board. This acknowledgment will contain the file or case number assigned to the claim. This file/claim number should be written on all further correspondence forwarded to the employer, the carrier, the Commission/Board, and, of course, on all billings sent to the carrier.

BILLING INFORMATION NOTES

The following is a summary of the general nationwide billing information for workers' compensation claims. Local requirements will vary by state. Be sure to follow all the regulations established by your state commission.

Eligibility

For-profit company/corporation or state employees with a work-related injury are eligible for workers' compensation benefits. Coal miners, longshoremen, harbor workers, and all federal employees, except those in the uniformed services, with a work-related injury are eligible for federal compensation plans.

Fiscal Agent

State Plans
Any one of the following can be designated the fiscal agent by state law and the corporation involved.

Practice Letter Head

PATIENT PROGRESS REPORT   DATE_____

RE: PATIENT:
       EMPLOYER:
       DATE OF INJURY:
       CLAIM NUMBER:
       DATE OF FIRST TREATMENT:
TREATMENT NOW BEING GIVEN: _____

_____

_____

_____

_____

DIAGNOSIS: _____

IS UNDER MY CARE: ☐ YES   ☐ NO

IS TOTALLY DISABLED: ☐ YES   ☐ NO

IS PARTIALLY DISABLED: ☐ YES   ☐ NO

IS WORKING: ☐ YES   ☐ NO

MAY BE ABLE TO RETURN TO WORK: WEEKS:_____
(ESTIMATE)   MONTHS: _____
                                             SPECIFIC DATE:_____

WORK LIMITATIONS: NONE: _____
                                             CANNOT WORK:_____
                                             LIGHT WORK: _____
                                             WEIGHTLIFTING: _____

PRESENT CONDITION: IMPROVED: _____
                                             UNCHANGED:_____
                                             WORSENING:_____

ANTICIPATED DATE OF MAXIMUM MEDICAL   WEEKS:_____
IMPROVEMENT OR DISCHARGE: MONTHS: _____
                                             SPECIFIC DATE:_____
                                             UNDETERMINED: _____

ANTICIPATED PERMANENT PARTIAL
DISABILITY (BASED ON _____   NONE: _____

_____   PER CENT:_____

_____   UNDETERMINED: _____

_____

SIGNATURE OF ATTENDING PHYSICIAN_____
TAX ID #_____

FIGURE 17-2 Sample workers' compensation narrative progress/supplemental report

1. State Compensation Fund (Do not confuse with the states' Compensation Board or Commission.)
2. A private, commercial insurance carrier
3. The employer's special company capital funds set aside for compensation cases

Federal Plans

Information may be obtained from the human resources officer at the agency where the patient is employed.

Underwriter

The federal or state government is the plan's underwriter, depending on the case.

Forms Used

The forms used include:

- First Report of Injury form.
- HCFA-1500 (12-90) claim form.

Filing Deadline

The filing deadline for the first injury report is determined by state law. The deadline for filing of the claim form for services performed will vary from carrier to carrier.

Deductible

There is no deductible for workers' compensation claims.

Copayment

There is no copayment with workers' compensation cases.

Premium

The employer pays all premiums.

Approved Fee Basis

The State Compensation Board establishes a schedule of approved fees. Many states use a Relative Value Study (RVS) unit value scale. Contact the State Commission/Board for information.

Accept Assignment

All providers must accept the compensation payment as payment in full.

Special Handling

Contact the employer immediately when an injured worker presents for the first visit without a written or personal referral from the employer. Contact the Workers' Compensation Board/Commission of the state where the work-related injury occurred if treatment is sought in another state.

No patient signature is needed on the First Report of Injury, Progress Report, or billing forms. If an established patient seeks treatment of a work-related injury, a separate compensation chart and ledger/account must be established for the patient.

The First Report of Injury requires a statement from the patient describing the circumstances and events surrounding the injury. Progress Reports should be filed when there is any significant change in the patient's condition and when the patient is discharged. Prior authorization may be necessary for nonemergency treatment.

WORKERS' COMPENSATION CLAIM INSTRUCTIONS— PATIENT AND POLICY IDENTIFICATION

Refer to Figure 17-3 for Blocks 1 through 13 of HCFA-1500 claim form.

Place Post-It® Notes or other markers on pages 486 and 488. You will be referring to them frequently.

Block 1   Enter an "X" in the FECA box for ALL WORK-RELATED INJURY claims.

■ **NOTE:** FECA is the Federal Employee Compensation Act. ■

Block 1a   *First claim:* Enter the patient's social security number.
Subsequent claims: Enter the insurance company assigned claim number if it is known. Otherwise, enter the patient's social security number.

Block 2   Enter the complete name (last name first, followed by the first name and middle initial). Use of nicknames or typographical errors will cause rejection of the claim.

Block 3   Enter the patient's name, birth date, (MM DD YYYY format), and gender.

Block 4   Enter the employer's name, if known.

Block 5   Enter patient's home address and phone number.

Block 6   Enter an "X" in the "OTHER" box.

Block 7   Enter address and telephone number of employer, if known.

FIGURE 17-3 Blocks 1 through 13 of the HCFA-1500 claim form

Block 8	Enter an "X" in the "EMPLOYED" box..
Blocks 9-9d	Leave blank.
Blocks 10a-10c	Enter an "X" in the "YES" box in Block 10a. Answer 10b and 10c as appropriate.
Block 10d	Leave blank.
Blocks 11-11a	Leave blank.
Block 11b	Enter name of the patient's employer.
Block 11c	Enter the name of the workers' compensation carrier.
Block 11d	Leave blank.
Block 12	Leave blank. Patient's signature and date are not required for workers'·compensation claims.
Block 13	Leave blank.
	Refer to the John Q. Public encounter form in Figure 17-4 and then review the completed HCFA-1500 claim form in Figure 17-5 (Blocks 1 through 13).

EXERCISE 17-1 Completing the Comparison Chart

■ **NOTE:** Complete all the steps in this exercise if you have not completed Exercise 12-1 prior to working in this chapter. If you have already completed Exercise 12-1, take out the Comparison Chart used in that exercise and proceed to Step 4 below. ■

ASSIGNMENT OBJECTIVE: To create a useful reference sheet as an aid to mastering the details of completing claim forms for six major insurance programs.

Step 1. Make five copies of the Comparison Chart in Appendix III.

Step 2. Record the following titles in the wide columns at the top of each page:
Commercial
BCBS
TRICARE Standard
Workers' Compensation

Step 3. Record the following numbers in the first column:

Page 1	Blocks	1 through 9d
Page 2		10 through 16
Page 3		17 through 23
Page 4		24A through 24K
Page 5		25 through 33

Step 4. Record abbreviated instructions in Blocks 1 through 13 of the workers' compensation column.

DATE 01/03/YYYY		REMARKS			
PATIENT John Q. Public			CHART # 17-1	SEX M	BIRTHDATE 10/10/1959
MAILING ADDRESS 10A Senate Avenue	CITY Anywhere	STATE ZIP US 12345	HOME PHONE (101) 201 7891		WORK PHONE
EMPLOYER BIO Laboratory		ADDRESS Nowhere US 12367	PATIENT STATUS MARRIED DIVORCED SINGLE STUDENT OTHER		
INSURANCE: PRIMARY High Risk, Inc.		ID# BL3636B	GROUP	SECONDARY POLICY	

POLICYHOLDER NAME BIO Laboratory	BIRTHDATE	RELATIONSHIP	POLICYHOLDER NAME	BIRTHDATE	RELATIONSHIP
SUPPLEMENTAL PLAN			EMPLOYER		
POLICYHOLDER NAME	BIRTHDATE	RELATIONSHIP	DIAGNOSIS		CODE
EMPLOYER			1. Whiplash		847.0
			2. Motor vehicle accident		E819.0
			3.		
REFERRING PHYSICIAN UPIN/SSN			4.		

PLACE OF SERVICE		
PROCEDURES	CODE	CHARGE
1. 01/03/YYYY Est, Office visit level III	99213	$40—
2.		
3.		
4.		
5.		
6.		

SPECIAL NOTES Injured driving delivery car 12/29/YYYY Return to work 01/04/YYYY			
TOTAL CHARGES $40—	PAYMENTS 0	ADJUSTMENTS 0	BALANCE $40—
RETURN VISIT PRN		PHYSICIAN SIGNATURE *Erin A. Helper, M.D.*	

ERIN A. HELPER, M.D.   101 MEDIC DRIVE, ANYWHERE, US 12345
PHONE NUMBER (101) 111-1234
EIN # 11-123452   SSN # 111-22-3333
UPIN EH8888   NPI 00818810   Medicaid # EBH8881   BC/BS # EH11881 GRP: 1204-P

FIGURE 17-4 John Q. Public encounter form

If the step-by-step instructions in this chapter indicate a particular block to be left blank, record the word "Blank."

Use horizontal arrows to indicate that the instructions in a specific block in the workers' compensation column are repeated in the next column (Figure 12-4).

If consecutive blocks are to be left blank, enter the word "Blank" in the first block and draw a vertical arrow down through the other blocks that have similar treatment.

Step 5. Save this form. It will be used in additional exercises in this chapter and other chapters mentioned in Step 2.

FIGURE 17-5 Completed Blocks 1 through 13 for John Q. Public encounter form in Figure 17-4

EXERCISE 17-2 HCFA-1500 Claim Form Blocks 1 through 13

This exercise requires 2 blank copies of a HCFA-1500 claim form. You may either make photocopies of the form in Appendix III or print copies of the blank form using the CD-ROM in the back of the text. (Instructions for installing the CD-ROM are printed in Appendix V.)

Step 1. Obtain two copies of the HCFA-1500 claim form.

Step 2. Review the instructions for Blocks 1 through 13 on your comparison chart.

Step 3. Review the Mary Sue Patient Encounter Form (Figure 17-6). Place a page marker at the encounter form.

Step 4. Abstract the information needed for Blocks 1 through 13 from the Encounter Form and enter the required information on the second claim form using Optical Scanning Guidelines. This may be completed by handwriting the information, using the Blank Form Mode on the disk, or typing the data.

Step 5. Review Blocks 1 through 13 of the claim form to be sure all required blocks are properly completed.

■ **NOTE:** This same encounter form and claim form will be used for Exercise 17-4. ■

DATE 01/20/YYYY	REMARKS							
PATIENT Mary Sue Patient					CHART # 17-2	SEX F	BIRTHDATE 10/10/1959	
MAILING ADDRESS 91 Home Street	CITY Nowhere	STATE US	ZIP 12367	HOME PHONE (101) 201 8989		WORK PHONE		
EMPLOYER A1 Grocery	ADDRESS Anywhere US 12345		PATIENT STATUS MARRIED DIVORCED SINGLE STUDENT OTHER					
INSURANCE: PRIMARY State Insurance Fund MSP9761		ID#	GROUP	SECONDARY POLICY				
POLICYHOLDER NAME	BIRTHDATE	RELATIONSHIP	POLICYHOLDER NAME		BIRTHDATE	RELATIONSHIP		

SUPPLEMENTAL PLAN

EMPLOYER

POLICYHOLDER NAME BIRTHDATE RELATIONSHIP	DIAGNOSIS	CODE
EMPLOYER	1. Lt upper & medial trapezius muscle spasms	728.85
	2. Weakness both arms	728.9
REFERRING PHYSICIAN UPIN/SSN	3. Cervical osteoarthritis	721.90
	4.	

PLACE OF SERVICE

PROCEDURES		CODE	CHARGE
1. 01/27/YYYY	Est. Office visit Level II	99212	$45—
2. 01/27/YYYY	Trigger Point Injection x2	20550	75—
3.			
4.			
5.			
6.			

SPECIAL NOTES
Injured at work 01/20/YYYY

TOTAL CHARGES $120.00	PAYMENTS	ADJUSTMENTS	BALANCE $120.00
RETURN VISIT		PHYSICIAN SIGNATURE *Erin A. Helper, M.D.*	

ERIN A. HELPER, M.D.   101 MEDIC DRIVE, ANYWHERE, US 12345
PHONE NUMBER (101) 111-1234
EIN # 11-123452   SSN # 111-22-3333
UPIN EH8888   NPI 00818810   Medicaid # EBH8881   BC/BS # EH11881 GRP: 1204-P

FIGURE 17-6 Mary Sue Patient encounter form

DIAGNOSTIC AND TREATMENT DATA

Refer to Figure 17-7 for Blocks 14 through 23 of the HCFA-1500 claim form.

Block 14   Enter the date the symptoms began or the on-the-job injury occurred.

Block 15   Enter the date a prior episode of the same or similar illness began, if it appears in the patient documentation.

Block 16   Enter the dates the patient was unable to work, if information is available in the chart or on the encounter form.

Block 17   Enter the name and title of any referring health care provider, if applicable.

14. DATE OF CURRENT: MM DD YY ◀ ILLNESS (First symptom) OR INJURY (Accident) OR PREGNANCY (LMP)	15. IF PATIENT HAS HAD SAME OR SIMILAR ILLNESS, GIVE FIRST DATE MM DD YY	16. DATES PATIENT UNABLE TO WORK IN CURRENT OCCUPATION MM DD YY MM DD YY FROM TO
17. NAME OF REFERRING PHYSICIAN OR OTHER SOURCE	17a. I.D. NUMBER OF REFERRING PHYSICIAN	18. HOSPITALIZATION DATES RELATED TO CURRENT SERVICES MM DD YY MM DD YY FROM TO
19. RESERVED FOR LOCAL USE		20. OUTSIDE LAB? $ CHARGES ☐ YES ☐ NO
21. DIAGNOSIS OR NATURE OF ILLNESS OR INJURY. (RELATE ITEMS 1, 2, 3, OR 4 TO ITEM 24E BY LINE) 1.⌐ . ⌐ 3.⌐ . ⌐ 2.⌐ . ⌐ 4.⌐ . ⌐		22. MEDICAID RESUBMISSION CODE ORIGINAL REF. NO. 23. PRIOR AUTHORIZATION NUMBER

FIGURE 17-7 Blocks 14 through 23 of the HCFA-1500 claim form

Block 17a   Enter the Social Security Number (SSN), with no spaces or hyphens, of the provider named in Block 17. If there is no referring provider, leave it blank.

Block 18   Enter the admission date and the discharge date (MM DD YYYY) if any procedure/service is rendered to a patient with inpatient status. If the patient is still hospitalized, leave the "TO" block blank.

Block 19   Leave blank.

Block 20   Enter an "X" in the "NO" box if all laboratory procedures included on this claim form were performed in the provider's office.

Enter an "X" in the "YES" box if laboratory procedures listed on the claim form were performed by an outside laboratory and billed to the referring health care provider.

Enter the total amount charged for all tests performed by the outside laboratory. The charge for each test should be entered as a separate line in Block 24D and the name and address of the outside laboratory included in Block 32.

Block 21   Enter the ICD-9-CM code number for the diagnoses or conditions treated on this claim.

■ **NOTE:** Detailed instructions for treatment of this block appear in Chapter 11. ■

Block 22   Leave blank.

Block 23   Enter any assigned managed care preauthorization number. Some carriers may also require that copies of any written authorization the provider received be attached to the claim.

Refer to Figure 17-8 for completed Blocks 14 through 23 for encounter form in Figure 17-4.

EXERCISE 17-3 Continuation of Work on Comparison Chart

Review the instructions for completing Blocks 14 through 23. As you read each block, record a description of the instructions in the appropriate block in the "workers' compensation" column of the Comparison Chart.

EXERCISE 17-4 Continuation of Exercise 17-2

Step 1. Review the Mary Sue Patient encounter form found in Figure 17-6 to find the diagnostic and treatment data.

14. DATE OF CURRENT: MM DD YY 12 29 YYYY ◀ ILLNESS (First symptom) OR INJURY (Accident) OR PREGNANCY (LMP)	15. IF PATIENT HAS HAD SAME OR SIMILAR ILLNESS, GIVE FIRST DATE MM DD YY	16. DATES PATIENT UNABLE TO WORK IN CURRENT OCCUPATION MM DD YY MM DD YY FROM 12 29 YYYY TO 01 04 YYYY
17. NAME OF REFERRING PHYSICIAN OR OTHER SOURCE	17a. I.D. NUMBER OF REFERRING PHYSICIAN	18. HOSPITALIZATION DATES RELATED TO CURRENT SERVICES MM DD YY MM DD YY FROM TO
19. RESERVED FOR LOCAL USE		20. OUTSIDE LAB? $ CHARGES ☐ YES ☒ NO
21. DIAGNOSIS OR NATURE OF ILLNESS OR INJURY. (RELATE ITEMS 1, 2, 3, OR 4 TO ITEM 24E BY LINE) 1. 847.0 3. 2. E819.0 4.		22. MEDICAID RESUBMISSION CODE ORIGINAL REF. NO. 23. PRIOR AUTHORIZATION NUMBER

FIGURE 17-8 Completed Blocks 14 through 23 for John Q. Public encounter form in Figure 17-4

Step 2. Abstract the information needed for Blocks 14 through 23 and complete the required information on a new claim form using Optical Scanning Guidelines. This may be done using the disk or handwriting or typing the data.

Step 3. Review Blocks 14 through 23 of the claim form to be sure all required blocks are properly completed.

Step 4. Compare your claim form with the completed form in Figure 17-13 (page 496).

■ **NOTE:** The same claim form will be used for Exercise 17-6. ■

Refer to Figure 17-9 for Block 24 of the HCFA-1500 claim form.

Block 24A

Enter the date the procedure was performed in the "FROM" column. Do not fill in the "TO" column for a single procedure entry unless you have special instructions to do so from a specific carrier. Use MMDDYYYY date format (no spaces).

To list similar procedures and charges performed on consecutive days, indicate the last day the procedure was performed in the "TO" column. Also, enter the number of consecutive days or units in the "Days/Units" column, Block 24G.

Block 24B

Use the appropriate two-digit code from the list below.

Provider's office	11
Patient's home	12
Inpatient hospital	21
Outpatient hospital	22
Emergency department—hospital	23
Ambulatory surgical center	24
Military treatment facility or	26
Uniformed service treatment facility	26
Skilled nursing facility	31
Nursing facility	32
Custodial care facility	33
Hospice	34

FIGURE 17-9 Blocks 24A through 24K of the HCFA-1500 claim form

Inpatient psychiatric facility	51
Psychiatric facility—partial hospitalization	52
Community mental health center	53
Intermediate care facility/mentally retarded	54
Residential substance abuse treatment facility	55
Psychiatric residential treatment center	56
Comprehensive inpatient rehabilitation facility	61
Comprehensive outpatient rehabilitation facility	62
End-stage renal disease treatment facility	65
State/local public health clinic	71
Rural health clinic	72
Independent laboratory	81
Other unlisted facility	99

Block 24C Use the appropriate code from the list below.

Medical care	1
Surgery	2
Consultation	3
Diagnostic Xray	4
Diagnostic laboratory	5
Radiation therapy	6
Other medical services	9
Durable medical equipment rental/purchase	A
Drugs	B
Ambulatory surgery	C
Hospice	D
Second opinion on elective surgery	E

■ **NOTE:** Number 9, other medical services, is a category for services that do not fit into any of the other codes, such as rehabilitation or occupational therapy. ■

Block 24D	Enter the appropriate five-digit CPT code or HCPCS Level II/III code number and any required CPT or HCPCS modifiers for the procedure being reported in this block. Enter a blank space, not a hyphen, to separate the code number from the modifier or multiple modifiers.
Block 24E	Enter the *reference number* (1 through 4) for the ICD-9 code number listed in Block 21 that justifies the medical necessity for each procedure listed in Block 24D.
Block 24F	Enter the fee for the procedure charged to the patient's account. If identical, consecutive procedures are reported on this line, enter the total fee for the combined procedures.
Block 24G	Enter the number of units/days for services reported in Block 24D. (Review the discussion on units in Chapter 11, page 283, if necessary.)
Block 24H	Leave blank.
Block 24I	Enter an "X" if the patient was administered emergency care before any required authorization was obtained.
Blocks 24J-24K	Leave blank.
	Refer to Figure 17-10 for completed Blocks 24A through 24K for the encounter form in Figure 17-4.

24. A						B	C	D		E	F		G	H	I	J	K
DATE(S) OF SERVICE						Place of Service	Type of Service	PROCEDURES, SERVICES, OR SUPPLIES (Explain Unusual Circumstances)		DIAGNOSIS CODE	$ CHARGES		DAYS OR UNITS	EPSDT Family Plan	EMG	COB	RESERVED FOR LOCAL USE
From			To														
MM	DD	YY	MM	DD	YY			CPT/HCPCS	MODIFIER								
1	0103YYYY					11		99213		1	40	00	1				
2																	
3																	
4																	
5																	
6																	

FIGURE 17-10 Completed Blocks 24A through 24K for John Q. Public encounter form in Figure 17-4

EXERCISE 17-5   Continuation of Work on Comparison Chart

Review the instructions for completing Blocks 24A through 24K. As you read each block, record a concise description of the instructions in the appropriate block in the "workers' compensation" column of the Comparison Chart.

EXERCISE 17-6   Continuation of Exercise 17-2

Step 1. Read the procedure data on the Mary Sue Patient encounter form found in Figure 17-6.

Step 2. Abstract the information needed for Blocks 24A through 24K and record the required information on a new claim form using Optical

Scanning Guidelines. This may be completed by using the disk or handwriting or typing the data.

Step 3. Review Blocks 24A through 24K of the three claim forms to be sure all required blocks are properly completed.

■ **NOTE:** This same claim form will be used for Exercise 17-8. ■

PROVIDER/BILLING ENTITY IDENTIFICATION

Refer to Figure 17-11 for Blocks 25 through 33 of the HFCA-1500 claim form.

Block 25
Enter the billing entity's Employer Tax Identification Number, if available. Otherwise, enter the provider's Social Security Number. In addition, be sure to enter an "X" in the appropriate box to indicate which is being reported.

■ **NOTE:** While third-party payers will accept the number with or without hyphens, when completing claim forms in this text (and while using the CD-ROM), be sure to enter hyphens. ■

Block 26
Enter the number assigned to the patient's account if the practice uses a numerical identification number to identify the patient's account or ledger card, or if the claim is filed electronically. Leave blank if the practice files patient accounts by patient name.

When working with case studies in this text and workbook, enter the case study number in this block. If the case requires primary and secondary forms, add the appropriate term.

Block 27
Leave blank.

Block 28
Total all charges on this claim form and enter the total in this block. This figure should never reflect negative charges or show a credit due the patient.

If multiple claims for one patient are generated by the computer because more than six services were reported, be sure the total charge recorded on each claim form accurately represents the total of the items on each separate claim form submitted.

Blocks 29 and 30
Leave blank.

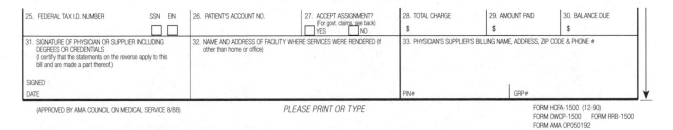

FIGURE 17-11 Blocks 25 through 33 of the HCFA-1500 claim form

Block 31

Paper claims: Most health care providers have arranged with major health insurance carriers to permit use of either a signature stamp or a typed name and professional credential. If these special arrangements have not been made, the provider must sign each claim.

■ **NOTE:** When arrangements are made to transmit claims electronically to an insurance company, a certification letter must be filed with the insurance company to replace the signature usually required in this space. ■

When working with case studies in this text and workbook, enter the provider's full name, credential, and the date the claim is completed.

Block 32

Enter this item when services listed on the claim form were performed at a site other than the provider's office or the patient's home. If the "YES" box in Block 20 contains an "X," enter the name and address of the laboratory that performed the laboratory procedures.

Block 33

Enter the phone number, including area code, to the right of the phrase "& PHONE #." It may overlap into the above printing.

Enter the official name of the billing entity on the first line below the phone number. Enter the mailing address of the billing entity on the next three lines. The zip code must appear on the same line as the city and state.

Out-of network provider claims: Leave blank the line with the abbreviations "PIN# and GRP#."

In-network provider claims: Enter any carrier-assigned participating provider identification number (PIN #) and/or group practice identification number (GRP #) in the appropriate space.

When working with case studies in this text and workbook, leave both the "PIN" and "GRP" spaces blank.

Refer to Figure 17-12 for the completed Blocks 25 through 33 for the encounter form in Figure 17-4.

EXERCISE 17-7 Continuation of Work on Comparison Chart

Review the instructions for completing Blocks 25 through 33. As you read each block, enter a concise description of the instructions in the appropriate block of the "workers' compensation" column of the Comparison Chart.

EXERCISE 17-8 Continuation of Exercise 17-2

Additional information you need for this case:

Dr. Helper's Social Security Number is 111-22-3333. She is on the medical staff and admits patient at Anywhere General Hospital, 222 Hospital Drive, in Anywhere, US.

Step 1. Review the Mary Sue Patient encounter form found in Figure 17-6.

Step 2. Abstract the information needed for Blocks 25 through 33 from the encounter form and the additional data provided and enter it on the claim form.

PLEASE
DO NOT
STAPLE
IN THIS
AREA

(SAMPLE ONLY - NOT APPROVED FOR USE)

◻◻◻ PICA

UNDERSTANDING HEALTH INSURANCE CLAIM FORM PICA ◻◻◻

1.						
MEDICARE	MEDICAID	CHAMPUS	CHAMPVA	GROUP HEALTH PLAN	FECA BLK LUNG	OTHER
◻ (Medicare #)	◻ (Medicaid #)	◻ (Sponsor's SSN)	◻ (VA File #)	☒ (SSN or ID)	◻ (SSN)	◻ (ID)

1a. INSURED'S I.D. NUMBER   (FOR PROGRAM IN ITEM 1)
BL3636A

2. PATIENT'S NAME (Last Name, First Name, Middle Initial)
PUBLIC JOHN Q

3. PATIENT'S BIRTH DATE   SEX
MM | DD | YY
10 | 10 | 1959   M ☒   F ◻

4. INSURED'S NAME (Last Name, First Name, Middle Initial)

5. PATIENT'S ADDRESS (No. Street)
10A SENATE AVENUE

6. PATIENT RELATIONSHIP TO INSURED
Self ◻   Spouse ◻   Child ◻   Other ☒

7. INSURED'S ADDRESS (No. Street)

CITY
ANYWHERE

STATE
US

8. PATIENT STATUS
Single ◻   Married ◻   Other ◻

CITY

STATE

ZIP CODE
12345

TELEPHONE (Include Area Code)
101 201 7891

Employed ☒   Full-Time Student ◻   Part-Time Student ◻

ZIP CODE

TELEPHONE (INCLUDE AREA CODE)
(   )

9. OTHER INSURED'S NAME (Last Name, First Name, Middle Initial)

10. IS PATIENT'S CONDITION RELATED TO:

11. INSURED'S POLICY GROUP OR FECA NUMBER

a. OTHER INSURED'S POLICY OR GROUP NUMBER

a. EMPLOYMENT? (CURRENT OR PREVIOUS)
☒ YES   ◻ NO

a. INSURED'S DATE OF BIRTH
MM | DD | YY   SEX
M ◻   F ◻

b. OTHER INSURED'S DATE OF BIRTH
MM | DD | YY   SEX
M ◻   F ◻

b. AUTO ACCIDENT?   PLACE (State)
☒ YES   ◻ NO   US

b. EMPLOYER'S NAME OR SCHOOL NAME
BIO LABORATORY

c. EMPLOYER'S NAME OR SCHOOL NAME

c. OTHER ACCIDENT?
◻ YES   ☒ NO

c. INSURANCE PLAN NAME OR PROGRAM NAME
HIGH RISK INC

d. INSURANCE PLAN NAME OR PROGRAM NAME

10d. RESERVED FOR LOCAL USE

d. IS THERE ANOTHER HEALTH BENEFIT PLAN?
◻ YES   ◻ NO   If yes, return to and complete item 9 a – d.

READ BACK OF FORM BEFORE COMPLETING & SIGNING THIS FORM.
12. PATIENT'S OR AUTHORIZED PERSON'S SIGNATURE I authorize the release of any medical or other information necessary to process this claim. I also request payment of government benefits either to myself or to the party who accepts assignment below.

SIGNED _____   DATE _____

13. INSURED'S OR AUTHORIZED PERSON'S SIGNATURE I authorize payment of medical benefits to the undersigned physician or supplier for services described below.

SIGNED _____

14. DATE OF CURRENT: ILLNESS (First symptom) OR INJURY (Accident) OR PREGNANCY (LMP)
MM | DD | YY
12 | 29 | YYYY

15. IF PATIENT HAS HAD SAME OR SIMILAR ILLNESS, GIVE FIRST DATE   MM | DD | YY

16. DATES PATIENT UNABLE TO WORK IN CURRENT OCCUPATION
MM | DD | YY   MM | DD | YY
FROM 12 | 29 | YYYY   TO 01 | 04 | YYYY

17. NAME OF REFERRING PHYSICIAN OR OTHER SOURCE

17a. I.D. NUMBER OF REFERRING PHYSICIAN

18. HOSPITALIZATION DATES RELATED TO CURRENT SERVICES
MM | DD | YY   MM | DD | YY
FROM   TO

19. RESERVED FOR LOCAL USE

20. OUTSIDE LAB? $ CHARGES
◻ YES   ☒ NO

21. DIAGNOSIS OR NATURE OF ILLNESS OR INJURY. (RELATE ITEMS 1, 2, 3, OR 4 TO ITEM 24E BY LINE)
1. 847 0
2. E819 0
3. ___.___
4. ___.___

22. MEDICAID RESUBMISSION CODE   ORIGINAL REF. NO.

23. PRIOR AUTHORIZATION NUMBER

24. A. DATE(S) OF SERVICE		B. Place of Service	C. Type of Service	D. PROCEDURES, SERVICES, OR SUPPLIES (Explain Unusual Circumstances)		E. DIAGNOSIS CODE	F. $ CHARGES	G. DAYS OR UNITS	H. EPSDT Family Plan	I. EMG	J. COB	K. RESERVED FOR LOCAL USE
From MM DD YY	To MM DD YY			CPT/HCPCS	MODIFIER							
0103YYYY		11		99213		1	40 00	1				

25. FEDERAL TAX I.D. NUMBER   SSN ◻ EIN ☒
11-123452

26. PATIENT'S ACCOUNT NO.
17-1

27. ACCEPT ASSIGNMENT? (For govt. claims, see back)
◻ YES   ◻ NO

28. TOTAL CHARGE
$ 40 00

29. AMOUNT PAID
$

30. BALANCE DUE
$ 40 00

31. SIGNATURE OF PHYSICIAN OR SUPPLIER INCLUDING DEGREES OR CREDENTIALS
(I certify that the statements on the reverse apply to this bill and are made a part thereof.)
ERIN A HELPER MD
SIGNED   DATE MMDDYYYY

32. NAME AND ADDRESS OF FACILITY WHERE SERVICES WERE RENDERED (If other than home or office)

33. PHYSICIAN'S SUPPLIER'S BILLING NAME, ADDRESS, ZIP CODE & PHONE #
(101) 111 1234
ERIN A HELPER MD
101 MEDIC DRIVE
ANYWHERE US 12345
PIN#   GRP#

(SAMPLE ONLY - NOT APPROVED FOR USE)

PLEASE PRINT OR TYPE

SAMPLE FORM 1500
SAMPLE FORM 1500 SAMPLE FORM 1500

FIGURE 17-12 Completed Blocks 25 through 33 for John Q. Public encounter form in Figure 17-4

PLEASE
DO NOT
STAPLE
IN THIS
AREA

(SAMPLE ONLY - NOT APPROVED FOR USE)

CARRIER

☐☐ PICA

UNDERSTANDING HEALTH INSURANCE CLAIM FORM PICA ☐☐

| 1. MEDICARE ☐ (Medicare #) MEDICAID ☐ (Medicaid #) CHAMPUS ☐ (Sponsor's SSN) CHAMPVA ☐ (VA File #) GROUP HEALTH PLAN ☐ (SSN or ID) FECA BLK LUNG ☒ (SSN) OTHER ☐ (ID) | 1a. INSURED'S I.D. NUMBER (FOR PROGRAM IN ITEM 1) MSP9761 |

2. PATIENT'S NAME (Last Name, First Name, Middle Initial)
PATIENT MARY SUE

3. PATIENT'S BIRTH DATE MM 10 | DD 10 | YY 1959 SEX M☐ F☒

4. INSURED'S NAME (Last Name, First Name, Middle Initial)

5. PATIENT'S ADDRESS (No. Street)
91 HOME STREET

6. PATIENT RELATIONSHIP TO INSURED
Self ☐ Spouse ☐ Child ☐ Other ☒

7. INSURED'S ADDRESS (No. Street)

CITY NOWHERE STATE US

8. PATIENT STATUS
Single ☐ Married ☐ Other ☐

CITY STATE

ZIP CODE 12367 TELEPHONE (Include Area Code) 101 201 8989

Employed ☒ Full-Time Student ☐ Part-Time Student ☐

ZIP CODE TELEPHONE (INCLUDE AREA CODE) ( )

9. OTHER INSURED'S NAME (Last Name, First Name, Middle Initial)

10. IS PATIENT'S CONDITION RELATED TO:

11. INSURED'S POLICY GROUP OR FECA NUMBER

a. OTHER INSURED'S POLICY OR GROUP NUMBER

a. EMPLOYMENT? (CURRENT OR PREVIOUS) ☒ YES ☐ NO

a. INSURED'S DATE OF BIRTH MM | DD | YY SEX M☐ F☐

b. OTHER INSURED'S DATE OF BIRTH MM | DD | YY SEX M☐ F☐

b. AUTO ACCIDENT? ☐ YES ☒ NO PLACE (State)

b. EMPLOYER'S NAME OR SCHOOL NAME
A1 GROCERY

c. EMPLOYER'S NAME OR SCHOOL NAME

c. OTHER ACCIDENT? ☐ YES ☒ NO

c. INSURANCE PLAN NAME OR PROGRAM NAME
STATE INSURANCE FUND

d. INSURANCE PLAN NAME OR PROGRAM NAME

10d. RESERVED FOR LOCAL USE

d. IS THERE ANOTHER HEALTH BENEFIT PLAN? ☐ YES ☐ NO If yes, return to and complete item 9 a – d.

READ BACK OF FORM BEFORE COMPLETING & SIGNING THIS FORM.
12. PATIENT'S OR AUTHORIZED PERSON'S SIGNATURE I authorize the release of any medical or other information necessary to process this claim. I also request payment of government benefits either to myself or to the party who accepts assignment below.
SIGNED _____ DATE _____

13. INSURED'S OR AUTHORIZED PERSON'S SIGNATURE I authorize payment of medical benefits to the undersigned physician or supplier for services described below.
SIGNED _____

14. DATE OF CURRENT: MM 01 | DD 20 | YY YYYY ◄ ILLNESS (First symptom) OR INJURY (Accident) OR PREGNANCY (LMP)

15. IF PATIENT HAS HAD SAME OR SIMILAR ILLNESS, GIVE FIRST DATE MM | DD | YY

16. DATES PATIENT UNABLE TO WORK IN CURRENT OCCUPATION FROM MM | DD | YY TO MM | DD | YY

17. NAME OF REFERRING PHYSICIAN OR OTHER SOURCE

17a. I.D. NUMBER OF REFERRING PHYSICIAN

18. HOSPITALIZATION DATES RELATED TO CURRENT SERVICES FROM MM | DD | YY TO MM | DD | YY

19. RESERVED FOR LOCAL USE

20. OUTSIDE LAB? ☐ YES ☒ NO $ CHARGES

21. DIAGNOSIS OR NATURE OF ILLNESS OR INJURY. (RELATE ITEMS 1, 2, 3, OR 4 TO ITEM 24E BY LINE)
1. 728 85
2. 728 9
3. 721 90
4. _____

22. MEDICAID RESUBMISSION CODE ORIGINAL REF. NO.

23. PRIOR AUTHORIZATION NUMBER

24. A DATE(S) OF SERVICE From MM DD YY To MM DD YY	B Place of Service	C Type of Service	D PROCEDURES, SERVICES, OR SUPPLIES (Explain Unusual Circumstances) CPT/HCPCS	MODIFIER	E DIAGNOSIS CODE	F $ CHARGES	G DAYS OR UNITS	H EPSDT Family Plan	I EMG	J COB	K RESERVED FOR LOCAL USE
1	0127YYYY	11	1	99212		1	45 00	1				
2	0127YYYY	11	2	20550		1	75 00	2				
3												
4												
5												
6												

25. FEDERAL TAX I.D. NUMBER 11-123452 SSN ☐ EIN ☒

26. PATIENT'S ACCOUNT NO. 17-2

27. ACCEPT ASSIGNMENT? (For govt. claims, see back) ☐ YES ☐ NO

28. TOTAL CHARGE $ 120 00

29. AMOUNT PAID $

30. BALANCE DUE $ 120 00

31. SIGNATURE OF PHYSICIAN OR SUPPLIER INCLUDING DEGREES OR CREDENTIALS (I certify that the statements on the reverse apply to this bill and are made a part thereof.)
ERIN A HELPER MD
SIGNED _____ DATE MMDDYYYY

32. NAME AND ADDRESS OF FACILITY WHERE SERVICES WERE RENDERED (If other than home or office)

33. PHYSICIAN'S SUPPLIER'S BILLING NAME, ADDRESS, ZIP CODE & PHONE #
(101) 111 1234
ERIN A HELPER MD
101 MEDIC DRIVE
ANYWHERE US 12345
PIN# GRP#

(SAMPLE ONLY - NOT APPROVED FOR USE) PLEASE PRINT OR TYPE SAMPLE FORM 1500 SAMPLE FORM 1500 SAMPLE FORM 1500

PATIENT AND INSURED INFORMATION

PHYSICIAN OR SUPPLIER INFORMATION

FIGURE 17-13 Completed HCFA-1500 claim form for Mary Sue Patient encounter form in Figure 17-6

Step 3. Review Blocks 25 through 33 of the three claim forms to be sure all required blocks are properly completed.

Step 4. Compare your claim form with the completed claim form in Figure 17-13.

Additional workers' compensation case studies are found in Appendix II.

Case studies found in Appendix II require reading the case study chart entries and abstracting and coding the diagnostic information. Necessary hospital, clinic, and physician data is included in the Clinic Billing Manual in Appendix II.

REVIEW

DEFINITION EXERCISE

Read the definitions carefully. If the statement is true, place a check mark to the left of the number. If the statement is false, correct it without rewriting the statement.

1. Workers' compensation: Provision by employers to compensate their employees for medical expenses incurred from work-related injuries or illnesses.

2. State Compensation Fund: Regulates the workers' compensation program within a state.

3. State Compensation Board/Commission: A state-administered insurance program for on-the-job injury cases.

4. Temporary disability: The worker will be able to fully recover from the disorder and return to his or her regularly assigned job.

5. Permanent disability: The inability to be gainfully employed.

CHALLENGE EXERCISE

Answer the following:

1. List four types of workers' compensation programs that were created by state governments to meet mandates of the federal law.

2. Name four groups of workers covered solely by the federal workers' compensation program.

3. List the five classifications of compensation cases as stipulated by federal law.

4. Four copies must be made of the physician's First Report of Injury form. Explain where each copy must be sent or filed.

5. Explain why it is necessary to keep a patient's treatment and financial data covering a work-related injury separate from the patient's medical record for treatment of all other medical problems.

6. State the deadline for filing the physician's First Report of Injury.

7. Explain where billing for treatment of a workers' compensation case should be sent.

8. State the name of the form used for filing a claim for treatment of a workers' compensation case.

9. Match the description of the patient's capability listed in Group One with the accepted compensation terminology describing the employee's diminished capacity as stated in Group Two. Enter the number corresponding to the compensation terminology to the left of the matching letter in Group One, which describes the patient's condition.

GROUP ONE

_____ A. Patient is capable of working in a standing or walking position that demands minimal effort.

_____ B. Patient has lost 50% capacity to perform activities such as repeated bending and stooping.

_____ C. Patient has lost 50% capacity for lifting.

_____ D. Patient is able to work while sitting with minimal demands for physical effort and may do some standing and walking.

_____ E. Patient's pain is an annoyance but will not handicap the performance of work.

_____ F. Patient can work in a position that allows sitting part of the time and standing or walking half of the time when minimal physical effort is demanded.

_____ G. Patient's pain is tolerable but may cause some limitation in performance.

_____ H. Patient has lost 50% capacity to perform bending, stooping, lifting, pushing, or pulling activities.

_____ I. Patient's pain is so bad that the patient is precluded from any activity that will precipItate pain.

GROUP TWO

1. Disability resulting in limitation to light work

2. Disability precluding heavy work

3. Disability precluding heavy lifting, repeated bending, and stooping

4. Disability precluding heavy lifting

5. Disability precluding very heavy work

6. Disability precluding very heavy lifting

7. Disability resulting in limitation to sedentary work

8. Disability resulting in limitation to semi-sedentary work

9. Minimal pain

10. Slight pain

11. Moderate pain

12. Severe pain

Case Studies: Set One

One

CASE STUDIES 1-1 THROUGH 1-15

■ **NOTE:** All the information needed for completing the claim forms is provided on the encounter forms. Review carefully, and note changes in provider information. ■

Case Study 1-1

DATE	REMARKS			
01/10/YYYY	Outpatient Service			

PATIENT			CHART #	SEX	BIRTHDATE
Hightower, Mary Sue			1-1	F	08/07/51

MAILING ADDRESS	CITY	STATE	ZIP	HOME PHONE	WORK PHONE
61 Water Tower Street	Anywhere	US	12345	(101) 201 6987	

EMPLOYER	ADDRESS	PATIENT STATUS
Homemaker		(MARRIED) DIVORCED SINGLE STUDENT OTHER

INSURANCE: PRIMARY	ID#	GROUP	SECONDARY POLICY
Aetna	272034109	NPW	

POLICYHOLDER NAME	BIRTHDATE	RELATIONSHIP	POLICYHOLDER NAME	BIRTHDATE	RELATIONSHIP
Walter W	04/09/51	Spouse			

SUPPLEMENTAL PLAN	EMPLOYER

POLICYHOLDER NAME	BIRTHDATE	RELATIONSHIP	DIAGNOSIS	CODE
			1. Coronary Artery Disease in grafted vein	414.02
EMPLOYER			2.	
Anywhere Water Co			3.	
REFERRING PHYSICIAN UPIN/SSN			4.	
I. M. Gooddoc	777 70 7070			

PLACE OF SERVICE	Goodmedicine Hospital Provider Street Anywhere US 12345

PROCEDURES		CODE	CHARGE
1. Left Heart Catheterization	1/10/YYYY	93510	$2000—
2. Injection for Catheterization	1/10/YYYY	93540	250—
3. Angiography, venous bypass grafts	1/10/YYYY	93556	750—
4.			
5.			
6.			

SPECIAL NOTES
Patient originally diagnosed with CAD five years ago (6/15/YYYY)

TOTAL CHARGES	PAYMENTS	ADJUSTMENTS	BALANCE
$3000—	-0-	-0-	$3000—

RETURN VISIT	PHYSICIAN SIGNATURE
5 days	*Irmina M. Brillant, M.D.*

IRMINA M. BRILLANT, M.D.   25 MEDICAL DRIVE, INJURY, US 12347
PHONE NUMBER (101) 201 3145
EIN 11-765431   UPIN IB9821   NPI 76534410
TRICARE PIN IBM7791   BC PIN 99531

Case Study 1-2

DATE	REMARKS				
03/01/YYYY					

PATIENT			CHART #	SEX	BIRTHDATE
Gayle, I.M.		SSA 210 01 0121	1-2	F	09/30/45

MAILING ADDRESS	CITY	STATE	ZIP	HOME PHONE	WORK PHONE
101 Happy Dr	Anywhere	US	12345	(101) 111-9876	111-9820

EMPLOYER	ADDRESS	PATIENT STATUS
Mail Boxes Inc.	Injury US	MARRIED DIVORCED ⟨SINGLE⟩ STUDENT OTHER

INSURANCE: PRIMARY	ID#	GROUP	SECONDARY POLICY
Conn General	210010121	101	

POLICYHOLDER NAME	BIRTHDATE	RELATIONSHIP	POLICYHOLDER NAME	BIRTHDATE	RELATIONSHIP
I.M. Gayle		Self			

SUPPLEMENTAL PLAN	EMPLOYER

POLICYHOLDER NAME	BIRTHDATE	RELATIONSHIP

DIAGNOSIS — CODE

1. Numbness, Lt arm — 782.0
2. Osteoarthritis, cervical — 715.98
3.
4.

EMPLOYER

REFERRING PHYSICIAN UPIN/SSN

PLACE OF SERVICE **Office**

PROCEDURES	CODE	CHARGE
1. OV, Est, Level III	99213	$60—
2. 2 Trigger point injections, Left upper & mid trapezius	20550	$75—
3.	20550-51	$75—
4.		
5.		
6.		

SPECIAL NOTES

TOTAL CHARGES	PAYMENTS	ADJUSTMENTS	BALANCE
$210—	$50—	0	$160—

RETURN VISIT	PHYSICIAN SIGNATURE
Return 2 wks if substantial improvement with injections	*Sejal Raja, M.D.*

SEJAL RAJA, M.D.   1 MEDICAL DRIVE, INJURY, US 12347
PHONE NUMBER (101) 202 2923
EIN 11-139799   UPIN SR1298   NPI 13944466
Conn. General PIN SR9919   BC PIN 994321   Medicaid SR2995

Case Study 1-3

DATE 03/01/YYYY		REMARKS			

PATIENT			CHART #	SEX	BIRTHDATE
Tiger, Katlyn			1-3	F	01/03/54

MAILING ADDRESS	CITY	STATE	ZIP	HOME PHONE	WORK PHONE
2 Jungle Road	Nowhere	US	12346	(101) 111-2222	111-3333

EMPLOYER	ADDRESS	PATIENT STATUS
John Lion CPA	Nowhere US 12346	MARRIED DIVORCED (SINGLE) STUDENT OTHER

INSURANCE: PRIMARY	ID#	GROUP	SECONDARY POLICY
BC/BS	ZJW334444	W310	None

POLICYHOLDER NAME	BIRTHDATE	RELATIONSHIP	POLICYHOLDER NAME	BIRTHDATE	RELATIONSHIP
Katlyn Tiger		Self			

SUPPLEMENTAL PLAN	EMPLOYER

POLICYHOLDER NAME	BIRTHDATE	RELATIONSHIP	DIAGNOSIS	CODE
			1. Bronchopneumonia	485
EMPLOYER			2.	
			3.	
REFERRING PHYSICIAN UPIN/SSN			4.	
I.M. Gooddoc				

PLACE OF SERVICE   Goodmedicine Hospital   Provider Street   Anywhere US   12345

PROCEDURES	CODE	CHARGE
1. Initial observation care, comprehensive 02/28/YYYY	99220	$175—
2. DC home 03/01/YYYY	99217	$65—
3.		
4.		
5.		
6.		

SPECIAL NOTES

Report 2 days   Return 03/07/YYYY

TOTAL CHARGES	PAYMENTS	ADJUSTMENTS	BALANCE
$240—	0	0	$240—

RETURN VISIT	PHYSICIAN SIGNATURE
03/07/YYYY	*Arnold J. Younglove, M.D.*

ARNOLD J. YOUNGLOVE, M.D.   21 PROVIDER STREET, INJURY, US 12347
PHONE NUMBER (101) 202 7754
EIN 11-123463   UPIN AY9999   NPI 00919919
Cigna PIN AY9999   BC PIN 991123

Case Study 1-4

DATE	REMARKS			
03/10/YYYY	Mrs. White housekeeper			

PATIENT		CHART #	SEX	BIRTHDATE
Green, Jeffrey A		1-4	M	02/03/87

MAILING ADDRESS	CITY	STATE	ZIP	HOME PHONE	WORK PHONE
103 Mountain View Road	Nowhere	US	12367	(101) 117-8765	Father 117-8543

EMPLOYER	ADDRESS	PATIENT STATUS
Student		MARRIED DIVORCED (SINGLE) (STUDENT) OTHER

INSURANCE: PRIMARY	ID#	GROUP	SECONDARY POLICY
BC BS	XWV7794483	876	BC BS XWV21928

POLICYHOLDER NAME	BIRTHDATE	RELATIONSHIP	POLICYHOLDER NAME	BIRTHDATE	RELATIONSHIP
Jeffrey G Green	07/01/55	Father	Janine	12/24/57	Mother

SUPPLEMENTAL PLAN	EMPLOYER
	Goodmedicine Clinic

POLICYHOLDER NAME	BIRTHDATE	RELATIONSHIP	DIAGNOSIS	CODE
			1. Bronchitis, acute	466.0
EMPLOYER			2. Purulent rhinitis	472.0
Self-employed			3.	
REFERRING PHYSICIAN UPIN/SSN			4.	

PLACE OF SERVICE	Office

PROCEDURES	CODE	CHARGE
1. OV, Est, Level II	99212	$26—
2.		
3.		
4.		
5.		
6.		

SPECIAL NOTES

TOTAL CHARGES	PAYMENTS	ADJUSTMENTS	BALANCE
$26—	$15—	0	$11—

RETURN VISIT	PHYSICIAN SIGNATURE
PRN	*Sejal Raja, M.D.*

SEJAL RAJA, M.D.   1 MEDICAL DRIVE, INJURY, US 12347
PHONE NUMBER (101) 202 2923
EIN 11-139799   UPIN SR1298   NPI 13944466
Conn. General PIN SR9919   BC PIN 994321   Medicaid SR2995

Case Study 1-5

DATE	REMARKS			
03/01/YYYY				

PATIENT		CHART #	SEX	BIRTHDATE
Noel, Christine		1-5	F	09/03/77

MAILING ADDRESS	CITY	STATE	ZIP	HOME PHONE	WORK PHONE
100 Christmas Tree Ln	Anywhere	US	12345	(101) 115-8123	115-8593

EMPLOYER	ADDRESS	PATIENT STATUS
Student (full time)		(MARRIED) DIVORCED SINGLE STUDENT OTHER

INSURANCE: PRIMARY	ID#	GROUP	SECONDARY POLICY
BC BS	ZJW35834	624	BC BS 123W476 X23

POLICYHOLDER NAME	BIRTHDATE	RELATIONSHIP	POLICYHOLDER NAME	BIRTHDATE	RELATIONSHIP
Noel, Henry	02/21/75	spouse	Christine Noel	09/03/77	Self

SUPPLEMENTAL PLAN	EMPLOYER
	Nowhere School District

POLICYHOLDER NAME	BIRTHDATE	RELATIONSHIP	DIAGNOSIS	CODE
			1. Pharyngitis, acute	462
EMPLOYER			2. Urinary frequency	788.41
Nowhere University			3.	
REFERRING PHYSICIAN UPIN/SSN			4.	

PLACE OF SERVICE

PROCEDURES	CODE	CHARGE
1. OV, Est, Level II	99212	$45—
2. UA dipstick c̄ microscopy	81000	8—
3. Quick Strep Test	86588	12—
4.		
5.		
6.		

SPECIAL NOTES

TOTAL CHARGES	PAYMENTS	ADJUSTMENTS	BALANCE
$65—	$20—	0	$45—

RETURN VISIT	PHYSICIAN SIGNATURE
PRN	*Arnold J. Younglove, M.D.*

ARNOLD J. YOUNGLOVE, M.D. 21 PROVIDER STREET, INJURY, US 12347
PHONE NUMBER (101) 202 7754
EIN 11-123463 UPIN AY9999 NPI 00919919
Cigna PIN AY9999 BC PIN 991123

Case Study 1-6

DATE 03/01/YYYY		REMARKS BCBS Medigap Plan ID 965432990			
PATIENT Blueberry, Elaine			CHART # 1-6	SEX F	BIRTHDATE 10/02/25

MAILING ADDRESS 101 Bust St	CITY Anywhere	STATE US	ZIP 12345	HOME PHONE	WORK PHONE

EMPLOYER	ADDRESS	PATIENT STATUS
		MARRIED DIVORCED SINGLE STUDENT OTHER

INSURANCE: PRIMARY Medicare	ID# 102 62 3434B	GROUP	SECONDARY POLICY None

POLICYHOLDER NAME Same	BIRTHDATE	RELATIONSHIP	POLICYHOLDER NAME	BIRTHDATE	RELATIONSHIP

SUPPLEMENTAL PLAN BC BS Medigap XWY123456	EMPLOYER

POLICYHOLDER NAME Same	BIRTHDATE	RELATIONSHIP	DIAGNOSIS	CODE
EMPLOYER			1. GI bleeding	578.9
			2. Perianal rash	691.0
REFERRING PHYSICIAN UPIN/SSN	UPIN IG 7777		3.	
I.M. Gooddoc, M.D.	NPI 00717717		4.	

PLACE OF SERVICE

PROCEDURES	CODE	CHARGE
1. InPt Consult, initial, Level III	99253	$125—
2.		
3.		
4.		
5.		
6.		

SPECIAL NOTES   Admission Date 03/01/YYYY   Discharge Date 03/05/YYYY
Goodmedicine Hospital, Anywhere Street, Anywhere, US 12345

TOTAL CHARGES $125—	PAYMENTS 0	ADJUSTMENTS 0	BALANCE $125—

RETURN VISIT	PHYSICIAN SIGNATURE *Irmina M. Brilliant, M.D.*

IRMINA M. BRILLANT, M.D.   25 MEDICAL DRIVE, INJURY, US 12347
PHONE NUMBER (101) 201 3145
EIN 11-765431   UPIN IB9821   NPI 76534410
TRICARE PIN IBM7791   BC PIN 99531

Case Study 1-7

DATE		REMARKS	Daughter Emma J. Peach		
03/02/YYYY			1234 Beneficiary Street Faraway US 99999		

PATIENT		SSA 888 44 1234	CHART #	SEX	BIRTHDATE
Berry Emma			1-7	F	03/08/05

MAILING ADDRESS	CITY	STATE	ZIP	HOME PHONE	WORK PHONE
Good Life Retirement Community Golden Age Road Anywhere US 12345				(101) 111 7700	

EMPLOYER	ADDRESS	PATIENT STATUS
Retired Nowhere School Dist		MARRIED DIVORCED (SINGLE) STUDENT OTHER

INSURANCE: PRIMARY	ID#	GROUP	SECONDARY POLICY
Medicare	888 44 1234A		

POLICYHOLDER NAME	BIRTHDATE	RELATIONSHIP	POLICYHOLDER NAME	BIRTHDATE	RELATIONSHIP

SUPPLEMENTAL PLAN		EMPLOYER
Aetna Medigap 888 44 1234		

POLICYHOLDER NAME	BIRTHDATE	RELATIONSHIP	DIAGNOSIS	CODE
Self			1. Stable, uncomplicated senile dementia	290.0
EMPLOYER			2. Peripheral edema	782.3
			3.	
REFERRING PHYSICIAN UPIN/SSN			4.	

PLACE OF SERVICE Skilled Nursing Facility at Good Life

PROCEDURES	CODE	CHARGE
1. Skilled Nursing Facility care, subsequent Level II	99312	$45—
2.		
3.		
4.		
5.		
6.		

SPECIAL NOTES
Aetna Medigap Plan ID 995432992

TOTAL CHARGES	PAYMENTS	ADJUSTMENTS	BALANCE
$45—	0	0	$45—

RETURN VISIT	PHYSICIAN SIGNATURE
Return 1 mo	*Arnold J. Younglove, M.D.*

ARNOLD J. YOUNGLOVE, M.D.   21 PROVIDER STREET, INJURY, US 12347
PHONE NUMBER (101) 202 7754
EIN 11-123463   UPIN AY9999   NPI 00919919
Cigna PIN AY9999   BC PIN 991123   Medicare PIN A9999

Case Study 1-8

DATE 03/20/YYYY		REMARKS					
PATIENT Cartwheel, Stella		SSA 332 99 9999	CHART # 1-8	SEX F		BIRTHDATE 01/02/27	
MAILING ADDRESS Red Wagon Rd		CITY Nowhere	STATE US	ZIP 12346	HOME PHONE (101) 113 6666		WORK PHONE
EMPLOYER Retired, Nowhere Univ		ADDRESS		PATIENT STATUS (MARRIED) DIVORCED SINGLE STUDENT OTHER			
INSURANCE: PRIMARY BC BS		ID# XYZ 33299 9009	GROUP 201	SECONDARY POLICY Medicare 332 99 9999A			
POLICYHOLDER NAME Fred W Cartwheel	BIRTHDATE 01/03/30	RELATIONSHIP Spouse	POLICYHOLDER NAME		BIRTHDATE	RELATIONSHIP	

SUPPLEMENTAL PLAN	EMPLOYER

POLICYHOLDER NAME BIRTHDATE RELATIONSHIP	DIAGNOSIS	CODE
EMPLOYER Nowhere University	1. Uncontrolled hypertensive crisis, malignant	401.0
	2. Vertigo, acute	780.4
REFERRING PHYSICIAN UPIN/SSN Yellow pages	3.	
	4.	

PLACE OF SERVICE Goodmedicine Hospital 1 Provider Street Anywhere US 12345

PROCEDURES	CODE	CHARGE
1. Initial Hosp. Visit, Level III (03/14/YYYY)	99223	$165—
2. Subsq. Hosp, Level III (03/15/YYYY)	99233	60—
3. Subsq. Hosp, Level II (03/16/YYYY)	99232	50—
4. Subsq. Hosp, Level II (03/17/YYYY)	99232	50—
5. Subsq. Hosp, Level I (03/18 & 19/YYYY)	99231	80—
6. Discharge, 30 min (03/20/YYYY)	99238	55—

SPECIAL NOTES Onset 03/12/YYYY Discharge home	Hospital PIN 1234GH	

TOTAL CHARGES $460—	PAYMENTS -0-	ADJUSTMENTS -0-	BALANCE $460—

RETURN VISIT	PHYSICIAN SIGNATURE *Angela DiLalio, M.D.*

ANGELA DILALIO, M.D.   99 PROVIDER STREET, INJURY, US 12347
PHONE NUMBER (101) 201-4321
EIN 11-198234   SSN # 111-99-6599
UPIN AD9101   NPI 00991234   TRICARE PIN ADL1982   BC PIN 991234   Medicare PIN D2112

Case Study 1-9

DATE 03/03/YYYY		REMARKS	Authorization GTM 18645-1		

PATIENT Makebetter, Geraldine T.			CHART # 1-9	SEX F	BIRTHDATE 06/20/45

MAILING ADDRESS 7866A Memory Lane	CITY Injury	STATE US	ZIP 12346	HOME PHONE (101) 111 9855	WORK PHONE

EMPLOYER None	ADDRESS	PATIENT STATUS MARRIED (DIVORCED) SINGLE STUDENT OTHER

INSURANCE: PRIMARY Medicare	ID# 101 27 8769W	GROUP	SECONDARY POLICY Medicaid 1198555W

POLICYHOLDER NAME self	BIRTHDATE	RELATIONSHIP	POLICYHOLDER NAME self	BIRTHDATE	RELATIONSHIP

SUPPLEMENTAL PLAN	EMPLOYER

POLICYHOLDER NAME	BIRTHDATE	RELATIONSHIP

DIAGNOSIS | **CODE**

1. Annual Physical Exam — V70.0
2. Bladder Infection — 595.9
3.
4.

EMPLOYER

REFERRING PHYSICIAN UPIN/SSN

PLACE OF SERVICE   office

PROCEDURES	CODE	CHARGE
1. Prevent Med, Est patient	99396	$75—
2. Est Office Visit, Level II	99212-25	40—
3. UA with microscopy	81000	8—
4. Hemoccult	82270	8—
5. CBC auto	85024	40—
6. Health Risk Assessment	99420	25—

SPECIAL NOTES
Sigmoid 1 mo — get preauthorization

TOTAL CHARGES $196—	PAYMENTS 0	ADJUSTMENTS 0	BALANCE $196—

RETURN VISIT	PHYSICIAN SIGNATURE *Arnold J. Younglove, M.D.*

ARNOLD J. YOUNGLOVE, M.D.   21 PROVIDER STREET, INJURY, US 12347
PHONE NUMBER (101) 202 7754
EIN 11-123463   UPIN AY9999   NPI 00919919
Cigna PIN AY9999   BC PIN 991123   Medicare PIN A9999

Case Study 1-10

DATE	REMARKS			
03/10/YYYY				

PATIENT			CHART #	SEX	BIRTHDATE
Phish, Gladys			1-10	F	11/21/30

MAILING ADDRESS	CITY	STATE	ZIP	HOME PHONE	WORK PHONE
21 Windwhisper Drive	Injury	US	12347	(101) 111 2397	

EMPLOYER	ADDRESS	PATIENT STATUS
Retired		(MARRIED) DIVORCED SINGLE STUDENT OTHER

INSURANCE: PRIMARY	ID#	GROUP	SECONDARY POLICY
Medicare	101 89 1701A		

POLICYHOLDER NAME	BIRTHDATE	RELATIONSHIP	POLICYHOLDER NAME	BIRTHDATE	RELATIONSHIP

SUPPLEMENTAL PLAN	EMPLOYER

POLICYHOLDER NAME	BIRTHDATE	RELATIONSHIP	DIAGNOSIS	CODE
			1. Cellulitis, Rt. Hand	682.4

EMPLOYER	
	2.
	3.

REFERRING PHYSICIAN UPIN/SSN	UPIN IG7771	
I.M. Gooddoc, MD	NPI 00717717	4.

PLACE OF SERVICE Goodmedicine Hospital 1 Provider Street Anywhere US 12345

PROCEDURES	CODE	CHARGE
1. I & D, abscess, subcutaneous 03/10/YYYY	10060	$450—
2.		
3.		
4.		
5.		
6.		

SPECIAL NOTES
Admit 03/10/YYYY   Discharge 03/11/YYYY

TOTAL CHARGES	PAYMENTS	ADJUSTMENTS	BALANCE
$450—	-0-	-0-	$450—

RETURN VISIT	PHYSICIAN SIGNATURE
3 days	*Angela DiLalio, M.D.*

ANGELA DiLALIO, M.D.   99 PROVIDER STREET, INJURY, US 12347
PHONE NUMBER (101) 201-4321
EIN 11-198234   SSN # 111-99-6599
UPIN AD9101   NPI 00991234   TRICARE PIN ADL1982   BC PIN 991234   Medicare PIN D2112

Case Study 1-11

DATE	REMARKS				
03/10/YYYY					

PATIENT			CHART #	SEX	BIRTHDATE
Filbert, Fiona J.			1-11	F	03/08/77

MAILING ADDRESS	CITY	STATE	ZIP	HOME PHONE	WORK PHONE
1 Butternut Street	Anywhere	US	12345	(101) 791 8645	

EMPLOYER	ADDRESS	PATIENT STATUS
		MARRIED (DIVORCED) SINGLE STUDENT OTHER

INSURANCE: PRIMARY	ID#	GROUP	SECONDARY POLICY
Medicaid	119850B		

POLICYHOLDER NAME	BIRTHDATE	RELATIONSHIP	POLICYHOLDER NAME	BIRTHDATE	RELATIONSHIP

SUPPLEMENTAL PLAN	EMPLOYER

POLICYHOLDER NAME	BIRTHDATE	RELATIONSHIP	DIAGNOSIS	CODE
			1. Papilloma c̄ cystic changes, benign, Lt breast, 3.0 x 1.5 x 0.2 cm	217
EMPLOYER			2.	
			3.	
REFERRING PHYSICIAN UPIN/SSN			4.	

PLACE OF SERVICE	Hospital Outpatient Dept Anywhere Street Anywhere US 12345

PROCEDURES	CODE	CHARGE
1. Excision, mass, left breast	19120	$75—
2.		
3.		
4.		
5.		
6.		

SPECIAL NOTES
Goodmedicine Hospital Medicaid PIN 9HO19076
Referred by Arnold J. Younglove, M.D. Medicaid PIN 00919919

TOTAL CHARGES	PAYMENTS	ADJUSTMENTS	BALANCE
$75—	$10—	0	$65—

RETURN VISIT	PHYSICIAN SIGNATURE
4 days	*Sejal Raja, M.D.*

SEJAL RAJA, M.D. 1 MEDICAL DRIVE, INJURY, US 12347
PHONE NUMBER (101) 202 2923
EIN 11-139799   UPIN SR1298   NPI 13944466
Conn. General PIN SR9919   BC PIN 994321   Medicaid PIN SR2995

Case Study 1-12

DATE 03/20/YYYY	REMARKS Injury date 03/17/YYYY			

PATIENT Willowtree, Gregory		CHART # 1-12	SEX M	BIRTHDATE 12/12/42

MAILING ADDRESS 150 Tree Lane	CITY Nowhere	STATE US	ZIP 12347	HOME PHONE	WORK PHONE

EMPLOYER Retired Army Capt	ADDRESS same	PATIENT STATUS MARRIED DIVORCED (SINGLE) STUDENT OTHER

INSURANCE: PRIMARY TRICARE	ID# 071 26 9845	GROUP	SECONDARY POLICY

POLICYHOLDER NAME self	BIRTHDATE	RELATIONSHIP	POLICYHOLDER NAME	BIRTHDATE	RELATIONSHIP

SUPPLEMENTAL PLAN	EMPLOYER

POLICYHOLDER NAME	BIRTHDATE	RELATIONSHIP	DIAGNOSIS	CODE
			1. Tear, medial meniscus, Rt knee	836.0
EMPLOYER			2. Plica, Rt knee	717.9
			3.	
REFERRING PHYSICIAN UPIN/SSN			4.	

PLACE OF SERVICE Goodmedicine Hospital 1 Provider Street Anywhere US 12345

PROCEDURES	CODE	CHARGE
1. Arthroscopy with medial meniscectomy 03/19/YYYY	29881	$2000—
2.		
3.		
4.		
5.		
6.		

SPECIAL NOTES

Discharge 03/20/YYYY

TOTAL CHARGES $2000—	PAYMENTS 0	ADJUSTMENTS 0	BALANCE $2000—

RETURN VISIT 3 days	PHYSICIAN SIGNATURE *Angela DiLalio, M.D.*

ANGELA DILALIO, M.D.   99 PROVIDER STREET, INJURY, US 12347
PHONE NUMBER (101) 201-4321
EIN 11-198234   SSN # 111-99-6599
UPIN AD9101   NPI 00991234   TRICARE PIN ADL1982   BC PIN 991234

Case Study 1-13

DATE		REMARKS	Duty Station USS George Bush CVN-02				
03/01/YYYY			Mail Address FPO AE 00599-2871				

PATIENT	SSA 103 24 6565		CHART #	SEX	BIRTHDATE
Patty, Agnes	(Gerry)		1-13	F	09/03/47

MAILING ADDRESS	CITY	STATE	ZIP	HOME PHONE	WORK PHONE
1 Patty Cake Drive	Nowhere	US	12367	(101) 112 2701	

EMPLOYER	ADDRESS	PATIENT STATUS
Domestic engineer		(MARRIED) DIVORCED SINGLE STUDENT OTHER

INSURANCE: PRIMARY	ID#	GROUP	SECONDARY POLICY
TRICARE Standard	103 23 6666		

POLICYHOLDER NAME	BIRTHDATE	RELATIONSHIP	POLICYHOLDER NAME	BIRTHDATE	RELATIONSHIP
Gerry Patty	03/09/40	Spouse			

SUPPLEMENTAL PLAN	EMPLOYER

POLICYHOLDER NAME	BIRTHDATE	RELATIONSHIP	DIAGNOSIS		CODE
			1. Cardiac arrhythmia		427.9
EMPLOYER			2. Epistaxis		784.7
			3.		
REFERRING PHYSICIAN UPIN/SSN			4.		
None					

PLACE OF SERVICE	Office

PROCEDURES	CODE	CHARGE
1. OV, new pt, level III	99203	$100—
2. Nasal cautery	30901	65—
3. EKG c̄ interpretation	93000	50—
4.		
5.		
6.		

SPECIAL NOTES
First symptoms 02/10/YYYY

TOTAL CHARGES	PAYMENTS	ADJUSTMENTS	BALANCE
$215—	$35— ck	0	$180—

RETURN VISIT	PHYSICIAN SIGNATURE
	Irmina M. Brilliant, M.D.

IRMINA M. BRILLANT, M.D.   25 MEDICAL DRIVE, INJURY, US 12347
PHONE NUMBER (101) 201 3145
EIN 11-765431   UPIN IB9821   NPI 76534410
TRICARE PIN IBM7791   BC PIN 99531

Case Study 1-14

DATE 03/10/YYYY		REMARKS Pt may return to work 03/31/YYYY				
PATIENT Million, Iona J.				CHART # 1-14	SEX F	BIRTHDATE 01/01/70

MAILING ADDRESS 100A Follish Pleasures Court	CITY Anywhere	STATE US	ZIP 12345	HOME PHONE (101) 759 0839	WORK PHONE

EMPLOYER Anywhere Golf Course	ADDRESS Anywhere MD	PATIENT STATUS MARRIED DIVORCED (SINGLE) STUDENT OTHER

INSURANCE: PRIMARY High Risk Ins.	ID# 10173	GROUP AGD	SECONDARY POLICY

POLICYHOLDER NAME	BIRTHDATE	RELATIONSHIP	POLICYHOLDER NAME	BIRTHDATE	RELATIONSHIP

SUPPLEMENTAL PLAN	EMPLOYER

POLICYHOLDER NAME	BIRTHDATE	RELATIONSHIP	DIAGNOSIS		CODE
			1. Retained Hardware		V54.0
EMPLOYER			2. Status Post Fx Surgery		V45.89
			3. Pain, healed fx site		719.47
REFERRING PHYSICIAN UPIN/SSN			4.		905.4

PLACE OF SERVICE Goodmedicine Hospital 1 Provider Street Anywhere US 12345

PROCEDURES	CODE	CHARGE
1. Removal, internal fixation, left ankle, deep	20680	$650—
2.		
3.		
4.		
5.		
6.		

SPECIAL NOTES   Admit 03/10/YYYY   Original date of injury 9/8/YYYY

Discharge same day

TOTAL CHARGES $650—	PAYMENTS -0-	ADJUSTMENTS -0-	BALANCE $650—

RETURN VISIT PRN	PHYSICIAN SIGNATURE *Angela DiLalio, M.D.*

ANGELA DILALIO, M.D.   99 PROVIDER STREET, INJURY, US 12347
PHONE NUMBER (101) 201-4321
EIN 11-198234   SSN # 111-99-6599
UPIN AD9101   NPI 00991234   TRICARE PIN ADL1982   BC PIN 991234

Case Study 1-15

DATE		REMARKS				
03/20/YYYY		WC Claim #BL3636				

PATIENT	SSN 163 63 3636		CHART #	SEX	BIRTHDATE
Scope, Mike Roe			1-15	M	06/20/72

MAILING ADDRESS	CITY	STATE	ZIP	HOME PHONE	WORK PHONE
10 Laboratory Ct	Nowhere	US	12347	(101) 214 1414	214 2072

EMPLOYER	ADDRESS	PATIENT STATUS
Bio Labs Inc	Nowhere US	MARRIED DIVORCED (SINGLE) STUDENT OTHER

INSURANCE: PRIMARY	ID#	GROUP	SECONDARY POLICY
High Risk Ins			

POLICYHOLDER NAME	BIRTHDATE	RELATIONSHIP	POLICYHOLDER NAME	BIRTHDATE	RELATIONSHIP
Bio Labs					

SUPPLEMENTAL PLAN	EMPLOYER

POLICYHOLDER NAME	BIRTHDATE	RELATIONSHIP

DIAGNOSIS   CODE

1. Strain, cervical   847.0
2. Low back strain   847.2
3.
4.

EMPLOYER

REFERRING PHYSICIAN UPIN/SSN

PLACE OF SERVICE	Office

PROCEDURES	CODE	CHARGE
1. OV, est, level II	99212	$26—
2.		
3.		
4.		
5.		
6.		

SPECIAL NOTES Work-related car accident Nowhere US 03/16/YYYY
Return to work 1 week

TOTAL CHARGES	PAYMENTS	ADJUSTMENTS	BALANCE
$26—	0	0	$26—

RETURN VISIT	PHYSICIAN SIGNATURE
3 wks	*Angela DiLalio, M.D.*

ANGELA DILALIO, M.D.   99 PROVIDER STREET, INJURY, US 12347
PHONE NUMBER (101) 201-4321
EIN 11-198234   SSN # 111-99-6599
UPIN AD9101   NPI 00991234   TRICARE PIN ADL1982   BC PIN 991234

Clinic Billing Manual and Case Studies: Set Two

Two

INTRODUCTION

This is a simulation using a variety of physician specialists that might be found in a small clinic practice.

This appendix is divided into two sections:

Section I contains portions of the Goodmedicine Clinic Billing Manual. Provider and billing entity identifiers necessary for completing claim form data blocks 17, 17a, 24B, 24C, 24K, 25, 32, and 33 for case studies in this appendix are included. **Section II** contains simulated clinic notes and encounter forms to be used in Chapter 10, Exercise 10-5, Part B, and additional claim form completion exercises for Chapters 12 through 17.

SECTION I CLINIC BILLING MANUAL

Welcome to the Goodmedicine Clinic, a small inner city clinic located in Anytown, USA. You are the Coding & Insurance Specialist for this clinic.

Clinic Data

GOODMEDICINE CLINIC, 1 Provider St., Anywhere, US 12345

Phone Number	(101) 111-2222
EIN	11-123456
BCBS Group #	GC12340
Medicare Group #	J1110
Group NPI	99123678

All physicians on staff in the clinic are participating providers for Medicare, Medicaid, and BCBS.

Hospital Data

All Goodmedicine Clinic physicians are on the medical staff of
GOODMEDICINE HOSPITAL
Anywhere Street
Anywhere, USA 12345

Medicare/Medicaid PIN	GHA123
Group NPI	90123478

Clinic Physicians

GAIL R. BONES, M.D.
Orthopedic Surgeon

SSN	555 55 5555
BCBS	12345
TRICARE	NonPAR
Medicare	G5555
UPIN	GB5555
NPI	00515515
Medicaid	GRB5555

HENRY C. CARDIAC, M.D.
Family Practice

SSN	444 44 4444
BCBS	12344
Medicare	H4444
UPIN	HC4444
NPI	00314414
Medicaid	HCC4444

NANCY J. HEALER, M.D.
Internal Medicine

SSN	333 33 3333
BCBS	12343
Medicare	N3333
UPIN	NH3333
NPI	00313313
Medicaid	NJH3333

R. K. PAINFREE, M.D.
Physiatric/Rehabilitation Medicine

SSN	666 66 6666
BCBS	12346
Medicare	R6666
UPIN	RP6666
NPI	00616616
Medicaid	RKP6666

T. J. STITCHER, M.D.
General Surgery

SSN	222 22 2222
BCBS	12342
TRICARE	NonPAR
Medicare	T2222
UPIN	TS2222
NPI	00212212
Medicaid	TJS2222

JANET B. SURGEON, M.D.
General Surgery

SSN	000 11 1111
BCBS	12341
TRICARE	NonPAR
Medicare	J1111
UPIN	JS1111
NPI	00111111
Medicaid	JBS1111

Referring Physicians

DAVID R. BANDAID, M.D.

EIN	11-123485
SSN	212 20 2002
UPIN	DB1212
NPI	01010111

I. M. GOODDOC, M.D.

EIN	11-123441
SSN	777 70 7070
UPIN	IG7777
NPI	00717717

ERIN HELPER, M.D.

EIN	11-123452
SSN	888 80 8080
UPIN	EH8888
NPI	00818818
Medicaid	EBH8881

X. N. RAES, M.D.

EIN	11-123496
SSN	313 30 3003
UPIN	XN1313
NPI	01111110

GOODEN REFLEXS, M.D.

EIN	11-123474
SSN	101 10 1001
UPIN	GR10101
NPI	01001011

ARNOLD YOUNGLOVE, M.D.

EIN	11-123463
SSN	999 90 9090
UPIN	AY9999
NPI	00919919

Insurance Carrier PlanID Numbers

Aetna	115432601	Conn. General Medigap	661234992
Aetna Medigap	115432992	High Risk Insurance	770123451
Bankers Life	222543601	Industrial Indemnity	880012341
Bankers Life Medigap	222543992	Kaiser	990022121
BC/BS	335432601	Mailhandlers	101234561
BC/BS Medigap	335432992	Medicaid	001234561
TRICARE	445612341	Metropolitan	201235671
Cigna	556712341	Metropolitan Medigap	201234992
Cigna Medigap	556712992	Prudential	301432111
Conn. General	661234001	Workers' Compensation Fund	401445671

Place of Service

CPT Evaluation and Management (E&M) codes are linked to **place of service (POS)**, and government payers (e.g., Medicare and Medicaid) require the appropriate place of service code (see Table 1) to be entered on the HCFA-1500 claim form. While previous versions of the HCFA-1500 claim form listed HCFAs POS descriptions and codes on the reverse, these have been deleted from the form currently in use.

✶ CAUTION: Check with private insurers to determine their requirements for POS codes on the HCFA-1500 claim form. Codes may differ from those required by government payers. ✶

Table 1 HCFAs Place of Service Codes

PLACE OF SERVICE DESCRIPTION	CODE
Office	11
Patient's home	12
Inpatient hospital	21
Outpatient hospital	22
Emergency department–hospital	23
Ambulatory surgical center	24
Birthing center	25
Military treatment facility	26
Uniformed service treatment facility	26
Skilled nursing facility	31
Nursing facility	32
Custodial care facility	33
Hospice	34
Ambulance–land	41
Ambulance–air or water	42
Federally qualified health center	50
Inpatient psychiatric facility	51

(Continued)

Table 1 HCFAs Place of Service Codes (continued)

PLACE OF SERVICE DESCRIPTION	CODE
Psychiatric facility–partial hospitalization	52
Community mental health center	53
Intermediate care facility/mentally retarded	54
Residential substance abuse treatment facility	55
Psychiatric residential treatment facility	56
Mass immunization center	60
Comprehensive inpatient rehabilitation facility	61
Comprehensive outpatient rehabilitation facility	62
End-stage renal disease treatment facility	65
State or local public health clinic	71
Rural health clinic	72
Independent laboratory	81
Other unlisted facility	99

Type of Service

Although Block 24C, type of service (TOS), remains on the HCFA-1500 claim form, not all government and private payers require TOS codes to be reported. Medicare, in particular, does *not* require the reporting of TOS codes. Check with individual payers to determine requirements for the entry of type of service codes on the HCFA-1500 claim form. For example, the TRICARE TOS code numbers (see Table 2) differ from the list developed by HCFA (see Table 3). In addition, previous versions of the HCFA-1500 claim form included HCFA's TOS descriptions and codes, but these have been deleted from the form currently in use.

Table 2 TRICARE–Type of Service Codes

TYPE OF SERVICE	CODE
Medical care	1
Surgery	2
Consultation	3
Diagnostic xray	4
Diagnostic laboratory	5
Radiation therapy	6
Anesthesia	7
Assistant at surgery	8
Other medical service	9
DME rental/purchase	A
Drugs	B
Ambulatory surgery	C

Table 2 *TRICARE–Type of Service Codes (continued)*

TYPE OF SERVICE	CODE
Hospice	D
Second opinion on elective surgery	E
Maternity	F
Dental	G
Mental health care	H
Ambulance	I
Program for persons with disability	J

Table 3 *HCFAs Type of Service Codes (not required by Medicare)*

TYPE OF SERVICE	CODE
Medical care	01
Surgery	02
Consultation	03
Diagnostic xray	04
Diagnostic laboratory	05
Radiation therapy	06
Anesthesia	07
Surgical assistance	08
Other medical services	09
Blood or packed red blood cells	10
Used durable medical equipment (DME)	11
DME purchase	12
Ambulatory surgical center facility	13
Renal supplies in home	14
Alternate method of dialysis	15
CDR equipment	16
Pre-admission testing	17
DME rental	18
Pneumonia vaccine	19
Second surgical opinion	20
Third surgical opinion	21
Hospice	H
Injections	I
Dental	T
Maternity	X
Other, for prescription drugs	99

HCFAs Evaluation & Management Documentation Guidelines

The first column of Block 24D on the HCFA-1500 claim form requires entry of a CPT or National (Level II) HCPCS code. Assigning Evaluation & Management (E&M) Services codes causes the most confusion for providers and insurance specialists because of the documentation criteria on which code selection is based. HCFA released the **1995 Documentation Guidelines for Evaluation and Management Services** to clarify E&M code assignment, but this version was widely criticized by specialists because the guidelines were too general. HCFA then released the **1997 Documentation Guidelines for Evaluation and Management Services**, which were also criticized. In response, HCFA announced that providers could assign E&M codes using the documentation guidelines version that resulted in the most appropriate reimbursement for services rendered. In addition, HCFA drafted a new set of documentation guidelines, entitled the **2000 Draft E&M Documentation Guidelines for Evaluation and Management Services**, scheduled for implementation in 2002.

■ **NOTE:** The 1995, 1997, and draft 2000 E&M documentation guidelines are available on the disk that accompanies this textbook. Each set can be viewed on-screen or printed. In addition, the guidelines are available as free, downloadable files at www.hcfa.gov/medicare/mcarpti.htm. The disk also contains an **E&M CodeBuilder** form, based on the 1997 E&M documentation guidelines, which can be printed for use with each case study in this textbook. ■

Many offices develop preprinted forms for providers to use during an E&M encounter, which allows the provider to select the CPT code(s) to be reported on the HCFA-1500 claim form. While this is a timesaver for a practice, it is important that health insurance specialists review and revise the form when new coding manuals are published. In addition, audits should be performed to ensure that codes selected by providers are supported by appropriate documentation in the patient's record. Another issue associated with CPT E&M coding is the reference to *levels* when assigning codes. For example, a provider or payer may refer to code 99211 as a Level I code. Table 4 contains a partial listing of E&M codes categorized according to level. Only those codes found on textbook and workbook encounter forms are included in the table.

■ **NOTE:** It is important to refer to a current CPT coding manual for complete descriptions of CPT codes. ■

Table 4 *Partial Listing of CPT Evaluation & Management Codes and Levels*

SUBSECTION (CATEGORY)	SUBCATEGORY	CODE	LEVEL
Office or Other Outpatient Services	New Patient	99201	I
		99202	II
		99203	III
		99204	IV
		99205	V
	Established Patient	99211	I
		99212	II
		99213	III
		99214	IV
		99215	V
Hospital Inpatient Services	Initial Hospital Care	99221	I
		99222	II
		99223	III
	Subsequent Hospital Care	99231	I
		99232	II
		99233	III
Consultations	Office or Other Outpatient Consultations	99241	I
		99242	II
		99243	III
		99244	IV
		99245	V
Preventive Medicine Services	New Patient	99381	I
		99382	II
		99383	III
		99384	IV
		99385	V
		99386	VI
		99387	VII
	Established Patient	99391	I
		99392	II
		99393	III
		99394	IV
		99395	V
		99396	VI
		99397	VII
Nursing Facility Services	Comprehensive Nursing Facility Assessments	99301	I
		99302	II
		99303	III
	Subsequent Nursing Facility Care	99311	I
		99312	II
		99313	III
Home Services	New Patient	99341	I
		99342	II
		99343	III
		99344	IV
		99345	V
	Established Patient	99347	I
		99348	II
		99349	III
		99350	IV

— SECTION II CASE STUDIES 2-1 THROUGH 2-16

Introduction

Before working with the Case Studies, review the Clinic Billing Manual for an overview of the required billing data necessary for completing the Insurance Case Studies.

For *Case Studies 2-1 through 2-16*, assign the appropriate ICD-9-CM and CPT code(s) by using current editions of each coding manual. To assign the appropriate level of service Evaluation & Management (E&M) Services codes, print and review HCFA *Documentation Guidelines for Evaluation and Management*, which are located on the disk that accompanies this textbook.

■ **NOTE:** All three versions of HCFA *Documentation Guidelines for Evaluation and Management* are included on the disk because the 1995 and 1997 guidelines remain in effect until implementation of the 2000 guidelines (scheduled for 2002). ■

While assigning the appropriate level of E&M code is the provider's responsibility, insurance specialists review patient chart documentation to determine whether the level of E&M service reported on the HCFA-1500 claim form is supported. Because *Case Studies 2-1 through 2-16* require assignment of appropriate E&M level-of-service codes, an E&M *CodeBuilder* form (based on the 1995 and 1997 documentation guidelines) is located on the disk that accompanies this textbook. Print a form for each case study and complete it according to the instructions located on the form.

You also have the option of assigning E&M codes according to your review of the narrative E&M documentation guidelines (located on the disk). Because each version of the guidelines varies, with the most significant difference between the 1995 and 1997 versions (the 2000 guidelines are based on the 1995 version), HCFA instructed providers to use the version that results in the most appropriate reimbursement for services provided. Assigning E&M codes using the narrative guidelines allows for practice of this assignment method.

When completing a claim form, replace the year designation of YYYY on the encounter form with the current year, and enter the current date for all dates reported in Blocks 12, 13, and 31 on the claim form.

Case Study 2-1

DATE	REMARKS
06/20/YYYY	

PATIENT		CHART #	SEX	BIRTHDATE
Raul, Jose X.	SSA 222 20 4040	2-1	M	01/01/68

MAILING ADDRESS	CITY	STATE	ZIP	HOME PHONE	WORK PHONE
10 Mexico St	Anywhere	US	12345	(101) 111-5454	(101) 111-4545

EMPLOYER	ADDRESS	PATIENT STATUS
Anywhere Telephone Co	Anywhere US	MARRIED DIVORCED (SINGLE) STUDENT OTHER

INSURANCE: PRIMARY	ID#	GROUP	SECONDARY POLICY
Bell Atlantic	222 304040	MD1	

POLICYHOLDER NAME	BIRTHDATE	RELATIONSHIP	POLICYHOLDER NAME	BIRTHDATE	RELATIONSHIP

SUPPLEMENTAL PLAN	EMPLOYER

POLICYHOLDER NAME	BIRTHDATE	RELATIONSHIP	DIAGNOSIS	CODE
			1.	
EMPLOYER			2.	
			3.	
REFERRING PHYSICIAN UPIN/SSN			4.	
I.M. Gooddoc				

PLACE OF SERVICE	Office

PROCEDURES	CODE	CHARGE
1. Consultation, level II		$100—
2.		
3.		
4.		
5.		
6.		

SPECIAL NOTES

TOTAL CHARGES	PAYMENTS	ADJUSTMENTS	BALANCE
$100—	0	0	$100—

RETURN VISIT	PHYSICIAN SIGNATURE
3 months	*Henry C. Cardiac, M.D.*

GOODMEDICINE CLINIC
1 PROVIDER STREET, ANYWHERE, US 12345
PHONE NUMBER: (101) 111-2222

06/20/YYYY Office Consultation

S.   Jose is an adult Mexican-American, single male, referred by Dr. I. M. Gooddoc for a consultation. He noted an umbilical mass roughly 5 days ago, 2 days after the onset of pain in this area. There was no known etiology.

He had been physically active, but within the past 2 months he has not engaged in his normal physical activity. He has erratic bowel habits with defecation 2-3-4 days and has a history of having some bright red blood in the stool and on the toilet tissue. He has had no melanotic stool or narrowing of the stool. He denies episodic diarrhea. He has had bronchitis and sinus difficulties, particularly in the fall. He is a nonsmoker. He has no genitourinary symptoms of prostatism.

His health history reveals that he has had a chronic, nonspecific dermatitis of his eyes, ears, hands, and groin and, in fact, felt that the bleeding in his perianal area was secondary to this. He was a full-term delivery. His history reveals that his maternal uncle had a hernia similar to this. His medications include the use of a halogenated steroid for his skin condition. HE HAS ALLERGIES IN THE FALL TO POLLEN. HE HAS A SENSITIVITY TO PERCODAN OR PERCOCET CAUSING NAUSEA, although he has taken Tylenol #3 without difficulty. He takes penicillin without difficulty. The rest of the Family and Social History is noncontributory; details can be found on the History Questionnaire.

0:   Supraclavicular fossae are free from adenopathy. Chest is clear to percussion and auscultation. No cutaneous icterus is present. His abdomen is soft and nontender without masses or organomegaly. Penis is circumcised and normal. Testicles are scrotal and normal. No hernia is palpable in the groin. At the base of the umbilicus, there is suggestion of crepitus but no true hernia at this time. Rectal examination reveals normal tone. There is some induration of the perianal tissues. The prostate is 3 x 4 cm and normal in architecture.

Hemoccult testing of the formed stool is negative for blood.

A: 1. Umbilical mass; possible umbilical cyst, possible umbilical hernia.

2. Rectal bleeding.

P: 1. Schedule endoscopic evaluation of lower colon.

2. Schedule followup visit to evaluate the progression of the umbilical change.

3. Note dictated to Dr. Gooddoc.

Henry C. Cardiac, M.D.

Case Study 2-2

DATE 06/20/YYYY	REMARKS Authorization 76031			

PATIENT Moutaine, Kay	CHART # 2-2	SEX F	BIRTHDATE 06/01/55

MAILING ADDRESS 634 Goodview Ave	CITY Anywhere	STATE US	ZIP 12345	HOME PHONE (101) 115-1234	WORK PHONE

EMPLOYER Goodmedicine Pharmacy	ADDRESS Anywhere US	PATIENT STATUS (MARRIED) DIVORCED SINGLE STUDENT OTHER

INSURANCE: PRIMARY Connecticut General	ID# 877345567	GROUP V143	SECONDARY POLICY

POLICYHOLDER NAME Charles W. Moutaine	BIRTHDATE 03/04/52	RELATIONSHIP Spouse	POLICYHOLDER NAME	BIRTHDATE	RELATIONSHIP

SUPPLEMENTAL PLAN	EMPLOYER

POLICYHOLDER NAME	BIRTHDATE	RELATIONSHIP	DIAGNOSIS		CODE
			1.		
EMPLOYER (Charles) General Electric Somewhere, US			2.		
			3.		
REFERRING PHYSICIAN UPIN/SSN			4.		

PLACE OF SERVICE   Office

PROCEDURES	CODE	CHARGE
1. Office visit, level III		$75—
2.		
3.		
4.		
5.		
6.		

SPECIAL NOTES

TOTAL CHARGES $75—	PAYMENTS $30—	ADJUSTMENTS 0	BALANCE $45—

RETURN VISIT PRN	PHYSICIAN SIGNATURE *Henry C. Cardiac, M.D.*

GOODMEDICINE CLINIC
1 PROVIDER STREET, ANYWHERE, US 12345
PHONE NUMBER: (101) 111-2222

06/20/YYYY Office Preventive Medicine

S: This white female, who appears her stated age, is here to meet the physician for the first time and to undergo routine annual PE. She has a history of sensory seizure disorder for which she takes Tegretol. This was diagnosed on EEG exam when she saw a neurologist in California. Tegretol has been quite efficacious in controlling her symptoms. She has sensations that she is "slipping away," auditory hallucinations, and deja vu with these attacks which last for 45 seconds.

She also has a history of migraine headaches for which she takes Inderal, with no exacerbation in several years. She has a history of allergies and asthma for which she takes Vanceril daily and Ventolin on a p.r.n. basis. She has history of fibrocystic breast disease for which she takes Vitamin E and follows a low-caffeine diet.

Recently, she was found to have heme positive stools with negative colonoscopy, BE, sigmoidoscopy. Currently on Colace and Fiberal for hemorrhoids.

No complaints today. Had Pap smear and mammogram in October.

O: NAD. HEENT: PERRL, funduscopic benign. Sinuses nontender. Neck: Supple, no nodes or masses. Chest: Clear. COR: RRR without murmur. ABD: Soft, nontender. Neuro exam: Cranial nerves II-XII, sensory, motor, cerebellar grossly intact. Gait coordinated.

Lab: Peak expiratory flow equals 510 liters/second.

A: 1. Temporal lobe epilepsy, doing well on Tegretol. Recent normal CBC and liver profile in November.
2. Migraine headaches, doing well on prophylaxis. I discussed with her the advantages and disadvantages of discontinuing the prophylaxis in light of no recurrence of headaches.
3. Atopic illness
   A. Bronchial asthma doing well.
   B. Allergic rhinosinusitis doing well, currently on Vanceril.
4. Fibrocystic breast disease, no breast exam done today as it had been done in October, apparently doing well.
5. History of hemorrhoids.

P: Medications renewed:

Tegretol, 200 mg, 1 P.O. b.i.d. #100, 1 refill.

Henry C. Cardiac, M.D.

Case Study 2-3

DATE		REMARKS					
06/20/YYYY							

PATIENT				CHART #	SEX		BIRTHDATE
Ping, Chang Li				2-3	M		01/06/45

MAILING ADDRESS	CITY	STATE	ZIP	HOME PHONE	WORK PHONE
100 Dragon St	Injury	US	12347	(101) 111-4545	(101) 111-3266

EMPLOYER	ADDRESS	PATIENT STATUS
Good Growth Inc.	Injury US	(MARRIED) DIVORCED SINGLE STUDENT OTHER

INSURANCE: PRIMARY	ID#	GROUP	SECONDARY POLICY
Connecticut General	333 66 9999	93939	

POLICYHOLDER NAME	BIRTHDATE	RELATIONSHIP	POLICYHOLDER NAME	BIRTHDATE	RELATIONSHIP
Ling, Song	06/01/42	Spouse			

SUPPLEMENTAL PLAN	EMPLOYER
	Hunan Inc., Injury US

POLICYHOLDER NAME	BIRTHDATE	RELATIONSHIP	DIAGNOSIS	CODE
			1. See Path Report	
EMPLOYER			2.	
			3.	
REFERRING PHYSICIAN UPIN/SSN			4.	
Henry Cardiac				

PLACE OF SERVICE	Office/Goodmedicine Hosp Admit 06/16/YYYY DC 06/20/YYYY

PROCEDURES	CODE	CHARGE
1. Office visit, level II 06/14/YYYY		$75—
2. Proctectomy with one-stage colostomy 06/16/YYYY		800—
3.		
4.		
5.		
6.		

SPECIAL NOTES
Hold for Path   Refer to Dr. Chemo

TOTAL CHARGES	PAYMENTS	ADJUSTMENTS	BALANCE
$875—	0	0	$875—

RETURN VISIT	PHYSICIAN SIGNATURE
1 wk	*Janet B. Surgeon, M.D.*

GOODMEDICINE CLINIC
1 PROVIDER STREET, ANYWHERE, US 12345
PHONE NUMBER: (101) 111-2222

06/14/YYYY Office Visit

S: This patient, a mature adult Asian-American male, is currently off work because of hypertension. He is a planner and estimator. In mid-June, he noticed a change in the quality of his bowel movements in that they became segmented. Two weeks ago occult blood was found in his stool on Hemoccult testing x3. He has noticed that his stool has been flat and hemispheric. Bowel movements occur every 2-3 hours. He has had no weight loss except that following preparation for his barium enema. His appetite has been good. In June, he had cramping in his abdomen.

His health problems include hypertension, which has been present for over 20 years, and an episode of recent parotitis. He admits to NO ALLERGIES.

0: On physical examination, supraclavicular fossae are free from adenopathy. Chest is clear to percussion and auscultation. Diminished breath sounds are present. Cardiac examination revealed regular rhythm without extra sound. Abdomen is soft and nontender. Groin is free from adenopathy. Rectal examination revealed normal tone. There is an external hemorrhoid anteriorly. Prostate is 4x4 cm, normal in architecture.

Hemoccult testing of the stool is positive. There are no masses palpable in the rectum. It has not been sent to the office yet, but the verbal report on the BE is that of an apple core type lesion in the lower sigmoid colon, findings compatible with a carcinoma. The length of this lesion is 2 cm.

A: Constricting lesion, lower sigmoid colon.

P: 1. Admission to Goodmedicine Hospital ASAP. Complete colonoscopy tomorrow, and an evaluation to include CSR, CEΛ, and liver function.

2. Surgery to follow, if tests prove to be positive.

Janet B. Surgeon, M.D.

06/16/YYYY – 06/20/YYYY Inpatient Hospitalization

06/16/YYYY   Proctectomy, complete, with one-stage colostomy.

06/20/YYYY   Path Report: Duke's C Carcinoma, colon.

Discharged from hospital to be seen in the office in 1 week.

To see Dr. Chemo, oncologist, in 3 weeks.

Janet B. Surgeon, M.D.

Case Study 2-4

DATE			REMARKS			
06/20/YYYY						

PATIENT				CHART #	SEX	BIRTHDATE
Recall John J.				2-4	M	06/03/42

MAILING ADDRESS	CITY	STATE	ZIP	HOME PHONE	WORK PHONE
10 Memory Lane	Anywhere	US	12345	(101) 111-5555	(101) 111-4444

EMPLOYER	ADDRESS	PATIENT STATUS
Will Solve It Inc	Injury US	MARRIED (DIVORCED) SINGLE STUDENT OTHER

INSURANCE: PRIMARY	ID#	GROUP	SECONDARY POLICY
BC/BS	ZJW55544	650	

POLICYHOLDER NAME	BIRTHDATE	RELATIONSHIP	POLICYHOLDER NAME	BIRTHDATE	RELATIONSHIP
		Self			

SUPPLEMENTAL PLAN	EMPLOYER

POLICYHOLDER NAME	BIRTHDATE	RELATIONSHIP	DIAGNOSIS	CODE
			1.	
EMPLOYER			2.	
			3.	
REFERRING PHYSICIAN UPIN/SSN			4.	
Arnold Younglove				

PLACE OF SERVICE	Office/Goodmedicine Hosp Admit 06/19/YYYY DC 06/20/YYYY

PROCEDURES	CODE	CHARGE
1. Office visit, level II 06/18/YYYY		$75—
2. Open Cholecystectomy 6/19/YYYY		1360—
3.		
4.		
5.		
6.		

SPECIAL NOTES

TOTAL CHARGES	PAYMENTS	ADJUSTMENTS	BALANCE
$1435—	0	0	$1435—

RETURN VISIT	PHYSICIAN SIGNATURE
5 days	*Janet B. Surgeon, M.D.*

GOODMEDICINE CLINIC
1 PROVIDER STREET, ANYWHERE, US 12345
PHONE NUMBER: (101) 111-2222

06/18/YYYY   Office Visit

New patient referred by Arnold Younglove, M.D. for surgery.

S: This patient is a white adult, unmarried male research analyst who was well until approximately early December when he noted pain in the right upper quadrant with bloating. This did not radiate. He had possible fever with chills several weeks ago, but has had no recurrence of this.

He has chronically had increased gas that was relieved with belching and has had some heartburn. He does have fatty food intolerance dating back several years. His pain has been intermittent since the initial episode. He has been slightly constipated. He has no alcoholic stools, jaundice, or liver disease. He drinks 2 highballs per night and smokes 1 pack of cigarettes per day. His weight has decreased 55 lbs in the past 6 months.

As a child, he had jaundice. His family history is negative for gallbladder disease. He has NO KNOWN ALLERGIES. His other medical problems include diabetes, diagnosed 5 years ago; arteriosclerotic cardiovascular disease, without CVA or angina; status post-five coronary artery bypass 4 years ago without recurrent angina or congestive heart failure or arrhythmia.

Studies reveal cholelithiasis and a normal upper gastrointestinal series.

0: Supraclavicular fossae are free from adenopathy. Chest is clear to percussion and auscultation. Cardiac examination reveals a regular rhythm, which is slow, without murmur or extra sound. The abdomen is soft and nontender, without masses or organomegaly. There is a suggestion of a left inguinal hernia. Groin is free of adenopathy. Rectal examination reveals normal tone without masses. Stool was not tested.

A: Cholelithiasis and chronic cholecystitis.
Diabetes.
Arteriosclerotic cardiovascular disease.
Status post five-coronary artery bypass.

P: 1. Admission for cholecystectomy.
2. Obtain films for review.

Janet B. Surgeon, M.D.

06/19/YYYY – 06/20/YYYY   Inpatient Hospitalization

06/19/YYYY   Cholecystectomy, open, performed yesterday.

DX: Chronic gallbladder with stones.

DC: 10:00 AM today. To be seen in 5 days.

Janet B. Surgeon, M.D.

Case Study 2-5

DATE 06/20/YYYY	REMARKS				

PATIENT			CHART #	SEX	BIRTHDATE
Islander, Philamena			2-5	F	11/21/53

MAILING ADDRESS	CITY	STATE	ZIP	HOME PHONE	WORK PHONE
129 Coconut Ct	Anywhere	US	12345	(101) 111-7218	(101) 111-7744

EMPLOYER	ADDRESS	PATIENT STATUS
Nixon Modeling Agency	Injury US	(MARRIED) DIVORCED SINGLE STUDENT OTHER

INSURANCE: PRIMARY	ID#	GROUP	SECONDARY POLICY
BC/BS	XWJ473655	101	

POLICYHOLDER NAME	BIRTHDATE	RELATIONSHIP	POLICYHOLDER NAME	BIRTHDATE	RELATIONSHIP
Richard T. Islander	2/11/52	Spouse			

SUPPLEMENTAL PLAN	EMPLOYER

POLICYHOLDER NAME	BIRTHDATE	RELATIONSHIP	DIAGNOSIS	CODE
			1.	
EMPLOYER			2.	
Wonderful Photos (Richard)			3.	
REFERRING PHYSICIAN UPIN/SSN			4.	

PLACE OF SERVICE   Office

PROCEDURES	CODE	CHARGE
1. Anoscopy c̄ Bx		$100—
2.		
3.		
4.		
5.		
6.		

SPECIAL NOTES   Schedule BE at Goodmedicine
Sigmoidoscopy 1 wk later
Give preps

TOTAL CHARGES	PAYMENTS	ADJUSTMENTS	BALANCE
$100—	$25—	0	$75—

RETURN VISIT	PHYSICIAN SIGNATURE
See above	Henry C. Cardiac, M.D.

GOODMEDICINE CLINIC
1 PROVIDER STREET, ANYWHERE, US 12345
PHONE NUMBER: (101) 111-2222

06/20/YYYY Office Surgery

S: This patient had no complaints since her last visit until 3 weeks ago when she noted some intermittent soft stool and decrease in the caliber of stools, with some bleeding that discontinued 4 days ago. She has no crampy abdominal pain.

0: External examination of the anus revealed some external skin tags present in the left anterior position. Anal examination revealed an extremely tight anal sphincter. This was dilated manually to allow instrumentation with the anoscope, which was accomplished in a 360-degree orientation. There was some prominence of the crypts and some inflammation of the rectal mucosa, a portion of which was sent for biopsy. This was friable. In the left anterior position there was a fistula that was healing with some formation of a sentinel pile on the outside, which had been noticed on external examination.

A: Anal fissure, unusual position, nontraumatic.

P: Rule out inflammatory bowel disease with air contrast barium enema examination and reflux into terminal ileum. Patient to return for sigmoidoscopy after BE.

Henry C. Cardiac, M.D.

Case Study 2-6

DATE 06/20/YYYY	REMARKS Daughter Imogene Sweet 435 Injury MD

PATIENT Sugar, Imogene	SSA 678 90 4415	CHART # 2-6	SEX F	BIRTHDATE 03/09/24

MAILING ADDRESS 120 Young Street	CITY Injury	STATE US	ZIP 12345	HOME PHONE (101) 111-8675	WORK PHONE (101) 111-4422 (daughter)

EMPLOYER	ADDRESS	PATIENT STATUS
		MARRIED DIVORCED (SINGLE) STUDENT OTHER

INSURANCE: PRIMARY Medicare	ID# 777 22 8888W	GROUP	SECONDARY POLICY

POLICYHOLDER NAME	BIRTHDATE	RELATIONSHIP	POLICYHOLDER NAME	BIRTHDATE	RELATIONSHIP

SUPPLEMENTAL PLAN Medicaid	1155773388	EMPLOYER

POLICYHOLDER NAME	BIRTHDATE	RELATIONSHIP	DIAGNOSIS	CODE
			1.	
EMPLOYER			2.	
			3.	
REFERRING PHYSICIAN UPIN/SSN			4.	

PLACE OF SERVICE   Home visit

PROCEDURES	CODE	CHARGE
1. Home visit, level II		$45—
2.		
3.		
4.		
5.		
6.		

SPECIAL NOTES Call Dr. Bones & Report

TOTAL CHARGES $45—	PAYMENTS 0	ADJUSTMENTS 0	BALANCE $45—

RETURN VISIT	PHYSICIAN SIGNATURE Nancy Healer, M.D.

GOODMEDICINE CLINIC
1 PROVIDER STREET, ANYWHERE, US 12345
PHONE NUMBER: (101) 111-2222

06/20/YYYY Home Visit

S: Patient was visited at home in followup for her Type I uncontrolled diabetes with circulatory problems. On 05/10/YYYY, while visiting her daughter in Somewhere, MD, she saw an orthopedic surgeon who admitted her to the hospital and did a transmetatarsal amputation of her foot. She had not notified Dr. Bones or me that she had received a second opinion or that she had gone through with surgery.

O: Her blood pressure is 130/70; she looks well. Chest is clear and cardiac examination is unremarkable. Examination of the leg shows no edema, redness, or heat in the lower extremity. The patient had strict instructions not to allow me to unwrap the wound.

A: This patient underwent transmetatarsal amputation although neither Dr. Bones nor I felt a BKA was warranted. I encouraged the patient to be compliant with followup planned by her orthopedic surgeon. I will inform Dr. Bones she had gone ahead with surgery and if problems develop, she is to contact me.

P: Schedule office followup visit in 2 weeks.

Nancy J. Healer, M.D.

Case Study 2-7

DATE 06/20/YYYY	REMARKS			
PATIENT Gonzales, Esau		CHART # 2-7	SEX M	BIRTHDATE 09/10/33

MAILING ADDRESS 14 Adobe St	CITY Nowhere	STATE US	ZIP 12347	HOME PHONE (101) 111-7689	WORK PHONE

EMPLOYER	ADDRESS	PATIENT STATUS MARRIED DIVORCED (SINGLE) STUDENT OTHER

INSURANCE: PRIMARY Medicare	ID# 101234591A	GROUP	SECONDARY POLICY

POLICYHOLDER NAME self	BIRTHDATE	RELATIONSHIP	POLICYHOLDER NAME	BIRTHDATE	RELATIONSHIP

SUPPLEMENTAL PLAN	EMPLOYER

POLICYHOLDER NAME	BIRTHDATE	RELATIONSHIP	DIAGNOSIS	CODE
EMPLOYER			1. 2. 3.	
REFERRING PHYSICIAN UPIN/SSN			4.	

PLACE OF SERVICE   Office

PROCEDURES	CODE	CHARGE
1. Office visit, level IV		$100—
2. EKG, routine c̄ interp		65—
3.		
4.		
5.		
6.		

SPECIAL NOTES

TOTAL CHARGES $165—	PAYMENTS 0	ADJUSTMENTS 0	BALANCE $165—

RETURN VISIT 06/27/YYYY for Stress test	PHYSICIAN SIGNATURE *Henry C. Cardiac, M.D.*

GOODMEDICINE CLINIC
1 PROVIDER STREET, ANYWHERE, US 12345
PHONE NUMBER: (101) 111-2222

01/10/YYYY Office Visit

S: Elderly African-American male returns, after a two year hiatus, for followup of coronary artery disease and associated problems. Since triple coronary bypass surgery four years ago, he has had no chest discomfort. It should be noted that he had no chest discomfort during a markedly abnormal stress test performed just two weeks before the bypass surgery. He now reports intermittent dyspnea that occurs at rest, and spontaneously abates. He does not notice any discomfort on exertion, but he does report that his lifestyle is sedentary. He denies orthopnea, paroxysmal nocturnal dyspnea or edema. He has continued to followup with his internist, Dr. Gooddoc, for treatment of his dyslipidemia and hypertension. He is on Cholestin and Tenormin.

O: Patient is a mildly obese, African American male appearing his stated age, in no acute distress. Weight is 210. Height is 5'8". Pulse 16. BP 162/82, 172/82, and then 188/82 in the office. HEENT grossly unremarkable. Neck reveals normal jugular venous pressure, without hepatojugular reflux. Normal carotid pulses; no bruits present. Lungs are clear to A&P. Heart reveals regular rhythm, S1 and S2 are normal. There is no murmur, rub, click, or gallop. Cardiac apex is not palpable. No heaves or thrills are detected. Abdomen is soft, nontender, with normal bowel sounds, and no bruits. No organomegaly, including abdominal aorta, or masses noted. Extremities reveal a surgical scar in the right leg, presumably from saphenous venectomy. Femoral pulses are normal, without bruits. Dorsalis pedis and posterior tibial pulses are also normal. There is no cyanosis, clubbing, or edema. Neurological is grossly within normal limits.

IMPRESSION:

1. Status post aortocoronary bypass surgery four years ago.

2. Coronary artery disease. Today's abnormal EKG suggests, but does not prove, that an inferior myocardial infarction may have occurred sometime in the past. There is independent suggestion of this on stress-thallium test performed six months ago. Additionally, he still has symptoms of dyspnea.

3. Hypertension.

4. Hypercholesterolemia.

PLAN:

1. Patient was instructed to followup with Dr. Gooddoc for hypertension and dyslipidemia.

2. Schedule treadmill stress test for next week.

Henry C. Cardiac, M.D.

Case Study 2-8

DATE	REMARKS			
06/20/YYYY				

PATIENT		CHART #	SEX	BIRTHDATE
Blooming Bush, Mary		2-8	F	04/01/30

MAILING ADDRESS	CITY	STATE	ZIP	HOME PHONE	WORK PHONE
9910 Reservation Rd	Nowhere	US	12347	(101) 111-9922	

EMPLOYER	ADDRESS	PATIENT STATUS	
Retired			(Widowed)
		MARRIED DIVORCED (SINGLE) STUDENT OTHER	

INSURANCE: PRIMARY	ID#	GROUP	SECONDARY POLICY
Medicare	071 26 9645B		

POLICYHOLDER NAME	BIRTHDATE	RELATIONSHIP	POLICYHOLDER NAME	BIRTHDATE	RELATIONSHIP
self					

SUPPLEMENTAL PLAN	EMPLOYER
Cigna	

POLICYHOLDER NAME	BIRTHDATE	RELATIONSHIP	DIAGNOSIS	CODE
			1.	
EMPLOYER			2.	
			3.	
REFERRING PHYSICIAN UPIN/SSN			4.	

PLACE OF SERVICE

PROCEDURES	CODE	CHARGE
1. Office visit, level IV		$100—
2.		
3.		
4.		
5.		
6.		

SPECIAL NOTES

TOTAL CHARGES	PAYMENTS	ADJUSTMENTS	BALANCE
$100—	0	0	$100—

RETURN VISIT	PHYSICIAN SIGNATURE
2 days after hosp tests	*Nancy J. Healer, M.D.*

GOODMEDICINE CLINIC
1 PROVIDER STREET, ANYWHERE, US 12345
PHONE NUMBER: (101) 111-2222

06/20/YYYY Office Visit

S: This elderly, widowed Native American woman comes in today after having a possible seizure at dinner last night. She reports that she was sitting at the table and suddenly fell to the floor. She had urine incontinence at that time and awoke in a slightly confused state with a bad headache. She denies any recent trauma, blows to the head, chest pain, palpitation, paresthesias, aura, or other symptoms.

Her history is remarkable for a well-differentiated nodular lymphoma on the upper right arm that was diagnosed and treated with radiation by Dr. Raes in Anywhere, US. She has had no clinical evidence of recurrence. There has been no prior hospitalization other than for childbirth. Para: 1001. She has had mild COPD for the past 10 years. Her husband died of an unexpected myocardial infarction 2 years ago. She now lives with her daughter. The review of systems is noncontributory. She has no current medications and the only known **allergy is to penicillin.**

O: Physical exam shows a well-nourished, well-developed female in no acute distress at this time. Her clothed weight is 155 lbs. Blood pressure: 120/72, both arms, with no orthostasis. Pulse: 70 and regular. Respirations: Unlabored at 18. HEENT: Head is normocephalic and atraumatic. PEERLA with intact EOMs. Sclerae are white and the conjunctivae are pink. Funduscopic exam is benign. Ears are normal bilaterally. There is no evidence of Battle's sign. The mouth and throat are unremarkable. Tongue is midline without atrophy or fasciculation. Neck is supple without JVD, adenopathy, thyromegaly, or bruits. The lungs are clear to P&A. Breasts are pendulous with no masses, dimpling, or nipple retraction. Heart rate and rhythm is regular with a grade II/VI SEM along the LSB without gallop, rub, clicks, or other adventitious sounds. Abdomen is soft and nontender without organomegaly, masses, or bruits. Bowel sounds are normal. Rectum has good sphincter tone without masses. Stool is hemoccult negative. Extremities have no edema, cyanosis, jaundice, clubbing, or petechiae. The peripheral pulses are full and palpable. There is no significant cervical, supraclavicular, axillary, or inguinal adenopathy noted. The mental status is normal. Cranial nerves II-XII are intact. Motor, sensory and cerebellar function is normal. Romberg sign is normal. The Babinski is absent. Reflexes are 2+ and symmetrical in both upper and lower extremities.

A: New onset seizure disorder. Rule out tumor, metabolic and vascular etiologies.

P: The patient will be scheduled ASAP for MRI of the brain and an EEG at Goodmedicine Hospital. Obtain blood for electrolytes, calcium, albumin, LFTs, and CBC with platelet count and sed rate, and send to the lab.

Patient was instructed to call immediately if she has any further difficulty or questions.

Nancy J. Healer, M.D.

Case Study 2-9

DATE 06/20/YYYY		REMARKS Hold for discharge			
PATIENT Cadillac, Mary A.	SSA 061 26 6811		CHART # 2-9	SEX F	BIRTHDATE 04/30/29

MAILING ADDRESS 500 Carr St	CITY Anywhere	STATE US	ZIP 12345	HOME PHONE (101) 222-3333	WORK PHONE

EMPLOYER	ADDRESS	PATIENT STATUS (MARRIED) DIVORCED SINGLE STUDENT OTHER

INSURANCE: PRIMARY BC/BS	ID# XWY111111	GROUP GM103	SECONDARY POLICY Medicare 001266811B

POLICYHOLDER NAME James D. Cadillac	BIRTHDATE 06/6/33	RELATIONSHIP Spouse	POLICYHOLDER NAME	BIRTHDATE	RELATIONSHIP

SUPPLEMENTAL PLAN	EMPLOYER Anywhere Auto Dealer Assoc

POLICYHOLDER NAME	BIRTHDATE	RELATIONSHIP	DIAGNOSIS		CODE
			1.		
EMPLOYER Anywhere Auto Dealer Assoc.			2.		
			3.		
REFERRING PHYSICIAN UPIN/SSN			4.		

PLACE OF SERVICE Goodmedicine Hospital

PROCEDURES	CODE	CHARGE
1. Laparoscopic cholecystectomy c̄ cholangiogram		$1350—
2. Liver biopsy		100—
3.		
4.		
5.		
6.		

SPECIAL NOTES 06/22/YYYY Released from hospital

TOTAL CHARGES $1450—	PAYMENTS 0	ADJUSTMENTS 0	BALANCE $1450—
RETURN VISIT 4 days		PHYSICIAN SIGNATURE *T.J. Stitcher, M.D.*	

GOODMEDICINE CLINIC
1 PROVIDER STREET, ANYWHERE, US 12345
PHONE NUMBER: (101) 111-2222

GOODMEDICINE HOSPITAL OPERATIVE REPORT

DATE: 06/20/ YYYY
PATIENT: Mary A. Cadillac

PREOPERATIVE DIAGNOSIS: Chronic cholecystitis and cholelithiasis without obstruction.

POSTOPERATIVE DIAGNOSIS: Same.

SURGEON: T. J. Stitcher, M.D.

PROCEDURE: Laparoscopic cholecystectomy, intraoperative cholangiogram, lysis of adhesions, liver biopsy.

ANESTHESIA: General endotracheal.

OPERATIVE FINDINGS: Numerous adhesions around the gallbladder area. The gallbladder was found to be distended. The cystic duct is normal in caliber. The common bile duct is normal. No residual stone on cholangiogram. The patient has two nodules on each side of the inferior lobe, close to the gallbladder, proximally and distally.

OPERATIVE PROCEDURE: The patient was placed in the dorsal supine position after adequate anesthesia was obtained. The abdomen was prepped and draped in the usual fashion. A right lateral infraumbilical incision was made and dissected to the fascia. The fascia was entered and dissection of the pre-peritoneum was done to again enter the peritoneal cavity. Adhesions were lysed with blunt dissection. A Hasson trocar was then inserted and anchored to the fascia after #1-0 Vicryl was preset on each side of the fascia. Insufflation was started with CO_2 gas.

After adequate insufflation was obtained, the patient was placed in the Trendelenburg position wherein the other trocar was placed under direct visualization. The skin was infiltrated with 0.5% Marcaine. After adequate placement of trocars, grasping forceps was then inserted. The gallbladder was then grasped on the lateral port along the subcostal area, anterior axillary line to lift the gallbladder up for dissection and lysis of the adhesions around the gallbladder. After adequate lysis of adhesions, the neck of the gallbladder was grasped with the midclavicular subcostal grasping forceps to expose the triangle of Calot. Careful dissection of the cystic branch going to the gallbladder was then identified and skeletonized. This was then clipped distally and proximally twice before being divided. The cystic neck was skeletonized and a small clip was placed distal to the cystic duct toward the gallbladder, and a small opening was made.

A cholangiocath was introduced and cholangiogram was performed using 50% dye, completed with no evidence of retained stone. The cholangiocath was then removed.

The cystic duct was then clamped twice distally and proximally using endoclips, then divided. The gallbladder was subsequently excised from the liver bed using the spatula cautery. Copious irrigation on the liver bed was clear with no evidence of bile leak or bleeding. The gallbladder was subsequently removed from the liver bed and brought out toward the subxyphoid opening under visualization. Bile content was removed and some of the stones had to be crushed prior to removal of the gallbladder through the 1 cm opening.

The trocar was then reinserted and a biopsy of the nodule noted on the liver was made, using a true cut needle, cutting going through the skin under direct visualization. Two specimens were removed (two nodules). The patient was placed in reverse Trendelenburg position and irrigation fluid was removed. All the trocars and grasping forceps were removed under direct visualization. The gas was deflated. Subsequently the Hasson was then removed with the laparoscope. The fascia layer on the umbilical area was closed using the preset sutures and the figure of 8. The fascia and the subxyphoid were likewise closed using #0 Vicryl figure of 8. Subcuticular reapproximation using #4-0 Vicryl was completed and the skin was Steri-stripped after application of Benzoin Tincture. The patient tolerated the procedure well. Estimated blood loss was less than 25 cc. The Foley catheter was removed, and the nasogastric tube was removed prior to the patient being extubated. The patient left the Operating Room in satisfactory condition.

T. J. Stitcher, MD

Case Study 2-10

DATE 06/20/YYYY	REMARKS Irene Pine (101) 111-9191			

PATIENT Hammerclaw, John W	SSA 101 10 1010	CHART # 2-10	SEX M	BIRTHDATE 05/30/30

MAILING ADDRESS 111 Lumber St	CITY Anywhere	STATE US	ZIP 12345	HOME PHONE (101) 111-9191	WORK PHONE daughter (101)111-1919

EMPLOYER Retired	ADDRESS	PATIENT STATUS MARRIED DIVORCED (SINGLE) STUDENT OTHER

INSURANCE: PRIMARY Medicare 101101010A	ID#	GROUP	SECONDARY POLICY

POLICYHOLDER NAME	BIRTHDATE	RELATIONSHIP	POLICYHOLDER NAME	BIRTHDATE	RELATIONSHIP

SUPPLEMENTAL PLAN BC/BS Medigap #YXW10110	EMPLOYER

POLICYHOLDER NAME	BIRTHDATE	RELATIONSHIP Self	DIAGNOSIS	CODE
EMPLOYER			1.	
			2.	
			3.	
REFERRING PHYSICIAN UPIN/SSN Erin Helper			4.	

PLACE OF SERVICE Office

PROCEDURES	CODE	CHARGE
1. Excision, 4.1 cm cyst, benign, back		$360—
2. Excision, 2.5 cm cyst benign, neck		300—
3.		
4.		
5.		
6.		

SPECIAL NOTES

TOTAL CHARGES $660—	PAYMENTS 0	ADJUSTMENTS 0	BALANCE $660—

RETURN VISIT 3 days	PHYSICIAN SIGNATURE *T.J. Stitcher, M.D.*

GOODMEDICINE CLINIC
1 PROVIDER STREET, ANYWHERE, US 12345
PHONE NUMBER: (101) 111-2222

06/20/YYYY Office Operative Report

PATIENT: John W. Hammerclaw

PREOPERATIVE DIAGNOSIS: 4.1 cm infected sebaceous cyst, back; 2.5 cm infected sebaceous cyst, posterior neck.

POSTOPERATIVE DIAGNOSIS: Same.

OPERATION: Excision, 4.1 cm benign cyst, back. Excision, 2.5 cm benign cyst, neck.

PROCEDURE: The patient was placed in the prone position and the back and posterior neck were prepped with Betadine scrub and solution. Sterile towels were applied in the usual fashion, and 0.25% Marcaine was injected subcutaneously in a linear fashion transversely over each of the cysts asynchronously. The lower cyst was excised and the cavity was irrigated with copious amounts of Marcaine solution. The skin edges were loosely reapproximated throughout with #3-0 nylon suture. Following this, Marcaine was injected around the superior cyst, an incision was made transversely, and the cyst was completely excised. The wound was irrigated with Marcaine and packed with Iodoform, and sterile dressings were applied. The patient was discharged with verbal and written instructions, as well as Tylenol #3 for pain and a prescription for 30. Return visit in 3 days for packing removal.

T. J. Stitcher, M.D.

Case Study 2-11

DATE 06/20/YYYY	REMARKS			
PATIENT Fontaine, Germane		CHART # 2-11	SEX F	BIRTHDATE 5/7/65

MAILING ADDRESS 132 Canal St	CITY Injury	STATE US	ZIP 12346	HOME PHONE (101) 111-9685	WORK PHONE

EMPLOYER none	ADDRESS	PATIENT STATUS MARRIED DIVORCED (SINGLE) STUDENT OTHER

INSURANCE: PRIMARY Medicaid	ID# 11347765	GROUP	SECONDARY POLICY

POLICYHOLDER NAME	BIRTHDATE	RELATIONSHIP	POLICYHOLDER NAME	BIRTHDATE	RELATIONSHIP

SUPPLEMENTAL PLAN	EMPLOYER

POLICYHOLDER NAME	BIRTHDATE	RELATIONSHIP	DIAGNOSIS	CODE
			1.	
EMPLOYER			2.	
			3.	
REFERRING PHYSICIAN UPIN/SSN			4.	

PLACE OF SERVICE Office

PROCEDURES	CODE	CHARGE
1. Office visit, est pt, level II		$26—
2. Quick strep test		12—
3.		
4.		
5.		
6.		

SPECIAL NOTES
She is to report in 3 weeks—referral to ENT if not improved

TOTAL CHARGES $38—	PAYMENTS 0	ADJUSTMENTS 0	BALANCE $38—

RETURN VISIT prn	PHYSICIAN SIGNATURE *Henry C. Cardiac, M.D.*

GOODMEDICINE CLINIC
1 PROVIDER STREET, ANYWHERE, US 12345
PHONE NUMBER: (101) 111-2222

06/20/YYYY Office Visit

S: This patient has had a sore throat for the past several days, temp. to 101°F with pleuritic cough. She has had abundant postnasal drip.

0: NAD. Sinuses are tender about the maxillary and frontal areas. TMs, gray bilaterally. Pharynx is injected and there is obvious purulent material in the left posterior pharynx. Neck: Supple, no nodes. Chest: Clear. COR: RRR without murmur. Lab: Sinus films normal.

A: Clinical chronic sinusitis; her sore throat is probably from this, but will obtain a Strep test to rule out that possibility, at her request.

P: Beconase nasal spray, 1 whiff to each nostril q.i.d. for 1 week, then 1 whiff b.i.d. to each nostril. If she has not improved in 3 weeks, refer to ENT specialist.

Henry C. Cardiac, M.D.

Case Study 2-12

DATE	REMARKS			
06/20/YYYY	Parents Ann & York Apple			

PATIENT		CHART #	SEX	BIRTHDATE
Apple, James		2-12	M	11/12/84

MAILING ADDRESS	CITY	STATE	ZIP	HOME PHONE	WORK PHONE
1 Appleblossom Ct	Hometown	US	15123	(201) 111-2011	

EMPLOYER	ADDRESS	PATIENT STATUS
Student		MARRIED DIVORCED SINGLE (STUDENT) OTHER

INSURANCE: PRIMARY	ID#	GROUP	SECONDARY POLICY
Medicaid	1234567		

POLICYHOLDER NAME	BIRTHDATE	RELATIONSHIP	POLICYHOLDER NAME	BIRTHDATE	RELATIONSHIP

SUPPLEMENTAL PLAN	EMPLOYER

POLICYHOLDER NAME	BIRTHDATE	RELATIONSHIP	DIAGNOSIS	CODE
			1.	
EMPLOYER			2.	
			3.	
REFERRING PHYSICIAN UPIN/SSN			4.	
Erin Helper called Dr. Cardiac				

PLACE OF SERVICE   Goodmedicine Hospital

PROCEDURES	CODE	CHARGE
1. 6/19/YYYY Initial inpatient visit, level III (Dr Cardiac), preop		$165—
2. 6/19/YYYY Laparoscopic appendectomy (Dr Stitcher)		1400—
3. Surg Asst (Dr Surgeon)		280—
4.		
5.		
6.		

SPECIAL NOTES

JH Cutdown MD Hometown US will follow patient

TOTAL CHARGES	PAYMENTS	ADJUSTMENTS	BALANCE
separate billing see above	0	0	

RETURN VISIT	PHYSICIAN SIGNATURE
	Henry C. Cardiac, M.D.
	T.J. Stitcher, M.D.

GOODMEDICINE CLINIC
1 PROVIDER STREET, ANYWHERE, US 12345
PHONE NUMBER: (101) 111-2222

06/19/YYYY Emergency Department Visit

Called to Goodmedicine ER at 11:30 PM by Dr. Cardiac who has performed a complete physical on this patient and determined he has an acute appendix. After talking with the patient and his parents, surgery was scheduled for 12:45 AM.

See hospital dictation for details.

T. J. Stitcher, M.D.

06/20/YYYY Inpatient Day of Discharge Visit

Patient was unremarkable postoperatively. Discharged 9 AM today. Mother was given standard, written pediatric appendectomy discharge sheet. Patient is to be seen in the office of J.H. Cutdown, M.D. in 5 days for postoperative followup.

T. J. Stitcher, M.D.

Goodmedicine Hospital Operative Report

DATE: 06/20/YYYY
PATIENT: James Apple

PREOPERATIVE DIAGNOSIS: Acute appendicitis.

POSTOPERATIVE DIAGNOSIS: Acute appendicitis.

OPERATION: Laparoscopic exploration with appendectomy.

ANESTHESIA: General anesthesia via endotracheal tube.

PROCEDURE: The patient was anesthetized with general anesthesia via an endotracheal tube. The abdomen was prepped and draped in sterile fashion. Because of the patient's size, he is 9 years old and quite small, it was not possible to place a catheter in the bladder. The patient was put in the Trendelenburg position. The abdominal wall was palpated, no masses felt. An incision was made below the umbilicus and the Verres needle inserted toward the pelvis. This was tested with normal saline; when it appeared to be in the peritoneal cavity, the abdomen was insufflated with 3 liters of CO_2. A 1/2 cm camera was introduced through this opening. There was no evidence of injury from the needle or trocar, and the area of the appendix was visualized and some exudate and free fluid in the area noted. Under direct vision, a 1/2 cm trocar was passed through the right edge of the rectus sheath in the mid abdomen. Using blunt and sharp dissection, the appendix and cecum were mobilized. The mesoappendix was serially ligated with hemoclips and then divided and the appendix freed to its base. The base was identified by the fact it was supple and it lay at the convergence of the tinea. Next, two #1 PDS endolopps were placed at the base. A single 0 chromic suture was laced approximately 1 cm distally and then the appendix divided between and through the 11 mm trocar. The abdomen was irrigated with normal saline and the contents aspirated. The skin was closed with 4-0 Vicryl, and Benzoin and steristrips applied. The estimated blood loss was 10 cc. Sponge and needle counts were correct. The patient tolerated the procedure well and returned to the recovery room awake and in stable condition.

T. J. Stitcher, M.D.

Case Study 2-13

DATE	REMARKS
06/20/YYYY	Outpatient surgery

PATIENT		CHART #	SEX	BIRTHDATE
Banana, Stanley N		2-13	M	11/11/36

MAILING ADDRESS	CITY	STATE	ZIP	HOME PHONE	WORK PHONE
1 Barrack St	Anywhere	US	12345	(101) 111-7676	

EMPLOYER	ADDRESS	PATIENT STATUS
US Army Retired		MARRIED (DIVORCED) SINGLE STUDENT OTHER

INSURANCE: PRIMARY	ID#	GROUP	SECONDARY POLICY
TRICARE	123445555		none

POLICYHOLDER NAME	BIRTHDATE	RELATIONSHIP	POLICYHOLDER NAME	BIRTHDATE	RELATIONSHIP
Self	11/11/36	Self			

SUPPLEMENTAL PLAN	EMPLOYER
None	

POLICYHOLDER NAME	BIRTHDATE	RELATIONSHIP	DIAGNOSIS	CODE
			1.	
EMPLOYER			2.	
			3.	
REFERRING PHYSICIAN UPIN/SSN			4.	
Nancy Healer				

PLACE OF SERVICE Outpatient Surg Goodmedicine Hospital

PROCEDURES	CODE	CHARGE
1. Flexible Sigmoidoscopy		$600—
2.		
3.		
4.		
5.		
6.		

SPECIAL NOTES

TOTAL CHARGES	PAYMENTS	ADJUSTMENTS	BALANCE
$600—	0	0	$600—

RETURN VISIT	PHYSICIAN SIGNATURE
PRN	*Janet B. Surgeon, M.D.*

GOODMEDICINE CLINIC
1 PROVIDER STREET, ANYWHERE, US 12345
PHONE NUMBER: (101) 111-2222

06/20/YYYY Outpatient Surgery

PROCEDURE: Flexible left sigmoidoscopy was performed. The lining of the colon to this point was normal throughout. No signs of inflammation, ulceration, or mass formation were noted. Anoscope was introduced into the anal canal and this was examined in 4 quadrants. To the left of the midline posteriorly a 4-5 mm very small fissure was seen, apparently exposing an underlying vein that was slightly darker. There was no sign of heaped up margin or any true ulceration.

DIAGNOSIS: Fissure in ano.

PLAN: **1.** Dietary modification to increase fluid and bulk in diet.

2. Avoid straining.

3. Use simple measures such as Sitz baths and Tucks pads when the fissure is symptomatic.

4. Return visit on a prn basis should any additional bleeding be seen.

Janet B. Surgeon, M.D.

Case Study 2-14

DATE 06/20/YYYY	**REMARKS**				
PATIENT Karot, Reginald T	SSA 012 34 6543		**CHART #** 2-14	**SEX** M	**BIRTHDATE** 10/01/35

MAILING ADDRESS 15 Caring St	**CITY** Anywhere	**STATE** US	**ZIP** 12345	**HOME PHONE** (101) 222-2202	**WORK PHONE** (101) 222-0022

EMPLOYER Is A Construction Co	**ADDRESS** Nearby, US 13246	**PATIENT STATUS** (MARRIED) DIVORCED SINGLE STUDENT OTHER

INSURANCE: PRIMARY Metropolitan	**ID#** 222 22 222A	**GROUP** ASD1	**SECONDARY POLICY** TRICARE Standard

POLICYHOLDER NAME Louise Karot	**BIRTHDATE** 10/11/36	**RELATIONSHIP** Spouse	**POLICYHOLDER NAME** Reginald Capt (Navy) Ret	**BIRTHDATE** 10/10/35	**RELATIONSHIP** Self

SUPPLEMENTAL PLAN	**EMPLOYER** Anywhere School District

POLICYHOLDER NAME	**BIRTHDATE**	**RELATIONSHIP**	**DIAGNOSIS**		**CODE**
EMPLOYER			1.		
			2.		
REFERRING PHYSICIAN UPIN/SSN Nancy J. Healer			3. 4.		

PLACE OF SERVICE Office

PROCEDURES	**CODE**	**CHARGE**
1. Office visit, new pt, level III		$75—
2.		
3.		
4.		
5.		
6.		

SPECIAL NOTES Schedule for Bilateral inguinal herniorrhaphy in late July

TOTAL CHARGES $75—	**PAYMENTS** 0	**ADJUSTMENTS** 0	**BALANCE** $75—

RETURN VISIT 1 wk before surgery	**PHYSICIAN SIGNATURE** *Janet B. Surgeon, M.D.*

GOODMEDICINE CLINIC
1 PROVIDER STREET, ANYWHERE, US 12345
PHONE NUMBER: (101) 111-2222

06/20/YYYY Office Visit

S: Three years ago today, this patient was noted to have a bulge in his left side. He has had possible weakness on the right side, noted in Dr. Healer's evaluation today. He does not smoke; he runs frequently and does not do any heavy lifting or straining. He has had some minor changes in his urinary stream and has been noted to have an enlarged prostate in the past. He reports terminal dribbling, but has no difficulty with initiating a stream and has noticed no change in the force of the stream. He reports his bowel movements have been normal. There has been no blood or black stools. He has no other significant medical problems. See the attached Family and Social History Data Sheet elsewhere in this chart.

0: The supraclavicular fossae are free of adenopathy. The chest is clear to percussion and auscultation. The abdomen is soft and nontender, without masses or organomegaly. There is a right lower quadrant appendectomy incision that is well healed. The penis is circumcised without masses. The testicles are scrotal and normal. In the standing position, there is a left inguinal hernia that exits the external ring and a right inguinal external ring that is beginning to do this. Rectal examination revealed normal tone. The prostate is 4.0 x 4.0 cm and normal in architecture. The stool was hemoccult negative.

A: Bilateral inguinal hernias, left greater than right.

P: Schedule for bilateral inguinal herniorrhaphy in early July.

Janet B. Surgeon, M.D.

Case Study 2-15

DATE 06/20/YYYY	REMARKS	Workers' Compensation Fund 113 Insurance Ave Anywhere US 12345			

PATIENT Butcher, James Lawrence	SSA 321 45 8765	CHART # 2-15	SEX M	BIRTHDATE 02/29/77

MAILING ADDRESS 14 Pigsfeet Rd	CITY Anywhere	STATE US	ZIP 12345	HOME PHONE (101) 333-4567	WORK PHONE

EMPLOYER Piglet Meat Packers Anywhere US 12345	ADDRESS	PATIENT STATUS MARRIED DIVORCED (SINGLE) STUDENT OTHER

INSURANCE: PRIMARY Workers' Comp	ID#	GROUP	SECONDARY POLICY

POLICYHOLDER NAME Piglet Meat Packers	BIRTHDATE	RELATIONSHIP	POLICYHOLDER NAME	BIRTHDATE	RELATIONSHIP

SUPPLEMENTAL PLAN	EMPLOYER

POLICYHOLDER NAME	BIRTHDATE	RELATIONSHIP	DIAGNOSIS	CODE
			1.	
EMPLOYER			2.	
			3.	
REFERRING PHYSICIAN UPIN/SSN			4.	

PLACE OF SERVICE

PROCEDURES	CODE	CHARGE
1. Extensor tendon repair 6/19/YYYY		$1400—
2. Office visit, postop followup 6/20/YYYY		n/c
3.		
4.		
5.		
6.		

SPECIAL NOTES Hospital filed injury report

TOTAL CHARGES $1400—	PAYMENTS 0	ADJUSTMENTS 0	BALANCE $1400—

RETURN VISIT 06/22/YYYY	PHYSICIAN SIGNATURE *T.J. Stitcher, M.D.*

GOODMEDICINE CLINIC
1 PROVIDER STREET, ANYWHERE, US 12345
PHONE NUMBER: (101) 111-2222

6/20/YYYY Office Visit

Mr. Butcher comes to the office today after having removed a splint and rebandaging himself at home. He had been clearly instructed in the ER not to do this. The patient said he was afraid that when he bumped it, he had "busted the stitches out;" therefore, he took the splint and bandage off to see.

TREATMENT: The dressing and splint were removed, taking care to keep the finger in extension. It should be noted that when the dressing was removed, there was a slight flexion to the thumb as it was lying in the splint as the patient had replaced it. The wound was clean and healing. The wound was cleaned with Aqueous Zephiran; Betadine Ointment was then applied and it was redressed. A new splint was put on, holding the thumb in a fully extended position.

DISPOSITION OF CASE: The patient was instructed to keep the dressing clean and dry, and not remove the splint or the dressing. He is to continue his Augmentin. He will continue on Darvocet-N 100 as needed for pain. If he has any problems or difficulties he is to call me or return to the emergency department; otherwise, he will be seen in the office in 2 days.

06/18/YYYY Emergency Department Procedure

PATIENT: James L. Butcher

SURGEON: T. J. Stitcher, M.D.

PREOPERATIVE DIAGNOSIS: 2 cm laceration of the dorsum of the thumb.

POSTOPERATIVE DIAGNOSIS: 2 cm laceration of the dorsum of the thumb with laceration of the extensor tendon.

OPERATION: Repair of the extensor tendon and laceration to the dorsum of the left thumb.

BRIEF HISTORY: This 22-year-old male came to the ED, today, 6/18/YYYY, with a chief complaint of a 2 cm laceration of the back of his left thumb. The patient says: "I was cutting the feet off of hogs when the knife slipped and cut the back of my thumb." He has not been able to extend the thumb since the accident. He had some bleeding, which he stopped with pressure, and then came to the ED. History reveals that this patient had a stable wound of his forearm while at work about a year ago and received tetanus toxoid at that time. He has no past history of any serious illnesses, operations, or allergies. Social and Family History is noncontributory.

PHYSICAL FINDINGS: Examination at this time reveals a well-developed, well-nourished white male appearing his stated age and in no acute distress. He has no abnormal findings other than the left thumb, which shows a laceration of the dorsum of the thumb proximal to the interphalangeal joint. The patient cannot extend the thumb; he can flex, adduct, and abduct the thumb. Sensation at this time appears to be normal.

PROCEDURE: With the patient in the supine position the area was prepped and draped. A digital nerve block using 1% Carbocaine was carried out. When the block was totally effective, the wound was explored. The distal severed end of the tendon was located. The proximal end could not be found. A vertical incision was then made down the lateral aspect of the thumb starting at the corner of the original laceration, thus creating a flap. When the flap was retracted back, the proximal portion of the tendon was located. Both tendon ends had a very clean-cut surface; therefore, the tendon was not trimmed. Examination revealed the joint capsule had been lacerated. After thorough irrigation of the wound with normal saline the joint capsule was repaired with two sutures of 5-0 Dexon. The tendon repair was then carried out using 4-0 nylon. When the tendon repair was complete, the patient was allowed to flex the thumb gently and then fully extend it. The thumb was then held in full extension. The wound was again irrigated well and the skin was then closed with 4-0 nylon. Dressings were applied and a splint was applied holding the interphalangeal joint in neutral position, in full extension but not hyperextension. The patient tolerated the procedure well and left the surgical area in good condition.

DISPOSITION OF CASE: The patient was instructed to elevate the hand, to keep his fingers moving, to keep the dressing clean and dry, and not to remove the splint or dressing at home. He is to take Percocet, one q4h as needed for pain. He will take Augmentin, 250 mg t.i.d. If he has any problems or difficulties he is to call or return to the emergency department; otherwise, he will be seen in the office for followup in three days.

Case Study 2-16

DATE 06/20/YYYY	REMARKS	Industrial Indemnity Co 10 Policy St Anywhere US 12345			
PATIENT Hurts, David J.	SSA 112 10 2121	CHART # 2-16	SEX M	BIRTHDATE 02/28/55	

| MAILING ADDRESS 4321 Nowhere St | CITY Anywhere | STATE US | ZIP 12345 | HOME PHONE (101) 314-1414 | WORK PHONE |

| EMPLOYER UC Painters | ADDRESS Anywhere US | PATIENT STATUS MARRIED DIVORCED (SINGLE) STUDENT OTHER |

| INSURANCE: PRIMARY Workers Comp | ID# 112 10 2121 | GROUP | SECONDARY POLICY |

POLICYHOLDER NAME	BIRTHDATE	RELATIONSHIP	POLICYHOLDER NAME	BIRTHDATE	RELATIONSHIP

| SUPPLEMENTAL PLAN | EMPLOYER |

POLICYHOLDER NAME	BIRTHDATE	RELATIONSHIP	DIAGNOSIS		CODE
			1.		
EMPLOYER			2.		
			3.		
REFERRING PHYSICIAN UPIN/SSN			4.		

PLACE OF SERVICE

PROCEDURES	CODE	CHARGE
1. Xray, forearm, complete		$80—
2. Closed fracture, Lt radius c̄ manipulation		300—
3. Simple repair, 2 cm, medial mandible		80—
4.		
5.		
6.		

SPECIAL NOTES Prepare first report of injury

TOTAL CHARGES $460—	PAYMENTS 0	ADJUSTMENTS 0	BALANCE $460—

| RETURN VISIT | PHYSICIAN SIGNATURE *Gail R. Bones, M.D.* |

GOODMEDICINE CLINIC
1 PROVIDER STREET, ANYWHERE, US 12345
PHONE NUMBER: (101) 111-2222

06/20/YYYY Office Visit

At 10:30 this morning, Mr. Ima Boss presented himself at the front desk and announced that he was the supervisor at U.C. Painters, Inc., and he had an injured worker in the car.

The patient is David J. Hurts of 4321 Nowhere Street in Anywhere, US 12345. U.C. Painters, Inc. is located at 123 Color Street in Anywhere, MD. The patient was injured when he fell from a ladder while painting at 543 House St. in Anywhere. The injury occurred at 10:15 AM. The compensation carrier is Industrial Indemnity Company, 10 Policy St., in Anywhere, US.

The patient says he fell when a step broke on the ladder. He has multiple abrasions and lacerations, which were treated. A 2.0 cm medial mandible laceration was closed with 3 black silk sutures.

Xrays revealed a Colles' fracture of the left radius with only minor displacement. The fracture was reduced and a plaster cast applied. The patient was given a prescription for Tylenol #3, instructed in cast care, and told to return tomorrow for a cast check.

The supervisor and patient were told the patient would not be able to return to his regular painting job for approximately 6 weeks. The doctor stated she does not anticipate any permanent disability.

Gail R. Bones, M.D.

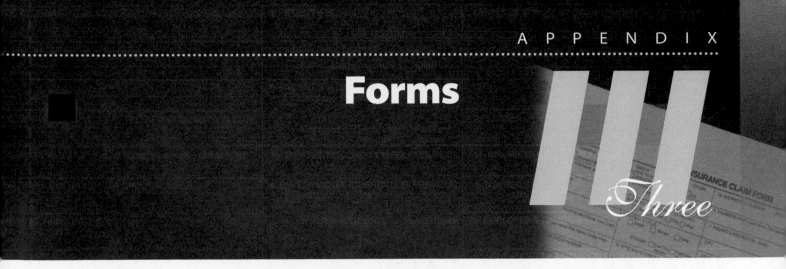

Forms

Three

You are welcome to copy the following forms for use when completing exercises in the textbook and workbook:

- HCFA-1500 claim form
- Coding Case Study Form (for Chapter 10 exercises)
- Claim Form Completion chart
- Workers' Compensation Commission form (for use with Case Studies: Set Two)
- E&M CodeBuilder

■ **NOTE:** These forms can also be printed from the disk that accompanies this textbook. ■

PLEASE
DO NOT
STAPLE
IN THIS
AREA

(SAMPLE ONLY - NOT APPROVED FOR USE)

□□ PICA

UNDERSTANDING HEALTH INSURANCE CLAIM FORM   PICA □□□

1.	MEDICARE	MEDICAID	CHAMPUS	CHAMPVA	GROUP HEALTH PLAN	FECA BLK LUNG	OTHER	1a. INSURED'S I.D. NUMBER	(FOR PROGRAM IN ITEM 1)
	□ (Medicare #)	□ (Medicaid #)	□ (Sponsor's SSN)	□ (VA File #)	□ (SSN or ID)	□ (SSN)	□ (ID)		

2. PATIENT'S NAME (Last Name, First Name, Middle Initial)

3. PATIENT'S BIRTH DATE   MM │ DD │ YY   SEX   M □   F □

4. INSURED'S NAME (Last Name, First Name, Middle Initial)

5. PATIENT'S ADDRESS (No. Street)

6. PATIENT RELATIONSHIP TO INSURED
Self □   Spouse □   Child □   Other □

7. INSURED'S ADDRESS (No. Street)

CITY   STATE

8. PATIENT STATUS
Single □   Married □   Other □

Employed □   Full-Time Student □   Part-Time Student □

CITY   STATE

ZIP CODE   TELEPHONE (Include Area Code)
(   )

ZIP CODE   TELEPHONE (INCLUDE AREA CODE)
(   )

9. OTHER INSURED'S NAME (Last Name, First Name, Middle Initial)

10. IS PATIENT'S CONDITION RELATED TO:

11. INSURED'S POLICY GROUP OR FECA NUMBER

a. OTHER INSURED'S POLICY OR GROUP NUMBER

a. EMPLOYMENT? (CURRENT OR PREVIOUS)
□ YES   □ NO

a. INSURED'S DATE OF BIRTH   MM │ DD │ YY   SEX   M □   F □

b. OTHER INSURED'S DATE OF BIRTH   MM │ DD │ YY   SEX   M □   F □

b. AUTO ACCIDENT?   PLACE (State)
□ YES   □ NO

b. EMPLOYER'S NAME OR SCHOOL NAME

c. EMPLOYER'S NAME OR SCHOOL NAME

c. OTHER ACCIDENT?
□ YES   □ NO

c. INSURANCE PLAN NAME OR PROGRAM NAME

d. INSURANCE PLAN NAME OR PROGRAM NAME

10d. RESERVED FOR LOCAL USE

d. IS THERE ANOTHER HEALTH BENEFIT PLAN?
□ YES   □ NO   If yes, return to and complete item 9 a - d.

READ BACK OF FORM BEFORE COMPLETING & SIGNING THIS FORM.
12. PATIENT'S OR AUTHORIZED PERSON'S SIGNATURE   I authorize the release of any medical or other information necessary to process this claim. I also request payment of government benefits either to myself or to the party who accepts assignment below.

SIGNED _____   DATE _____

13. INSURED'S OR AUTHORIZED PERSON'S SIGNATURE   I authorize payment of medical benefits to the undersigned physician or supplier for services described below.

SIGNED _____

14. DATE OF CURRENT: MM │ DD │ YY   ◄ ILLNESS (First symptom) OR INJURY (Accident) OR PREGNANCY (LMP)

15. IF PATIENT HAS HAD SAME OR SIMILAR ILLNESS, GIVE FIRST DATE   MM │ DD │ YY

16. DATES PATIENT UNABLE TO WORK IN CURRENT OCCUPATION   MM │ DD │ YY   FROM   TO   MM │ DD │ YY

17. NAME OF REFERRING PHYSICIAN OR OTHER SOURCE

17a. I.D. NUMBER OF REFERRING PHYSICIAN

18. HOSPITALIZATION DATES RELATED TO CURRENT SERVICES   MM │ DD │ YY   FROM   TO   MM │ DD │ YY

19. RESERVED FOR LOCAL USE

20. OUTSIDE LAB? $ CHARGES
□ YES   □ NO

21. DIAGNOSIS OR NATURE OF ILLNESS OR INJURY. (RELATE ITEMS 1, 2, 3, OR 4 TO ITEM 24E BY LINE)

1. └─── . ──   3. └─── . ──

2. └─── . ──   4. └─── . ──

22. MEDICAID RESUBMISSION CODE   ORIGINAL REF. NO.

23. PRIOR AUTHORIZATION NUMBER

24. A DATE(S) OF SERVICE						B Place of Service	C Type of Service	D PROCEDURES, SERVICES, OR SUPPLIES (Explain Unusual Circumstances)		E DIAGNOSIS CODE	F $ CHARGES	G DAYS OR UNITS	H EPSDT Family Plan	I EMG	J COB	K RESERVED FOR LOCAL USE
From MM	DD	YY	To MM	DD	YY			CPT/HCPCS	MODIFIER							
1																
2																
3																
4																
5																
6																

25. FEDERAL TAX I.D. NUMBER   SSN EIN   □ □

26. PATIENT'S ACCOUNT NO.

27. ACCEPT ASSIGNMENT? (For govt. claims, see back)
□ YES   □ NO

28. TOTAL CHARGE $

29. AMOUNT PAID $

30. BALANCE DUE $

31. SIGNATURE OF PHYSICIAN OR SUPPLIER INCLUDING DEGREES OR CREDENTIALS
(I certify that the statements on the reverse apply to this bill and are made a part thereof.)

SIGNED _____   DATE _____

32. NAME AND ADDRESS OF FACILITY WHERE SERVICES WERE RENDERED (If other than home or office)

33. PHYSICIAN'S SUPPLIER'S BILLING NAME, ADDRESS, ZIP CODE & PHONE #

PIN#   GRP#

(SAMPLE ONLY - NOT APPROVED FOR USE)

PLEASE PRINT OR TYPE

SAMPLE FORM 1500
SAMPLE FORM 1500   SAMPLE FORM 1500

(right margin, vertical text) CARRIER → PATIENT AND INSURED INFORMATION → PHYSICIAN OR SUPPLIER INFORMATION

Coding Case Study Form

Page ____

CASE STUDY NO.	DX (DIAGNOSIS)	CODE #	TX (PROCEDURE)	CODE #

Claim Form Comparison Chart

Page ___

BLOCK											

INSTRUCTIONS

1. Type answers to All questions and file original with the Workers' Compensation Commission within 72 hours after first treatment.
2. DO NOT FAIL to forward to the Workers' Compensation Commission PROGRESS REPORTS and FINAL REPORT upon discharge of patient.

DO NOT WRITE IN THIS SPACE

WORKERS' COMPENSATION COMMISSION
6 NORTH LIBERTY STREET, BALTIMORE, MD. 21201-3785
SURGEON'S REPORT

WCC CLAIM #

EMPLOYER'S REPORT Yes ☐ No ☐

This is First Report ☐   Progress Report ☐   Final Report ☐

EVERY QUESTION MUST BE ANSWERED AND FORM SIGNED

1. Name of Injured Person: Soc. Sec. No.   D.O.B.   Sex   M ☐   F ☐

2. Address: (No. and Street)   (City or Town)   (State)   (Zip Code)

3. Name and Address of Employer:

4. Date of Accident or Onset of Disease: Hour: A.M. ☐   P.M. ☐   5. Date Disability Began:

6. Patient's Description of Accident or Cause of Disease:

7. Medical description of Injury or Disease.

8. Will Injury result in:
(a) Permanent defect?   Yes ☐   No ☐   If so, what?   (b) Disfigurement   Yes ☐   No ☐

9. Causes, other than injury, contributing to patients condition:

10. Is patient suffering from any disease of the heart, lungs, brain, kidneys, blood, vascular system or any other disabling condition not due to this accident?
Give particulars:

11. Is there any history or evidence present of previous accident or disease? Give particulars:

12. Has normal recovery been delayed for any reason? Give particulars:

13. Date of first treatment: Who engaged your services?

14. Describe treatment given by you:

15. Were X-Rays taken: Yes ☐   No ☐   By whom? — (Name and Address)   Date

16. X-Ray Diagnosis:

17. Was patient treated by anyone else?   Yes ☐   No ☐   By whom? — (Name and Address)   Date

18. Was patient hospitalized?   Yes ☐   No ☐   Name and Address of Hospital   Date of Admission: Date of Discharge:

19. Is further treatment needed?   Yes ☐   No ☐   For how long?   20. Patient was ☐ will be ☐ able to resume regular work on:
Patient was ☐ will be ☐ able to resume light work on:

21. If death ensued give date: 22. Remarks: (Give any information of value not included above)

23. I am a qualified specialist in: I am a duly licensed Physician in the State of: I was graduated from Medical School (Name)   Year

Date of this report: (Signed)

(This report must be signed PERSONALLY by Physician)

Address: Phone:

E&M CODEBUILDER

(For use with 1995 and 1997 *HCFA Documentation Guidelines for Evaluation & Management Coding*)

Introduction

The E&M code reported to a third-party payer must be supported by documentation in the patient's record (e.g., SOAP or clinic note, diagnostic test results, operative findings). While providers are responsible for selecting the E&M code at the time patient care is rendered, insurance specialists audit records to make sure that the appropriate level of E&M code was reported to the third-party payer.

This E&M CodeBuilder form can be used for that purpose, and it can also be used as a tool to teach appropriate assignment of E&M level codes. To assign a code, just review the documentation in the patient's record, record your findings below (based on the directions provided), and refer to the CPT coding manual to select the E&M code to be reported.

E&M code selection is based on three key components: *history, examination,* and *medical decision making.* This CodeBuilder form emphasizes those components. It is important to be aware that contributory components (*counseling* and *coordination of care*) also play an important role in selecting the E&M code when documentation in the patient record indicates that counseling or coordination of care dominated the visit. In this situation, the contributory component of *time* can be considered a key or controlling factor in selecting a level of E&M service (code).

■ **NOTE:** *Time* and *nature of presenting problem* are listed in some E&M code descriptions to assist in determining which code number to report. ■

Selecting the Level of History

To select the level of history, review the following elements in the patient record. If an element is not documented, it cannot be considered when selecting the level of E&M service code.

- History of Present Illness (HPI)
- Review of Systems (ROS)
- Past, Family, and Social History (PFSH)

History of Present Illness (HPI)

Review the clinic or SOAP note in the patient's record, and for each documented HPI element listed below, enter an X in the box located in front of the element on this form. Then, total the Xs and enter that number in the box located in front of the Total Score (below). Finally, select the level of history based on the total number of elements documented, and enter an X in the appropriate box.

- ☐ **Location:** of pain/discomfort; is pain diffused/localized, unilateral/bilateral, does it radiate or refer?
- ☐ **Quality:** a description of the quality of the symptom (e.g., is pain described as sharp, dull, throbbing, stabbing, constant, intermittent, acute or chronic, stable, improving, or worsening).
- ☐ **Severity:** use of self-assessment scale to measure subjective levels (e.g., on a scale of 1-10, how severe is the pain?), or comparison of pain quantitatively with previously experienced pain.
- ☐ **Timing:** establishing onset of pain and chronology of pain development (e.g., migraine in the a.m.).
- ☐ **Context:** where was the patient and what was he doing when pain begins (e.g., was patient at rest or involved in an activity; was pain aggravated or relieved, or does it recur, with a specific activity; did situational stress or some other factor precede or accompany the pain)?
- ☐ **Modifying factors:** what has patient attempted to do to relieve pain (e.g., heat vs. cold; does it relieve or exacerbate pain; what makes the pain worse; have over-the-counter drugs been attempted—with what results)?
- ☐ **Associated signs/symptoms:** clinician's impressions formulated during the interview may lead to questioning about additional sensations or feelings (e.g., diaphoresis associated with indigestion or chest pain, blurred vision accompanying a headache, etc.).

____ **Total Score:** Enter the score for number of X's entered above (representing number of HPI elements), and enter an X in front of the HPI type below:

- ☐ Brief HPI (1-3 elements)
- ☐ Extended HPI (4 or more elements)

Review of Systems (ROS)

Review the clinic or SOAP note in the patient's record, and for each documented ROS element listed below, place an X in the box located in front of the element on this form. Then, total the Xs and enter that number in the box located in front of the Total Score (below). Finally, select the level of ROS based on the total number of elements documented, and enter an X in the appropriate box.

■ **NOTE:** To properly assess review of systems documentation, have *HCFA Documentation Guidelines for Evaluation & Management Coding* available as you review the patient's record. ■

- ☐ Constitutional symptoms
- ☐ Eyes
- ☐ Ears, nose, mouth, throat
- ☐ Cardiovascular
- ☐ Respiratory
- ☐ Gastrointestinal
- ☐ Integumentary (including skin & breast)
- ☐ Genitourinary
- ☐ Musculoskeletal
- ☐ Allergic/Immunologic
- ☐ Hematologic/Lymphatic
- ☐ Neurologic
- ☐ Psychiatric
- ☐ Endocrine

____ **Total Score:** Enter the score for number of Xs entered above (representing number of ROS elements), and enter an X in front of the ROS type below:
- ☐ None
- ☐ Problem Perinent (1 body system documented)
- ☐ Extended (2-9 body systems documented)
- ☐ Complete (all body systems documented)

Past, Family, and/or Social History (PFSH)

Review the clinic or SOAP note in the patient's record, and for each documented PFSH element listed below, place an X in the box located in front of the element on this form. Then, total the Xs and enter that number in the box located in front of the Total Score (below). Finally, select the level of PFSH based on the total number of elements documented, and enter an X in the appropriate box.

- ☐ Past history (patient's past experience with illnesses, operations, injuries, and treatments)
- ☐ Family history (review of medical events in the patient's family, including diseases that may be hereditary or place the patient at risk)
- ☐ Social history (an age appropriate review of past and current activities)

____ **Total Score:** Enter the score for number of Xs entered above (representing number of ROS elements), and enter an X in front of the PFSH type below:
- ☐ None
- ☐ Pertinent (1 history area documented)
- ☐ Complete (2 or 3 history areas documented)

Level of History

Circle the type of HPI, ROS and PFSH determined above; then circle the appropriate Level of History below

HPI	Brief	Brief	Extended	Extended
ROS	None	Problem Pertinent	Extended	Complete
PFSH	None	None	Pertinent	Complete
Level of History	Problem Focused	Expanded Problem Focused	Detailed	Comprehensive

Selecting the Level of Examination

To select the level of examination, first determine whether a *single organ examination* (specialist exam; e.g., ophthalmologist) or a *general multi-system examination* (e.g., family practitioner) was completed.

■ **NOTE:** To properly assess review of systems documentation, have *HCFA Documentation Guidelines for Evaluation & Management Coding* available as you review the patient's record. ■

Single Organ System Examination

Refer to the single organ system examination requirements in *HCFA Documentation Guidelines for Evaluation & Management Services*, and enter an X in front of the appropriate exam type below.

☐ PROBLEM FOCUSED EXAMINATION (1-5 elements identified by a bullet)

☐ EXPANDED PROBLEM FOCUSED EXAMINATION (at least 6 elements identified by a bullet)

☐ DETAILED EXAMINATION (at least 12 elements identified by a bullet) **Note:** For eye and psychiatric examinations, at least 9 elements in each box with a shaded border and at least one element in each box with a shaded or unshaded border is documented

☐ COMPREHENSIVE EXAMINATION (all elements identified by a bullet; document every element in each box with a shaded border and at least 1 element in each box with an unshaded box)

General Multisystem Exam

Refer to the General Multi-System Examination Requirements in *HCFA Documentation Guidelines for Evaluation & Management Services*. Enter an X in front of the organ system or body area for up to the total number of allowed elements (e.g., up to 2 elements can be documented for the Neck exam).

☐ Constitutional (2)   ☐ Respiratory (4)   ☐ Genitourinary (male–3; female–6)

☐ Eyes (3)   ☐ Gastrointestinal (5)   ☐ Musculoskeletal (6)

☐ Ears, nose, mouth, throat (6)   ☐ Chest (Breasts) (2)   ☐ Neurologic (3)

☐ Neck (2)   ☐ Skin (2)   ☐ Psychiatric (4)

☐ Cardiovascular (7)

_____ **Total Score:** Enter the score for number of X's entered above (representing number of Exam elements), and enter an X in front of the Exam type below:

☐ PROBLEM FOCUSED EXAMINATION (1-5 elements identified by a bullet on *HCFA Documentation Guidelines for Evaluation & Management Services*)

☐ EXPANDED PROBLEM FOCUSED EXAMINATION (at least 6 elements identified by a bullet on *HCFA Documentation Guidelines for Evaluation & Management Services*)

☐ DETAILED EXAMINATION (at least 2 elements identified by a bullet from each of 6 organ systems or body areas or at least 12 elements identified by a bullet in two or more systems or areas, on *HCFA Documentation Guidelines for Evaluation & Management Services*)

☐ COMPREHENSIVE EXAMINATION (documentation of all elements identified by a bullet in at least 9 organ systems or body areas, and documentation of at least 2 elements identified by a bullet from each of 9 organ systems or body areas, on *HCFA Documentation Guidelines for Evaluation & Management Services*)

Medical Decision Making

Select the appropriate level of medical decision making based upon the following criteria:

NUMBER OF DIAGNOSES OR MANAGEMENT OPTIONS	AMOUNT/COMPLEXITY OF DATA TO BE REVIEWED	RISK OF COMPLICATIONS AND/OR MORBIDITY/MORTALITY	MEDICAL DECISION MAKING
Minimal	Minimal or None	Minimal	Straightforward
Limited	Limited	Low	Low Complexity
Multiple	Moderate	Moderate	Moderate Complexity
Extensive	Extensive	High	High Complexity

E&M Code Selection

Select the E&M code based on selection of level of history, examination, and medical decision making:

History	Problem focused	Expanded problem focused	Expanded problem focused	Detailed	Comprehensive
Examination	Problem focused	Expanded problem focused	Expanded problem focused	Detailed	Comprehensive
Medical Decision Making	Straightforward	Low complexity	Moderate complexity	Moderate complexity	High complexity

Go to the appropriate E&M category/subcategory, and select the code based upon the information above.

Answers to Coding Exercises

ANSWERS TO ICD-9-CM CODING EXERCISES (CHAPTER 6)

■ **NOTE:** The underlined word is the condition found in the Index. ■

Exercise 6-1

1.	Bronchiole spasm	519.1
2.	Congenital candidiasis	112.9
3.	Irritable bladder	596.8
4.	Earthquake injury	E909
	(No site mentioned. See Injury in Index to External Causes)	
5.	Exposure to AIDS virus	V01.7
6.	Ground itch	126.9
7.	Nun's knees	727.2
8.	Mice, right knee joint	717.6

Exercise 6-2

1.	Acute purulent sinusitis	461.9 - (purulent) is a nonessential modifier.
2.	Fracture, mandible	802.20 - (closed) is a nonessential modifier
3.	Actinomycotic meningitis	039.8 and 320.7 - bracketed code is sequenced second
4.	Psychomotor akinetic epilepsy	345.40 - requires fifth digit
5.	3 cm laceration, right forearm	881.00 - See also wound, open
6.	Contusion, abdomen	868.00 - NEC
7.	Pneumonia due to H. influenzae	482.2 - Subcategory
8.	Delayed healing, open wound, abdomen	879.3 - Boxed Note describes "delayed healing" as "complicated"
9.	Bile duct cicatrix	576.8 - "Trust the index."
10.	Uncontrolled noninsulin dependent diabetes with osteomyelitis	250.82 & 731.8 - Bracketed code

Exercise 6-3

1.	515	Postinflammatory pulmonary fibrosis	C
2.	250.1	Noninsulin-dependent diabetes	250.00
3.	727.67	Nontraumatic rupture of Achilles tendon	C
4.	422.0	Acute myocarditis due to Coxsackie virus	074.23, 422.0
5.	813.22	Malunion, closed, right radial fracture	733.81
6.	483.0	Mycoplasmic pneumonia	C
7.	795.71	Positive HIV test, asymptomatic	V08
8.	796.2	Elevated blood pressure	C
9.	718.06	Old tear of right knee meniscus	C
		(Knee joint location is described in fifth-digit subclassification codes located above category 710)	

Exercise 6-4

1.	Pregnancy complicated by gonorrhea	647.10 - fifth digit bracket
2.	Benign neoplasm, ear cartilage	215.0 - ear cartilage is not excluded
3.	Cervicitis, tuberculous	016.70 - Includes

4. Uncontrolled Type II <u>diabetes</u>
   with polyneuropathy   250.62 and 357.2 - Use additional code
5. Congenital <u>hemangioma</u> on face   228.01 - Site is skin. Includes
6. <u>Hiss-Russell</u> shigellosis   004.1 - "Trust the Index."
7. Closed <u>fracture</u>, right leg   827.0 - NOS
8. Diabetic <u>cataract</u>   250.50 and 366.41 - Use additional code
9. Muscular <u>atrophy</u>, left leg   728.2 - NEC
10. Chronic smoker's bronchitis with   466.0 (the acute disorder) and
    acute <u>bronchitis</u>   491.0 - Includes (the underlying chronic condition)

Exercise 6-5

1. Essential hypertension with cardiomegaly   402.90 Includes
2. Transient hypertension due to pregnancy   642.30 (episode of care is not stated)
3. Malignant hypertensive crisis   401.0
4. Renal and heart disease due to hypertension   404.90 Hypertension, Cardiorenal

Exercise 6-6

1. <u>Kaposi's</u> sarcoma   /3 Malignant primary
2. <u>Lipoma</u>, skin, upper back   /0 Benign
3. <u>Carcinoma</u> *in situ*, skin, left cheek   /2 In situ
4. Scrotum <u>mass</u>   No M code
5. <u>Neurofibroma</u>   /0 benign
6. <u>Cyst</u> on left ovary   No M code
7. <u>Ganglion</u>, right wrist   No M code
8. <u>Yaws</u>, frambeside   /0 Benign
9. Breast, chronic <u>cystic</u> disease   No M code
10. Hurtle cell <u>tumor</u>   /0 Benign
11. Bile duct <u>cystadenocarcinoma</u>   /3 Malignant primary
12. Mixed <u>glioma</u>   /3 Malignant primary

Exercise 6-7

1. Ca (carcinoma) of the lung   162.9
2. Metastasis from the lung   162.9 (lung is primary) and
                                           199.1 (unknown secondary site)

3. Abdominal mass   789.30
4. Carcinoma of the breast (female) with   174.9 & 196.3
   metastasis to the axillary lymph nodes

5. Carcinoma of axillary lymph nodes and   174.9 (breast is primary)
   lungs, metastatic from the breast (female)   196.3 & 197.0 (secondary sites)
6. Astrocytoma (Unspecified site)   191.0 (/3)
7. Skin lesion, left cheek   709.9

Exercise 6-8

1. Adverse <u>reaction</u> to pertussis vaccine   995.2 (unspecified adverse effect) and E948.6
2. Cardiac arrhythmia caused by interaction   971.2 (poisoning, ephedrine),
   between prescribed ephedrine   980.0 (poisoning, alcohol),
   and alcohol, not prescribed   427.9 (arrhythmia), E980.4, and
                                           E980.9 (undetermined external cause)

3. Sinus bradycardia due to correctly prescribed   427.89 and E942.0
   dose of propranolol
4. Stupor due to overdose of Nytol   963.0 (poisoning, Nytol), 780.09 (stupor), and E950.4
   (suicide attempt)   (suicide attempt)

Exercise 6-9

1. Family <u>history</u> of epilepsy with no   V17.2
   evidence of seizures
2. Six-week postpartum <u>checkup</u>   V24.2
3. Premarital physical (<u>examination</u>, marriage)   V70.3
4. Consult with dietitian for patient with   V65.3 and 250.00
   diabetes mellitus (Consultation)
5. Rubella <u>screening</u>   V73.3
6. <u>Exposure</u> to TB   V01.1

Exercise 6-10

1. Patient is HIV positive with no symptoms   V08
2. AIDS patient treated for Candida   112.9 and 042
3. Open fracture maxilla   802.5
4. Greenstick fracture, third digit, right foot   826.0
5. Multiple fractures, right femur, distal end   821.29

Exercise 6-11

1. Malunion due to fracture, right ankle,   733.81 and 905.4 (Late Effect)
   9 months ago
2. Brain damage due to subdural hematoma,   348.9 and 438.9 (nontraumatic)
   18 months previously   or 907.0 (traumatic)
3. Second-degree burn, anterior chest wall   942.22 and 948.00 (extent of body surface
        burned is 9%)
4. Scalding with erythema, right forearm   943.11, 944.10, and 948.00
   and hand
5. Third-degree burn, back, 18% body surface   942.34 and 948.11

Exercise 6-12

1. Automobile accident, highway, passenger   E819.1 (Accident, motor vehicle)
2. Worker injured by <u>fall from</u> ladder   E881.0
3. Accidental <u>drowning</u>, fell from power boat   E832.1
4. Soft tissue <u>injury</u>, right arm, due to snow-   884.0, E820.9 (Accident,
   mobile accident in patient's yard   snow vehicle) and E849.0
        (Accident, occurring at or in)

ANSWERS TO CPT CODING EXERCISES (CHAPTER 7)

■ **NOTE:** The underlined words are found in the Index. Words in parentheses are substitutions to help you locate the procedure/service in the index, or provide explanations of special coding situations. ■

Exercise 7-1

1. True   Physician, Hospital Outpatient and Ambulatory Surgical Centers use two-digit modifiers.
2. False   The asterisk indicates a variable minor surgical procedure only. Pre- and postop services are billed separately.
3. False   The Evaluation and Management and Anesthesia sections are excluded from the list. Nuclear medicine is a subsection of Radiology. Pathology should be listed as Pathology and Laboratory.
4. False   The triangle indicates a code description revision in the current CPT coding manual.
5. False   CPT requires either a two-digit modifier attached to the five-digit CPT code or a five-digit modifier listed beneath the five-digit CPT code.
6. True   While parenthetical notes apply to specific codes or refer the reader to additional codes, blocked notes provide instruction for codes listed below the heading.
7. True   Semicolons save space in CPT where a series of related codes are found.
8. False   Qualifiers may appear in main and subordinate clauses.
9. False   Parenthetical statements beginning with "E.g." provide examples of terms that might be in the health care provider's description of the service performed. They do not have to be included in the documentation.

Exercise 7-2

B. Marsupialization means creating a pouch.
C. 47350   simple suture of liver wound or injury
    47360   complex suture of liver wound or injury, with or without hepatic artery ligation
    47361   exploration of hepatic wound, extensive debridement, coagulation, and/or suture with or without packing of the liver wound
    47362   re-exploration of the wound for removal of packing

Exercise 7-3

1. Closed treatment of wrist <u>dislocation</u>   25660, 25675, 25680
2. <u>Dilation</u> of cervix   57800-57820
   (<u>Dilation and Curettage</u> listed same code numbers)
3. <u>Placement</u> of upper GI feeding tube   No entry
   <u>Insertion</u>, Gastroscopy Tube   No entry
   <u>Insertion</u>, Tube, Gastrointestinal, Upper   43241
   <u>Insertion</u>, Catheter, Gastrointestinal, Upper   43241
   <u>Placement</u>, nasogastric tube   43752

4. Radiograph and fluoroscopy of chest, 4 views
   <u>Xray, Chest</u>, Complete (four views), with Fluoroscopy   71034
5. <u>Magnetic resonance imaging</u> (MRI), <u>Spine</u>, Lumbar   72148-72149, 72156-72158
6. Darrach <u>procedure</u>   No entry
   (<u>Darrach Procedure</u> - *See* Excision, Ulna, Partial)   25150-25151, 25240
7. Manual <u>CBC</u>—*See* Blood Cell Count, Complete   85022-85025, 85031
   Blood Count (CBC)
8. <u>Electrosurgical</u> removal, skin tags   No entry
   <u>Destruction</u>, Skin Lesion, Benign   17000-17004
   <u>Skin, Destruction</u>, Benign Lesions (number of lesions
   removed needed)
   <u>Skin, Tags</u>, Removal   11200-11201

Exercise 7-4

1. <u>Incision and drainage</u> (I&D) finger <u>abscess</u>   26010*
2. Percutaneous I&D, <u>abscess, appendix</u>   44901
3. Anesthetic agent injection, L-5   64475
   <u>paravertebral nerve</u>
4. Laparoscopic <u>cholecystectomy</u> with cholangiography   47563
5. Flexible esophagoscopy with brushing and specimen   43215 & 74235
   collection and removal of foreign body and radiologic supervision
   and interpretation (S&I) (Esophagus, Endoscopy, Removal,
   Foreign Body **or** Endoscopy, Esophagus, Removal, Foreign Body.
   See parenthetical note below 43215 for second code.)
6. Anterior interbody approach, arthrodesis   22558 & 22585
   with minimal diskectomy, L-1 through L-3 vertebrae
   (Arthrodesis, Vertebra, Lumbar, Anterior,
   Anterolateral Approach. There are two interspaces
   between L-1 & L-3. Use add-on code for the second interspace.)

Exercise 7-5

1. Diagnostic <u>arthroscopy</u>, right wrist, with biopsy (BX)   29840
2. Simple vaginal mucosal <u>biopsy</u>   57100
3. Diagnostic nasal <u>endoscopy</u>, bilateral and   31231
   Facial <u>chemical peel</u>   15788
4. Diagnostic <u>thoracoscopy</u>, pleural space and biopsy right lung   32602

Exercise 7-6

1. Excision, 2.5 cm malignant lesion, left cheek   11643
   (<u>Excision, Skin, Malignant</u>)
2. Excision 1-1/2 inch benign lesion, scalp   11424
   (Lesion is 3.81 cm. <u>Excision</u>, Lesion, Skin, benign)
3. Remove 10 <u>skin</u> tags upper back, 3 right   11200 (first 15 lesions)
   arm, 4 chest, 2 left thigh, 3 abdomen   11201 (remaining 7 lesions)
4. Suture, 1 inch simple laceration, left forearm, and 2-1/2 inch   12004
   simple laceration, right arm (<u>Repair</u>, Wound, Simple. Instructional
   note at Repair-Simple states "sum of lengths of repairs."
   Therefore, add 1 inch and 2-1/2 inch repairs together,
   convert to centimeters, and wound length is 8.89 cm)
5. <u>Excision</u> 2.5 cm malignant <u>lesion</u> forehead   11643
   with intermediate closure   12051
   (See parenthetical note regarding closure at
   Excision-Malignant Lesions)

Exercise 7-7

1. <u>Exploration</u> of right wrist with removal of deep foreign body   25248
2. <u>Manipulation</u> of right thumb <u>dislocation</u>   26641
3. Reapplication of short leg walking <u>cast</u>   29425
4. Open reduction with screws, compound <u>fracture</u>,   27758
   shaft, left tibia and fibula, and application of a long
   leg cast (No code for cast. See casting notes at
   beginning of Application of Casts and Strapping.)

5. Diagnostic <u>arthroscopy</u> followed by removal   29870
of the medial meniscus by <u>arthrotomy</u>.   27332
(Surgery was not performed through the arthroscope.)

Exercise 7-8

1. <u>Laparoscopy</u> cholecystectomy with cholangiography   47563
2. <u>Anoscopy</u> with removal of polyp by snare   46611
3. Diagnostic flexible bronchoscopy (Bronchi, Exploration)   31622
4. Fibroscopic full colonoscopy, with removal of polyps   45385
by snare (Endoscopy, Colon, Removal)
5. Nasal endoscopy with partial ethmoidectomy   31254

Exercise 7-9

1. Cardiac catheterization, right side only,   93501
(<u>Catheter</u>, Cardiac, Right Heart) with conscious <u>sedation</u>, IV   99141
2. Routine <u>EKG</u>, tracing only   93005
3. <u>Spirometry</u>   94010
4. <u>CPR</u>, in office   92950
5. <u>Psychiatric diagnostic</u> examination   90801
6. Influenza <u>vaccine</u>   90659 or 90660 and 90471
7. <u>Whirlpool</u> and   97022
<u>paraffin bath</u> therapy   97018
8. WAIS-R and MMPI psychological tests and report,   96100
1 hour (Psychiatric Diagnosis, Psychological Testing)
9. Office services on emergency basis (Office, Medical Service)   99058

Exercise 7-10

1. GI series <u>xray</u>, with small bowel and air studies, without KUB   74246
2. Chest <u>xray</u>, PA & Left Lateral   71020
3. Cervical spine, complete, with flexion and extension (xray, spine)   72052
4. <u>Xray</u> pelvis, AP only   72170
5. Abdomen, flat plate, AP (x-ray)   74000
6. BE, colon, with air (xray colon)   74280
7. Postoperative radiological supervision and   74305
interpretation of <u>cholangiography</u> by radiologist
8. <u>SPECT</u> exam of the liver   78205
9. Retrograde pyelography with KUB   74420

Exercise 7-11

1. Hepatic function <u>panel</u>   80076
2. Hepatitis <u>panel</u>   80074
3. <u>TB</u> skin test, PPD   86580
4. <u>Urinalysis</u> with microscopy, automated   81001
5. <u>CBC</u> w/Diff, manual   85031
6. Stool for <u>occult blood</u>   82270
7. Wet mount, vaginal <u>smear</u>   87210
8. <u>Glucose</u>/blood sugar, <u>quantitative</u>   82948
9. <u>Sedimentation</u> rate (Need method for definitive code)   85651 or 85652
10. Throat <u>culture</u>, bacterial   87070 or 87081
11. Urine <u>sensitivity, disk</u>   87184
12. Hematocrit, spun   85013
13. <u>Monospot</u>   86403
14. Strep test, rapid (<u>Streptococcus, Group A</u>, Direct
Optical Observation)   87880

Exercise 7-12

1. Home visit, problem focused, est pt   99347
2. Emer dept service, new pt, low complexity   99282
DX: Low-grade chest pain
3. Hosp visit, new pt, initial, high complexity   99223
4. Hospital care, subsequent, detailed   99233
5. Emergency care, hospital, est pt, problem focused,   99281
counseling 15 min. DX: Bladder infection.

6. Pt requested consult, new pt, moderate complexity,   99274
   no 3rd party confirmation requested
7. Office consult, high complexity, est pt,   99245
   surgery scheduled tomorrow
8. Followup consult, office, problem focused,   99214
   counseling 15 min. full encounter 25 min.
   (There is no follow-up outpatient consult; use
   Est. Office Visit. Counseling becomes the key factor,
   selection is based on time.)
9. Followup consult, inpatient, detailed, 35 min.   99263

Exercise 7-13

1. New pt, routine preventative medicine, age 11   99383
   Risk factor discussion, 20 min.
2. Critical care, 1.5 hr   99291 and 99292
3. NFS visit, subsequent visit, expanded
   problem focused H&PE   99312
4. Medical team conference, 50 min.   99362
5. Followup visit, ICU pt, stable, expanded   99232
   problem focused
   (Patient is stable, use subsequent inpatient category)
6. Resuscitation, newborn, initial   99440
7. Telephone call with social worker, brief   99371
8. Custodial care, est pt, detailed H&PE, high complexity   99333
9. Pediatrician on standby, high-risk birth, 65 min.   99360 X 2
10. Heart risk factor education, group counseling,   99412
    nonsymptomatic attendees, 65 min.
11. Prolonged care of subsequent inpatient level III   99233, 99356, 99357 X 2, and 92950
    with CPR, 1 hr 45 min.
    (Neither the inpatient visit nor CPR is bundled
    with prolonged care; code separately.)

Exercise 7-14

1. Assistant surgeon, cesarean section, delivery only   59514-80
2. Cholecystectomy, open, performed within the post-   47600-79
   operative period of a leg fracture
3. Level III OV, est pt workup, at time of a preventive   99213-25
   medicine visit, age 54
4. Abdominal hysterectomy, surgery only   58150-54
5. Level II, initial inpatient hospital visit by surgeon, with 99222-57
   decision to perform surgery tomorrow
6. OV consult, level IV, for surgical clearance   99244
7. Postoperative management of vaginal hysterectomy   58260-55
8. Repeat gallbladder xray series, same physician   74291
   (No modifier needed because the CPT description
   includes the word repeat.)
9. Reduction of closed fracture left wrist followed by   25680 and 29830-59
   diagnostic arthroscopy, right elbow
   (Reduction = manipulation)
10. Needle core biopsy, right and left breast   19100-50
11. Level II office consult requested by lawyer   99272-32
12. Unrelated level III OV, by surgeon during postoperative 99215-24
    period for an appendectomy

ANSWERS TO CHAPTER 10 EXERCISES

Exercise10-1

1. Acute pharyngitis
2. Musculoligamentous sprain, ankle
3. Benign prostatic hypertrophy with urinary retention
4. Bacterial endocarditis
5. Partial drop foot gait
6. Cervical osteoarthritis

Exercise 10-2

A. Primary DX: Carcinoma lower sigmoid colon
   (Specific location in the colon is given in item #4)

Procedures	**Ref #**	**Diagnoses**
Proctoscope	4	Apple core-type lesion, lower sigmoid
Proctectomy with biopsy	5	Carcinoma, colon

B. Primary DX: Strep throat

Procedures	**Ref #**	**Diagnoses**
Office visit	3	Strep throat
Rapid Strep Test	3	Strep throat
UA, manual	1	Urinary frequency and dysuria

C. Primary DX: Pneumonia

Procedures	**Ref #**	**Diagnoses**
Office visit	4	Pneumonia
Xray chest	4	Pneumonia

D. Primary DX: Influenza

Procedures	**Ref #**	**Diagnoses**
Nursing home visit	3	Influenza
Injection, Tigan	3	Influenza

E. Primary DX: Acute diverticulitis

Procedures	**Ref #**	**Diagnoses**
Inpatient consult	3	Diverticulitis, acute

Exercise 10-3

1.
Procedures	**Codes**	**Diagnoses**	**Codes**
Prevent Med, est, age 66	99397	Annual exam	V70.0
Outpatient visit, est, level III	99213-25	Elevated BP	796.2
CBC, auto	85025	Screening, blood	V78.9
UA, dipstick, auto, micro	81001	Screening, GU	V81.6
Chest Xray, 2 views		Exam, Radio, NEC	V72.5
Vaccination, influenza	90659	Vaccination	V04.8

Only disorder reported is the elevated BP. V codes are used to justify the screening tests.

2.
Procedures	**Codes**	**Diagnoses**	**Codes**
Arthroscopy, shoulder	29815	Pain, shoulder NOS	719.41
Outpatient, est pt	99212	Tired	780.7

3.
Procedure	**Code**	**Diagnosis**	**Code**
Inpatient, initial, level II	99222	Appendicitis with abscess	540.1

4.
Procedure	**Code**	**Diagnosis**	**Code**
inpatient, initial, level III	99223	Cholecystitis NOS	575.10

5.
Procedure	**Code**	**Diagnosis**	**Code**
Appendectomy, open	44900-55	Aftercare, surgery	V58.49

Do not code the office visit because you need to use a modifier 55 to get reimbursement for the postoperative care.

Do not code Appendicitis; the appendix is no longer present.

Exercise 10-4

	Diagnosis
1. Atrophic gastritis	535.10
2. Cholecystitis with cholelithiasis	574.00
Metastatic adenocarcinoma	197.7
3. Rheumatoid arthritis, NOS	714.0
4. Unstable angina	411.1

5. Exudative tonsillitis   463
6. Seizure disorder, onset   780.39

Exercise 10-5

Case 1

Diagnoses:	Granulation, tissue, skin	701.5
	History, personal, malignant, skin	V10.83
Procedure:	Excision, scalp, benign, 5.0 cm	11420

Case 2

Diagnosis:	Atypical neoplasm, skin (uncertain behavior)	238.2
	(Pathology ordered the reexcision because of atypical cells)	
Procedures:	Excision, skin, benign, with return to OR	11420-78
	Closure, intermediate	12032

Case 3

Diagnoses:	Neoplasm, benign, intestine, sigmoid	211.3
	Melanosis coli	569.89
Procedure:	Colonoscopy, with ablation	45384

Case 4

Diagnosis:	Serous otitis media, acute	381.01
Procedure:	Bilateral myringotomy with insertion of ventilating tubes	69421-50

Case 5

Diagnosis:	Lesion, buccal mucosa	528.9
	(If working in the office, diagnosis should not be coded until biopsy report received—it could be a malignant lesion.)	
Procedure:	Biopsy, buccal mucosa	40812

Case 6

Diagnosis:	Pilonidal cyst—no mention of abscess	685.1
Procedure:	Excision pilonidal cyst	11770

Case 7

Diagnosis:	Femoral hernia, incarcerated	552.00
	(Incarcerated equals strangulated)	
Procedure:	Herniorrhaphy, femoral	49553
	(Not stated as recurrent)	

Exercise 10-6

		Diagnosis Code(s)	**Procedure Code(s)**
A.	1. Office visit	569.3	99204
	Friday surgery	V64.1	45378-53 (or 45378-73, depending on setting)
		569.3	
	Monday surgery	562.10	45338
		211.3	
	2.	530.2	74241
	3.	427.9	93312
			99141 (or 99412, depending on method of administration)
	4.	436	99218 (or 99219 or 99220, depending on documentation)

B. Input the above answers into the coding case studies form.

Using the UHI Student Practice CD-ROM

USING THE UHI STUDENT PRACTICE CD-ROM

The Understanding Health Insurance (UHI) Student Practice CD-ROM, found inside the back cover of this textbook, is designed to help you practice completing HCFA-1500 claim forms. The CD-ROM Procedure Manual along with tutorials for using the Blank Form, Study, and Self Test modes are located on the disk. They can be viewed on your computer screen or printed. Brief instructions to get you started using the UHI software follow.

System Requirements

- 386 Processor or better, with hard drive, 3.5 floppy disk drive, and CD-ROM drive
- Windows 3.1, 95, 98, NT, 2000, or ME
- 4 MB RAM
- 2.5 MB free hard drive space
- Mouse
- Printer with 4 MB memory

Installing and Uninstalling the UHI Student Practice Software Program

1. Insert the UHI disk into the CD-ROM drive.

2. If you are using Windows 95/98/NT/2000/ ME, click **Start** and then click **Run**. If you are using Windows 3.1, select **Run** from the **File** menu in the Windows Program Manager.

3. Type **D:\SETUP** and click **OK**.

4. In a few moments, you will see an installation screen; click **Next** to start the installation.

5. A dialog box will appear, and you will be asked to identify the drive and directory to install the software. Click **Next** so that the default directory (**C:\DELMAR\UHI**) is selected. If you want to change the directory location, click Browse and enter the drive and directory name into which the program should be installed.

6. The installation will begin at this time; you can stop the installation at any time by clicking **Cancel**.

7. A Delmar UHI icon will be added to the Program Manager on your computer, and if you use Windows 95 or higher, a Start menu item will be created.

8. When you see the **Installation is complete** message, click **OK**.

To remove the program from your computer, you can uninstall it by selecting **Delmar Applications** from the **Programs** menu and then selecting **Uninstall UHI 6**.

General Hints

- Proofread each entry before moving to the next block of the HCFA-1500 claim form.
- Press the **Caps Lock** key on your keyboard to activate it.
- Follow Optical Scanning Guidelines (below) when completing the HCFA-1500 claim form.

- Enter reference numbers (not ICD code numbers) in Block 21.

- Enter the provider's full name and credentials in Block 31.

- Press the **Num Lock** key on your keyboard to activate it, before using the numeric keypad to enter long strings of numbers.

- Use the Study mode for Case Studies 1-1 through 1-15 (Appendix I of this textbook) when working in diagnosis and procedure **Skill Builders.**

Optical Scanning Guidelines

- Do not interchange a zero (0) with the alpha character O.

- When manually preparing the HCFA-1500 claim form, use pica type (10 characters per inch) and type all alphabetic characters in upper case (capital letters).

- Do not enter the dollar sign ($) for charges, payments, or balances due.

- Enter a space instead of any of the following:
  -Decimal point in charges, payments, or balances

  -Decimal point in a diagnostic code number

  -Dash in front of a procedure code number or a telephone number

- Do not type the parentheses when entering the area code of the telephone number (they are printed automatically on the form).

- Leave one blank space between the patient's/policyholder's last name, first name, and middle initial.

- Do not use any punctuation in a patient's/policyholder's name, except for a hyphen in a compound name.

- Do not use a patient's or policyholder's title or other designations such as Sr., Jr., II, or III on a claim form unless they appear on the patient's insurance ID card.

Example:

The name on the ID card reads:
  Wm. F. Goodpatient, IV

This name on the claim form is written:
  GOODPATIENT IV WILLIAM F

Exceptions:

- TRICARE/CHAMPUS active duty sponsor required rank or grade after the name.

- Use two zeros (00) in the cents column when a fee or a monetary total is expressed in whole dollars.

Examples:

Six dollars is written 6 00

Six thousand dollars is written 6 000 00

- All dates should be entered as eight digits with spaces between the digits representing the month, day, and year. Care should be taken to ensure that none of the digits fall on the vertical separations within the block.

Two-digit code numbers for the months are:

Jan	01	May	05	Sept	09
Feb	02	June	06	Oct	10
Mar	03	July	07	Nov	11
Apr	04	Aug	08	Dec	12

Examples:

03 04 1897 for March 4, 1897

03 04 1997 for March 4, 1997

Exception:

- Blocks 24A, 24B, and 31 do not allow for spacing between month/day and day/year.

- Enter the hyphen in all Employer Identification Numbers (EIN).

- Enter social security numbers as a continuous number, without the hyphens or spaces.

- In Block 31, enter the provider's full name and credentials.

- Review the claim form to be sure all blocks that require an "X" to be placed within the block are so marked.

Completing Case Study Claim Forms

When starting the program, you are asked to designate whether you want to store your data on a floppy disk or on the computer's hard drive. It is simpler to use a floppy disk, using the same disk every time you work, so that you have access to your previous work. Just insert the floppy disk before you start the program, and select **Use Floppy.**

1. YOU CAN USE THE CD-ROM TO:

- Print blank HCFA-1500 claim forms to manually complete a claim (e.g., handwritten or typewritten).

- Complete Case Studies 1-1 through 1-15 (Appendix I of this textbook) in the Blank Form mode, where no feedback is provided and completed forms can be printed.

- Complete Case Studies 2-1 through 2-15 (Appendix II of this textbook) using the Study mode, where feedback is provided as you enter information in each Block of the HCFA-1500 claim form, and reports can be printed.

- Complete Case Studies 2-1 through 2-15 (Appendix II of this textbook) using the Self Test mode, where *no* feedback is provided, the completed claim is graded, and reports can be printed.

- Use Skill Builders, in either the Study or Self Test mode, to practice coding diagnoses and procedures/services based on Case Studies 2-1 through 2-15 (Appendix II of this textbook). As you enter data, the software checks your entries against expected answers and either provides feedback immediately or upon completion of the case, depending on which feedback procedure you selected.

  Example:
  To print just your current work on a claim form, click off (deselect) the Print Summary Report options.

2. KEYSTROKES TO HELP MANEUVER AROUND THE CLAIM FORM:

Go To A Specific Block	Ctrl-G and key in the block number
Go To Next Block	Ctrl-N
Go To Previous Block	Ctrl-P
Go To Top Of Claim	Ctrl-T

To help you use these shortcuts, click on **View** in the toolbar and select the action you desire.

3. Using **Enter** or **Tab** keys when working on the claim form in the Study mode provides immediate feedback.

4. TO SAVE A CLAIM FORM: All case study claim forms must be saved manually to your floppy disk or hard disk after you have completed work with a claim form.

On the top menu bar, choose **File > Save As...**

In the **Save As...** dialog box, choose the desired disk drive and folder, and specify a filename. (Please review the File Naming Conventions discussion that follows.)

In the **Save file as type:** area on the dialog box, be sure that **Health Insurance (*.UHI)** is selected as the file type, and then click **OK**.

File Naming Conventions

- You should name each file to correspond with the case study it represents.

- If the case study you are working on requires two or more claims, be sure to indicate Primary (P) or Secondary (S) in your filename.

- Your filename can include hyphen (-) and underscore (_) characters, but it cannot include most other symbols.

- To maintain compatibility across operating systems, it is best to limit your filename to no more than eight (8) characters, plus the three-character .UHI file type extension.

Printing Blank and Completed HCFA-1500 Claim Forms

1. TO PRINT A BLANK HCFA-1500 CLAIM FORM:

- At the UHI main menu, click on **Blank HCFA-1500** in the Blank Form box.

- Click **OK** (you are not required to enter the form's destination).

- When the blank HCFA-1500 claim form appears on your computer screen, click **Print** and then click **OK**.

2. TO PRINT A COMPLETED HCFA-1500 CLAIM FORM:

- Once you have completed a HCFA-1500 claim form using either the Study or Self Test mode, click **Print**.

- A **Printing Options** dialogue box will appear, and you can click on any checked box to deselect a particular option.

- Note that the check mark disappears when you click on a box. To select that printing option again, click in the box and the check mark reappears.

Abbreviations

ABBREVIATIONS ORGANIZED BY CHAPTER

Chapter 1

HCFA	Health Care Financing Administration
EDI	Electronic data interchange
HCPCS	HCFA Common Procedure Coding System
CPT	Current Procedural Terminology

Chapter 2

HMO	Health Maintenance Organization
CHAMPVA	Civilian Health and Medical Program of Veterans Affairs
HCFA	Health Care Financing Administration
HCPCS	Health Care Financing Administration Common Procedure Coding System
CPT	*Current Procedural Terminology*
ICD-9-CM	*International Classification of Diseases–9th Revision–Clinical Modification*
CCI	Correct Coding Initiative
HIPAA	Health Insurance Portability and Accountability Act
APC	Ambulatory Payment Classification
PCP	Primary Care Provider
PlanID	National third-party payer identification number
NPI	National provider identifier
EIN	National standard employer identifier number
EDI	Electronic data interchange

Chapter 3

MCO	Managed Care Organization
HMO	Health Maintenance Organization
HMO Act of 1973	Health Maintenance Organization Assistance Act of 1973
ERISA	Employee Retirement Income Security Act of 1974
TEFRA	Tax Equity and Fiscal Responsibility Act of 1982

CMP	Competitive medical plan
OBRA	Omnibus Budget Reconciliation Act of 1981
COBRA	Consolidated Omnibus Budget Reconciliation Act of 1985
HEDIS	Health Plan Employer Data and Information Set
HIPAA	Health Insurance Portability and Accountability Act of 1996
PCP	Primary care provider
MSO	Management service organization
GPWW	Group practice without walls
IPO	Integrated provider organization
IPA	Individual practice association
IPA	Independent practice association
PPO	Preferred provider organization
NCQA	National Committee for Quality Assurance
JCAHO	Joint Commission on Accreditation of Healthcare Organizations

Chapter 4

PAR	Participating provider
PCP	Primary care physician
EOB	Explanation of Benefits
HCFA-1500	Insurance claim form, developed by the National Uniform Claims Committee (NUCC), for use by noninstitutional providers and suppliers to bill third-party payers
NonPAR	Nonparticipating provider

Chapter 5

FI	Fiscal intermediary
HIPAA	Health Insurance Portability and Accountability Act of 1996
CCI	Correct Coding Initiative
MSA	Medical savings account
NPI	National provider identifier
PlanID	National third-party payer identification number
EDI	Electronic data interchange

Chapter 6

ICD	International Classification of Diseases
ICD-9-CM	*International Classification of Diseases–9th revision–Clinical Modification*
NCHS	National Center for Health Statistics
HCFA	Health Care Financing Administration
ABN	Advance Beneficiary Notice
HCFA-1500	Insurance claim form, developed by the National Uniform Claims Committee (NUCC), for use by non-institutional providers and suppliers to bill third-party payers
HCFA-1450	also know as UB-92 (Uniform Bill, developed in 1992); insurance claim form, developed by the National Uniform Billing Committee (NUBC), for use by institutional providers and suppliers to bill third-party payers
NEC	Not elsewhere classifiable
HCPCS	HCFA Common Procedure Coding System
AHFS	American Hospital Formulary Service
Ca	Cancer or carcinoma

Chapter 7

CPT	*Current Procedural Terminology*
HCPCS	HCFA Common Procedure Coding System
ORIF	Open reduction with internal fixation

Chapter 8

HCPCS	HCFA Common Procedure Coding System
DME	Durable medical equipment
DMEPOS	Durable Medical Equipment, Prosthetic and Orthotic Supplies
DMERC	Durable Medical Equipment Regional Carriers
CIM	Coverage Issues Manual
MCM	Medicare Carriers Manual
ABN	Advance Beneficiary Notice
HPSA	Health Personnel Shortage Area

Chapter 9

RBRVS	Resource-Based Relative Value Scale system
RVU	Relative value units
CF	Conversion factor
GPCI	Geographic practice cost index
FR	*Federal Register*
LMC	Local Medicare Carrier
MFS	Medicare Fee Schedule
NonPAR	Nonparticipating provider
MSN	Medicare Summary Notice
DMEPOS	Durable Medical Equipment, Prosthetic and Orthotic Supplies
MFN	Most favored nation
NP	Nurse Practitioner
PA	Physician Assistant

DRG	Diagnosis Related Groups
MCO	Managed care organization
CIM	Coverage Issues Manual
MCM	Medicare Carriers Manual
TOS	Type of service
POS	Place of service

Chapter 10

HCFA-1500	Insurance claim form, developed by the National Uniform Claims Committee (NUCC), for use by noninstitutional providers and suppliers to bill third-party payers

Chapter 11

NPI	National Provider Identifier
EMC	Electronic media claim
KISS	Keep It Short and Simple
ASC	Ambulatory Surgical Center
OCR	Optical character reader
EIN	Employer tax identification number
PIN	Provider identification number
GRP #	Group practice identification number

Chapter 12

HCFA-1500	Insurance claim form, developed by the National Uniform Claims Committee (NUCC), for use by noninstitutional providers and suppliers to bill third-party payers

Chapter 13

BC	Blue Cross
BS	Blue Shield
AHA	American Hospital Association
BCBS	Blue Cross/Blue Shield
BCBSA	Blue Cross and Blue Shield Association
PAR	Participating provider
PPN	Preferred Provider Network
NonPAR	Nonparticipating provider
MM	Major Medical
DME	Durable medical equipment
PPA	Preferred provider arrangement
PPO	Preferred provider organization
EPO	Exclusive provider organization
POS	Point-of-service plan
PCP	Primary care provider
FEHBP	Federal Employee Health Benefits Program
FEP	Federal Employee Program
OMP	Office of Personnel Management
OPAP	Outpatient Pretreatment Authorization Plan
SSO	Second surgical opinion
HMO	Health maintenance organization
UCR	Usual, Customary, and Reasonable
TPA	Third-party administrator

Chapter 14

FI	Fiscal intermediary
SSA	Social Security Administration
IEP	Initial Enrollment Period
GEP	General Enrollment Period
QMB	Qualified Medicare Beneficiary
SLMB	Specified Low-income Medicare Beneficiary
ESRD	End-stage renal disease
PAR	Participating provider
NonPAR	Nonparticipating provider
LC	Limiting charge
LLC	Limited license practitioners
ABN	Advance Beneficiary Notice
RBRVS	Resource-Based Relative Value Scale system
MFS	Medicare Fee Schedule
MSP	Medicare Secondary-Payer
COBRA	Consolidated Omnibus Budget Reconciliation Act of 1985
MSN	Medicare Summary Notice
MSP	Medicare Supplemental Plan
PSO	Provider-Sponsored Organization
PPO	Preferred Provider Organization
MSA	Medical Savings Accounts Plan
DOD	Department of Defense
PFFS	Private Fee-For-Service Plan
DMERC	Durable Medical Equipment Regional Carrier
UPIN	Unique Provider Identification Number
NPI	National Provider Identification
CLIA	Clinical Laboratory Improvement Act
PIN	Provider Identification Number
PAYERID	Payer identification number (now known as PlanID)

Chapter 15

AFDC	Aid to Families with Dependent Children
TANF	Temporary Assistance for Needy Families
SCHIP	State Children's Health Insurance Program
ADA	American Disabilities Act
SSI	Supplemental Security Income
FPL	Federal poverty level
MN	Medically needy
EPSDT	Early and Periodic Screening, Diagnostic, and Treatment services
FMAP	Federal Medical Assistance Percentage
QMB	Qualified Medical Beneficiary
SLMB	Specified Low-Income Medicare Beneficiary

QI	Qualifying Individual
QDWI	Qualified Disabled and Working Individual

Chapter 16

CRI	CHAMPUS Reform Initiative
LA	Lead Agent
MHSS	Military Health Services System
HA	Health Affairs
TMA	TRICARE Management Activity
MTF	Military Treatment Facility
PPN	Preferred Provider Network
PCM	Primary Care Manager
DEERS	Defense Enrollment Eligibility Reporting System
PMO	Program Management Organization
NMOP	National Mail Order Pharmacy
BRAC	Base Realignment and Closure
TPR	TRICARE Prime Remote
FEHBP	Federal Employee Health Benefit Program
TSSD	TRICARE Senior Supplement Demonstration Program
DoD/NCI	Department of Defense/National Cancer Institute
TSC	TRICARE Service Center
BSR	Beneficiary Services Representative
HCF	Health Care Finder
BCAC	Beneficiary Counseling and Assistance Coordinator
NAS	Nonavailability statement
CT	Computed tomography
CAT	Computerized axial tomography
MRI	Magnetic resonance imaging
FI	Fiscal intermediary
DME	Durable medical equipment
DRG	Diagnosis related group
PFPWD	Program for Persons with Disabilities
CHAMPVA	Civilian Health and Medical Program of Veterans Affairs
OHI	Other Health Insurance

Chapter 17

OSHA	Occupational Safety and Health Administration
MSDS	Material Safety Data Sheet
FECA	Federal Employment Compensation Act
FELA	Federal Employment Liability Act
LHWCA	Longshore and Harbor Workers' Compensation Act

ABBREVIATIONS IN ALPHABETIC ORDER

(Chapter numbers in which terms appear are in parentheses.)

ABN	Advance Beneficiary Notice (6, 8, 14)
ADA	American Disabilities Act (15)
AFDC	Aid to Families with Dependent Children (15)
AHA	American Hospital Association (13)
AHFS	American Hospital Formulary Service (6)
APC	Ambulatory payment classification (2)
ASC	Ambulatory Surgical Center (11)
BC	Blue Cross (13)
BCAC	Beneficiary Counseling and Assistance Coordinator (16)
BCBS	Blue Cross/Blue Shield (13)
BCBSA	Blue Cross and Blue Shield Association (13)
BRAC	Base Realignment and Closure (16)
BS	Blue Shield (13)
BSR	Beneficiary Services Representative (16)
Ca	Cancer or carcinoma (6)
CAT	Computerized axial tomography (16)
CCI	Correct Coding Initiative (2)
CCI	Correct Coding Initiative (5)
CF	Conversion factor (9)
CHAMPVA	Civilian Health and Medical Program of Veterans Affairs (2, 16)
CIM	Coverage Issues Manual (8, 9)
CLIA	Clinical Laboratory Improvement Act (14)
CMP	Competitive medical plan (3)
COBRA	Consolidated Omnibus Budget Reconciliation Act of 1985 (3, 14)
CPT	*Current Procedural Terminology* (1, 2, 7)
CRI	CHAMPUS Reform Initiative (16)
CT	Computed tomography (16)
DEERS	Defense Enrollment Eligibility Reporting System (16)
DME	Durable medical equipment (8, 13, 16)
DMEPOS	Durable Medical Equipment, Prosthetic and Orthotic Supplies (8,9)
DMERC	Durable Medical Equipment Regional Carriers (8, 14)
DOD	Department of Defense (14)
DoD/NCI	Department of Defense/National Cancer Institute (16)
DRG	Diagnosis Related Groups (9, 16)
EDI	Electronic data interchange (1, 2, 5)
EIN	National standard employer identifier number (2)
EIN	employer tax identification number (11)
EMC	Electronic media claim (11)

EOB	Explanation of Benefits (4)
EPO	Exclusive provider organization (13)
EPSDT	Early and Periodic Screening, Diagnostic, and Treatment services (15)
ERISA	Employee Retirement Income Security Act of 1974 (3)
ESRD	End-stage renal disease (14)
FECA	Federal Employment Compensation Act (17)
FEHBP	Federal Employee Health Benefits Program (13, 16)
FELA	Federal Employment Liability Act (17)
FEP	Federal Employee Program (13)
FI	Fiscal intermediary (5, 14, 16)
FMAP	Federal Medical Assistance Percentage (15)
FPL	Federal poverty level (15)
FR	*Federal Register* (9)
GEP	General Enrollment Period (14)
GPCI	Geographic practice cost index (9)
GPWW	Group practice without walls (3)
GRP #	Group practice identification number (11)
HA	Health Affairs (16)
HCF	Health Care Finder (16)
HCFA	Health Care Financing Administration (1, 2, 6)
HCFA-1500	Insurance claim form, developed by the National Uniform Claims Committee (NUCC), for use by noninstitutional providers and suppliers to bill third-party payers (4, 6, 10, 12)
HCFA-1450	also known as the UB-92; insurance claim form, developed by the National Uniform Billing Committee (NUBC), for use by institutional and other selected providers to bill third-party payers (6)
HCPCS	HCFA Common Procedure Coding System (1, 6, 7, 8)
HEDIS	Health Plan Employer Data and Information Set (3)
HIPAA	Health Insurance Portability and Accountability Act of 1996 (2, 3, 5)
HMO	Health Maintenance Organization (2, 3, 13)
HMO Act of 1973	Health Maintenance Organization Assistance Act of 1973 (3)
HPSA	Health Personnel Shortage Area (8)
ICD	International Classification of Diseases (6)
ICD-9-CM	*International Classification of Diseases–9th Revision–Clinical Modifications* (2, 6)
IEP	Initial Enrollment Period (14)
IPA	Individual practice association (3)
IPA	Independent practice association (3)
IPO	Integrated provider organization (3)
JCAHO	Joint Commission on Accreditation of Healthcare Organizations (3)

KISS	Keep It Short and Simple (11)		PAYERID	Payer identification number (now known as PlanID) (14)
LA	Lead Agent (16)		PCM	Primary Care Manager (16)
LC	Limiting charge (14)		PCP	Primary Care Provider (2, 3, 13)
LHWCA	Longshore and Harbor Workers' Compensation Act (17)		PCP	Primary care physician (4)
LLC	Limited license practitioners (14)		PFFS	Private Fee-For-Service Plan (14)
LMC	Local Medicare Carrier (9)		PFPWD	Program for Persons with Disabilities (16)
MCM	Medicare Carriers Manual (8, 9)		PIN	Provider identification number (11, 14)
MCO	Managed Care Organization (3, 9)		PlanID	National Health PlanID (2, 5)
MFN	Most favored nation (9)		PMO	Program Management Organization (16)
MFS	Medicare Fee Schedule (9, 14)		POS	Place of service (9)
MHSS	Military Health Services System (16)		POS	Point-of-service plan (13)
MM	Major Medical (13)		PPA	Preferred provider arrangement (13)
MN	Medically needy (15)		PPN	Preferred Provider Network (13, 16)
MRI	Magnetic resonance imaging (16)		PPO	Preferred Provider Organization (3, 13, 14)
MSA	Medical savings account (5, 14)		PSO	Provider-Sponsored Organization (14)
MSDS	Material Safety Data Sheet (17)		QDWI	Qualified Disabled and Working Individual (15)
MSN	Medicare Summary Notice (9, 14)			
MSO	Management service organization (3)		QI	Qualifying Individual (15)
MSP	Medicare Secondary-Payer (14)		QMB	Qualified Medicare Beneficiary (14, 15)
MSP	Medicare Supplemental Plan (14)		RBRVS	Resource-Based Relative Value Scale system (9, 14)
MTF	Military Treatment Facility (16)			
NAS	Nonavailability statement (16)		RVU	Relative value units (9)
NCHS	National Center for Health Statistics (6)		SCHIP	State Children's Health Insurance Program (15)
NCQA	National Committee for Quality Assurance (3)			
			SLMB	Specified Low-income Medicare Beneficiary (14, 15)
NEC	Not elsewhere classifiable (6)			
NMOP	National Mail Order Pharmacy (16)		SSA	Social Security Administration (14)
NonPAR	Nonparticipating provider (4, 9, 13, 14)		SSI	Supplemental Security Income (15)
NP	Nurse Practitioner (9)		SSO	Second surgical opinion (13)
NPI	National Provider Identifier (2, 5, 11, 14)		TANF	Temporary Assistance for Needy Families (15)
OBRA	Omnibus Budget Reconciliation Act of 1981 (3)			
			TEFRA	Tax Equity and Fiscal Responsibility Act of 1982 (3)
OCR	Optical character reader (11)			
OHI	Other Health Insurance (16)		TMA	TRICARE Management Activity (16)
OMP	Office of Personnel Management (13)		TOS	Type of service (9)
OPAP	Outpatient Pretreatment Authorization Plan (13)		TPA	Third-party administrator (13)
			TPR	TRICARE Prime Remote (16)
ORIF	Open reduction with internal fixation (7)		TSC	TRICARE Service Center (16)
OSHA	Occupational Safety and Health Administration (17)		TSSD	TRICARE Senior Supplement Demonstration Program (16)
PA	Physician Assistant (9)		UCR	Usual, Customary, and Reasonable (13)
PAR	Participating provider (4, 13, 14)		UPIN	Unique Provider Identification Number

Common Medical Terminology Prefixes, Suffixes, and Combining Forms

a-, an-	no; not
ab-	away from
abdomin-	abdomen
acr-	extremities; top
ad-	toward
-ad	toward
adip-	fat
-al	pertaining to
angi-	vessel
ankyl-	crooked; bent
anti-	against
arthr-	joint
-asis, -esis, -iasis, -isis, -sis	condition
bi	two
blephar-	eyelid
brachy-	short
brady-	slow
bronch-	bronchial tube
cardi-	heart
cephal-	head
cervic-	neck; cervix
colp-, kolp-	vagina
contra-	against; opposite
crani-	skull
cry-	cold
cyan-	blue
dacry-	tear
dactyl-	fingers; toes
de-	lack of; down
demi-	half
derm-, dermato-	skin
dextro-	right
di-	two
dis-	separation
-dynia	pain
dys-	bad; painful
-ectomy	excision; removal
-emesis	vomiting
-emia	blood condition
en-	in; within
end-, endo-	in; within
epi-, epi-	above; upon
erythr-, erythro-	red
-esis	condition
-esthesia	nervous sensation
etio-	cause
ex-	out; away from
extra-	outside
fibro-	fiber
fore-	before
galact-, galacto-, lact-	milk
gaster-, gastr-	stomach
genito-	genitals
glosso-	tongue
gluc-, glyc-	sugar, glucose
gram	record
-graph	instrument for reading
-graphy	process of recording
gyn-, gyne-, gyneco-, gyno-	women; female
hem-, hema-, hemato-, hemo-	blood
hemi-	half
hepat-, hepato-	liver
hyp-, hyph-, hypo-	below; under
hyper-	above; excessive
hyster-, hystero-	uterus; womb
-ia, -iasis	condition
-ic	pertaining to
ileo-	ileum (small intestine)
ilio-	ilium (hip bone)
in-	in; into; not
infra-	within; into
inter-	between
intra-, intro-	within; into
ipsi-	same
-isis	condition
-itis	inflammation
juxta-	near
laryng-, laryngo-	larynx (voice box)
latero-	side
leuk-, leuko-	white
linguo-	tongue

lip-, lipo-	fat; lipid	pneum-, pneuma-, pneumato-	lung; air
-lith, -litho	stone	-poiesis, -poietic	formation
-lysis	breakdown	poly-	many; much
mal-	bad	post-	after; behind
-mania	obsessive preoccupation	postero-	back; behind
med-, medi-, medio-	middle	pro-	before; forward
mega-, megal-, megalo-	large	pseud-, pseudo-	false
melan-, melano-	black	psych-, psycho-	mind
meta-	change; beyond	pyelo-	renal pelvis
metr-, metra-, metro-	uterus; measure	re-	back; again
mon-, mono-	one; single	ren-, reno-	kidney
musculo-, my-, myo-	muscle	retro-	behind; back
myel-, myelo-	spinal cord; bone marrow	rheo-, -rrhea	flow
naso-	nose	rhino-	nose
necr-, necro-	death	-rrhage, --rhagia	bursting forth of blood
neo-	new	-rrhaphy	suture
nephr-, nephra-, nephro-	kidney	salping-, salpingo-	fallopian tube; auditory tube
non-	not; no	scirrho-	hard
normo-	rule; order	-sclerosis	hardening
ob-	obstetrics	-scope	instrument for visual examination
oculo-, optico-, opto-	eye	-scopy	visual examination
-oma	tumor; mass	semi-	half
omphal-, omphalo-	umbilicus (navel)	soma-, somato-	body
onych-, onycho-	nail	sphygmo-	pulse
oo-, ovi-, ovo-	egg	spleno-	spleen
oophor-, oophoro-, oophoron-	ovary	spondyl-, spondylo-	vertebra
-osis	condition—usually abnormal	steno-	narrowness
		stetho-	chest
oste-, osteo-	bone	sub-	below
-ostomosis, -ostomy, -stomosis, -stomy	new opening	super-	above, superior
		supra-	above, upper
ot-, oto-	ear	tachy-	fast
-otomy	incision	tel-, tele-	complete
-ous	pertaining to	tendo-, teno-	tendon
pach-, pachy-	heavy; thick	thorac-, thoraci-, thoraco-	chest; pleural cavity
pan-	all	thrombo-	clot
para-, -para	near; besides	-tomy	process of cutting
path-, patho-, -path, -pathic, -pathy	disease	trans-	across
		trich-, trichi-, tricho-	hair
per-	through	tympano-	tympanic membrane
peri-	surrounding	ultra-	beyond; excess
-pexy	fixation	uni-	one
pharyng-, pharyngo-	throat (pharynx)	uretero-	ureter
phlebo-	vein	urethro-	urethra
-phobia	fear	-uria	urination
-plegia	paralysis	vaso-	vessel; duct
pleur-, pleuro-	pleura	veno-	vein
		vesico-	urinary bladder

Web Sites

Eight

WEBSITES ORGANIZED BY CHAPTER
(IN ORDER OF APPEARANCE
WITHIN EACH CHAPTER)

Chapter 1

HCFA – What's New	www.hcfa.gov/whatsnew
AAMA – Code of Ethics	www.aama-ntl.org/mission.html
AHIMA – Code of Ethics	www.ahima.org/infocenter/guidelines/ethics.html
AHIMA	www.ahima.org
AAPC	www.aapcnatl.org
ACAP	www.claims.org

Chapter 2

No Web sites

Chapter 3

Kaiser Permanente	www.kaiserpermanente.org
Medical Data International, Inc.	www.medicaldata.com
NCQA – Report Card	hprc.ncqa.org
HealthEast	www.healtheast.org
NCQA	www.ncqa.org
JCAHO	www.jcaho.org

Chapter 4

No Web sites

Chapter 5

US DOH listing	www.fsis.usda.gov/ophs/stategov.htm
NARA	www.access.gpo.gov/nara
Federal Register	www.nara.gov/fedreg
HCFA Press Releases	www.hcfa.gov/news/news.htm
Trailblazer Health Enterprises	www.the-medicare.com
CodeCorrect.com	www.codecorrect.com
HCFA Internet Security Policy	www.hcfa.gov/security/isecplcy.htm
Record Retention Laws by State	www.ahima.org/journal/pb/99.06.html
HIPAA Administrative Simplification	aspe.os.dhhs.gov/admnsimp
HIPAA Insurance Reform	www.hcfa.gov/Medicaid/hipaa/default.asp
HIPAA-REGS Listserv	aspe.os.dhhs.gov/admnsimp/lsnotify.htm
Medicare Computer-Based Training	www.medicaretraining.com
Mx City	www.mxcity.com

Physician Compliance Program	www.hhs.gov/progorg/oig/modcomp/webcpg.txt
OIG Compliance Programs	www.hhs.gov/progorg/oig/modcomp
Correct Coding Initiative Edits	www.ntis.gov/product/correct-coding.htm
CodeCorrect.com CCI Edits	www.codecorrect.com
HCFA and DHHS Initiatives	www.hcfa.gov/hcfainit.htm
HIPAA EDI Downloads	hipaa.wpc-edi.com/HIPAA_40.asp

Chapter 6

Delmar Thomson Learning	www.delmaralliedhealth.com
ICD-9-CM Updates	www.cdc.gov/nchs/icd9.htm
ICD-9-CM on CD-ROM	bookstore.gpo.gov
Delmar's Insurance & Coding Center	www.delmaralliedhealth.com/ins_cod/index.html
National Uniform Claim Committee	www.nucc.org
National Uniform Billing Committee	www.nubc.org
ASC X12 (HIPAA Administrative Simplification)	www.x12.org
HIPAA Administrative Simplification Provision (DHHS)	aspe.os.dhhs.gov/admnsimp
Federal Register (NARA)	www.access.gpo.gov/su_docs/aces/aces140.html
ICD-9-CM and ICD-10-CM development (NCHS)	www.cdc.gov/nchs/icd9.htm
ICD-10-PCS development (NCVHS)	hcfa.hhs.gov/stats/icd10/icd10.htm
ICD-10 development (WHO)	www.who.int/whosis/icd10
Coding Updates (Medicode)	www.medicode.com/icdupdate.html

Chapter 7

CPT Coding Manual (Delmar)	www.delmaralliedhealth.com/ins_cod/index.html
CPT Coding Manual (AMA)	www.ama-assn.org/catalog
E&M Documentation Guidelines	www.hcfa.gov/medicare/mcarpti.htm
E&M Coding Tools	www.donself.com/doc-nomusic.html
Family Practice Management newsletter	www.aafp.org/fpm
Documentation Issues	www.bcm.tmc.edu/compliance/jun99reged.html
CPT-5 Project	www.ama-assn.org/med-sci/cpt/cpt5.htm
CPT-5 Slide Presentation	www.wedi.org/htdocs/meetings/National/presentations beebe_files/frame.htm

Chapter 8

HCFA Public Use Files (e.g., physician fee schedule)	www.hcfa.gov/stats/pufiles.htm
HCFA (Medicare regulations)	www.hcfa.gov
Medicare Payment Systems	www.hcfa.gov/medicare/payment.htm
E&M Documentation Guidelines	www.hcfa.gov/medicare/mcarpti.htm

Chapter 9

National Physician Fee Schedule Relative Value File	www.hcfa.gov/stats/pufiles.htm
HCFA	www.hcfa.gov
Medicare payment systems	www.hcfa.gov/medicare/payment.htm
HCFA (*Documentation Guidelines for E&M Services*)	www.hcfa.gov/medicare/mcarpti.htm

Chapter 10

No Web sites

Chapter 11

No Web sites

Chapter 12

No Web sites

Chapter 13

| BlueCard® Doctor and Hospital Search | www.bcbs.com |
| BlueCard Health Care News | www.bcbshealthissues.com |

WEBSITES IN ALPHABETIC ORDER BY NAME OF SITE

Downloadable Medicare files	www.hcfa.gov/medicare/mcarpti.htm
EDI PowerPoint presentation at Remora Bay	www.remorabay.com/ub.html
E&M Coding Tools	www.donself.com/doc-nomusic.html
E&M Documentation Guidelines	www.hcfa.gov/medicare/mcarpti.htm
E&M Documentation Guidelines	www.hcfa.gov/medicare/mcarpti.htm
Family Practice Management newsletter	www.aafp.org/fpm
Federal Register (NARA)	http://www.access.gpo.gov/su_docs/aces/aces140.html
Federal Register	www.nara.gov/fedreg
HCFA	www.hcfa.gov
HCFA (*Documentation Guidelines for E&M Services*)	www.hcfa.gov/medicare/mcarpti.htm
HCFA (Medicare regulations)	www.hcfa.gov
HCFA-1450 (UB-92) training software	www.medicaretraining.com
HCFA and DHHS Initiatives	www.hcfa.gov/hcfainit.htm
HCFA Internet Security Policy	www.hcfa.gov/security/isecplcy.htm
HCFA's Intermediary-Carrier Directory	www.hcfa.gov/medicare/incardir.htm
HCFA-mandated EDI transaction formats	www.hcfa.gov/medicare/edi/edi3.htm
HCFA Press Releases	www.hcfa.gov/news/news.htm
HCFA Public Use Files (e.g., physician fee schedule)	www.hcfa.gov/stats/pufiles.htm
HCFA–What's New	www.hcfa.gov/whatsnew
HealthEast	www.healtheast.org
HIPAA Administrative Simplification Provision (DHHS)	http://aspe.os.dhhs.gov/admnsimp
HIPAA Adminstrative Simplification	aspe.os.dhhs.gov/admnsimp
HIPAA EDI Downloads	hipaa.wpc-edi.com/HIPAA_40.asp
HIPAA Insurance Reform	www.hcfa.gov/Medicaid/hipaa/default.asp
HIPAA-REGS Listserv	aspe.os.dhhs.gov/admnsimp/lsnotify.htm
ICD-10 development (WHO)	http://www.who.int/whosis/icd10
ICD-10-PCS development (NCHVS)	http://hcfa.hhs.gov/stats/icd10/icd10.htm
ICD-9-CM and ICD-10-CM development (NCHS)	http://www.cdc.gov/nchs/icd9.htm
ICD-9-CM on CD-ROM	bookstore.gpo.gov
ICD-9-CM Updates	www.cdc.gov/nchs/icd9.htm
JCAHO	www.jcaho.org
Kaiser Permanente	www.kaiserpermanente.org
Medicaid Publications (for download)	www.hcfa.gov/medicaid/mcaidpti.htm
Medicaid-West Virginia UB-92 Instructions	www.wvdhhr.org/bms/y2k/y2k_new_billing_instructions.htm
Medicaid-South Dakota UB-92 Instructions	www.state.sd.us/social/medicaid/hosp%20manual/hospiii.html
Medical Data International, Inc.	www.medicaldata.com
Medicare Computer-Based Training	www.medicaretraining.com
Medicare Consumers website	www.medicare.gov
Medicare EDI information	www.hcfa.hhs.gov/medicare/edi/edi.htm
Medicare-General Instructions	www.hcfa.gov/medicare/edi/edi5.htm
Medicare Payment Systems	www.hcfa.gov/medicare/payment.htm
Medicare payment systems	www.hcfa.gov/medicare/payment.htm
Medicare-SNF Information	www.hcfa.gov/pubforms/12_snf/sn560.htm
Medicare Summary Notice	www.medicare.gov/basics/summary notice_howtoread.asp
Mx City	www.mxcity.com
NARA	www.access.gpo.gov/nara
National Physician Fee Schedule Relative Value File	www.hcfa.gov/stats/pufiles.htm
National Uniform Billing Committee	www.nubc.org
National Uniform Claim Committee	www.nucc.org
NCQA - Report Card	www.ncqa.org/pages/hprc/index.asp
NCQA	hprc.ncqa.org
Occupational Safety and Health Administration	www.osha.gov
OIG Compliance Programs	www.hhs.gov/progorg/oig/modcomp
Physician Compliance Program	www.hhs.gov/progorg/oig/modcomp/webcpg.txt
Record Retention Laws by State	www.ahima.org/journal/pb/99.06.html
Trailblazer Health Enterprises	www.the-medicare.com
TRICARE Fact Sheets	www.tricare.osd.mil/factsheets
TRICARE Manuals	www.tricare.osd.mil/tricaremanuals
US DOH listing	www.fsis.usda.gov/ophs/stategov.htm
Workers' Compensation-Texas	www.workerscompensation.com/texas/forms/

Electronic Data Interchange and the UB-92

INTRODUCTION

This appendix provides an introductory approach to the concept of electronic data interchange as it relates to submitting **UB-92** (Uniform Bill, implemented in 1992) claim form information for institutional services (e.g., hospitals and skilled nursing facilities). **Electronic data interchange** is used by organizations to exchange information in a computerized format. Issues associated with the impact that HIPAA has had on EDI are also discussed.

UB-92

The UB-92 claim form contains data entry blocks called **Form Locators (FLs)** that are similar to the HCFA-1500 claim form blocks used to input information about procedures or services provided to a patient. While some institutions actually complete the UB-92 claim form and submit it to third-party payers for reimbursement purposes, most perform data entry of UB-92 information using commercial software (*see* Figure IX-1). What this means is most institutions do *not* actually complete a UB-92 claim form for submission to a third-party (unlike providers who usually complete the HCFA-1500 claim form either manually or on-screen using a software package). Instead, personnel who render services to institutional patients (e.g., nursing, laboratory or radiology) enter UB-92 data into a commercial software product. The data resides in the patient's computerized account, and upon discharge of the patient from the institution, the data is verified by billing office personnel and transmitted electronically either directly to the third-party payer or (more likely) to a clearinghouse. A **clearinghouse** is an organization that processes electronic claims by editing and validating them to ensure that they are error-free, reformatting them to the specifications of the payer, and submitting them electronically to the appropriate payer.

EXAMPLE

During an inpatient admission, the attending physician writes an order in the patient's record for a blood glucose level to be performed by the laboratory. The patient's nurse processes the order by contacting the laboratory (e.g., telephone or computer message), which sends a technician to the patient's room to perform a venipuncture (blood draw, or withdrawing blood from the patient's arm using a syringe). The blood specimen is transported to the laboratory by the technician where the blood glucose test is completed. The technician enters the results into the patient record information technology (IT) system using a computer terminal. At the same time, the UB-92 data elements are input into the patient account IT system using a computer terminal. This data resides in the patient's computerized account until it is verified by the billing office (at patient discharge) and is then transmitted to a clearinghouse that processes the claim and submits it to the third-party payer. The clearinghouse also uses the network to send an acknowledgment to the institution upon receipt of the submitted claim.

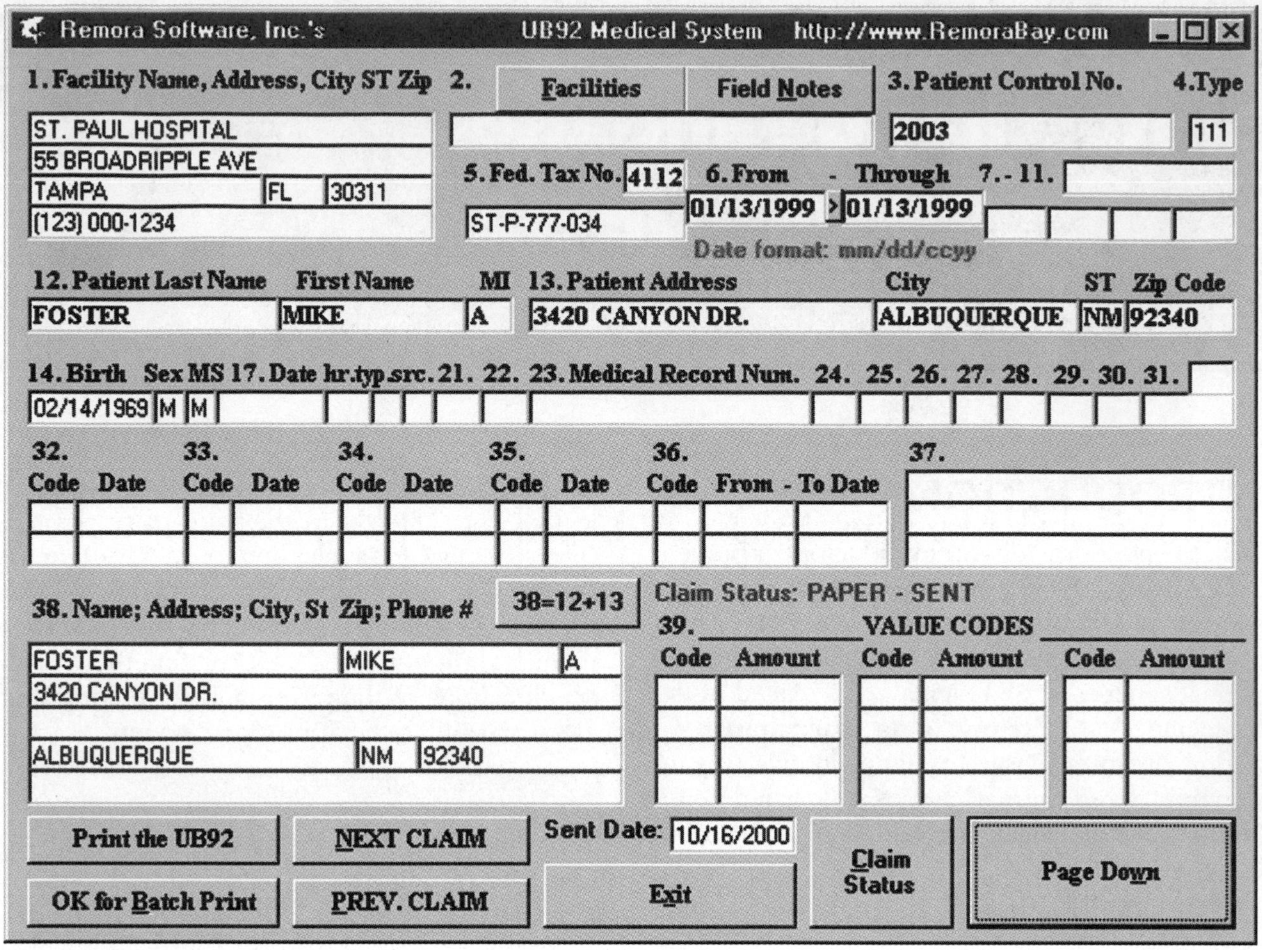

Figure IX-1 Sample data entry screen using UB-92 electronic data interchange software (Permission to reprint granted by Remora Software, Inc.)

UB-92 Claim Form Development and Implementation

Institutional and other selected providers submit UB-92 (HCFA-1450) claim form (see Figure IX-2) data to third-party payers for reimbursement of patient services. The National Uniform Billing Committee (NUBC) is responsible for developing data elements reported on the UB-92 in cooperation with State Uniform Billing Committees (SUBCs).

■ **NOTE:** UB-92 claim data for Medicare Part A reimbursement is submitted to **fiscal intermediaries (FIs)**, which are private insurance companies contracted by HCFA to serve as the financial agent between providers and the federal government for the purpose of handling Medicare Part A reimbursement. The FI processes payments for hospitals, skilled nursing facilities, home health and hospice agencies, dialysis facilities, rehabilitation facilities, and rural health clinics. ■

◆ **HINT:** The role of the FI is similar to that of the Medicare carrier associated with Medicare Part B claims processing. ◆

National Uniform Billing Committee (NUBC)

Like the role of the National Uniform Claims Committee (NUCC) in the development of the HCFA-1500 claim form, the **National Uniform Billing Committee (NUBC)** is responsible for identifying and revising **data elements** (information entered into UB-92 form locators or submitted by institutions using electronic data interchange),

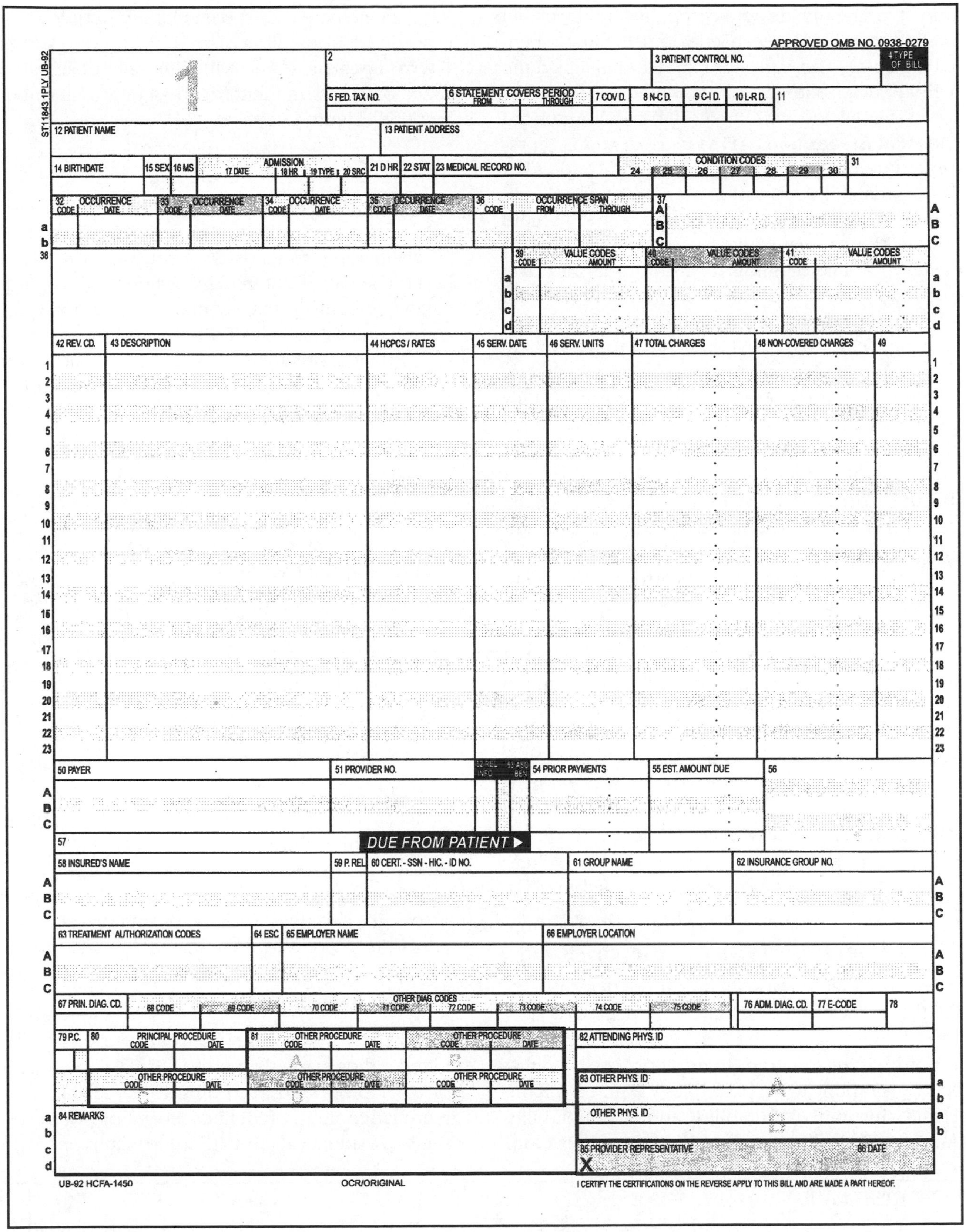
APPROVED OMB NO. 0938-0279

ST11843 1PLY UB-92

1 | 2 | 3 PATIENT CONTROL NO. | 4 TYPE OF BILL

5 FED. TAX NO. | 6 STATEMENT COVERS PERIOD FROM THROUGH | 7 COV D. | 8 N-C D. | 9 C-I D. | 10 L-R D. | 11

12 PATIENT NAME | 13 PATIENT ADDRESS

14 BIRTHDATE | 15 SEX | 16 MS | ADMISSION 17 DATE 18 HR 19 TYPE 20 SRC | 21 D HR | 22 STAT | 23 MEDICAL RECORD NO. | CONDITION CODES 24 25 26 27 28 29 30 | 31

32 OCCURRENCE CODE DATE | 33 OCCURRENCE CODE DATE | 34 OCCURRENCE CODE DATE | 35 OCCURRENCE CODE DATE | 36 OCCURRENCE SPAN CODE FROM THROUGH | 37 A B C

38 | 39 VALUE CODES CODE AMOUNT | 40 VALUE CODES CODE AMOUNT | 41 VALUE CODES CODE AMOUNT

42 REV. CD. | 43 DESCRIPTION | 44 HCPCS / RATES | 45 SERV. DATE | 46 SERV. UNITS | 47 TOTAL CHARGES | 48 NON-COVERED CHARGES | 49

1–23

50 PAYER | 51 PROVIDER NO. | 52 REL INFO | 53 ASG BEN | 54 PRIOR PAYMENTS | 55 EST. AMOUNT DUE | 56

57 DUE FROM PATIENT ▶

58 INSURED'S NAME | 59 P. REL | 60 CERT. - SSN - HIC. - ID NO. | 61 GROUP NAME | 62 INSURANCE GROUP NO.

63 TREATMENT AUTHORIZATION CODES | 64 ESC | 65 EMPLOYER NAME | 66 EMPLOYER LOCATION

67 PRIN. DIAG. CD. | OTHER DIAG. CODES 68 CODE 69 CODE 70 CODE 71 CODE 72 CODE 73 CODE 74 CODE 75 CODE | 76 ADM. DIAG. CD. | 77 E-CODE | 78

79 P.C. | 80 PRINCIPAL PROCEDURE CODE DATE | 81 OTHER PROCEDURE CODE DATE A | OTHER PROCEDURE CODE DATE B | 82 ATTENDING PHYS. ID

OTHER PROCEDURE CODE DATE C | OTHER PROCEDURE CODE DATE D | OTHER PROCEDURE CODE DATE E | 83 OTHER PHYS. ID A | OTHER PHYS. ID B

84 REMARKS | 85 PROVIDER REPRESENTATIVE X | 86 DATE

UB-92 HCFA-1450 | OCR/ORIGINAL | I CERTIFY THE CERTIFICATIONS ON THE REVERSE APPLY TO THIS BILL AND ARE MADE A PART HEREOF.

Figure IX-2 Sample UB-92 claim form (Reprinted according to HCFA's reuse policy at www.hcfa.gov)

and it originally designed the first uniform bill (called the UB-82 because of its 1982 implementation date). The current claim form is called the UB-92 because it was implemented in 1992.

The NUBC was created by the American Hospital Association (AHA) in 1975 and is represented by major national provider (e.g., AHA State Hospital Association Representatives) and payer (e.g., Blue Cross and Blue Shield Association) organizations. The intent was to develop a single billing form and standard data set that could be used by all institutional providers and payers for health care claims processing. In 1982, the NUBC voted to accept the UB-82 and its **data set** (a compilation of data elements that are reported on the uniform bill) for implementation as a national uniform bill. Once the UB-82 was adopted, the focus of the NUBC shifted to the state level, and a **State Uniform Billing Committee (SUBC)** was created in each state to handle implementation and distribution of state-specific UB-82 manuals (that contained national guidelines along with unique state billing requirements).

When the NUBC established the UB-82 data set design and specifications, it also implemented an evaluation process through 1990 to determine whether the UB-82 data set was appropriate for third-party payer claims processing. The NUBC surveyed SUBCs to obtain suggestions for improving the design of the UB-82, and the UB-92 was implemented in 1992 to incorporate the best of the UB-82 with data set design improvements (e.g., providers no longer need to include as many attachments to UB-92 claims submitted).

Data Specifications for the UB-92

When reviewing data specifications for the UB-92, the NUBC balances the payers' need to collect information against the burden of providers to report that information. In addition, the administrative simplification principles required of the Health Insurance Portability and Accountability Act of 1996 (HIPAA) are applied when develop-ing data elements. Each data element required for reporting purposes is assigned to a unique UB-92 **Form Locator (FL)**, which is the designated space on the form identified by a unique number and title (Figure IX-3).

UB-92 Claim Form Submission

Whether completed manually (Figure IX-2) or using on-screen software (Figure IX-1), the UB-92 claim form contains 86 form locators (Table IX-1). The data is entered according to third-party payer guidelines that contain instructions for completing the UB-92 (Table IX-2).

Providers that submit the UB-92 claim form (or UB-92 data elements in EDI format) include:

- ambulance companies
- ambulatory surgery centers (ASC)
- home health care agencies (HHA)
- hospice organizations
- hospitals (emergency department, inpatient, and outpatient services)
- psychiatric drug/alcohol treatment facilities (inpatient and outpatient services)
- skilled nursing facilities (SNFs)
- subacute facilities
- stand-alone clinical/laboratory facilities
- walk-in clinics

The UB-92 (HCFA-1450) and its data elements serve the needs of many third-party payers, and while some payers do not collect certain data elements, it is important to capture all NUBC-approved data elements for audit trail purposes. In addition, NUBC-approved data elements are reported by facilities that have established coordination of benefits agreements with the payers.

■ **NOTE:** All Medicare claims are currently submitted either manually on the UB-92 paper claim form, or processed according to electronic data interchange (EDI) guidelines. Form locator definitions are identical and in some situations, the

12 PATIENT NAME	

Figure IX-3 UB-92 Form Locator 12–Patient Name

Table IX-1 UB-92 Form locators and brief description of information to be entered

FORM LOCATOR	BRIEF DESCRIPTION OF INFORMATION TO BE ENTERED ON THE UB-92	FORM LOCATOR	BRIEF DESCRIPTION OF INFORMATION TO BE ENTERED ON THE UB-92
1	Provider Name, Address & Telephone #	46	Units of Service
2	Unlabeled Field - State Use	47	Total Charges (by Revenue Code Category)
3	Patient Control Number (Account Number)	48	Non-Covered Charges
4	Type of Bill	49	Unlabeled Field - National Use
5	Federal Tax Number	50A-C	Payer Identification
6	Statement Covers Period	51A-C	Provider Number
7	Covered Days	52A-C	Release of Information Certification Indicator
8	Non-Covered Days	53A-C	Assignment of Benefits Certification Indicator
9	Coinsurance Days	54A-C, P	Prior Payments - Payers and Patient
10	Lifetime Reserve Days	55A-C, P	Estimated Amount Due
11	Unlabeled Field - State Use	56	DRG Number and Grouper ID
12	Patient Name	57	Unlabeled Field - National Use
13	Patient Address	58A-C	Insured's Name
14	Patient Birthdate	59A-C	Patient's Relationship to Insured
15	Patient Sex	60A-C	Health Insurance Claim Identification Number
16	Patient Marital Status	61A-C	Insured Group Name
17	Admission Date	62A-C	Insurance Group Number
18	Admission Hour	63A-C	Treatment Authorization Code
19	Type of Admission	64A-C	Employment Status Code
20	Source of Admission	65A-C	Employer Name
21	Discharge Hour	66A-C	Employer Location
22	Patient Status	67	Principal Diagnosis Code
23	Medical/Health Record Number	68-75	Other Diagnosis Codes
24-30	Condition Codes	76	Admitting Diagnosis
31	Unlabeled Field - National Use	77	External Cause of Injury Code (E-Code)
32-35a,b	Occurrence Codes and Dates	78	Principal Diagnosis Code
36a,b	Occurrence Span Codes and Dates	79	Procedure Coding Method Used
37	Internal Control Number (ICN)	80	Principal Procedure Code and Date
38	Responsible Party Name and Address	81A-E	Other Procedure Codes and Dates
39-41a-d	Value Codes and Amounts	82a-b	Attending Physician ID
42	Revenue Code	83a-b	Other Physician ID
43	Revenue Description	84	Remarks
44	HCPCS/Rates	85	Provider Representative Signature
45	Service Date	86	Date Bill Submitted

(Reprinted according to content reuse policy at www.hcfa.gov)

Table IX-2 Partial list of UB-92 claims form completion instructions according to third-party payer and State or type of health care organization

THIRD PARTY PAYER – STATE/TYPE OF HEALTH CARE ORGANIZATION	WEB SITE CONTAINING UB-92 CLAIMS FORM COMPLETION INSTRUCTIONS
BLUE CROSS/BLUE SHIELD – Illinois	www.bcbsil.com/provider/ec/ub92Specs.htm
MEDICAID – West Virginia	www.wvdhhr.org/bms/Y2K/y2k_new_billing_instructions.htm
MEDICAID – South Dakota	www.state.sd.us/social/Medicaid/Hosp%20manual/HOSPIII.html
MEDICARE – General Instructions	www.hcfa.gov/medicare/edi/edi5.htm
MEDICARE – SNF	www.hcfa.gov/pubforms/12_SNF/sn560.htm
WORKERS' COMPENSATION – Texas	www.workerscompensation.com/texas/forms/

electronic claim contains more characters than the corresponding item on the paper form. ■

ELECTRONIC DATA INTERCHANGE (EDI)

Electronic Data Interchange (EDI) is the electronic exchange of business documents (e.g., UB-92 data elements) from one organization's computer to another organization's computer according to standard data formats. For example, the exchange of data between a Medicare fiscal intermediary and a provider is considered EDI.

■ **NOTE:** EDI involves submissions from modem to modem or by other electronic means. Computer-generated paper claims are not categorized as electronic claims. ■

History of Electronic Data Interchange (EDI)

Electronic data interchange (EDI) originated in the 1980s when a number of industries decided to save costs and reduce waste through the electronic transmission of business information. EDI is based on approved standard formats that define **transaction sets** (electronic messages) that are used to send data from one computer to another. These transaction sets replace paper documents such as claim forms and explanation of benefit forms.

■ **NOTE:** An organization called the **Workgroup for Electronic Data Interchange (WEDI)**, a HIPAA designated advisor to the Secretary of the Department of Health and Human Services, was formed in 1991 to develop standards for the transmission of electronic health care data and work toward a government mandate that would require all hospitals to implement standardized electronic billing during the 1990s. ■

The EDI formats currently supported by Medicare include the following:

- **Electronic Media Claim (EMC)**—a health care claim (e.g., UB-92) processed according to electronic billing record formats that require data elements consistent with the UB-92 data set (so that one processing system can handle both formats). Form locator definitions are identical and, in some situations, the electronic

record contains more characters than the corresponding item on the paper form. The **EMC Submission** is a transaction used to send health care claim billing information, encounter information, or both, from health care service providers to third-party payers, either directly or through intermediary billers and claim clearinghouses. **Intermediary billers** are individuals or organizations contracted by providers to process electronic claims (e.g., third-party administrators, or TPAs). Clearinghouses (discussed earlier in this appendix) are companies that serve as "one-stop service centers" and process providers' health care claims for a number of payers; they can process as many as 100,000 electronic claims per month.

- **Coordination of Benefits (COB) Exchange** —a transaction set used to transmit health care claims and billing payment information between payers of health care with different payment responsibilities. It allows for the coordination of benefits between payers and regulatory agencies that monitor the rendering, billing, and/or payment of health care services within a specific health care/insurance industry segment.

- **Eligibility Transaction**—a transaction used to inquire about the eligibility, coverage, or benefits associated with a health care plan, employer, plan sponsor, subscriber, or a dependent under the subscriber's policy. It also can be used to communicate information about, or changes to, eligibility, coverage, or benefits from information sources (e.g., insurers, sponsors, and payers) to information receivers (e.g., physicians, hospitals, third-party administrators, and government agencies).

- **File Transmission Acknowledgment**—a transaction that is used to provide a telecommunications acknowledgment of the receipt of an electronic UB-92 or National Standard Format claims transaction.

- **Health Care Payment/Remittance Advice Transaction**—a transaction set used to make a payment and/or send an explanation of benefits (EOB) remittance advice to a health care provider either directly or via a financial institution.

- **Attachments**—a transaction set used to transmit health care service information, (e.g., subscriber, patient, demographic, diagnosis, or treatment data) for the purpose of requests for review, certification, notification, or reporting the outcome of a health care services review.

HIPAA ADMINISTRATIVE SIMPLIFICATION (AS) PROVISIONS

The **Administrative Simplification (AS)** provisions of the Health Insurance Portability and Accountability Act of 1996 (HIPAA) require the Secretary of Health and Human Services (HHS) to adopt standards for electronic health care transactions. The AS provisions are intended to reduce the costs and administrative burdens of health care by making possible the standardized, electronic transmission of many manual administrative and financial transactions that are currently carried out on paper.

In August 2000, HHS Secretary Donna E. Shalala announced the adoption of standard formats and data content for the submission of electronic media claims and other administrative health transactions. All health care providers will be able to use the electronic format to bill for their services, and all health care plans will be required to accept these standard electronic claims, referral authorizations, and other transactions. Presently, different insurers require different electronic and paper forms from health care providers who file claims. Under the new regulation all electronic claims transactions must follow the single standardized format. Providers will still be allowed to use paper forms, but the simplified process is expected to encourage more electronic filing.

By law, health care plans (except for small self-administered plans), clearinghouses, and providers that choose to transmit transactions in electronic form must comply with these rules within 26 months from the date of publication of this final rule. Small plans have one additional year in which to comply. The final rule, entitled the National Standards for Electronic Transactions, was published in the *Federal Register* on August 17, 2000, and the effective date for implementation is October 16, 2000 with a the compliance date of October 16, 2002 (2003 for small health care plans).

INTERNET LINKS

Download the free HCFA-1450 (UB-92) training software from www.medicaretraining.com.

Medicare Electronic Data Interchange (EDI) information is located at hcfa.hhs.gov/medicare/edi/edi.htm.

Administrative Simplification information can be found at aspe.os.dhhs.gov/admnsimp/.

A PowerPoint presentation about EDI can be downloaded from Remora Software Inc.'s Web site at www.RemoraBay.com/UB.html.

SUMMARY

Electronic Data Interchange (EDI) is the computer-to-computer exchange of information between organizations in a standardized format. This information includes claims submissions, payments to providers and institutions, eligibility verification, and other transactions related to the operation of a health care organization. The Health Insurance Portability and Accountability Act of 1996 (HIPAA) included Administrative Simplification (AS) provisions to establish code sets for data elements reported during health claims transactions, which directly impacted EDI upon its implementation in 2000. HCFA has identified standard electronic formats acceptable for the processing of Medicare claims, which include the following: UB-92 flat-file format, National Standard Format (NSF), and ANSI ASC X12 837 format. The **UB-92 flat-file format** is defined as a fixed-length format that is used to bill institutional services, such as those performed in hospitals. The **National Standard Format (NSF)** is also a fixed-length format, used to bill physician and noninstitutional services, such as those performed by a general practitioner. The **ANSI ASC X12 837 format** is a variable-length format used to bill both institutional and noninstitutional services.

INTERNET LINK

Go to www.hcfa.gov/medicare/edi/edi3.htm to download HCFA-mandated EDI transaction formats for HCFA-1500 and UB-92 electronic media claims submission, coordination of benefits exchange, eligibility determination, file transmission acknowledgment, health care payment and remittance advice, and attachments.

Bibliography

BOOKS AND MANUALS

American Medical Association. (2000). *CPT 2001.* Chicago, IL: Author.

Austin, M. S. (2000). *Managed health care simplified: A glossary of terms.* Albany, NY: Delmar.

Blue Cross Association. (1972). *The Blue Cross story.* Chicago, IL: Author.

Blue Cross and Blue Shield Association. (1987). *The history of Blue Cross and Blue Shield plans.* Chicago, IL: Author.

Davis, J. B. (2000). *Reimbursement manual for the medical office: A comprehensive guide to coding, billing & fee management.* Practice Management Information Corporation.

Davison, J., & Lewis, M. (2000). *Working with insurance and managed care plans: A guide for getting paid.* Practice Management Information Corporation.

Garrett, T. M., Baillie, H. W., & Garrett, R. M. (2001). *Health care ethics: Principles and problems.* Upper Saddle River, NJ: Prentice Hall.

Ingenix Publishing. (2000). *2001 HCPCS.* Salt Lake City, UT: Author.

Ingenix Publishing. (2000). *2001 hospital & payer ICD-9-CM.* Salt Lake City, UT: Author.

Johnson, S. L. (2000). *Understanding medical coding: A comprehensive guide.* Albany, NY: Delmar.

Medicode. (1999). *2000 coder's desk reference.* Salt Lake City, UT: Ingenix Publishing.

Medicode. (1999). *2000 Medicode's encoder pro,* Salt Lake City, UT: Medicode.

Medicode. (2000). *Code It Right 2000.* Salt Lake City, UT: Ingenix Publishing.

Medicode. (2000). *Coders' desk reference 2001.* Salt Lake City, UT: Ingenix Publishing.

Medicode. (2000). *Encoder pro 2001.* UT: Ingenix Publishing.

Medicode. (2000). *ICD-10 made easy.* Salt Lake City, UT: Ingenix Publishing.

Medicode. (1999). *Medicare billing guide 2000.* Salt Lake City, UT: Ingenix Publishing.

Medicode. (2000). *Modifiers made easy 2001.* Salt Lake City, UT: Ingenix Publishing.

National Association of Blue Shield Plans. *The Blue Shield story: All of us helping each of us.* Chicago, IL: Blue Cross and Blue Shield Association.

Rizzo, C. D. (2000). *Uniform billing: A guide to claims processing.* Albany, NY: Delmar.

St. Anthony's. (2000). *St. Anthony's complete guide to coverage issues: A reference to covered and noncovered services.* Salt Lake City, UT: Ingenix Publishing.

BROCHURES AND BULLETINS

2000 guide to health insurance for people with Medicare. Washington, D.C: Health Care Financing Administration.

Coverage policy bulletins. Hartford, CT: Aetna US Healthcare, Aetna Life Insurance Company.

Federal Employees Program (FEP) claim form Completion Instructions. Chicago, IL: Blue Cross and Blue Shield Federal Employees Program.

FEP service benefit plan brochure. Chicago, IL: Blue Cross and Blue Shield Federal Employees Program.

HCFA-1500 claim filing instructions. Albuquerque, NM: BlueCross BlueShield of New Mexico.

Health Insurance Portability and Accountability Act of 1996—Administrative simplification care fact sheet. Washington, D.C.: Health Care Financing Administration.

Health insurance, the history. Seattle, WA: Health Insurance Association of America.

Medicare & you 2001. Washington, D.C.: Health Care Financing Administration.

Medicare and other health benefits: Your guide to who pays first. Washington, D.C.: Health Care Financing Administration.

Medicare fraud and abuse. Washington, D.C.: Health Care Financing Administration.

Medicare savings for qualified beneficiaries. Washington, D.C.: Health Care Financing Administration.

Medigap policies and protections. Washington, D.C.: Health Care Financing Administration.

TRICARE grand rounds. Falls Church, VA: TRICARE Management Activity.

Understanding your Medicare choices. Washington, D.C.: Health Care Financing Administration.

Your Medicare benefits. Washington, D.C.: Health Care Financing Administration.

INSURANCE MANUALS

Blue Cross and Blue Shield of Maryland guide to programs & benefits. (2001). Owings Mills, MD: Blue Cross and Blue Shield of Maryland, Inc.

CHAMPVA handbook. (2001). Denver, CO: VA Health Administration Center.

HCFA's state Medicaid manual. (2001). Washington, D.C.: Health Care Financing Administration.

Medicare & Medicaid program manuals. (2001). Washington, D.C.: Health Care Financing Administration.

TRICARE/CHAMPUS policy manuals. (2001). Falls Church, VA: TRICARE Management Activity.

TRICARE Standard provider handbook. (2001). Falls Church, VA: TRICARE Management Activity.

JOURNALS, NEWSMAGAZINES AND NEWSLETTERS FOR ADDITIONAL READING

Advance for health information professionals. King of Prussia, PA: Merion Publications.

American medical news. Chicago, IL: American Medical Association.

BlueReview for BlueCross and BlueShield of Illinois institutional & professional providers. Chicago, IL: Blue Cross and Blue Shield of Illinois.

Claims for compensation under the Federal Employees' Compensation Act, Final Rule, 11/25/1998. Federal Register. Washington, D.C: National Archives and Records Administration.

CodeCorrect news. Yakima, WA: CodeCorrect.com.

Coding edge. San Clemente, CA: Laguna Medical Systems.

CPT assistant. Chicago, IL: American Medical Association.

Family practice management. Leawood, KS: American Academy of Family Physicians.

For the record. Valley Forge, PA: Great Valley Publishing.

HealthInk. Owings Mills, MD: CareFirst Blue Cross and Blue Shield.

Journal of the American health information management association. Chicago, IL: American Health Information Management Association.

Medical office management. Pensacola, FL: Professional Association of Health Care Office Managers.

Medicare part B news. Denison, TX: Trailblazer Health Enterprises, LLC., a HCFA Contracted Intermediary/Carrier.

Medicare part B special bulletins. Denison, TX: Trailblazer Health Enterprises, LLC., a HCFA Contracted Intermediary/Carrier.

Part B news, Rockville, MD:United Communications Group.

Professional medical assistant. Chicago, IL: American Association of Medical Assistants.

Provider news brief. Albuquerque, NM: BlueCross BlueShield of New Mexico.

Solutions for health care providers. Camp Hill, PA: Healthcare Management Solutions, Inc.

INTERNET-BASED REFERENCES

CodeCorrect.com – CPT, ICD-9, CCI, Coding Crosswalk and APC data, and searchable Medicare newsletters and *Federal Register.*

FirstGov.gov – resource for locating government information on the Internet

medicaretraining.com – self-paced Medicare training by downloading free interactive courses and attending free satellite programs designed to teach Medicare billing guidelines.

MediRegs.com – Legislation, Code of Federal Regulations, *Federal Register* notices, HCFA and SSA manuals and memoranda, CPT-4, CCI, RVU, and DRG updates, CPT Assistant, UPIN and DEA Registration List, Fraud Materials from OIG and DOJ.

MxCity.com – a gateway to up-to-date reimbursement, coding, and compliance information.

the-medicare.com – Medicare Part A and Part B Newsletter and Special Bulletins.

NOTE: Number(s) following a term indicate chapter(s) in which terms are listed.

1995 DGs (7): *see* 1995 Evaluation and Management Documentation Guidelines.

1995 Evaluation and Management Documentation Guidelines (DGs) (7): guidelines developed by the Health Care Financing Administration (HCFA) to supplement and clarify the assignment of codes from the E&M Section of CPT.

1997 DGs (7): *see* 1997 Evaluation and Management Documentation Guidelines.

1997 Evaluation and Management Documentation Guidelines (DGs) (7): an alternate set of guidelines developed by HCFA for use by providers who perform single-system exams (e.g., ophthalmologists).

2000 DGs (draft version) (7): *see* 2000 Evaluation and Management Documentation Guidelines.

2000 Evaluation and Management Documentation Guidelines (7): revised guidelines developed by HCFA to simplify the 1997 DGs and clarify assignment of codes from the E&M Section of CPT; implementation is scheduled for 2002.

abuse (5, 9): practices that result in unnecessary costs to the Medicare program; abuse is characterized by the fact that it is not possible to establish whether practices were committed knowingly or willfully.

accept assignment (4, 9): the provider agrees to accept Medicare's fee as payment-in-full.

accidental poisoning (6): associated with the ICD-9-CM Table of Drugs and Chemicals; indicates that a substance was taken/given accidentally (as opposed to intentionally as in a suicide attempt or assault).

accreditation (3): voluntary process that a health care facility or organization undergoes to show it has met standards in addition to requirements imposed by law.

active duty personnel (17): government service personnel on current assignment with one of the uniformed services.

Advance Beneficiary Notice (ABN) (6, 8, 14): *see* waiver of liability.

adverse effect (reaction) (6): a pathological reaction following the ingestion of or exposure to drugs or other chemical substances. These effects may result from the cumulative effects of a drug/substance, the patient's hypersensitivity to the substance, unexpected side effects, or an interaction between two or more prescribed drugs.

adverse selection (3): the problem of covering members who are sicker than the general population.

Aid to Families with Dependent Children (AFDC) (Welfare) (15): a welfare program covering pregnant women and young children who are members of households where income falls below the poverty level.

á la carte billing (7): the breaking down of an integrated major surgical package into various components for the purpose of differential coding and obtaining a higher reimbursement.

allogenic bone marrow transplant (14): type of bone marrow transplant where a portion of a healthy donor's stem cells or bone marrow is used.

allowable charge (4): *see* allowed charge.

allowed charge (4): the maximum amount, according to the individual policy, that insurance will pay for each procedure or service performed.

ambulatory payment classifications (APCs) (2): a prospective payment system (PPS) modeled on Ambulatory Patient Groups (APGs), a program developed by 3M Health Information Systems under a contract with HCFA. In 2000, APCs are implemented for hospital outpatient services, certain Part B services furnished to hospital inpatients who have no Part A coverage, and partial hospitalization services furnished by community mental health centers. It was enacted as part of the Balanced Budget Act of 1997 (BBA) that authorized the Health Care

Financing Administration (HCFA) to implement the system. Also under development is a reimbursement system to be used for payment of surgeries performed by ambulatory surgery centers (ASCs); it is anticipated that this system will collapse back to the surgical APCs.

Ambulatory Surgical Center (ASC) (11): an independent surgical facility certified and licensed by state health departments for the purpose of performing surgery on patients who are expected to be discharged the same day surgery is performed. ASCs performing surgery on Medicare patients must also be approved by HCFA.

Amendment to the HMO Act of 1973 (3): legislation that allows members (subscribers) to occasionally seek care from non-HMO physicians and be partially reimbursed.

American Disabilities Act of 1990 (ADA) (15): law that prohibits discrimination of individuals with disabilities.

American Hospital Association (AHA) (13): professional organization promoting the ideal performance and functions of acute care hospitals in the United States.

ANSI ASC X12N 837 (2): abbreviations for the National Standards Institute (ANSI), Accredited Standards Committee (ASC), Insurance Subcommittee (X12N), claims validation tables (837); represents a format to be used when submitting electronic claims.

aplastic anemia (14): deficient red blood cell production due to bone marrow disorders.

assault (6): associated with the ICD-9-CM Table of Drugs and Chemicals; indicates a substance was administered with the intent to harm or kill.

assessment (10): process by which a patient's condition is appraised or evaluated.

assignment of benefits (13): authorization granted by the patient to allow the insurance company to pay claim benefits directly to the provider of care. It is to the provider's benefit to have the patient sign the "assignment of benefits" statement on each claim form. All benefits due to the provider will be mailed directly to the provider rather than to the patient.

autologous bone marrow transplant (14): type of bone marrow transplant in which the patient's own, previously stored marrow is used.

Away From Home Care Program (13): a "guest membership" offered by participating Blue Cross and Blue Shield HMOs.

axis of classification (6): organizing entities, diseases, and other conditions according to etiology, anatomy, or severity.

balance billing (9, 14, 16): charging the patient for the difference between the physician's fee and the insurance carrier's allowed fee.

Balanced Budget Act of 1997 (3): federal legislation that enacted significant changes to the Medicare and Medicaid

Programs and expanded services provided by HCFA through the Child Health Insurance Program (Title XXI); provisions impacted Medicare Parts A & B, Medicare+ Choice, Prevention Initiatives, Rural Initiatives, Anti-Fraud and Abuse Provisions, and Improvements in Protecting Program Integrity, Medicaid, Programs of All-Inclusive Care for the Elderly (PACE), State Children's Health Insurance Program, Welfare, and related provisions.

Base Realignment and Closure (BRAC) Pharmacy Benefit (16): TRICARE benefit available to Medicare-eligible enrollees who had been using pharmacies at military bases that have closed.

basic coverage (Blue Cross/Blue Shield) (13): insurance coverage limited to basic inpatient medical and diagnostic care, and both inpatient and outpatient surgery services.

beneficiary (4, 9): a person eligible to receive the benefits of a specific policy or program.

Beneficiary Counseling and Assistance Coordinator (BCAC) (16): beneficiary advocates and problem solvers located at Lead Agent offices and military treatment facilities.

Beneficiary Services Representative (BSR) (16): TRICARE Service Centers personnel who provide information about TRICARE plans.

benefit period (14): a Medicare designation for the period of time covered by the inpatient deductible. A benefit period starts with the first day of hospitalization and ends when the patient has been out of the hospital for 60 consecutive days. (Also known as "spell of illness.")

benign (6): a tumor that is noninvasive (not affecting deeper tissue), localized, and nonspreading.

billing entity (11): a legal business name of a practice or organization.

birthday rule (4): guideline for the designation of the primary insurance policy when dependents are concurrently enrolled in two or more policies. The rule states the following: the primary policy is the one taken out by the policyholder with the earliest birthday occurring in the calendar year. In cases where the birthdays of the policyholders occur on the same day, the policy that has been in effect the longest is considered primary. The year of birth is not considered.

black box edits (5): coding edits implemented by HCFA and used by commercial insurance carriers; if the edits are not used by a local payer, office staff may not be familiar with them.

Black Lung Benefits Act (17): federal legislation that provides workers' compensation coverage for miners suffering from black lung disease (pneumoconiosis).

blocked indented notes (7): used in CPT at the beginning of heading to provide general information.

BlueCard PPO (13): a program that offers "guest memberships" to subscribers at participating BCBS PPOs.

BlueCard Program (13): a BC/BS program that eases the processing of claims from PAR and PPN providers when they provide medical services to BC/BS patients enrolled in plans outside the health care provider's local service area. This program was formerly known as the "Out-Of-Area Program."

BlueCard Worldwide (13): a program that allows subscribers who travel or live abroad to receive covered inpatient hospital care and physician services from a network of hospitals and doctors around the world.

Blue Cross (BC) (13): a medical insurance corporation organized for the purpose of offering prepaid hospital care plans to people living and working in a specific geographic region.

Blue Cross and Blue Shield Association (BCBSA) (13): corporation created when the Board of Directors of the separate National Blue Cross and Blue Shield associations merged.

Blue Cross/Blue Shield (BCBS) (13): originally created as two separate prepaid medical plans, most have merged resulting in the creation of names that no longer have regional designations.

Blue Shield (BS) (13): a medical insurance corporation organized for the purpose of offering prepaid medical and surgical care plans to people living and working in a specific geographic region.

boldface type (6, 7): in CPT, indicates major divisions under a code.

brace (6): terms in the ICD-9-CM Tabular List that are located to the right of the brace, modify the statement located at the left of the brace; these terms must be present in the provider's diagnostic statement to assign the code which includes a brace.

brackets (6): in the ICD-9-CM index, bracketed codes appear in slanted brackets, follow an unbracketed code, and are to be reported along with the primary code to fully describe the cause and effect relationship stated in the diagnosis.

breach of confidentiality (5): failure to safeguard the privacy of patient records; disclosure (breaches) can occur inadvertently or intentionally. It involves the unauthorized release of confidential patient information to a third party.

budget neutral (9): adjustments made to the fee schedules by local Medicare carriers to keep Medicare Part B within a $20 million limit or budget neutral.

bundled codes (7): CPT codes for procedures and services that are included in other service and procedure codes.

cafeteria plan (3): *see* triple option plan.

cancer (Ca) *in situ* (6): *see* carcinoma *in situ*.

capitation (2, 3): a reimbursement system used by HMOs and some other managed care plans to pay the health care provider a fixed fee on a per capita basis that has no relationship to type of services performed or the number of services each patient receives.

carcinoma (Ca) *in situ* (6): a malignant tumor that is localized, circumscribed, and noninvasive (not affecting deeper tissue).

care plan oversight service (7): a CPT evaluation and management service for the purpose of reporting the physician's time spent coordinating multidisciplinary patient care plans, and integrating or adjusting the patient's medical treatment plans.

case law (5): laws based on court decisions that establish a standard.

case management (3, 7, 16): development of patient care plans for the management of complicated cases in a cost-effective manner.

case management service (7): a CPT evaluation and management service for the process in which the attending physician or agent coordinates the care given to a patient by other health care providers and/or community organizations.

case manager (4): a nurse or other medically-trained person who coordinates the care of patients with long-term chronic conditions.

catastrophic cap benefit (16): established limits on a serious illness or long-term treatment.

catchment area (a TRICARE term) (16): a region which is defined by postal zip code boundaries that fit roughly within a 40-mile radius of the government medical treatment facility and is used to determine the need for preauthorization for any civilian medical care.

category (6): in CPT, the six major sections are subdivided into subsections and then categories. In ICD-9-CM, categories are printed in bold upper and lowercase type and preceded by a three-digit number.

CHAMPUS (2, 16): *see* TRICARE.

CHAMPUS Reform Initiative (CRI) (16): a demonstration project that offers military families a choice of how their health care benefits could be used.

CHAMPVA (2, 16): a healthcare benefits program for (1) dependents of veterans who were rated by the VA as having a total and permanent disability; (2) survivors of veterans who died from VA-rated service-connected conditions, or who at the time of death, were rated permanently and totally disabled from a VA-rated service-connected condition; and (3) survivors of persons who died in the line of duty and not due to misconduct. CHAMPVA refers to Civilian Health and Medical Program of Veterans Affairs.

chapter heading (6): (associated with ICD-9-CM) printed in uppercase letters and preceded by a chapter number.

charge slip (4): summary of services rendered to the patient during a visit. Includes the date, patient's name, and list of all services rendered on that particular date.

check digit (5): a one-digit character (either alphabetic or numerical) used to verify the validity of a unique identifier.

Civilian Health and Medical Program of the Uniformed Services (CHAMPUS)(16): *see* TRICARE.

Civilian Health and Medical Program of Veterans Affairs (CHAMPVA)(16): a separate program from TRICARE Standard that covers dependents and survivors of veterans.

claim attachment (11): additional claims documentation needed to adjudicate the claim.

Classification of Drugs by AHFS List (6): located in ICD-9-CM, Appendix C; contains the American Hospital Formulary Services drug list number and equivalent code number, organized in straight numerical order by AHFS List number.

Classification of Industrial Accidents According to Agency (6): located in ICD-9-CM, Appendix D; contains a listing of external cause codes (E-codes) created from employment injury statistics adopted by the Tenth International Conference of Labor Statisticians.

clearinghouse (5): an organization that performs centralized claims processing for health care providers and plans.

Clinical Laboratory Improvement Act (CLIA) certification number (14): issued to clinical laboratories so that procedures performed are covered by Medicare; effective date for implementation of CLIA was 9/1/92.

clinical trial (16): a test of a new treatment in patients.

closed fracture treatment (7): alignment of a fracture without surgical intervention.

closed-panel HMO (3): an established insurance program that allows members to receive nonemergency health services from contracted providers at specified facilities.

COBRA insurance (3): the Consolidated Omnibus Budget Reconciliation Act (COBRA) of 1985 gave employees who leave a company with employer-sponsored group health insurance the right to continue their health insurance coverage for up to eighteen months, if they are willing to pay the entire cost of premiums. Medicare is primary to COBRA insurance.

cochlear implant (16): electronic device surgically implanted in the ear to assist hearing.

code first (6, 7): in ICD-9-CM, indicates that two codes are required, one of which is to be sequenced first.

code modifier (5): a two-digit code added to CPT main codes or a two-character code added to HCPCS Level II and III codes to indicate a deviation from the provider's normal fee. Use of a code modifier will keep the specific procedure out of the profile determination calculation.

code pairs (edit pairs) (5): multiple codes that, if reported together, would either be excluded from payment or paid at a reduced price.

coding (1, 5): a method of assigning numeric or alphanumeric codes to procedures/services for reimbursement.

coding conventions (6, 7): rules that apply to the assignment of codes; *see* conventions.

coding conventions for ICD-9-CM Index to Diseases (6): rules that apply to entries in the ICD-9-CM Index to Diseases.

   a. **codes in slanted brackets (6):** secondary codes that classify manifestations (results) of other conditions; these codes are listed below the primary code number on the HCFA-1500 claim form (Block 21).

   b. **eponym (6):** diseases (and procedures) named for an individual.

   c. **essential modifier (6):** subterms that are indented below the index entry for the main term.

   d. **NEC (not elsewhere classifiable)(6):** abbreviation that indicates a code is to be assigned but cannot be located in the ICD-9-CM coding book.

   e. **nonessential modifier (6):** subterm(s) that are enclosed in parentheses and follow the main term to clarify the code selection; they do not have to be present in the provider's diagnostic statement.

   f. **notes (6):** boxed narrative explanations that define terms, clarify index entries, and list choices for additional digits (e.g., fifth-digits).

   g. ***see* (6):** instruction that directs a coder to a more specific term in the index under which the code can be found.

   h. ***see also* (6):** instruction that directs a coder to additional terms in the index where the code can be found.

   i. ***see category* (6):** instruction that directs a coder to a Tabular List category (three-digit code) where a code can be located.

coding conventions for ICD-9-CM Tabular List of Diseases (6): rules that apply to disease and condition codes in the ICD-9-CM Tabular List of Diseases (including supplementary classifications).

   a. **and (6):** interpreted as "and/or" in the Tabular List and indicates that either of the two disorders is associated with the code number.

   b. **bold type (6):** all category and subcategory codes and descriptions are printed in bold type.

   c. **braces (6):** enclose a series of terms, each of which modifies the statement that appears to the right of the brace.

   d. **brackets (6):** enclose synonyms, alternate wording, or explanatory phrases.

   e. **code first underlying disease (6):** appears when the referenced code is to be listed second on the HCFA-1500 claim form; the code, title, and instructions are italicized.

   f. **colon (6):** used after an incomplete term and is followed by one or more modifiers (additional terms that clarify the tabular entry).

g. **Excludes (6):** a note that directs the coder to another location in the codebook where the code is located.

h. **format (6):** subterms are indented below the term to which they are linked, and if a definition or disease requires more than one line, that text is printed on the next line and further indented.

i. **fourth- and fifth digits (6):** the assignment of fourth and fifth digits is indicated by an instructional note located below the category or subcategory description.

j. **Includes (5):** notes that appear below a three-digit category code description to further define, clarify, or provide an example.

k. **NOS (not otherwise specified) (6):** an abbreviation that indicates the code is unspecified and the coder should ask the provider for a more specific diagnosis before assigning a code.

l. **parentheses (6):** enclose supplementary words that may be present or absent in the diagnostic statement, without affecting assignment of the code.

m. **use additional code (6):** a note that indicates a second code is to be reported to provide more information about the diagnosis.

n. **with (6):** when codes combine one disorder with another, the provider's diagnostic statement must clearly indicate that both conditions are present and that a relationship exists between the conditions.

coding conventions for ICD-9-CM Index to Procedures and Tabular List (6): rules that apply to the ICD-9-CM Index to Procedures and Tabular List.

a. *omit code* **(6):** instruction that identifies procedures or services that may be components of other procedures and directs the coder not to assign a separate code.

b. **code also any synchronous procedures (6):** an instruction that indicates an additional code should be assigned to completely code the procedure.

coinsurance (2, 4): *see* coinsurance payment.

coinsurance payment (4): a specified percentage of insurance determined for each service the patient must pay the health care provider.

colon (6): a punctuation mark found in the Tabular List of ICD-9-CM; terms located after the colon complete the statement.

combination programs (a Workers' Compensation term) (17): a mix of different style Workers' Compensation programs from which employers can choose to insure employees against injuries/disorders acquired within the scope of their employment.

combined medical/surgical case (11): an inpatient hospitalization where the patient was first admitted as a medical case but, after testing, required surgery.

common data file (4): an abstract of all recent insurance claims filed for a patient.

common law (5): *see* case law.

community spouse (15): the spouse that remains at home while the other resides in a nursing facility.

comorbidity (6): *see* concurrent condition.

competitive medical plan (CMP) (3): an HMO that meets federal eligibility requirements for a Medicare risk contract.

complication (6): condition that develops subsequent to inpatient admission.

component/comprehensive codes (9): in CPT, the component code is a subset of the comprehensive code; e.g., 49000 (exploratory laparotomy) is a component of 47610 (open cholecystectomy).

comprehensive examination (7): an extensive physical examination of all body systems or a single organ system.

comprehensive history (7): a CPT Evaluation and Management Service requiring a documented patient history that includes the chief complaint; an extended discussion of the history of the present illness; a complete review of the patient's past, family, and social histories; a comprehensive review of all body systems.

comprehensive assessment (7): a nursing care plan for patients in skilled nursing facilities that includes the patient's functional capacity and identification of potential problems and nursing plan to enhance or maintain the patient's physical and psychosocial functions.

computed tomography (CT) scan (16): special radiological exam that gathers anatomical information about the patient.

computerized axial tomography (CAT) scan (16): *see* computed tomography.

concurrent condition (6): disorders present at the same time as the primary diagnosis that complicates the treatment required or lengthens the expected recovery time of the primary condition.

concurrent review (3): review, during inpatient hospitalization, of services and procedures ordered on a patient to determine if they are medically necessary.

conditional primary payer status (14): a Medicare phrase indicating that Medicare will pay an assigned claim as a primary payer under the following circumstances: 1) the normally designated primary payer denied payment; 2) the patient who is physically or mentally impaired failed to file a claim with the regular primary carrier; 3) a claim has been filed with a liability carrier, but 120 or more days have passed without a response from the carrier.

confidentiality (5): restricting patient information access to those with proper authorization.

confirmatory consultation (7): an examination of a patient for the purpose of giving an opinion about the necessity or appropriate nature of the patient's treatment plan. Most insurance carriers require these second opinion consultations prior to the authorization of nonemergency hospital admission.

Consolidated Omnibus Budget Reconciliation Act of 1985 (COBRA) (3): legislation that allows employees to continue health care coverage beyond the benefit termination date; *see* COBRA insurance.

constant attendance (9): a requirement for coding CPT critical care services; the physician must be with the patient constantly to report this code.

consultation (7): an examination of a patient by a health care provider to assist the referring/attending physician in the evaluation and/or management of a specific case. Consultants may initiate diagnostic and/or therapeutic services as necessary.

contiguous sites (overlapping sites) (6): when the origin of a tumor (primary) involves two adjacent sites.

contract (5): an agreement between two or more parties to perform specific services or duties.

contributory components (7): in CPT, components include counseling, coordination of care, nature of presenting problem, and time that helps determine the code when more than 50% of the provider's time is spent on such components.

conventions (6, 7): special terms, punctuation marks, abbreviations, or symbols used as shorthand in a coding system to efficiently communicate special instructions to the coder. If the conventions are ignored, the code number established may be incorrect.

conversion factor (CF) (9): amount of money established for one unit as applied to a service rendered.

Coordinated Care Plans (14): Medicare categories of HMOs, PSOs, and PPOs.

Coordinated Home Health and Hospice Care Program (13): a BCBS managed care option that allows the patients to elect an alternative to the acute care setting. If elected, the patient's physician must file a treatment plan with the BCBS case manager, and all authorized services must be rendered by personnel from a licensed home health agency or approved hospice facility.

coordination of care (7): arrangements made with other providers or agencies for the provision of services to a patient.

copay (2, 3, 4): *see* copayment.

copayment (2, 3, 4): a provision in an insurance policy requiring the policyholder or patient to pay a specified dollar amount to a health care provider for each visit or medical service received. HMO contracts state the copayment should be made at the time the service is performed. (Also known as copay.)

Correct Coding Initiative (CCI) (2, 5): *see* National Correct Coding Initiative.

cost-based HMO (14): a Medicare-HMO plan that allows the Medicare beneficiary to receive care through the HMO without loss of the traditional Medicare program. If the patient goes outside the HMO network for care, the claim is submitted to the traditional Medicare carrier for processing.

cost-share (16): TRICARE term for *copayment*.

counseling (7): a discussion with a patient and/or family concerning the diagnosis, prognosis, risks, treatment, and care of the patient.

Coverage Issues Manual (CIM) (8, 9): a reference to Medicare's covered and non-covered services; contains national coverage policies as published in HCFA regulations, contained in a HCFA ruling, or issued as a program instruction.

covered lives (3): a managed care term describing the number of persons enrolled in the program.

CPT-5 (7): an updated version of CPT being undertaken by the American Medical Association to support electronic data interchange and the electronic medical record keeping.

CPT (Current Procedural Terminology) (1, 7): a medical procedure coding system maintained and published by the American Medical Association.

critical care services (7): medical care for critically ill patients who require the constant attention of physicians; this care is usually, but not exclusively, administered in the emergency or critical care facilities of the hospital.

Current Procedural Terminology (CPT) (7): the coding system published by the American Medical Association, used for coding outpatient procedures and services performed by health care providers.

custodial care (16): care provided in an institution or home that covers daily needs, such as eating and dressing, but not medical care.

cystourethroscopy (7): insertion of an endoscope through the urethra to visualize the urinary bladder.

day sheet (4): chronological summary of all the practice's financial transactions posted to individual patient ledgers/accounts on a specific day.

death of the worker claims (17): death benefits are computed according to the earning capacity of the worker at the time of injury; benefits are paid to the workers' dependents.

deductible (2, 3, 4, 16): a specified amount of annual out-of-pocket expense for covered medical services that the insured must incur and pay each policy year to a health care provider before the insurance company will pay benefits.

Defense Enrollment Eligibility Reporting System (DEERS) (16): the TRICARE computerized listing of all TRICARE/CHAMPVA-eligible dependents. Verification of eligibility may be obtained by calling the HBA and asking for a DEERS check on a patient.

Demonstration Program for Retirees (16): tests a new program during a trial period, after which the program is further evaluated, modified, and/or abandoned.

demonstration project (16): tests and establishes feasibility of implementing a new program during a trial period, after which the program is evaluated, modified, and/or abandoned.

Department of Defense/National Cancer Institute (DoD/NCI) Cancer Prevention and Treatment Clinical Trials Demonstration Project (16): offers TRICARE beneficiaries the latest in cancer preventive care and treatment.

Department of Defense (DoD)/TRICARE (demo) Plan (14): an alternative to Medicare's original fee-for-service program that was created as part of the BBA 1997; eligible sponsors can select the DoD/TRICARE (demo) Plan; other BBA 1997 alternate plans include HMOS, MSAs, PPOs, PSOs, Private fee-for-service Plans, and Religious Fraternal Benefit Plans.

descriptive qualifiers (CPT) (7): words in the middle of a clause and located after the semicolon (may or may not be enclosed in parentheses) that further describes a word.

detailed examination (7): an extended physical examination of the involved body systems and related organs.

detailed history (7): a CPT evaluation and management service requiring a documented patient history that includes the chief complaint; an extended discussion of the present illness; a review of the involved body systems plus limited number of other systems, the pertinent past, family, and/or social histories that are related to the patient's problem.

diagnosis reference numbers (11): the item numbers 1 through 4 that are preprinted in Block 21 of the HCFA-1500 claim form.

Diagnosis Related Groups (DRG) (9, 16): inpatient reimbursement system based on a patient's age, gender, admitting diagnosis, ICD-9-CM diagnosis and procedure codes, and patient's condition upon discharge; each DRG is worth a specific amount of money and is multiplied by a DRG weight that is specific to a particular geographic region (e.g., if the DRG amount is $3,840 and the weight 3.000, reimbursement to the facility is calculated as $11,520 ($3,840 x 3.000). *See also* episode of care reimbursement.

dialysis (14): a process by which waste products are removed from the body.

direct-contract model (HMO) (3): an IPA HMO that contracts directly with the individual physicians rather than with an intermediary or association of physicians.

direct laryngoscopy (7): visual exam of larynx using a laryngoscope.

direct patient contact (7): face-to-face contact with a patient.

disability (14): an illness or injury that affects an individual's ability to continue in the job previously held.

disability insurance (2): reimbursement for lost income resulting from a temporary or permanent illness or injury.

discharge planning (3): arrangements made for the provision of health care services after a patient is discharged from the hospital (e.g. home health care).

Disease Index (6): the alphabetical listing of diseases and disorders in ICD-9-CM.

disease oriented panel (7): a series of laboratory tests conducted to investigate a specific organ or a disorder.

Disease Tabular List (6): the numerical listing of diseases found in ICD-9-CM. Also known as Volume I or Tabular List.

domiciliary care (7): medical services provided to patients who reside in custodial care facilities that do not have 24-hour nursing care.

drug formulary (3): a published list of approved drugs.

dual eligibles (15): individuals eligible for full Medicare coverage and some type of Medicaid benefit.

durable medical equipment (DME) (8, 13, 16): nondisposable medical devices.

durable medical equipment, prosthetic and orthotic supplies (DMEPOS) (8, 9): reusable medical equipment ordered by a physician for use by the patient in the home (e.g., walkers, wheelchairs, or hospital beds); DMEPOS is reimbursable under Medicare Part B.

durable medical equipment, prosthetic, and orthotic supplies (DMEPOS) dealers (8): suppliers of DMEPOS that submit claims for reimbursement to one of four DMERCs (durable medical equipment regional carriers).

Durable Medical Equipment Regional Carrier (DMERC) (8, 14): the regional fiscal agent that processes Medicare claims for durable medical equipment.

E codes (6): ICD-9 codes for the external causes of injury, poisoning, or other adverse reactions that explain how the injury occurred.

E&M codes (Evaluation and Management codes) (7): CPT codes that describe patient encounters with health care professionals for the purpose of evaluation and management of general health status.

E&M Documentation Guidelines (9): developed with the assistance of the American Medical Association and released by HCFA; specify documentation elements needed to justify CPT Evaluation and Management code selection.

Early and Periodic Screening Diagnostic and Treatment Services (EPSDT) (15): a Medicaid program to uncover and treat chronic physical and/or mental disorders in beneficiaries under the age of 21.

electronic claim (5): replaces the paper claim submitted to third-party payers, resulting in faster claim processing and payment to providers.

electronic claims processing (1): electronic transmission (e.g., modem) of health care claims to third-party payers, which shortens the provider's reimbursement cycle, reduces administrative and clerical costs, and eliminates postage.

electronic data interchange (EDI) (1, 2, 5): the process of electronically transferring data (e.g., health insurance claim) from one location to another using a standardized format (e.g., ANSI ASC X12N 837).

electronic explanation of benefits (5): electronic transmission of remittance advice (details reimbursement to provider as a result of electronic claims processing) in one of two forms: ANSI ASC X12 835 Health Care Claim Payment/Advice Transaction or HCFA Part B National Standard Format for Electronic Remittance Advice (ERN).

electronic mail (11): more commonly called *e-mail*, the electronic transmission of information transferred from one party to another through the Internet.

electronic media claim (EMC) (5, 11): a claim that is transferred electronically from health care providers' offices to insurance carriers.

electronic transaction standards (2): implemented as part of HIPAA, national standards for electronic health care transactions will encourage electronic commerce and simplify the processes involved; a national standard for electronic claims and other transactions (e.g., electronic EOBs) will allow health care providers to submit the same transaction to any third-party payer in the U. S. and the payer must accept it.

eligible amount (4): *see* allowed charge.

emergency (16): sudden and unexpected onset of a medical condition that is life threatening.

emergency department services (7): medical services provided in an organized hospital-based emergency room facility that is open 24 hours a day for the provision of unscheduled, episodic services to patients requiring immediate medical attention.

Employee Retirement Income Security Act of 1974 (ERISA) (3): federal legislation that establishes requirements for group life and health care plans, permits large employers to self-insure, and exempts large employers from taxes on insurance premiums.

employer self-insured programs (17): programs whereby employers with sufficient capital insure their own employees against loss of medical expenses and/or wages without contracting with a commercial carrier for coverage.

Employer-Sponsored Retirement Plan (14): a health insurance conversion plan offered to employees of certain companies at the time of their retirement. These plans are intended to complement the retiree's Medicare coverage, and are not regulated by the federal government.

employer tax identification number (EIN) (11): the federal tax number assigned to all employers for the purpose of reporting and depositing of federal tax and Social Security money withheld from the employee salaries. The EIN is also used as the billing entity identifier in Block 25 on the HCFA-1500 claim form.

encounter form (4): this is the financial record source document used by health care providers and other personnel to record the patient's treated diagnoses and services rendered to the patient. Also known as the charge slip, routing form or superbill.

encrypt (5): conversion of information to a secure language format for data transmission purposes.

endoscopic guide-wire dilation (7): after passage of a guide-wire through an endoscope, the endoscope is removed and dilators are inserted to dilate a constricted area.

end-stage renal disease (ESRD) (14): a chronic kidney disorder that requires long-term hemodialysis or kidney transplantation because the patient's filtration system in the kidneys has been destroyed. Workers who have paid into the Social Security/Medicare Fund and their dependents with ESRD who meet specific ESRD requirements are covered by Medicare.

enrollees (3): employees and dependents who join a managed care plan.

enteral therapy (8): also called enteral tube feeding; feeding provided to a patient through a tube passed through the alimentary canal (from nasal passage into stomach or duodenum), or by a gastrostomy or jejunostomy tube.

episode of care (9): hospital services provided and limited by the admission and discharge date for that hospitalization.

episode of care reimbursement (2): a payment method in which the health care provider receives one lump sum for all services rendered to the patient for a specific illness or injury.

eponym (6): diseases, disorders, and syndromes that are identified by the name of a person who conducted an early, detailed study on a topic, the name of a patient, or a location name.

errata (6): published document that contains corrections for errors in the coding manual.

essential modifiers (6): subterms listed below the main term and indented two spaces, located in the alphabetical index of ICD-9-CM.

established patient (4, 7): according to CPT, one who has received professional services from the physician or another physician of the same specialty who belongs to the same group practice, within the past three years.

ethics (1): rules or standards governing the conduct of members of a profession.

evaluation and management (E&M) section (7): a CPT classification of services covering patient encounters with physicians for the purpose of evaluating and managing the patient's health status.

excess income (15): the difference between an individual's income and the amount allowed for Medicaid eligibility.

excludes (6): note used in the ICD-9-CM Tabular List (Volume I) to indicate that the coder should look elsewhere for the proper code number.

exclusive provider organization (EPO) (3, 13): a closed-panel PPO plan where enrollees receive no benefits if they opt to receive care from a provider who is not in the EPO.

expanded problem focused examination (7): a physical examination limited to the affected body systems and related organ system(s).

expanded problem focused history (7): a CPT evaluation and management service requiring a documented patient history that includes the chief complaint, a brief discussion of the present illness and review of the pertinent body system.

explanation of benefits (EOB) form (4): an insurance report accompanying all claim payments which explains how the insurance company adjudicated a claim.

Explanation of Medicare Benefits (EOMB) (5, 14): a notice sent to the patient and provider after a Part B claim for services is filed under the Original Medicare Plan. This notice explains what the provider is billed for, the approved amount, how much Medicare paid, and what the patient must pay. The EOMB is being replaced by the Medicare Summary Notice (MSN), which summarizes all services over a certain period of time, generally monthly. This can also be processed electronically.

extent of examination (7): an assessment of the patient's organ and body systems on physical examination.

extent of history (7): a CPT evaluation and management service requiring a documented patient history that includes the chief complaint; an extended discussion of the present illness; a review of the involved body systems plus limited number of other systems, the pertinent past, family, and/or social histories that are related to the patient's problem.

extra coverage plan (14): specialized insurance plans which cover specific diagnoses or which fall into the special hospital indemnity class.

face-to-face time (7): time the provider spends with the patient and/or family during an office visit.

false claim (9): refers to the Federal False Claims Amendments Act of 1986.

Federal Employee Health Benefits Program (FEHBP) (13, 16): a program administered by the federal office of Personnel Management to provide medical insurance for federal employees as authorized under the Federal Employee Health Benefits law.

Federal Employee Health Benefits Program (FEHBP) Demonstration Program for Retirees (16): 1999 Defense Authorization Act three-year demonstration project (January 1, 2000 through December 31, 2002) that allows up to 66,000 Medicare-eligible uniformed services retirees and their families in selected areas to enroll in the Federal Employees Health Benefits Program (FEHBP)—the same program available to federal civilian employees and retirees; enrollees select from FEHBP plans in their area and pay the required premium; the beneficiary pays 28% of the total premium, and the Department of Defense pays 72%.

Federal Employee Program (FEP) (13): the BC/BS Federal Employee Plan. One of the many nationwide health benefit plans available to employees of the federal government. *See* Federal Employee Health Benefit Program.

Federal Employment Compensation Act (FECA) (17): federal legislation that requires workers' compensation coverage for nonmilitary federal employees.

Federal Employment Liability Act (FELA) (17): federal legislation that mandates liability for employee injuries by railroads engaged in interstate commerce.

Federal False Claims Act (5): law passed during the Civil War to regulate fraud by military contractors selling supplies and equipment to the Union Army.

Federal Health Maintenance Organization Assistance Act of 1973 (HMO Act of 1973) (3): legislation that provides grants and loans; defines a federally qualified HMO, and requires most employers with more than 25 employees to offer HMO coverage.

Federal Medical Assistance Percentage (FMAP) (15): the portion of the Medicaid program paid by the federal government.

Federal Medical Care Recovery Act of 1970 (16): law that requires the federal government to pursue repayment of medical expenses reimbursed by TRICARE when third-party liability insurance is available or the injured party successfully sues a third party for damages.

federal poverty level (FPL) (15): poverty guidelines issued each year in the *Federal Register* by the Department of Health and Human Services (HHS) and used to determine financial eligibility for certain federal programs.

***Federal Register* (5, 9):** daily federal publication that contains a record of proposed and final rules from many federal agencies.

federally qualified HMO (3): health care providers certified to offer services to enrollees.

fee-for-service (3, 7): a method whereby the physician or other health care provider bills for each visit or service rendered rather than on an all-inclusive or prepaid fee basis.

fee-for-service plan (2): a contract where the carrier allows the patient complete freedom of the choice of health care providers. The reimbursement is made either according to a set fee or agreed upon percentage of the charge for each covered health care service rendered to a plan enrollee.

fee-for-service reimbursement (2): the longstanding traditional form of reimbursement in which the individual service performed is itemized, priced, and charged to the patient's account. Payment is made by the patient or a third-party payer.

fee-for-service with utilization (2): a form of the traditional fee-for-service reimbursement method that adds some form of prospective and/or retrospective review of the provider's treatment and discharge planning to the individual itemization and pricing of each service.

fee schedule (2, 9): the listing in an insurance policy stating the maximum dollar amount the insurance company will allow for specific medical procedures performed on a patient. (Also called a schedule of benefits.)

fee ticket (4): *see* encounter form.

Final Rule: Standards for Electronic Transactions (6): implements requirements of the Administrative Simplification provisions of HIPAA.

first party (5): the person designated in a contract to receive the contracted service.

First Report of Injury (17): a form filed by the health care provider when a patient initially seeks treatment for a work-related injury or disorder.

fiscal agent: *see* fiscal intermediary.

fiscal intermediary (FI) (5, 14, 16): an insurance company selected by competitive bidding to process claims payments for a government insurance program.

fiscal year (16): any 12-month period used by government or a business entity for its annual financial accounting cycle.

for-profit corporation (13): enterprises that pay taxes on profits generated by the corporate's for-profit enterprises and pay dividends to shareholders on the after-tax profits.

fourth- and fifth-digit code number (6): CPT codes that describe services and procedures.

fragmented surgery (7): the breaking down of an integrated major surgical package into its various components for the purpose of differential coding and obtaining higher reimbursement. (Also called unbundling.)

fraud (5, 9): deliberate misrepresentation of facts.

full disability: classification of disability where the patient has lost full capacity to earn a living.

gag clause (3): Medicare and some state managed care contract requirement that prevents providers from discussing all treatment options with patients.

gatekeeper (2, 3): primary physician or other health care professional assigned by the insurer to review the medical management of plan enrollees.

General Enrollment Period (GEP) (14): the period of time during which all who turn 65 in a given year are eligible to enroll in Medicare.

geographic adjustment factor (GAF) (14): used to address regional differences in the cost of furnishing health care services, the GAF is designed to account for geographic variations in the costs of practicing medicine and obtaining malpractice insurance.

geographic practice cost index (GPCI) (9): payment adjustments based on the cost of operating a medical practice (e.g., work and practice expenses).

global service (9): also called global fee, global surgery, or surgical package; as defined by Medicare, a 0-, 10-, or 90-day period during which all services related to a procedure are covered including, but not limited to, suture removal, postoperative office visits, and dressing changes. Office visits for services *not* related to a procedure are reported using modifier –79 (procedure or service is unrelated to the original service); e.g., complications of surgery.

global surgery (7): a Medicare billing term that requires an all-inclusive fee for the following services: preoperative services performed by the surgeon within 24 hours of surgery, all interoperative procedures, treatment of surgical complications not requiring a return to the operating room, and 90 days of surgery-related postoperative care.

global surgical fee (2): the fee for total care of a surgical case including all pre/postoperative care. This applies to surgical cases listed in the CPT code book which do not have an asterisk (*) at the end of the code number.

Glossary of Mental Disorders (ICD-9-CM) (6): Appendix B of ICD-9-CM that contains a list of mental disorders and definitions.

Government-Wide Service Benefit Plan (13): a plan in which government employees elect to enroll.

group health insurance (4): health care coverage available through employers and other organizations (e.g., labor unions, rural and consumer health cooperatives); employers usually pay part, or all, of premium costs.

group model (HMO) (3): an HMO that contracts with an already existing multispecialty group practice to perform all services for the HMO. In some cases the providers contract to work exclusively for the HMO and treat patients within the plan's facilities. In other cases, they are free to accept private, non-HMO patients and see both categories of patients in their private offices.

group practice (2): three or more health care providers joined to provide health care who jointly use equipment, supplies, personnel, and divide income by a prearranged formula.

group practice identification number (GRP#) (11): assigned by HCFA or the insurance carrier.

group practice without walls (GPWW) (3): a managed care contract that allows physicians to maintain their own offices and share services.

guardian (5): person who has legal responsibility for a minor child or an incompetent adult.

guest membership (13): allows subscribers and their dependents to become a "guest member" of another local BCBS PPO for a given period of time.

guidelines (CPT) (7): define terms and clarify the assignment of codes for procedures and services in a particular section of CPT.

HCFA-1500 (1-90) claim form (2, 4, 6): the standard insurance form used to report outpatient services to insurance carriers.

HCFA Common Procedure Coding System (8, 9): *see* HCPCS.

HCFA ICD-9-CM Coding Guidelines (6): companion document developed for use with ICD-9-CM coding manuals and approved by the cooperating parties for ICD-9-CM (AHA, AHIMA, HCFA, and HCHS); guidelines assist in coding and reporting diagnoses and procedures where the ICD-9-CM manual does not provide direction.

HCFA outpatient coding guidelines (6): guidelines developed by HCFA that address the assignment of ICD-9-CM codes for services and procedures provided in outpatient departments and provider offices.

HCFA Place of Service codes (13): HCFA's official listing of places of service and corresponding codes for reporting on the HCFA-1500 claim form.

HCFA's Office of Managed Care (3): the HCFA component responsible for facilitating innovation and competition among Medicare managed care plans.

HCPCS (1, 6, 7): the HCFA Common Procedural Coding System used for reporting outpatient health care services provided to Medicare beneficiaries. This coding system is arranged in three levels. Level I contains the CPT codes; level II contains HCFA-developed alphanumeric codes for reporting physician and nonphysician services not included in CPT; level III contains Medicare carrier codes covering Medicare reimbursement issues.

Health Affairs (HA) (16): the Office of the Assistant Secretary of Defense for Health Affairs; is responsible for military readiness and peacetime health care.

health care (2): the performance of diagnostic, therapeutic, and preventive services and procedures by health care providers to persons who are sick, injured, or concerned about their health status.

Health Care Financing Administration (HCFA) (1, 2, 6): a federal administrative agency charged with primary responsibility for Medicare and the federal portion of the Medicaid programs.

Health Care Financing Administration Common Procedure Coding System (2, 7): *see* HCPCS.

health care finder (HCF) (16): a referral program to encourage the use of civilian TRICARE participating providers by TRICARE patients.

health care fraud (2): knowingly and willfully executing, or attempting to execute, a plan to 1) defraud any health care benefit program; or 2) obtain, by false or fraudulent pretenses, representations, or promises, any of the money or property owned by, or under the custody or control of, a health care benefit program.

health care provider (1): physician or other supplier of medical services or equipment.

health care specialist (4): a health care provider who is not a primary care physician.

health insurance (2): a contract between the policyholder and an insurance carrier or government program to reimburse the policyholder for all or a portion of the cost of medically necessary treatment or preventive care rendered by health care professionals.

health insurance claim (1): demand for payment of covered medical expenses that is sent to a third-party payer.

Health Insurance Portability and Accountability Act (HIPAA) (2, 3, 5): legislation passed by Congress in the summer of 1996 that contains provisions for insured persons enrolled in employer-sponsored insurance programs to retain the right to new health insurance when they change jobs without regard to their current health status; a prohibition on the use of genetic testing information to deny health insurance coverage; and strengthens existing fraud, abuse and confidentiality issues. This law is also known as the Kennedy-Kassebaum bill or the Kassebaum-Kennedy bill.

health maintenance organization (HMO) (2, 3, 13, 14): a prepaid, managed care, health care provider group practice with responsibility for providing health care services for a fixed fee to subscribers in a given geographical area.

Health Personnel Shortage Area (HPSA) (8): physicians providing services in established rural HPSAs add a modifier to CPT codes submitted on claims.

Health Plan Employer Data and Information Set (HEDIS) (3): federal legislation that created standards to assess managed care systems using data elements that are collected, evaluated, and published to compare the performance of managed health care plans.

HEDIS (3,): *see* Health Plan Employer Data and Information Set.

hemodialysis (14): a process that passes the patient's blood through an artificial kidney machine to remove waste products, and the cleansed blood is returned to the patient.

history (7): describes the patient's present illness from the onset of symptoms to the present.

hold harmless clause (1): an insurance contract provision that requires preauthorization for certain services and/or procedures; if the service/procedure is performed without preauthorization, the health care provider may be unable to collect fees from the patient.

home plan (13): a BC/BS term used in the BlueCard Program literature when discussing the provider's local plan.

home services (7): services provided in a private residence.

hospice (14): *see* hospice care.

hospice care (16): a style of care, sometimes called *palliative care*, which is the active total care of patients whose disease is not responsive to curative treatment; according to the World Health Organization, hospice care affirms life and regards dying as a normal purpose, neither hastens nor postpones death, provides relief from pain and other distressing symptoms, integrates the psychological and spiritual aspects of patient care, offers a support system to help patients live as actively as possible until death, and offers a support system to help the family cope during the patient's illness and in bereavement.

hospital inpatient (7): someone who is admitted and discharged and who has a length of stay of one or more days.

hospital observation service (7): a CPT outpatient E&M service, provided by the attending physician, for patients who are "admitted for observation."

host plan (13): a BC/BS term used in the BlueCard Program literature when discussing the patient's out-of-area plan.

iatrogenic illness (6): conditions that result from medical intervention.

ICD-9 (6): International Classification of Diseases, 9th Revision, published by the World Health Organization.

ICD-9-CM (1, 6): an extension of the World Health Organization's ICD-9 coding system developed for use in the United States for reporting diseases and indexing hospital records to the U.S. Public Health Service and HCFA.

identifier (5): a series of numerical or alphanumerical characters assigned to providers, health plans, employers, and patients.

"incident to" (9): services that must be performed in a physician's office.

includes (6): notes in ICD-9-CM that clarify a main disorder.

indented parenthetical note (7): immediately follows a CPT code number description or an indented code description to provide special instructions.

independent practice association (IPA) (3): a group of individual health care providers who join together to provide prepaid health care to individuals or groups who purchase coverage. This is a closed-panel HMO that has no common facilities.

Index to Diseases (Volume 2) (ICD-9-CM) (6): an alphabetical index to diseases and injuries, along with a table of drugs and chemicals, and an index to external causes of injury and poisoning.

indexing (6): cataloging diseases and procedures by code number.

indirect laryngoscopy (7): visual exam of larynx using a mirror.

individual case management (16): allows TRICARE-eligible enrollees who have extraordinary medical or psychological disorders to receive health care benefits that would normally be limited or not covered.

Individual Practice Association (IPA) (3): *see* independent practice association.

inferred words (7): CPT terms that save space when subterms are referenced.

Initial Enrollment Period (IEP) (14): the seven-month waiting period after an individual applies for Medicare Part A or B.

initial hospital care (7): the first hospital inpatient encounter the admitting physician has with the patient for each admission.

injury (6): traumatic wound or some other damage to an organ.

in-network provider (4): *see* participating provider.

inpatient (6): a person who is admitted to the hospital for treatment with the expectation that the patient will remain in the hospital for a period of 24 hours or more. The inpatient admission status is stipulated by the admitting physician.

inpatient discharge service (7): a CPT code that includes final examination of the patient, discussion with the patient and/or caregiver about the hospitalization, instructions for continuing care, and preparation of discharge records.

inpatient medical case (11): a patient who is admitted to the hospital for medical care and billed on a fee-for-service basis.

instructional notes (7): CPT notes that appear throughout the book in the following formats: blocked/unindented, indented/parenthetical and as parenthetical statements within the five-digit code description.

insurance (2): protection against risk, loss, or ruin by a contract in which an insurer or underwriter guarantees in return for the payment of a premium to pay a sum of money to the insured in the event of some contingency such as death, accident, or illness.

insured (4): a policyholder; the subscriber; the person who contracts with an insurance company for insurance coverage.

integrated delivery system (3): a health care organization of affiliated provider sites combined under a single ownership that offers the full spectrum of managed health care.

integrated provider organization (IPO) (3): manages the delivery of health care services offered by hospitals, physicians, and other organizations.

International Classification of Diseases **(ICD) (6):** *see* ICD-9.

International Classification of Diseases, 9th Revision, Clinical Modification **(ICD-9-CM) (2, 5):** the numerical coding system used by all health care providers in the United States to classify and report diagnoses, external causes of injury and other medically justifiable reasons for seeking health care.

itemized pricing (7): *see* unbundling.

Joint Commission on Accreditation of Healthcare Organizations (JCAHO) (3): an organization that accredits hospitals, nursing homes, and other health care facilities.

June 2000 DGs (draft version) (7): *see* 2000 Evaluation and Management Documentation Guidelines.

key components (CPT) (7): extent of history, extent of examination, and complexity of medical decision making that are considered when assigning CPT E&M codes.

kidney transplantation (14): harvesting of a healthy kidney from a donor and implanting it into the patient with a lack of kidney function.

KISS (11): Keep It Short and Simple.

KISS letter (11): a medical report written in plain English rather than technical terms that describes an unusual procedure, special operation, or a patient's medical condition that warrants performing surgery in a site different from the HCFA-stipulated surgical site.

laboratory panel (CPT) (7): *see* disease oriented panel.

late effect (6): an adverse residual effect (sequela) of a previous illness, injury, or surgery.

layered closure (7): an intermediate repair or closure classified in CPT.

Lead Agent (LA) (TRICARE) (16): military treatment facilities selected to provide care to TRICARE enrollees.

legislation (3, 9): laws.

lesion (6): any discontinuity of the skin or an organ.

leukemia (14): an atypically progressive growth of abnormal white blood cells resulting in a form of cancer.

level of service (7): reflects the amount of work involved in providing health care to patients.

liability insurance (2): insurance which covers losses to a third-party caused by the insured; or by an object owned by the insured; or on the premises owned by the insured. Malpractice, auto, and homeowners insurance are all specific types of liability insurance.

lifetime reserve days (Medicare) (14): an additional 60 days of inpatient hospitalization that may be elected by the patient when the normal 90-day hospitalization stay per spell of illness has been exhausted. Each patient is allotted 60 additional days per life time.

limited license practitioner (LLP) (14): a health care professional who is licensed to perform specific medical services in an independent practice.

limiting charge (LC) (9, 14, 16): *see* limiting fee.

limiting fee (14): the maximum fee a nonparticipating provider may charge for a covered service.

> **Medicare:** nonparticipating health care providers' approved rate is 5% below the Medicare participating fee schedule. The nonparticipating provider is limited to charging a patient a maximum of 15% above the participating provider approved rate.

> **Federal Employee Health Benefit Program:** charges on claims for retired federal employees who are not eligible for Medicare are limited to the Medicare Fee Schedule.

> **TRICARE:** nonparticipating health care providers are limited to charging a patient no more than 15% above the TRICARE fee schedule for participating providers.

liquid assets (15): cash and property a person possesses that can immediately be converted to cash.

List of Three-Digit Categories (ICD-9-CM) (6): Appendix E of ICD-9-CM that contains a list of three-digit categories and descriptions.

listserv (5): a subscriber-based question and answer forum that is available through e-mail.

local codes (1): HCPCS Level 3 alphanumeric codes developed by local carriers that are scheduled for elimination;

providers will report CPT and HCPCS Level 2 (national) codes instead.

Local Medicare Carrier (LMC) (8, 9): fiscal intermediary (FI) that processes Medicare claims.

lock-in provision (14): a Medicare-HMO provision restricting payment for unauthorized nonemergency services provided by out-of-network providers to patients enrolled in risk-restricted plans.

Longshore and Harbor Workers' Compensation Act (LHWCA) (17): federal legislation that provides workers' compensation to specified employees of private maritime employers.

M codes (6): morphology of neoplasms (tissue type) codes in the ICD system used to gather statistical data on the occurrences of specific tumors on the general population. These codes should not appear on physicians' office insurance claims.

magnetic resonance imaging (MRI) (16): test that uses nuclear magnetic resonance technology to scan an image of the body's anatomy.

main term (6): bold-faced terms found in the alphabetical index of ICD-9-CM.

Major Medical (MM) coverage (13): a policy designed to cover some or all of the following outpatient medical services: durable medical equipment, prescription drugs, dental care services, and private duty nursing.

major surgery case (11): a CPT term referring to surgery procedures that do not have asterisks after the code number, and therefore are billed on a global service basis. *See* global service.

major surgical procedure (7): the surgery reimbursed at 100% by the insurance carrier.

major topic headings (ICD-9-CM) (6): subdivisions in ICD-9-CM that are printed in bold uppercase letters and followed by a range of codes enclosed in parentheses.

malignant (6): a tumor that is invasive (has spread to deeper tissue) and is capable of spreading to other, remote parts of the body.

managed care (3): patients receive care from a set group of doctors and providers. Usually they pay a copayment for each service.

managed care organization (MCO) (3, 9): a health insurance organization that adheres to the principles of strong dependence on selective contracting with health care providers, the use of primary care physicians or case managers as gatekeepers, prospective and retrospective utilization management, use of treatment guidelines for high cost chronic disorders, and an emphasis on preventive care, education, and patient compliance with treatment plans.

managed fee-for-service (2): adds prospective and retrospective review of the health care provider's treatment plan and/or discharge planning.

managed health care (3): *see* managed care.

management service organization (MSO) (3): organization that provides practice support to individual physician practices (an MSO is usually a hospital or a physician group practice that has the resources to coordinate and offer support).

mandates (3): laws.

mandatory categorically needy eligibility groups (15): categories of people whose income prohibits them from obtaining health insurance on their own (e.g., SSI recipients whose income prevents them from purchasing insurance).

Mandatory Second Surgical Opinion (SSO) (13): this is a managed care option that requires a second surgical opinion be obtained by the patient before they undergo elective, nonemergency surgical care.

manipulation of a fracture (7): reduction of a fracture.

manual daily accounts receivable journal (4): *see* day sheet.

Material Safety Data Sheets (MSDS) (17): all employers are required to obtain and retain the manufacturer's data sheets on all chemicals and hazardous substances used on site. They are also required by the OSHA Act of 1970 to give all employees training in the safe handling of these substances.

maximum allowed amount (4): *see* allowed charge.

Medicaid (2, 15): combined federal/state program designed to help people on welfare or medically indigent persons with medical expenses. (Also known as Medical Assistance Program.)

MediCal (15): title that the state of California gives to its Medicaid Program.

Medical Assistance Program (15): medical coverage provided by Medicaid/MediCal programs.

medical care (2): diagnostic and treatment measures provided by health care professionals to persons who are sick, injured, or concerned about their health status.

medical claims with no disability (17): workers' compensation classification for a minor injury/disorder where a worker is treated by a physician and is able to continue working or returns to work within a few days.

medical decision making (7): making a judgment about the complexity of establishing the diagnoses and the selection of treatment options.

medical emergency care rider (13): an insurance clause that covers immediate treatment sought and received for sudden, severe, and unexpected conditions which, if not treated, would place the patient's health in permanent jeopardy, or would lead to permanent impairment or dysfunction of an organ or body part.

medical foundation (3): nonprofit organization that contracts with and acquires clinical and business assets of physician practices.

medical necessity (6, 10): proving the need to perform a service or procedure based upon accepted standards of medical practice.

medical necessity denial (14): denial of otherwise covered services that were found to be not "reasonable and necessary."

medical savings account (MSA) (5): a tax-exempt savings account with a financial institution (e.g., bank, insurance company) that contains money to be used for qualified medical expenses; an MSA must be used in conjunction with a *high deductible health plan (HDHP)*, which has a higher annual deductible than typical health care plans and a maximum limit on annual out-of-pocket medical expenses.

medically indigent (15): *see* medically needy.

medically needy (MN) optional groups (15): includes those eligible for Medicaid under one of the mandatory or optional groups, except that their income and/or resources exceeds the eligibility level established by their state.

Medicare (2): a federal health insurance program for people 65 years of age or over and retired on Social Security, Railroad Retirement, or federal government retirement programs, individuals who have been legally disabled for more than 2 years, and persons with end-stage renal disease.

Medicare Bulletin (5): publication produced by a Medicare fiscal intermediary.

Medicare Carriers Manual (MCM) (8, 9): a HCFA manual containing Medicare carrier national coverage policies; Medicare carriers are requested to apply all statutory provisions, regulations, and national coverage policies during claims processing.

Medicare Fee Schedule (MFS) (9, 14): schedule of Medicare fees based on RBRVS factors. NonPARs are restricted to the limiting fees on this schedule.

Medicare-Medicaid Crossover (MCD) (14): a combination of the Medicare and Medicaid Programs that is available to Medicare-eligible persons with income below the federal poverty level.

Medicare MSA (14): authorized by the BBA 1997, a tax-exempt savings account with a financial institution (e.g. bank, insurance company) into which Medicare deposits money to be used for qualified medical expenses; a Medicare MSA must be used in conjunction with a *Medicare MSA Health Policy*, which has a higher annual deductible than typical health plans, and must have been designed to work as part of a Medicare MSA plan.

Medicare MSA Health Policy (14): a special health insurance policy that has a high deductible; together, the medicare MSA and the Medicare MSA Health Policy create the Medicare MSA Plan for a medicare beneficiary.

Medicare Part A (14): benefits covering inpatient hospital and skilled nursing facility services, hospice care, home health care, and blood transfusions.

Medicare Part B (14): benefits covering outpatient hospital and health care provider services.

Medicare private contract (14): agreement between physician and beneficiary in which Medicare payments for services are relinquished and the patient accepts responsibility for payment of all charges.

Medicare Risk Program (3): created by Congress in 1992 as a way to increase choices in health care delivery systems and reduce utilization rates without affecting quality of care; HMOs assume responsibility for providing all Medicare-covered services to beneficiaries in return for a capitated payment (predetermined amount for each enrollee), and the HMO pays for all covered health care services used by Medicare enrollees; thus, the HMO accepts the risk that it will be able to provide health services within the capitated amount.

Medicare Medical Savings Account (MSA) plan (14): BBA of 1997 options that allow for private, fee-for-service plans; provider sponsored organizations and Medicare Savings Accounts.

Medicare Secondary-Payer (MSP) (14): an insurance plan that is primary to Medicare.

Medicare subvention (16): *see* TRICARE Senior Prime.

Medicare Summary Notice (MSN) (9, 14): *see* Explanation of Medicare Benefits (EOMB).

Medicare Supplemental Plan (13, 14): an insurance plan that covers the Medicare patient's deductible and copayment obligations. These policies may be purchased individually (Medigap policies) or premiums may be paid through an employer-sponsored program for retirees of the company.

Medicare+Choice: a new Medicare program that allows for more choices among Medicare health plans (all who have Medicare Parts A and B, except those with end-stage renal disease, are eligible).

Medigap policy (14): an individual plan covering the patient's Medicare deductible and copayment obligations that fulfills the federal government standards for Medicare supplemental insurance.

Medi/Medi claim (14): a combined Medicare and Medicaid claim.

member (13): *see* subscriber.

member hospital (13): hospital that has signed a contract with a medical plan to provide special rates.

Merchant Marine Act (Jones Act) (17): provides seamen with protection from employer negligence.

metastasize (6): spread of cancer from the primary site to a second site (regional or distant).

metastatic (6): describes the spread of cancer from a primary to secondary site. *see also* metastasis (noun)

Military Health Services System (MHSS) (16): health care system of the U. S. uniformed services and includes military treatment facilities and various programs in the civilian health care market.

military treatment facility (MTF) (16): a clinic and/or hospital located on a United States military base.

minor surgery case (11): *see* minor surgical procedure.

minor surgical procedure (7): defined in the CPT as a relatively small surgical service too variable to be billed as an all-inclusive surgical package and identified with an asterisk following the code number.

modifier (5, 6, 7): *see* code modifier.

morbidity (6): disease (*note:* mortality means death).

morphology (6): structure, form, and tissue type of a neoplasm.

Morphology of Neoplasms (6): ICD-9-CM classifies *morphology of neoplasms* according to histologic (tissue) type and behavior (e.g., benign, malignant) of the neoplasm.

mortality (6): number of deaths in a population, as in *mortality rate*; condition of being mortal, or being subject to death.

most favored nation (MFN) (9): an entity that receives the most beneficial contract or price available to anyone. This status would be attributed to Medicare if legislation is passed that requires providers to adjust Medicare billings to the lowest amount they would be willing to accept from one of their contracted managed care plans; as a result, Medicare payments would be reduced.

multiple myeloma (14): malignant disease of bone and bone marrow.

multiple surgical procedures (7): two or more surgeries performed on a patient during the same operative session.

National Account (13): a health insurance contract that covers company employees who are located in more than one geographic area.

National Center for Health Statistics (NCHS) (6): the organization that gathers information on diseases and injuries and determines the future changes in federally sponsored insurance programs.

National Codes (1): HCPCS Level 2 alphanumeric codes are created by HCFA for use by ambulatory care settings (e.g., physician offices) to report medical equipment, injectable drugs, and other services not classified by CPT.

National Committee for Quality Assurance (NCQA) (3): a nonprofit organization that evaluates and accredits HMOs according to a set of standards designed to measure the HMO's ability to deliver good health care.

national conversion factor (CF) (14): a multiplier that transforms relative values adjusted by *geographic practice cost indices* (GCPI) into payment amounts for physician services.

National Correct Coding Initiative (CCI) (2, 9): a program developed by HCFA to correct procedural coding billing errors on government claims.

national health plan ID (PlanID) (2, 5, 14): identifiers that will eventually be assigned to third-party payers by HCFA, under HIPPA provisions.

National Individual Identifier (5): *see* patient identifier.

National Mail Order Pharmacy (NMOP) (16): program allows enrollees to receive a 90-day supply on non-narcotic medications or a 30-day supply of narcotic medications, mailed to the enrollee's home address.

national provider identifier (NPI) (2, 5, 11, 14): a HCFA-assigned health care provider number that is to be used on all claim forms to aid in the detection and tracking of fraudulent and abusive claims submissions.

national standard employer identifier number (EIN) (2, 5): unique identification number, assigned by the Internal Revenue Service to employers for reporting health care transactions (e.g., HCFA-1500 claim form).

nationwide account (13): an insurance contract for employers that have workers based in more than one region of the country, where the benefits are the same throughout the country.

nature of the presenting problem (CPT) (7): disease, condition, illness, injury, symptom, sign, finding, complaint, or other reason for encounter, with or without a diagnosis being established at the time of the encounter.

NEC (6): in ICD-9-CM, NEC is an index convention that means not elsewhere classifiable; NEC indicates that the code assignment for a condition is vague. Codes designated by the NEC abbreviation are to be used only when the coder lacks information necessary to code the diagnosis to a more specific category, subcategory or subclassification.

neonatal intensive care (7): services provided to critically ill newborns.

neoplasm (6): new growth.

network model (HMO) (3): health care services provided to subscribers by two or more physician multispecialty group practices.

newborn care (7): the initial and subsequent examination of neonates in a hospital or other birthing facility setting.

new patient (as used in CPT coding) (4, 7): a person who has not received any professional service from the health care provider or another provider of the same specialty in the same group practice within the last 36 months.

new patient intake interview (4): an interview between the office staff and a prospective patient to gather preliminary data to ensure that the patient has called the appropriate health care office for an appointment and check on the patient's insurance eligibility and benefit status before giving the patient an initial appointment.

nonavailability statement (NAS) (16): preauthorization for nonemergency civilian health care issued by the base commander when medical care required for a TRICARE-eligible person is not available at a government medical treatment facility within the patient's catchment area.

noncovered procedure (4): *see* uncovered procedure.

nonessential modifiers (6): subterms that follow the main term and are enclosed in parentheses, located in the alphabetical index of ICD-9-CM.

nonparticipating limited fee (2): a stipulation in the Medicare and CHAMPUS/TRICARE laws that forbids the nonparticipating health care provider to charge a patient more than 15 percent above the program's approved fee.

nonparticipating provider (nonPAR) (4, 9, 13, 14): a health care provider that has not signed a participating provider contract with an insurance carrier and has the right to bill the patient for the difference between the amount charged for a service and the insurance company's determined allowed fee. (Also known as an out-of-network provider.)

nonphysician provider (8): caregiver other than a physician; e.g., dentist, physical therapist, speech therapist, etc.

nonprofit corporation (13): *see* not-for-profit corporation.

NOS (6): in ICD-9-CM, NOS is a Tabular List convention that means not otherwise specified; the provider's diagnostic statement is not specific and therefore the code selected is unspecified.

not medically necessary service (4): *see* uncovered benefit.

Nurse Advisor (16): professional staff member available to answer questions 24 hours/day, 7 days/week; provides advice and assistance regarding treatment alternatives and discusses treatment options.

nurse practitioner (NP) (9): state licensed health care professional whose scope of practice is determined by state law.

nursing facility services (NFS) (7): services performed in skilled-care, intermediate-care, or long-term care facilities, as well as nonpsychotherapeutic visits to patients in a residential psychiatric treatment facility.

objective (10): an element of SOAP notes that documents findings observed by the provider (e.g., physical exam).

observation care discharge (7): a CPT E&M service used when a patient is discharged to home or another institution from observation status in the hospital.

observation or inpatient care services (7): CPT E&M category that contains codes for reporting observation or inpatient care services to third-party payers for patients who are admitted and discharged from observation or inpatient care on the same day.

observation services (7): furnished in a hospital outpatient setting to determine whether further treatment or inpatient admission is needed.

Occupational Safety and Health Administration (OSHA) Act of 1970 (17): legislation designed to protect all employees against injuries from occupational hazards in the workplace. It has special significance for health care workers because any worker who might come into contact with human blood and infectious materials must be given specific training in the handling of infectious materials and the strict use of standard precautions to avoid contamination. Each person who might have exposure to infectious material must be given hepatitis B vaccinations. The law also stipulates that comprehensive records must be kept for 20 years of all vaccinations given and any accidental exposure incidents such as needle sticks. *See* Material Safety Data Sheets.

Office of Inspector General (OIG) (5): provides policy direction and conducts, supervises, and coordinates all audits, investigations, and other activities in the U.S. Department of the Interior designed to promote economy and efficiency or prevent and detect fraud, waste and abuse.

Office of Personnel Management (OPM) (13): the federal government's human resources agency.

Olmstead v. L.C. (15): 1999 Supreme Court decision that challenged federal, state, and local governments to develop more accessible services for individuals with disabilities.

Omnibus Budget Reconciliation Act of 1981 (OBRA) (3): federal legislation that expanded Medicare and Medicaid programs.

on-the-job injury (17): injury sustained by an employee while working within the scope of his or her job description or while performing a service required by the employer. The worker does not have to be on company property at the time of the injury to qualify for Workers' Compensation.

open reduction with internal fixation (ORIF) (7): surgical manipulation of a fracture with placement of a prosthetic device (e.g., pin).

open treatment of fracture (7): a surgical procedure required to properly reduce a fracture (open or closed).

open treatment of closed fracture (7): an incision is made over the fracture and some type of fixation device is applied.

operative report (10): also called op notes; documentation of a surgical procedure by the responsible physician (e.g., surgeon) that is included in the patient record.

optical character reader (OCR) (11): equipment that scans specially prepared forms (e.g., HCFA-1500 completed according to HCFA's OCR guidelines).

optional categorically related needy eligibility groups (15): Medicaid coverage to groups that fall into defined categories but whose eligibility criteria are more liberally defined.

ordering physician (14): the doctor who is responsible for coordinating the patient's care and for ordering appropriate diagnostic tests (e.g., lab, x-ray, and so on) and arranging for therapeutic interventions (e.g., surgery, evaluation by a specialist, and so on).

organ panel (7): *see* disease oriented panel.

Original Medicare Plan (14): also known as "fee-for-service" and "traditional pay-per-visit" where beneficiaries pay a fee for each health care service or procedure received.

OSHA Act of 1970 (17): *see* Occupational Safety and Health Administration (OSHA) Act of 1970.

Other Health Insurance (OHI) (16): an insurance policy that is considered primary to TRICARE.

out-of-network provider (4): *see* nonparticipating provider.

outpatient (6): a person who falls into one of the following classifications depending on where the encounter took place: 1) health care provider's office, 2) hospital clinic, emergency room or same day surgery unit, 3) admitted to a hospital for observation.

Outpatient Pretreatment Authorization Plan (OPAP) (13): a BC/BS managed care program requiring preauthorization of outpatient physical, occupational and speech therapy service that requires the filing of periodic treatment forms.

oversight (3): supervising committee of physicians who analyze accreditation findings.

package concept (7): CPT concept whereby a code includes the procedure, certain supplies, preoperative anesthesia, and so on.

palliative care (16): relief, such as pain medication, with no attempt to prolong life.

PAR provider (4): *see* participating provider.

parenteral therapy (8): medication/feeding route other than through the alimentary canal, such as intravenous (IV), subcutaneous, intramuscular (IM), or mucosal.

intravenous (IV)—within or into a vein.

subcutaneous—beneath the skin; also called hypodermic.

intramuscular (IM)—within or into a muscle.

mucosal—refers to mucous membranes (moist tissue layer that lines hollow organs and body cavities); e.g., the medicine from nitroglycerin tablets that are placed sublingually (below the tongue) is absorbed mucosally.

parenthetical statements within code description (7): in CPT, these statements are nonessential modifiers and do not need to be present in the provider's statement.

partial disability (17): disability cases where the patient has permanently lost a specific percentage of his or her earning capacity.

partial hospitalization (16): the patient spends a minimum of three hours on-site at the treatment facility, five days per week, including weekends and/or evenings, then goes home overnight (e.g., substance abuse centers).

participating provider (PAR) (4, 13, 14): a health care provider who has entered into a contract with the government or an insurance company to provide medical services to enrolled subscribers. In the contract, it is agreed that the health care provider will accept the insurance company's approved fee for each medical service and will bill the subscriber for only the deductible subscriber copayments, and any uncovered services as stated in the subscriber's policy. (Also known as an in-network provider.)

patient account record (4): a permanent record of all financial transactions between the patient and the practice. All charges, personal payments, and third-party payments are posted to the patient's individual account record.

patient base (1): number of patients who receive health care services from a practice.

patient-health care provider contract (5): a contract between the patient or their guardian and the health care provider for performance of medical services in exchange for the patient's/guardian's agreement to promptly pay that physician's usual fee for the services performed.

patient identifier (5): HIPAA provisions called for the assignment of patient identifiers, an issue that is presently on hold pending privacy legislation.

patient ledger (4): *see* patient account record.

payer of last resort (15): an insurance carrier that is billed only if the patient has no other medical benefits, or if the patient's other insurers deny responsibility for some or all payment or have lower payment schedules for benefits covered by the payer of last resort.

per capita (2): Latin phrase meaning *per person*.

per capita payments (2): *see* capitation.

percutaneous skeletal fixation (7): surgical procedure involving implantation of a skeletal prosthesis (e.g., wire) through the skin.

performance measures (7): criteria on which the assessment of providers and facilities is based.

peritoneal dialysis (14): the passage of waste products from the patient's body through the peritoneal membrane into the peritoneal cavity, where a solution is introduced and periodically removed.

permanent disability (17): a legal term referring to an injured employee's diminished capacity to return to the work force. The employee is not expected to be able to return to the job held before the illness or injury or to have any other form of employment.

Personal Responsibility and Work Opportunity Reconciliation Act of 1996 (15): implemented to halt open-ended federal entitlement programs for persons who qualified for other such programs.

Pharmacy Redesign Pilot Program (16): the equivalent of TRICARE Extra pharmacy benefits, which includes access to military treatment facility pharmacies, TRICARE retail network pharmacies, and the national mail order pharmacy program.

physical examination (7): medical examination performed by a health care provider to assess a patient's condition or health status.

physician assistant (PA) (9): state licensed health care professional whose scope of practice is determined by state law.

Physician's *Current Procedural Terminology* (CPT) (2): the official title of the procedural coding system developed and maintained by the AMA for use in reporting health care services performed in the outpatient setting. It is also known as Level I HCPCS codes.

physician extender provider (14): nonphysician employees of a medical practice who are licensed by the state to perform specific medical procedures under the direct supervision of a physician.

physician-hospital organization (PHO) (3): a business entity in which the hospital and selected physicians form a health care network for the purpose of contracting with managed care organizations to render health care for subscribers.

physician incentive (3): payments made directly or indirectly to health care providers to serve as encouragement to reduce or limit services.

Physician Incentive Plan (3): requirement that Medicare/Medicaid managed care plans disclose information about physician incentive plans to HCFA or state Medicaid agencies before a new or renewed contract receives final approval.

physician standby service (7): a CPT E&M service used to report the time a physician was immediately available to perform a specialized service for another physician. To qualify for this service the standby physician may not be providing care to another patient during the specified time, or the physician performed a service that is part of a global surgical procedure.

place of service (POS) (7, 9): indicators that replaced type of service (TOS) codes.

plan (9, 10): an element of SOAP notes that documents the provider's plan for work-up and medical management of the patient.

plan identification number (PlanID) (14): *see* National Health PlanID.

plastic repair (7): use of plastic surgery to repair tissue.

PMPM payment (2): a designation in discussions on capitation contract or literature that informs the reader that the per capita payment method is based on a "per member per month" formula.

point-of-service option (16): allows members of an HMO the flexibility to receive certain services outside the plan's established provider network, with higher cost-sharing by the patient and the HMO providing partial reimbursement for out-of-network services.

point-of-service plan (POS) (3, 13, 16): a plan that is either an open panel HMO or PPO that allows the enrollees to choose between using the in-network or out-of-network providers whenever they need medical care. The plan benefits are higher and the patients' out-of-pocket payments are lower if they use a network provider. An option available to TRICARE Prime enrollees and will result in out of pocket expenses for the patient.

poisoning (6): an adverse medical state caused by an overdose of medication, the prescription and use of a medicinal substance prescribed in error, or a drug mistakenly ingested or applied.

policyholder (4): *see* insured.

PPN provider (13): a health care provider who has signed a participating provider network agreement with a medical insurance company or managed care program.

PPO provider (13): a health care provider who has signed a participating provider agreement with a medical insurance company or managed care program.

preadmission certification (PAC) (3): a review for the medical necessity of inpatient care prior to a patient's admission.

preadmission review (3): *see* preadmission certification.

preauthorization (1, 3, 16): prior approval for reimbursement of health care services by a third-party payer.

precedent (5): legal decision that is based on an established case.

precertification (13): third-party payer requirement that certain health care services be preapproved before services are provided (also called prospective authorization).

pre-existing conditions (4): medical conditions under active treatment at the time the application is made for an insurance policy.

preferred provider arrangement (PPA) (13): contract between a third-party payer and a health care provider or group to provide services to individuals covered under that contract.

Preferred Provider Health Care Act of 1985 (3): legislation that reduced restrictions on PPOs.

preferred provider network (PPN) (13, 16): a provider-driven managed care plan where the provider, not the patient, is responsible for adhering to the managed care provisions of the plan.

Preferred Provider Organization (PPO) (3, 13, 14): pre-paid managed care, open panel, non-HMO affiliated plan that provides more patient management than is available under regular fee-for-service medical insurance plans and contracts to provide medical care for PPO patients for a special reduced rate.

preferred provider organization plan (13): *see* Preferred Provider Organization (PPO).

premium: the periodic payment made by the policyholder to an insurance company to initiate or to keep existing insurance coverage.

preoperative clearance (7): an evaluation and management service performed by a specialist at the request of a surgeon, to clear the patient for surgery.

prepaid health plan (2): contracts to individuals or groups for coverage of specified medical expenses.

prepaid medical plan (13): *see* prepaid health plan.

preventive medicine services (7): coding category used when the patient sees the physician for a routine examination (such as an annual physical or for well-baby care), or when risk management counseling is provided to patients who are exhibiting no signs or symptoms of a disorder.

preventive services (2): services rendered to a patient that are designed to help the individual avoid health and injury problems.

primary care manager (PCM) (16): the TRICARE title for the managed care gatekeeper or primary care physician.

primary care physician (PCP) (2, 4): a family practice, internal medicine, pediatric, and, in some plans, gynecology specialist responsible for providing all routine primary health care for the patient.

primary care provider (PCP) (2, 3, 13): *see* primary care physician (PCP).

primary care referral form (4): a form prepared by the primary care physician referring the patient to a specialist and authorizing specific services.

primary diagnosis (6, 11): the condition considered to be the major health problem for the patient for the submitted claim. This condition is always listed and coded first on the insurance claim form.

primary insurance (4): insurance responsible for paying first on a claim, often subject to deductible, copayment, and/or coinsurance amounts that are the responsibility of the patient.

primary malignancy (6): the original tumor site where the new growth began.

principal diagnosis (6): the diagnosis determined after study to be the major cause of the patient's admission to the hospital. The principal diagnosis may or may not be the same as the primary diagnosis.

principal procedure (6): a procedure performed for therapeutic rather than diagnostic purposes; or that procedure performed to treat a complication; or that procedure that most closely relates to the principal diagnosis.

prior authorization (3): consent obtained by a health care provider from an insurance company to proceed with described treatment. Some companies will not pay benefits for specific procedures without prior approval.

privacy (5): the right of individuals to keep their information from being disclosed to others.

privacy standards (5): legislation that will authorize the creation and implementation of regulations to protect a patient's privacy.

private, commercial Workers' Compensation programs (17): employer-purchased policy that meets state-determined requirements for Workers' Compensation coverage.

private contract (2): Medicare term used to describe situations where a patient and physician agree not to submit a claim for a service that would otherwise be covered and paid by Medicare.

Private Fee-for-Service Plan (14): a Medicare beneficiary who opts to use a regular fee-for-service insurance plan will receive assistance from Medicare for payment of premiums.

private health insurance (4): commercial health insurance coverage that is categorized as individual insurance (providing health care coverage for the policyholder and/or family) or group contract (providing health care coverage for a group of people as a single unit, such as employees).

problem focused examination (7): a physical examination of the patient that is limited to the affected body or organ system.

problem focused history (7): a CPT evaluation and management service requiring a documented patient history that includes the chief complaint, and a brief discussion of the present problem.

procedural code (7, 8): a statistical code system designed to communicate procedural data to insurance companies or other third-party payers.

> **Current Procedural Terminology (CPT):** the coding system published by the American Medical Association.
>
> **Health Care Financing Administration Common Procedural Coding System (HCPCS):** an alphanumeric coding system devised by the federal Health Care Financing Administration (HCFA) as a supplement to the CPT code and distributed by the regional fiscal agents for Medicare, TRICARE, and Medicaid.
>
> **Relative Value System (RVS) Code (referred to as California Standard Nomenclature System):** a coding system that originated with the California Medical Society; now used by many State Workers' Compensation carriers.

Procedures Tabular List and Alphabetical Index (6): *see* Volume III (ICD-9-CM).

professional component (CPT term) (7): the portion of a diagnostic health care service that represents providers' responsibility for the supervision of technical staff, the interpretation of results, and the writing of the diagnostic report results.

Program for Persons with Disabilities (PFPWD) (16): financial assistance program for active duty dependents with severe physical disabilities or moderate-to-severe mental retardation who cannot obtain specialized training or care through public resources.

prolonged services (7): a CPT evaluation and management service used to describe unusual services beyond the normal E&M encounter service that is provided in either the inpatient or outpatient setting.

prospective authorization (13): *see* precertification.

provider identification number (PIN) (11, 14): a computer number assigned to a health care provider by an insurance company to be used on all claims filed by that provider.

provider-sponsored organization (PSO) (14): a business entity that is owned and operated by a network of physicians and hospitals in a specific region.

qualified diagnosis (6): diagnosis stated in the records that is not yet proven and includes words such as: "suspected," "possible," "questionable," "suspicious of," or "ruled out."

Qualified Disabled and Working Individual (QDWI) (15): an individual whose income is below the poverty level and who is not otherwise eligible for Medicaid benefits may qualify for Medicaid to pay monthly Medicare Part A premiums.

Qualified Individual (QI) (15): an individual ineligible for full Medicaid benefits and whose resources are at or below twice the standard allowed under the SSI program receives assistance with all or a small part of monthly Medicare Part B premiums.

Qualified Medicare Beneficiary (QMB) (14, 15): a program designed to pay Medicare premiums, deductibles, and patient copayments for all Medicare-eligible persons of all ages who have income at or below the federally set poverty level.

quality assurance program (3): assessment of the quality of care provided in a health care setting.

Quality Improvement System for Managed Care (QISMC) (3): established by Medicare to assure managed care plan accountability in terms of objectives and requirements.

radiographic (16): image produced by Xrays.

radiologic views (7, 16): Xrays taken from different angles.

reduction of a fracture (7): manipulation of a fracture.

re-excision (6): associated with cancer surgery; a surgeon performs a second excision to widen the margins of the original tumor site.

referral (16): total transfer of a patient's medical care to another physician for treatment limited to a specific disorder.

regulation (5, 9): rules; laws; legislation.

relative value units (RVU) (9, 14): payment components of physician work/practice expense and malpractice cost.

Religious Fraternal Benefit Society Plans (14): a plan that may restrict enrollment to members of a church, convention, or group with which the society is affiliated.

remission (14): disease free, as in cancer.

report card (3): contains data regarding a managed care plan's quality, utilization, customer satisfaction, administrative effectiveness, financial stability, and cost control.

Resource-Based Relative Value Scale (RBRVS) system (9, 14): a payment system implemented in 1992 that reimburses physicians' practice expenses based on relative values for three components of each physician's service: physician work, practice expense, and malpractice insurance expense.

respite care (14, 16): the temporary hospitalization of a hospice patient for the purpose of giving relief from duty for the nonpaid person who has the major day-to-day responsibility for the care of a chronically ill, dependent patient.

review of systems (ROS) (7): part of the patient's history that consists of an interview by body system.

rider (13): an amending clause added to the original policy which may increase or decrease policy coverage.

risk-based HMO (14): this is a capitated Medicare-HMO plan that serves Medicare-eligible persons in a specific geographic area in lieu of their regular Medicare coverage. The patient is subjected to all the regular HMO constraints and procedures. Some plans have a lock-in provision that means neither the HMO nor Medicare will pay for unauthorized nonemergency care provided by out-of-network health care providers.

risk contract (3): arrangement among providers to provide fixed, prepaid health care.

risk pool (3): group of people whose insurance coverage costs are effected by health status, age, sex, and occupation.

routing form (4): *see* encounter form.

same day admit/discharge service (7): ambulatory or outpatient who is treated and released the same day.

same day surgery (ambulatory surgery) (16): surgery is performed and the patient is sent home the same day.

scope of practice (9): health care services that may be practiced by professionals (e.g., nurse practitioners) as determined by each state.

second party (5): the person or organization in a contract that is designated to provide the service.

second surgical opinion (SSO) (3): prior to surgery, a second physician is asked to evaluate the necessity of surgery and make recommendations.; some insurance plans require another opinion about the necessity for elective surgery prior to authorizing the surgery.

secondary condition (6): a disorder running concurrently with the primary diagnosis that does not overtly affect the prognosis of the primary condition.

secondary diagnosis (6, 11): *see* concurrent condition.

secondary malignancy (6): a tumor that has metastasized; cells have broken away from the primary site and a tumor mass is now found in a new location.

Section Guidelines (7): in CPT, each major section contains several pages of guidelines that provide instruction for coding from that section.

security (5): safekeeping of patient information by various means.

See (6, 7): a mandatory index convention in ICD-9-CM and CPT that instructs the coder to look elsewhere in the index.

See also (6, 7): an index convention in ICD-9-CM and CPT that refers the coder to a second main term before selecting a code.

See category (6): in ICD-9-CM, an index convention that indicates the category specified should be reviewed before a code is assigned.

See condition (6): in ICD-9-CM, an index convention that indicates the coder has focused on the wrong term.

self-referral (managed care) (3): a patient who sees an out-of-network provider without a referral from the primary care physician or case manager.

self-referral (Start II Regulations) (5): under Stark II federal regulations, self-referral involves providers ordering services to be performed for patients by organizations in which the provider has a financial interest.

separate procedure (7): CPT term describing a surgical procedure that was performed as a completely independent procedure not related to any other procedure performed in the same operative session.

sequelae (6): late effects of an injury or illness.

service location (13): the location where the patient received health care services.

severe combined immunodeficiency disease (SCID) (14): syndrome marked by decreased immunity and increased susceptibility to fungal, bacterial, and viral infections.

site of service differential (9): reduction in payment when services are performed at a facility other than the physician's office.

skin lesion (7): any discontinuity of the skin.

SOAP note (10): a medical charting system.

    S: subjective (patient's complaint).

    O: objective clinical data.

    A: assessment of the problem and diagnosis.

    P: plan for treatment, further studies and case management.

Social Security Administration (SSA) (14): an agency of the federal government.

Social Security Administration (SSA) benefits (14): the support a person receives when they meet specific requirements and have paid into the retirement, old age, survivors, disability, and hospital insurance programs run by the federal government.

Social Security number (SSN) (11): a federal identification number assigned by the Social Security Administration for the purpose of tracking an individual's eligibility for designated governmental services, individual payroll tax withholding accounts, etc. Insurance companies, banks, schools, and business corporations also use the SSN to identify individual clients.

source document (4): the hard copy document (routing slip, charge slip, encounter form, superbill, etc.) from which a claim is generated.

special accidental injury rider (13): a clause added to an insurance policy that covers 100 percent of nonsurgical care sought and rendered within 24 to 72 hours of an accidental injury.

Special Enrollment Period (SEP) (14): period of time when individuals can enroll in Medicare Part B if they did not enroll during the initial enrollment period.

special income level (15): an income amount established by each state that enables people to receive health care benefits.

Specified Low-Income Medicare Beneficiary (SLMB) (14, 15): a program designed to pay Medicare Part B premium for persons whose income falls in the federally designated "near poor" program.

spell of illness (14): *see* benefit period.

spend down (15): a process of determining an individual's excess income and demonstrating that medical expenses are equal to or greater than the excess income.

sponsor (a TRICARE/CHAMPVA term) (16): the individual who is a member of the Armed Forces or the uniformed branch of the Public Health Service, the National Oceanic and Atmospheric Administration (NOAA), or the North Atlantic Treaty Organization (NATO).

Spousal Impoverishment Protection Legislation (15): federal legislation that curbs the need for married couples to "spend down" income and other liquid assets (cash and property immediately convertible to cash) before one of the partners can be declared eligible for Medicaid coverage for nursing home care.

staff model (HMO) (3): a closed-panel multispecialty group practice where all physicians are employees and all health care services, including ancillary services such as physical therapy, pharmacy, and central supplies, are provided within a corporate building.

standards (3): requirements developed by accrediting organizations (e.g., JCAHO and NCQA).

State Children's Health Insurance Program (SCHIP) (15): federal legislation that provides states with grants to provide health coverage for children who are dependents of low-income families (also called Children's Health Insurance Program, or CHIP).

State Compensation Board/Commission (17): an administrative agency set up by the state legislature to oversee the Workers' Compensation program within the state.

State Compensation Fund (17): a state government agency functioning as the insuring body to cover workers' compensation claims.

statute (5): laws passed by legislative bodies.

statutory law (5): *see* statute.

subcategory (6): in CPT, the six major sections are subdivided into subsections, categories, and subcategories or headings. In ICD-9-CM, subcategories are indented and printed in bold upper and lowercase type and are preceded by a four-digit number.

subclassification (6): in ICD-9-CM, fifth-digit subclassification codes are indented below fourth-digit subcategory codes; they are printed in bold upper and lowercase type and are preceded by a five-digit number.

subjective (10): an element of SOAP notes that documents the patient's symptom in his/her own words.

subrogation (15): the assumption of an obligation for which another party is primarily liable.

subscriber (4, 13): the insured; the insurance policyholder.

subsequent hospital care (7): inpatient encounter for the purpose of conferring with the patient to update the patient's progress, reviewing the patient's medical chart, writing new orders for diagnostic tests and treatment orders, and consulting with other health care professionals about the case.

subsequent nursing facility care (7): an encounter with an NFS patient for the purpose of assessing the patient's current status when no major, permanent change of status is present.

subterm (6): terms located below main terms and indented two spaces, found in the alphabetical index of ICD-9-CM.

suicide attempt (6): associated with the ICD-9-CM Table of Drugs and Chemicals; indicates a self-inflicted poisoning.

Sunshine Law (14): this law is officially known as the Privacy Act of 1979. One of its provisions forbids the regional government program carriers from disclosing the status of any unassigned claim to NonPAR providers.

superbill (4): *see* encounter form.

supplemental plan (11): *see* supplemental insurance.

Supplemental Security Income (SSI) (15): a federally administered income assistance welfare program authorized under Title 16 of the Social Security Act; this program provides cash payments to needy, aged, blind, or disabled persons.

surgery or surgical procedure (as used by the insurance industry) (7): any treatment that breaks the normal skin barrier, such as injections, incisions, and excisions; examination with the aid of a scope that goes beyond the normal body orifice; a laryngeal mirror or vaginal speculum does not fit this definition because there is no penetration beyond the regular body orifice; bronchoscopy, proctosigmoid examinations, and dilation of the cervix are examples that qualify for the surgery definition; treatment for burns; treatment for fractures, both open and closed; and any procedure fitting the popular definition of surgery.

surgical package (CPT definition) (7): surgical procedures where one fee covers the surgery, normal, uncomplicated follow-up care, and the injection of local anesthesia.

surgical procedure (CPT definition) (7): those procedures that carry a CPT code number assigned from 10000 through 69999.

survey (3): assessment, examination, or investigation.

Tabular List (as used in ICD-9-CM coding) (6): a numerical listing of diseases and their assigned code numbers. *See* Disease Tabular List.

Tabular List and Index to Procedures (ICD-9-CM) (6): listing of procedure codes and descriptions used for inpatient classification.

Tax Equity and Fiscal Responsibility Act of 1982 (TEFRA) (3): federal legislation that established risk contracts, created Medicare risk programs, and defined a competitive medical plan.

Technical component (-TC) (7): a HCPCS Level II modifier used to indicate the charge is for the technical portion of a diagnostic test (cost of running a machine, the supplies and the technical supervision portion) without the professional component.

Temporary Assistance for Needy Families Act (TANF) (15): provided block grants to states offering time-limited cash assistance to persons eligible for federal entitlement programs.

temporary disability (17): workers' compensation classification describing a situation where the worker is unable to perform his or her usual duties for a limited period of time. It is expected that the worker will fully recover from the disorder and be able to return to the job after a short-term disability leave.

therapeutic use (6): associated with the ICD-9-CM Table of Drugs and Chemicals; indicates that a substance was taken/administered correctly.

third party (5): someone other than the persons directly involved in an action or contract; an outsider with no direct, binding, legal interest in a case.

third-party administrator (TPA) (3, 13): an administrator or corporation appointed by the insurer to oversee the authorization of medical treatment, performance of retrospective utilization, review of treatment plans, and payment of claims. This administrator has no direct interest in the health insurance contract.

third-party payer (2): an individual or corporation that makes a payment on an obligation/debt but is not a party to the contract that created the obligation/debt.

total disability (17): a 100% loss assignment is rendered because the injured employee is unable to perform duties associated with his/her occupation.

traditional health insurance coverage (3): fee-for-service basis reimbursement for health care services provided.

TRICARE (2, 16): a comprehensive federal civilian medical care program for spouses and dependents of those in the uniformed services, either active duty personnel or those who died while on active duty, as well as retired personnel, their spouses, and dependents. TRICARE is the government's health insurance program for all seven of the uniformed services. It is also known as CHAMPUS (Civilian Health and Medical Program for the Uniformed Services).

TRICARE contractor (16): an insurance company that serves as the fiscal intermediary (FI) for TRICARE and processes health claims.

TRICARE Extra (16): under this option, the sponsor chooses a doctor, hospital, or other medical provider listed in the TRICARE Provider Directory. If the sponsor needs assistance, they can call the Health Care Finder (HCF) at their nearest TRICARE Service Center. Anyone who is CHAMPUS eligible may enroll in TRICARE Extra. (Active duty personnel are not CHAMPUS eligible and are enrolled in TRICARE Prime).

TRICARE Management Activity (TMA) (16): new name for OCHAMPUS, the office that coordinates and administers the TRICARE program.

TRICARE Prime (16): in this option, most health care will come from a military treatment facility (MTF), augmented by the TRICARE contractor's Preferred Provider Network (PPN). All active duty service members will be enrolled in TRICARE Prime and will continue to receive most of their care from military medical personnel. For active duty families, there is no enrollment fee for TRICARE Prime, but they must complete an enrollment form.

TRICARE Prime Remote (16): provides benefits similar to TRICARE Prime to active duty service members who reside and work outside of a military treatment facility (MTF) catchment area (region defined by code boundaries within a 40-mile radius of an MTF).

TRICARE Program Management Organization (PMO) (16): organization responsible for managing TRICARE programs and demonstration projects.

TRICARE Retail Network Pharmacy (16): provides discount prescription drugs to enrollees and is a member of a network of civilian pharmacies established as part of the TRICARE program.

TRICARE Retiree Dental Program (16): provides dental care coverage for uniformed services retirees, certain surviving spouses, and their family members.

TRICARE Selected Reserve Dental Program (16): provides dental care coverage for uniformed services, National Guard, and Reserve personnel who are also members of the Selected Reserve.

TRICARE Senior Prime (16): authorized in the BBA of 1997 for the purpose of establishing an alternate health care delivery system for retirees and their spouses who are age 65+ and who are covered by Medicare Parts A and B.

TRICARE Senior Supplement Demonstration Program (TSSD) (16): offers affordable coverage, secondary to Medicare, and includes a pharmacy benefit for enrollees.

TRICARE Service Center (TSC) (16): an office located in an area with large concentrations of military families; questions are answered about TRICARE health services.

TRICARE sponsor (16): uniformed services personnel who are either on active duty, have retired, or have died while in the service.

TRICARE Standard (16): this is the new name for traditional CHAMPUS. Sponsors can choose any physician they want. Treatment may also be available at a military treatment facility, if space allows and after TRICARE Prime patients have been served. Furthermore, TRICARE Standard may be the only coverage available in some areas.

triple option plan (3): offered by either a single insurance plan or as a joint venture between two or more insurance carriers to provide subscribers with a choice among HMO, PPO, and traditional health insurance plans.

type of service (TOS) (7, 9): indicator used with CPT codes that has been replaced with procedure code modifiers or place of service (POS) codes.

UB-92 (HCFA-1450) (6): uniform bill adopted by HCFA to standardize the processing of hospital inpatient and outpatient claims.

UCR policy (Usual, Customary, and Reasonable policy) (13): a policy that uses the usual, customary, and reasonable average fee profiles to determine the "allowable" reimbursement for each procedure.

unauthorized service (4): service provided to a managed care patient without proper authorization or a current authorization from the patient's primary care physician or case manager.

unbundling (5, 7): the breaking down of an integrated major surgical package into various components for the purpose of differential coding and obtaining higher reimbursement. (Also known as fragmented surgery.)

uncertain behavior (6): the designation for a tumor where the morphology or behavior of the tumor cannot be stated with certainty.

uncovered benefit (4): *see* uncovered procedure.

uncovered procedure (4): any service determined not to be a benefit of the insurance policy, therefore disallowed for payment.

uniformed services (16): the Army, Navy, Coast Guard, Air Force, Marines, Public Health Service, and National Oceanic and Atmospheric Administration.

Unique Provider Identification Number (UPIN) (14): assigned by HCFA and given to the physician for purposes of identification on forms and claims.

unit/floor time (7): the amount of time the provider spends at the patient's bedside as well as managing the patient's care.

unspecified nature (6): a descriptive qualifier for a neoplasm when the histology or nature of the tumor has not been determined.

upcoding (5): practice of assigning a procedure or service code that does not match patient record documentation for the purpose of illegally increasing reimbursement.

usual and reasonable payments (2): *see* reasonable fee.

Usual, Customary and Reasonable (UCR) (13): *see* UCR policy.

utilization management (UM) (3): evaluation of necessity, quality, effectiveness, and efficiency of health care services, procedures, and facilities.

utilization review organization (URO) (3): an organization responsible for authorization of treatment, payment of claims, and performance of retrospective utilization review for an insurance program. The organization has no direct interest in the insurance contract it administers or reviews.

V codes (6): ICD codes representing either factors that influence a person's health status or legitimate reasons for contacting the health facility when the patient has no definitive diagnosis or active symptoms of any disorder.

verbal contract (5): an agreement established between the patient and the health care provider when the patient asks a provider to perform medical services.

vocational rehabilitation (17): training in new job skills to enable a person receiving Workers' Compensation or disability funds to become gainfully employed in a new position.

Volume 1 (ICD-9-CM) (6): the tabular (numerical) listing of diseases in the International Classification of Diseases coding system.

Volume 2 (ICD-9-CM) (6): the alphabetical index to Volume I (tabular listing of the International Classification of Diseases coding system).

Volume 3 (ICD-9-CM) (6): the tabular and alphabetical index of procedures in the International Classification of Disease coding system; used exclusively by hospital coders for inpatient procedure coding.

waiver of liability (8): statement on file with the provider's office that indicates the patient has agreed to pay for a service that is likely to be rejected by Medicare; also called Advance Beneficiary Notice (ABN).

welfare (2): federal and state financial and other assistance given to persons whose income falls near or below the federally designated poverty level. Also known as public assistance.

without direct patient contact (7): non-face-to-face time spent by the physician on an outpatient or inpatient basis and occurring before and/or after direct patient care.

Wiskott-Aldrich syndrome (14): x-lined immune deficiency syndrome (group of symptoms that characterize disease) characterized by decreased resistance to infection and eczema, decreased T lymphocytes, reduced immunoglobulins M (IgM), and inadequate response to antigens.

workers' compensation (17): an insurance program mandated by federal/state governments that requires employers to cover medical expenses and loss of wages for workers who are injured on the job or who have developed job-related disorders.

Index